T0202469

Lecture Notes in Computer Science **13440**

More information about this series at https://link.springer.com/bookseries/558

José Cano · Phil Trinder (Eds.)

Euro-Par 2022: Parallel Processing

28th International Conference on Parallel and Distributed Computing Glasgow, UK, August 22–26, 2022 Proceedings

Editors
José Cano
University of Glasgow
Glasgow, UK

Phil Trinder
University of Glasgow
Glasgow, UK

ISSN 0302-9743 ISSN 1611-3349 (electronic)
Lecture Notes in Computer Science
ISBN 978-3-031-12596-6 ISBN 978-3-031-12597-3 (eBook)
https://doi.org/10.1007/978-3-031-12597-3

This Springer imprint is published by the registered company Springer Nature Switzerland AG
The registered company address is: Gewerbestrasse 11, 6330 Cham, Switzerland

Preface

This volume contains the papers presented at Euro-Par 2022, the 28th International European Conference on Parallel and Distributed Computing, held in Glasgow, Scotland, during August 22–26, 2022. As the coronavirus pandemic receded Euro-Par 2022 was primarily an in-person event, but with some provision for authors and delegates to present, attend, and interact online.

For over 25 years, Euro-Par has consistently brought together researchers in parallel and distributed computing. Founded by pioneers as a merger of the three thematically related European conference series PARLE and CONPAR-VAPP, Euro-Par started with the aim to create the main annual scientific event on parallel and distributed computing in Europe and to be the primary choice of professionals for the presentation of their latest results.

Since its inception, Euro-Par has covered all aspects of parallel and distributed computing, ranging from theory to practice, scaling from the smallest to the largest parallel and distributed systems, from fundamental computational problems and models to full-fledged applications, from architecture and interface design and implementation to tools, infrastructures, and applications. Euro-Par's unique organization into topics provides an excellent forum for focused technical discussion as well as interaction with a large, broad, and diverse audience of researchers in academic institutions, public and private laboratories, and industry. Euro-Par's topics were always oriented towards novel research issues and the current state of the art. Most topics became constant entries, while new themes emerged and were included in the conference. Euro-Par selects new organizers and chairs for every edition, giving opportunity to young researchers and leading to fresh ideas while ensuring tradition. Organizers and chairs of previous editions support their successors. In this sense, Euro-Par also promotes networking across borders, leading to the unique spirit of Euro-Par.

Previous conference editions took place in Stockholm, Lyon, Passau, Southampton, Toulouse, Munich, Manchester, Paderborn, Klagenfurt, Pisa, Lisbon, Dresden, Rennes, Las Palmas, Delft, Ischia, Bordeaux, Rhodes, Aachen, Porto, Vienna, Grenoble, Santiago de Compostela, Turin, Göttingen, Warsaw, and Lisbon.

Thus Euro-Par in Scotland followed the well-established format of its predecessors. The 28th edition of Euro-Par was organized by the School of Computing Science at the University of Glasgow, with support from Heriot-Watt University, the University of Edinburgh, and the University of Stirling.

Euro-Par 2022 accepted papers in the following nine topic areas:

- Compilers, Tools, and Environments
- Performance and Power Modeling, Prediction and Evaluation
- Scheduling and Load Balancing
- Data Management, Analytics, and Machine Learning
- Cluster and Cloud Computing
- Theory and Algorithms for Parallel and Distributed Processing

– Parallel and Distributed Programming, Interfaces, and Languages
– Multicore and Manycore Parallelism
– Parallel Numerical Methods and Applications

Submissions were also sought in two other topics areas. The High-performance Architectures and Accelerators topic received and reviewed five submissions, but none was considered strong enough for inclusion in the conference. The Parallelism in IoT/Edge Computing topic received just two submissions, and these were considered under other topics.

A total of 102 full papers were submitted by authors from 25 different countries. The number of submitted papers, the range of topics, and the requirement to obtain high-quality reviews mandated careful selection using a large pool of experts. The 102 members of the Program Committee (PC) combined with 108 external reviewers, to give a total of 210 reviewers from 39 countries. The reviewers submitted 405 reviews, with all but three papers receiving four or more reviews. The accepted papers were selected in a two-phase process. Following discussion, each topic PC proposed sets of papers for acceptance, discussion, and rejection. The papers from all topics were reviewed and discussed in an online paper selection meeting on April 22, 2022. The outcome was to select 25 papers to be presented at the conference and published in these proceedings, a 24.5% acceptance rate.

To increase reproducibility of the research Euro-Par encourages authors to submit artifacts, such as source code, data sets, and reproducibility instructions. In the notification of acceptance authors were encouraged to submit artifacts for evaluation. A total of 12 artifacts were submitted in support of accepted papers and were evaluated by the Artifact Evaluation Committee (AEC). The AEC successfully reproduced results for 11 artifacts, or 44% of accepted papers. These papers are marked in the proceedings by a special stamp, and the artifacts are available online in the Figshare repository. For the first time, selected artifacts will also be published in a Euro-Par Special Issue of the Journal of Open Source Software.

In addition to the technical program, we had the pleasure of hosting three distinguished keynotes.

– Ewa Deelman, USC Information Sciences Institute, USA
– José Duato, Polytechnic University of Valencia, Spain
– Domenico Talia, DIMES, University of Calabria, Italy

The conference program started with two days of workshops on specialized topics, an Intel tutorial, and a Doctoral Symposium. Yehia Elkhatib coordinated the Doctoral Symposium. Dora Blanco Heras and Jeremy Singer coordinated and organized the workshops and tutorial as workshop co-chairs. After the conference, a selection of the papers presented at the workshops will be published in a separate Springer LNCS proceedings.

We would like to thank the authors, chairs, PC members, and reviewers for contributing to the success of Euro-Par 2022. Similarly, we would like to extend our appreciation to the Euro-Par Steering Committee for its support. Our mentor, Paul Kelly, provided valuable support and direction, and we are grateful for the wisdom and resources shared by the Euro-Par 2021 team.

August 2022

José Cano
Phil Trinder

Organization

Steering Committee

Full Members

Luc Bougé (Chair)	ENS Rennes, France
Fernando Silva (Vice-chair)	University of Porto, Portugal
Dora Blanco Heras (Workshops Chair)	University of Santiago de Compostela, Spain
Marco Aldinucci	University of Turin, Italy
Christos Kaklamanis	Computer Technology Institute, Greece
Paul Kelly	Imperial College London, UK
Thomas Ludwig	University of Hamburg, Germany
Maciej Malawski (Virtualization Chair)	AGH University of Science and Technology, Poland
Tomàs Margalef	Autonomous University of Barcelona, Spain
Wolfgang Nagel	Dresden University of Technology, Germany
George Papadopoulos	University of Cyprus, Cyprus
Francisco Fernández Rivera	University of Santiago de Compostela, Spain
Krzysztof Rządca	University of Warsaw, Poland
Rizos Sakellariou	University of Manchester, UK
Henk Sips (Finance Chair)	Delft University of Technology, The Netherlands
Leonel Sousa	University of Lisbon, Portugal
Domenico Talia	University of Calabria, Italy
Massimo Torquati (Artifacts Chair)	University of Pisa, Italy
Phil Trinder	University of Glasgow, UK
Felix Wolf	Technical University of Darmstadt, Germany
Ramin Yahyapour	GWDG, Germany

Honorary Members

Christian Lengauer	University of Passau, Germany
Ron Perrott	Oxford e-Research Centre, UK
Karl Dieter Reinartz	University of Erlangen-Nürnberg, Germany

General Chair

Phil Trinder	University of Glasgow, UK

Workshop Chairs

Jeremy Singer — University of Glasgow, UK
Dora Blanco Heras — University of Santiago de Compostela, Spain

PhD Symposium Chair

Yehia Elkhatib — University of Glasgow, UK

Submissions Chair

José Cano — University of Glasgow, UK

Publicity Chairs

Patrick Maier — University of Stirling, UK
Lito Michala — University of Glasgow, UK

Web Chair

Michel Steuwer — University of Edinburgh, UK

Virtual/Local Chairs

Waqar Nabi — University of Glasgow, UK
Rob Stewart — Heriot-Watt University, UK
Lauritz Thamsen — University of Glasgow, UK

Artifact Evaluation Chairs

Hans-Wolfgang Loidl — Heriot-Watt University, UK
Massimo Torquati — University of Pisa, Italy
Wim Vanderhauwhede — University of Glasgow, UK

Scientific Organization

Topic 1: Compilers, Tools, and Environments

Global Chair

George Papadopoulos — University of Cyprus, Cyprus

Local Chair

Nick Brown — University of Edinburgh, UK

Members

Vicenç Beltran	Barcelona Supercomputing Center, Spain
Tobias Grosser	University of Edinburgh, UK
Valeria Bartsch	Fraunhofer, Germany
Artur Podobas	KTH Royal Institute of Technology, Sweden

Topic 2: Performance and Power Modeling, Prediction and Evaluation

Global Chair

Jorge G. Barbosa	University of Porto, Portugal

Local Chair

Horacio González-Vélez	National College of Ireland, Ireland

Members

Alexey Lastovetsky	University College Dublin, Ireland
Horst Simon	LBNL, USA
Paul Kelly	Imperial College London, UK
Maciej Malawski	AGH University of Science and Technology, Poland
Gordana Rakic	University of Novi Sad, Serbia
Helen Karatza	Aristotle University of Thessaloniki, Greece
Andreas Knuepfer	TU Dresden, Germany
Arnaud Legrand	CNRS/Inria/University of Grenoble, France

Topic 3: Scheduling and Load Balancing

Global Chair

Dimitrios S. Nikolopoulos	Virginia Tech, USA

Local Chair

Wolfgang Schreiner	Johannes Kepler University Linz, Austria

Members

Ioannis E. Venetis	University of Piraeus, Greece
Carlos Reaño	Universitat de València, Spain
Imre Varga	University of Debrecen, Hungary
Thomas Fahringer	University of Innsbruck, Austria

Topic 4: Data Management, Analytics, and Machine Learning

Global Chair

Ruggero G. Pensa	University of Turin, Italy

Local Chair

Nikos Ntarmos	Huawei Technologies R&D, UK

Members

Maurizio Drocco	IBM, USA
Robert Birke	ABB Research, Switzerland
Reza Akbarinia	Inria, France
Tania Cerquitelli	Politecnico di Torino, Italy
Peter Pietzuch	Imperial College London, UK

Topic 5: Cluster and Cloud Computing

Global Chair

Ivona Brandic	Vienna University of Technology, Austria

Local Chair

Blesson Varghese	Queen's University Belfast, UK

Members

Alexandra Carpen-Amarie	Fraunhofer ITWM, Germany
Rizos Sakellariou	University of Manchester, UK
Atakan Aral	University of Vienna, Austria
David Bermbach	TU Berlin, Germany
Vlado Stankovski	University of Ljubljana, Slovenia

Topic 6: Theory and Algorithms for Parallel and Distributed Processing

Global Chair

Henning Meyerhenke	Humboldt-Universität zu Berlin, Germany

Local Chair

Ciaran McCreesh	University of Glasgow, UK

Members

Francesco Silvestri	University of Padua, Italy
Flavio Vella	University of Trento, Italy
Yihan Sun	University of California, Riverside, USA
Marek Klonowski	Wroclaw University of Technology, Poland
Johannes K. Fichte	TU Wien, Austria
Gianluca De Marco	University of Salerno, Italy

Fredrik Manne	University of Bergen, Norway
Christopher Jefferson	University of St Andrews, UK
Thoma Sauerwald	University of Cambridge, UK

Topic 7: Parallel and Distributed Programming, Interfaces, and Languages

Global Chair

Gabriele Keller	Utrecht University, The Netherlands

Local Chair

Hans Vandierendonck	Queen's University Belfast, UK

Members

Polyvios Pratikakis	FORTH, Greece
Sergei Gorlach	University of Muenster, Germany
Giorgis Georgakoudis	Lawrence Livermore National Laboratory, USA
Zhenjiang Hu	Peking University, China
Xavier Martorell	Universitat Politècnica de Catalunya, Spain

Topic 8: Multicore and Manycore Parallelism

Global Chair

Massimo Torquati	University of Pisa, Italy

Local Chair

Chris Brown	University of St Andrews, UK

Members

Valeria Cardellini	Tor Vergata University of Rome, Italy
Peter Kilpatrick	Queen's University Belfast, UK
Herbert Kuchen	University of Muenster, Germany
Arturo Gonzalez-Escribano	University of Valladolid, Spain

Topic 9: Parallel Numerical Methods and Applications

Global Chair

Paolo Bientinesi	Umeå University, Sweden

Local Chair

Michael Bane	Manchester Metropolitan University, UK

Members

Davor Davidovic	Rudjer Boskovic Institute, Croatia
Fabienne Jezequel	Sorbonne University, France
Francisco D. Igual	Universidad Complutense de Madrid, Spain
Jonas Thies	Delft University of Technology, The Netherlands
Adrian Tate	NAG, UK

Topic 10: High-performance Architectures and Accelerators

Global Chair

Pedro Trancoso	Chalmers University of Technology, Sweden

Local Chair

Tom Spink	University of St Andrews, UK

Members

Francesca Palumbo	University of Sassari, Italy
Alexandra Jimborean	University of Murcia, Spain
M. Waqar Azhar	Chalmers University of Technology, Sweden
Mario Porrmann	Osnabrueck University, Germany
Bhavishya Goel	Chalmers University of Technology, Sweden
Jing Chen	Chalmers University of Technology, Sweden

Topic 11: Parallelism in IoT/Edge Computing

Global Chair

Rosa Badia	Barcelona Supercomputing Center, Spain

Local Chair

Paul Keir	University of the West of Scotland, UK

Members

Dejan Milojicic	Hewlett Packard Enterprise, USA
James Riordan	University of the West of Scotland, UK
Massimo Villari	University of Messina, Italy
Xavier Masip	Universitat Politècnica de Catalunya, Spain

PhD Symposium

Chair

Yehia Elkhatib	University of Glasgow, UK

Members

Marco Aldinucci	University of Turin, Italy
Georgios Bouloukakis	Télécom Sud Paris, France
Thaleia-Dimitra Doudali	IMDEA Software, Spain
Maya G. Neytcheva	Uppsala University, Sweden
Pavlos Petoumenos	University of Manchester, UK
Minyar Mokhtar Sassi	Imam Abdulrahman Bin Faisal University, Saudi Arabia
Sameer Shende	University of Oregon, USA
Zheng Wang	University of Leeds, UK

Artifact Evaluation

Chairs

Hans-Wolfgang Loidl	Heriot-Watt University, UK
Massimo Torquati	University of Pisa, Italy
Wim Vanderbauwhede	University of Glasgow, UK

Members

Iacopo Colonnelli	University of Turin, Italy
Daniele De Sensi	ETH Zurich, Switzerland
Marko Doko	Heriot-Watt University, UK
Dejice Jacob	University of Glasgow, UK
Dominic Lindsay	Lancaster University, UK
Alberto R. Martinelli	University of Turin, Italy
Youssef Moawad	University of Glasgow, UK
Ole Stubben	University of Glasgow, UK
Robert Szafarczyk	University of Glasgow, UK
Nicolò Tonci	University of Pisa, Italy
Alois Zoitl	Johannes Kepler University Linz, Austria
Cocoa Xu	University of Glasgow, UK

Additional Reviewers

José L. Abellán
Sabtain Ahmad
Usman Akhtar
Francisco J. Andújar
Eugenio Angriman
Jonatha Anselmi
Blair Archibald
Moiz Arif
Kevin Assogba
Reid Atcheson
Elias Athanasopoulos
Olivier Aumage
Martin Aumüller
Erna Begovic
Paolo Bethaz
Luca Buratti
Tamás Bérczes
Franck Cappello
Rocío Carratalá-Sáez
Bruno Casella
Paolo Castagno
Sandra Catalan
Juan M. Cebrian
José M. Cecilia
Soteris Constantinou
Raphaël Couturier
Rossana Damiano
Vincent Danjean
Vincenzo De Maio
Ivo Gabe de Wolff

David Defour
Augustin Degomme
Matthias Diener
Konstantinos Dogeas
Roger Ferrer Ibanez
Pierre Fortin
Zoltan Gal
Chryssis Georgiou
Gramoz Goranci
Martin Grambow
Salvatore Greco
Yan Gu
Ishaan Gulati
Koby Hayashi
Markus Hecher
Edvin Hopkins
Guillaume Huard
Markus Höhnerbach
Roman Iakymchuk
Maurice Jamieson
Ahmet-Serdar Karakaya
Oguz Kaya
Jason Kennedy
Gergely Kocsis
Sai Charan Koduru
Alexandros Kouris
Vladyslav Kucher
Martin Kuehn
Attila Kuki
Svetlana Kulagina
Moreno La Quatra
Kenneth Langedal
Ning Li
Dominik Marek Loroch
Daniel Luger
Yasir Mahmood
Loris Marchal
Theo Mary
Ilias Mavridis
Trevor L. McDonell
Charles McGuffey
Lucas Mello Schnorr
Gabriele Mencagli
Milan Mihajlovic
Simone Monaco
Daichi Mukunoki
Orestis Papadigenopoulos
Zafeirios Papazachos
Stefan Pedratscher
Tobias Pfandzelter
Javier Prades
Christos Psarras
Sasko Ristov
Valentin Roland
Dominik Rusovac
Philip Salzmann
Aravind Sankaran
Tim Schmielau
Zheqi Shen
Jessica Shi
Dimitrios Siakavaras
Fedor Smirnov
Hari Subramoni
Jozsef Suto
Paolo Sylos Labini
Moisis Symeonidis
Jakub Szewczyk
Lauritz Thamsen
Andres Tomas
Phil Tooley
Yuri Torres de La Sierra
Dimitris Tychalas
Ádám Tóth
Bartolomeo Vacchetti
David van Balen
Paolo Viviani
Frédéric Vivien
Haris Volos
Yiqiu Wang
Xinzhe Wu
Yuan Yao

Euro-Par 2022 Invited Talks

Living in a Heterogenous World: How Scientific Workflows Help Automate Science and What We Can Do Better?

Ewa Deelman

University of Southern California, USA
deelman@isi.edu

Scientific workflows are now a common tool used by domain scientists in a number of disciplines. They are appealing because they enable users to think at high level of abstraction, composing complex applications from individual application components. Workflow management systems (WMSs), such as Pegasus (http://pegasus.isi.edu) automate the process of executing these workflows on modern cyberinfrastructure. They take these high-level, resource-independent descriptions and map them onto the available heterogeneous resources: campus clusters, high-performance computing resources, high-throughput resources, clouds, and the edge.

WMSs can select the appropriate resources based on their architecture, availability of key software, performance, reliability, availability of cycles, storage space, among others. With the help of compiler-inspired algorithms, they can determine what data to save during execution, and which are no longer needed. Similarly to compiler solutions, they can generate an executable workflow that is tailored to the target execution environment, taking into account reliability, scalability, and performance. WMS use workflow execution engines to run the executable workflows on the target resources providing scalability and reliability.

This talk will describe the key concepts used in the Pegasus WMS to help automate the execution of workflows in distributed and heterogeneous environments. It will explore potential use of artificial intelligence and machine learning approaches to enhance automation. The talk will also help identify challenges that exist in adopting novel approaches for science at the technological and social levels.

Effective Congestion Management for Large-Scale Datacenters

José Duato

Universitat Politècnica de València, Camino de Vera s/n, 46022 Valencia, Spain
jduato@disca.upv.es

Datacenters are essential for providing Internet services. As the number of client requests per time unit and their complexity keep increasing, datacen-ters are adopting computing solutions to scale with the demand, and provide appropriate support for interactive services. In particular, computing accelerators (mostly GPUs, but also TPUs, FPGAs, etc) have become very popular, and some recent designs even incorporate network ports in those devices to directly attach them to the interconnection network. As system size increases, the cost of the interconnection network grows faster than system size, thus becoming increasingly important to carefully design it to prevent over-provisioning. However, by doing so, the network operation point moves closer to saturation and sudden traffic bursts may lead to congestion. This situation is aggravated by the recent introduction of flow control in datacenter networks to cope with RDMA requirements, and network power management. The result is massive performance degradation whenever some network region becomes congested. Moreover, performance degradation may remain for long even after the traffic bursts that congested the network have already been transmitted.

This keynote will show why congestion appears in an interconnection network, how it propagates, and why performance may degrade so dramatically. Different kinds of congestion will be identified. Also, a global solution to effectively address the congestion problem will be proposed. It consists of several complementary mechanisms that accurately identify the congestion sources and cooperate to address all kinds of congestion, operating at different time scales. Some of these mechanisms have been recently incorporated into commercial products and are being standardized.

Programming Big Data Analysis: Towards Data-Centric Exascale Computing

Domenico Talia

University of Calabria, Rende (CS) 87036, Italy
talia@dimes.unical.it

Software applications today are strongly data driven. For this reason programming models and tools and novel architectures have been recently studied and developed to extract valuable information from Big Data, addressing data complexity, scalability, and/or high velocity. Analytics and machine learning on Big Data sources are not feasible through sequential algorithms to obtain in a reasonable time models and patterns from huge volumes of data. For this reason, parallel computers, such as many- and multicore systems, Clouds, and multi-clusters, along with parallel and decentralized algorithms and systems are required to analyze Big Data sources and repositories. In this direction Exascale computing systems represent the next step. Exascale systems refer to high performance computing systems capable of at least one exaFLOPS, so their implementation is representing a very significant research and technology move. In fact, cluster computers and Cloud platforms used today can store very large amounts of data, however they do not provide the high performance expected from massively parallel Exascale systems. This is the main motivation for developing Exascale platforms that will represent the most advanced model of supercomputers.

Data analysis solutions advance by exploiting the power of data mining and machine learning techniques and are changing several scientific and industrial areas. Therefore, it is vital to design scalable solutions for processing and analysis such massive datasets. Scalability and performance requirements are challenging conventional data storages, file systems and database management systems. Architectures of such systems have reached limits in handling very large processing tasks involving petabytes of data because they have not been built for scaling after a given threshold. This condition claims for new hardware architectures and data analysis software solutions that must process Big Data for extracting complex predictive and descriptive models. To reach Exascale size, it is in fact required to define new programming models and languages that combine abstraction with both scalability and performance Hybrid models (shared/distributed memory) and communication mechanisms based on locality and grouping are currently designed as promising approaches. Parallel applications running on Exascale systems require to control millions of threads running on a very large set of cores. Such applications need to avoid or limit synchronization, use less communication and remote memory, and handle with software and hardware faults that could occur.

Implementing scalable data analysis applications in Exascale computing systems is a very complex job and it requires high-level fine-grain parallel models, appropriate programming constructs and skills in parallel and distributed programming.

Mechanisms are needed for expressing task dependencies and inter-task parallelism, for designing synchronization and load balancing, handling failures, and properly manage distributed memory and concurrent communication among a very large number of tasks. Moreover, when the target computing infrastructures are heterogeneous and require different libraries and tools to program applications on them, the programming issues are even more complex. One of the most important aspects to ponder in applications that run on Exascale systems and analyze big datasets is the tradeoff between sharing data among computing elements and processing data locally to reduce communication and energy costs, while keeping performance and fault-tolerance levels. Scalable programming models based on basic operations for data intensive/data-driven applications must include mechanisms and functions for parallel data access, data-driven local communication, near-data synchronization, in-memory querying, fault resiliency, data aggregation, and locality-based data selection. Reliable and high-level programming models and their associated runtime must be able to manage and provide implementation solutions for those operations through the exploitation of a very large amount of parallelism on hundred thousand or millions of cores.

Exascale systems raise new requirements on application developers and programming systems to target architectures composed of a very large number of homogeneous and heterogeneous cores. General issues like energy consumption, multitasking, scheduling, reproducibility, and resiliency must be addressed together with other data-oriented issues like data distribution and mapping, data access, data communication and synchronization. Programming constructs and runtime systems will play a crucial role in enabling future data analysis programming models, runtime models, and hardware platforms to address these challenges, and in supporting the scalable implementation of real-world big data analysis applications. This keynote aims at addressing these topics and issues.

Euro-Par 2022 Topic Overviews

Topic 1: Compilers, Tools, and Environments

George A. Papadopoulos and Nick Brown

This topic addresses programming tools and system software for all kinds of parallel computer architectures, ranging from low-power embedded high-performance systems, multi- and manycore processors, and accelerators to large-scale computers and cloud computing. Focus areas include compilation and software testing to design well-defined components and verify their necessary structural, behavioral, and parallel interaction properties. It deals with tools, analysis software, and runtime environments to address the challenges of programming and executing the parallel architectures mentioned above. Furthermore, the topic deals with methods and tools for optimizing non-functional properties such as performance, programming productivity, robustness, energy efficiency, and scalability.

The topic received eight submissions across the aforementioned subjects and papers were thoroughly reviewed by the seven topic Program Committee members and external reviewers. Each submission was subjected to rigorous review from at least four peers and, after intensely scrutinizing the reviews, we were pleased to select three high-quality papers for the technical program, corresponding to a per-topic acceptance rate of 37.5%.

The first accepted paper “CrossDBT: An LLVM-based User-level Dynamic Binary Translation Emulator” by Wei Li et al. deals with dynamic binary translation. A novel LLVM-based emulator has been developed which enables guest machine code to be directly lifted to LLVM IR and this produces high-quality machine code, ultimately reducing runtime overhead compared against state of the art approaches. The second paper “AutomaticMARTINI: The Little Match and Replace Tool for Automatic Application Rewriting With Code Examples” by Alister Johnson et al. is concerned with automated refactoring via metaprogramming. Specifically, this work describes a new approach to code rewriting by providing advanced and semantic-driven rewrite capabilities to users in a simple and natural way. Finally, the third accepted paper, “Accurate Fork-join Profiling on the Java Virtual Machine” by Matteo Basso et al. addresses the fork-join model for parallel programming. It presents a novel approach for analyzing fork-join computations on the JVM, addressing the peculiarities of the Java fork-join framework, including features such as task unforking and task reuse.

We would like to thank the authors who responded to our call for papers, the members of the Program Committee and the additional external reviewers who, with their opinion and expertise, ensured a program of the highest quality. Many thanks to Phil Trinder for the tremendous overall organization of Euro-Par 2022 and his engaging interaction.

Topic 2: Performance and Power Modeling, Prediction and Evaluation

Jorge G Barbosa and Horacio González–Vélez

In recent years, a range of novel methods and tools have been developed for the evaluation, design, and modeling of parallel and distributed systems and applications. Furthermore, in addition to the classic resource-oriented notion, the term 'performance' has now been broadened to also encompass scalability and energy efficiency, as well as system reliability and robustness.

The papers submitted to this topic represent progressive research on different aspects of performance modeling, evaluation, and prediction, both for systems and applications running on the whole range of parallel and distributed systems (e.g. multicore and heterogeneous architectures, HPC systems, and clouds). That is to say, the accepted papers provide an interesting horizon of novel research in distinct areas of performance modeling, prediction, and evaluation, helping to bring together current theory and practice.

This topic received 15 submissions, which were thoroughly reviewed by the 11 members of the topic Program Committee and external reviewers. Out of all submissions, and after a careful and detailed discussion among committee members, we finally decided to accept three papers, resulting in a per-topic acceptance rate of 20%.

We would like to thank the authors for their submissions, the Euro-Par 2022 Organizing Committee for their help throughout, and the Program Committee members and the reviewers for providing timely and detailed reviews, and for participating in the discussion and consensus carried out after the reviews were received.

Topic 3: Scheduling and Load Balancing

Dimitrios Nikolopoulos and Wolfgang Schreiner

New computing systems offer the opportunity to reduce the response times and the energy consumption of the applications by exploiting the levels of parallelism. Modern computer architectures are often composed of heterogeneous compute resources and exploiting them efficiently is a complex and challenging task. Scheduling and load balancing techniques are key instruments to achieve higher performance, lower energy consumption, reduced resource usage, and real-time properties of applications.

This topic attracts papers on all aspects related to scheduling and load balancing on parallel and distributed machines, from theoretical foundations for modeling and designing efficient and robust scheduling policies to experimental studies, applications, and practical tools and solutions. It applies to multi- and manycore processors, embedded systems, servers, heterogeneous and accelerated systems, and HPC clusters as well as distributed systems such as clouds and global computing platforms.

In this track 11 full papers were submitted, each of which received four reviews from the eight Program Committee (PC) members and 25 external reviewers. On the basis of this thorough feedback, we accepted three submissions, resulting in a per-topic acceptance rate of 27%.

The chairs would like to sincerely thank all the authors for their high quality submissions, the Euro-Par 2022 Organizing Committee for all their valuable help, and the PC members and external reviewers for their excellent work. They all contributed to making this topic and Euro-Par an excellent forum to discuss scheduling and load balancing challenges.

Topic 4: Data Management, Analytics, and Machine Learning

Ruggero G. Pensa and Nikos Ntarmos

Many areas of science, industry, and commerce are producing extreme-scale data that must be processed—stored, managed, analyzed—in order to extract useful knowledge. This topic seeks papers in all aspects of distributed and parallel data management and data analysis. For example, cloud and grid data-intensive processing, parallel and distributed machine learning, HPC in situ data analytics, parallel storage systems, scalable data processing workflows, federated learning, and distributed stream processing are all in the scope of this topic.

This year, the topic received nine submissions, which were thoroughly reviewed by the seven members of the topic Program Committee (PC) and external reviewers. Out of all the submissions, and after a careful and detailed discussion among committee members, we finally decided to accept three papers, resulting in a per-topic acceptance rate of 33%.

We would like to express our thanks to the authors for their submissions, the Euro-Par 2022 Organizing Committee for their help throughout, the PC members and the external reviewers for providing timely and detailed reviews, and for participating in the discussion of the reviews were received.

Topic 5: Cluster and Cloud Computing

Ivona Brandic and Blesson Varghese

Cluster computing research deals with the efficient organization of large computer systems at single geographic locations. Cloud computing, on the other hand, addresses questions on the effective delivery of services that run across geographically distributed clusters. Thus, there is an overlap of interests and problems addressed by both research areas, which is the focus of this topic.

Important research topics on cluster computing focus on performance, reliability, energy efficiency, and the design and use of novel processor architectures. Cloud computing abstracts the hardware and system software details from the users and, therefore, research issues include various forms of virtualization and their impact on performance, resource management, and business models that address service provider and user interests. Further, employing Cloud data centres and their advantages with respect to reliability and load balancing along with the consideration of networks is of interest to the community.

Leveraging local computing resources along with the Cloud, referred to as edge or fog computing, has received growing interest in recent times.

This year, 10 papers were submitted to the track. Following a thorough discussion of the reviews obtained from experts, the topic chairs accepted three submissions resulting in a per-topic acceptance rate of 33%. The papers accepted address relevant challenges in container, delay tolerance, and microservices-based cluster and cloud/edge systems.

The topic chairs acknowledge the contributions of all authors who submitted their research, the Euro-Par 2022 Organizing Committee for their support, the reviewers for providing timely and high-quality reviews, and all who participated in the discussions.

Topic 6: Theory and Algorithms for Parallel and Distributed Processing

Henning Meyerhenke and Ciaran McCreesh

Nowadays parallel and distributed processing is ubiquitous. Multicore processors are available on smartphones, laptops, servers, and supercomputing nodes. Also, many devices cooperate in fully distributed and heterogeneous systems to provide a wide array of services. Despite recent years having witnessed astonishing progress in this field, many research challenges remain open concerning fundamental issues as well as the design and analysis of efficient, scalable, and robust algorithmic solutions with provable performance and quality guarantees.

This year, a total of 16 submissions were received in this topic. Each submission received four reviews from the 11 Topic Program Committee members. Following the thorough discussion of the reviews, four original and high-quality papers were accepted, giving a per-topic acceptance rate of 25%.

We would like to thank the authors for their excellent submissions, the Euro-Par 2022 Organizing Committee for their help throughout, and the PC members and the external reviewers for providing timely and detailed reviews, and for participating in the discussions that helped reach the decisions.

Topic 7: Parallel and Distributed Programming, Interfaces, and Languages

Gabriele Keller and Hans Vandierendonck

Parallel and distributed applications require appropriate programming abstractions and models, efficient design tools, parallelization techniques, and practices. This topic attracted papers presenting new results and practical experience in this domain: efficient and effective parallel languages, interfaces, libraries, and frameworks, as well as solid practical and experimental validation.

The accepted papers emphasize research on high-performance, resilient, portable, and scalable parallel programs via appropriate parallel and distributed programming model, interface, and language support. Contributions that assess programming abstractions and automation for usability, performance, task-based parallelism, or scalability were valued.

This year, the topic received 11 submissions, which were thoroughly reviewed by the six members of the topic Program Committee and external reviewers. After careful and detailed discussion among committee members, we decided to accept three of the submissions, giving a per-topic acceptance rate of 27%.

The topic chairs would like to thank all the authors who submitted papers for their contribution to the success of this track, the Euro-Par 2022 Committee for their support, and the external reviewers for their high-quality reviews and their valuable feedback.

Topic 8: Multicore and Manycore Parallelism

Massimo Torquati and Chris Brown

Multicore and manycore architectures are nowadays pervasive in all computing fields. Yet, their intrinsic complexity creates several programming challenges when performance, portability, and power efficiency are the most important metrics to optimize. Programming complexity is further exacerbated when considering heterogeneous platforms comprising thousands of heterogeneous cores. To use such systems efficiently, algorithms must scale to a large degree of parallelism, utilize optimized data structures and synchronization mechanisms, and leverage fine-tuned parallel runtimes and frameworks capable of reducing parallel overheads. This topic seeks to explore the programming of homogeneous and heterogeneous multicore and manycore systems. It focuses on novel research and solutions in the form of programming models, algorithms, concurrent data structures, libraries, runtime systems, and tools capable of increasing programmability and performance of multi- and manycore systems in the context of general-purpose, high-performance, and embedded parallel computing.

This year, six papers covering some of these issues were submitted. Each of them was reviewed by four reviewers. Finally, one regular paper was selected. It focuses on prediction models to estimate the slowdown effect of executing multiple concurrent kernels on GPU devices. It proposes an enhancement of the Simultaneous Multikernel distribution model to reduce the prediction error.

We would like to express our gratitude to all the authors for submitting their work. We also thank the reviewers for their great job and useful comments. Finally, we would like to thank the Euro-Par organization and steering committees for their continuous support.

Topic 9: Parallel Numerical Methods and Applications

Paolo Bientinesi and Michael Bane

The need for high-performance computing grows hand-in-hand with the need for simulations and data analyses, ubiquitous across all domains of science, engineering, finance, and life sciences. In turn, large-scale computations and analyses have to be supported by efficient, scalable, and reliable algorithms and implementations that are able to exploit modern computer architectures. Ultimately, end users will face a range of algorithmic requirements regarding performance, accuracy, and energy consumption. These requirements may potentially span a range of architectures including CPUs, GPUs, and FPGAs, typically in a heterogeneous environment.

This topic provides a forum to discuss recent developments in the design and implementation of parallel numerical algorithms. The submissions address algorithmic design, performance analysis, and accuracy study, as well as integration of parallel numerical methods in real-world and industrial applications. This year, the topic received 12 submissions, which were carefully reviewed by the seven members of the topic Program Committee with the help of external reviewers. Each submission received four reviews which were then discussed among committee members. Ultimately, two papers were accepted.

We would like to sincerely thank all the authors for their submissions, the Euro-Par 2022 Organizing Committee for all their valuable help, and especially all the reviewers for their efforts. We feel that this topic and Euro-Par as a whole is an excellent forum to discuss parallel numerical methods and applications.

Contents

Compilers, Tools, and Environments

Performance and Power Modeling, Prediction and Evaluation

Scheduling and Load Balancing

Data Management, Analytics, and Machine Learning

Cluster and Cloud Computing

Theory and Algorithms for Parallel and Distributed Processing

Compilers, Tools and Environments

CrossDBT: An LLVM-Based User-Level Dynamic Binary Translation Emulator

Wei Li, Xiaohui Luo, Yiran Zhang, Qingkai Meng, and Fengyuan Ren(✉)

Beijing National Research Center for Information Science and Technology (BNRist), Tsinghua University, Beijing, China
renfy@tsinghua.edu.cn

Abstract. Emulation of Instruction Set Architecture (ISA) is necessary for a wide variety of use cases, such as providing the compatibility to execute programs compiled for a different ISA. This issue is usually solved using Dynamic Binary Translation (DBT), where guest machine code is translated to host ISA on runtime and Just-in-time (JIT) compilation is performed to achieve high-performance emulation. QEMU, a famous emulator, is developed to solve this issue, where Tiny Code Generator (TCG) is constructed to translate guest binary code to TCG Intermediate Representation (IR), and then generate target ISA machine code from TCG IR. Due to the limitations of TCG, some extensions, such as HQEMU, use LLVM as the backend to optimize programs and generate high-performance machine code. However, HQEMU is limited by its underlying implementation. That is, HQEMU still translates guest binary code to TCG IR at first. In this paper, we develop a novel, LLVM-based emulator, where guest machine code is directly lifted to LLVM IR to reduce the extra overhead and produce high-quality machine code. We evaluate our DBT emulator using BYTEmark benchmark and demonstrating its ability to outperform the de facto standard QEMU DBT system. The evaluation results confirm that our emulator delivers an average speedup of 3.3x over QEMU across BYTEmark benchmark compiled for x86-64 running on an ARMv8 platform, meanwhile, demonstrate that our user-level DBT emulator can significantly reduce the overhead to run a program on a cross-ISA system.

Keywords: Dynamic binary translation · Optimization · LLVM

1 Introduction

Over the past several decades, many popular ISAs have been created and the CPU diversity in high performance computing has been increasing, for example, PowerPC, x86, ARM and RISC-V. How to run programs compiled for one ISA, especially closed-source programs, on another ISA platform is a technical issue. User-level DBT is widely used to run Linux/BSD programs compiled for one architecture on another target architecture and plays a prominent role in the transition of ISA. Motivated by the need for ISA transition, a great amount

J. Cano and P. W. Trinder (Eds.): Euro-Par 2022, LNCS 13440, pp. 3–18, 2022.
https://doi.org/10.1007/978-3-031-12597-3_1

of work focus on constructing a user-level/system-level DBT emulator such as QEMU [3]. Apple develops Rosetta based on QuickTransit for PowerPC to x86 and Rosetta2 for x86-64 to ARM64. Intel also releases IA-32 execution layer to improve the performance of 32-bit applications running on IA-64 systems. The DBT emulator is also convenient for users to emulate some architectures which they cannot access currently, especially as new features come into these architectures which are not widely available for physical use yet, for example, ARM releases an emulator for users to access SVE feature. A DBT system for user-programs like QEMU works as follows: for initialization, the guest code is mapped into the address space of the emulator and the virtual CPU state is initialized. For translation, the guest code is divided and decoded to many instruction basic blocks, lifting to a low-level IR. Code optimization can be applied on IR and we compile IR to host architecture machine code, which will be cached for performing JIT. Due to the limitation of TCG IR, QEMU utilizes few optimizations and lacks the support of modern SIMD instructions (e.g. AVX, AVX2, AVX512), resulting in the inefficiency of the generated code.

LLVM [19] is a compiler framework that can optimize programs during their whole lifetime, including compile-time, link-time and run-time, where many pass managers and JIT compilers are provided for optimization.

In this work, we present CrossDBT, our novel user-level DBT emulator, which splits the whole process into two stages: the offline stage and the online stage to overcome these issues. In the offline stage, architecture instructions are realized by C++ functions and CrossDBT uses Clang to compile C++ functions to LLVM IR functions. In the online stage, CrossDBT analyzes binary code by an interpreter and divides guest instructions into basic blocks. With LLVM IR functions from the offline stage, guest instructions are mapped into LLVM IR. CrossDBT utilizes LLVM as a backend to optimize LLVM IR, generate high-quality host machine code, and run the code by LLVM JIT.

We evaluate CrossDBT using an x86-64 guest model and a 64-bit ARMv8 host model and implement a DBT emulator outperforming QEMU by an average speedup of 3.3x in BYTEmark benchmark.

Our main contributions are the following:

- We propose an efficient LLVM-based user-level DBT framework called CrossDBT, where guest machine code is directly lifted to LLVM IR in order to avoid the extra overhead and loss of local information caused by translating guest machine code to TCG IR at first.
- We design a two-stage process: offline stage and online stage in a DBT to reduce the cost of compilation while maintaining code quality.
- We build an x86-64-to-ARMv8 user-level DBT emulator to demonstrate the performance of CrossDBT. The x86-64-to-ARMv8 CrossDBT emulator is 3.3 times faster than QEMU in BYTEmark benchmark on average.

This paper is structured as follows: Sect. 2 introduces related works. Section 3 illustrates the CrossDBT architecture in details including the two stages. Section 4 presents the performance evaluation. Finally, we summarize our findings in Sect. 5.

2 Related Work

DBT [24] is a compilation technique to support the execution of binary code for a guest ISA on a host ISA. When the guest ISA and the host ISA are the same, we call it as a same-ISA translator. A general purpose of the same-ISA translator is to instrument binary code, which is referred as dynamic binary instrumentation (DBI). When the guest ISA and the host ISA are different, we call it as a cross-ISA emulator. There are two types of the cross-ISA emulator: system-level DBT emulator running operating systems for any machine and user-level DBT emulator running programs on any supported architecture (on the same OS).

Dynamic Binary Instrumentation. Valgrind [22] lifts code with superblock granularity to VEX IR, where optimizations and modifications can be performed. The instrumenter runs in the same address space as the instrumented program. Dynamo [1] is a software dynamic optimization system that is capable of improving the performance of an instruction stream. DynamoRIO [5,6] allows for heavy-weight transformations and represents programs' code in a low-level, architecture-dependent IR with no optimizations applied. Pin [20] allows inserting calls to functions in the instrumenting tool at any point in the program. DBILL [21] first lifts the machine code to TCG, and then uses LLVM as backend to conduct optimizations. Instrew [14] overcomes the limitations of TCG through directly lifting machine code to LLVM IR overcoming the limitations of TCG IR.

System-Level DBT Emulator. QEMU [3], as a de facto industry standard, is a typical system-level emulator. QEMU is composed of several subsystems: CPU emulator (with software memory management unit), emulated devices, generic devices, machine descriptions, debugger and user interface. For the translation of machine code, QEMU lifts machine code to TCG IR with basic block granularity and then can be compiled to target architecture machine code. For complex instructions like SIMD instruction, QEMU uses helper C function to emulate. Embra [30] is a machine simulator for the processors, caches, and memory systems of uniprocessors and cache-coherent multiprocessors. Transmeta CMS [11] is a system-level implementation of x86 architecture comprising a native VLIW microprocessor with aggressive speculation, hardware support and adaptive recompilation. MagiXen [7] is a prototype implementation of a Xen [2] virtual machine monitor with an integrated binary translation that can run IA-32 virtual machines on Itanium platforms. PQEMU [12], an extension of QEMU, tries to support multi-processor emulations to effectively utilize the underlying parallelism presented by multi-core processors. HyperMAMBO-X64 [10] runs the translator as a user program under the hypervisor and works with complete transparency with regard to the virtualized system. Captive (2016) [27] exploits existing hardware virtualization technology for improving the performance of full-system cross-ISA emulation. Captive [28] performs DBT within the generated JIT compiler in a virtual bare-metal environment provided by a KVM [17] hypervisor, which enables us to realize the system-related and system-privileged features not accessible to other DBT systems operating as user processes.

User-Level DBT Emulator. QuickTransit[18] allows software compiled for one specific processor and operating system combination to be executed on a different processor and/or operating system architecture without source code or binary changes. Harmonia [23], an ARM-to-IA DBT tool, is based on open-source QEMU utilizing register mapping and condition-code optimization. ISAMAP [26] is a flexible instruction mapping driven by DBT, whose mapping mechanism providing a fast translation between ISAs under an easy-to-use description. Walkabout [9] develops DBT techniques based on retargetability, separation of machine-dependent from machine-independent concerns and JIT compilation. Walkabout is a framework for experimenting with DBT, as well as other techniques such as interpreters, DBI tools and optimization. Yirr-Ma [29] is an extension to a generated Walkabout machine emulator. Yirr-Ma is used to experiment with two different DBT techniques: (1) translates hot source machine traces using dynamic partial inlining of interpretation functions, (2) translates hot source machine traces by JIT compiling an IR of the trace's dynamic operational semantics. LLVM QEMU [8] addresses the limitation of TCG IR. The guest machine code is first lifted to micro-operations, which are compiled to LLVM IR. Then LLVM QEMU utilizes LLVM backend to optimize IR and generate host machine code. HQEMU [16] solves the performance problem of QEMU by using a hybrid approach where only performance-sensitive sections are optimized using LLVM. LnQ [16] achieves the performance improvement by directly lifting machine code to LLVM IR and applying the chaining optimization such as caches for predicting indirect jump and function returns. Due to the limitations of TCG, HQEMU is not possible to further increase translation granularity to allow more complex control flows and exploits more semantic information for optimization. [13] implements a novel approach that adapts the Instrew/Rellume [14] framework which directly lifts machine code to LLVM IR with function-level granularity.

Summary. Many approaches are based on QEMU's DBT [8,15,16] and other binary translation systems [4,25] use LLVM as the backend to generate host machine code from scratch. We further discuss these emulators and compare them with our work. LLVM QEMU [8] lifts machine code to micro operations of TCG IR at first. Each micro operation is implemented by C and compiled into LLVM IR, which is used to generate host machine code by LLVM backend. HQEMU [15] uses a hybrid approach where the entire code is also first translated using TCG and only performance-sensitive sections are then optimized using LLVM. LnQ [16] achieves performance improvements over QEMU by lifting guest code to LLVM IR. But they still have some limitations. As the machine code is lifted first to TCG IR, LLVM QEMU and HQEMU suffer from two problems: (1) TCG IR loses the local context information of the original code, which can be used for LLVM to optimize code, (2) The performance improvements are provided by LLVM and using TCG IR only costs more time with no benefit. LnQ, which is an extension of QEMU, faces another problem that QEMU focuses more on compatibility not performance and then doesn't utilize many specific optimizations for user-level DBT emulator. Table 1 describes the differences between CrossDBT and related work, clearly shows the novel features of CrossDBT.

Table 1. The comparison between CrossDBT and related works

Tool	Frontend	Backend	Translation Path	Main Contributions
QEMU	TCG	TCG	Guest code→TCG IR→ Host code	System-level emulation
LLVM QEMU	TCG	LLVM	Guest code→TCG IR→ LLVM IR→Host code	Lifting TCG IR to LLVM IR
HQEMU	TCG	LLVM	Guest code→TCG IR→ LLVM IR→Host code	Optimizing hot-spot sections
LnQ	TCG	LLVM	Guest code→LLVM IR→ Host code	Lifting binary code to LLVM IR
CrossDBT	Interpreter	LLVM	Guest code→LLVM IR→ Host code	Two-stage translation

3 DBT Emulator

3.1 Overview

In this section, we describe the main concepts of CrossDBT, which are composed of two main stages as shown in Fig. 1: offline stage and online stage.

In offline stage, we implement the instructions of the target architecture by C++ functions and then compile them to LLVM IR, which is discussed in Sect. 3.2. The instructions are described in LLVM IR files for mapping in the runtime. The online stage is discussed in Sect. 3.3. The DBT system itself runs in host system as a process holding the heap and stack memory for the guest application. The purpose to separate the DBT system into the offline stage and online stage is for hiding the overhead of translating C++ functions to LLVM IR and utilizing optimization. In online stage, CrossDBT only needs to load the LLVM IR files produced on the offline stage. We use an x86-64-to-ARMv8 user-level emulator as an example to explain our CrossDBT framework in this section. It is not difficult to port it to a new ISA. What we should do is to emulate the instructions according to the manual of the new ISA without the support of the vendors.

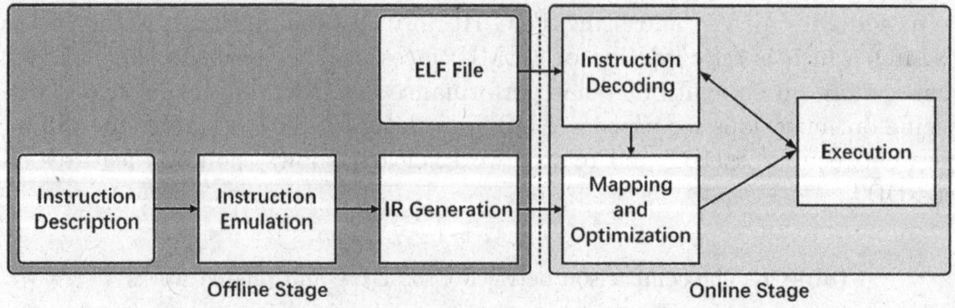

Fig. 1. Overview of CrossDBT.

3.2 Offline Stage

ISA Description. To support a new ISA in CrossDBT, we first have to acknowledge the ISA description according to the ISA developer's manual such as Intel 64 and IA-32 architectures software developer's manual for x86-64. A classical ISA includes these features:

- instruction types: data handling and memory operations, arithmetic and logic operations, control flow operations, coprocessor instructions, complex instructions (e.g. floating-point arithmetic operations, atomic instructions and single instruction multiple data (SIMD) instructions).
- instruction encoding: opcode formats, number and type of operands, immediate value formats, operand addressing.
- instruction length: fixed length, variable length.
- register pressure: the availability of free registers at any point in time during the program execution.
- register type: general-purpose registers, special registers (e.g. segment registers and EFLAGS registers in x86-64).

We should consider these features when designing the vCPU structure, which includes general-purpose registers, extend control registers, system registers, model-specific registers, SIMD registers and x87 registers for x86-64 ISA.

Instruction Emulation. We use the high-level programming language C++ to define instruction syntax and semantics. The instruction function is identified by opcode, operand type and size. For simple instructions, we implement them as shown in Fig. 2. For complex instructions, we design specific approach for each type of complex instruction. For example, we utilize the interface provided by LLVM to construct our atomic instructions. LLVM provides a uniformed interface to realize atomic instructions for different ISA such as __atomic_fetch_add and __atomic_add_fetch. SIMD and floating-point instructions, system calls are discussed in Sect. 3.4 and Sect. 3.5.

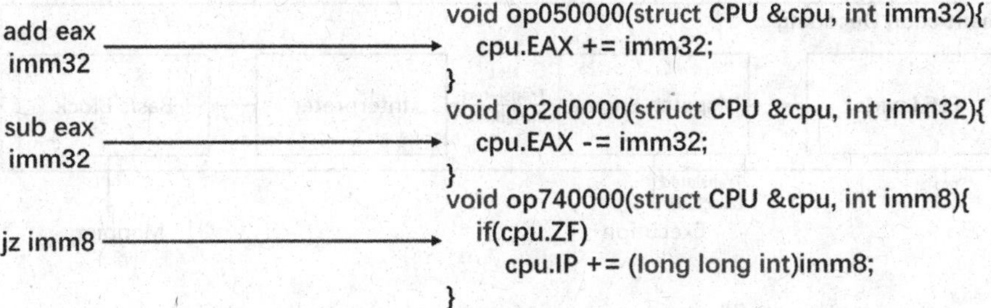

Fig. 2. The C++ functions for emulating instructions.

```
void op2d0000(struct CPU &cpu, int imm32) {
  cpu.EAX -= imm32;
}
                    ↓
define dso_local void @_Z4op2d0000R3CPUi
(%struct.CPU* nonnull align 8 dereferenceable(16) %0, i32 %1) #0 {
  %3 = alloca %struct.CPU*, align 8;                    %4 = alloca i32, align 4;
  store %struct.CPU* %0, %struct.CPU** %3, align 8;
  store i32 %1, i32* %4, align 4;                       %5 = load i32, i32* %4, align 4;
  %6 = load %struct.CPU*, %struct.CPU** %3, align 8;
  %7 = getelementptr inbounds %struct.CPU, %struct.CPU* %6, i32 0, i32 1
  %8 = load i32, i32* %7, align 8;                      %9 = sub nsw i32 %8, %5;
  store i32 %9, i32* %7, align 8;                       ret void;
}
```

Fig. 3. The LLVM IR function compiled from the C++ function.

IR Generation. In order to get LLVM IR functions, we use Clang to compile these instruction C++ functions to LLVM IR functions stored in LLVM IR files. The LLVM IR functions are named, which can be loaded by name in online stage.. Figure 3 shows that a C++ function is compiled to a corresponding LLVM IR function. Due to the implementation of C++ static polymorphism, the name of the LLVM IR function is not the same as the name of C++ function. Thus, an instruction description table is needed, where CrossDBT can get the LLVM IR function of any instruction.

3.3 Online Stage

The online stage of CrossDBT involves the analysis and running of the guest application and is composed of three main phases: Instruction Decoding (ELF Loader, Dispatch Engine, Interpreter), Mapping and Optimization, Execution as shown in Fig. 4.

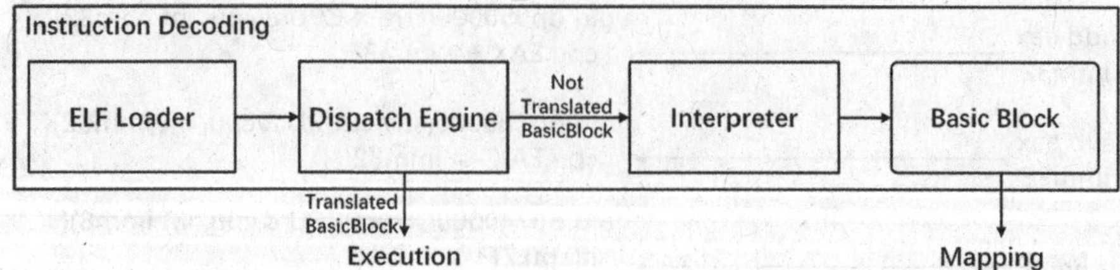

Fig. 4. The architecture of instruction decoding phase.

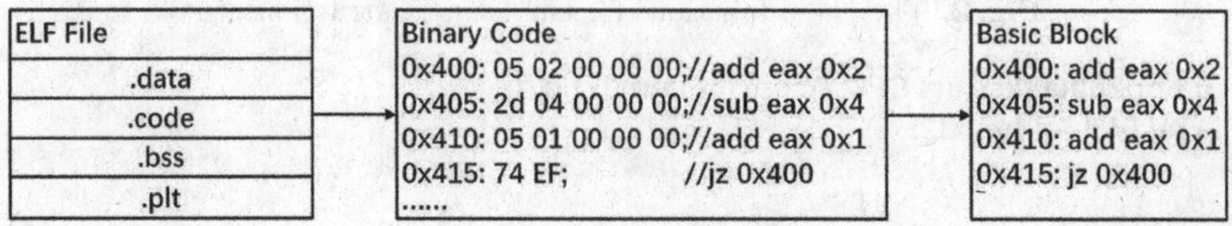

Fig. 5. Instruction decoding phase analyzes ELF files and decodes instructions.

Instruction Decoding. The first phase in online stage is instruction decoding, which is composed of ELF Loader, Dispatch Engine, Interpreter as shown in Fig. 4. ELF Loader loads ELF files and extracts useful information like code segment, data segment, the relocation table. After loading files, CrossDBT uses dispatch engine to check whether this basic block of instructions has been cached, where basic block is identified by the Program Counter (PC) of the first instruction. If the basic block is cached, the next phase is the execution phase. If not, CrossDBT decodes instruction by the interpreter and the next phase is mapping phase. The interpreter analyzes binary code according to ISA developers' manual. As a user-level emulator, CrossDBT only focuses on the emulation of normal operations and ignores the privilege instructions, I/O operations. Figure 5 gives an example to show how instruction decoding works.

Mapping and Optimization. During the mapping and optimization phase, CrossDBT creates an empty LLVM IR function representing a basic block. For each decoded function in the basic block, CrossDBT puts the corresponding LLVM IR function (which was produced in the offline stage) in it. We should optimize the LLVM IR function to generate high performance host machine code. LLVM provides various kinds of LLVM IR pass manager for optimization such as function inlining pass, instruction combining pass, loop vectorize pass. In Fig. 6, we give an example to show the pipeline mapping the instructions in a basic block to LLVM IR functions and optimizing LLVM IR functions by LLVM pass managers.

Execution. There are two situations that CrossDBT gets into the execution phase. The first situation is that CrossDBT tries to generate host machine code

```
Basic Block
0x400: add eax 0x2
0x405: sub eax 0x4
0x410: add eax 0x1
0x415: jz 0x400
```

```
LLVM IR function
define void @PC_0x400(ptr %0) {
BasicBlock:
  call void @_Z4op050000R3CPURi(ptr %0, i32 2);
  call void @_Z4op2d0000R3CPURi(ptr %0, i32 4)
  call void @_Z4op050000R3CPURi(ptr %0, i32 1);
  call void @_Z4op740000R3CPURi(ptr %0, i32 -17)
  ret void
}
```

```
Optimized LLVM IR function
define void @PC_0x400(ptr %0) local_unnamed_addr {
BasicBlock:
  %1 = getelementptr inbounds %struct.CPU, ptr %0, i64 0, i32 1
  %2 = load i32, i32* %1, align 8
  %3 = add nsw i32 %2, -1
  store i32 %3, i32* %1, align 8
  %4 = getelementptr inbounds %struct.CPU, ptr %0, i64 0, i32 2
  %5 = load i8, i8* %4, align 4
  %6 = and i8 %5, 1
  %.not.i = icmp eq i8 %6, 0
  br i1 %.not.i, label %_Z4op74R3CPUi.exit, label %7
7:                                        ; preds = %BasicBlock
  %8 = getelementptr inbounds %struct.CPU, ptr %0, i64 0, i32 0
  %9 = load i64, i64* %8, align 8
  %10 = add nsw i64 %9, -17
  store i64 %10, i64* %8, align 8
  br label %_Z4op74R3CPUi.exit
_Z4op74R3CPUi.exit:                       ; preds = %BasicBlock, %7
  ret void
}
```

Fig. 6. Mapping and optimization phase generates LLVM IR from instructions.

```
.text                        .globl PC_0x400              .p2align 2
.type PC_0x400,@function     .globl PC_0x400
PC_0x400:
.cfi_startproc               ldr  w8, [x0, #8]            ldrb w9, [x0, #12]
sub w8, w8, #1               str  w8, [x0, #8]            tbz w9, #0, .LBB0_2
ldr x8, [x0]                 sub x8, x8, #17              str x8, [x0]
.LBB0_2:
ret
.Lfunc_end0:
.size PC_0x400,              .Lfunc_end0-PC_0x400         .cfi_endproc
```

Fig. 7. The generated host machine code from LLVM IR in Fig. 6.

by LLVM backend after finishing mapping phase. CrossDBT passes the LLVM IR function to LLVM JIT for code generation and code cache, notifies dispatch engine that this basic block has been cached now. The next time coping with this basic block, CrossDBT does not need to translate it again. The second case is that CrossDBT tries to run the host machine code by the LLVM JIT for the basic block cached. For this case, we don't have to utilize extra operations. Figure 7 shows an example of the generated host machine code.

LLVM has several JIT methods for users: JIT, MCJIT, ORCJIT. ORCJIT is the newest JIT method provided by LLVM, which has many new technical features such as JIT-linking, LLVM IR compilation, eager and lazy compilation, concurrent JIT'd code and concurrent compilation. These features provide more flexibility to organize the ORC layers to achieve better performance. Thus, the JIT in CrossDBT is built by LLVM ORCJIT.

3.4 SIMD and Floating Point

SIMD instructions are widely used to process 3D graphics, although modern graphics cards with embedded SIMD have largely taken over this task from the CPU. Some systems also include permute functions that re-pack elements inside vectors, making them particularly useful for data processing and compression. They are also used in cryptography. The trend of general-purpose computing on GPUs may lead to wider use of SIMD in the future. Even some glibc functions (e.g. memcpy) use SSE instructions as default in x86-64 architecture. QEMU 6.0.0 supports MMX, SSE, SSE2, SSE3, SSSE3, SSE4 instruction sets by using helper functions to emulate. Due to the limitation of helper functions, QEMU cannot utilize the hardware to accelerate SIMD instruction. CrossDBT also implements MMX, SSE, SSE2, SSE3, SSSE3, SSE4 instructions by emulation. However, with the optimization of LLVM backend, CrossDBT makes use of the hardware for SIMD instruction to a certain degree.

x87 is a floating-point-related subset of x86 ISA. It originated as an extension of the 8086 instruction set in the form of optional floating-point coprocessors that worked in tandem with corresponding x86 CPUs. Most x86 processors since the Intel 80486 have had these x87 instructions implemented in the main CPU, but the term is sometimes still used due to the feature of providing 80-bit floating-point number or the compatibility for 32-bit application. Modern processors have SSE/AVX instruction set extension providing floating-point instructions which operate on a new independent registers, the XMM and YMM registers. CrossDBT supports the floating-point operations supplied by x87 and SSE instructions. There are notable differences in the method that floating-point flags, NaNs, rounding modes and infinities are handled in specific architecture. This incompatibility between floating point needs to be considered in some cases. CrossDBT ensures that the guest vCPU state is accurate with how the guest machine would normally operate. For example, a precision mismatch is handled by utilizing software floating-point library such as 128-bit floating-point number provided by compiler. Another example is about rounding modes that Fused Multiply Add (FMA) instructions calculate $a * b + c$ with only once intermediate value rounding while using normal arithmetic operations would operate twice intermediate value rounding.

3.5 System Call

A system call is the programmatic way in which a computer program requests a service from the kernel of the operating system on which it is executed. System calls provide an essential interface between a process and the operating system. Implementing system calls requires a transfer of control from user space to kernel space, which involves some sort of architecture-specific feature. Thus, system calls are different for x86-64 and ARMv8 architecture. CrossDBT needs an immediate layer to translate system call and only deals with the situation that guest and host both use the Linux OS. There are three cases about how to translate a system call.

Directly Use Host System Call. The most part of system calls have the same interface and the same semantics such as read and write. CrossDBT can get the arguments from the guest registers and directly invoke the host system call to achieve the goal.

Emulate by Host System Call. For some system calls, they have different interface between x86-64 and ARMv8 such as stat, for which we should prepare the arguments to call the host system call. For system calls having special features such as clone, we need to pay more effort. CrossDBT uses fork to create a new process and sets thread local storage, child tid, parent tid, child stack of the child process. For creating a new thread, CrossDBT utilizes pthread libs to construct a new thread and sets the necessary data of the thread, where a new translation main loop is established to continue the translation. When the task of thread or process is finished, CrossDBT uses exit syscall to close and sets child_tidptr to zero if needed.

Linux vDSO and Vsyscall. The vsyscall and vDSO (virtual Dynamic Shared Object) are two mechanisms used to accelerate certain system calls in Linux. The vsyscall is added as a way to execute specific system calls which do not need any real level of privilege to run in order to reduce the system call overhead. The kernel maps into user space a page containing the fast implementation of some system calls. However, this vsyscall mechanism has some limitations: the memory allocated is small and allows only 4 system calls, and, more important and serious, the vsyscall page is statically allocated to the same address in each process, which causes a security problem. Then the vDSO offers the same functionality as the vsyscall, while overcoming its limitations. The vDSO is a memory area allocated in user space which exposes some kernel functionalities at user space in a safe manner. For Linux kernel, if vDSO is not supported, kernel falls back to the traditional system calls, which means

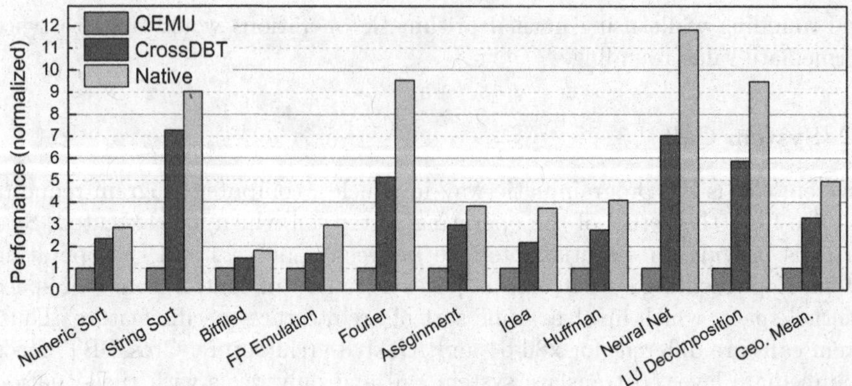

Fig. 8. Performance of QEMU, CrossDBT and Native on BYTEmark (higher is better).

we don't need to do anything. For glibc functions like gettimeofday, if vDSO is not supported, these functions try to use vsyscall in x86-64, which we need to cope with. The vsyscall always maps system calls into process space from 0xFFFFFFFFFF600000 to 0xFFFFFFFFFF600C00, where the gettimeofday, time, getcpu system calls locate. They are emulated by the corresponding host system calls in CrossDBT.

4 Experiment Results

To evaluate the performance of CrossDBT, we apply it on the BYTEmark benchmark, which is designed to expose the capabilities of a system's CPU, FPU, and memory system and also used to for the evaluation of similar systems [3]. We use x86-64 as guest architecture and ARMv8 as host architecture. The performance of CrossDBT is compared against a native compilation for ARMv8 as well as against QEMU 4.2.0.

4.1 Setup

We conduct the following experiments in a single thread mode. Our ARMv8 target platform is based on Kunpeng 920-4826 CPUs, 64 KB L1 instruction cache, 64 KB L1 data cache, 512 KB L2 cache, 48 MB L3 cache, 2.6 GHz frequency and 192 GB memory, running Ubuntu Linux 18.04 with Linux Kernel 5.0.0-23. The native code is compiled with Clang+LLVM 11.0.0 and –O3.

4.2 Results

We first compare the running performance of QEMU, CrossDBT and native ARMv8. The result is shown in Fig. 8. The performance ranges from 1.46X to 7.26X, and CrossDBT is 3.3 times faster than QEMU on a geometric average of BYTEmark benchmark.

On the one hand, the improvement is significant in benchmarks that have heavy floating-point operations such as String Sort, Fourier, Neural Net and LU Decomposition. On the other hand, CrossDBT doesn't reach high improvement on the benchmarks that have few floating-point operations.

The main reason of this improvement is the insufficient translation ability of QEMU. TCG, the compiler of QEMU's DBT, doesn't support floating-point operations or SIMD instructions and translates them into helper function calls, which causes huge performance loss. Thus, CrossDBT gains much performance improvement than QEMU on floating-point-intensive benchmark because CrossDBT utilizes LLVM backend to generate high quality code and make use of the host hardware to accelerate SIMD instructions and floating-point operations.

Comparing CrossDBT with the native ARMv8, the extra overhead ranges 18.2% to 46.1% and 33.1% on geometric average. Coincidentally, the largest gap is also happening on floating-point-intensive benchmark. This phenomenon indicates that we need pay more effort on how to translate floating-point operations and SIMD instructions better.

5 Conclusion

In this article, we developed a novel user-level DBT emulator, CrossDBT, that directly lifts guest machine code to LLVM IR and utilizes LLVM backend to optimize and generate target host machine code. CrossDBT is composed of two stages: offline stage, where we implement guest instructions by C++ functions and compile them into LLVM IR, and online stage, where we lift binary code to LLVM IR and generate host machine code.

We demonstrate the performance of CrossDBT by using an x86-64 guest running normal environment on ARMv8 host, where CrossDBT outperforms the widely used QEMU across BYTEmark benchmark with on average 3.3 times.

Acknowledgments. The authors gratefully acknowledge the anonymous reviewers for their constructive comments. This work is supported in part by the National Key Research and Development Program of China (No.2018YFB1700203), and by National Natural Science Foundation of China (NSFC) under Grant No. 62132007 as well as gifts from Huawei.

References

1. Bala, V., Duesterwald, E., Banerjia, S.: Dynamo: a transparent dynamic optimization system. SIGPLAN Not. **35**(5), 1–12 (2000). https://doi.org/10.1145/358438.349303

2. Barham, P., et al.: Xen and the art of virtualization. In: Proceedings of the Nineteenth ACM Symposium on Operating Systems Principles, SOSP 2003, pp. 164–177. Association for Computing Machinery, New York (2003). https://doi.org/10.1145/945445.945462
3. Bellard, F.: QEMU, a fast and portable dynamic translator. In: 2005 USENIX Annual Technical Conference (USENIX ATC 2005), Anaheim, CA. USENIX Association, April 2005
4. Brandner, F., Fellnhofer, A., Krall, A., Riegler, D.: Fast and accurate simulation using the LLVM compiler framework. In: Proceedings of the 1st Workshop on Rapid Simulation and Performance Evaluation: Methods and Tools, RAPIDO, vol. 9, pp. 1–6 (2009)
5. Bruening, D., Amarasinghe, S.: Efficient, transparent, and comprehensive runtime code manipulation. Ph.D. thesis, Massachusetts Institute of Technology, Department of Electrical Engineering and Computer Science (2004)
6. Bruening, D., Garnett, T., Amarasinghe, S.: An infrastructure for adaptive dynamic optimization. In: Proceedings of the International Symposium on Code Generation and Optimization: Feedback-Directed and Runtime Optimization, CGO 2003, pp. 265–275. IEEE Computer Society, USA (2003). https://doi.org/10.5555/776261.776290
7. Chapman, M., Magenheimer, D.J., Ranganathan, P.: Magixen: combining binary translation and virtualization. HP Enterprise Systems and Software Laboratory, pp. 1–15 (2007)
8. Chipounov, V., Candea, G.: Dynamically translating x86 to LLVM using QEMU. Technical report, EPFL (2010)
9. Cifuentes, C., Lewis, B., Ung, D.: Walkabout-a retargetable dynamic binary translation framework. In: Workshop on Binary Translation, pp. 22–25 (2002)
10. d'Antras, A., Gorgovan, C., Garside, J., Goodacre, J., Luján, M.: Hypermambo-x64: using virtualization to support high-performance transparent binary translation. In: Proceedings of the 13th ACM SIGPLAN/SIGOPS International Conference on Virtual Execution Environments, VEE 2017, pp. 228–241. Association for Computing Machinery, New York (2017). https://doi.org/10.1145/3050748.3050756
11. Dehnert, J.C., et al.: The transmeta code morphing^{TM} software: using speculation, recovery, and adaptive retranslation to address real-life challenges. In: Proceedings of the International Symposium on Code Generation and Optimization: Feedback-Directed and Runtime Optimization, CGO 2003, pp. 15–24. IEEE Computer Society, USA (2003). https://doi.org/10.5555/776261.776263
12. Ding, J.H., Chang, P.C., Hsu, W.C., Chung, Y.C.: PQEMU: a parallel system emulator based on QEMU. In: 2011 IEEE 17th International Conference on Parallel and Distributed Systems, pp. 276–283 (2011). https://doi.org/10.1109/ICPADS.2011.102
13. Engelke, A., Okwieka, D., Schulz, M.: Efficient LLVM-based dynamic binary translation. In: Proceedings of the 17th ACM SIGPLAN/SIGOPS International Conference on Virtual Execution Environments, VEE 2021, pp. 165–171. Association for Computing Machinery, New York (2021). https://doi.org/10.1145/3453933.3454022
14. Engelke, A., Schulz, M.: Instrew: leveraging LLVM for high performance dynamic binary instrumentation. In: Proceedings of the 16th ACM SIGPLAN/SIGOPS International Conference on Virtual Execution Environments, VEE 2020, pp. 172–184. Association for Computing Machinery, New York (2020). https://doi.org/10.1145/3381052.3381319

15. Hong, D.Y., et al.: HQEMU: a multi-threaded and retargetable dynamic binary translator on multicores. In: Proceedings of the Tenth International Symposium on Code Generation and Optimization, CGO 2012, pp. 104–113. Association for Computing Machinery, New York (2012). https://doi.org/10.1145/2259016.2259030
16. Hsu, C.C., et al.: LNQ: building high performance dynamic binary translators with existing compiler backends. In: 2011 International Conference on Parallel Processing, pp. 226–234 (2011). https://doi.org/10.1109/ICPP.2011.57
17. Kivity, A., Kamay, Y., Laor, D., Lublin, U., Liguori, A.: KVM: the Linux virtual machine monitor. In: Proceedings of the Linux Symposium, Dttawa, Dntorio, Canada, vol. 1, pp. 225–230 (2007)
18. Knowles, P.: Transitive and quicktransit overview (2008). https://www.linux-kvm.org/images/9/98/KvmForum2008%24kdf2008_2.pdf
19. Lattner, C., Adve, V.: LLVM: a compilation framework for lifelong program analysis and transformation. In: Proceedings of the International Symposium on Code Generation and Optimization: Feedback-Directed and Runtime Optimization, CGO 2004, p. 75. IEEE Computer Society, USA (2004). https://doi.org/10.5555/977395.977673
20. Luk, C.K., et al.: Pin: building customized program analysis tools with dynamic instrumentation. In: Proceedings of the 2005 ACM SIGPLAN Conference on Programming Language Design and Implementation, PLDI 2005, pp. 190–200. Association for Computing Machinery, New York (2005). https://doi.org/10.1145/1065010.1065034
21. Lyu, Y.H., et al.: DBILL: an efficient and retargetable dynamic binary instrumentation framework using LLVM backend. In: Proceedings of the 10th ACM SIGPLAN/SIGOPS International Conference on Virtual Execution Environments, VEE 2014, pp. 141–152. Association for Computing Machinery, New York (2014). https://doi.org/10.1145/2576195.2576213
22. Nethercote, N., Seward, J.: Valgrind: a framework for heavyweight dynamic binary instrumentation. In: Proceedings of the 28th ACM SIGPLAN Conference on Programming Language Design and Implementation, PLDI 2007, pp. 89–100. Association for Computing Machinery, New York (2007). https://doi.org/10.1145/1250734.1250746
23. Ottoni, G., Hartin, T., Weaver, C., Brandt, J., Kuttanna, B., Wang, H.: Harmonia: a transparent, efficient, and harmonious dynamic binary translator targeting the intel® architecture. In: Proceedings of the 8th ACM International Conference on Computing Frontiers, CF 2011. Association for Computing Machinery, New York (2011). https://doi.org/10.1145/2016604.2016635
24. Probst, M.: Dynamic binary translation. In: UKUUG Linux Developer's Conference, vol. 2002 (2002)
25. Shigenobu, K., Ootsu, K., Ohkawa, T., Yokota, T.: A translation method of arm machine code to LLVM-IR for binary code parallelization and optimization. In: 2017 Fifth International Symposium on Computing and Networking (CANDAR), pp. 575–579 (2017). https://doi.org/10.1109/CANDAR.2017.75
26. Souza, M., Nicácio, D., Araújo, G.: ISAMAP: instruction mapping driven by dynamic binary translation. In: Varbanescu, A.L., Molnos, A., van Nieuwpoort, R. (eds.) ISCA 2010. LNCS, vol. 6161, pp. 117–138. Springer, Heidelberg (2011). https://doi.org/10.1007/978-3-642-24322-6_11
27. Spink, T., Wagstaff, H., Franke, B.: Hardware-accelerated cross-architecture full-system virtualization. ACM Trans. Archit. Code Optim. **13**(4), 1–25 (2016). https://doi.org/10.1145/2996798

28. Spink, T., Wagstaff, H., Franke, B.: A retargetable system-level DBT hypervisor. ACM Trans. Comput. Syst. **36**(4), 1–24 (2020). https://doi.org/10.1145/3386161
29. Tröger, J.: Specification-driven dynamic binary translation. Ph.D. thesis, Queensland University of Technology (2005)
30. Witchel, E., Rosenblum, M.: Embra: fast and flexible machine simulation. In: Proceedings of the 1996 ACM SIGMETRICS International Conference on Measurement and Modeling of Computer Systems, SIGMETRICS 1996, pp. 68–79. Association for Computing Machinery, New York (1996). https://doi.org/10.1145/233013.233025

MARTINI: The Little Match and Replace Tool for Automatic Application Rewriting with Code Examples

Alister Johnson[1(✉)], Camille Coti[2], Allen D. Malony[1], and Johannes Doerfert[3]

[1] University of Oregon, Eugene, OR, USA
{ajohnson,malony}@cs.uoregon.edu
[2] Université du Québec à Montréal, Montréal, QC, Canada
coti.camille@uqam.ca
[3] Argonne National Laboratory, Lemont, IL, USA
jdoerfert@anl.gov

Abstract. Rewriting code for cleanliness, API changes, and new programming models is a common, yet time-consuming task. Localized or syntax-based changes are often mechanical and can be automated with text-based rewriting tools, like `sed`. However, non-localized or semantic-based changes require specialized tools that usually come with complex, hard-coded rules that require expertise in compilers. This means techniques for source rewriting are either too simple for complex tasks or too complex to be customized by non-expert users; in either case, developers are often forced to manually update their code instead.

This work describes a new approach to code rewriting which exposes complex and semantic-driven rewrite capabilities to users in a simple and natural way. Rewrite rules are expressed as a pair of parameterized "before-and-after" source code snippets, one to describe what to match and one to describe what the replacement looks like. Through this novel and user-friendly interface, programmers can automate and customize complex code changes which require a deep understanding of the language without any knowledge of compiler internals.

As our prototype, MARTINI, is built on top of Clang, we can (conceptually) handle all Clang's input languages, including CUDA, SYCL, and many other C/C++-based interfaces, like Kokkos and OpenMP. To showcase usability, we implemented the `clang-tidy` rule "modernize-use-nullptr" and a simple instrumentation example. To further illustrate the potential of MARTINI, we reimplemented `HIPIFY`, which translates CUDA to HIP. Compared to `hipify-perl` and `hipify-clang` from `HIPIFY`, our version is easier to implement, more understandable, and customizable. The latter allows us to outperform `HIPIFY`-generated code by slightly modifying the translation rules of MARTINI-HIPIFY.

Keywords: refactoring · metaprogramming · AST matchers

A. Johnson—Work done while at Argonne National Laboratory.

J. Cano and P. W. Trinder (Eds.): Euro-Par 2022, LNCS 13440, pp. 19–34, 2022.
https://doi.org/10.1007/978-3-031-12597-3_2

1 Introduction

Rewriting and refactoring are common tasks that can take a great deal of time if performed by hand on a large code base. Some of these tasks are easily automated with existing text-based search-and-replace tools, like the GNU stream editor, `sed`, or C preprocessor macros. This is especially true if the rewrite is localized and does not require any semantic information that is not also present through syntax. However, once rewrites span code ranges or require semantic reasoning, text-based tooling is inadequate or requires complex implementations (for example, tracking balanced parentheses with extended regular expressions). Traditionally, this is where compiler-based tooling comes in [10]. The compiler's frontend has parsing and semantic analysis capabilities that allow more complete understanding of the source code and, consequently, semantic-based rewriting over most arbitrary code ranges. However, developing and customizing such tooling requires a deep understanding of the compiler and its rewriting infrastructure (if it has one), which restricts the developer pool drastically [7,17]. In the past, as long as the number of desired rewrites was small and customization was not required, hard-coded rules in a compiler-based rewriting tool were sufficient. Today, however, language standards are changing more rapidly and new parallel programming models are constantly being developed.

Programmers who wish to keep their applications up-to-date must use a streamlined refactoring process [19]. For instance, testing a new programming model is an intriguing and often difficult proposition; parts might be a simple matter of replacing one API with another, but most often complex changes have to be made as well, especially the new model has any kind of parallelism. Other rewriting tasks, such as adding instrumentation or error-checking asserts, are just as time-consuming and important. These changes often follow patterns, however, and if programmers are able to capture those patterns in some way, these tasks seem like they *should* be able to be automated.

The complexity of capturing these patterns in the form of rewrite rules or tasks is closely tied to the complexity of the semantic context necessary to

```
int* test() {
 int* a = 0;
 double b, *c;
 b = 0;
 c = 0;
 return 0;
}
```

(a) Example snippet in which the `0`-literal is used for pointer and non-pointer values.

```
int* test() {
 int* a = nullptr;
 double b, *c;
 b = 0;
 c = nullptr;
 return nullptr;
}
```

(b) The same snippet with the `0`-literal replaced by `nullptr` in all pointer contexts.

Fig. 1. Example to showcase the "modernize-use-nullptr" `clang-tidy` rewrite rule, which replaces `0`-literal pointers with `nullptr`. While the initialization of `a` can be reasonably found with text-based search-and-replace techniques, the other two replacements require non-local, semantic reasoning.

perform the transformation (e.g., nesting level of loops, lambda handling). A tool to automate code rewriting must have the ability to access and understand semantic context, allow the user to easily contribute semantic knowledge, and utilize both in code replacements.

As an example, consider the "simple" rewriting task done by the `clang-tidy` rule "modernize-use-nullptr"[1]. This rule replaces constants, like `NULL` and `0`, assigned to pointer variables with the C++11 `nullptr` keyword, which is both safer and more readable. Figure 1 illustrates the changes `clang-tidy` can perform. The first replacement, where `a` is initialized to `0`, could be done with a text-based tool, like `sed`, although constructing a generic regular expression to match arbitrary types and variable names could be tricky. However, the other two replacements, in the assignment to `c` and the return statement, are difficult if not impossible to handle without semantic context. The physical distance between the type of the variable and the `0`-literal can cross file boundaries, and most languages allow for various other complexities, like shadowing declarations with different types. This semantic context is out of reach for purely text-based search-and-replace tools.

Once a rewriting task reaches a complexity beyond the capabilities of search-and-replace tools, programmers are often left with no choice but to develop specialized modules in a compiler, where the semantic information needed is most readily available. The "modernize-use-nullptr" `clang-tidy` rule shown above is one of many such modules implemented using the Clang compiler's tooling infrastructure, which provides access to semantic information from the Clang AST. The code for this rule, though, is roughly 125 lines of complex C++ and Clang AST matchers (excluding comments and code to handle `NULL` macros) which require Clang AST specific knowledge. Other rewriting software (ref. Sect. 6) expects similar specialized knowledge, as it also directly operates on the AST.

For sophisticated code transformations, using a compiler front end is often the only solution. However, we believe that this does not preclude a user-friendly approach, since developers can often write *what* they want to happen, though maybe not *how* it should happen. To this end, we developed a system built on Clang and based on *semantic matching* and user-provided *code replacements* that is accessible to the average programmer. Similar to regular expressions, users can describe and customize code transformations naturally as "before-and-after" snippets of C++ code, which correspond to the two expressions used in search-and-replace schemes. The available context for searching and replacing is not restricted to syntax, though; it also contains semantic information extracted by a compiler. Our interface is designed to be intuitive for C++ developers by restricting its syntax to modern C++ and requiring no knowledge of compiler internals, unlike previous rewriting tools. It is also designed to give users a great deal of control over which changes are applied and where.

Continuing the above example, we can mimic most of the functionality of `clang-tidy`'s "modernize-use-nullptr" rule (except `NULL` macros) through the three code pairs shown in Fig. 2. On the left hand side are the "matchers" which describe what should be replaced, and on the right hand side are corresponding

[1] https://clang.llvm.org/extra/clang-tidy/checks/modernize-use-nullptr.html.

```
template <typename T>
[[clang::matcher("nullptr-decl")]]
auto null_match() {
  [[clang::matcher_block]]
  T* var = 0;
}
```

(a) Matcher for initializing a pointer-typed variable to a 0-literal.

```
template <typename T>
[[clang::replace("nullptr-decl")]]
auto null_replace() {
  [[clang::matcher_block]]
  T* var = nullptr;
}
```

(b) Replacement using `nullptr` for the matcher in Fig. 2a.

```
template <typename T>
[[clang::matcher("nullptr-asgn")]]
auto null2_match() {
  T* var = nullptr;
  [[clang::matcher_block]]
  var = 0;
}
```

(c) Matcher for a 0-literal assignment to a pointer-typed variable.

```
template <typename T>
[[clang::replace("nullptr-asgn")]]
auto null2_replace() {
  T* var = nullptr;
  [[clang::matcher_block]]
  var = nullptr;
}
```

(d) Replacement using `nullptr` for the matcher in Fig. 2c.

```
template <typename T>
[[clang::matcher("nullptr-ret")]]
T* null3_match() {
  [[clang::matcher_block]]
  return 0;
}
```

(e) Matcher for a pointer-typed return statement using a 0-literal.

```
template <typename T>
[[clang::replace("nullptr-ret")]]
T* null3_replace() {
  [[clang::matcher_block]]
  return nullptr;
}
```

(f) Replacement using a `nullptr` for the matcher in Fig. 2e.

Fig. 2. The three matcher-replacer pairs we used to mimic (most of) the functionality of clang-tidy's "modernize-use-nullptr" rule. Applied to Fig. 1a, the "modernized" version in Fig. 1b is produced. The variable name `var` is a parameter of the matcher block, and the original variable name in the matched program fragment (e.g., `a`, `b`, and `c` in Fig. 1) is bound to it for use in the replacement. While our matchers are by default type-agnostic, and hence fully polymorphic, we enable type-based reasoning for template type parameters, here `T`. As a result, the matchers on the left are restricted to pointer-typed values.

"replacers" which contain the desired code with references back to the matched input. This example demonstrates how our approach provides semantic context for code rewriting and allows the average programmer to automate more complex rewriting tasks.

The main contributions of our work are:

- MARTINI, the Little Match and Replace Tool, an open-source[2], extensible code rewriting tool built on top of Clang's tooling infrastructure.
- A C++ user interface, similar to an embedded DSL, that is both user-friendly *and* customizable, unlike many previous similar tools.

[2] https://github.com/ajohnson-uoregon/llvm-project/tree/feature-ajohnson/clang-tools-extra/clang-rewrite.

- A prototype alternative to the `HIPIFY` tool [11], which rewrites CUDA into HIP, that is both easier to understand and customizable by the user.
- Further examples that showcase the versatility of MARTINI: custom `clang-tidy`-like rewrite rules that do not require Clang AST knowledge, and instrumentation code placement in 20 lines of code.

Known limitations of our prototype implementation include:

- The inability to describe generic type matching rules; our prototype generally ignores types, which makes it fully polymorphic, however we honor certain type constraints (e.g., is a pointer type) for template type parameters.
- The inability to declare optional expressions; for our case study we automatically generated matcher and replacer pairs with varying argument counts.
- No support for matching function, class, or struct declarations.
- Very limited support for matching sequences of statements.

The rest of this paper is organized as follows. In Sect. 2 the design and implementation of MARTINI are described. The instrumentation example follows in Sect. 3 before we discuss our HIPIFY clone in Sect. 4 with an evaluation in Sect. 5. The discussion of future work in Sect. 7 follows the comparison to related work in Sect. 6. Section 8 concludes.

2 Design and Implementation

We present MARTINI, a source-to-source transformation tool implemented using Clang's front end tooling infrastructure. To specify code modifications, users provide two sets of C++ functions containing parameterized code snippets: *matchers* and *replacers* (or *transformations*, which are a special form of replacer, though we use the two terms interchangeably). Matchers describe which code snippets to modify, and are distinct from Clang's *AST* matchers. We will always refer to the latter as AST matchers in this work to avoid ambiguity. Replacers (and transformations) describe how matched code should be rewritten. Figure 3 illustrates the workflow of MARTINI. Our contributions, which include the AST matcher generator, the replacer transform generator, and code rewriting functionality, are highlighted through bold green outlines. We reused Clang's AST generation and AST matcher utilities, as well as some rewriting functionality. The user provides the program source to be rewritten as well as the matchers and replacers. The latter is shown as separate files but one file can contain any number of matchers and replacers.

To declare matchers and replacers, we introduce the C++ attributes described in Fig. 4 to Clang. Through the use of native C++ to embed control annotations, we can work with an otherwise unmodified Clang. Similarly, users can verify the validity of their snippets through existing source code verification in the Clang front end (e.g., via `clang++ -cc1 -verify`). This is important as we expect the user-given code to be valid in its respective language, e.g., CUDA, since a Clang AST can only be generated for such inputs.

Our AST matcher generator, shown in Fig. 3, "compiles" the statements in the matcher block (ref. [[clang::matcher_block]] in Fig. 4) of functions annotated as matchers (ref. [[clang::matcher("...")]] in Fig. 4) into a Clang AST matcher. These AST matchers will match source code that has the same semantic structure as the input code snippet, regardless of syntactic differences. Consequently, potential hazards like arbitrarily complex sub-expressions, line breaks and spacing, and inline comments, are automatically dealt with. Matchers are by default parametric, but can also look for literal names (through the hasName() AST matcher). Parameters are bound (via the bind() AST matcher) to the source code they match.

To turn a code snippet into an AST matcher, the snippet's AST is traversed and converted node-by-node based on the node's semantics. For example, the AST matchers generated for the operands of a CallExpr node (function call) are connected via a hasArgument() AST matcher to the CallExpr's AST matcher.

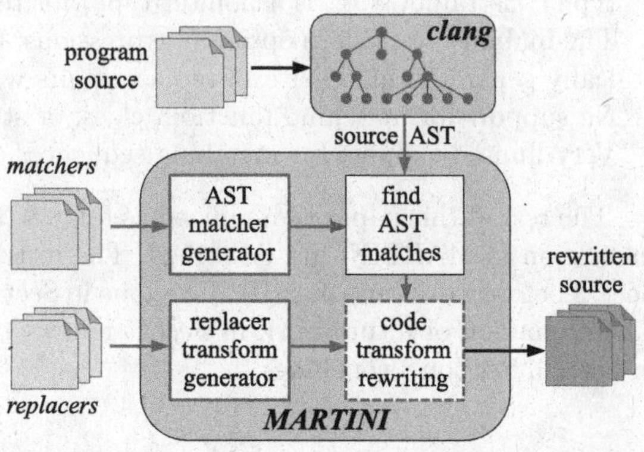

Fig. 3. The workflow of MARTINI. Our contributions are denoted with bold, green outlines. The dashed green outline indicates we significantly expanded existing functionality. Note that the matchers and replacers need not be in separate files. (Color figure online)

Replacers are read by the replacer transform generator also shown in Fig. 3. The AST of the replacer does not need to be stored as it can be regenerated as needed. Thus, only the source code of the matcher block in a replacer (ref. [[clang::replace("...")]] in Fig. 4) is kept.

Matchers and replacers are tied together through names in their respective attributes written as string literals (ref. "<matcher_name>" and "<matcher␣list>" in Fig. 4). Replacers and transformations can be tied to any number of matchers, and a single matcher can be tied to multiple replacers, e.g., both insert_before and insert_after. A match found by a matcher will be rewritten with the code of the replacer with the matcher's name in its list, with appropriate names and values in the code replaced with those from the match.

MARTINI takes in a specification file describing matchers and replacers, performs AST matcher generation, parses the replacers, then uses the existing AST matcher framework to search the user's source code for matches. Matches are processed in the order they are found, which is by top-down AST traversal. When it finds a match, it uses Clang's existing Rewriter utilities to replace any identifiers in the replacement code with the code bound to that identifier by the matcher. Finally, the location of the match in the source file is modified by replacing the matched code range with the replacement code. An entirely new

[[clang::matcher("<matcher_name>")]]
for matchers; identifies a function as a matcher specification with the given name.

[[clang::replace("<matcher␣list>")]]
for replacers; identifies a function as a replacer associated with all listed matchers.

[[clang::insert_before("<matcher␣list>")]]
for transformations; identifies a function as replacer that inserts code before a match.

[[clang::insert_after("<matcher␣list>")]]
for transformations; identifies a function as replacer that inserts code after a match.

[[clang::matcher_block]]
for matchers, replacers, and transformations; identifies statement(s) to be matched, replaced, or inserted. Outside code can provide declarations to ensure valid C++. If not present, all statements are used, though support for this is incomplete.

Fig. 4. The MARTINI-specific C++ attributes used to declare matchers and replacers in user-provided code snippets. Through use of native C++, MARTINI control attributes are naturally embedded in the source and can be handled by an otherwise unmodified Clang.

source file is produced to simplify experimentation with different transformation specifications and preserve the original source in case of mishaps. We put very few restrictions on the kinds of transformations users can write, even those that may produce invalid C++ output, to give users as much flexibility as possible. We have implemented a few safety checks for insert_before and insert_after (for example, we will not insert code into the conditions of an if statement), but in general users must verify the correctness of their rewritten code.

As mentioned, all identifiers, such as variables and function names, are treated as matcher parameters unless they are marked as *literals* by the user. This means users can choose to, e.g., match all functions that take two arguments and use the name of the matched function as a parameter in the replacer. Alternatively, a user can choose to match all calls to a specific function named foo that takes two arguments by making foo a literal. An identifier is marked as literal through a declaration in a special namespace (i.a., namespace clang_rewrite_literals void foo(int a, int b); – note a and b are *not* literals as they are parameters, not explicitly declared in the namespace), or by putting it in a special vector (i.a., vector<string> clang_rewrite_literal_names "foo";). We are considering adding another attribute for declaring literals for users that do not want to use the namespace or vector.

3 Case Study: Instrumentation

Profiling, for one reason or another, is something every application developer wants to do at some point. However, maintaining a program version that performs any form of logging is costly, especially given the varied kinds of logging one might want to perform. While abstractions like templates, macros, and #ifdef can help, applications making heavy use of them often redesign a multi-level DSL with severe implications for long-term maintainability and readability. Given

```
auto fn(auto);
auto LOG_FN(auto, auto) {}
auto LOG_LAMBDA(auto, auto) {}

[[clang::matcher("log_fn")]]
auto fn_call_matcher(int arg) {
  fn(arg);
}
[[clang::replace("log_fn")]]
auto fn_call_replacer(int arg) {
  LOG_FN(fn, arg);
}
[[clang::matcher("log_lambda")]]
auto lambda_call_matcher(int arg) {
  auto lambda = [&](int){};
  [[clang::matcher_block]]
  lambda(arg);
}
[[clang::replace("log_lambda")]]
auto lambda_call_replacer(int arg) {
  auto lambda = [&](int){};
  [[clang::matcher_block]]
  LOG_LAMBDA(lambda, arg);
}
```

(a) Matcher and replacer pairs for instrumenting a single argument function ("log_fn") and a single argument lambda ("log_lambda").

```
int g(int);
void test() {
  [&](int _){
    g(g(_));
  }(g(0));
}
```

(b) Non-trivial input example with nested calls and a lambda invocation which make it complex for text-based search-and-replace tools. Such tools would also struggle with newlines, comments, and (malicious) strings, such as: `f(g("\"),q(\""))`.

```
int g(int);
void test() {
  LOG_LAMBDA([&](int _){
      LOG_FN(g, LOG_FN(g, _));
    }, LOG_FN(g, 0));
}
```

(c) The input from Fig. 5b rewritten by MARTINI with the shown example-based rewrite rules. All three function calls are replaced by the "log_fn" rule while the lambda invocation was modified by the "log_lambda" rule.

Fig. 5. Example of how MARTINI can effectively instrument a code base with simple example-based rewrite rules that are semantic context-aware.

easy to use, customizable, and fully automatic code rewriting, however, developers can instead create short-lived, special-purpose code versions on-demand while keeping the core application code clean.

While we do not provide a full-fledged instrumentation suite yet, we showcase the benefits of MARTINI for instrumentation tasks in Fig. 5. Through the two simple before-and-after code snippets shown in Fig. 5a, users can easily create a one-off program version that will log every call, including lambdas. As shown in Fig. 5b and 5c, function calls and lambda invocations are replaced by the macros `LOG_FN` and `LOG_LAMBDA`, respectively. Note that, to MARTINI, there is no semantic difference between declaring a variable as an argument to a matcher or replacer and declaring it outside a `[[clang::matcher_block]]`. We demonstrate the former in this example.

Though contrived, this example clearly shows how the power of semantic matching and the simplicity of example-based rewriting come together. Since the rules are reusable, easily customizable, and maintainable by non-expert users, instrumented code can be produced from the original application at any point. Thus, one-off rewriting effectively reduces the maintenance burden while offering more powerful capabilities than "baked-in" instrumentation solutions.

4 Case Study: HIPIFY

For a realistic evaluation we performed a case study against `HIPIFY` [11], a state-of-the-art source code rewriting tool that ports CUDA codes to the (very similar, but more portable) HIP programming model. `HIPIFY` exists in two versions, as a "legacy" perl script, `hipify-perl`, and as an extension to the Clang front end, `hipify-clang`. Both versions have been used by researchers and application developers to port code, with generally positive results [1,4,16].

To bootstrap our `HIPIFY` clone, we used the rewrite rules already defined in the `hipify-clang` source. We limited our `HIPIFY` to CUDA's runtime API for now to keep the number of matchers and replacers manageable for debugging our prototype. The existing tables from `hipify-clang` allowed us to automatically generate matcher-replacer pairs for CUDA runtime calls and types, including all simple renames, such as `cudaMalloc` to `hipMalloc`. However, `hipify-clang` requires that transformations more complex than renaming, such as kernel calls, be implemented explicitly with strong coupling to the Clang AST. Figure 6 illustrates this with an excerpt of the `hipify-clang` source code for rewriting CUDA kernel launches. These particular lines pretty-print the thread grid and block dimensions to the output stream (`OS`). For brevity we omit 62 lines of this function, as well as all helpers and the logic that creates and applies the AST matcher. Still, all of this complexity is required just to replace CUDA kernel calls.

```
// 31 lines of C++ code (removed)
OS << kern;
if (caleeDecl->isTemplateInstantiation())
  OS << ")";
OS << ",␣";

// Next up are the four kernel configur-
// ation parameters, the last two of
// which are optional and default to 0.

// Copy the two dimensional arguments
// verbatim.
for (unsigned int i = 0; i < 2; ++i) {
  string sArg = readSourceText(*SM, config
      ->getArg(i)->getSourceRange()).str()
      ;
  bool bDim3 = equal(sDim3.begin(), sDim3.
      end(), sArg.c_str());
  OS << (bDim3 ? "" : sDim3) << sArg << (
      bDim3 ? "" : ")") << ",␣";
}
// 31 lines of C++ code (removed)
```

Fig. 6. Excerpt of `hipify-clang` source translating CUDA kernel launches to HIP. The replacement function alone (`HipifyAction::cudaLaunchKernel`) is 73 lines (excluding comments and helper functions). This snippet pretty-prints the grid and block dimensions to the output file. It still inspects the input code string (e.g., by scanning for the string `sDim3 = "dim3("`), despite AST matching of CUDA kernels being done earlier elsewhere. This kind of string matching code is hard to read, hard to modify, and overall fragile as typedefs or syntactic deviations (e.g., spaces) impact it easily.

In Fig. 7 we illustrate our alternative approach, which does not require any interaction with an AST, or any other complexity. In Fig. 7a, the matcher for a CUDA kernel launch with two kernel arguments and three launch parameters is shown. Since we currently do not support optional arguments, we automatically generate matchers and replacers for all supported numbers of arguments and launch parameters explicitly with a script. While we will support such variability more concisely in the future, one can already see how our approach is fundamentally simpler and more natural to non-compiler experts. Neither the matcher nor the replacer require interaction with the AST or other compiler internals, but all benefits over text-based search-and-replace approaches are preserved. For example, all matcher parameters (e.g., `kern` and `nthreads`) can bind to arbitrary complex expressions in the user's code. Figure 7b shows the associated replacer pattern. The kernel name (`kern`), together with the launch parameters (`nthreads` converted to `dim3`), are moved to argument positions in HIP's kernel launch function.

Importantly, the replacer pattern is written directly in the target language, which makes it easy for any developer to change the argument order, adjust default values (here, 0 in the HIP kernel launch), or modify the transformation in other ways. As an example, the shown replacer will not only port a CUDA kernel launch to HIP, but also double the number of threads to account for the (usually) larger wave size on AMD GPUs compared to the warp size on NVIDIA GPUs. The two characters added for this modification are highlighted in the definition of `nthreads3D` in Fig. 7b.

While our prototype emits the literal code in the `clang::matcher_block`, including the conditional that converts integer grid sizes to `dim3` types, we intend to add further capabilities to replacers such that compile-time constant expressions like this can be simplified. In this example, the `is_integer` condition can be determined at replacement time, which would allow the ternary expression to be simplified.

5 Evaluation

Our evaluation machine has two 14-core, hyperthreaded Intel Xeon(R) E5-2680 v4 CPUs running at 2.40 GHz, 128 GB of RAM, and two AMD Instinct MI100 GPUs. HIP codes were compiled using `hipcc` 4.4.21432-f9dccde4 based on AMD Clang 13.0.0 and ROCm 4.5.2 and the same version of `hipify-perl`. We used `hipify-clang` with git hash `61241a4` compiled using gcc 9.3.0 and the same LLVM version as MARTINI, which is hash `4c2b57ae` from LLVM's main branch.

We compare translating a simple gravitational N-body simulation code[3] from CUDA to HIP with MARTINI-HIPIFY and AMD's HIPIFY. It features four variants: unoptimized (nbody-orig), struct-of-arrays (SOA) data layout (nbody-soa), cache blocked (nbody-block), and unrolled loops (nbody-unroll).

[3] https://github.com/harrism/mini-nbody.

```
__global__ void kern(int a1 = 0,
    int a2 = 0, /* more args */) {}

template<int nblocks, int nthreads,
        int shmem, int a1, int a2>
[[clang::matcher("launch2a3p")]]
auto launch_2_3_matcher() {
 [[clang::matcher_block]]
 kern<<<nblocks, nthreads, shmem
    >>>(a1, a2);
}
```

(a) Matcher for a CUDA kernel launch with three launch parameters and two kernel arguments. As our prototype is a work in progress, we opted to generate the matchers for varying numbers of launch parameters and arguments explicitly with a script. A matcher has to be valid in the source language, here CUDA, to allow (an unmodified) Clang to generate an AST. Depending on the situation, the user also needs to provide additional declarations, e.g., the `kern` (dummy) function, for the same reason.

```
template<int nblocks, int nthreads,
        int shmem, int a1, int a2>
[[clang::replace("launch2a3p")]]
auto launch_2_3_replacer() {
 [[clang::matcher_block]] {
  bool nthreadsIs1D = numeric_limits
      <decltype(nthreads)>
      ::is_integer;
  auto nthreads3D = nthreadsIs1D
      ? dim3(nthreads * 2 )
      : nthreads;
  hipLaunchKernelGGL(kern, nblocks,
      nthreads3D, shmem, 0,
      a1, a2);
}}
```

(b) HIP kernel launch replacement code for the matcher in 7a. Replacers and matchers are linked by the name, here `"launch2a3p"`. Non-literal variables that are used in both act like capture groups in regular expressions. The expression in the source code that is bound to them by the matcher is substituted into the end result at use locations in the replacer.

Fig. 7. Matcher/replacer pair for CUDA kernel launches with two kernel arguments and three launch parameters.

5.1 Performance

Since we cannot compile and run both CUDA and HIP on the same device on our testing machine, it would be unfair to compare the performance obtained by the original CUDA and translated HIP codes. Therefore, we only compare the performance of the automatically translated HIP codes created by `hipify-perl`, `hipify-clang`, and MARTINI.

The performance we obtained for each translation is given in Table 1. Each version was run for ten iterations, and the average and standard deviation run times per iteration are presented in ms. As expected, all three translators generate very similar code with very similar performance for both medium and larger-size problems, regardless of application version.

Interestingly, when we generated code that multiplied the number of threads by two ("#Threads x2" columns in Table 1), as done in Fig. 7, performance greatly improved on the larger problem size for all versions of the application except nbody-orig (which is a naive implementation where little performance gain is expected). Performance also improved on the smaller problem size for nbody-block and nbody-unroll. These numbers are bolded in the table. This is due to the wider thread waves on AMD GPUs compared to thread warps on NVIDIA GPUs. `hipify-perl` and `hipify-clang` are unable to make these kinds of changes easily, as we will discuss in Sect. 5.2.

5.2 Usability

Both MARTINI-HIPIFY and AMD's `hipify-clang` are command line compiler tools, but while the core of `hipify-clang`[4] is approximately 1,000 lines (excluding comments and newlines) of AST matchers and C++ making heavy use of Clang internals, MARTINI-HIPIFY is 5,672 lines of simple CUDA/C++ (again excluding comments and newlines), the vast majority of which was automatically generated using tables in `hipify-clang` that convert CUDA names to HIP names. Of the 712 matchers and replacers generated, 212 were for kernel launches with varying numbers of launch parameters and arguments (this will be reduced by at least an order of magnitude once optional arguments are implemented), and the remaining 500 were for CUDA runtime functions and types. Of those 500, only 46 needed to be fixed by hand due to problems our generator script had getting the correct types from the CUDA headers. As a rough comparison of code complexity, all of the matchers and replacers in our `HIPIFY` have a McCabe cyclomatic complexity [6] of 1, while AMD's `hipify-clang` has an average cyclomatic complexity of 6.7 (calculated with `pmccabe`).

Table 1. Execution time in ms of the HIP output code for the N-body benchmark.

		MARTINI-HIPIFY				AMD HIPIFY			
	Number	Unmodifed		#Threads x2		hipify-perl		hipify-clang	
Benchmark	Particles	Mean	Stddev	Mean	Stddev	Mean	Stddev	Mean	Stddev
nbody-block	30000	319.65	5.42	**104.62**	0.11	319.62	3.44	318.73	6.34
	300000	457.65	1.35	**210.60**	0.90	453.55	1.63	449.20	2.71
nbody-orig	30000	171.99	0.47	172.43	0.35	171.63	0.78	172.63	0.89
	300000	415.97	2.11	418.35	0.75	414.98	2.72	416.91	2.38
nbody-soa	30000	198.45	1.66	197.19	1.78	205.60	1.19	205.38	2.40
	300000	426.05	0.42	**363.84**	2.67	429.44	0.54	428.72	2.76
nbody-unroll	30000	332.87	2.08	**180.71**	0.61	334.45	1.98	335.24	2.36
	300000	470.70	0.95	**229.27**	0.64	471.06	0.51	469.65	1.59

For a more concrete comparison, consider a user who wants to make a simple modification to the translation of CUDA kernel calls into HIP: multiplying the number of threads by two to improve performance on AMD devices, which generally have wider threading than NVIDIA devices. To do so with `hipify-clang`, that user would have to 1) determine that HipifyAction.cpp is where most of the translation is done, 2) find the function `HipifyAction::cudaLaunchKernel()`, 3) analyze the 73 lines of code in that function to find where the kernel configuration is handled, and 4) determine where in the relevant string manipulation code (shown in Fig. 6) to insert their `*2`. Without knowledge of the Clang AST and Clang's source manipulation libraries this is incredibly difficult, time-consuming, and highly dependent on the (in-source) documentation of `hipify-clang`.

[4] HipifyAction.cpp/.h and main.cpp.

To do the same thing with MARTINI-HIPIFY, the user would only have to modify the kernel call replacers similarly to what is shown in Fig. 7b. The replacers are easy to find by searching for the HIP kernel launch function name, and the modification could be done with a traditional search-and-replace tool. No understanding of Clang internals is necessary to modify MARTINI-HIPIFY. (It was a simple matter for us to modify the script that generated MARTINI-HIPIFY so all kernel call replacers looked like the one in Fig. 7b.) Other modifications, for example, printing the size of all arrays allocated on the device, are similarly intuitive.

6 Related Work

The most similar work to our own is Nobrainer [12,13], which also uses C/C++ code snippets and AST matchers to match application code and describe how to modify it, and inspired some of our user interface. As the Nobrainer project has existed for longer than ours, it supports more of the C++ standard. However, Nobrainer uses more restrictive and specialized syntax (e.g., to match a single expression, the expression must be returned) and generally enforces more restrictions on transformations than we do. They do this to ensure their transformations are (type-)safe, but we opted to take a more lenient approach both to simplify the implementation of our prototype and to give users more flexibility in the transformations they can define. It's easy to imagine cases where users may want to change the type of an expression – in fact, we make heavy use of this in our `HIPIFY` case study – but this is nearly impossible in Nobrainer. Nobrainer rewrite rules are strictly before-and-after code snippets; ours allow for more nuance with both insert and replace rules and the potential for adding more control and logic around which transformations happen when. Nobrainer's design philosophy is to make matchers as specific as possible and force users to add generality – they assume all names in a matcher are literals unless they are specified as parameters and do their best to enforce safety. Our philosophy is almost precisely opposite of that: our matchers are as general as possible and users must add specificity, e.g., with literals, and we allow users to define any transformations they wish with minimal restrictions on safety.

ClangMR [19] and the Clang Transformer library [2] are similar code rewriting tools implemented in Clang, but both of these use AST matchers (with a few additions) as a user interface. Our tool is designed to provide similar functionality but be usable by non-compiler experts.

Other code rewriting frameworks include the ROSE compiler [10], Xevolver [17] (built on ROSE), and the Omni source-to-source compiler [7]. These tools provide more low-level interfaces than ours, and thus more precise control over rewriting, but at the cost of requiring users to be compiler experts. In particular, Xevolver provides an XML-based AST pattern matching interface for describing code transformations and Omni requires users to write Java classes that perform transformations on an XML representation of the AST. Neither of these are very user-friendly, as users have to directly describe AST manipulations and use syntax specific to each tool. Our tool, on the other hand, only requires knowledge of C++ and the semantics of a few new attributes.

7 Future Work

As mentioned earlier, our tool currently has very little support for types and only supports the subset of Clang AST nodes necessary for `HIPIFY`, which mostly focuses on CallExprs and their arguments. As more use cases and example matcher/replacer sets are created, support for the full Clang AST, including type matching, will be added, as well as an "easy mode" that does not require the `[[clang::matcher_block]]` attribute for one-line transformations, as done in Fig. 5a. More interestingly, we plan to implement a way to denote parameters in matchers as optional, e.g., for default arguments or overloaded functions, and other ways to include more complex logic in transformations. For example, returning to the transformation described in Fig. 7 and Sect. 5.2, if a user wished to double `nthreads` only when the value of `nthreads` is small, that logic could be encoded in the transformation itself, not in the code the transformation produces. This would allow more complex rewriting tasks to be implemented succinctly in one matcher/replacer pair, instead of multiple matcher/replacer sets, and also decrease the complexity needed in the code output.

Once we have support for more of the Clang AST and the tool is more mature, we would like to conduct user studies for feedback on how we could make the interface more user-friendly. We would like to do a direct comparison to Nobrainer for these studies, but sadly Nobrainer is not open-source. We are also looking at a few real-world use cases where we could work with application developers to get their feedback. Other future use cases we are currently considering include:

- Instrumentation, e.g. inserting calls to an instrumentation API [14] around "interesting" code snippets (as defined by the user), or call stack tracing.
- Translating to/from other programming models, such as OpenMP → Kokkos, or pragma translation for OpenACC ↔ OpenMP (which is not as simple as it seems [3,9,15,18]).
- Common compiler optimizations, like loop unrolling.
- Other in-flight data analyses, such as checkpointing or in situ compression.

We are particularly interested in translating between various programming models and adding support for pragmas, since this would open up many interesting use cases such as users defining custom pragmas.

Since MARTINI is based on the Clang AST and front end infrastructure, there is also the possibility of expanding it to include other languages that use Clang as a front end, including Cilk, Objective C/C++, and even Fortran once the Flang [8] tooling infrastructure has matured.

8 Conclusion

We have presented a new automatic code rewriting tool, MARTINI, built on Clang, and provided a prototype re-implementation of `HIPIFY` that is easier to understand and customize than the original. The user interface is pure C++ and designed for ease of use so that the average C++ programmer can write their own code transformations without needing to resort to specialized compiler tools. While our new tool currently only supports a subset of the Clang AST, we are working to add more support and upstream our work into Clang. Our implementation can be found at https://github.com/ajohnson-uoregon/llvm-project/tree/feature-ajohnson/clang-tools-extra/clang-rewrite.

Acknowledgements and Data Availability Statement. The authors would like to thank our anonymous reviewers for their very helpful feedback.

The version of MARTINI used in this paper and instructions for generating our results are available in the Figshare repository: https://doi.org/10.6084/m9.figshare.19993454 [5].

Part of this research was supported by the Exascale Computing Project (17-SC-20-SC), a collaborative effort of two U.S. Department of Energy organizations (Office of Science and the National Nuclear Security Administration) responsible for the planning and preparation of a capable exascale ecosystem, including software, applications, hardware, advanced system engineering, and early testbed platforms, in support of the nation's exascale computing imperative.

Part of this research was supported by the Lawrence Livermore National Security, LLC ("LLNS") via MPO No. B642066.

References

1. Brown, C., Abdelfattah, A., Tomov, S., Dongarra, J.J.: Design, optimization, and benchmarking of dense linear algebra algorithms on AMD GPUs. In: High Performance Extreme Computing Conference, HPEC (2020). https://doi.org/10.1109/HPEC43674.2020.9286214
2. Clang Developers: clang::tooling::Transformer class reference. https://clang.llvm.org/doxygen/classclang_1_1tooling_1_1Transformer.html
3. Denny, J.E., Lee, S., Vetter, J.S.: CLACC: Translating OpenACC to OpenMP in Clang. In: Workshop on the LLVM Compiler Infrastructure in HPC (LLVM-HPC) (2018). https://doi.org/10.1109/LLVM-HPC.2018.8639349
4. Dufek, A.S., et al.: Case study of using Kokkos and SYCL as performance-portable frameworks for Milc-Dslash benchmark on NVIDIA, AMD and Intel GPUs. In: Workshop on Performance, Portability and Productivity in HPC, P3HPC@SC (2021). https://doi.org/10.1109/P3HPC54578.2021.00009
5. Johnson, A., Coti, C., Malony, A.D., Doerfert, J.: Artifact instructions for MARTINI: The little match and replace tool. https://doi.org/10.6084/m9.figshare.19993454
6. McCabe, T.: A complexity measure. Trans. Softw. Eng. **SE-2**(4) (1976). https://doi.org/10.1109/TSE.1976.233837

7. Murai, H., Sato, M., Nakao, M., Lee, J.: Metaprogramming framework for existing HPC languages based on the Omni compiler infrastructure. In: International Symposium on Computing and Networking Workshops (CANDARW) (2018). https://doi.org/10.1109/CANDARW.2018.00054
8. Osmialowski, P.: How the Flang frontend works: Introduction to the interior of the open-source Fortran frontend for LLVM. In: Proceedings of the Fourth Workshop on the LLVM Compiler Infrastructure in HPC. LLVM-HPC 2017. Association for Computing Machinery, New York (2017). https://doi.org/10.1145/3148173.3148183
9. Pino, S., Pollock, L., Chandrasekaran, S.: Exploring translation of OpenMP to OpenACC 2.5: Lessons learned. In: International Parallel and Distributed Processing Symposium Workshops (IPDPSW) (2017). https://doi.org/10.1109/IPDPSW.2017.84
10. Quinlan, D., Liao, C.: The ROSE source-to-source compiler infrastructure. In: Cetus Users and Compiler Infrastructure Workshop @PACT (2011)
11. ROCm Developers: HIPIFY: Tools to translate CUDA source code into portable HIP C++ automatically. https://github.com/ROCm-Developer-Tools/HIPIFY
12. Savchenko, V.V., et al.: NOBRAINER: A tool for example-based transformation of C/C++ code. Program. Comput. Softw. **46**(5), 362–372 (2020). https://doi.org/10.1134/S0361768820040052
13. Savchenko, V., et al.: Nobrainer: An example-driven framework for C/C++ code transformations. In: Bjørner, N., Virbitskaite, I., Voronkov, A. (eds.) PSI 2019. LNCS, vol. 11964, pp. 140–155. Springer, Cham (2019). https://doi.org/10.1007/978-3-030-37487-7_12
14. Shende, S.S., Malony, A.D.: The TAU parallel performance system. Int. J. High Perform. Comput. Appl. **20**(2) (2006). https://doi.org/10.1177/1094342006064482
15. Sultana, N., Calvert, A., Overbey, J.L., Arnold, G.: From OpenACC to OpenMP 4: Toward automatic translation. In: Proceedings of the XSEDE16 Conference on Diversity, Big Data, and Science at Scale, XSEDE 2016 (2016). https://doi.org/10.1145/2949550.2949654
16. Sun, Y., et al.: Evaluating performance tradeoffs on the Radeon Open Compute platform. In: International Symposium on Performance Analysis of Systems and Software, ISPASS 2018 (2018). https://doi.org/10.1109/ISPASS.2018.00034
17. Takizawa, H., Hirasawa, S., Hayashi, Y., Egawa, R., Kobayashi, H.: Xevolver: An XML-based code translation framework for supporting HPC application migration. In: 2014 21st International Conference on High Performance Computing (HiPC) (2014). https://doi.org/10.1109/HiPC.2014.7116902
18. Wolfe, M.: Compilers and more: OpenACC to OpenMP (and back again) (2016). https://www.hpcwire.com/2016/06/29/compilers-openacc-openmp-back/
19. Wright, H.K., Jasper, D., Klimek, M., Carruth, C., Wan, Z.: Large-scale automated refactoring using ClangMR. In: International Conference on Software Maintenance (2013). https://doi.org/10.1109/ICSM.2013.93

Accurate Fork-Join Profiling on the Java Virtual Machine

Matteo Basso(✉), Eduardo Rosales, Filippo Schiavio, Andrea Rosà, and Walter Binder

Faculty of Informatics, Università della Svizzera italiana (USI), Lugano, Switzerland
{matteo.basso,rosale,filippo.schiavio,andrea.rosa,walter.binder}@usi.ch

Abstract. The fork-join model for parallel computing has become very popular and is included in the Java class library since Java 7. While understanding and optimizing the performance of fork-join computations is of paramount importance, accurately profiling them on the Java Virtual Machine (JVM) is challenging due to the complexity of the API. In this paper, we present a novel model for analyzing fork-join computations on the JVM, addressing the peculiarities of the Java fork-join framework, including features such as task unforking and task reuse. We implement our model in a profiler that detects every spawned fork-join task, capturing all task dependencies and aiming at collecting cycle-accurate task-granularity data. We evaluate our profiler against a dedicated fork-join profiler for the JVM, showing that our tool achieves higher profile accuracy and introduces less overhead.

Keywords: Fork-join Parallelism · Work Stealing · Accurate Profiling · Task Granularity · Task Dependencies · Java

1 Introduction

The fork-join model for parallel computing has first been described in the 1960s [5,18] and has become popular with languages such as Cilk [2,8], implementing an execution mechanism based on work stealing [3,4]. The Java class library includes an implementation of the fork-join model since Java 7 [13], which has become very popular. It is used not only for application-level fork-join computations, but it is also at the core of many frameworks both for Java (e.g., it is used in the Java Stream framework [19] for executing parallel streams) and for other languages targeting the Java Virtual Machine (JVM), including Scala (e.g., Scala actors [10]), Groovy (e.g., GPars [31]), and Clojure (e.g., Reducers [30]).

As related work demonstrates [1,14,23,27], to understand the performance of fork-join computations and optimize them, one needs dedicated profilers able to capture metrics specific to the fork-join framework (e.g., focusing on task stealing, nested task executions, and parent/child task relationships) as well as task-granularity information (i.e., a measure of the amount of computations performed by every task). Regarding the former category, to the best of our

J. Cano and P. W. Trinder (Eds.): Euro-Par 2022, LNCS 13440, pp. 35–50, 2022.
https://doi.org/10.1007/978-3-031-12597-3_3

knowledge, there is no profiler for the JVM that can collect such metrics on the Java fork-join framework. Regarding the latter, while there are dedicated tools for task-granularity profiling on the JVM [23,25], they suffer from high overhead, resulting in serious measurement perturbations and inaccurate (and possibly misleading) task-granularity profiles.

To bridge this gap, in this paper, we present a novel technique to accurately and efficiently profile fork-join computations on the JVM. Differently from programming languages such as Cilk, where the simplicity of the underlying fork-join model facilitates the development of related profilers [11,14,27], in the case of Java, accurately profiling fork-join computations is challenging, because the fork-join framework is complex, supporting not only forking and joining of tasks, but also task unforking and task cancellation, as well as task reinitialization (i.e., the reuse of task instances). These features are also commonly used in practice (e.g., task unforking and task reuse are employed in some benchmarks [6]). Hence, existing formal models for fork-join computations in Cilk cannot be used to correctly model the execution of an arbitrary fork-join computation permitted by the Java API.

For this reason, we propose a new profiling model that captures any legitimate use of the Java fork-join framework and allows a variety of relevant metrics to be computed, such as e.g. number of workers, number of tasks stolen from/by a given thread (task-stealing rate), task execution nesting, and task-reuse rate, in addition to task granularity. Our model accurately detects the parent/child relationships between tasks even when multiple fork-join computations concurrently execute in the same fork-join pool. Moreover, similarly to other established profilers [14,28], our model allows one to analyze high-level information related to load balancing and task dependencies. Such metrics and information greatly enhance program comprehension and guide developers to optimize fork-join computations, e.g., by identifying source-code locations where task reuse is applicable.

We implement our model in a novel fork-join profiler for the JVM, named wosp. Our tool minimizes data collection at profiling time and calculates key metrics in a post-processing phase. Our profiles include task-granularity information in terms of elapsed reference cycles[1].

We compare the profiling accuracy and the overhead of wosp with FJProf [25]. To the best of our knowledge, FJProf is the only profiler specific to the Java fork-join framework able to collect task-granularity data on fork-join tasks[2]. Our evaluation results demonstrate that wosp achieves a much higher accuracy of the collected profiling information while introducing a much lower profiling overhead.

In summary, this paper makes the following contributions. We present a novel profiling model that accurately captures a variety of relevant metrics on

[1] Reference cycles are the clock cycles elapsed during an operation, collected at the nominal processor frequency (regardless of frequency scaling). The paper uses the term "cycles" to indicate "reference cycles" for short.

[2] FJProf is a fork-join-specific version of the task-granularity profiler tgp [24].

the Java fork-join framework as well as task-granularity data. We also present wosp, an efficient profiler implementing our model (Sect. 3). We evaluate accuracy and overhead of our profiler and compare it with the task-granularity profiler FJProf [25], demonstrating that our profiler results in superior accuracy and a much lower overhead than FJProf (Sect. 4). We complement the paper with the necessary background information (Sect. 2), a discussion on related work (Sect. 5), and our concluding remarks (Sect. 6).

2 Background

The Java implementation of the fork-join framework [13] is based on work-stealing [3,4] and adopts a work-first [9] approach to scheduling. The main entities composing the framework are *tasks* (implemented in class ForkJoinTask) and the *fork-join pool* (implemented in class ForkJoinPool), to which tasks are submitted.

The ForkJoinPool API allows developers to perform advanced tuning and scheduling customizations by offering a rich set of features that go beyond the fork-join primitives offered by other languages such as Cilk [2,8]. In this section, we summarize these additional features, namely task reuse, unforking, and cancellation, and we describe their specifications. Unless otherwise noted, we use the term *task* to indicate an instance of class ForkJoinTask [20], and we refer to the execution of method ForkJoinTask.exec as *task execution*. Given two tasks p and c such that p forks c (i.e., while a thread is executing p, it calls c.fork), we refer to p as the *parent* of c and to c as the *child* (or *subtask*) of p.

Task Reuse. It is the reusage of the same task instance to perform multiple executions instead of frequently allocating new tasks. This feature may be useful when executing pre-constructed trees of tasks in loops. Internally, a call to the method ForkJoinTask.reinitialize resets the internal state of the task, allowing a subsequent fork. Note that the Java fork-join framework allows executing multiple forks on the same task instance only if the task is reinitialized (by calling reinitialize) between each pair of forks [20]. Reinitialization is allowed only if the task either 1) has never been forked, or 2) has been forked, executed, and all joins of the task have completed. The API does not specify the behavior of reinitialization if the above conditions do not hold. As an example, reinitialization is used in the implementation of the well-known task-parallel benchmark nbody evaluated in Sect. 4.

Task Unforking. It is the unscheduling of a task which was previously forked locally (i.e., in the parent task) which can help reduce the task-management overhead of the framework. According to the Java documentation, a call to method task.tryUnfork may return true (but is not guaranteed to do so) if task is the most recently forked task by the current thread, and its execution has not already started in another thread. A typical use of this method is to locally process tasks that could have been—but actually were not—stolen. As an example, task unforking is used in the implementation of the benchmarks integrate and lud evaluated in Sect. 4.

Task Cancellation. It is the cancellation of the execution of a task by the user. This features enables optimizations related to specific problems, such as short-circuiting a computation. A call to task.cancel may fail depending on the internal state of the task, e.g., if the task has already completed. If successful, and the task has not started executing when the method cancel is called, the execution of the task is unscheduled and suppressed. After method cancel returns successfully, the task cannot be used anymore, unless there is an intervening call to task.reinitialize. Moreover, trying to join a cancelled task is not allowed (it will result in a CancellationException). Note that this method is designed to be invoked by other tasks. To terminate the current task, users can just use a return statement or throw an unchecked exception from its computation method.

3 Profiling Technique

In this section, we present our technique for profiling the Java fork-join framework. We first present our profiling model (Sect. 3.1) and then we outline its implementation in the wosp profiler (Sect. 3.2).

3.1 Profiling Model

Here, we first define the focus and goals of our technique and describe the underlying profiling model using high-level events. With the model, we explain how we produce execution traces, i.e., sequences of records which represent the profiled events in an application. Our traces track the minimum amount of information that allow a reconstruction of the parent/child relationship and the granularity of each task offline, i.e., after the application has terminated. Then, we detail how to compute task granularity and detect work stealing by reconstructing the parent/child relationship using the generated traces. Finally, we map high-level events (used in the model description) to concrete methods of the fork-join framework.

Focus and Goals. Our goal is representing the parallel task computation taking place at runtime. Hence, we focus on the execution of tasks that have been forked, i.e., tasks that have been arranged for parallel execution. We disregard the sequential execution of children tasks, i.e., direct synchronous method invocations. We incorporate the granularity of any direct synchronous method invocations into the granularity of their parent tasks. On the other hand, a forked task that happens to be sequentially executed by the forking thread would be profiled separately. Also, we detect tasks that are forked, subsequently unforked, and manually executed or canceled by the user. In addition, we detect reused

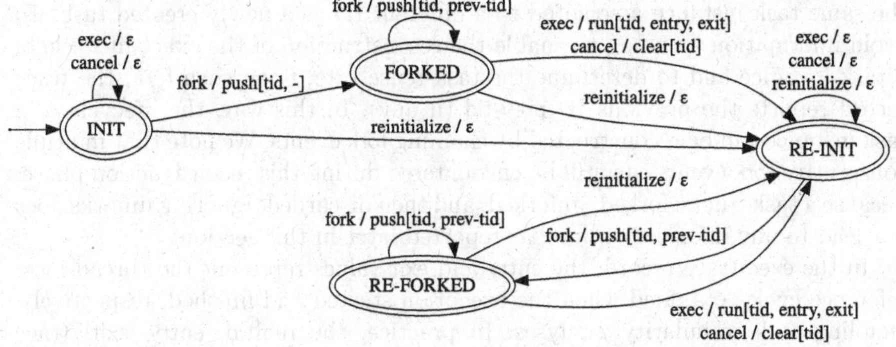

Fig. 1. Finite state machine modeling the lifetime of a fork-join task.

tasks, too. We focus on legitimate and meaningful usages of the fork-join framework; we do not model erroneous API usages. For example, we assume that a task is not forked more than once unless the task has been completed and reinitialized (which would be an illegal usage).

Task State Machine. We model each fork-join task as a finite state machine. Figure 1 shows a graphical representation of the finite state machine where states are represented using ellipses and transitions are represented with arrows. Transitions produce *trace record* as output. The state machine consists of four states, all of them final: *INIT*, *FORKED*, *RE-INIT*, and *RE-FORKED*. Above each state transition, the notation "*event/trace record*" specifies the event that triggered the transition and the produced trace record. State transitions are triggered by four events: fork, exec, cancel, and reinitialize. Event fork indicates task forking, or, at a lower level, a push to a work queue, i.e., to the thread-local deque of tasks owned by each fork-join thread that executes tasks in the fork-join pool (called *worker*). Events exec, cancel, and reinitialize indicate task execution, cancellation, and reinitialization, respectively.

After instantiation, a task begins its lifecycle in the initial state *INIT*. State *FORKED* indicates that a newly created task has been forked due to the occurrence of a fork. State *RE-INIT* indicates that a task has been either reset due to the occurrence of a reinitialize, executed due to the occurrence of an exec, or cancelled due to the occurrence of a cancel. State *RE-FORKED* indicates that a task has been forked after a reset, allowing us to track reused tasks.

Our model considers three different trace records: push[tid, prev-tid], clear[tid], and run[tid, entry, exit]. We report the runtime values that each trace record encapsulates within squared brackets. In Fig. 1, a special value "–" indicates that a record value is not present for a specific transition. The notation ϵ indicates that, for that transition, no profiling trace record is produced. In trace records, tid refers to a unique ID associated to each task usage, i.e., to each sequence of events that starts with a fork and may end with an exec or a cancel. Unique IDs are newly generated upon the occurrence of each fork. This allows us to consider the same task instance associated to a different ID as a newly created task. To avoid information loss, i.e., to enable the reconstruction of the exact lifecycle of a task instance and to determine the task-reuse rate, upon each fork, the trace record reports the previous ID prev-tid (if any). In this way, the lifecycle of a task instance can be reconstructed by chaining fork events. We note that multiple consecutive fork events can still be encountered during this reconstruction phase, because a task can be forked, unforked, and then discarded. Ignoring unforks does not lead to any information loss, as reported later in this section.

In the exec trace record, the entry and exit values represent the thread-local reference cycles obtained when the execution started and finished, respectively, enabling task-granularity analyses. In practice, the run[tid, entry, exit] trace record is composed of two sub-records run_begin[tid, entry] and run_end[exit]. This allows us to reconstruct parent/child task relationships, as explained later. We note that, even in case of nesting, i.e., run occurring within another run, trace records run_begin and run_end are always balanced and hence it is not necessary to report tid in run_end.

We note that our model does not employ an unfork event since an unforked task will be either executed (producing an exec and hence a transition) or discarded (producing no events and hence no information). Not explicitly considering task unforking allows us to reduce runtime overhead without information loss. Under the assumption that a fork-join pool terminates and cancels all the tasks that were forked but not executed before the shutdown of the JVM (as the common pool automatically instantiated by the JVM does), the quantity $\#push - \#cancel - \#exec$ gives the number of scheduled tasks that have neither been cancelled nor executed.

Work Stealing and Parent/Child Relationship. Since state transitions may take place in different executing threads during the lifecycle of a task, each trace record contains a reference to the thread that produced it. In practice, instead of collecting traces per task, traces can be collected more efficiently per thread. This allows us not only to analyze load balancing by manipulating run trace records and the corresponding cycles, but also to determine when work stealing takes place. If a push and a run associated to the same ID π are produced by different threads t0 and t1, respectively, we can conclude that t1 has stolen the task associated to π from t0.

Trace records of different tasks may be nested within the traces of the same thread, i.e., trace records of a task c may appear between the run_begin and the run_end records of another task p. We refer to the particular case of nested run records as *nested task executions*. We refer to p as the *outer task*, and to c as the *inner task*. Nested executions may take place in the fork-join framework either because of nested parent/child executions (in wosp, in case of forking, unforking, and subsequent execution) or because of helping. Indeed, in the fork-join framework, workers help complete other tasks until the task being joined is done. As a consequence, outer tasks may not be parent tasks of their corresponding inner tasks. While nested executions provide insightful information about the actual

Table 1. Java methods corresponding to events in the task state machine (Fig. 1).

Event	Triggering Java Methods	
fork	ForkJoinTask.fork	ForkJoinPool.submit
	ForkJoinTask.invokeAll	ForkJoinPool.invokeAny
	ForkJoinPool.invokeAll	ForkJoinPool.execute
	ForkJoinPool.invoke	
exec	ForkJoinTask.exec	ForkJoinTask.quietlyJoin
	ForkJoinTask.invoke	ForkJoinTask.quietlyInvoke
	ForkJoinTask.invokeAll	ForkJoinPool.invoke
	ForkJoinTask.join	ForkJoinPool.invokeAll
	ForkJoinTask.get	ForkJoinPool.invokeAny
cancel	ForkJoinTask.cancel	ForkJoinPool.invokeAny
	ForkJoinTask.invokeAll	ForkJoinPool.shutdown
	ForkJoinPool.invokeAll	ForkJoinPool.shutdownNow
reinitialize	ForkJoinTask.reinitialize	

execution taking place at runtime, they do not allow to reconstruct parent/child task relationships. In our model, a push of a task c occurring within the run of another task p indicates that p is the parent task of c.

Mapping Java Methods to Events. For each event of the task state machine, Table 1 reports the methods of the ForkJoinTask and ForkJoinPool classes that may trigger such event. Internally, methods that map to fork invoke ForkJoinTask.fork, methods that map to exec invoke ForkJoinTask.exec, and methods that map to cancel invoke ForkJoinTask.cancel. Methods that map to both fork and exec (e.g., ForkJoinPool.invoke) first trigger fork and then exec. We note that some methods (e.g., ForkJoinPool.invokeAll) trigger fork and exec/cancel for several different tasks. We also note that cancel is conditionally triggered by some methods that trigger also exec. For example, in ForkJoinTask.invokeAll, if any task encounters an exception, the others may be cancelled.

We emphasize that the invocation of some methods, such as ForkJoinTask.join, may lead not only to the execution of the task currently being joined but—because of helping—also to the execution of other tasks, as previously explained.

Finally, the default implementation of methods ForkJoinPool.shutdown and ForkJoinPool.shutdownNow (i.e., the methods used to terminate the ForkJoinPool) cancel forked tasks that were not executed.

3.2 Implementation

We implemented our profiling technique in a novel profiler for the Java fork-join framework called wosp. Here, we outline implementation details of our profiler.

wosp is composed of three main components: the instrumentation, the tracing agent, and the postprocessor. The instrumentation implements the state machine and invokes the tracing agent to produce profiling traces. Then, after application execution, the postprocessor decodes the traces to extract task information and metrics. Below, we detail each component separately.

Instrumentation. To instrument the target application according to the model, wosp relies on DiSL [16], a load-time out-off-process Java bytecode instrumentation framework that guarantees full bytecode coverage. To minimize runtime perturbation and data collection, we perform minimal instrumentation. In particular, we profile fork events by instrumenting the low-level methods push and lockedPush defined in class ForkJoinPool.WorkQueue. We profile the events exec, cancel, and reinitialize instrumenting methods exec, cancel, and reinitialize defined in all the subtypes of class ForkJoinTask, respectively. We note that all the methods associated to the events listed in Table 1, internally call the methods we instrument. Hence, we do not need to instrument all of them individually. To avoid expensive runtime typechecks, we efficiently determine all subtypes of class ForkJoinTask at instrumentation-time leveraging the DiSL Reflection API [26].

Tracing Agent. Traces are produced by invoking native primitives of a JVMTI agent attached to the executing JVM via JNI. To reduce contention, similarly to related work [14], wosp produces thread-local traces. Our implementation stores trace records in thread-local buffers that are pre-allocated (i.e., a certain number of buffers is allocated at VM startup) and acquired the first time a thread needs to store a trace record during the application execution. When an acquired buffer is full, the executing thread can acquire another pre-allocated buffer. The buffered data is dumped to files only at the shutdown of the JVM to avoid I/O overheads during the execution of application code. Only if the pre-allocated buffers are not enough, the agent dumps and allocates new buffers at runtime (although none of the analyzed workloads required runtime buffer dumping and allocation). While unique IDs associated to task usages are provided to the agent via JNI calls, reference cycles are collected per thread directly in native code using the PAPI [12] library. Binary files can be decoded by external applications to perform analyses.

Postprocessor and Metrics. To analyze the traces, we implement a Java application that reads the binary files and decodes their content by applying the rules reported in Sect. 3.1. During trace decoding, the postprocessor keeps a stack of run_begin records. Every time a run_begin record is encountered, it is pushed on the stack; when a run_end record is encountered, the corresponding run_begin record is popped from the stack, and the pair run_begin-run_end allows calculating the task granularity. We measure task-granularity as the exclusive measurement of reference cycles, i.e., the difference between the cycles stored in the run_end and run_begin records, minus the sum of task granularity of the nested inner tasks. When a push[child-id] is encountered, if a run_begin[parent-id] is on the top of the stack we can create the parent/child relation among tasks (parent-id, child-id). Once the whole parent/child relation has been built, we can reconstruct stolen tasks, i.e., a task is stolen if 1) it has a parent and 2) the thread who executed the parent task is different from the thread who executed the child task. After postprocessing, we report runtime metrics and information including but not limited to: number of workers, task granularity, parent/child task relationships (task dependencies), number of tasks stolen from/by a given thread (task-stealing rate), load balance, task execution nesting, and task-reuse rate.

4 Evaluation

In this section, we present our evaluation. We first describe our experimental setup (Sect. 4.1). Then, we evaluate the accuracy of the profiles produced by wosp and its profiling overhead (Sect. 4.2). In both cases, we compare our tool with FJProf [25], a fork-join task profiler for the JVM, allowing dedicated task-granularity profiling.

4.1 Experimental Setup

Here, we describe the benchmarks used in our evaluation and the testbed.

Benchmarks. Our evaluation targets the Renaissance [21] and Aeminium [6] benchmark suites. We use the latest releases of Renaissance (v.0.14.0, released on Jan. 31, 2022) and Aeminium (latest commit on the open-source repository [7], dated Oct. 19, 2016) at the time of writing.

Renaissance includes one workload exercising fork-join computations, fj-kmeans. From Aeminium, we consider all workloads which either make use of the peculiar features of the Java fork-join framework (described in Sect. 2) or execute a large number of fork-join tasks. For each workload, we focus only on the *steady-state* iteration, i.e., a complete execution of the workload after garbage-collector ergonomics and dynamic compilation have stabilized. We run as many warm-up iterations as suggested by the developers of Renaissance [22] and Aeminium [7].

Testbed. We run all the experiments on two machines M_1 and M_2. M_1 is equipped with an 8-core Intel Xeon E5-2680 (2.7 GHz) and 128 GB of RAM, while M_2 with a 18-core Intel i9-10980XE (3.00 GHz) with 256 GB of RAM. M_1 and M_2 run under Linux, generic kernel versions 4.15.0-147 and 5.4.0-89, respectively. We disable Turbo Boost and Hyper-Threading. The CPU governor is set to "performance". We use OpenJDK 17 (build 17.0.2+8-LTS) and PAPI 6.

4.2 Accuracy and Overhead Evaluation

Here, we evaluate the profiling accuracy and overhead of wosp and FJProf.

Table 2. Results of the accuracy and overhead evaluation.

Workload	Machine	#Workers	#Tasks		Overhead factor		Accuracy[%]	
			FJProf	wosp	FJProf	wosp	FJProf	wosp
fj-kmeans	M_1	19	666,200	666,200	**2.12**	**1.02**	**79.58**	**99.68**
	M_2	19	666,200	666,200	**2.75**	**1.02**	**78.19**	**98.84**
fft	M_1	9	65,535	32,768	**1.34**	**1.01**	**90.51**	**99.90**
	M_2	19	65,535	32,768	**1.13**	**1.02**	**97.56**	**99.70**
doall	M_1	23	1,572,861	786,432	**4.26**	**1.02**	**56.23**	**99.27**
	M_2	23	1,572,861	786,432	**10.43**	**1.04**	**41.42**	**98.47**
heat	M_1	17	102,913	102,712	**2.53**	**1.04**	**94.20**	**99.07**
	M_2	19	102,913	102,712	**4.95**	**1.09**	**74.76**	**99.95**
integrate	M_1	20	731	501	**3.60**	**1.07**	**55.61**	**97.31**
	M_2	22	747	892	**9.42**	**1.20**	**34.86**	**93.86**
lud	M_1	18	28,367	39,853	**4.51**	**1.05**	**55.14**	**99.95**
	M_2	19	39,250	56,187	**12.83**	**1.10**	**32.91**	**99.80**
matrixmult	M_1	17	131,071	65,536	**1.11**	**1.01**	**96.90**	**99.64**
	M_2	20	131,071	65,536	**1.77**	**1.11**	**85.66**	**99.47**
mergesort	M_1	9	262,143	131,072	**4.53**	**1.06**	**45.25**	**99.32**
	M_2	19	262,143	131,072	**8.59**	**1.09**	**28.43**	**99.58**
quicksort	M_1	21	1,487,767	1,487,767	**6.21**	**1.04**	**36.60**	**97.18**
	M_2	25	1,487,767	1,487,767	**10.54**	**1.02**	**23.74**	**97.82**
pi	M_1	16	32,767	16,384	**1.04**	**1.01**	**96.84**	**98.19**
	M_2	20	32,767	16,384	**1.03**	**1.01**	**97.34**	**98.54**
fibonacci	M_1	14	11,405,773	5,702,887	**20.45**	**1.12**	**16.86**	**90.20**
	M_2	19	11,405,773	5,702,887	**65.40**	**1.21**	**9.28**	**83.88**
nbody	M_1	9	351	176	**1.10**	**1.08**	**99.02**	**99.77**
	M_2	9	351	176	**1.18**	**1.14**	**99.10**	**99.99**

Accuracy. We aim at comparing the total task granularity (i.e., the total number of cycles elapsed during task executions) accounted for all the profiled tasks as reported by wosp and FJProf with the cycles elapsed by all fork-join computations in a non-instrumented execution of a workload, i.e., the *baseline*. The smaller the difference between the total cycles and the baseline, the higher the profile accuracy.

Baseline Computation. Since all the selected workloads perform exclusively fork-join computations, our baseline is computed as the total cycles elapsed in the execution of a workload, which we approximate to the total fork-join-computation cycles. We compute the baseline using PAPI, reading cycle counters of the main thread and the workers, before and after the steady-state iteration. Hence, our baseline reflects the total cycles elapsed by all threads involved in fork-join computations.

Results. Table 2 shows the results of our evaluation on M_1 and M_2. For each workload, we first report the number of workers (*#Workers*) and then the total number of tasks (*#Tasks*) as reported by FJProf and wosp. Both values correspond to the mean of 51 runs (rounded to integers).

We then report the profiling overhead, which is computed as the *overhead factor*, i.e., the execution time of an instrumented workload divided by the execution time of the workload without any profiling (considering also the means of 51 runs). To estimate accuracy, we use the *relative error (RE)*, which is computed from the mean of the baseline and the total cycles reported by each profiler. We define accuracy as the quantity 1 - RE (shown as percentage). A RE of zero would indicate the highest possible accuracy (100%).

Both FJProf and wosp, for the same workload and machine, report the same number of workers. We note that the number of workers that execute tasks does not depend only on the number of cores (and hence on the machine) but also on the parent/child task relationships (and hence on the workload). While the number of cores determines the number of preallocated workers that can steal tasks, the fork-join pool creates a new worker whenever a task cannot be executed because all the existing workers are blocked.

We note that the number of tasks reported by FJProf is twice (minus one) the number reported by wosp for fft, doall, matrixmult, mergesort, pi, fibonacci, and nbody. This is explained by the key differences in the profiling models implemented by the two profilers. In the model of FJProf, a new fork-join task execution (and hence, a new task) is always detected upon a call to method ForkJoinTask.exec. In the model of wosp, a new fork-join task execution is detected upon a call to method ForkJoinTask.exec, provided that the task has been previously forked (as explained in Sect. 3.1). Indeed, differently from FJProf, our model focuses only on the execution of tasks that have been arranged for parallel execution (i.e., explicit submission of a task to a fork-join pool). In the aforementioned workloads, tasks split the work into two parts, creating two subtasks to carry them out. One subtask is executed sequentially in the currently executing thread while the other is forked and later joined. Since FJProf profiles the execution of both subtasks whereas wosp disregards the execution of the first one (that is not forked), the number of tasks profiled by wosp is half (minus one) the number reported by FJProf. wosp detects less tasks than FJProf for all the evaluated workloads, except in lud, which particular case is discussed later in this section.

For all the evaluated workloads, wosp always achieves both a higher accuracy and lower overhead than FJProf. Our evaluation results show that FJProf introduces a notably higher average[3] profiling overhead (2.91× on M_1 and 5.01× on M_2) than wosp (1.04× on M_1 and 1.09× on M_2). The highest overheads are experienced while profiling fibonacci (wosp: 1.12× on M_1 and 1.21× on M_2, FJProf: 20.45× on M_1 and 65.36× on M_2). These overheads can be explained by the presence of many tasks, all of which have to be tracked by both profilers, leading to the execution of substantial instrumentation code (in addition to the original application code). In general, for the workloads that do not exercise peculiar features of the Java fork-join API (which are discussed below), we find that the higher the number of tasks, the higher the overhead.

[3] Average overheads and accuracies across multiple workloads are computed using the geometric mean.

We note that both integrate and lud (i.e., the benchmarks that exercise task unforking) show relatively high overheads for both profilers even if the reported number of tasks is low. This is because both wosp and FJProf profile a substantial number of forks (approx. 340 thousands for integrate and approx. 588 thousands for lud, considering the average of 51 runs), indicating that most of the tasks are unforked successfully and executed sequentially for both workloads. Both wosp and FJProf avoid tracking tasks executed sequentially through methods that are not ForkJoinTask.exec. As the execution of these tasks is sequential, their cycles are included in the parent task but their execution does not increase the number of tasks reported in Table 2. In summary, the profiling overhead of both profilers increases in integrate and lud because they instrument abundant forking. Despite the low number of tasks, the executed instrumentation code to detect the forking is relevant and increases the profiling overhead.

We remark that lud is the only workload where wosp detects more tasks than FJProf. We inspected the root causes that lead to this peculiarity and determined that the overhead of FJProf can significantly affect the execution of the workloads that internally rely on task unforking. Concretely, when lud is being profiled by FJProf, method ForkJoinTask.tryUnfork succeeds more frequently as threads are busy executing instrumentation code, instead of actively stealing (the latter action is the behavior expected in an uninstrumented execution of the workload). Since unforked tasks are executed sequentially and not via ForkJointTask.exec, they are not accounted by both wosp and FJProf (and thus FJProf does not increase the number of tasks as reported in Table 2 for this profiler).

The average accuracy achieved by wosp is 98.25% and 97.38% on M_1 and M_2, respectively. In contrast, the average accuracy achieved by FJProf is 61.69% on M_1 and 47.74% on M_2. The lowest accuracies are observed for fibonacci (wosp: 90.20% on M_1 and 83.88% on M_2, FJProf: 16.86% on M_1 and 9.28% on M_2). Similarly to the overhead, the low accuracies are explained by the large number of tasks that the workload executes (wosp: 5,702,887 tasks, FJProf: 11,405,773 tasks), whose execution has to be detected by both evaluated profilers, causing the execution of significant instrumentation code. In general, we can see that the higher the overhead, the lower the accuracy, as significant profiling overheads result in more cycle-measurement perturbations.

Accuracies are generally lower and overheads higher on M_2 than on M_1. This is explained by the number of CPU cores available in the respective machines (M_1 has 8 cores and M_2 has 18), which may lead to higher contention on M_2 (for some workloads, this is exacerbated by the increased number of workers that need to be tracked by both tools). For instance, the overhead of FJProf for fibonacci on M_2 is more than three times the one experienced on M_1. This is explained because the tracing of task creation, forking, and execution in FJProf is supported by ShadowVM [15], a system for instrumentation-based dynamic analyses which aims at improving isolation and coverage. The ShadowVM is executed on a separate JVM, such that there is inter-thread communication for notifying relevant events (task creation, forking and execution). Via a Java API, FJProf invokes primitives through an agent of the ShadowVM, which is attached to the JVM executing the profiled application. Even though this agent employs thread-local buffers, the agent internally employs many threads, which under contention compete with the workers of the Java fork-join framework for resources. Moreover, these ShadowVM-related threads perform lock-based synchronization, potentially generating a contention that can slow the profiled application down, in particular when a large number of tasks is executed. In contrast, wosp is less sensitive to contention, as it uses a minimal and specialized tracing agent that reduces runtime work and contention via efficient buffer handling.

Overall, our evaluation results show that wosp achieves a notably higher accuracy than FJProf, while incurring much less overhead. This highlights the effectiveness of our profiling technique which uses a minimal instrumentation and efficient tracing to reduce the perturbation of cycle measurements. We have shown that reducing application perturbation is key to provide developers accurate task-granularity profiles, which otherwise would report inaccurate (and potentially misleading) information describing fork-join parallelism. Concretely, the low accuracy achieved by FJProf may lead to profiles that do not reflect the actual granularity of the profiled tasks. The profiles may wrongly indicate a task as too fine-grained or too coarse-grained, or may miss the actual tasks with suboptimal granularity, making it impossible to locate and optimize performance problems related to task granularity. On the other hand, wosp does not suffer from this problem, given its high accuracy.

5 Related Work

Many tools originated both in industry and in academia to analyze various aspects of parallel applications [17,29]. Most of these tools report low-level metrics from which it is hard to extract high-level aggregated metrics on fork-join computations on the JVM, as these tools are not specific to profiling fork-join tasks. Existing tools like CilkView [11], CilkProf [27], HPCToolkit [1], and steal-tree [14] profile (or trace) high-level events in the application code (e.g., task forking) to establish a parent/child relationship. Unfortunately, the profiling model used by the aforementioned tools is not suitable for collecting detailed metrics on fork-join computations the JVM, as it considers a simpler fork-join model that lacks more complex features that are instead supported by the Java fork-join framework (such as task reuse, unforking and cancellation).

To the best of our knowledge, only two existing tools target task-granularity profiling on the JVM, i.e., tgp [23] (which targets generic tasks) and FJProf [25], a version of tgp [23] specific to fork-join tasks. Due to their limited task model, none of the two tools is able to track parent/child relationships between tasks, making it impossible to reconstruct the whole tree of tasks' execution. However, it has been shown [1] that such a tree reconstruction is helpful in understanding performance issues in fork-join applications. Moreover, due to their heavyweight infrastructure, these tools incur high overhead and yield low profile accuracy. While our evaluation focuses on FJProf, we expect comparable results on tgp, as it employs a similar profiling model and infrastructure.

Overall, our work is the first effort in modeling a profiler for the Java fork-join framework that considers complex features, such as task unforking, task cancellation, and task reinitialization. Moreover, wosp is the first tool capable of low-overhead and cycle-accurate profiling of Java fork-join applications.

6 Conclusions

In this paper, we presented a novel profiling technique for fork-join applications on the JVM. Our technique allows measuring the computations performed by parallel task executions in terms of elapsed reference cycles, producing metrics that ease understanding the behavior and performance of a Java fork-join application.

The profiling model implemented in wosp minimizes the instrumentation required to collect all the relevant profiling events from which many important metrics can be computed. Our evaluation results show that the profile accuracy is 97.82% on average, while achieving an average overhead factor of 1.06×, considering all evaluated workloads on two different machines. Our experiments demonstrate that wosp notably outperforms FJProf, a fork-join task profiler for the JVM (which shows an average accuracy of 54.27% and an average overhead factor of 3.82×).

As part of our future work, we plan to conduct a large-scale characterization of Java fork-join applications used in publicly available code repositories along with exploring ways to optimize them, e.g., by identifying source-code locations where task reuse is applicable. We also plan to extend wosp with a visualization tool which can ease program comprehension. Moreover, we plan to release wosp as open-source software.

Acknowledgments. This work has been supported by Oracle (ERO project 1332) and by the Swiss National Science Foundation (project 200020_188688).

References

1. Adhianto, L., et al.: HPCTOOLKIT: tools for performance analysis of optimized parallel programs. Concurrency Comput. Pract. Exp. **22**(6), 685–701 (2010). https://doi.org/10.1002/cpe.1553
2. Blumofe, R.D., Joerg, C.F., Kuszmaul, B.C., Leiserson, C.E., Randall, K.H., Zhou, Y.: Cilk: an efficient multithreaded runtime system. J. Parallel Distrib. Comput. **37**(1), 55–69 (1996). https://doi.org/10.1145/209936.209958
3. Blumofe, R.D., Leiserson, C.E.: Scheduling multithreaded computations by work stealing. J. ACM **46**(5), 720–748 (1999). https://doi.org/10.1145/324133.324234
4. Chen, S., et al.: Scheduling threads for constructive cache sharing on CMPs. In: SPAA, pp. 105–115 (2007). https://doi.org/10.1145/1248377.1248396
5. Conway, M.E.: A multiprocessor system design. In: AFIPS, pp. 139–146 (1963). https://doi.org/10.1145/1463822.1463838
6. Fonseca, A., Cabral, B.: Evaluation of runtime cut-off approaches for parallel programs. In: VECPAR, pp. 121–134 (2016). https://doi.org/10.1007/978-3-319-61982-8_13

7. Fonseca, A., Stork, S.: AeminiumBenchmarks (2016). https://github.com/AEminium/AeminiumBenchmarks
8. Frigo, M., Leiserson, C.E., Randall, K.H.: The implementation of the Cilk-5 multithreaded language. SIGPLAN Not. **33**(5), 212–223 (1998). https://doi.org/10.1145/277650.277725
9. Guo, Y., Barik, R., Raman, R., Sarkar, V.: Work-first and help-first scheduling policies for async-finish task parallelism. In: IPDPS, pp. 1–12 (2009). https://doi.org/10.1109/IPDPS.2009.5161079
10. Haller, P., Tu, S.: The Scala Actors API (2022). https://docs.scala-lang.org/overviews/core/actors.html
11. He, Y., Leiserson, C.E., Leiserson, W.M.: The Cilkview scalability analyzer. In: SPAA, pp. 145–156 (2010). https://doi.org/10.1145/1810479.1810509
12. ICL: PAPI (2021). http://icl.utk.edu/papi
13. Lea, D.: A Java Fork/Join framework. In: JAVA, pp. 36–43 (2000). https://doi.org/10.1145/337449.337465
14. Lifflander, J., Krishnamoorthy, S., Kale, L.V.: Steal tree: low-overhead tracing of work stealing schedulers. In: PLDI, pp. 507–518 (2013). https://doi.org/10.1145/2499370.2462193
15. Marek, L., et al.: ShadowVM: robust and comprehensive dynamic program analysis for the Java platform. ACM SIGPLAN Not. **49**(3), 105–114 (2013). https://doi.org/10.1145/2517208.2517219
16. Marek, L., Villazón, A., Zheng, Y., Ansaloni, D., Binder, W., Qi, Z.: DiSL: a domain-specific language for bytecode instrumentation. In: AOSD, pp. 239–250 (2012). https://doi.org/10.1145/2162049.2162077
17. Mohr, B., Brown, D., Malony, A.: TAU: a portable parallel program analysis environment for pC++. In: CONPAR – VAPP VI, pp. 29–40 (1994). https://doi.org/10.1007/3-540-58430-7_4
18. Nyman, L., Laakso, M.: Notes on the history of Fork and Join. IEEE Ann. Hist. Comput. **38**(3), 84–87 (2016). https://doi.org/10.1109/MAHC.2016.34
19. Oracle: Package java.util.stream (2021). https://docs.oracle.com/en/java/javase/17/docs/api/java.base/java/util/stream/Stream.html
20. Oracle: ForkJoinTask (2022). https://docs.oracle.com/en/java/javase/17/docs/api/java.base/java/util/concurrent/ForkJoinTask.html
21. Prokopec, A., et al.: Renaissance: benchmarking suite for parallel applications on the JVM. In: PLDI, pp. 31–47 (2019). https://doi.org/10.1145/3314221.3314637
22. Renaissance Suite: Documentation Overview. https://renaissance.dev/docs (2019)
23. Rosà, A., Rosales, E., Binder, W.: Analysis and optimization of task granularity on the java virtual machine. ACM Trans. Program. Lang. Syst. **41**(3) (2019). https://doi.org/10.1145/3338497
24. Rosà A.: TGP (2022). https://github.com/fithos/tgp
25. Rosales, E., Rosà, A., Binder, W.: FJProf: profiling Fork/Join applications on the Java Virtual Machine. In: VALUETOOLS, pp. 128–135 (2020). https://doi.org/10.1145/3388831.3388851
26. Rosà, A., Binder, W.: Optimizing type-specific instrumentation on the JVM with reflective supertype information. J. Vis. Lang. Comput. **49**, 29–45 (2018). https://doi.org/10.1016/j.jvlc.2018.10.007
27. Schardl, T.B., Kuszmaul, B.C., Lee, I.T.A., Leiserson, W.M., Leiserson, C.E.: The Cilkprof scalability profiler. In: SPAA, pp. 89–100 (2015). https://doi.org/10.1145/2755573.2755603

28. Tallent, N.R., Mellor-Crummey, J.M.: Identifying performance bottlenecks in work-stealing computations. Computer **42**(12), 44–50 (2009). https://doi.org/10.1109/MC.2009.396
29. Teng, Q.M., Wang, H.C., Xiao, Z., Sweeney, P.F., Duesterwald, E.: THOR: a performance analysis tool for Java applications running on multicore systems. IBM J. Res. Dev. **54**(5), 4:1–4:17 (2010). https://doi.org/10.1147/JRD.2010.2058481
30. The Clojure Team: Reducers (2019). https://clojure.org/reference/reducers
31. The GPars Team: GPars - A Concurrency & Parallelism Framework for Groovy and Java (2016). http://www.gpars.org

Performance and Power Modeling, Prediction and Evaluation

Characterization of Different User Behaviors for Demand Response in Data Centers

Maël Madon(✉), Georges Da Costa, and Jean-Marc Pierson

IRIT, Université de Toulouse,
CNRS, Toulouse INP, UT3, Toulouse, France
{mael.madon,georges.da-costa,
jean-marc.pierson}@irit.fr

Abstract. Digital technologies are becoming ubiquitous while their impact increases. A growing part of this impact happens far away from the end users, in networks or data centers, contributing to a rebound effect. A solution for a more responsible use is therefore to involve the user. As a first step in this quest, this work considers the users of a data center and characterizes their contribution to curtail the computing load for a short period of time by solely changing their job submission behavior.

The contributions are: (i) an open-source plugin for the simulator Batsim to simulate users based on real data; (ii) the exploration of four types of user behaviors to curtail the load during a time window, namely *delaying*, *degrading*, *reconfiguring* or *renouncing* their job submissions. We study the impact of these behaviors on four different metrics: the energy consumed during and after the time window, the mean waiting time and the mean slowdown. We also characterize the conditions under which the involvement of users is the most beneficial.

Keywords: Demand response · User involvement · User-aware · Reproducible research · Parallel workload · Data center

1 Introduction

Digital technologies are increasingly contributing to global warming, for instance through mining of their components, transport along their supply chains or electricity consumed during their use phase. A recent review of estimates [6] puts this impact at 1.0-1.7 $GtCO_2e$ in 2020, i.e., 1.8%–2.8% of global greenhouse gas emissions. The authors also argue that although progress in energy efficiency of these technologies will probably continue, it will likely be outbalanced by growth in usage, leading to an overall increase of the carbon footprint. This so-called "rebound effect" seems difficult to fight within our research area (scheduling and distributed computing) where the focus is on energy optimization that must be effortless to end-users. On the contrary, we argue that users of digital technologies must be brought back into the loop, made aware of their impact and empowered to mitigate it.

J. Cano and P. W. Trinder (Eds.): Euro-Par 2022, LNCS 13440, pp. 53–68, 2022.
https://doi.org/10.1007/978-3-031-12597-3_4

Involving the user for environmental-aware scheduling in data centers has two aspects. One is to consider user *requests* for more environment-friendly services (e.g., guarantees, green labels) and try to achieve them. The other is to consider the users as a *lever* for flexibility in the scheduling, i.e., they accept to compromise occasionally on their quality of service to allow some optimizations. The degradation can be spatial [9] (reducing the amount of resources allocated for the jobs), temporal [16] (delaying their execution) or both [8].

This paper proposes an experimental analysis of such user levers in a context of demand response management by investigating the following question: from the users' perspective, what is the room for maneuver to curtail the load on the data center for a short period of time?

The rest of the article is organized as follows. We start by giving some background and discuss related works in Sect. 2. Section 3 presents our data center model and lists the user behaviors studied for demand response. Section 4 describes the experimental setup for characterizing these behaviors. The results are presented in Sect. 5 while Sect. 6 provides a discussion on the results and the limitations of the study. Finally, we conclude in Sect. 7 and provide perspectives for future works.

2 Background and Related Works

Context: Demand Response. Data centers are viewed as good candidates to participate in demand response programs [17]. Large consumers of electricity, they also have a more flexible load than other industrial facilities. Demand response consists of adapting the electricity *consumption* in response to the availability of *production*. For example, some electricity markets have Coincident Peak Pricing programs, where industrial consumers are charged a very high price during the time window when the most electricity is requested overall in the grid. These peak pricing events last typically 15 min [18] or one hour [14] but are only known *afterwards*, e.g., at the end of the month. The electricity supplier would only send warnings to the consumer that a peak load event may happen in the next few hours.

Involving the Users. Among the large body of work on energy-aware scheduling in data centers, some authors have studied strategies involving the users. Some works aim at providing guarantees to their users ("green offers" [7], "green SLA" [1,10]) and commit to fulfilling them by classical methods (self-supply of renewable energy [10], geo-distributed data centers with variable PUE and energy mix [1,7]). More related to this paper, some works study user flexibility as a *lever* for energy efficiency. For example, Guyon et al. [9] give to the users the choice between three execution modes (big, medium, little) for their jobs. Small execution modes request fewer resources but take longer to complete. They achieve gains through spatial consolidation with a bin-packing algorithm. Orgerie et al. [16] save energy through thermal-aware scheduling and smart resource switch off by letting the users choose between different submission times on the basis of energy consumption estimations for each of the alternatives. A combination of both spatial and thermal consolidation is proposed in another work by Guyon et al. [8] or in the All4Green project [2], where user involvement is leveraged through contracts between the energy supplier, the data center and the user. The latter work, also in a context of demand response, is the closest to our approach. However, it integrates demand response mechanisms affecting the user with mechanisms transparent to them (use of batteries, precooling, geographical workload migration) so much so that the contribution of each user behavior to the final results is difficult to identify.

The originality of our work is to focus on the user behaviors, which allows providing a characterization of them. To the best of our knowledge, we are also the only ones to consider the behavior of simply *renouncing* job submissions. It is a radical behavior, but to be considered in a sufficiency approach.

3 Model

In our model, a demand response event will be represented by a time window of few hours (called "demand response window") during which the objective is to reduce electricity consumption. The event is supposed unknown in advance. In order to characterize the efficiency of different user behaviors to react to such demand response event, we consider a data center to which users can submit their jobs. At the interface between the two is the RJMS (Resource and Job Management System), the scheduler in charge of job placement and resource management. In this section, we describe the different components of our system.

3.1 Data Center

In the data center, we only take into account the energy consumption of the multicore homogeneous machines. The power of a machine is P_{off}, P_{son} or P_{soff} if the machine is switched off, switching on or switching off, respectively. When a machine is switched on, its power is equal to $P_{idle} + N * P_{core}$ with P_{idle} the power drawn by an idle machine, N the number of cores in use (i.e., with a job running on it) and P_{core} the power drawn by each core.

A job is completely defined by its *submission time*, *execution time* and number of requested cores that we denote by *size* in the rest of this paper. The scheduler decides the starting time for the job and the machine it will be executed on. Note that the scheduler in our model only execute jobs on single machines. We suppose perfect communication without latency.

3.2 Scheduler

The scheduler is a bin-packing scheduler with shutdown (same as Guyon et al. [8, 9]). It is a greedy algorithm trying to schedule ("pack") all the jobs in the least possible machines and shut down idle machines. To do so, it maintains and updates two data structures: a queue of waiting jobs and a list of switched-on machines. The queue of jobs is sorted by *decreasing* size order – and by increasing submission time (first come, first served) in case of a tie. The list of machines is sorted by *increasing* order of available cores. Every time one (or more) job is submitted or finishes, the scheduler goes through the job queue in order and tries to find for each job the smallest machine where it fits. If no machine is found that way, a new machine (if any) is powered on and the job is scheduled on this machine. After that, we immediately shut down all idle machines.

3.3 Users

During the demand response window, users are asked to make an effort to curtail the load in the data center. They do so by adopting different behaviors described below and illustrated in Fig. 1.

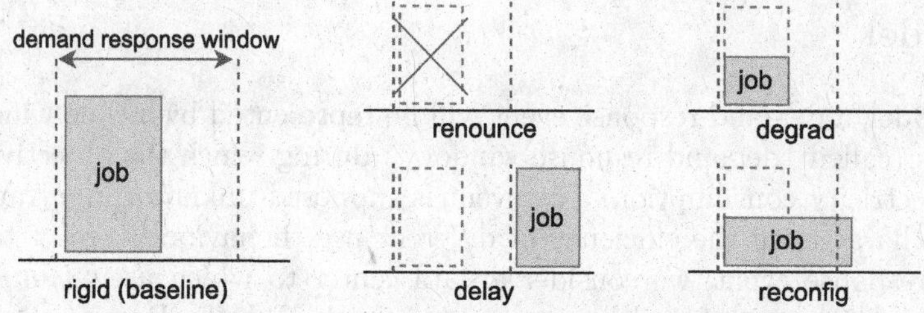

Fig. 1. The five user behaviors studied

- **rigid**: replay jobs as in the original workload; Baseline for comparison.
- **renounce**: do not submit jobs originally submitted during the window.
- **delay**: delay all job submissions to the end of the window.
- **degrad**: divide the size of the jobs by two, rounded up. The execution time stays the same. Note that the rounding implies that when only one core is requested for a job, the job remains unchanged.
- **reconfig**: also divide the size by two, rounded up, but increase the execution time to match the original computing mass. We make the hypothesis of perfect speedup, i.e., a job executing on one core completes in exactly twice the time than on two cores.

4 Experimental Setup

4.1 Software Used for Simulation

To simulate our system, we use Batsim [4], an open-source infrastructure and resource management system simulator[1] based on SimGrid[2]. We implemented

[1] Batsim: https://batsim.org/.

[2] SimGrid: https://simgrid.org with the energy plugin https://simgrid.org/doc/latest/Plugins.html?highlight=energy#host-energy.

the bin-packing scheduler for Batsim in C++. We also developed a plugin called "batmen" to interact with simulated users and receive their job submissions. For the purpose of this study, users replay an input workload trace except in the demand response window, where they act according to their behavior. We therefore implemented five user classes corresponding to the five behaviors of Fig. 1. Our code is open source[3]. With this simulation tool, we designed and conducted an experimental campaign, whose main details are given below. All scripts are available to reproduce and analyze our results, either in our gitlab[4] or in the Figshare repository [15].

4.2 Workload

We replay a real public workload trace containing the information about the submitting user for each recorded job. We chose the 2-year trace from MetaCentrum (national grid of the Czech Republic), available in the Parallel Workload Archive[5]. The platform is very heterogeneous and underwent majors changes during the logging period [12]. For the purpose of our study, we perform the following selection:

1. We truncate the workload to keep only 6 months (June to November 2014) where no major change was performed in the infrastructure, and we remove all the clusters whose nodes have more than 16 cores;
2. From this truncated workload, we remove all jobs with an execution time greater than one day and all jobs with a size greater than 16. It leaves us with a workload manageable with machines of a usual size, and without more than one day of inertia.

4.3 Platform

The first selection step keeps a total of 6304 cores. The second selection step excludes 2.7% of jobs from the truncated workload, representing 73.7% of the mass (in core-hour). Consequently, we create a simulated platform adapted to this load with $6304 * (1 - 0.737)/16 =$ **104 homogeneous 16-core machines**. Power constants ($P_{idle} = 100\,\text{W}$, $P_{core} = 7.3125\,\text{W}$, $P_{off} = 9.75$, $P_{son} = 100\,\text{W}$ and $P_{soff} = 125\,\text{W}$) for the servers and time to switch on ($T_{son} = 150\,\text{s}$) and switch off ($T_{son} = 6\,\text{s}$) are measurements in Taurus Grid'5000 cluster from existing work [9].

4.4 Experimental Campaign

For the evaluation, we consider the following scenario. We imagine a data center functioning at nominal load: some jobs are currently running and users can

[3] Batmen repository: https://gitlab.irit.fr/sepia-pub/mael/batmen.

[4] Experiments repository: https://gitlab.irit.fr/sepia-pub/open-science/demand-response-user/-/tree/europar2022.

[5] METACENTRUM-2013-3.swf available at https://www.cs.huji.ac.il/labs/parallel/workload/l_metacentrum2/index.html.

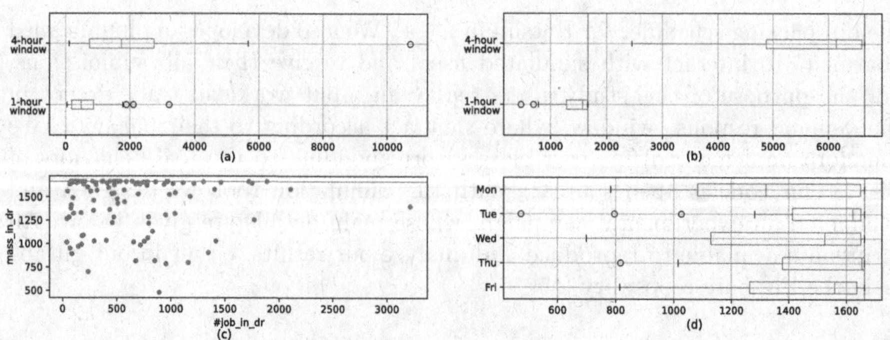

Fig. 2. Descriptive statistics for the 105 experiments. Red lines corresponds to the infrastructure (1664 cores). (a) number of jobs submitted in window; (b) computing mass (in core-hour) in window; (c) computing mass in window by number of submitted jobs (1-h window); (d) computing mass in window by weekday (1-h window) (Color figure online)

submit new jobs to the scheduler. Suddenly, the electrical grid sends an alert to warn the data center manager that a consumption peak is detected in the grid. The manager forwards this alert to his users who adapt their submission behavior. At the end of the alert, the users return to a normal behavior (after submitting all their delayed jobs, if any).

We conduct an experimental campaign on 105 different input data (the number of weekdays between Jun 1, 2014 and Oct 23, 2014). For each input data, we simulate the aforementioned scenario, assuming that all users adopt the same behavior during the demand response window. On three days of data center operation, we make the demand response event arise at 16:00 on day 2, chosen to be a weekday. This choice is justified by a characterization of 26 years' coincident peak pricing data [14], given that the MetaCentrum trace also displays diurnal and weekday/weekend patterns. We study two lengths for the demand response window: one and four hours. We also tried other starting times (drawn at random) and other window lengths (0.5 and 2 h) but decided not to report their results here as they are not leading to different conclusions.

The simulation starts one day before the event and stops one day after, to ensure that the infrastructure runs at nominal load on day 2 and has absorbed the event by the end of day 3 (the selected jobs in the workload having an execution time lower than one day). In total, we launch nine simulations per experiment (= input data): the baseline simulation with all users having a "rigid" behavior, and the four other behaviors on the two window lengths. Descriptive statistics on the experiments are displayed in Fig. 2.

The campaign launched in parallel on a 2×8-core Intel Xeon E5-2630 v3 machine finished in less than two hours. Launched in France, and ran 2 times in total, this has a carbon footprint of around 50 g CO2e (calculated using https://green-algorithms.org v2.1 [13]).

5 Results

5.1 Energy Metrics

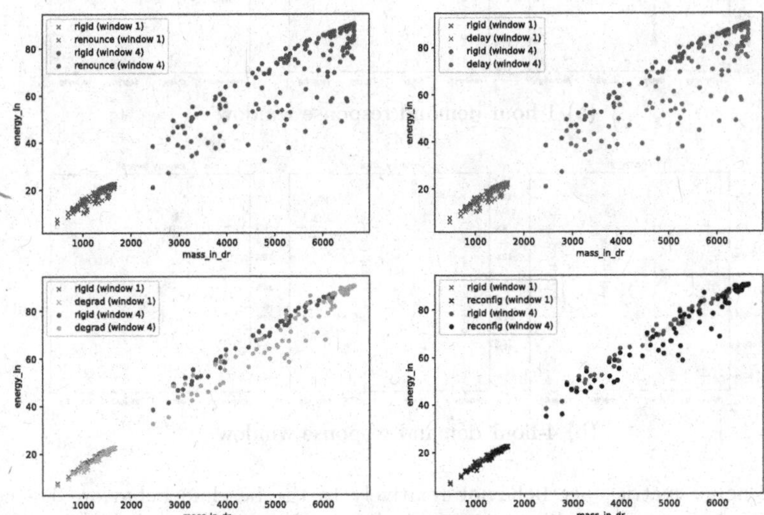

Fig. 3. Energy consumed in each simulation. Y-axis: energy consumed (in kWh) during the demand response window. X-axis: computing mass (in core-hour) during the demand response window for the baseline behavior.

We recall our research question: by intervening only on the user's side, what energy gains can be expected by adapting one's behavior for a few hours? Figure 3 displays the **energy consumed during the demand response window** for every experiment and every behavior. Values are scattered by the total load of the infrastructure during the window for the baseline behavior. For that behavior, we note an almost linear relationship between infrastructure load and consumed energy. Deviations from the linear line are due to situations favoring a more or less good packing from the scheduler inside the 16-core machines. Behaviors "renounce" and "delay" perform identically for this metric: users of both behaviors stop submitting inside the demand response window, resulting in a lower energy consumption compared to the baseline. This gain is the best we can expect. Behaviors "degrad" and "reconfig" display similar results. In addition, one would expect a positive correlation between the load of the platform and the relative energy gains of the four behaviors compared to the baseline. It would translate into an increasing distance between the colored dots and the blue dots in the graphs, as the load increases. Counter-intuitively, this does not seem to happen.

The experimental campaign showing very scattered results, Fig. 4 displays the relative energy gains for each experiment as box plots. We can read for

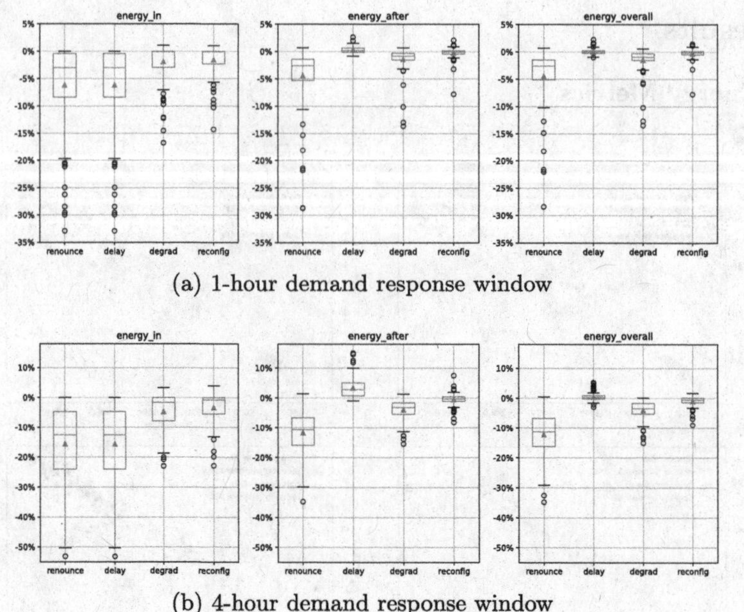

(a) 1-hour demand response window

(b) 4-hour demand response window

Fig. 4. Energy metrics per behavior relatively to the baseline behavior. The green triangle in the box plots indicates the mean. (Color figure online)

example that "renounce", the most radical behavior, allows energy savings of up to 33% in the window for a one-hour window, and 53% for a four-hour window. The savings do not go up to 100% because jobs that were already there before the window are still running in the infrastructure, which consumes energy.

In addition to the energy consumed *within* the window, Fig. 4 shows the impact of the different behaviors on the energy consumed *after* the demand response event, i.e., from 17:00 or 20:00 on day2 (depending on the window length) to 24:00 on day3. For this second metric, "delay" performs very differently compared to "renounce". All the jobs within the window get postponed, resulting in an extra power consumption at the end of the window: +0.3% (resp. +3.4%) on average for a 1-h (resp. 4-hour) window. This behavior remains neutral with respect to overall energy consumption (*within* + *after* the window). The behavior "reconfig", which also keeps a constant mass of jobs compared to the baseline, allows some optimizations. Up to 10% overall energy consumption could be saved because the reconfigured jobs "fit better in the holes" left by the available cores in the switched on machines. "Degrad" performs unsurprisingly better in all respects, the users having accepted to reduce the mass of job submitted.

Finally, we notice that **the bigger the window, the better the energy gains**. This is due to inertia of the system: with a longer window, a behavior on the submitted jobs has more time to make a difference compared to the residual jobs that are still running in the infrastructure.

5.2 Perceived Impact on the Scheduling

We use two usual metrics: mean waiting time and mean slowdown. Waiting time is the time a user has to wait until her job starts running:

$$waiting_{time} = starting_{time} - submission_{time}$$

Slowdown divides this extended completion time by the execution time:

$$slowdown = (finish_{time} - submission_{time})/execution_{time}.$$

For each experiment, we take the average waiting time (resp. slowdown) on all jobs submitted between the beginning of the demand response window and the end of the experiment (same period as metric *energy_in* + *energy_after*). Figure 5 shows these results for the “rigid” behavior. We observe that for half of the experiments, the mean waiting time is below one hour (3600 s) and the mean slowdown below 25. These are experiments with an unsaturated infrastructure and an often empty queue of waiting job. On the other hand, there are also cases of high congestion (e.g., the seven outliers at more than 6h mean waiting time).

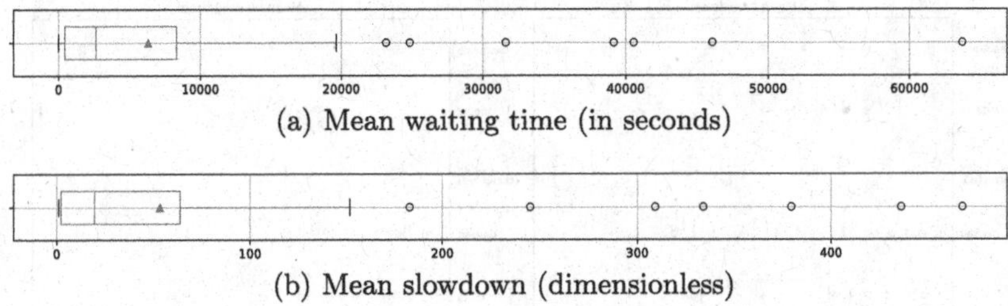

(a) Mean waiting time (in seconds)

(b) Mean slowdown (dimensionless)

Fig. 5. Scheduling metric distribution for the 105 experiments, baseline behavior.

The results for the other behaviors are plotted in Fig. 6, as a percentage of gain/loss compared to the baseline. Specifically for the behavior “delay”, we provide both *corrected* and *uncorrected* metrics. The uncorrected slowdown and waiting time are calculated in relation to the *new* (delayed) submission times, while the corrected ones use the *original* submission times (from the baseline). Note also that for the behavior “renounce” some jobs have been canceled, thus the mean waiting time and slowdown is calculated on a subset of the jobs compared to the other behaviors. From Fig. 6 it can be observed that the behaviors “renounce”, “degrad” and “reconfig” (in this order) affect the scheduling positively on average. This is not surprising, as the first two behaviors reduce the total mass of jobs to compute, and the third allows a better packing. Yet, the scheduling gets worsened in a significant number of cases (around 50% for “reconfig” and 25% for “degrad” and “renounce”), due to bad choices of the scheduler.

The behavior “delay” stands out from the others as it affects the scheduling negatively in most cases, even for the uncorrected metrics. It gets even worse when including the extra waiting time from the delayed job in the calculation of the corrected metrics. In fact, it is preferable in terms of waiting time and slowdown that the job submissions are spread out throughout the time.

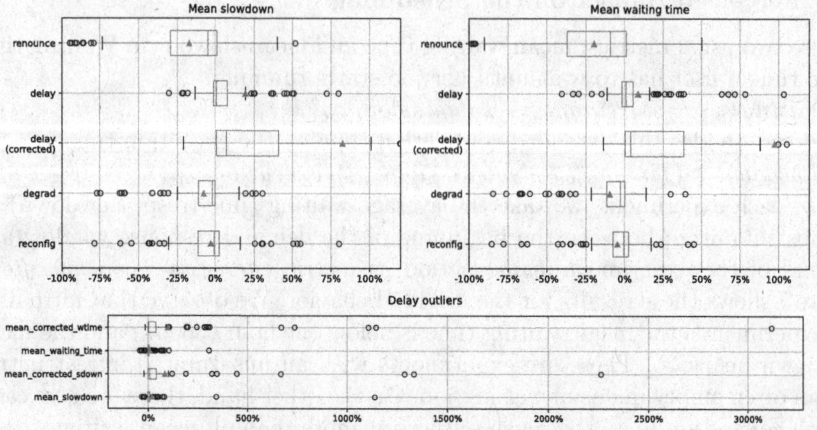

(a) 1-hour demand response window

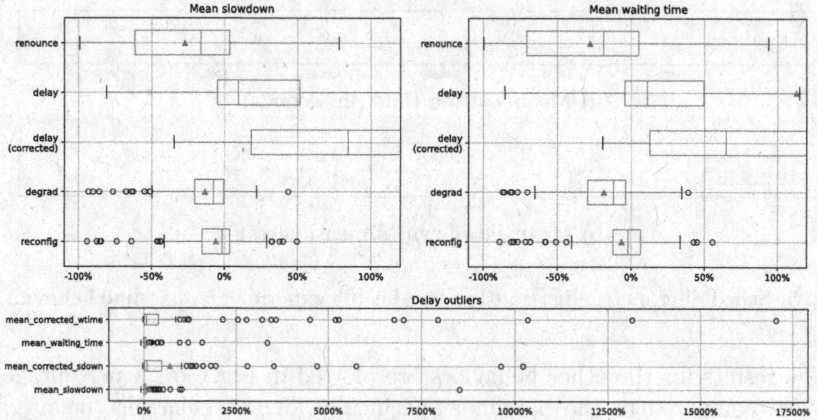

(b) 4-hour demand response window

Fig. 6. Scheduling metrics per behavior relatively to the baseline behavior

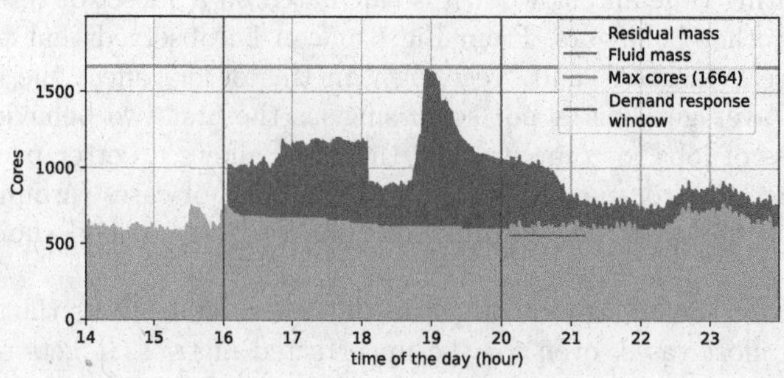

Fig. 7. Example of fluid and residual mass. *(Thursday Jun 26 2014)*

6 Discussion

6.1 The Fluid-Residual Ratio: An Explanation of the Results

As seen previously in Fig. 3, the achievable energy savings in the demand response window cannot be explained by the infrastructure load during that window. In fact, it is possible that the load is very high because of a large mass of job submitted *before* the window, although the load on which the users have an influence is the mass submitted *during* the window. We call these two quantities the **residual mass**, submitted outside the window, and the **fluid mass**, submitted inside the window (Fig. 7).

Users, by accepting to "renounce" or "delay" their jobs, allow cutting the energy consumption due to the fluid mass, which is roughly proportional to the mass itself, as we saw before. In other terms, **the gains during the window are at most equal to the proportion of fluid mass in that window.** This is exactly what we see in Fig. 8 displaying the energy gains as a function of the fluid-residual ratio. The red line indicates the best possible gains, which are almost achieved by "renounce" and "delay" behavior (the non-linearity of the energy model explaining the gap).

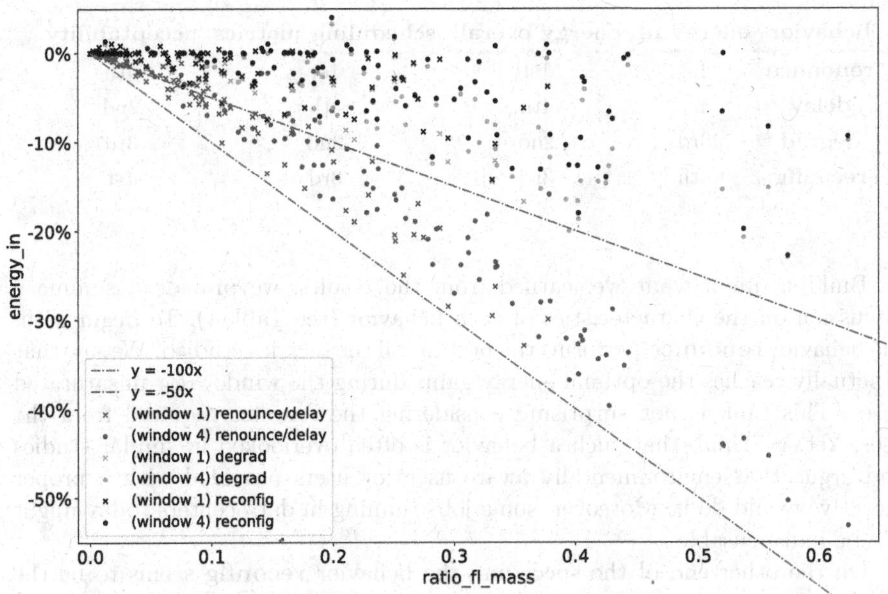

Fig. 8. Energy gains in function of the fluid-residual ratio. Only one plot for the behaviors "renounce" and "delay" because they are identical for this metric.

In some cases, however, these behaviors don't realize that gain: they are cases of **saturation**, when many jobs are waiting in the queue. The removal of the fluid mass is compensated by the execution of the awaiting residual mass.

For the "degrad" behavior, gains are expected to be of half the fluid mass at most, as users divide their submitted mass by two. In practice, the results are even more scattered and further away from their optimal (magenta line). This is partially due to the saturation effect, but also to rounding (e.g., a job with an original size of 3 will be submitted with size 2 and a job with size 1 remains unchanged) and imperfect packing. The analysis for the behavior "reconfig" is similar, with even less expected gains. Some experiments even make negative gains: they are due to the greedy and non-clairvoyant scheduler taking bad decisions for the future, like switching off a machine just before the submission of new jobs.

6.2 Pros and Cons of Each Behavior

Table 1. Summary ranking of the four behaviors according to their impact on energy consumption and scheduling metrics. The column "acceptability" is opinion-based, it reflects the size of the effort asked from the user.

behavior	energy in	energy overall	scheduling metrics	acceptability
renounce	1st	1st	1st	4th
delay	1st	4th	4th	2nd
degrad	3rd	2nd	2nd	3rd
reconfig	4th	3rd	3rd	1st

Building upon what we learned from the results, we provide a summary discussion on the characteristics of each behavior (see Table 1). To begin with, the behavior **renounce** performs the best for all the metrics studied. We saw that it actually reaches the optimal energy gains during the window for unsaturated cases. This rank is not surprising considering the sacrifice required from the user. Yet, we think that such a behavior is often overlooked in similar studies and argue that environmentally aware users or users provided with a proper incentive would do it. Moreover, some jobs running in data centers today might not be indispensable.

On the other end of the spectrum, the behavior **reconfig** seems to be the most acceptable to the users, as it does not decrease the mass initially submitted and provides better waiting time and slowdown than "delay" for both the jobs within and after the window. "Reconfig" is a good trade-off to achieve some optimizations with a low effort from the user, especially in combination with bin-packing schedulers and on/off policies (see [9]).

Delay also keeps the mass constant, which ranks it second behind "reconfig" in terms of acceptability. Same as "renounce", it reaches the optimal energy gains during the window. However, it introduces an overhead in overall energy consumption and slowdown compared to the baseline behavior. Note that this overhead would probably be less important in real life due to users adapting their behavior if they experience congestion in the infrastructure. This is the limit of blindly replaying past workload traces in simulations, as pointed by Feitelson [5].

Finally, the behavior **degrad** ranks second or third in all the categories of Table 1. It remains an interesting trade-off between simply renouncing a job and reconfiguring it at constant mass. Practical applications of this behavior are optional features in an application that can be cut off if needed (e.g., recommendations for e-commerce, alternative paths for mapping apps).

6.3 Interactions with Scheduling Systems

The work presented in this paper is rather theoretical and abstracts part of the reality of production systems. For example, in real-world schedulers, it is commun to have job priorities. In that case, the degradation of a low-priority job would be less costly to the user compared to a high-priority job. The priority of a job could be considered along with other criterias (e.g., magnitude of the delay, size of the degradation) to define a *utility* metric in an attempt to quantify the acceptability of a given behavior.

All in all, user submission behaviors remain one lever for energy saving among others. It has the particularity of having some latency, which makes it not optimal in a context of demand response without prediction. Therefore, **taking into account these behaviors inside the scheduler** seems essential to make the best of their potential and go beyond the fluid-residual limit. For example, by allowing the scheduler to kill jobs, checkpoint them [3], or to suspend the waiting queue. Decisions could be taken on behalf of the users, with a mecanism of contract with the data center operator specifying the degradation the user is willing to accept [2]. Nevertheless, it seems crucial for us to make these decisions transparent to the user and involve them as much as possible, as this appears as the main path towards a *sufficient* [11] use of our technologies.

6.4 Limitations

Model Simplifications. In our data center simulations, we do not take into account the latency and bottleneck effects in the communications. Also, we suppose perfect speedup in the model, i.e., a job executed on two cores will take exactly twice longer than the same job executed on four cores. Finally, we accounted only for the energy consumption of the CPUs, and neglected others like memory, network or cooling. Hopefully, the powerful simulation tools that we use (Batsim and SimGrid) will help us to overcome these simplifications in future works.

Methodological Limitations. We see three major threats to the validity of our method to answer the research question. First, we study only one scheduler (bin-packing) while results with other common schedulers (FCFS, easy-backfilling...)

would have been of interest. Second, we use only one input trace (MetaCentrum) which comes from a research infrastructure and not a production cloud, and we perform a selection from it (see Sect. 4.2) that might make us miss the big picture. Finally, our study includes all the limitations related to the use of a simulation, especially when dealing with human behaviors which are unpredictable.

7 Conclusion and Future Works

In this paper, we study four different ways for a user of a data center to curtail her load for a certain period of time by changing submission behavior. These behaviors are delaying, degrading, reconfiguring or renouncing the jobs during the time period. We show experimentally through simulation on real world data that these behaviors have a certain latency for decreasing the load on the infrastructure. Indeed, they cannot decrease the load due to jobs that are already running on the infrastructure. Therefore, we define two quantities, the *fluid* and *residual* mass, and discuss the experimental results according to the ratio of these two quantities. We also discuss the pros and the cons of each behavior in the light of their energy saving potential, impact on scheduling and acceptability to the user. We hope that this work will pave the way for studies involving the user more intensely.

Future work will focus on (i) improving the data center model to deal with the model simplifications listed in Subsect. 6.4, (ii) proposing schedulers capable of leveraging the efforts made by the user (e.g., through "green SLA"), (iii) elaborating on the user model to more realistically account for submission patterns and response to feedback from the infrastructure (as proposed by Feitelson [5]) and (iv) going beyond the limited scope of demand response to reason on the sustainability of the infrastructure as a whole.

Acknowledgements and Data Availability Statement.. Experiments presented in this paper were carried out using the Grid'5000 testbed, supported by a scientific interest group hosted by Inria and including CNRS, RENATER and several Universities as well as other organizations (see https://www.grid5000.fr). The scripts and instructions necessary to reproduce and analyze our result are available in a Figshare repository [15].

This work was partly supported by the French Research Agency under the project Energumen (ANR-18-CE25-0008) and DataZero2 (ANR-19-CE25-0016).

References

1. Amokrane, A., Langar, R., Zhani, M.F., Boutaba, R., Pujolle, G.: Greenslater: on satisfying green SLAs in distributed clouds. IEEE Trans. Netw. Serv. Manag. **12**(3), 363–376 (2015). https://doi.org/10.1109/TNSM.2015.2440423
2. Basmadjian, R., Botero, J.F., Giuliani, G., Hesselbach, X., Klingert, S., De Meer, H.: Making data centers fit for demand response: introducing GreenSDA and GreenSLA contracts. IEEE Trans. Smart Grid **9**(4), 3453–3464 (2018). https://doi.org/10.1109/TSG.2016.2632526

3. Dupont, B., Mejri, N., Da Costa, G.: Energy-aware scheduling of malleable HPC applications using a particle swarm optimised greedy algorithm. Sustain. Comput. Inf. Syst. **28**, 100447 (2020). https://doi.org/10.1016/j.suscom.2020.100447
4. Dutot, P.-F., Mercier, M., Poquet, M., Richard, O.: Batsim: a realistic language-independent resources and jobs management systems simulator. In: Desai, N., Cirne, W. (eds.) JSSPP 2015-2016. LNCS, vol. 10353, pp. 178–197. Springer, Cham (2017). https://doi.org/10.1007/978-3-319-61756-5_10
5. Feitelson, D.G.: Resampling with feedback — a new paradigm of using workload data for performance evaluation. In: Dutot, P.-F., Trystram, D. (eds.) Euro-Par 2016. LNCS, vol. 9833, pp. 3–21. Springer, Cham (2016). https://doi.org/10.1007/978-3-319-43659-3_1
6. Freitag, C., Berners-Lee, M., Widdicks, K., Knowles, B., Blair, G.S., Friday, A.: The real climate and transformative impact of ICT: a critique of estimates, trends, and regulations. Patterns **2**(9), 100340 (2021). https://doi.org/10.1016/j.patter.2021.100340
7. Garg, S.K., Yeo, C.S., Buyya, R.: Green cloud framework for improving carbon efficiency of clouds. In: Jeannot, E., Namyst, R., Roman, J. (eds.) Euro-Par 2011. LNCS, vol. 6852, pp. 491–502. Springer, Heidelberg (2011). https://doi.org/10.1007/978-3-642-23400-2_45
8. Guyon, D., Orgerie, A.C., Morin, C.: Energy - efficient IaaS-PaaS co-design for flexible cloud deployment of scientific applications. In: 2018 30th International Symposium on Computer Architecture and High Performance Computing (SBAC-PAD), pp. 69–76, September 2018. https://doi.org/10.1109/CAHPC.2018.8645888
9. Guyon, D., Orgerie, A.C., Morin, C., Agarwal, D.: Involving users in energy conservation: a case study in scientific clouds. Int. J. Grid Util. Comput. **10**(3), 272–282 (2019). https://doi.org/10.1504/IJGUC.2019.099667
10. Haque, M.E., Le, K., Goiri, Í., Bianchini, R., Nguyen, T.D.: Providing green SLAs in high performance computing clouds. In: 2013 International Green Computing Conference Proceedings, pp. 1–11, June 2013. https://doi.org/10.1109/IGCC.2013.6604503
11. Hilty, L.: Computing efficiency, sufficiency, and self-sufficiency: a model for sustainability? In: LIMITS 2015, First Workshop on Computing within Limits. s.n., Irvine, CA, USA, June 2015. https://doi.org/10.5167/uzh-110766
12. Klusáček, D., Tóth, Š, Podolníková, G.: Real-life experience with major reconfiguration of job scheduling system. In: Desai, N., Cirne, W. (eds.) JSSPP 2015-2016. LNCS, vol. 10353, pp. 83–101. Springer, Cham (2017). https://doi.org/10.1007/978-3-319-61756-5_5
13. Lannelongue, L., Grealey, J., Inouye, M.: Green algorithms: quantifying the carbon footprint of computation. Adv. Sci. **8**(12), 2100707 (2021). https://doi.org/10.1002/advs.202100707
14. Liu, Z., Wierman, A., Chen, Y., Razon, B., Chen, N.: Data center demand response: avoiding the coincident peak via workload shifting and local generation. Perform. Eval. **70**(10), 770–791 (2013). https://doi.org/10.1016/j.peva.2013.08.014
15. Madon, M., Da Costa, G., Pierson, J.M.: Artifact and instructions to generate experimental results for Euro-Par'2022 paper: characterization of different user behaviors for demand response in data centers, June 2022. https://doi.org/10.6084/m9.figshare.19948352
16. Orgerie, A., Lefèvre, L., Gelas, J.: Save watts in your grid: green strategies for energy-aware framework in large scale distributed systems. In: 2008 14th IEEE International Conference on Parallel and Distributed Systems, pp. 171–178, December 2008. https://doi.org/10.1109/ICPADS.2008.97

17. Wierman, A., Liu, Z., Liu, I., Mohsenian-Rad, H.: Opportunities and challenges for data center demand response. In: International Green Computing Conference, pp. 1–10, November 2014. https://doi.org/10.1109/IGCC.2014.7039172
18. Zarnikau, J., Thal, D.: The response of large industrial energy consumers to four coincident peak (4CP) transmission charges in the Texas (ERCOT) market. Utilities Policy **26**, 1–6 (2013). https://doi.org/10.1016/j.jup.2013.04.004

On-the-Fly Calculation of Model Factors for Multi-paradigm Applications

Joachim Protze[1(✉)], Fabian Orland[1], Kingshuk Haldar[2], Thore Koritzius[1], and Christian Terboven[1]

[1] IT Center, RWTH Aachen University, Aachen, Germany
{protze,orland,terboven}@itc.rwth-aachen.de,
thore.koritzius@rwth-aachen.de
[2] HLRS, University of Stuttgart, Stuttgart, Germany
haldar@hlrs.de

Abstract. Model factors provide initial insight into fundamental issues of parallel applications. These metrics elaborate beyond conventional HPC metrics to indicate whether an application suffers from systemic or local load imbalances, or high cost for synchronization or data transfer. The metrics are also useful to compare the parallel characteristics of different versions of the same application. This work proposes a model of separating the impact factors of different layered parallelism paradigms. In contrast to previous work in this area, we successfully separate all factors and can prove all efficiency values to be between 0 and 1. While we use MPI + OpenMP as an example in this work, the general concepts also apply to layering other parallel programming paradigms. As a proof of concept, we present a tool that collects the necessary performance data and determines different critical paths in the execution without measurable runtime overhead. We evaluate the methodology with synthetic source code examples but also with a real-world application and an application using the latest or future MPI and OpenMP features in order to evaluate the methodology on applications with an overlap of asynchronous computation and communication at the highest possible concurrency.

1 Introduction

Multiple programming paradigms are becoming more common in contemporary HPC codes than only relying on a single one [6]. While MPI, by and large, has become a de facto for distributed memory parallelization, with increasing cores fitted per node, combining it with shared memory paradigms has become crucial. On the one hand, this reduces memory requirement per node as codes can look at the subset of a problem at the MPI level while allowing cores on the same node to use the shared resources.

Optimal use of these resources is a foremost concern of the relatively newer hybrid codes. While performance metrics of each paradigm individually are well studied, describing their interactions simply and predictably remains an open

J. Cano and P. W. Trinder (Eds.): Euro-Par 2022, LNCS 13440, pp. 69–84, 2022.
https://doi.org/10.1007/978-3-031-12597-3_5

question. More often than not, the second paradigms get introduced after the codes are relatively mature to take advantage of more modern architectures. As a result, usually, one of them suffers more from the resulting inefficiencies.

The model-factors (Sect. 2) provide self-explaining components and are well adapted for MPI and OpenMP separately. There are multiple methods to derive the metrics (e.g., critical path analysis in Dimemas [5]). These methods use a post-mortem simulation to derive the metrics. While these are the most accurate with their model, they require significant computation.

Previous work [4] to quantify efficiency metrics of hybrid codes with hierarchical interactions between two HPC paradigms has proposed a subset of equivalent hybrid metrics. However, this does not resolve the metrics fully and, in principle, is not applicable for non-hierarchical codes yet. We propose a methodology to resolve the hybrid metrics to the full extent of such separate equivalent metrics, also applicable to non-hierarchical codes. Our method works on the fly with memory overheads in the order of a flat profiler, no measurable runtime overhead, and the result is readily available right after the end of execution. Furthermore, we show that the resulting breakdown is consistent.

This work constitutes of

- a proposed method for on-the-fly resolution of the communication efficiency in a hybrid regime;
- a theoretical validation with synthetic examples of various possible scenarios;
- an implementation for OpenMP + MPI regime; and
- its applications on real-life codes and evaluation of overhead and performance.

In the following, Sect. 2 presents the fundamentals of model factors, and Sect. 3 presents concept and our extension of the critical path technique. Section 4 describes our methodology based on the terminologies described in Sect. 3. Section 5 presents the extension of the model factors based on the methodology described in the past sections. Section 6 contains the evaluation by validation experiments with synthetic and real-life examples, and Sect. 8 presents the conclusions from this.

2 Model Factors

Model factors or fundamental performance factors as introduced by C. Rosas et al. [11] describe parallel efficiency as product of the impact factors *load balance*, *serialization efficiency*, and *transfer efficiency*.

Load balance (LB) quantifies the balance of work load between the different execution units. If all execution units have the same amount of work during the observed time interval, load balance is 100%.

$$LB = \frac{avg(t_i)}{max(t_i)} \tag{1}$$

The value t_i represents the aggregated quantity (usually time) for each execution unit i. Figure 1 shows execution traces with 75% load balance in (a) and 100% in (b).

Transfer efficiency (TE) reflects the cost of actual data transfer or synchronization introduced by the parallel programming paradigms. On an ideal network/bus with zero cost for synchronization, transfer efficiency would always be 100%.

$$TE = \frac{runtime_{ideal}}{runtime_{real}} = \frac{runtime_{ideal}}{runtime} \tag{2}$$

In this context, $runtime_{ideal}$ is a simulated runtime from the application when executed on an ideal network or bus with no latency and infinite bandwidth. Also, thread-level synchronization has no latency on such a machine. Nevertheless, this machine model does not impact the latency to shared memory from application code. Both execution traces in Fig. 1 have an ideal runtime of 2 s and a real runtime of 2.2 s. Therefore the transfer efficiency in both traces is 91%.

Serialization efficiency (SerE) reflects local load imbalances with synchronizing dependencies to other execution units. The overall load balance can be perfect, while locally alternating execution units wait for each other to proceed. If the execution units always wait for the same unit to proceed, serialization efficiency is 100% as this is accounted for in the load balance metric.

$$SerE = \frac{max(t_i)}{runtime_{ideal}} \tag{3}$$

Trace (a) in Fig. 1 has 100% serialization efficiency because the second process needs to wait on the first process consistently. In (b), the dependency chain switches from the first to the second process, which results in 75% serialization efficiency.

Parallel efficiency (PE) is the product of load balance, serialization efficiency, and transfer efficiency.

$$PE = LB * SerE * TE = \frac{avg(t_i)}{runtime} \tag{4}$$

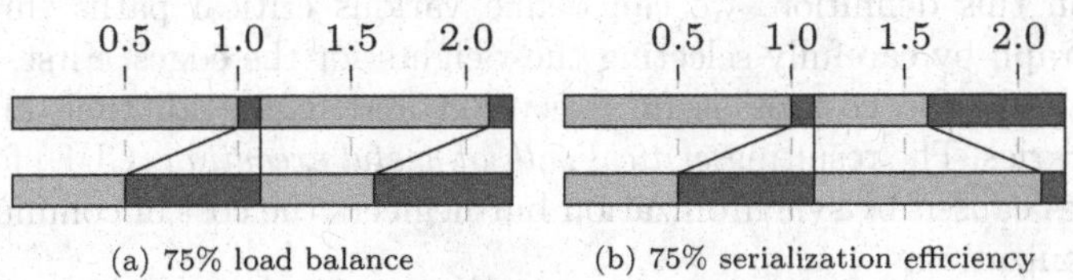

(a) 75% load balance (b) 75% serialization efficiency

Fig. 1. Examples with two processes, two phases of useful execution (blue) and MPI synchronization (red). Both cases show ideal runtime of 2 s and 91% transfer efficiency. (Color figure online)

Both execution traces in Fig. 1 have the same parallel efficiency of 68% as the product of 91%, 75%, and 100%. They differ is just the ordering of the factors.

In this work, we use the term *useful execution* (UE) to characterize time spent to execute the application code distinguished from time spent in parallel runtime libraries such as OpenMP and MPI. For applications where parallel execution does not require additional, possibly redundant calculations, the above definition of parallel efficiency matches the commonly used understanding of parallel efficiency. All aggregated useful execution is equivalent to serial execution for these applications.

Besides $runtime_{ideal}$, all of the values are directly measured and can be collected locally on each of the executing threads. The following section will explain how we derive $runtime_{ideal}$ using critical path analysis.

3 Critical Path

Critical path analysis is used in different performance analysis tools targeting parallel applications [1,8,13]. In these tools, critical path analysis aims to determine the critical path in parallel execution, possibly highlighting the critical path in an execution trace and identifying bottlenecks on the critical path. The tools need to explicitly identify the critical path through the application and apply different algorithms to identify the critical path in the execution graph to reach these goals. Often this analysis involves a forward and backward replay. In contrast, it is sufficient to determine the critical path implicitly for our use case, which significantly simplifies the problem.

Yang et al. [13] characterize the critical path as the "event path in the execution history of the program that has the longest duration". In our work, we want to use the term *critical path* in a broader sense and define the critical path for the execution graph of an actually observed execution of the application. The edges in the execution graph represent: a) thread-level synchronization, e.g., from OpenMP, b)process-level synchronization, e.g., from MPI communication, or c) sequential execution within a process unit, e.g., executing application code or parallel runtime code. Such execution graph is always directed and acyclic.

The *critical path* between two connected nodes in a directed acyclic graph is the path with the highest sum of weights on the edges of the path.

Based on this definition, we can define various critical paths through an execution graph by carefully selecting the weights for the edges. First, we want to consider only the cost of useful execution and ignore all time in parallel runtime libraries. The resulting *critical path of useful execution* (CUE) follows all dependencies caused by synchronization but neglects the cost of communication and synchronization.

Similarly, we can define graphs, where only time in the MPI or time in the OpenMP runtime library is ignored. The *critical path of outside MPI time* (COM) has zero weights for time spent in the MPI runtime. The *critical path of outside OpenMP time* (COO) has zero weights for time spent in the OpenMP runtime.

In the following, we will not only consider the global execution graph (G-), but also process-local execution graphs (PL-) limited to the specific process and ignoring synchronization with other processes. For symmetry, we also consider thread-local execution (TL-) as a special case that ignores all synchronization with other execution units.

An important observation is that the critical path can follow a different path for the same observed execution if the metric selected for the weights is changed. As an example, we can look at the execution trace in Fig. 2(a). The metric PL-CUE for this region is 2.0 and follows the second thread, which can be easier seen in Fig. 2(b) where the MPI time is removed from the trace. The metric PL-COO for this region is 2.5 and follows the first thread. The metric ignores just the yellow OpenMP time.

4 On-the-Fly Critical Path Analysis

We are only interested in the sum of weights along the critical path for our use case. Therefore, we can implement the critical path metric following the concept of a Lamport clock [7]. Each execution unit has a local value of the metric. The weight is added to the local value for each step in the execution graph. Concrete synchronization in the execution graph can have different characteristics. The simplest form is point-to-point synchronization, like a pair of send and receive calls in MPI. Another form is barrier synchronization, where each execution unit needs to arrive before all can continue. Finally, OpenMP has several forms of channeled signal-wait synchronization, where the signaling execution unit and the waiting execution unit do not know all synchronization partners. An example is the synchronization of task execution with any of the task synchronization constructs like `barrier`, `taskwait`, `taskgroup`, or dependencies with other tasks. To evaluate the proposed metrics, we implemented a prototype tool[1] that supports all means of OpenMP and MPI synchronization.

4.1 Measuring Time

Each thread maintains a set of clocks to account for the different critical path metrics introduced in the previous section. Depending on the instance of the clock, the clock is stopped when entering an MPI API call (useful execution, outside MPI) and started when leaving the MPI call. Similarly, useful execution and outside OpenMP clocks are stopped and started when the execution enters and leaves the OpenMP runtime code. For a parallel region, the primary thread enters the runtime with the parallel-begin event. All threads start the execution of the parallel region with the implicit-task-begin event. At the end of the region, all threads encounter the implicit barrier and enter the runtime. Finally, the primary thread continues execution after the parallel-end event.

[1] https://github.com/RWTH-HPC/llvm-project/tree/criticalPath-Euro-Par.

4.2 Critical Path in OpenMP

The Archer runtime [9] solves a similar challenge for OpenMP-aware data race detection, translating OpenMP synchronization into vector clock semantics, that the data race detection tool ThreadSanitizer can understand. Following the concept of synchronization clocks, initially introduced by FastTrack [3], all synchronization with *signal* semantic updates the thread-local clock towards the synchronization clock, and all synchronization with *wait* semantic updates the thread-local clock from the synchronization clock. We adapt and extend the Archer runtime to implement the Lamport clock updates for the OpenMP part of our analysis. All clock updates are implemented as a maximum operation using a compare-and-swap (CAS) loop.

In addition to tracking the synchronization, we integrate the time measurement for time spent in the OpenMP runtime library into these OMPT callbacks.

4.3 Critical Path in MPI

For MPI, we implement the Lamport clock updates using communication piggybacking with additional communication calls on shadow communicators to avoid interference with application communication. For collective communication with barrier semantics in the application (e.g., `barrier`, `allreduce`, or `alltoall`) we use a maximum all-reduction on all participating threads' clocks. Similarly, we use a broadcast of the root's clocks for application calls like `bcast` or `scatter` and a reduction on all participating threads' clocks towards root's clock for application calls like `reduce` or `gather`. In contrast to OpenMP, time measurement in MPI can simply be implemented by an RAII class with the scope of the whole MPI wrapper function.

4.4 Implementation Challenges

In implementing the time measurement for G-COO and PL-COM/G-COM we encountered two challenges. For G-COO, we conceptually need to measure time intervals that start on one process and end on another process following the MPI synchronization paths. Therefore, this metric is impacted by the problem of timer offset (different timer value at the same moment) and dilation (different clock rate, possibly changing over time) like all distributed time measurements [2]. Our prototype accounts for timer offsets with a simple clock exchange during startup but ignores timer dilation. All other metrics used in this work are process-local and therefore only slightly affected by timer dilation. The ratio of values in average calculations might not be exact. Since the local counter value and the incoming counter value contain a started value, we can simply apply the max function to the two running counters without stopping both counters before the comparison.

For PL-COM and G-COM, we want to measure the time spent executing anything besides MPI code. These metrics should explicitly contain the OpenMP synchronization cost. Suppose the metric contains waiting time in barriers. In that case, the result can overestimate the synchronization cost if the MPI communication happens on the critical path within the OpenMP parallel region as in Fig. 2. Rather than considering the whole waiting time, the metric should only capture the synchronization overhead. This overhead might be estimated by the time the last thread arrives in the barrier until the first thread leaves the barrier. Unfortunately, OpenMP barriers are also task scheduling points. The tasks might also contain MPI communication leading to more skewed results.

5 Hybrid Model Factors

The general concept of the hybrid model factors is to break down the global model factors into factors for each level of parallelism. In this paper, we focus on the combination of MPI and OpenMP. The same concepts would also apply to combinations of MPI and CUDA or the combination of more parallel programming paradigms. Because of the implementation issues for critical outside MPI (COM) described in the previous section, we focus on using critical outside OpenMP (COO) to separate the cost for MPI and OpenMP parallelization.

5.1 Definition of Separated Model Factors

In the following, t_i indicates TL-CUE on thread $i \in T$ with T the set of all threads in the execution. $PT_i \subset T$ contains all threads of process $i \in P$ with P being the set of all processes in the execution.

For load balance, we can calculate the threading load balance for each process and then take the weighted average across all processes. The weighted average of process-local averages in the numerator of the LB formula is equal to the global average across all threads. Under this consideration, we can split the global load balance into these two factors:

$$LB_{omp} = \frac{|T| \cdot \operatorname{avg}(t_{i \in T})}{\sum\limits_{j \in P} (|PT_j| \cdot \max(t_{k \in PT_j}))} \quad \text{and} \quad LB_{mpi} = \frac{\sum\limits_{j \in P} (|PT_j| \cdot \max(t_{k \in PT_j}))}{|T| \cdot \max(t_{i \in T})} \tag{5}$$

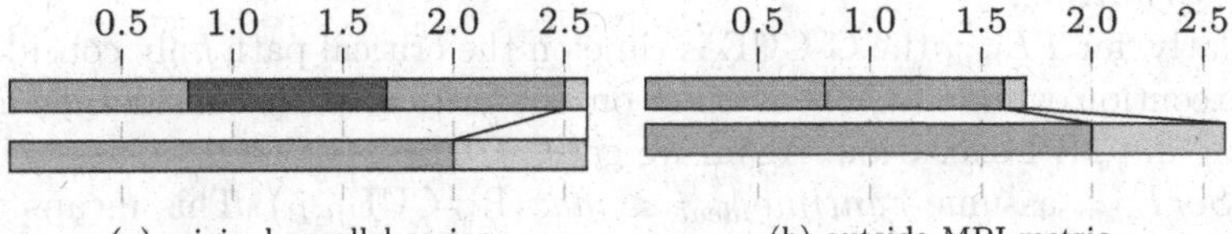

(a) original parallel region (b) outside MPI metric

Fig. 2. Example with two threads with a final barrier at the end (yellow). (a) The upper thread contains some MPI communication (red). (b) Naive calculation of COM would result in the same value for critical path as the actual runtime. (Color figure online)

For serialization efficiency, the question is what would be the maximum runtime of the different MPI processes, if MPI data transfers took no time. At the same time, this value should indicate the ideal process-local runtime of all processes. Based on this consideration, we can use PL-CUE to split the global serialization efficiency into two factors:

$$SerE_{omp} = \frac{\max(t_{i\in T})}{\max(PL\text{-}CUE_{j\in P})} \quad \text{and} \quad SerE_{mpi} = \frac{\max(PL\text{-}CUE_{j\in P})}{runtime_{ideal}} \tag{6}$$

G-COO contains all potential waiting time for MPI communication, and all synchronization, while OpenMP synchronization cost is dropped. Therefore, we can use this metric to split the transfer efficiency into the following two factors:

$$TE_{omp} = \frac{G\text{-}COO}{runtime} \quad \text{and} \quad TE_{mpi} = \frac{G\text{-}CUE}{G\text{-}COO} \tag{7}$$

5.2 Properties of Separated Model Factors

We want to highlight that all of our hybrid model factors are values from 0 to 1. In order to prove this claim, we first note that all values $t_{i\in T}$ = TL-CUE on thread $i \in T$, PL-CUE, G-COO, and G-CUE represent time on different critical paths of the execution. As such, they are always non-negative (zero or larger) since execution can only evolve forward in time. The same holds for *runtime* and $runtime_{ideal}$ of course. In the split of global load balance (5), we sum over products of TL-CUE either with $|T|$, the number of all threads in the execution, or with $|PT_i|$, the number of threads of a process i. Since both thread counts cannot be negative, the resulting products will always be non-negative. Note that the average or maximum of a set of non-negative times is trivially also non-negative. As all model factors in the split of global serialization efficiency (6) and transfer efficiency (7) are simply quotients of non-negative times they are also non-negative. To further prove that all of our model factors cannot be larger than 1.0, we have to show that for each quotient, the numerator is less than or equal to the denominator.

For TE_{omp} we know that G-COO is the time on the global critical path only considering useful execution and MPI execution. In contrast, *runtime* is the time on the critical path additionally considering OpenMP execution. Thus we have G-COO $\leq runtime$.

Similarly, for TE_{mpi} the G-CUE is time on the critical path only considering useful execution while G-COO is time on the critical path considering useful execution and MPI execution. Again we get G-CUE $\leq$ G-COO.

For $SerE_{mpi}$ assume $runtime_{ideal} < max(\text{PL-CUE}_{j\in P})$. This means there exists a process $j \in P$ that needs more time to perform its useful execution than given by $runtime_{ideal}$. By definition of ideal runtime, this cannot be as each process has to be finished with useful execution before the execution of the whole application can end. So by contradiction we get $max(\text{PL-CUE}_{j\in P}) \leq runtime_{ideal}$.

For $SerE_{omp}$ we can argue analogously assuming $max(\text{PL-CUE}_{j \in P}) < max(t_{i \in T})$. This means there exists at least one thread that spends more time on useful execution than any of the processes. However, this is not possible as each thread cannot spend more time on useful execution than the corresponding process it belongs to. So by contradiction we get $max(t_{i \in T}) \leq max(\text{PL-CUE}_{j \in P})$.

For LB_{omp} we can argue by definition of the average

$$|T| \cdot avg(t_{i \in T}) = \sum_{i \in T} t_i = \sum_{j \in P} \left(\sum_{k \in PT_j} t_k \right) \leq \sum_{j \in P} \left(|PT_j| \cdot \max(t_{k \in PT_j}) \right).$$

For LB_{mpi} we can argue that we have

$$\text{for each } j \in P : \max(t_{k \in PT_j}) \leq \max(t_{i \in T_i})$$

and thus also

$$\sum_{j \in P} \left(|PT_j| \cdot \max(t_{k \in PT_j}) \right) \leq \sum_{j \in P} \left(|PT_j| \cdot \max(t_{i \in T}) \right) = |T| \cdot \max(t_{i \in T}).$$

6 Evaluation

In Figs. 3, 5, and 7 we show a breakdown of model factors in the way they impact the overall parallel efficiency. From top to bottom, an additional model factor is multiplied and plotted. We show transfer efficiency, serialization efficiency, load balance, and parallel efficiency from top to bottom in all figures. The differently colored areas highlight the loss in efficiency caused by the specific model factor. The larger plot on the left shows the hybrid breakdown, where the corresponding OpenMP factor is on top of the MPI factor. The two smaller plots on the right show the separated breakdown for OpenMP and MPI. The parallel efficiency at the bottom still separates the OpenMP from the MPI parallel efficiency. Multiplying the two efficiencies results in the hybrid parallel efficiency shown in the left plot. For randomly selected measurements we compared execution time with and without tool. In no case we could see an overhead exceeding the variation of execution time of these non-deterministic parallel applications.

6.1 Experiment Setup

All experiments are executed on exclusively reserved nodes of the Claix 2018 cluster with two Intel Xeon Platinum 8160 processors and 192 GB main memory. Hyperthreads are disabled; therefore, a node has 48 cores. Furthermore, sub-NUMA clustering is enabled, leading to four NUMA nodes. In all cases threads are pinned using `OMP_PLACES=cores` and `OMP_PROC_BIND=close`. Therefore, experiments with 6 and 12 threads execute on a single sub-NUMA domain.

We use IntelMPI 2018, which is the default MPI on Claix. To compile JuKKR we use Intel 19.0 compilers. To compile the Blocked Cholesky Factorization use a custom-built version of LLVM/clang derived from the `main` branch (`0fd5f696`) just before the recent 14.0 release branch.

6.2 Real-World Application JuKKR

We demonstrate the applicability of our methodology to real-world applications by applying it to the KKRhost code of the Juelich KKR suite (JuKKR)[2]. The JuKKR suite is a collection of codes solving problems in the field of density functional theory by implementing the Korringa-Kohn-Rostoker Green function method. The KKRhost code is a main building block of the whole JuKKR suite to perform electronic structure calculations on periodic systems, for example, crystalline solids. It is a highly parallel Fortran application with a hybrid of MPI + OpenMP [12]. Thus it is a perfect candidate to evaluate our proposed split of *Load Balance*, *Serialization Efficiency* and *Transfer Efficiency* into the different levels of parallelism. The code iteratively computes the electron density of the periodic crystal lattice under investigation until self-consistency. In each self-consistency iteration cycle solving the algebraic Dyson equation constitutes the hotspot of the application.

In the following, we analyze our prototype tool's performance results for the KKRhost code. Based on previous measurements, that are not shown here, choosing 6 threads per process already showed a significant inefficiency due to load imbalances on the OpenMP level, which increased even more, when further scaling up the number of OpenMP threads. Thus, for the experiment shown in this work we decided to fix the number of OpenMP threads per process to 6 and vary the number of MPI processes. The resulting breakdown of our hybrid model factors for this strong-scaling experiment of the KKRhost code are shown in Fig. 3. Keeping the number of OpenMP threads fixed also results in a constant

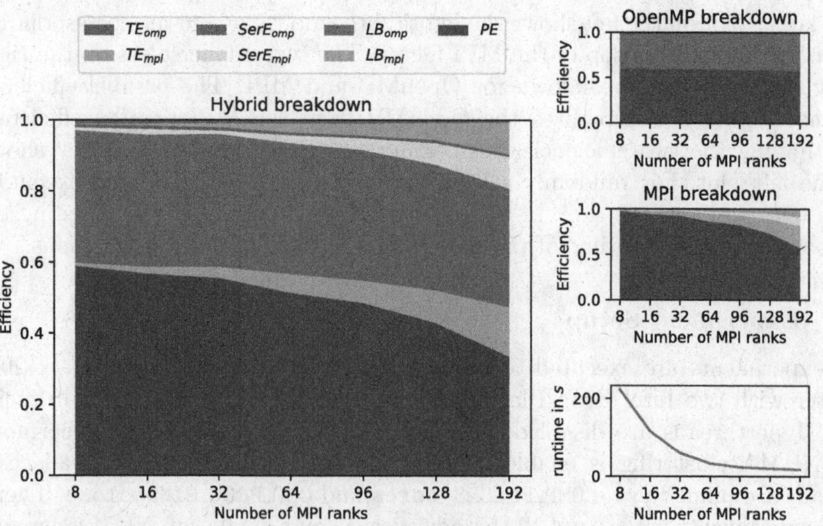

Fig. 3. Breakdown of hybrid model factors for JuKKR executed with 6 threads and varying number of MPI processes

[2] https://jukkr.fz-juelich.de/.

OpenMP load balance of 60%, as the OpenMP breakdown in the top right of Fig. 3 reveals. This inefficiency is caused by the parallelization of the k-point integration loop in the hotspot region of the code. In our 3D test case of a unit cell containing four gold atoms, we have 1536000 k-points. For each k-point, an LU decomposition of a small 32×32 matrix is computed using the multithreaded version of the Intel Math Kernel Library (MKL). We found out that due to the small matrix size, the Intel MKL does not make use of all 6 OpenMP threads. In addition, the loop over all k-points is not parallelized with OpenMP so that other parts of this loop are executed only by the main thread of the corresponding MPI process. All in all, this leads to the observed load imbalances on the OpenMP level.

6.3 Distributed Block Cholesky Factorization

In previous work [10] we proposed the concept of actual asynchronous MPI communication. The proposal gets currently refined in the MPI forum with the goal to introduce the feature as *MPI continuations* with MPI 5. To showcase the benefits of such asynchronous MPI communication that can interact with OpenMP tasks and task dependencies, we developed different versions of distributed Block Cholesky Factorization. For all experiments, we use a matrix with rank $2^{16} \approx 131k$, which is distributed into blocks of rank $2^9 = 512$. The blocks are distributed block-cyclic in both decomposition dimensions.

The base version of the code is *block-synchronous*. The execution trace in Fig. 4 illustrates the execution of a smaller problem size with four processes and four threads each. It alternates between communication and computation phases to ensure that communication cannot conflict with reading and writing data during communication. Only a single thread per process performs all communication. Such parallelization can often be found in hybrid MPI + OpenMP codes. In previous work, we studied the node-level behavior of the code and found it to be sensitive to NUMA effects. Therefore we execute the code with 12 threads per process and scale the number of processes. Four processes fit on a single node, while 128 processes are distributed to 32 nodes. The breakdown of model factors in Fig. 5 highlights the minimal overhead introduced at the threading level. At the same time, transfer efficiency is responsible for most

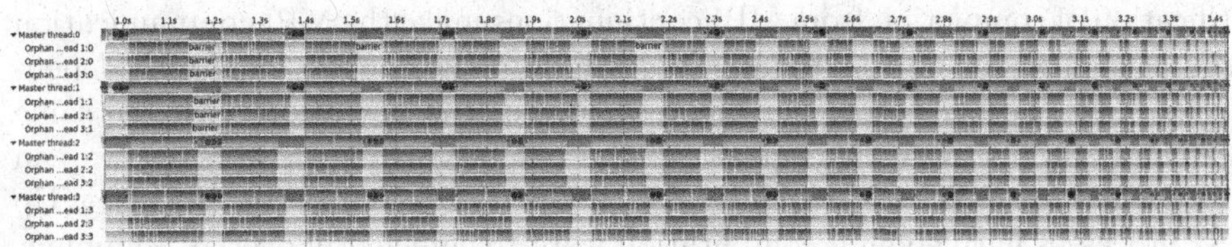

Fig. 4. Execution trace of block-synchronous version of Block Cholesky Factorization executed with four threads and four MPI processes. Red shows MPI communication, light blue is OpenMP synchronization, purple represents dgemm tasks and green are other tasks (Color figure online)

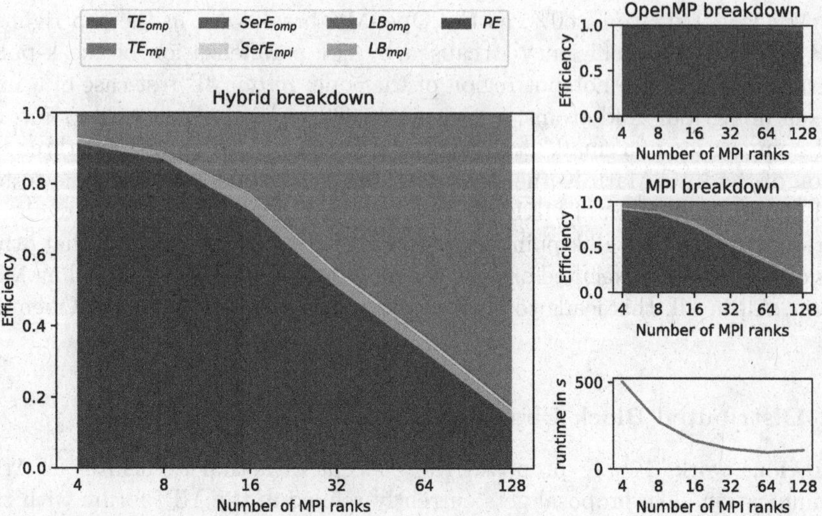

Fig. 5. Breakdown of hybrid model factors for block-synchronous version of Block Cholesky Factorization executed with 12 threads and varying number of MPI processes

of the drop in parallel efficiency. The observed MPI load imbalance is a result of the block-cyclic domain distribution, where some processes consistently have an extra block of work below the main diagonal. In this code version, the single communicating thread blocks the other threads from running calculations. Looking at the number of messages sent with increasing process count, we observe a significant increase in data transfers. At the same time, the calculation time per iteration scales down. This impact on the ratio of computation to communication is reflected in the transfer efficiency.

The second version we consider for this evaluation makes use of the future *MPI continuations* concept in combination with the OpenMP 5.0 concept of detached tasks. Generally speaking, this combination allows to span a task dependency graph across distributed memory nodes by treating MPI communication as dependency edges. Task dependencies enforce an ordering of communicating blocks and computing with blocks. Detached tasks combined with the notification of completion from MPI continuations make the MPI communication really asynchronous and fit them seamlessly into the process-local task dependencies. The execution trace in Fig. 6 illustrates the execution with the same parameters as in Fig. 4. In contrast to the block-synchronous version, we can observe the impact of task dependencies on OpenMP serialization efficiency. Up to 32 processes have enough computation work to sufficiently overlap communication and computation. Starting with 64 processes, the growing communication time combined with reduced calculation time impacts the transfer efficiency and, therefore, the parallel efficiency. To quantify the tool overhead, we execute the 16 nodes experiment 10 times with and without our tool. The mean execu-

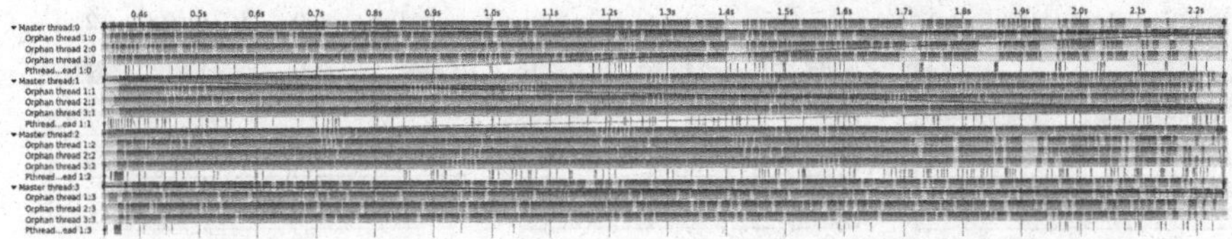

Fig. 6. Execution trace of the asynchronous version of Block Cholesky Factorization executed with four threads and four MPI processes. The prototype implementation of MPI continuations spawns an extra thread to notify the OpenMP tasks about completion of MPI communication.

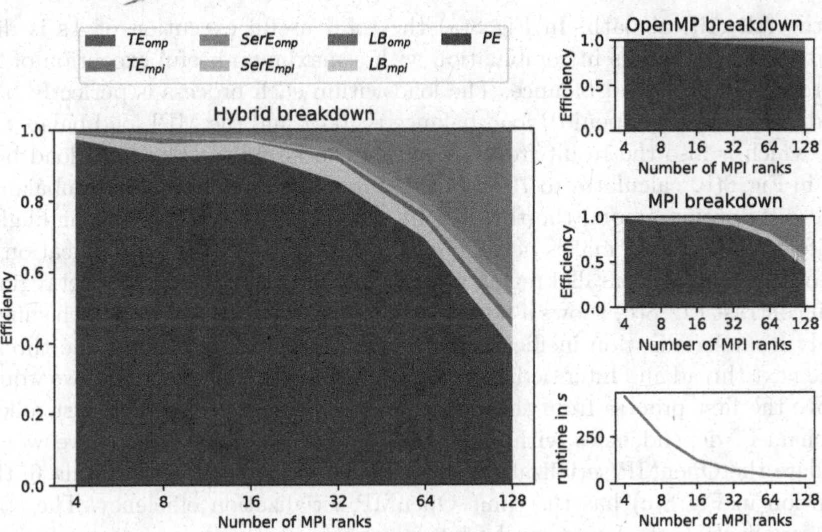

Fig. 7. Breakdown of hybrid model factors for the asynchronous version of Block Cholesky Factorization using detached OpenMP tasks executed with 12 threads and a varying number of MPI processes

tion time and standard deviation with tool is 44.72 ± 0.92 s and without tool is 44.68 ± 0.48 s. This means that the average tool overhead is smaller than the spread of execution times caused by non-deterministic execution and influence from hardware and network variances.

6.4 Synthetic Benchmark

To complement the evaluation of actual application codes, we also designed synthetic benchmark codes to evaluate the expressiveness of the separated model factors. Figure 8 shows three execution traces of hybrid execution with asymmetric thread counts. In all cases we will ignore transfer efficiency mainly because the MPI waiting time is only added to highlight the communication pattern. Figures 8(a) and (b) have 100% serialization efficiency, because the first process

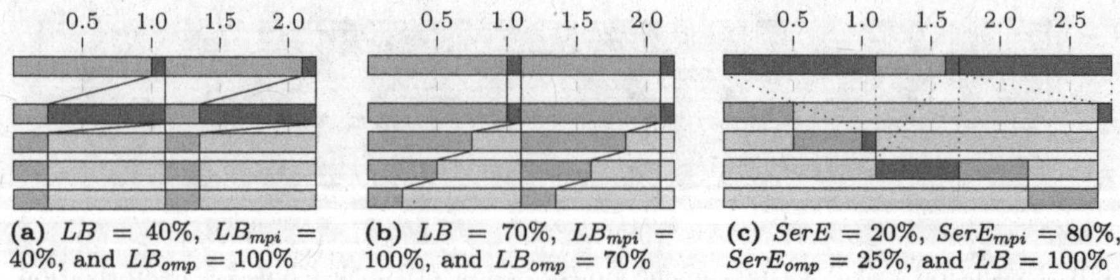

(a) $LB = 40\%$, $LB_{mpi} = 40\%$, and $LB_{omp} = 100\%$ **(b)** $LB = 70\%$, $LB_{mpi} = 100\%$, and $LB_{omp} = 70\%$ **(c)** $SerE = 20\%$, $SerE_{mpi} = 80\%$, $SerE_{omp} = 25\%$, and $LB = 100\%$

Fig. 8. Examples with two processes, where the second process executes four threads.

has the full critical path. In Fig. 8(a) the total useful execution of 4 s is distributed to five threads in combination with a maximum useful execution of 2 s this results in 40% load balance. The load within each process is perfectly balanced, therefore the OpenMP load balance is 100% and the MPI load balance is 40%, which is also the result from consulting the formulas. The total load balance in Fig. 8(b) calculates to 70%. In this case the source of all load imbalance is the distribution among the threads. In this figure we furthermore highlight, that for the metrics it makes no difference, whether the MPI communication is part of the OpenMP parallel region or in serial code outside any parallel region.

In contrast Fig. 8(c) shows a perfectly balanced execution trace, which suffers mainly from serialization inefficiency. The critical path moves from one thread to the next thread and intermediately also moves to the first process. If we would remove the first process from the execution, the critical path would just follow the chain of dependencies within the second process. In such case, we would calculate the OpenMP serialization efficiency to 25%. Based on Formula 6, the execution in Fig. 8(c) has the same OpenMP serialization efficiency. The 80% MPI serialization efficiency can be interpreted as one process executes 80% of the critical path. As a comparison, the separation proposed by Giménez et al. [4] would calculate $LB_{mpi} = \frac{\frac{0.5+2.7*4}{5}}{2.7} = 83.7\%$ for the latter trace, which is the weighted average of time outside MPI at the primary threads divided by the maximum time outside MPI. With $LB = 100\%$, we would get $LB_{omp} = 119\%$ while we would expect all model factors not to exceed 100%.

7 Future Work

In the following we will discuss two main topics for future work. The first aspect is how an application developer might identify regions of interest. The other aspect is how our approach might extent to other hybrid programming models like offloading to accelerators.

7.1 Region-based Analysis

The default behavior of our prototype tool is to observe the whole execution of a program. The starting point is either the `MPI_Init` call or the initialization of the OpenMP runtime. Similarly, the end point is either the `MPI_Finalize` call or the finalization of the OpenMP runtime. Currently, our tool implementation also allows the user to redefine the start and end point for the analysis. By calling `MPI_Pcontrol(1)` or `omp_control_tool(1)` the user can mark the start point of the analysis. Respectively, calling `MPI_Pcontrol(0)` or `omp_control_tool(4)` marks the user-defined end of the analysis.

However, it is not possible to mark multiple regions right now. In the future we plan to extend the capabilities of our tool to support collection of our proposed model factors for multiple, possibly overlapping, regions, at the same time. We also plan to allow aggregation of same regions that occur inside an iterative loop, for example. In principle the user will be free to define arbitrary regions for the analysis. For very small regions, e.g., a single OpenMP parallel region, the expressiveness of our approach might be questionable because in this case global synchronization between all processes is missing. Since our approach relies on the critical path global synchronization is necessary to determine the critical path correctly. These kind of use-cases will need a thorough investigation in the future.

7.2 Accelerator Support

Many applications offload parts of their computation to accelerator devices by using CUDA, OpenACC, OpenMP target offloading or others. In the current state our approach does not support accelerator offloading. However, we can identify similar synchronization points such as kernel launches or explicit waits on memory copies. Based on these synchronization points we can also track the implicit critical path along accelerator devices similar to a hybrid MPI+OpenMP execution. Our separated model factors then need to be redefined to include load balance, serialization- and transfer efficiency for accelerator execution accordingly. In order to implement this extension in our prototype tool the popular accelerator programming models mentioned above offer suitable interfaces that can be used to track the required synchronization points. CUDA offers the CUDA Profiling Tools Interface (CUPTI), OpenACC also offers a callback-based tool interface for profiling and tracing events and for OpenMP target offloading we can build upon our existing implementation of the OMPT interface.

8 Conclusions

Although our prototype collects the metrics on the fly, a post-mortem analysis tool can calculate the same metrics from execution traces and therefore calculate the separated model factors based on the formulas. As we showed in the evaluation, collecting the metrics on the fly does not introduce measurable runtime overhead since we store even less data than a stack profiling tool. We believe that any tracing tool should be able to collect the information while tracing the application without additional runtime overhead. We proved that all separated model factors stay in the range between 0 and 1 as expected for efficiency values.

In one example, our separation approach shows more consistent results than previous work. Finally, we used real-world applications as well as synthetic parallel kernels to evaluate the expressiveness of the separated model factors.

Acknowledgements. Parts of this work has received funding from the European Union's Horizon 2020 research and innovation programme under grant agreement 824080. Parts of this work are funded by the Federal Ministry of Education and Research (BMBF) and the state of North Rhine-Westphalia as part of the NHR Program. We gracefully thank the reviewers for their valuable feedback.

References

1. Böhme, D., Wolf, F., de Supinski, B.R., Schulz, M., Geimer, M.: Scalable critical-path based performance analysis. In: IPDPS (2012)
2. Doleschal, J., Knüpfer, A., Müller, M.S., Nagel, W.E.: Internal timer synchronization for parallel event tracing. In: Lastovetsky, A., Kechadi, T., Dongarra, J. (eds.) EuroPVM/MPI 2008. LNCS, vol. 5205, pp. 202–209. Springer, Heidelberg (2008). https://doi.org/10.1007/978-3-540-87475-1_29
3. Flanagan, C., Freund, S.N.: Fasttrack: efficient and precise dynamic race detection. In: Proceedings of the 2009 ACM SIGPLAN Conference on Programming Language Design and Implementation, PLDI (2009)
4. Giménez, J., Mercadal, E., Llort, G., Mendez, S.: Analyzing the efficiency of hybrid codes. In: 2020 19th International Symposium on Parallel and Distributed Computing (ISPDC) (2020)
5. Labarta, J., Girona, S., Cortes, T.: Analyzing scheduling policies using dimemas. Parallel Comput. **23**, 23–34 (1997)
6. Laguna, I., Marshall, R., Mohror, K., Ruefenacht, M., Skjellum, A., Sultana, N.: A large-scale study of MPI usage in open-source HPC applications. In: Proceedings of the International Conference for High Performance Computing, Networking, Storage and Analysis. SC 2019 (2019)
7. Lamport, L.: Time, clocks, and the ordering of events in a distributed system. Commun. ACM **21**(7), 558–565 (1978)
8. Pillet, V., Labarta, J., Cortes, T., Girona, S.: Paraver: A tool to visualize and analyze parallel code. In: Proceedings of WoTUG-18: Transputer and OCCAM Developments (1995)
9. Protze, J., Hahnfeld, J., Ahn, D.H., Schulz, M., Müller, M.S.: OpenMP tools interface: Synchronization information for data race detection. In: International Workshop on OpenMP (2017)
10. Protze, J., et al.: MPI detach - towards automatic asynchronous local completion. Parallel Comput. **109**, 102859 (2022)
11. Rosas, C., Giménez, J., Labarta, J.: Scalability prediction for fundamental performance factors. Supercomput. Front. Innov. **1**(2), 4–19 (2014)
12. Rüßmann, P.: Spin scattering of topologically protected electrons at defects. Dissertation, RWTH Aachen University (2018)
13. Yang, C., Miller, B.P.: Critical path analysis for the execution of parallel and distributed programs. In: ICDCS. IEEE Computer Society (1988)

Relative Performance Projection on Arm Architectures

Clément Gavoille[1,3(✉)], Hugo Taboada[1,2], Patrick Carribault[1,2], Fabrice Dupros[4], Brice Goglin[3], and Emmanuel Jeannot[3]

[1] CEA, DAM, DIF, 91297 Arpajon, France
{clement.gavoille,hugo.taboada,patrick.carribault}@cea.fr
[2] Université Paris-Saclay, CEA, Laboratoire en Informatique Haute Performance pour le Calcul et la simulation, 91680 Bruyères le Chatel, France
[3] Inria, LaBRI, Univ. Bordeaux, CNRS, Bordeaux-INP, Bordeaux, France
{brice.goglin,emmanuel.jeannot}@inria.fr
[4] ARM, Paris, France
fabrice.dupros@arm.fr

Abstract. With the advent of multi- many-core processors and hardware accelerators, choosing a specific architecture to renew a supercomputer can become very tedious. This decision process should consider the current and future parallel application needs and the design of the target software stack. It should also consider the single-core behavior of the application as it is one of the performance limitations in today's machines. In such a scheme, performance hints on the impact of some hardware and software stack modifications are mandatory to drive this choice. This paper proposes a workflow for performance projection based on execution on an actual processor and the application's behavior. This projection evaluates the performance variation from an existing core of a processor to a hypothetical one to drive the design choice. For this purpose, we characterize the maximum sustainable performance of the target machine and analyze the application using the software stack of the target machine. To validate this approach, we apply it to three applications of the CORAL benchmark suite: LULESH, MiniFE, and Quicksilver, using a single-core of two Arm-based architectures: Marvell ThunderX2 and Arm Neoverse N1. Finally, we follow this validation work with an example of design-space exploration around the SVE vector size, the choice of DDR4 and HBM2, and the software stack choice on A64FX on our applications with a pool of three source architectures: Arm Neoverse N1, Marvell ThunderX2, and Fujitsu A64FX.

Keywords: Performance Projection · Design space exploration · Arm architecture · Roofline model

1 Introduction

In the pursuit of reaching the exaflops target, the CPUs are becoming more complex both from hardware and software perspectives. Even when working on a

J. Cano and P. W. Trinder (Eds.): Euro-Par 2022, LNCS 13440, pp. 85–99, 2022.
https://doi.org/10.1007/978-3-031-12597-3_6

multicore processor, it is essential to consider the single-core performance when exploring all the possibilities in its design. Indeed, there are multiple choices to make on the memory hierarchy side and the computational part with, for example, vector units. Therefore, it is meaningful to study the impact of those choices on the software stack and the applications. Considering we have access to a source machine and the software stack of a hypothetical target machine, how can we evaluate the impact of the differences between the machines and software stacks on the application performance?

This paper proposes a methodology to evaluate this impact of single-core performance from a source machine to a hypothetical target machine with a dedicated software stack. By analyzing the differences between two architectures and two binaries, this approach evaluates the performance from one machine to another with a roofline-based model, leading to an interval of performance. The obtained intervals analysis led to a study of the relevance of some hardware modifications and their impact on software. We present such an exploration around hardware vector sizes, various memory types, and different compilers on 3 Arm architectures (Marvell ThunderX2, Neoverse N1, and Fujitsu A64FX) and 3 CORAL mini-apps (Lulesh, MiniFE, and Quicksilver).

Section 2 presents the related work while Sect. 3 describes the methodology and its implementation. Then Sect. 4 presents the experimental environment used for approach validation in Sect. 5 and parameter exploration on 3 Arm architectures in Sect. 6.

2 Related Work

There are various approaches for evaluating the performance impact regarding design-space exploration. The first one relies on cycle-accurate simulators [11] leading to precise prediction but significant overhead (10000×). This drawback is too limiting for exploring the performance impact on a whole mini-app.

Hence, analytical models can be used, leading to less precise but much faster estimation. The main difficulty lies in defining the relevant metrics and obtaining them. The choices and approximations made to obtain these metrics are different in each model and result in differences in precision and speed. Some analytical approaches choose to reduce the problem by being application-dependent [4]. However, our model can explore different applications as we want to characterize diverse behavior in our applicative workload. Some of the application-independent approaches choose to use simulation on a small scale [14] to have a good prediction and limit the analysis time compared to a complete simulation. Our approach does not rely on a simulator to get metrics but only on the emulation of non-native ISA, which is much faster than fully simulating the application. Furthermore, it allows exploring parameters on applications with a larger input size. While it is possible to consider a hardware-independent representation of the application [8,9], it is essential to look at the impact of software stack targeting an architecture in an environment as recent and diverse as the Arm HPC environment. The choices in the software stack have a non-negligible impact on performance, as shown on A64FX [5]. Therefore, our approach considers that having access to the target machine software stack is necessary for our model.

The idea of projecting the performance from a source machine to a target machine is behind some machine-learning-oriented approaches [7]. One of the current limitations is the low number of machines in the Arm environment, making it hard to have a sufficient dataset necessary for training. However, we could consider coupling our approach with machine learning as more and more machines appear in the Arm HPC environment.

This article presents an analytical performance projection approach used for design space exploration. It allows to take into account the differences in hardware and in software stack when targeting a particular architecture. The exploration around different hardware parameters in this article leads to a discussion on the effectiveness and the limitations of the approach.

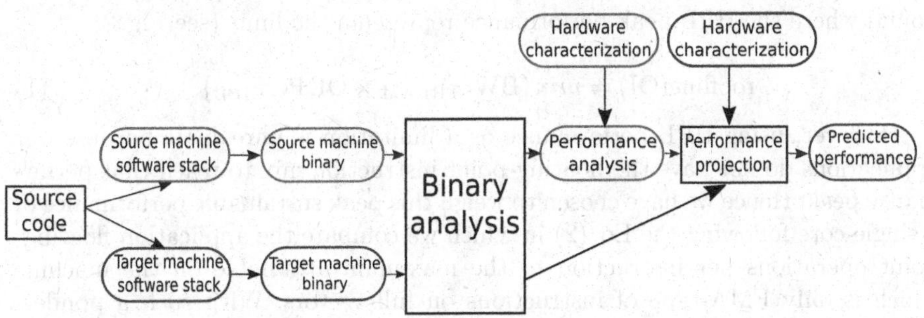

Fig. 1. Our performance-estimation workflow (Color figure online)

3 Workflow Presentation and Implementation

This section presents our approach and the methodology and its implementation for validation and design-space exploration. Figure 1 presents the main workflow in which the target and source machine characterization are represented in green and red while the model analysis running on the source machine is black. The first step is to get two binaries with the same source code: one with the software stack of the source machine and the other for the target architecture. Both binaries are then analyzed to gather the metrics directly on the source machine.

In the field of performance analysis, the Roofline model [18] is a well-known representation to characterize the behavior of an application according to the hardware limitations. So, we have chosen to use this representation to analyze performance on our source machine and evaluate a target one. The model output is a performance interval on the roofline representation of the target machine. Moreover, it helps to understand the impacts of the software stack on the target architecture.

3.1 Hardware and Software Characterization

Our approach relies on two binaries (source and target) obtained through a dedicated software stack. We consider the hardware differences thanks to the maximum available bandwidth and peak sustainable performance of the machine. In contrast, the differences brought by the software stack are visible in the metrics we obtain by analyzing the binaries. We have chosen to consider their Operational Intensities (OI) and their floating-point instruction mix. Once we have considered these hardware and software differences, we project the roofline analysis from the source machine to a hypothetical target architecture.

Hence, the first study is to obtain these hardware limitations imposed by the peak memory bandwidth of all memory levels and the peak sustainable performance of our core. These limitations are represented by the roofline (1) of the Stream Triad bandwidth of each memory level $\mathrm{BW_{STREAM}}$ [13] and the peak performance of High Performance Linpack ($\mathrm{Perf_{HPL}}$) [15]. This leads to two regions: (i) memory-bound limited by the memory bandwidth and (ii) compute-bound where the HPL peak performance represents the limit (see Fig. 2).

$$\mathrm{roofline(OI)} = min\{\mathrm{BW_{STREAM}} \times \mathrm{OI}, \mathrm{Perf_{HPL}}\} \tag{1}$$

However, using HPL performance as a limitation is unrealistic because our applications do not have the floating-point instruction mix to reach that performance peak. Hence we have chosen to weigh this peak sustainable performance of a single-core following the Eq. (2) in which we compare the application floating-point operations per instruction to the maximum attainable on the machine which is only FMA-type of instructions on full vectors. With such a ponderation, the compute part of the roofline represents the maximum sustainable performance for our application instruction mix.

$$\mathrm{Perf_{HPL_{ponderated}}} = \frac{\mathrm{Perf_{HPL}}}{2 \times \frac{\text{vector size}}{\text{datasize}}} \times \frac{N_{\text{floating point operations}}}{N_{\text{floating point instructions}}} \tag{2}$$

The next main component in our model is the Operational Intensity (OI). Because we want to consider the bandwidth of the different memory levels, we need to assess the bytes accessed in these memory levels in the OI as presented in the Cache-Aware Roofline Model [6]. Hence, in a two cache-level machine, we obtain the OI from L1 using the Eq. (3) with B_i the total of bytes accessed in the cache level i.

$$\mathrm{OI}_{L1} = \frac{N_{\text{floating } point \text{ operations}}}{B_{L1} + B_{L2} + B_{\text{Main Memory}}} \tag{3}$$

The OI from the L1 memory level is the same OI defined in the CARM approach, and the OI of the main memory is the one used in the Original Roofline Model.

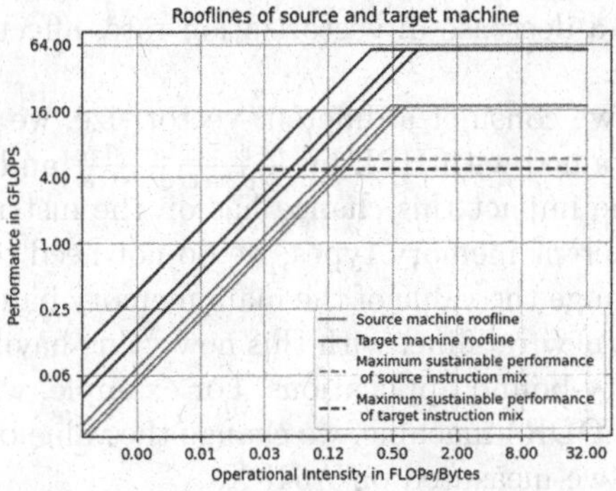

Fig. 2. Roofline representation: plain lines represent, from left to right, the rooflines of L1, L2, and Main Memory for each machine (green is source machine, red is target machine) with the peak sustainable performance obtained with HPL. The maximum attainable performance weighted by instruction mix is in dotted for both machines. (Color figure online)

3.2 Performance Projection

The projection uses the same idea as Kwack et al. for roofline projection [12]: it considers the ratio between the performance ($\text{Perf}_{\text{source}}$) and one roofline on the source machine at the $\text{OI}_{\text{source}}$ ($\text{roofline}_{\text{source}}(\text{OI}_{\text{source}})$), and projects this ratio on the target machine using the new OI and the new roofline ($\text{roofline}_{\text{target}}(\text{OI}_{\text{target}})$). This is presented in Eq. (4). Thus depending on the OI value, the application is limited by the memory-level bandwidth or the core peak performance.

$$\text{Perf}_{\text{target}} = \frac{\text{Perf}_{\text{source}}}{\text{roofline}_{\text{source}}(\text{OI}_{\text{source}})} \times \text{roofline}_{\text{target}}(\text{OI}_{\text{target}}) \tag{4}$$

This analysis results in multiple values because of all the OIs and rooflines, forming a projection interval.

3.3 Methodology for Design-Space Exploration

We want to use this model to explore the parameters best reflected by this projection approach. We can make such an exploration around different software stacks and instruction mixes of the application. But we also consider hardware parameters such as the memory type and bandwidth and the hardware vector length. In the Arm environment, the exploration of the different vector sizes is allowed by the vector-length-agnostic approach of the SVE (Scalable Vector Extension) ISA of Arm architectures [17].

The model translates the hardware differences into rooflines used for projection, whereas the software stack and instruction mix changes are shown in the OI and its peak compute performance.

However, hardware and software changes are often not dissociated because one modification can impact the other. When we change the hardware vector size, we often observe a decrease in vectorization rate, affecting the instruction mix of the application.

Technically, when we consider a different vector size, we multiply the maximum performance obtained with HPL by $\frac{new\ vector\ size}{old\ vector\ size}$ and analyze the target binary again to see the impact this change has on the instruction mix and OI. When we consider different memory types, we do not need to run a new binary analysis as we only change the value of the main memory bandwidth and project performance with this new roofline, with this new value having the most significant impact on memory-bound applications. For example, when we introduce a HBM2 of A64FX on a DDR4 machine, we change the value of the main memory bandwidth to the one we measured on A64FX.

Hence, when running the model with each of the new parameters, we will obtain a different, or not, prediction interval. By comparing these intervals, we can analyze the impact of the evolution of diverse parameters and their impact on the performance of the application we study.

3.4 Implementation

As explained before, the machine characterization is obtained by running Stream and HPL on our source machine. We assume we have access to these benchmarks results or extrapolate this information on the source machine. For the analysis of the binaries we obtain with the different software stacks, we need to gather two kinds of metrics:

1. Instruction mix: number of floating-point instructions, total number of accessed bytes, number of flops. We rely on the dynamic code instrumentation with DynamoRIO [3] and ArmIE for SVE emulation [1] when changing the vector length. ArmIE instrumentation client allows for an easy floating-point instructions, FLOPs and bytes accessed count instruction per instruction, even for emulated SVE instructions on a non-SVE architecture.
2. Memory usage: percentage of hits in every memory level. We rely on hardware counters on the source machine but it is also possible to modelize a cache thanks to an ArmIE memory instruction trace client.

Our implementation is explained in Fig. 3 adding precision to Fig. 1 with the tool and benchmark used in our implementation.

4 Experimental Environment

This section describes the architectures and the benchmark applications used to validate and experiment our model.

4.1 Architectures

We chose to use three different Arm CPUs to experiment with our approach: a single-core of Marvell ThunderX2 (TX2), Arm Neoverse N1 (N1), and Fujitsu

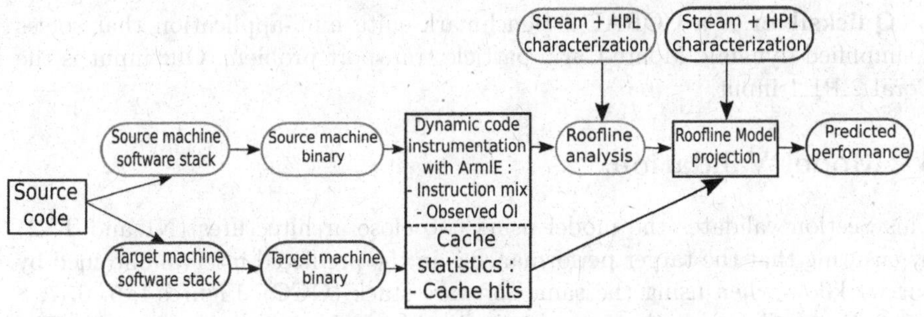

Fig. 3. Description of the implementation flow.

Table 1. Single-Core Characteristics the 3 Test Machines.

Machine	TX2	N1	A64FX
Performance (GFLOPS)	17.53	18.22	56.71
MM bandwidth (GB/s)	25.43	21.14	65.52
Vector size and ISA	NEON 128 bits	NEON 128 bits	SVE 512 bits
Memory type	DDR4	DDR4	HBM2
Compiler	g++ 10.3.0	g++ 10.3.0	g++ 10.3.0 FCC 4.6.3 (clang mode)
Flags	-O3 -ffast-math -mcpu=thunderx2t99	-O3 -ffast-math -mcpu=neoverse-n1	-O3 -ffast-math mcpu=a64fx

A64FX (A64FX). Table 1 summarizes their characteristics and the results of HPL and Stream benchmarks running alone on a full node we obtained. These three architectures cover different parts of the Arm HPC environment, from the server market (N1 and TX2 processors) to the HPC focus (Fujitsu A64FX). The latter is currently the only Arm processor in production to use SVE vectors of 512 bits. With HBM2 and longer vectors than N1 and TX2, the single-core performance of a A64FX node is much higher when running STREAM and HPL benchmarks.

4.2 Applications

We use three benchmarks of the CORAL and CORAL-2 Benchmark suites: LULESH [10] , MiniFE [2] and Quicksilver [16].

LULESH (Livermore Unstructured Lagrangian Explicit Shock Hydrodynamics) approximates hydrodynamic equations by using a regular cartesian mesh to partition the spatial problem. Our test's input is a mesh of size 100^3.

MiniFE is a mini-application based on finite element methods that implement an iterative conjugate gradient solver. Our test's input is a mesh of size 256^3.

Quicksilver is a CORAL-2 Benchmark suite mini-application that solves a simplified dynamic Monte-Carlo particle transport problem. Our input is the Coral_2_P1_1 input.

5 Model Validation

This Section validates the model using two close architectures (N1 and TX2) by ensuring that the target performance is in the predicted interval obtained by our workflow when using the same software stack (GCC). Figures 4, 5, 6, 7, 8 and 9 display the prediction interval obtained with the different projections. The blue crosses represent these projections creating the interval depicted by the blue dotted box. The source machine rooflines are green, and the target machine ones are red. We analyze each application after initialization and before finalization.

5.1 LULESH

Figures 4 and 5 present the projection of LULESH from one machine to the other. The maximum sustainable performance weighted by the floating-point instruction mix (corresponding to the dotted rooflines) is a bit higher on TX2 than N1 despite having a lower maximum performance on HPL. The OIs of the L1 memory level are similar on both machines. Situated in the TX2 memory-bound region, the differences between the bandwidth and the projections in this region create an interval that is not modified by the projections from the OIs of L2 and main memory. This interval is higher when projecting from TX2 because of the difference in L1 and L2 cache bandwidth. Because performances on both machines are nearly equal, we are closer to the TX2 roofline hence we obtain a better ratio which is then translated into a higher prediction interval. In both figures, the interval we predict includes the actual performance measured on the target machine, validating our approach in this application.

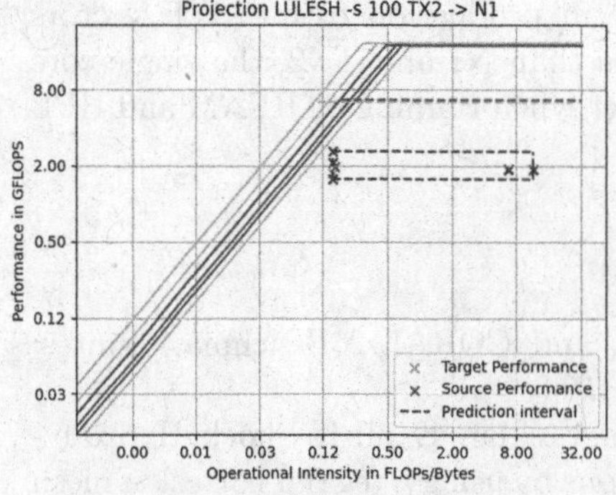

Fig. 4. Results on LULESH TX2 → N1. (Color figure online)

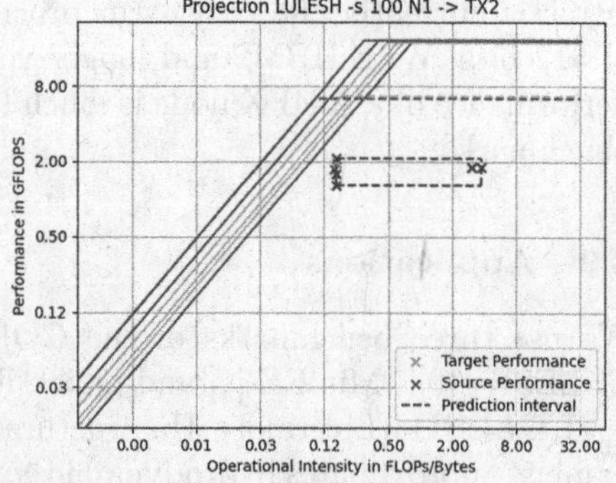

Fig. 5. Results on LULESH N1 → TX2. (Color figure online)

5.2 MiniFE

MiniFE exploits vectorization on the two architectures. This better vectorization rate is translated into a good performance of its instruction mix (see Figs. 6 and 7). Compared to LULESH, the OI of L1 is in the memory-bound region of all rooflines on both machines. Once again, the interval we predict, only being affected by the OI of L1, does not change whether we project from N1 or TX2. However, the N1 performance is higher (1.87 GFLOPS) than the TX2 performance (1.04 GFLOPS). Despite this difference in performance, our interval includes the measured performance. We can suppose that, because we are in the memory-bound region of the L1 and L2 cache levels, the better performance of MiniFE on N1 may result from the higher bandwidth of these levels.

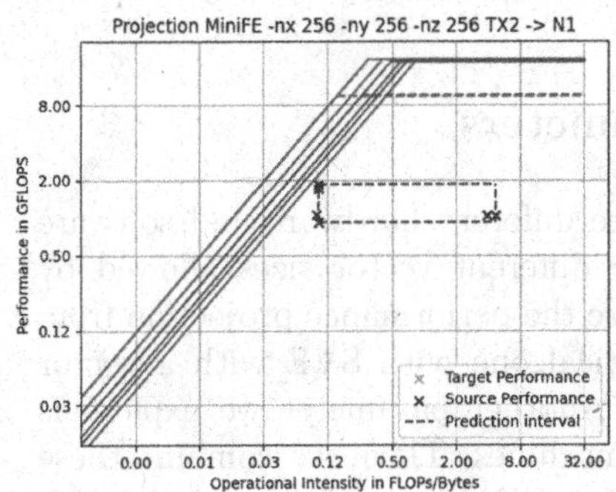

Fig. 6. Results miniFE TX2 → N1. (Color figure online)

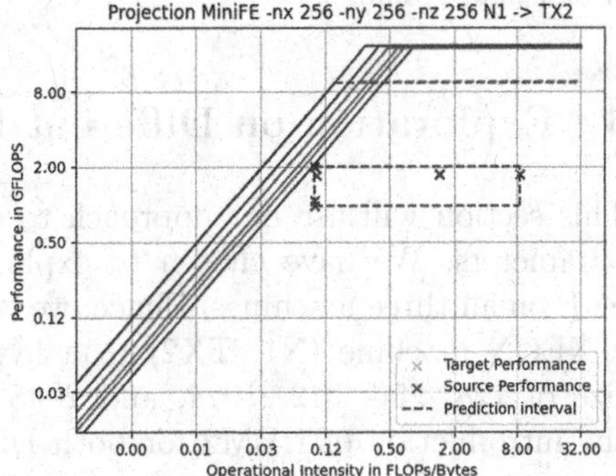

Fig. 7. Results miniFE N1 → TX2. (Color figure online)

5.3 Quicksilver

Quicksilver is our application with the lowest OI and measured performances on both machines (Figs. 8 and 9). The low performance may result from the poor vectorization rate of this application, shown in the maximum performance attainable by the instruction mix of both binaries. All the OI deducted from the L1 are in the memory-bound region of all rooflines, while the OIs derived from other memory levels are in the compute-bound regions. The prediction interval is obtained because of the OI from L1, which includes the measured performances. We observe higher performance on N1 (0.5 GFLOPS) than TX2 (0.4 GFLOPS). This difference in performance may be due to the difference in cache bandwidth, giving an advantage to the N1 core.

To conclude this validation, when we apply our model on the most similar machine in our machine pool, the prediction interval we obtain always includes the measured performance of our application. For the most memory-bound application (MiniFE and Quicksilver), we also observe higher performance when running on an N1 core that may be enabled by the higher bandwidth of the cache levels.

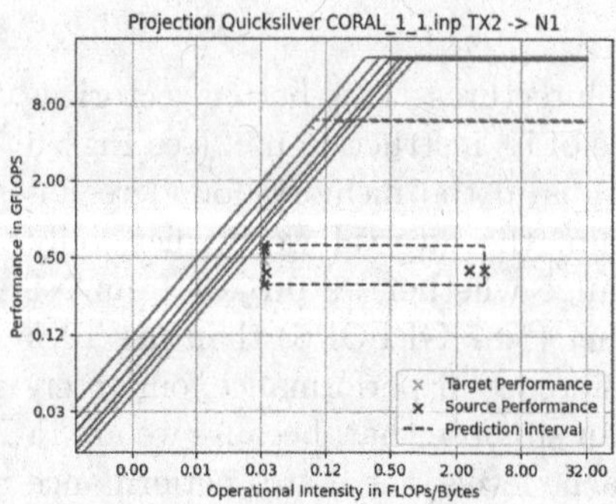

Fig. 8. Results Quicksilver TX2 → N1. (Color figure online)

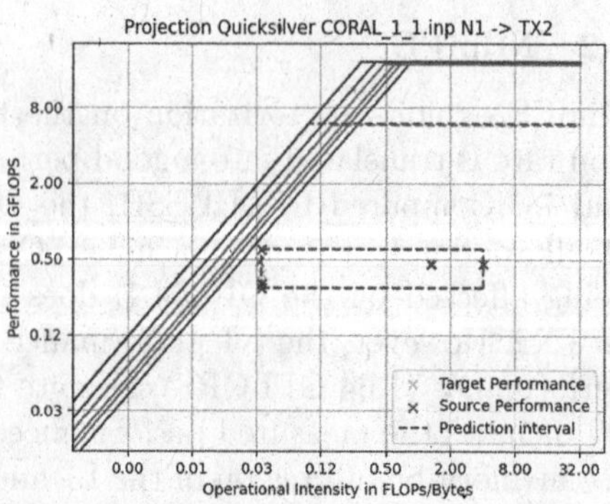

Fig. 9. Results Quicksilver N1 → TX2. (Color figure online)

6 Exploration on Different Parameters

This section will use our approach to explore different hardware and software parameters. We have chosen to explore the different vector sizes allowed by SVE on all three machines. Hence, we compare the performance projection from a NEON machine (N1, TX2) to a hypothetical one with SVE with a vector size of 128, 256, 512, 1024, and 2048 bits. Another parameter we explore is the introduction of HBM2 for both DDR4 machines. Then, we combine these parameters to compare hypothetical SVE512 + HBM2 machines with A64FX. Finally, we observe the differences a change of software stack creates in exploring different vector sizes on A64FX. The SVE512 value is not a projection for A64FX in the following figures as it is native on this core.

6.1 Exploration on SVE vector sizes

One of the challenges in the design of future Arm core is the size imposed by the hardware on SVE vectors and the impact this choice has on the performance of the applications. We can obtain such a characterization with our model by looking at how such a change impacts the maximum performance imposed by hardware and the software stack.

Figure 10 shows that the impact of the vector size on LULESH depends on the source machine. We observe that, when targeting A64FX and TX2 architecture, the binary's predicted performance benefits more from this increase in vector size than when targeting N1. GCC does not vectorize LULESH as much when targeting N1. Despite having a very similar source performance on native N1 and TX2, this difference in vectorization predicts lower performance on N1 than TX2 with longer SVE vectors.

When doing this exercise on MiniFE (Fig. 11), we observe here a similar behavior on all machines. A change in vector size impacts all the predicted performances of our architectures. But this impact is not equivalent for all our architectures. When comparing TX2 and N1, the predicted interval upper bound of TX2 gains more performance at each step to reach a maximum of 10.2 GFLOPS.

The behavior of MiniFE when exploring vector size is opposed to Quicksilver (Fig. 12). This application does not benefit from the change of vector size on any architectures. On all architectures, GCC cannot vectorize the application, meaning they do not benefit from this change of vector size. If we want to gain performance on Monte-Carlo applications, increasing the vector size is not the solution.

The predicted interval is smaller on A64FX than on the other two machines on all these figures. This shows that there are not many differences when projecting performances with different bandwidths of these machines. We can suppose it is because of the bandwidths of the A64FX being much higher, meaning the OIs of our application are closer to the compute-bound region for all bandwidths.

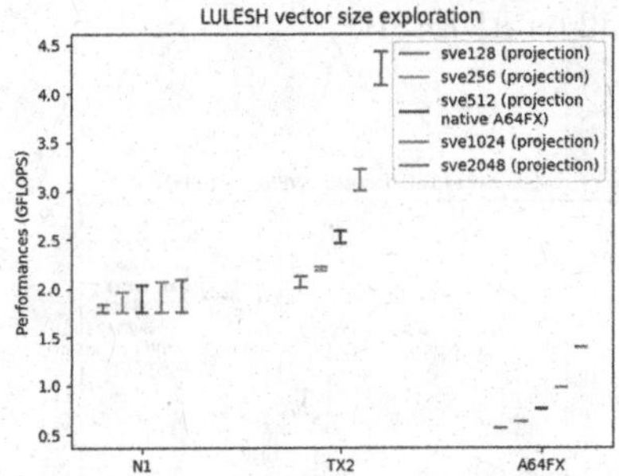

Fig. 10. Exploration of different SVE vector sizes on LULESH

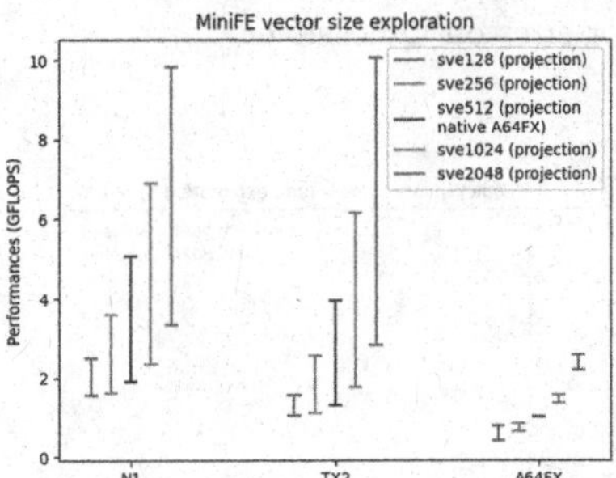

Fig. 11. Exploration of different SVE vector sizes on MiniFE

6.2 Exploration on the Introduction of HBM2 on DDR4 Machines

Another characterization we make with our approach is to analyze the introduction of the HBM2 memory of A64FX on N1 and TX2, creating a hypothetical machine with the same characteristics as our source machine with only the main memory bandwidth being different in our model. The first observation on Figs. 13 and 14 is that the N1 core can be the one that benefits the most from this change of main memory bandwidth on LULESH and Quicksilver. This leads to a higher predicted upper bound on both applications on N1 despite LULESH having less performance with DDR4 on this machine. We suppose this is due to the N1 core having higher cache bandwidth and lower memory bandwidth than TX2. So the memory bandwidth gain is higher for the N1 core, leading to more performance gain for these applications. We also see that the lower bound of our predicted interval does not change on both applications compared to DDR4. This is due to the cache bandwidth of our hypothetical machine not being adapted to this main memory bandwidth increase. Finally, our model cannot characterize the latency aspect of our applications, which may be an issue with the introduction of HBM2 because of its latency access being higher than DDR4.

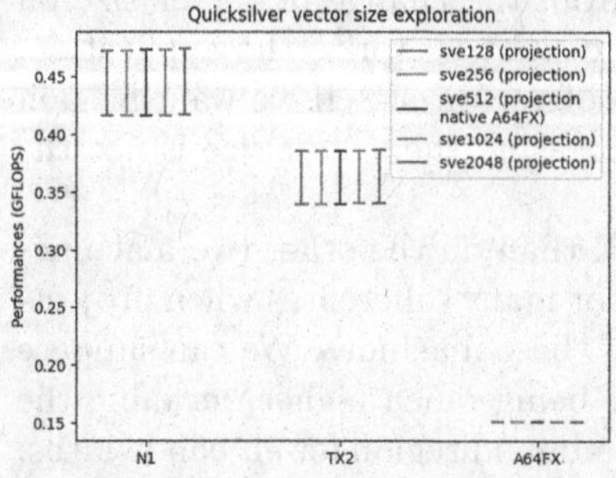

Fig. 12. Exploration of different SVE vector sizes on Quicksilver

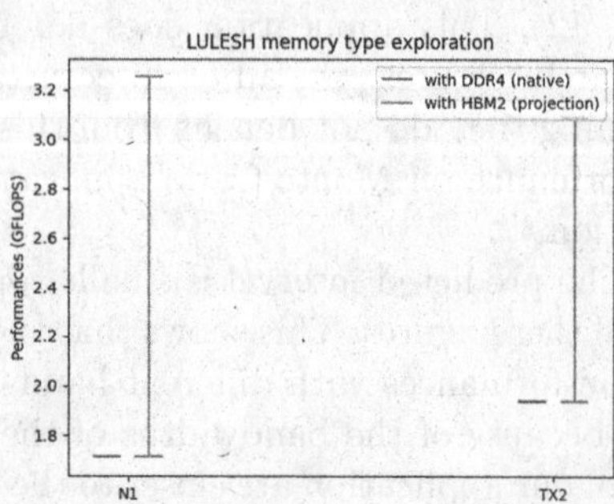

Fig. 13. Exploration of introduction of HBM2 on LULESH

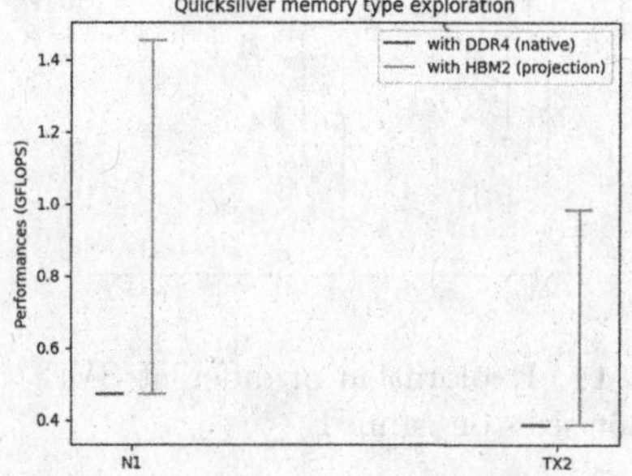

Fig. 14. Exploration of introduction of HBM2 on Quicksilver

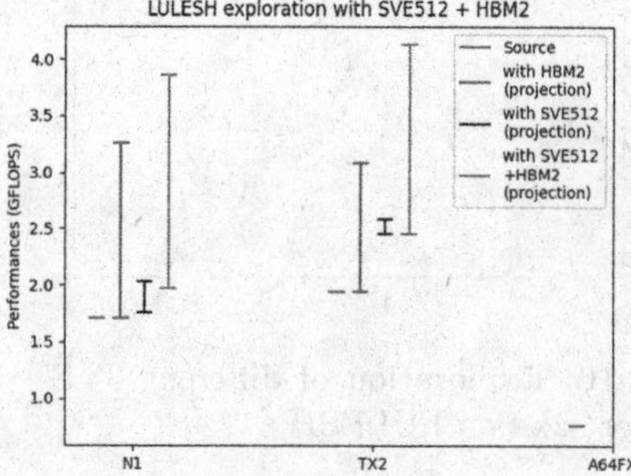

Fig. 15. Exploration of introduction of HBM2 and SVE512 on LULESH

6.3 Comparison of Projections from N1 and TX2 with SVE 512 and HBM2 to A64FX

We combine both changes of parameters we made in the two previous subsections to compare the introduction of SVE 512 bits and HBM2 on N1 and TX2 and compare it with the A64FX architecture on two applications: LULESH and Quicksilver. We choose to use GCC 10.3 on all 3 machines for this comparison presented in the Figures 15 and 16. We can observe the change introduced by HBM2 to the interval predicted only with SVE512. Similarly, the use of HBM2 impacts the N1 core the most on LULESH, even with SVE512. Even if both machines can gain more performance, this leads to similar predicted performance between N1 and TX2 despite LULESH not benefitting from vectorization on N1. On MiniFE, the predicted performance is not as impacted on both applications.We only observe the predicted upper bound being higher by 0.6 GFLOPS on N1 and no change on TX2. This analysis shows it can be more impactful on performance to increase vector size than increasing the main memory bandwidth for MiniFE.

When we compare the projection on both applications to the performance on the A64FX machine, we predict performance to be higher on N1 and TX2 architecture. We can suppose the introduction of HBM2 and SVE512 on these machines changed their single-core roofline to be on par with A64FX, and GCC is more efficient when targeting N1 and TX2 architecture than A64FX, causing this higher predicted performance.

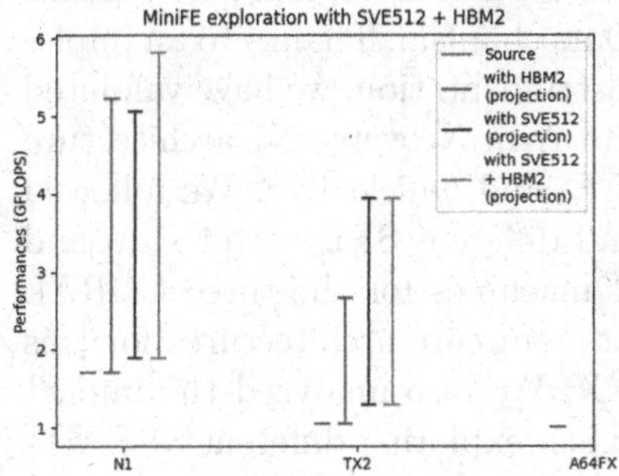

Fig. 16. Exploration of introduction of HBM2 and SVE512 on MiniFE

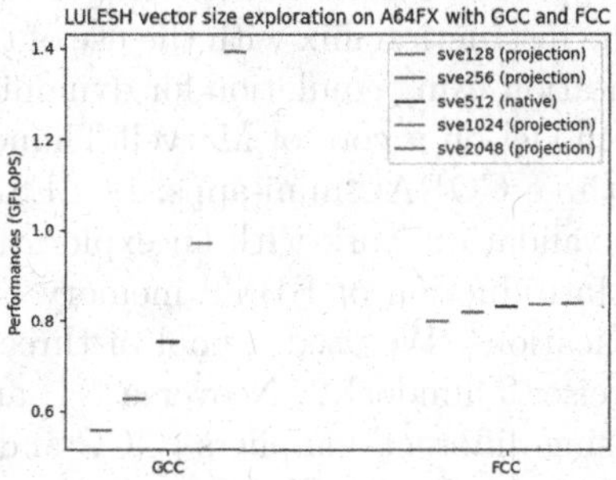

Fig. 17. Vector sizes exploration with GCC and FCC on A64FX on LULESH

6.4 Vector Sizes Exploration on A64FX with Different Software Stacks

We have seen that GCC has a hard time obtaining performance on a single-core of A64FX, and we want to compare it with the use of the Fujitsu Compiler (FCC). Figure 17 presents this comparison when changing the vector sizes on LULESH with GCC and FCC compilers. We do not have an interval with both software stacks, meaning the OIs of both binaries are in the compute-bound region of A64FX. However, we observe a different evolution of the predicted value when increasing the SVE vector size. GCC binary gains more performance when increasing vector size when compared to the FCC binary because it has more vector usage. Despite this difference in vectorization, we observe higher performance on FCC with SVE vectors from 128 bits to 512 bits, with the last being the native vector size. We can suppose that FCC is more careful when vectorizing the application because of its insight of the microarchitecture impact of the A64FX, whereas GCC vectorizes a loop without considering it as much. So we have better usage of an A64FX when compiling with the Fujitsu Compiler than with GCC.

7 Conclusion and Future Work

This article presents an approach for core design space exploration of a single processor core using performance projection from a source machine. We have chosen to consider the impact of the software stack of the target machine. The workflow relies on binary analysis, hardware characterization, and the Roofline model to obtain a performance interval on the target machine. Thanks to this projection, we can characterize the impact of the differences between a single core maximum performance, the bandwidth of all memory levels, and the cache efficiency. We can also analyze the differences brought by the software stack on the application with metrics such as the observed OI and maximum performance of the instruction mix with the use of the SIMD mechanism. Thanks to an implementation using emulation for dynamic code instrumentation, we have validated our model on a core of Marvell ThunderX2 and Arm Neoverse N1 architecture for three CORAL mini-apps: LULESH, MiniFE, and Quicksilver. We followed this validation work with an exploration around different SVE vector sizes and the introduction of HBM2 memory on DDR4 machines for the three CORAL applications. We used a pool of three different Arm core architectures for this exercise: ThunderX2, Neoverse N1, and A64FX. We also analyzed the impact of using different compilers (GCC and FCC) when exploring different SVE vector lengths on A64FX. To enhance the model, we plan to characterize some microarchitectural features and parallelism at a full-node level.

RIKEN Acknowledgment:. The work presented in this paper has been executed in the context of the CEA and RIKEN collaboration on High Performance Computing, Artificial Intelligence and Quantum Computing.

We thank the RIKEN team for granting us access to the Fugaku supercomputer in the context of our bilateral collaboration.

Authors' Contributions:

Clément Gavoille. Conceptualization, Methodology, Software, Validation, Investigation, Writing - Original Draft, Writing - Review & Editing, Visualization

Hugo Taboada. Conceptualization, Methodology, Resources, Writing - Original Draft, Supervision

Patrick Carribault. Conceptualization, Methodology, Resources, Writing - Original Draft, Supervision

Fabrice Dupros. Resources, Writing - Original Draft, Supervision.

Brice Goglin. Conceptualization, Writing - Original Draft, Supervision.

Emmanuel Jeannot. Conceptualization, Writing - Original Draft, Supervision.

References

1. ARM: Arm instruction emulator. https://developer.arm.com/tools-and-software/server-and-hpc/compile/arm-instruction-emulator
2. Barrett, R.F., Heroux, M.A.: The mantevo projectmini-applications: vehicles for co-design. (2013)
3. Bruening, D., Garnett, T., Amarasinghe, S.: An infrastructure for adaptive dynamic optimization. In: Proceedings of the International Symposium on Code Generation and Optimization: Feedback-Directed and Runtime Optimization. CGO 2003 (2003)
4. Davis, J., Mudalige, G., Hammond, S., Herdman, A., Miller, I., Jarvis, S.: Predictive analysis of a hydrodynamics application on large-scale CMP clusters. Computer Science - Research and Development, vol. 26 (2011)
5. Domke, J.: A64fx - your compiler you must decide! (2021)
6. Ilic, A., Pratas, F., Sousa, L.: Cache-aware roofline model: upgrading the loft. IEEE Comput. Architect. Lett. **13**, 21–24 (2014)
7. Ipek, E., de Supinski, B.R., Schulz, M., McKee, S.A.: An approach to performance prediction for parallel applications. In: Cunha, J.C., Medeiros, P.D. (eds.) Euro-Par 2005. LNCS, vol. 3648, pp. 196–205. Springer, Heidelberg (2005). https://doi.org/10.1007/11549468_24
8. Jongerius, R., Anghel, A., Dittmann, G., Mariani, G., Vermij, E., Corporaal, H.: Analytic multi-core processor model for fast design-space exploration. IEEE Trans. Comput. **67**, 755–770 (2018)
9. Jongerius, R., Mariani, G., Anghel, A., Dittmann, G., Vermij, E., Corporaal, H.: Analytic processor model for fast design-space exploration. In: 2015 33rd IEEE International Conference on Computer Design (ICCD) (2015)
10. Karlin, I., Keasler, J., Neely, R.: Lulesh 2.0 updates and changes. Technical report, LLNL-TR-641973 (2013)
11. Kodama, Y., Odajima, T., Asato, A., Sato, M.: Evaluation of the riken post-k processor simulator, April 2019
12. Kwack, J.H., Arnold, G., Mendes, C., Bauer, G.: Roofline analysis with cray performance analysis tools (CrayPat) and roofline-based performance projections for a future architecture. Pract. Exp. Concurr Comput. **31**, e4963 (2018)
13. McCalpin, J.: Memory bandwidth and machine balance in high performance computers. IEEE Technical Committee on Computer Architecture Newsletter (1995)
14. Obaida, M.A., Liu, J., Chennupati, G., Santhi, N., Eidenbenz, S.: Parallel application performance prediction using analysis based models and HPC simulations. In: Proceedings of the 2018 ACM SIGSIM Conference on Principles of Advanced Discrete Simulation, SIGSIM-PADS 2018 (2018)
15. Petitet, A., Whaley, R., Dongarra, J., Cleary, A.: HPL - a portable implementation of the high-performance LINPAC benchmark for distributed-memory computers (2008)
16. Richards, D., Brantley, P., Dawson, S., Mckenley, S., O'Brien, M.: Quicksilver, version 00
17. Stephens, N., et al.: The arm scalable vector extension. IEEE Micro **37**, 26–39 (2017). https://doi.org/10.1109/MM.2017.35
18. Williams, S., Waterman, A., Patterson, D.: Roofline: an insightful visual performance model for multicore architectures. ACM Commun. **52**, 65–74 (2009)

Scheduling and Load Balancing

Exploring Scheduling Algorithms for Parallel Task Graphs: A Modern Game Engine Case Study

Mustapha Regragui[1], Baptiste Coye[1,2], Laércio L. Pilla[1(✉)], Raymond Namyst[1], and Denis Barthou[1]

[1] Univ. Bordeaux, CNRS, Bordeaux INP, Inria, LaBRI, 5800 Talence, France
mustapha.regragui@bordeaux-inp.fr, {laercio.pilla,raymond.namyst, denis.barthou}@inria.fr
[2] Ubisoft Bordeaux, Bordeaux, France
baptiste.coye@ubisoft.com

Abstract. Game engines are at the heart of the design of modern video games. One of their functions is to keep a high frame rate by scheduling the tasks required to generate each frame (image). These tasks are organized in a soft real-time, parallel task graph, which is a scenario very few works have focused on, or adapted scheduling algorithms to. In this paper, we study the scheduling problem of game engines. We model the tasks and the scheduling problem by profiling a commercial game engine, adapt and compare different scheduling algorithms, and propose two additional optimizations regarding the micro-scheduler and the parallelization of targeted tasks.

Keywords: Scheduling · Video Game engine · Soft real-time · Task programming

1 Introduction

The video game market is valued at over 100 billion USD [15], making it larger than the HPC market, or even the movie and music industries combined. This industry impacts computing both at the hardware and software levels. It produces and sells tens of millions of video game consoles yearly. Its games are run on personal computers, consoles, smartphones, and even on Cloud gaming servers. These games are more easily developed and ported to different platforms thanks to a key software component called the game engine.

The **game engine** serves as a framework for game development. Video game companies can license game engines, such as Unity, Unreal Engine 4, or Game Maker: Studio, or produce their own. A game engine contains core software components (such as the 3D rendering system or the collision detection system) that can be extended and combined with different art assets and game logic to

J. Cano and P. W. Trinder (Eds.): Euro-Par 2022, LNCS 13440, pp. 103–118, 2022.
https://doi.org/10.1007/978-3-031-12597-3_7

produce different games [12]. Moreover, game engines are responsible for managing resources such as the memory, and for scheduling tasks. This makes the optimization of game engines essential for the gaming experience of players.

The problem of scheduling in game engines has not been previously studied in detail, and we have noticed that this problem includes uncommon characteristics. For instance, although video games are soft real-time systems (with a video frame being displayed every few milliseconds), their recurring tasks do not match exactly with the models of periodic or sporadic task systems [16, Chapter 28]. Additionally, although their tasks are parallel, they are neither malleable nor moldable [16, Chapter 25]. With a better understanding of this problem, we could optimize the schedule in game engines for the benefit of players and developers alike: with fewer dropped frames, players can have a better gaming experience; with some extra free time before having to display a frame, developers can include more detailed graphics, physics, or AI, while mobile devices can operate at lower frequencies and save battery, and Cloud gaming servers can dedicate less computing resources to a game.

In this paper, our goal is to understand and find solutions to the scheduling problem of game engines. Working with a modern game engine as a case study, we are able to model this problem and to adapt several scheduling algorithms to it. Our experimental evaluation reveals performance improvements in the game engine when answering the following three research questions: (I) "*Can scheduling strategies from the state of the art improve the performance of game engines?*"; (II) "*Can changes in the scheduling mechanism of a game engine reduce the performance gap between schedulers and the critical path?*"; and (III) "*Can small changes to the task graph lead to performance improvements?*". Our contributions include the model and evaluation metrics, the list of algorithms adapted for this problem, and their experimental evaluation, which are all presented in Sects. 3, 4, and 5, respectively. Section 2 covers information on game engines and related work, and Sect. 6 provides concluding remarks.

2 Background and Related Work

2.1 Background on Video Games and Game Engines

Video games work as soft real-time interactive simulations [12]. The frequency of interactions is given by the *frame rate*, which defines how many *frames* (images) are presented *per second*. Nowadays, the de facto standard dictates a frame rate of 60fps, giving $\frac{1}{60}$ s $\approx$ 16.667 ms for producing each frame. If this time is surpassed, a frame is *dropped*. Frequent frame drops degrade the gaming experience.

As a video game is built on a game engine, engineers will add, remove, or adapt functionalities to their needs. Given the complexity of developing a game engine, it is very common for large companies to maintain their own engines for over a decade to capitalize on their know-how. Still, the cost of hand-tuning all their features is exacerbated by the variety of gaming platforms and their evolution (e.g., increase in the number of CPU cores available).

One way of reducing the required hand-tuning comes with the game engine scheduler, which manages the execution of tasks (functionalities) by itself. For instance, Unity provides its Job System [21] so engineers can write their own tasks with dependencies and let Unity schedule them. Meanwhile, Unreal Engine 4 includes Tick Groups [22] to set when a task should be executed (e.g., before or after physics simulations). Our case study contains a task graph that is executed for each frame. The structure of the graph is static for a single game. Moreover, considering the transfer of knowledge through developer recruitment in the video game industry [7] and game engines' needs in order to create frames (e.g., light, physics) [12], this results in a standardized architecture. In this context, the graph's structure changes very little between games (e.g., gameplay) and companies, making our graph representative. This organization makes it easier for multiple teams of engineers to work on their own functionalities. Additionally, each task is composed of one or more parallel subtasks, which is also recommended on Intel's Games Task Scheduler (GTS) [3].

2.2 Scheduling Problems and Algorithms

The game engine's scheduler may find issues to keep the frame rate due to resources being used by others (e.g., the operating system), for other tasks (loading assets), or due to changes in the **load of the game** (e.g., additional objects to render or AI agents to simulate). A change in load may mean not only a change in the execution time of a task, but also to its number of subtasks. Although high load episodes may be hard to anticipate (given the dynamic and interactive nature of video games), load changes are usually gradual. A scheduler could benefit from this by estimating the behavior of tasks based on recent frames in a way similar to the use of the principle-of-persistence in periodic load balancing [1]. Conversely, estimations are avoided by GTS through work stealing [3].

Given the lack of studies on this scheduling problem, our efforts have been dedicated to finding and adapting algorithms and heuristics proposed in other contexts [2,8,10,13,14] (cf. Sect. 4). We find that there is value in bringing to light new applications and knowledge on existing algorithms, as have done Benoit et al. [5] for the asymptotic performance of the longest processing time (LPT) heuristic for the case of tasks originating from uniform integer compositions.

Our scheduling problem has distinct characteristics that block the use of techniques and heuristics used for scheduling traditional real-time or parallel tasks [16]. Real-time scheduling most often considers independent, recurring tasks. Such is the case on the work of Nascimento and Lima [17], where earliest deadline first (EDF) heuristics are employed for scheduling soft and hard real-time tasks in parallel resources. Nonetheless, the game engine contains dependent tasks with an entire task graph to be computed for each frame. Additionally, the absence of individual deadlines for tasks induces the frame's end as a shared due date, obstructing the use of EDF heuristics. Moreover, strong limitations regarding memory and differences of constructions between video and 3D rendering restrains our capacity to treat several frames simultaneously or to split the image to render in block as done by Zhao and Liang [23]. Meanwhile, parallel task scheduling usually models tasks that use multiple resources simultaneously, but the game engine's tasks follow a fork-join model internally. These levels of tasks and subtasks are also reflected on GTS [3] with its **macro-** and

micro-schedulers. An algorithm called DynFed was proposed to schedule parallel tasks with dependencies in real-time systems by Dai, Mohaqeqi, and Yi [9]. Nonetheless, it focuses on periodic, independent tasks whose parallel subtasks have dependencies, while our scheduling problem contains tasks with dependencies whose parallel subtasks are independent.

3 Scheduling in Game Engines

Our discussion of the scheduling problem in game engines is organized in three parts: the task model; the scheduling problem at the scale of a single frame; and the problem for multiple frames.

3.1 Task Model

A game engine performs multiple tasks to produce each frame (e.g., graphics rendering and physics simulations [12]). These tasks have precedence constraints that must be respected for their correct execution, which leads to their organization as a directed acyclic graph (DAG). Figure 1 represents the task graph of our case study. It was extracted from a modern video game from Ubisoft and its structure is reflected in other game engines and video games. The leftmost task is the start of the frame and the rightmost its end. The path on the bottom of Fig. 1 is composed of graphic tasks (all run in the same CPU core to dispatch work to the GPU), while the other paths represent simulation and control tasks.

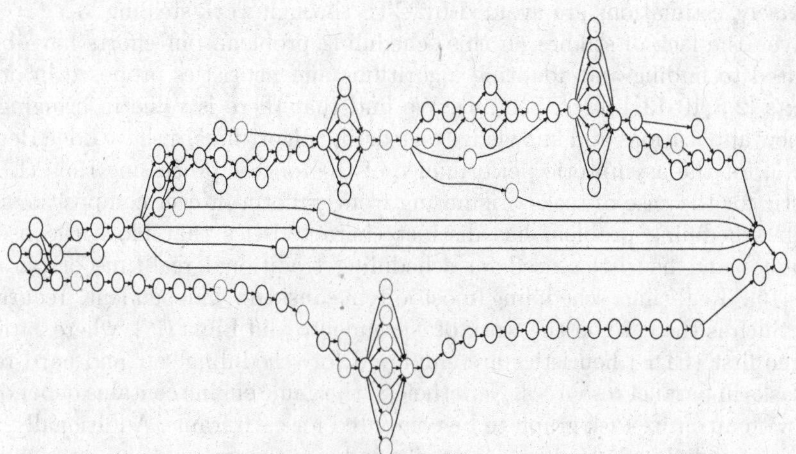

Fig. 1. A DAG representing game engine tasks (vertices) and their precedence constraints (edges, from left to right). Tasks in red are composed of multiple sequential subtasks. (Color figure online)

Each task represents a functionality written by a given team in a given moment in the lifetime of the game engine, so task interactions have to be kept simple. Internally, each task contains one or more independent, sequential subtasks following a fork-join model as illustrated in Fig. 2. For our $\approx$ 100 tasks, over 1000 subtasks can be computed at each frame. Both their number and execution time may change during the game execution. We refer to this effect as the *load* of the frame.

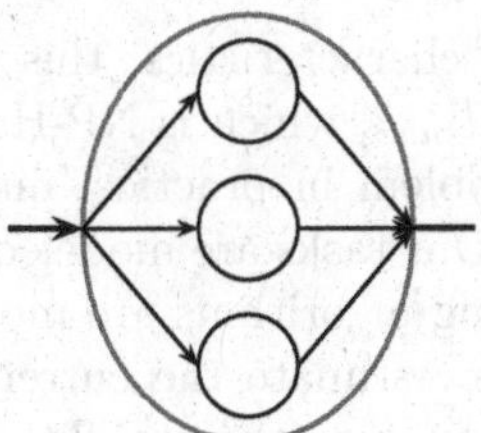

Fig. 2. Fork-join parallelism inside a task. Each small circle represents one sequential subtask.

In order to model and simulate the behavior of the game engine under different loads, we profiled its tasks and subtasks on varied executions (>10 on different maps of the game) and different phases (over 3000 frames). We obtained their minimum, maximum, mean, and standard deviation values, and used them to model timings as log-normal distributions [20] depending on the load. Equation 1 defines the processing time p_j^{sub} of a subtask of task j with load $l \in [0,1]$ depending on $p_j^{min}(l)$, $p_j^{max}(l)$, $\mu_j(l)$, and $\sigma_j(l)$ that are resp. the minimal, maximal, mean, and standard deviation of the execution time under load l. Each value was obtained for *low* ($l = 0$) and *high* ($l = 1$) loads, and intermediary values are computed by a linear interpolation in l. We compute the processing time $p_j(l)$ of task j by adding together the times of its subtasks in Eq. 2. In it, $s_j(l)$ represents the number of subtasks of task j with load l, which is computed in a similar fashion to other load-dependent parameters—i.e., $s_j(l) = \lceil (1-l) \cdot s_{j,low} + l \cdot s_{j,high} \rceil$.

$$p_j^{sub}(l) = p_j^{min}(l) + (p_j^{max}(l) - p_j^{min}(l)) \log \mathcal{N}(\mu_j(l), \sigma_j(l)) \quad (1)$$

$$p_j(l) = \sum_{k=1}^{s_j(l)} p_j^{sub}(l) \quad (2)$$

3.2 Scheduling Problem for a Single Frame

A simplified description of the scheduling problem for a frame can be shown using Graham's notation [11]. The machine environment is composed of parallel and identical resources (CPU cores). The task characteristics and scheduling constraints follow the model of Sect. 3.1. In short, our tasks have precedence constraints, different processing times, and the same due date. For the objective function, we define C_j as the completion time of task j, its lateness L_j in Eq. 3 and its tardiness T_j in Eq. 4, where d_j represents the due date of the task.

$$L_j = C_j - d_j \quad (3)$$

$$T_j = \max(L_j, 0) \quad (4)$$

Given the aforementioned characteristics, this scheduling problem can be represented as $P|prec, d_j = d|T_{max}$, which is NP-Hard. Still, this does not capture all the details of our problem in practice, mainly due to imprecision on the processing times of tasks. Our tasks are modeled using stochastic processing times, and time-ware scheduling algorithms are mostly dependent on measurements from previous frames to estimate the current frame's behavior (i.e., its load). This is not an issue thanks to the stability of the game engine and to the minor effects of slight prediction disturbances in similar contexts [4]. In this sense, using the notation P_j to represent stochastic processing times [6, Chapter 1], our scheduling problem would be closer to $P|P_j, prec, d_j = d|T_{max}$.

3.3 Scheduling Problem for Multiple Frames

The quality of a scheduling solution for multiple frames is based on its results for each frame. Consider the total number of frames F and a given frame $f \in [1, F]$. We denote the maximum tardiness of frame f as T^f_{max}. Using this information, we define three possible optimization metrics to minimize, namely the **Slowest Frame** (SF), the number of **Delayed Frames** (DF), and the **Cumulative Slowdown** (CS), represented in Eqs. 5, 6, and 7. The Slowest Frame represents the moment with the worst frame rate to be noticed by a player. The number of Delayed Frames quantifies the periods of reduced frame rate that can be noticed. Lastly, the Cumulative Slowdown qualifies these periods with the amount of time that surpasses the due date of each frame. Using these three metrics, we can compare different scheduling algorithms for game engines.

$$SF = \max_{f \in [1,F]} T^f_{max} + d \quad (5)$$

$$DF = \sum_{f \in [1,F] \wedge T^f_{max} > 0} 1 \quad (6)$$

$$CS = \sum_{f \in [1,F]} T^f_{max} \quad (7)$$

4 Exploring List Scheduling Algorithms

Given the absence of known solutions for our scheduling problem, we have selected—and, sometimes, adapted—several scheduling algorithms used in other contexts to our experiments. All of them follow a list scheduling strategy: Whenever a resource becomes available, the macro-scheduler takes the task with the highest priority and the micro-scheduler executes one of its subtasks. Besides its known benefits, list scheduling is also attractive for its ability to adapt to changes in the number of resources available.

Table 1 lists the chosen algorithms, which we believe cover a wide range of the behaviors seen in the literature. The algorithms are ordered according to the way they compute task priorities. *Local* algorithms use only information from the task to compute its priority, which leads to a lower complexity or overhead. The opposite are *global* algorithms that tend to consider the paths in the task graph. *Online* algorithms require information obtained at run time, while *offline* algorithms can pre-compute task priorities. Finally, *time*-aware algorithms use timing information to compute priorities.

The First In, First Out scheduler represents the original implementation in the game engine and serves as the baseline. Regarding online algorithms, SLPT (and SSPT) follows the same logic of LPT [10] (SPT [13]), but at a subtask level (i.e., using $p_{j,k}^{sub}$ to choose which task has the priority). Instead of using processing times to compute priorities, HRRN and WT use information related to the moments a task becomes available in the priority queue in the current frame (r_j), its first subtask starts executing (b_j), and its last subtask finishes executing (C_j). HRRN uses these values to compute a *response ratio* for the priorities as $\frac{C_j - b_j}{C_j - r_j}$. WT computes the difference between the moment a task becomes ready and the moment it starts executing ($b_j - r_j$). In both cases, tasks with higher values are given a higher priority.

Offline algorithms try to prioritize tasks that may delay the completion of the last task (*exit node*). HLF [14] prioritizes tasks in the longest paths to the exit node, while HLFET [2] extends it with processing time estimations (the mean times used in our model). CG [8] uses a labeling algorithm that has been shown to be optimal for the problem $P2|p_j = p, prec|C_{max}$.

Our last algorithm, named DCP, combines global information online. It computes the priority of a task in two ways. If task j is identified as part of the critical path in the previous frame, it is added to the head of the priority queue.

Table 1. Characterization of tested scheduling algorithms.

Acronym	Ref.	Meaning	Info. scale	Priority comp.	Time-awareness
FIFO		First In, First Out	—	—	—
LPT	[10]	Longest processing time first	Local	Online	Previous frame
SPT	[13]	Shortest processing time first	Local	Online	Previous frame
SLPT		LPT at a subtask level	Local	Online	Previous frame
SSPT		SPT at a subtask level	Local	Online	Previous frame
HRRN		Highest response ratio next	Local	Online	Prev. & curr. frame
WT		Longest waiting time first	Local	Online	Prev. & curr. frame
HLF	[14]	Highest level First	Global	Offline	—
HLFET	[2]	HLF with estimated times	Global	Offline	Mean
CG	[8]	Coffman-Graham's algorithm	Global	Offline	—
DCP		Dynamic critical path	Global	Online	Previous frame

Else, task j is added to the queue with priority $prio(j)$ after all tasks in the critical path. $prio(j)$ is computed in Eq. 8 using information from the previous frame, the set of successors of task j in the graph as $succ(j)$, and the number of resources m. In short, the priority of a task is computed based on the highest priority among its successors and the maximum between an estimation of its parallel execution and its slowest subtask.

$$prio(j) = \max_{i \in succ(j)} prio(i) + \max\left(\frac{\sum_{k=1}^{s_j} p_{j,k}^{sub}}{\min(m, s_j)}, \max_{k \in [1, s_j]} p_{j,k}^{sub}\right) \quad (8)$$

5 Experimental Evaluation

We conducted a series of experiments using an in-house simulator covering three different scenarios based on the research questions brought up in Sect. 1. Following the methods described in Sect. 5.1, the results of the experimental scenarios are presented in Sects. 5.2, 5.3, and 5.4.

5.1 Details Regarding the Simulation and Statistical Evaluation

The experiments use an in-house scheduling simulator written in C++. Given a complete description of the task graph (Sect. 3.1), the number of frames to simulate, the number of resources, a scheduling algorithm, and a random number generator (RNG) seed, it deterministically simulates the scheduling and execution of all tasks. This enables direct comparisons between scheduling algorithms and experimental scenarios. The simulation represents an ideal environment with no overhead from the scheduling algorithm, data locality, or other sources of interference, trading realism for understandability. All parameters required to model the tasks (Eq. 1) were obtained in a development machine from Ubisoft.

To test load variations, each simulation runs 200 frames with the load parameter starting at 0 and increasing linearly up to 1 in the 101st frame and then decreasing linearly until it reaches 0.01 for the last frame. This provides a gradual change of load while also generating a load peak. For each scenario and scheduling strategy, we ran simulations using from 4 up to 20 resources. By regarding results with fewer resources, we can also anticipate the effects of external interference (Sect. 2.2). Our standard case is set to 12 resources, as this is a common number of cores in current gaming processors. In each situation, we varied the RNG seed in the interval $[1, 50]$. Excluding Critical Path simulations, this represents a total of $200 \times 50 \times 17 \times 11 \times 3 = 5,610,000$ frames.

For the statistical evaluation of our experiments, we first employed descriptive methods to understand our results and to verify that no errors were present. We then followed with inferential methods. Setting our tests to a 5% significance level, we used Kolmogorov-Smirnov tests to check if samples came from normal distributions for all metrics whenever relevant. In all tested cases, we could not reject the null hypothesis that the results came from a normal distribution (all p-values > 0.05). We then ran F-tests to compare the variances of relevant pairs of samples. Again, in all cases, we could not reject the null hypothesis that the samples had the same variance. Given these statistical results, we used Student's T-test for all relevant comparisons discussed in the next sections.

All results were obtained on an Intel Core i7-1185G7 processor, with 32 GB of LPDDR4 RAM (3200 MHz). The machine ran on Ubuntu 20.04.3 LTS (5.13.0-1022-oem), and g++ 9.3.0 was used for the simulator's compilation (−O3 flag). The code used for this study is available online [18], as is a dataset containing all simulation results and evaluation scripts [19].

5.2 Scenario I - Employing Scheduling Algorithms

We summarize the main performance results when scheduling tasks on 12 resources in Table 2 and Fig. 3 (small values the better). Table 2 shows the values of Slowest Frame, Delayed Frames, and Cumulative Slowdown (rows) computed for each scheduling algorithm (columns). These values represent the averages over 50 executions. The first column presents FIFO (our baseline) and the last column shows the values for the Critical Path. The general distribution of values for the different metrics is illustrated as boxplots in Fig. 3.

The smallest improvements are achieved for the SF metric. This indicates that, under the worst load conditions, no algorithm is able to avoid the large increase in frame duration. Still, even the minor improvements achieved by WT and CG are still statistically significant (p-values $= 5.12 \times 10^{-33}$ and 9.64×10^{-30}, resp.). This is not the case for LPT (p-value = 0.69). In any case, the average SF for the Critical Path is only better than FIFO's by a factor of 1.159, and still 1.70 times larger than the desired frame duration (16.667 ms).

The scheduling algorithms provide more noticeable improvements for the DF and CS metrics. This happens for strategies both local and global, online and offline (Table 1). For instance, WT (local, online) reduced DF by a factor of 1.054 over the baseline (p-value $= 4.16 \times 10^{-21}$), as did CG (global, offline) (p-value $= 5.65 \times 10^{-21}$). DCP (global, online) did the same by a factor of 1.055 (p-value $= 4.21 \times 10^{-21}$). Interestingly enough, we cannot say that these three strategies perform differently for the DF metric (all p-values > 0.05), but we can do so for CS (all p-values < 0.05).

In order to better understand the effects of the scheduling algorithms on the duration of the frames, Fig. 4 shows the frame duration reductions achieved by LPT, WT, CG, and DCP as histograms. These values are obtained by subtracting the duration of each frame scheduled by FIFO by the respective value for each algorithm. These subtractions are done for each pair of frame number and

Table 2. Average metrics for all scheduling strategies on 12 resources.

	FIFO	LPT	SPT	SLPT	SSPT	HRRN	WT	HLF	HLFET	CG	DCP	Crit. Path
SF (ms)	32.88	32.87	32.40	32.37	32.78	32.37	32.39	32.48	32.54	32.38	32.38	28.37
DF (frames)	72.48	72.86	68.82	68.70	72.02	68.50	68.74	69.52	69.98	68.74	68.70	45.50
CS (ms)	375.30	376.83	344.37	343.12	370.86	342.99	342.52	349.52	353.69	343.17	342.87	171.40

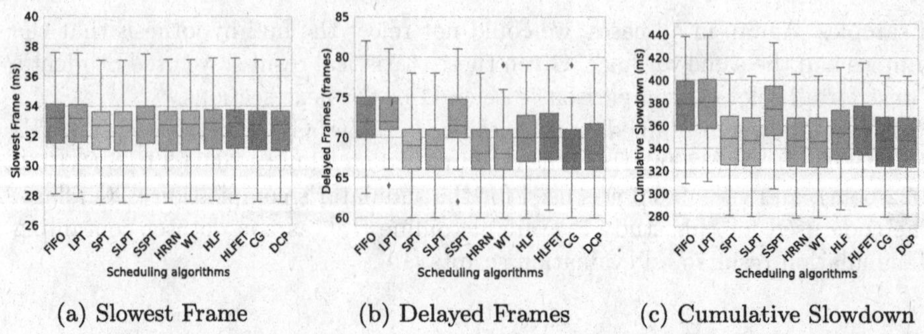

(a) Slowest Frame (b) Delayed Frames (c) Cumulative Slowdown

Fig. 3. Boxplots for the 3 metrics on 12 resources. Vertical axes start at different points to emphasize differences.

RNG seed. The horizontal axis is organized in bins of 20 µs truncated in a range of −1000 µs to 1000 µs[1]. A positive reduction means that the algorithm reduces the duration of a specific frame, thus improving performance.

Three relevant aspects can be noticed here. First, LPT (Fig. 4a) has most of its frame duration reductions centered around 0ms, indicating that its decisions lead to schedules very similar to FIFO. Second, the other illustrated strategies have results mostly centered around 500 µs with slightly different curves. Although they make different decisions with varied effects on the duration of each frame, they are still able to improve the performance of the game engine in their own ways. Third, all scheduling strategies show values that are below 0 µs, demonstrating that no single algorithm is able to always improve performance.

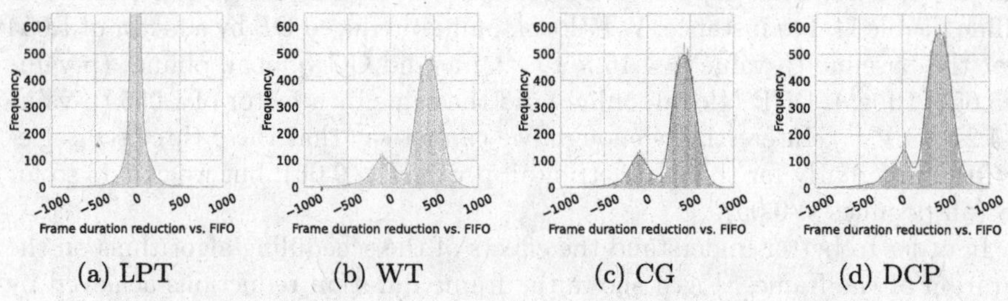

(a) LPT (b) WT (c) CG (d) DCP

Fig. 4. Histograms presenting frame duration reductions (in µs) compared to FIFO (positive values mean shorter frame durations by the algorithms). Lines represent kernel density estimations.

[1] Some frame duration changes fall outside the illustrated range.

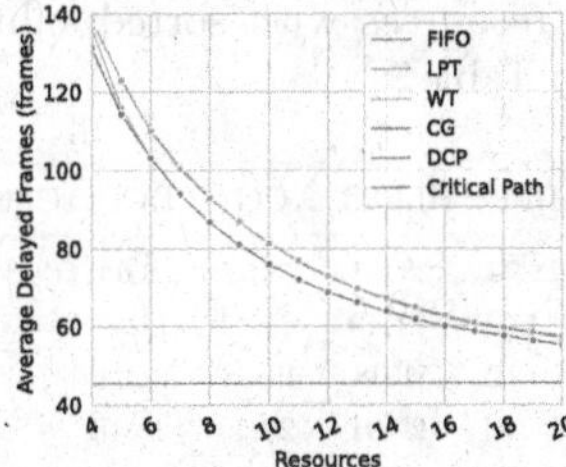

Fig. 5. Average number of delayed frames on different number of resources. The vertical axis starts at 40 frames to emphasize differences.

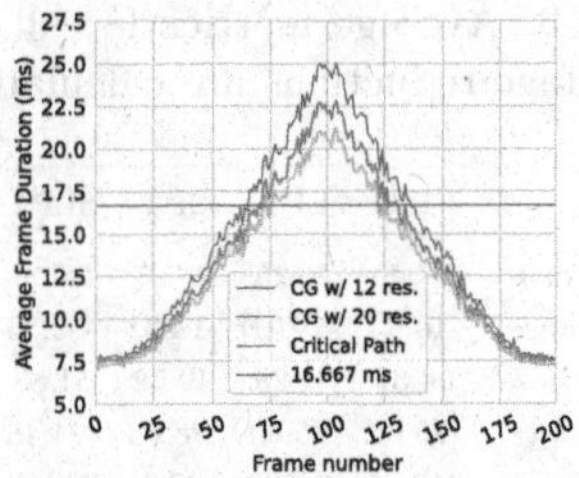

Fig. 6. Average duration of each frame for CG on 12 and 20 resources, and for the Critical Path.

Performance improvements can also be seen across different numbers of resources. This is illustrated in Fig. 5, where the average DF of selected algorithms (vertical axis) is shown from 4 up to 20 resources (horizontal axis). In general, we can see that FIFO and LPT perform similarly, as do WT, CG, and DCP among themselves with 6 or more resources. The absolute difference between FIFO and other strategies tends to decrease when more resources are available, going from about 7 frames on 4 resources down to under 2 frames on 20 resources. This shows that it becomes harder to saturate resources as their numbers increase, which in turn reduces the delay seen on important tasks from the critical path.

Even when scheduling tasks on 20 resources, a noticeable gap remains between some of the best schedulers and the Critical Path. To better illustrate this difference, Fig. 6 contrasts the frame duration of the Critical Path and CG. The horizontal axis represents the simulated frames in order, while the vertical axis represents their average durations for CG with 12 and 20 resources, and for the Critical Path. Figure 6 exposes the change in frame duration following the change in load (which peaks around frame 100). While the Critical Path starts surpassing the due date with a load around 0.75, CG has the same issue for even smaller loads depending on the number of resources. Although the increase from 12 to 20 resources reduces the gap between its timing and the optimal one from 4 ms down to 2 ms for the slowest frames, we were surprised that such a gap still remained. This motivated the changes presented in the next scenario.

5.3 Scenario II - Subtask Scheduling

In search of a way to overcome the previous limitations, we have moved our attention from the macro-scheduler to the micro-scheduler (cf. Sect. 4). Originally, the micro-scheduler takes the first non-executed subtask from the highest priority task available. We have instead chosen to sort the subtasks in a task by non-increasing order of execution time. We consider this is a feasible change to the game engine because it does not affect the actual execution of the subtasks nor the dependencies in the task graph. Additionally, developers can provide

Table 3. Average metrics for all schedulers over 12 resources with sorted subtasks. Percentage reductions are calculated in comparison to Table 2.

	FIFO	LPT	SPT	SLPT	SSPT	HRRN	WT	HLF	HLFET	CG	DCP	Crit. Path
SF (ms)	29.29	29.25	28.67	28.96	29.15	28.65	28.63	28.74	28.80	28.63	28.64	28.37
(% change)	-10.93	-11.01	-11.52	-10.53	-11.08	-11.49	-11.60	-11.51	-11.49	-11.57	-11.57	-
DF (frames)	54.32	54.28	49.52	51.88	53.62	49.12	48.98	50.12	51.08	49.38	49.34	45.50
(% change)	-25.06	-25.50	-28.04	-24.48	-25.55	-28.29	-28.75	-27.91	-27.01	-28.16	-28.18	-
CS (ms)	217.91	217.32	189.36	203.24	212.60	187.71	186.62	192.86	197.13	187.81	187.84	171.40
(% change)	-41.94	-42.33	-45.01	-40.77	-42.67	-45.27	-45.52	-44.82	-44.27	-45.27	- 45.22	-

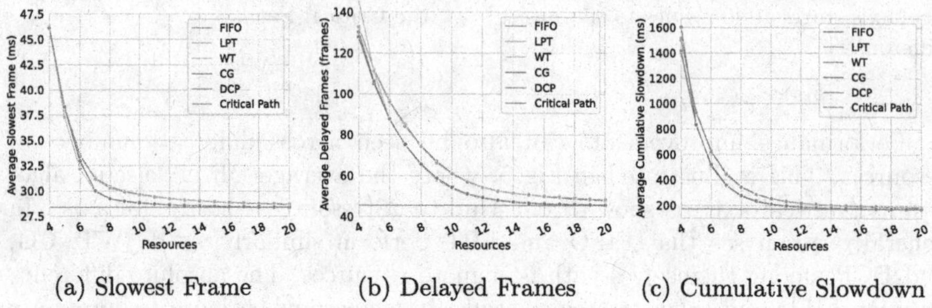

(a) Slowest Frame (b) Delayed Frames (c) Cumulative Slowdown

Fig. 7. Average values for all metrics for schedulers using sorted subtasks on different numbers of resources.

clues of the most important subtasks statically or using simple internal parameters.

The performance results achieved in this scenario are summarized in Table 3. Its additional rows show how much the metrics have been reduced in comparison to Scenario I (Table 2). The improvements are noticeable for all scheduling algorithms and metrics. For instance, the average SF for FIFO changed from 32.88 ms to 29.29 ms, representing a 10.93% decrease in time (an improvement factor of 1.123). This is greater than the benefits previously achieved by changing the scheduling algorithms only. Still, in many cases, the algorithms show even better gains, leading to greater cumulative improvements over FIFO.

If we focus our attention on strategies LPT, WT, CG, and DCP, we can verify that their improvements over FIFO are all statistically significant (p-values < 0.05), with the exception of the DF metric for LPT (p-value $= 0.73$). WT leads to the same average SF as CG and DCP (p-values $= 0.52$ and 0.23, resp.) while differing in the other metrics. Also, CG and DCP results cannot be differentiated (p-values > 0.05), which contrasts with the results in Scenario I.

Table 3 also shows that the performance gap to the Critical Path is much smaller than before, even though these results use 12 resources only. A better visualization for different numbers of resources can be seen in Fig. 7. The best schedulers here (WT, CG, and DCP) show trends similar to before, as they create a gap between their performance and the baseline that decreases when many resources are available. Yet, in this situation, the absolute differences in values are not strictly decreasing anymore, as FIFO seems to benefit more from the sorted subtasks for small numbers of resources. For instance, comparing Figs. 7b and 5, we can see that changing the micro-scheduler reduces DF on 4 resources by about 5 frames for FIFO (from 138.26 to 132.9) but only 3 for CG (from 131 to 127.9). This effect later disappears when more resources are available. Another difference from Scenario I comes from the fading gap between the best schedulers and the Critical Path. If we consider CG running over 16 resources, the average differences are 0.09, 0.82, and 3.97 for the SF, DF, and CS metrics, respectively. The proximity of these results to the optimal solution highlights the benefits of using scheduling algorithms and internal scheduling mechanisms that are well-adapted to the problem being faced. It does not, however, lead by itself to a situation where 60 fps can be achieved under the worst load situations. We investigate additional means to improve performance in our final scenario.

5.4 Scenario III - Subtask Splitting

Given the near-optimal performance of the modified game engine scheduler, the only way to achieve further improvements requires a new optimal. That, in turn, demands changing the task graph. We have identified the two tasks with the longest processing times and changed them to increase their parallelism. For each of their subtasks, we run two subtasks, each with half of the original processing time. This local transformation has no impact on the global task graph nor to the total processing time of the tasks, and it does not affect the majority of the tasks. Nevertheless, we are aware that these changes may not be feasible in some game engines due to the nature of the tasks being computed.

The new performance results are summarized in Table 4. The additional parallelism leads to improvements for all scheduling strategies and metrics. When compared to Scenario I, SF is decreased by about one quarter, DF is reduced by over one half, and CS is reduced by about three quarters. When comparing FIFO's results in Scenarios II and III, these metrics are improved by factors of 1.174, 1.602, and 2.390, resp., which are proportionally larger than the improvements seen from Scenario I to II.

When comparing the algorithms to FIFO, their general behavior remains the same. For example, WT, CG, and DCP show better results than FIFO (p-values

Table 4. Average metrics over 12 resources with sorted subtasks and additional parallelism in two tasks. Reductions are calculated in comparison to Table 2.

	FIFO	LPT	SPT	SLPT	SSPT	HRRN	WT	HLF	HLFET	CG	DCP	Crit. Path
SF (ms)	24.94	24.92	24.32	24.60	24.81	24.31	24.29	24.40	24.45	24.30	24.32	22.99
(% change)	-24.13	-24.18	-24.92	-24.02	-24.31	-24.90	-25.01	-24.86	-24.87	-24.97	-24.92	-18.97
DF (frames)	33.90	33.88	28.74	31.10	32.94	28.40	28.30	29.54	30.44	28.48	28.62	17.92
(% change)	-53.23	-53.50	-58.24	-54.73	-54.26	-58.54	-58.83	-57.51	-56.50	-58.57	-58.34	-60.62
CS (ms)	91.19	90.80	73.35	81.35	87.45	72.39	71.87	75.47	77.65	72.42	72.75	41.81
(% change)	-75.70	-75.90	-78.70	-76.29	-76.42	-78.89	-79.02	-78.41	-78.05	-78.90	-78.78	-75.60

< 0.05). WT performed better than DCP (p-values < 0.05), but it performed the same as CG for metrics SF and DF (p-values $= 0.31$ and 0.06, resp.).

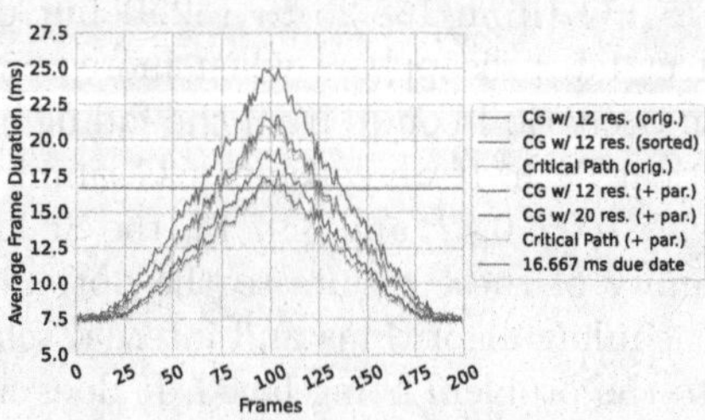

Fig. 8. Average duration of each frame for CG and the Critical Path on different numbers of resources and scenarios.

The additional parallelism increases the gap between the algorithms and the new Critical Path. In general, the best performing algorithms running over 12 resources still show absolute differences of ≈1.5, 10.5, and 30.5 for the SF, DF, and CS metrics, respectively. This is mainly caused by a lack of resources, as 12 is not enough to profit from the extra parallelism. Meanwhile, when using 20 resources, these differences are reduced to 0.2, 1.3, and 4.0, respectively. This evolution can be visualized in Fig. 8, which shows the change in average frame duration throughout the simulations for the three scenarios (similarly to Fig. 6). The first gap between CG and the Critical Path is overcome just by sorting subtasks, while the new gap requires using more resources. Overall, we can clearly see that the improvements brought in each scenario makes the game engine more robust to high loads, leading to a better gaming experience.

6 Conclusion and Future Work

In this paper, we have examined the scheduling problem of game engines. Using as a case study a game engine extracted from a modern Ubisoft video game, we have modeled the problem, chosen and adapted scheduling algorithms, and ran an extensive experimental evaluation with an in-house simulator. Compared to the original FIFO scheduler on 12 resources, the use of well-adapted algorithms improved the proposed metrics of Slowest Frame, Delayed Frames, and Cumulative Slowdown up by factors of 1.015, 1.058, and 1.096, resp. The proposed change to the micro-scheduler increased these gains to factors of 1.148, 1.480, and 2.011, with near-optimal results when using more resources. Finally, the additional parallelism in two tasks led to total improvements by factors of 1.354, 2.561, and 5.222.

These results establish the potential contributions that well-adapted scheduling algorithms (local and global, online and offline) and techniques can have on the video game industry. Further research should be dedicated to see how these results extend to other game engines, video games, and even other interactive simulations. An implementation of the algorithms and techniques in an actual game engine would enable an evaluation of the overhead of run time profiling, online algorithms, and the management of the priority queue. Finally, the effects of hardware heterogeneity (both for uniform and unrelated resources) remains to be studied.

Acknowledgments and Data Availability.. The code used for this study is available online in Figshare [18]. The dataset containing all simulation results and evaluation scripts is available online in Zenodo [19].

References

1. Acun, B., et al.: Power, reliability, and performance: one system to rule them all. Computer **49**(10), 30–37 (2016). https://doi.org/10.1109/MC.2016.310
2. Adam, T.L., Chandy, K.M., Dickson, J.R.: A comparison of list schedules for parallel processing systems. Commun. ACM **17**(12), 685–690 (1974). https://doi.org/10.1145/361604.361619
3. Alfieri, B.: Intel games task scheduler, January 2019. https://github.com/GameTechDev/GTS-GamesTaskScheduler. Accessed 04 Jan 2022
4. Beaumont, O., Eyraud-Dubois, L., Gao, Y.: Influence of tasks duration variability on task-based runtime schedulers. In: 2019 IEEE International Parallel and Distributed Processing Symposium Workshops (IPDPSW), pp. 16–25 (2019). https://doi.org/10.1109/IPDPSW.2019.00013
5. Benoit, A., Canon, L.-C., Elghazi, R., Héam, P.-C.: Update on the asymptotic optimality of LPT. In: Sousa, L., Roma, N., Tomás, P. (eds.) Euro-Par 2021. LNCS, vol. 12820, pp. 55–69. Springer, Cham (2021). https://doi.org/10.1007/978-3-030-85665-6_4
6. Cai, Xiaoqiang, Wu, Xianyi, Zhou, Xian: Optimal Stochastic Scheduling. ISORMS, vol. 207. Springer, Boston (2014). https://doi.org/10.1007/978-1-4899-7405-1
7. Chaminade, C., Martin, R., McKeever, J.: When regional meets global: exploring the nature of global innovation networks in the video game industry in southern Sweden. Entrepreneurs. Reg. Deve. **33**(1-2), 131–146 (2021). https://doi.org/10.1080/08985626.2020.1736184
8. Coffman, E.G., Graham, R.L.: Optimal scheduling for two-processor systems. Acta inform. **1**(3), 200–213 (1972). https://doi.org/10.1007/BF00288685
9. Dai, G., Mohaqeqi, M., Yi, W.: Timing-anomaly free dynamic scheduling of periodic DAG tasks with non-preemptive nodes. In: 2021 IEEE 27th International Conference on Embedded and Real-Time Computing Systems and Applications (RTCSA), pp. 119–128 (2021). https://doi.org/10.1109/RTCSA52859.2021.00022
10. Graham, R.L.: Bounds on multiprocessing timing anomalies. SIAM J. Appl. Math. **17**(2), 416–429 (1969). https://doi.org/10.1137/0117039
11. Graham, R., Lawler, E., Lenstra, J., Kan, A.: Optimization and approximation in deterministic sequencing and scheduling: a survey. In: Discrete Optimization II, Annals of Discrete Mathematics, vol. 5, pp. 287–326. Elsevier (1979). https://doi.org/10.1016/S0167-5060(08)70356-X
12. Gregory, J.: Game Engine Architecture, 3rd edn. Taylor and Francis Ltd., Milton Park (2018)
13. Horn, W.A.: Technical note-minimizing average flow time with parallel machines. Oper. Res. **21**(3), 846–847 (1973). https://doi.org/10.1287/opre.21.3.846

14. Hu, T.C.: Parallel sequencing and assembly line problems. Oper. Res. **9**(6), 841–848 (1961). https://doi.org/10.1287/opre.9.6.841
15. Intelligence, M.: Global Gaming Market - Growth, Trends, Covid-19 Impact, and Forecasts (2022–2027). https://www.mordorintelligence.com/industry-reports/global-gaming-market. Accessed 26 Jan 2022
16. Leung, J.Y.: Handbook of Scheduling: Algorithms, Models, and Performance Analysis. CRC Press, Boca Raton (2004)
17. Nascimento, F.M.S., Lima, G.: Effectively scheduling hard and soft real-time tasks on multiprocessors. In: 2021 IEEE 27th Real-Time and Embedded Technology and Applications Symposium (RTAS), pp. 210–222 (2021). https://doi.org/10.1109/RTAS52030.2021.00025
18. Regragui, M., Coye, B., Lima Pilla, L., Namyst, R., Barthou, D.: Artifact and instructions to generate experimental results for the Euro-Par 2022 paper "Exploring scheduling algorithms for parallel task graphs: a modern game engine case study", June 2022. https://doi.org/10.6084/m9.figshare.19961210
19. Regragui, M., Coye, B., Pilla, L.L., Namyst, R., Barthou, D.: Performance results of different scheduling algorithms used in the simulation of a modern game engine (2022). https://doi.org/10.5281/zenodo.6532252
20. Trietsch, D., Mazmanyan, L., Gevorgyan, L., Baker, K.R.: Modeling activity times by the Parkinson distribution with a lognormal core: theory and validation. Eur. J. Oper. Res. **216**(2), 386–396 (2012). https://doi.org/10.1016/j.ejor.2011.07.054
21. Unity User Manual 2020.3 (LTS). https://docs.unity3d.com/Manual/UnityManual.html. Accessed 26 Jan 2022
22. Unreal Engine 4 Documentation. https://docs.unrealengine.com/4.27/en-US/. Accessed 26 Jan 2022
23. Zhao, Z., Liang, P.: Data partition for wavefront parallelization of h.264 video encoder. In: 2006 IEEE International Symposium on Circuits and Systems (ISCAS), pp. 4, 2672 (2006). https://doi.org/10.1109/ISCAS.2006.1693173

Decentralized Online Scheduling of Malleable NP-hard Jobs

Peter Sanders(✉) and Dominik Schreiber

Karlsruhe Institute of Technology, 76131 Karlsruhe, Germany
{sanders,dominik.schreiber}@kit.edu

Abstract. In this work, we address an online job scheduling problem in a large distributed computing environment. Each job has a priority and a demand of resources, takes an unknown amount of time, and is malleable, i.e., the number of allotted workers can fluctuate during its execution. We subdivide the problem into (a) determining a fair amount of resources for each job and (b) assigning each job to an according number of processing elements. Our approach is fully decentralized, uses lightweight communication, and arranges each job as a binary tree of workers which can grow and shrink as necessary. Using the NP-complete problem of propositional satisfiability (SAT) as a case study, we experimentally show on up to 128 machines (6144 cores) that our approach leads to near-optimal utilization, imposes minimal computational overhead, and performs fair scheduling of incoming jobs within a few milliseconds.

Keywords: Malleable job scheduling · Load balancing · SAT

1 Introduction

A parallel task is called *malleable* if it can handle a fluctuating number of workers during its execution. In the field of distributed computing, malleability has long been recognized as a powerful paradigm which opens up vast possibilities for fair and flexible scheduling and load balancing [13,17]. While most previous research on malleable job scheduling has steered towards iterative data-driven applications, we want to shed light on malleability in a very different context, namely for NP-hard tasks with unknown processing times. For instance, the problem of propositional satisfiability (SAT) is of high practical relevance and an important building block for many applications including automated planning [26], formal verification [18], and cryptography [20]. We consider malleable scheduling of such tasks highly promising: On the one hand, the description of a job can be relatively small even for very difficult problems, and the successful approach of employing many combinatorial search strategies in parallel can be made malleable without redistribution of data [27]. On the other hand, the limited scalability of these parallel algorithms calls for careful distribution of computational resources. We believe that a cloud-like on-demand system for

J. Cano and P. W. Trinder (Eds.): Euro-Par 2022, LNCS 13440, pp. 119–135, 2022.
https://doi.org/10.1007/978-3-031-12597-3_8

resolving NP-hard problems has the potential to drastically improve efficiency and productivity for many organizations and environments. Using malleable job scheduling, we can schedule new jobs within a few milliseconds, resolve trivial jobs in a fraction of second, and rapidly resize more difficult jobs to a fair share of all resources – as far as the job can make efficient use of these resources.

To meet these objectives, we propose a fully decentralized scheduling approach which guarantees fast, fair, and bottleneck-free scheduling of resources without any knowledge on processing times. In previous work [27], we briefly outlined initial algorithms for this purpose while focusing on our award-winning scalable SAT solving engine which we embedded into our system. In this work, we shed more light on our earlier scheduling algorithms and proceed to propose significant improvements both in theory and in practice.

We address two subproblems. The first problem is to let m workers compute a fair number of workers v_j for each active job j, accounting for its priority and maximum demand, which result in optimal system utilization. In previous work [27] we outlined this problem and employed a black box algorithm to solve it. The second problem is to assign v_j workers to each job j while keeping the assignment as stable as possible over time. Previously [27], we proposed to arrange each job j as a binary tree of workers which grows and shrinks depending on v_j, and we described and implemented a worker assignment strategy which routes request messages randomly through the system. When aiming for optimal utilization, this protocol leads to high worst-case scheduling latencies.

In this work, we describe fully distributed and bottleneck-free algorithms for both of the above problems. Our algorithms have $\mathcal{O}(\log m)$ span and are designed to consistently achieve optimal utilization. Furthermore, we introduce new measures to preferably reuse existing (suspended) workers for a certain job rather than initializing new workers. We then present our scheduling platform *Mallob*[1] which features simplified yet highly practical implementations of our approaches. Experiments on up to 128 nodes (6144 cores) show that our system leads to near-optimal utilization and schedules jobs with a fair share of resources within tens of milliseconds. We consider our theoretical as well as practical results to be promising contributions towards processing malleable NP-hard tasks in a more scalable and resource-efficient manner.

2 Preliminaries

We now establish important preliminaries and discuss work related to ours.

2.1 Malleable Job Scheduling

We use the following definitions [10]: A *rigid* task requires a fixed number of workers. A *moldable* task can be scaled to a number of workers at the time of its scheduling but then remains rigid. Finally, a *malleable* task is able to adapt to a fluctuating number of workers *during* its execution. Malleability can be a

[1] https://github.com/domschrei/mallob.

highly desirable property of tasks because it allows to balance tasks continuously to warrant fair and optimal utilization of the system at hand [17]. For instance, if an easy job arrives in a fully utilized system, malleable scheduling allows to shrink an active job in order to schedule the new job immediately, significantly decreasing its response time. Due to the appeal of malleable job scheduling, there has been ongoing research to exploit malleability, from shared-memory systems [13] to HPC environments [6,9], even to improve energy efficiency [25].

The effort required to transform a moldable (or rigid) algorithm into a malleable algorithm depends on the application at hand. For iterative data-driven applications, redistribution of data is necessary if a task is expanded or shrunk [9]. In contrast, we demonstrated in previous work [27] for the use case of propositional satisfiability (SAT) that basic malleability is simple to achieve if the parallel algorithm is composed of many independent search strategies: The abrupt suspension and/or termination of individual workers can imply the loss of progress, but preserves completeness. Moreover, if workers periodically exchange knowledge, the progress made on a worker can benefit the job even if the worker is removed. For these reasons, we have not yet considered the full migration of application processes as is done in adaptive middlewares [9,16] but instead hold the application itself responsible to react to workers being added or removed.

Most prior approaches rely on known processing times of jobs and on an accurate model for their execution time relative to the degree of parallelism [5,24] whereas we do not rely on such knowledge. Furthermore, most approaches employ a centralized scheduler, which implies a potential bottleneck and a single point of failure. Our approach is fully decentralized and uses a small part of each processes' CPU time to perform distributed scheduling, which also opens up the possibility to add more general fault-tolerance to our work in the future. For instance, this may include continuing to schedule and process jobs correctly even in case of network-partitioning faults [2], i.e., failures where sub-networks in the distributed environment are disconnected from each another. Other important aspects of fault-tolerance include mitigation of simple node failures (i.e., a machine suddenly goes out of service) and of Byzantine failures [7] (i.e., a machine exhibits arbitrary behavior, potentially due to a malicious attack).

2.2 Scalable SAT Solving

The propositional satisfiability (SAT) problem poses the question whether a given propositional formula $F = \bigwedge_{i=1}^{k} \left(\bigvee_{j=1}^{c_i} l_{i,j} \right)$ is satisfiable, i.e., whether there is an assignment to all Boolean variables in F such that F evaluates to `true`. SAT is the archetypical NP-complete problem [8] and, as such, a notoriously difficult problem to solve. SAT solving is a crucial building block for a plethora of applications such as automated planning [26], formal verification [18], and cryptography [20]. State-of-the-art SAT solvers are highly optimized: The most popular algorithm named Conflict-Driven Clause Learning (CDCL) performs depth-first search on the space of possible assignments, backtracks and restarts its search frequently, and derives redundant *conflict clauses* when encountering a dead end in its search [19]. As these clauses prune search space and can help to derive unsatisfiability, remembering important derived clauses is crucial for modern SAT solvers' performance [3].

The empirically best performing approach to parallel SAT solving is a so-called *portfolio* of different solver configurations [14] which all work on the original problem and periodically exchange learned clauses. In previous work, we presented a highly competitive portfolio solver with clause sharing [27] and demonstrated that careful periodic clause sharing can lead to respectable speedups for thousands of cores. The malleable environment of this solver is the system which we present here. Other recent works on decentralized SAT solving [15,21] rely on a different parallelization which generates many independent subproblems and tends to be outperformed by parallel portfolios for most practical inputs [11].

2.3 Problem Statement

We consider a homogeneous computing environment with a number of interconnected machines on which a total of m *processing elements*, or PEs in short, are distributed. Each PE has a *rank* $x \in \{0, \ldots, m-1\}$ and runs exclusively on $c \geq 1$ cores of its local machine. PEs can only communicate via message passing.

Jobs are introduced over an interface connecting to some of the PEs. Each job j has a job description, a priority $p_j \in \mathbb{R}^+$, a *demand* $d_j \in \mathbb{N}^+$, and a *budget* b_j (in terms of wallclock time or CPU time). If a PE participates in processing a job j, it runs an execution environment of j named a *worker*. A job's demand d_j indicates the maximum number of parallel workers it can currently employ: d_j is initialized to 1 and can then be adjusted by the job after an initial worker has been scheduled. A job's priority p_j may be set, e.g., depending on who submitted j and on how important they deem j relative to an average job of theirs. In a simple setting where all jobs are equally important, assume $p_j = 1 \ \forall j$. A job is cancelled if it spends its budget b_j before finishing. We assume for the active jobs J in the system that the number $n = |J|$ of active jobs is no higher than m and that each PE employs at most one worker at any given time. However, a PE can preempt its current worker, run a worker of another job, and possibly resume the former worker at a later point.

Let T_j be the set of active workers of $j \in J$. We call $v_j := |T_j|$ the *volume* of j. Our aim is to continuously assign each $j \in J$ to a set T_j of PEs subject to:

(C1) (Optimal utilization) Either all job demands are fully met or all m PEs are working on a job: $(\forall j \in J : v_j = d_j) \ \vee \ \sum_{j \in J} v_j = m$.

(C2) (Individual job constraints) Each job must have at least one worker and is limited to d_j workers: $\forall j \in J : 1 \leq v_j \leq d_j$.

(C3) (Fairness) Resources allotted to each job j scale proportionally with p_j except if prevented by C2:
For each $j, j' \in J$ with $p_j \geq p_{j'}$, there are *fair assignments* $\omega, \omega' \in \mathbb{R}^+$ with $\omega/\omega' = p_j/p_{j'}$ and some $0 \leq \varepsilon \leq 1$ such that $v_j = \min(d_j, \max(1, \lfloor \omega + \varepsilon \rfloor))$ and $v_{j'} = \min(d_{j'}, \max(1, \lfloor \omega' \rfloor))$.

Due to rounding, in C3 we allow for job volumes to deviate by a single unit (see $\varepsilon \leq 1$) from a fair distribution as long as the job of higher priority is favored.

3 Approach

We subdivide the problem at hand into two subproblems: First, find *fair volumes* v_j for all currently active jobs $j \in J$ subject to C1–C3. Secondly, identify pairwise disjoint sets T_j with $|T_j| = v_j$ for each $j \in J$. In this section, we present fully decentralized and highly scalable algorithms for both subproblems. In Sect. 4.1 we describe how our practical implementation differs from these algorithms.

To assess our algorithms, we consider two important measures from parallel processing. Given a distributed algorithm, consider the dependency graph which is induced by the necessary communication among all PEs. The *span* (or *depth*) of the algorithm is the length of a critical path through this graph. The *local work* is the complexity of local computations summed up over all PEs.

3.1 Calculation of Fair Volumes

Given jobs J with individual priorities and demands, we want to find a fair volume v_j for each job j such that constraints C1–C3 are met. Volumes are recomputed periodically taking into account new jobs, departing jobs, and changed demands. In the following, assume that each job has a single worker which represents this (and only this) job. We elaborate on these representants in Sect. 3.2.

We defined our problem such that $n = |J| \leq m$. Similarly, we assume $\sum_{j \in J} d_j > m$ since otherwise we can trivially set $v_j = d_j$ for all jobs j. Assuming real-valued job volumes for now, we can observe that for any parameter $\alpha \geq 0$, constraints C2–C3 are fulfilled if we set $v_j = v_j(\alpha) := \max(1, \min(d_j, \alpha p_j))$. By appropriately choosing α, we can also meet the utilization constraint C1: Consider the function $\xi(\alpha) := m - \sum_{j \in J} v_j(\alpha)$ which expresses the unused resources for a particular value of α. Function ξ is a continuous, monotonically decreasing, and piece-wise linear function (see Fig. 1). Moreover, $\xi(0) = m - n \geq 0$ and

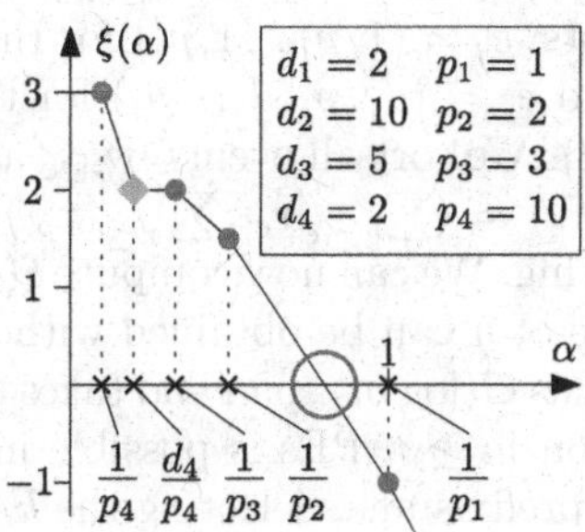

Fig. 1. Volume calculation example with four jobs and $m = 7$. Five of the eight points where $\xi(\alpha)$ is evaluated are depicted, three more (d_3/p_3, d_1/p_1, and d_2/p_2) are omitted. In the interval $[1/p_2, 1/p_1]$ we find $\alpha_0 = 0.8$ (red circle) where $\xi(\alpha) = 0$. Job 4 is capped at its demand ($v_4 = 2$) and job 1 is raised to $v_1 = 1$. The real-valued shares $\alpha_0 p_2 = 1.6$ and $\alpha_0 p_3 = 2.4$ are rounded to $v_2 = 1$ and $v_3 = 3$ as job 3 has the higher priority. (Color figure online)

$\xi(\max_{j\in J} d_j/p_j) = m - \sum_{j\in J} d_j < 0$. Hence $\xi(\alpha) = 0$ has a solution α_0 which represents the desired choice of α that exploits all resources, i.e., it also fulfills constraint C1. Once α_0 is found, we need to round each $v_j(\alpha_0)$ to an integer. Due to C1 and C3, we propose to round down all volumes and then increment the volume of the $k := m - \sum_j \lfloor v_j(\alpha_0) \rfloor$ jobs of highest priority: We identify $J' := \{j \in J : v_j(\alpha_0) < d_j\}$, sort J' by job priority, and select the first k jobs.

We now outline a fully distributed algorithm which finds α_0 in logarithmic span. We exploit that ξ', the gradient of ξ, changes at no more than $2n$ values of α, namely when $\alpha p_j = 1$ or $\alpha p_j = d_j$ for some $j \in J$. Since we have $m \geq n$ PEs available, we can try these $\mathcal{O}(n)$ values of $\xi(\alpha)$ in parallel. We then find the two points with smallest positive value and largest negative value using a parallel reduction operation. Lastly, we interpolate ξ between these points to find α_0.

The parallel evaluation of ξ is still nontrivial since a naive implementation would incur quadratic work – $\mathcal{O}(n)$ for each value of α. We now explain how to accelerate the evaluation of ξ. For this, we rewrite $\xi(\alpha) = m - \sum_{j\in J} v_j(\alpha)$ as:

$$\xi(\alpha) = m - \underbrace{\left(\sum_{j\,:\,\alpha p_j < 1} 1 + \sum_{j\,:\,\alpha p_j > d_j} d_j \right)}_{R} - \alpha \underbrace{\sum_{j\,:\,1 \leq \alpha p_j \leq d_j} p_j}_{P} \tag{1}$$

Intuitively, R sums up all resources which are assigned due to raising a job volume to 1 (if $\alpha p_j < 1$) and due to capping a job volume at d_j (if $\alpha p_j > d_j$); and αP sums up all resources assigned as $v_j = \alpha p_j$ (if $1 \leq \alpha p_j \leq d_j$).

This new representation only features two unknown variables, R and P, which can be computed efficiently. At $\alpha = 0$, we have $R = n$ and $P = 0$ since all job volumes are raised to one. If we then successively increase α, we pass $2n$ *events* where R and P are modified, namely whenever $\alpha p_j = 1$ or $\alpha p_j = d_j$ for some job j. Since each such event modifies R and P by a fixed amount, we can use a single prefix sum calculation to obtain *all* intermediate values of R and P.

Each event $e = (\alpha_e, r_e, p_e)$ occurs at point α_e and adds r_e to R and p_e to P. Each job j causes two events: $\underline{e}_j = (1/p_j, -1, p_j)$ for the point $\alpha p_j = 1$ where v_j stops being raised to 1, and $\overline{e}_j = (d_j/p_j, d_j, -p_j)$ for the point $\alpha p_j = d_j$ where v_j begins to be capped at d_j. We sort all events by α_e and then compute a prefix sum over r_e and p_e: $(R_e, P_e) = (\sum_{e' \preceq e} r_{e'}, \sum_{e' \preceq e} r_{p'})$, where "$\prec$" denotes the ordering of events after sorting. We can now compute $\xi(\alpha_e) = m - (n + R_e) - \alpha_e P_e$ at each event e.[2] The value of n can be obtained with a parallel reduction.

Overall, our algorithm has $\mathcal{O}(\log m)$ span and takes $\mathcal{O}(m \log m)$ work: Sorting $\mathcal{O}(n)$ elements in parallel on $m \geq n$ PEs is possible in logarithmic time,[3] as is computing reductions and prefix sums. Selecting the k jobs to receive additional volume after rounding down all volumes can be reduced to sorting as well.

[2] If there are multiple events at the same α, their prefix sum results can differ but will still result in the same $\xi(\alpha)$. This is due to the continuous nature of ξ: Note how each event modifies the gradient $\xi'(\alpha)$ but preserves the value of $\xi(\alpha)$.

[3] Asymptotically optimal sorting on communication networks [1] is of mostly theoretical value due to the large constant values involved. However there are quite practical algorithms when $n \in \mathcal{O}(\sqrt{m})$ or when spending $\mathcal{O}(\log^2 n)$ time is acceptable [4].

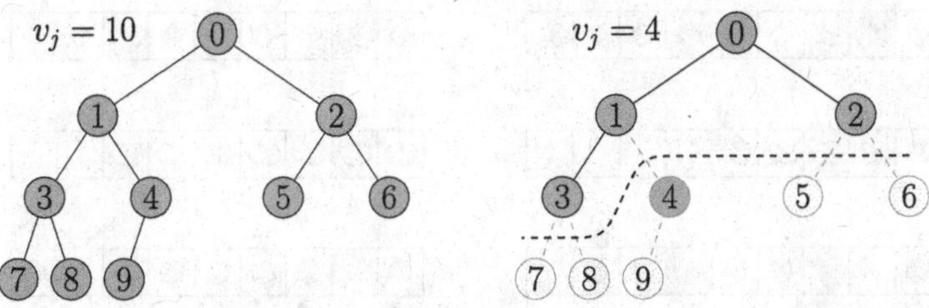

Fig. 2. Left: Job tree T_j features ten workers $\{w_j^0, w_j^1, \ldots, w_j^9\}$ due to the volume $v_j = 10$ assigned to j. Right: Volume update $v_j = 4$ arrives. Consequently, all workers with index ≥ 4 are suspended and the corresponding PEs can adopt another job.

3.2 Assignment of Jobs to PEs

We now describe how the fair volumes computed as in the previous section translate to an actual assignment of jobs to PEs.

Basic Approach. We begin with our basic approach as introduced in [27].

For each job j, we address the k current workers in T_j as $w_j^0, w_j^1, \ldots, w_j^{k-1}$. These workers can be scattered throughout the system, i.e., their *job indices* $0, \ldots, k-1$ within T_j are not to be confused with their ranks. The k workers form a communication structure in the shape of a binary tree (Fig. 2). Worker w_j^0 is the root of this tree and represents j for the calculation of its volume (Sect. 3.1). Workers w_j^{2i+1} and w_j^{2i+2} are the left and right children of w_j^i. Jobs are made malleable by letting T_j grow and shrink dynamically. Specifically, we enforce that T_j consists of exactly $k = v_j$ workers. If v_j is updated, all workers w_j^i for which $i \geq v_j$ are suspended and the corresponding PEs turn idle. Likewise, workers without a left (right) child for which $2i+1 < v_j$ $(2i+2 < v_j)$ attempt to find a child worker w_j^{2i+1} (w_j^{2i+2}). New workers are found via *request messages*: A request message $r = (j, i, x)$ holds index i of the requested worker w_j^i as well as rank x of the requesting worker. If a new job is introduced at some PE, then this PE emits a request for the root node w_j^0 of T_j. All requests for w_j^i, $i > 0$ are emitted by the designated parent node $w_j^{\lfloor (i-1)/2 \rfloor}$ of the desired worker.

In [27], we proposed that each request performs a random walk through a regular graph of all PEs and is resolved as soon as it hits an idle PE. While this strategy resolves most requests quickly, some requests can require a large number of hops. If we assume a fully connected graph of PEs and a small share ϵ of workers is idle, then each hop of a request corresponds to a Bernoulli process with success probability ϵ, and a request takes an expected $1/\epsilon$ hops until an idle PE is hit. Consequently, to improve worst-case latencies, a small ratio of workers should be kept idle [27]. By contrast, our following algorithm with logarithmic span does not depend on suboptimal utilization.

Matching Requests and Idle PEs. In a first phase, our improved algorithm (see Fig. 3) computes two prefix sums with one collective operation: the number

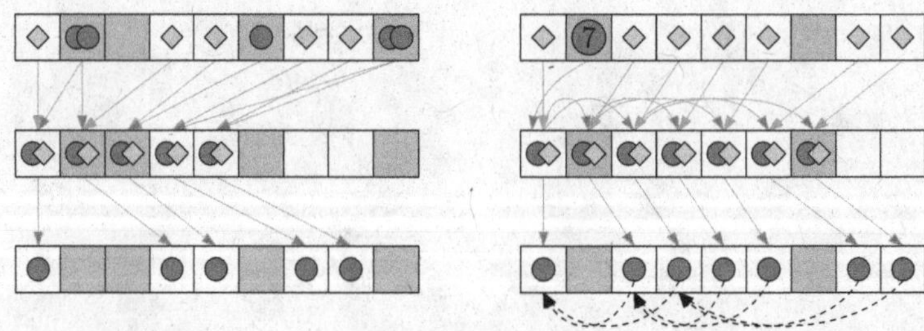

Fig. 3. Examples for matching requests and idle PEs. White (gray) squares represent idle (busy) PEs, spheres (diamonds) represent requests (idle tokens). Left: A prefix sum (not depicted) numbers all requests and idle tokens, and each request (token) of index i is sent to rank i. Each PE with a matching pair sends the request to the idle PE. Right: A job j grows by multiple layers of T_j. Requests are sent along a tree structure and child-parent relationships of T_j are encoded into the distributed requests.

of requests q_i being emitted by PEs of rank $< i$, and the number o_i of idle PEs of rank $< i$. We also compute the total sums, q_m and o_m, and communicate them to all PEs. The q_i and o_i provide an implicit global numbering of all requests and all idle PEs. In a second phase, the i-th request and the i-th token are both sent to rank i. In the third and final phase, each PE which received both a request and an idle token sends the request to the idle PE referenced by the token.

If the request for a worker w_j^i is only emitted by its designated parent $w_j^{\lfloor (i-1)/2 \rfloor}$, then our algorithm so far may need to be repeated $\mathcal{O}(\log m)$ times: Repetition l activates a worker which then emits requests for repetition $l+1$. Instead, we can let a worker emit requests not only for its direct children, but for all *transitive* children it deserves. Each worker w_j^i can compute the number k of desired transitive children from v_j and i. The worker then contributes k to q_i. In the second phase, the k requests can be distributed communication-efficiently to a range of ranks $\{x, \ldots, x+k-1\}$: w_j^i sends requests for workers w_j^{2i+1} and w_j^{2i+2} to ranks x and $x+1$, which send requests for corresponding child workers to ranks $x+2$ through $x+5$, and so on, until worker index $v_j - 1$ is reached. To enable this distribution, we append to each request the values x, v_j, and the rank of the PE where the respective parent worker will be initialized. As such, each child knows its parent within T_j (Fig. 3) for job-internal communication.

We now outline how our algorithm can be executed in a fully asynchronous manner. We compute the prefix sums within an In-Order binary tree of PEs [22, Chapter 13.3], that is, all children in the left subtree of rank i have a rank $< i$ and all children in the right subtree have a rank $> i$. This prefix sum computation can be made sparse and asynchronous: Only non-zero contributions to a prefix sum are sent upwards explicitly, and there is a minimum delay in between sending contributions to a parent. Furthermore, we extend our prefix sums to also include *inclusive* prefix sums q'_i, o'_i which denote the number of requests (tokens) at PEs of rank $\leq i$. As such, every PE can see from the difference $q'_i - q_i$ ($o'_i - o_i$) how many of its local requests (tokens) took part in the prefix sum. Last but not least, the number of tokens and the number of requests may not always match – a PE which receives either a request or an idle token (but not both) knows of this imbalance due to the total sums q_m, o_m. The unmatched message is sent to its origin and can re-participate in the next iteration.

Our matching algorithm has $\mathcal{O}(\log m)$ span and takes $\mathcal{O}(m)$ local work. The maximum local work of any given PE is in $\mathcal{O}(\log m)$ (to compute the above k), which is amortized by other PEs because at most m requests are emitted.

3.3 Reuse of Suspended Workers

Each PE remembers up to C most recently used workers (for a small constant C) and deletes older workers. Therefore, if a worker w_j^i is suspended, it may be resumed at a later time. Our algorithms so far may choose different PEs and hence create new workers whenever T_j shrinks and then re-grows. We now outline how we can increase the reuse of suspended workers.

In our previous approach [27], each worker remembers a limited number of ranks of its past (direct) children. A worker which desires a child queries them for reactivation one after the other until success or until all past children have been queried unsuccessfully, at which point a normal job request is emitted.

We make two improvements to this strategy. First, we remember past workers in a distributed fashion. More precisely, whenever a worker joins or leaves T_j, we distribute information along T_j to maintain the following invariant: Each current leaf w_j^i in T_j remembers the past workers which were located in a subtree below index i. As such, past workers can be remembered and reused even if T_j shrinks by multiple layers and re-grows differently.

Secondly, we adjust our scheduling to actively prioritize the reuse of existing workers over the initialization of new workers. In our implementation, each idle PE can infer from its local volume calculation (Sect. 4.1) which of its local suspended workers w_j^i are eligible for reuse, i.e., $v_j > i$ in the current volume assignment. If a PE has such a worker w_j^i, the PE will reject any job requests until it received a message regarding w_j^i. This message is either a query to resume w_j^i or a notification that w_j^i will not be reused. On the opposite side, a worker which desires a child begins to query past children according to a "most recently used" strategy. If a query succeeds, all remaining past children are notified that they will not be reused. If all queries failed, a normal job request is emitted.

4 The Mallob System

In the following, we outline the design and implementation of our platform named Mallob, short for **Mal**leable **Lo**ad **B**alancer. Mallob is a C++ application using the Message Passing Interface (MPI) [12]. Each PE can be configured to accept jobs and return responses, e.g., over the local file system or via an internal API. The application-specific worker running on each PE is defined via an interface with a small set of methods. These methods define the worker's behavior if it is started, suspended, resumed, or terminated, and allow it to send and receive application-specific messages at will. Note that we outlined some of Mallob's earlier features in previous work [27] with a focus on our malleable SAT engine.

4.1 Implementation of Algorithms

Our system features practical and simplified implementations solving the volume assignment problem and the request matching problem. We now explain how and why these implementations differ from the algorithms provided in Sect. 3.

Volume Assignment. Our implementation computes job volumes similar to the algorithm outlined in Sect. 3.1. However, each PE computes the desired change of root α_0 of ξ locally. All events in the system (job arrivals, departures, and changes in demands) are aggregated and broadcast periodically such that each PE can maintain a local image of all active jobs' demands and priorities [27]. The local search for α_0 is then done via bisection over the domain of ξ. This approach requires more local work than our fully distributed algorithm and features a broadcast of worst-case message length $\mathcal{O}(n)$. However, it only requires a single all-reduction. At the scale of our current implementation ($n < 10^3$ and $m < 10^4$), we expect that our simplified approach performs better than our asymptotically superior algorithm which features several stages of collective operations. When targeting much larger configurations in the future, it may be beneficial to implement and employ our fully distributed algorithm instead.

Request Matching. We did not yet implement asynchronous prefix sums as described in Sect. 3.2. Instead, we route requests directly along a communication tree R of PEs. Each PE keeps track of the *idle count*, i.e., the number of idle PEs, in each of its subtrees in R. This count is updated transitively whenever the idle status of a child changes. Emitted requests are routed upwards through R until hitting an idle PE or until a hit PE has a subtree with a non-zero idle count, at which point the request is routed down towards the idle PE. If a large number of requests (close to n) are emitted, the traffic along the root of R may constitute a bottleneck. However, we found that individual volume updates in the system typically result in a much smaller number of requests, hence we did not observe such a bottleneck in practice. We intend to include our bottleneck-free algorithm (Sect. 3.2) in a future version of our system.

4.2 Engineering

For good practical performance of our system, careful engineering was necessary. For instance, our system exclusively features asynchronous communication, i.e., a PE will never block for an I/O event when sending or receiving messages. As a result, our protocols are designed without explicit synchronization (barriers or similar). We only let the main thread of a PE issue MPI calls, which is the most widely supported mode of operation for multithreaded MPI programs.

As we aim for scheduling latencies in the range of milliseconds, each PE must frequently check its message queue and react to messages. For instance, if the main thread of a PE allocates space for a large job description, this can cause a prohibitively long period where no messages are processed. For this reason, we use a separate thread pool for all tasks which involve a risk of taking a long time. Furthermore, we split large messages into batches of smaller messages, e.g., when transferring large job descriptions to new workers.

5 Evaluation

We now present our experimental evaluation. All experiments have been conducted on the supercomputer SuperMUC-NG. If not specified otherwise, we used 128 compute nodes, each with an Intel Skylake Xeon Platinum 8174 processor clocked at 2.7 GHz with 48 physical cores (96 hardware threads) and 96 GB of main memory. SuperMUC-NG is running Linux (SLES) with kernel version 4.12 at the time of running our experiments. We compiled Mallob with GCC 9 and with Intel MPI 2019. We launch twelve PEs per machine, assign eight hardware threads to each PE, and let a worker on a PE use four parallel worker threads. Our system can use the four remaining hardware threads on each PE in order to keep disturbance of the actual computation at a minimum. Our software and experimental data are available at https://github.com/domschrei/mallob.

5.1 Uniform Jobs

In a first set of experiments, we analyze the base performance of our system by introducing a stream of jobs in such a way that exactly n_{par} jobs are in the system at any time. We limit each job j to a CPU time budget B inversely proportional to n_{par}. Each job corresponds to a difficult SAT formula which cannot be solved within the given budget. As such, we emulate jobs of fixed size.

We chose m and the values of n_{par} in such a way that $m/n_{\text{par}} \in \mathbb{N}$ for all runs. We compare our runs against a hypothetical rigid scheduler which functions as follows: Exactly m/n_{par} PEs are allotted for each job, starting with the first n_{par} jobs at $t = 0$. At periodic points in time, all jobs finish and each set of PEs instantly receives the next job. This leads to perfect utilization and maximizes throughput. We neglect any kind of overhead for this scheduler.

For a modest number of parallel jobs n_{par} in the system ($n_{\text{par}} \leq 192$), our scheduler reaches 99% of the optimal rigid scheduler's throughput (Table 1). This efficiency decreases to 97.6% for the largest n_{par} where $v_j = 2$ for each job. As the CPU time of each job is calculated in terms of its assigned volume and as the allocation of workers takes some time, each job uses slightly less CPU time than advertised: Dividing the time for which each job's workers have been active by its advertised CPU time, we obtained a work efficiency of $\eta \geq 99\%$. Lastly, we measured the CPU utilization of all worker threads as reported by the operating system, which averages at 98% or more. In terms of overall work efficiency $\eta \times u$, we observed an optimum of 98% at $n_{\text{par}} = 192$, a point where neither n_{par} nor the size of individual job trees is close to m.

Table 1. Scheduling uniform jobs on 1536 PEs (6144 cores) compared to a hypothetical optimal rigid scheduler. From left to right: Max. number n_{par} of parallel jobs; max. measured throughput θ, optimal throughput θ_{opt} (in jobs per second), throughput efficiency θ/θ_{opt}; work efficiency η; mean measured CPU utilization u of worker threads.

n_{par}	θ	θ_{opt}	$\frac{\theta}{\theta_{opt}}$	η	u
3	0.159	0.16	0.991	0.990	0.981
6	0.318	0.32	0.994	0.990	0.983
12	0.636	0.64	0.993	0.991	0.984
24	1.271	1.28	0.993	0.992	0.985
48	2.543	2.56	0.993	0.993	0.985
96	5.071	5.12	0.990	0.993	0.986
192	10.141	10.24	0.990	0.995	0.985
384	20.114	20.48	0.982	0.995	0.983
768	39.972	40.96	0.976	0.992	0.980

5.2 Impact of Priorities

In the following we evaluate the impact of job priorities. We use 32 nodes (1536 cores, 384 PEs) and introduce nine streams of jobs, each stream with a different job priority $p \in [0.01, 1]$ (see Fig. 4 right) and with a wallclock limit of 300 s per job. As such, the system processes nine jobs with nine different priorities at a time. Each stream is a permutation of 80 diverse SAT instances [27].

As expected, we observed a proportional relationship between priority and assigned volume, with small variations due to rounding (Fig. 4). By contrast, response times appear to decrease exponentially towards a certain lower bound, which is in line with the NP-hardness of SAT and the diminishing returns of parallel SAT solving [27]. The modest margin by which average response times decrease is due to the difficulty of the chosen SAT benchmarks, many of which cannot be solved within the imposed time limit at either scale.

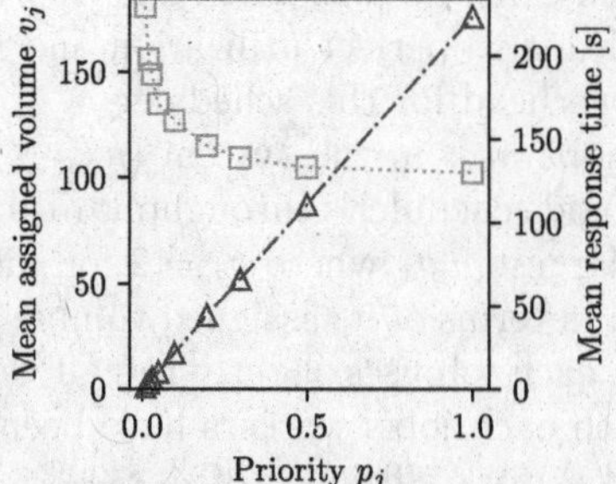

p_j	$\tilde{v}_j$	RT [s]
0.01	1.0	229.6
0.02	3.0	198.0
0.03	5.0	189.1
0.05	8.1	171.3
0.10	17.1	161.2
0.20	35.2	146.0
0.30	52.4	138.6
0.50	87.5	133.1
1.00	176.6	130.0

Fig. 4. Impact of job priority on mean assigned volume (left axis, blue triangles) and response time (right axis, orange squares). The table shows the used priorities p_j with the corresponding mean assigned volume $\tilde{v}_j$ and mean response times in seconds. (Color figure online)

5.3 Realistic Job Arrivals

In the next set of experiments, we analyze the properties of our system in a more realistic scenario. Four PEs introduce batches of jobs with poisson-distributed arrivals (inter-arrival time of $1/\lambda \in \{2.5\,\text{s}, 5\,\text{s}, 10\,\text{s}\}$) and between one and eight jobs per batch. As such, we simulate users which arrive at independent times and submit a number of jobs at once. We also sample a priority $p_j \in [0.01, 1]$, a maximum demand $d_j \in 1, \ldots, 1536$, and a wallclock limit $b_j \in [1, 600]$ s for each job. We ran this experiment with our current request matching (Sect. 4.1) and with each request message performing up to h random hops (as in [27]) until our request matching is employed, for varying values of h. In addition, we ran the experiment with three different suspended worker reuse strategies: No deliberate reuse at all, the basic approach from [27], and our current approach.

Figure 5(left) shows the number of active jobs in the system over time for our default configuration (our reuse strategy and immediate matching of requests). For all tested interarrival times, considerable changes in the system load can be observed during a job's average life time which justify the employment of a malleable scheduling strategy. Figure 5(right) illustrates for $1/\lambda = 5\,\text{s}$ that system utilization is at around 99.8% on average and almost always above 99.5%. We also measured the ratio of time for which each PE has been idle: The median PE was busy 99.08% of all time for the least frequent job arrivals ($1/\lambda = 10\,\text{s}$), 99.77% for $1/\lambda = 5\,\text{s}$, and 99.85% for $1/\lambda = 2.5\,\text{s}$. Also note that $\sum_j d_j < m$ for the first seconds of each run, hence not all PEs can be utilized immediately.

In the following, we focus on the experiment with $1/\lambda = 5\,\text{s}$. The latency of our volume calculation, i.e., the latency until a PE received an updated volume for an updated job, reached a median of 1 ms and a maximum of 34 ms for our default configuration. For the scheduling of an arriving job, Fig. 6(left) shows that the lowest latencies were achieved by our request matching ($h = 0$). For increasing values of h, the variance of latencies increases and high latencies ($\geq$50 ms) become more and more likely. Note that jobs normally enter a fully utilized system, and have $d_j = 1$. Therefore, the triggered balancing calculation may render only a single PE idle, which heavily disfavors performing a random walk. Regarding the latency of expanding a job tree by another layer,

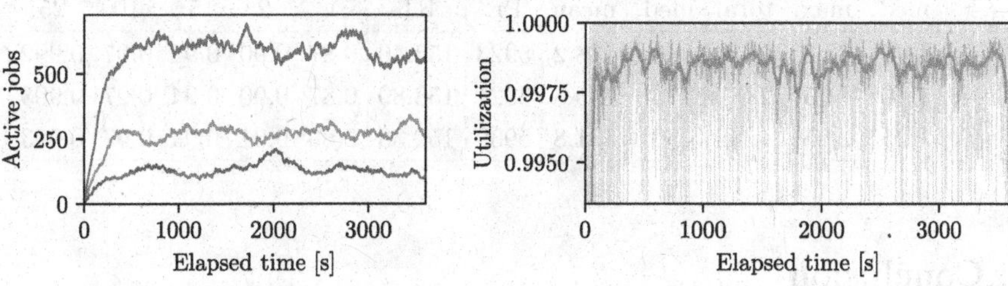

Fig. 5. Left: Number of active jobs for interarrival times $1/\lambda$ of 2.5 s (top), 5 s (middle), and 10 s (bottom). Right: System utilization (i.e., ratio of busy PEs) for $1/\lambda = 5\,\text{s}$ at a sliding average of window size 1 s, 15 s, and 60 s respectively.

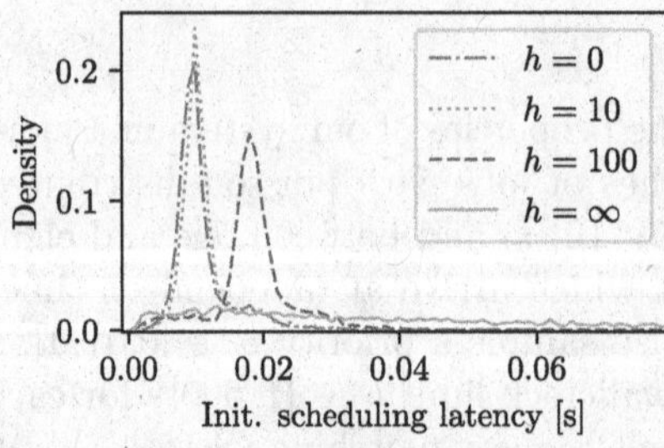

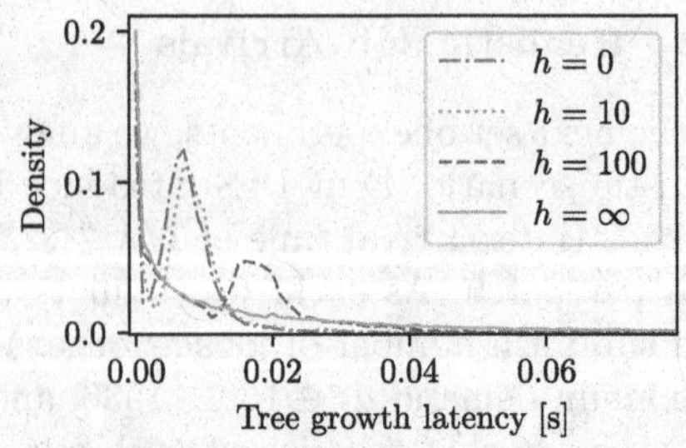

Fig. 6. Distribution over measured latency for the initial scheduling of a job (left) and the expansion of a job tree by another worker (right), for inter arrival rate $1/\lambda = 5$, for a varying number h of random hops until a request message is routed along R.

Fig. 6(right) indicates that requests performing random walks have a high chance to succeed quickly but can otherwise result in high latencies (>10 ms).

To compare strategies for reusing suspended workers, we divided the number of created workers for a job j by its maximum assigned volume v_j. This *Worker Creation Ratio* (WCR) is ideally 1 and becomes larger the more often a worker is suspended and then re-created at a different PE. We computed the WCR for each job and in total: As Table 2 shows, our approach reduces a WCR of 2.14 down to 1.8 (−15.9%). Context switches (i.e., how many times a PE changed its affiliation) and average response times are improved marginally compared to the naive approach. Last but not least, we counted on how many distinct PEs each w_j^i has been created: Our strategy initializes 89% of all workers only once, and 94% of workers have been created at most five times. We conclude that most jobs only feature a small number of workers which are rescheduled frequently.

Table 2. Comparison of worker reuse strategies in terms of worker creation ratio (WCR, per job – median, maximum – and in total), context switches (CS, median per PE and mean), the number of processed jobs within 1 h (Pr.), their mean response time (RT), and the fraction of workers created on at most $\{1, 2, 5, 10, 25\}$ distinct PEs.

	WCR			CS				Pr [WC ≤ ·]				
	med.	max.	total	med.	mean	Pr.	RT	1	2	5	10	25
None	1.43	33.0	2.14	136	138.2	5923	153.40	0.87	0.90	0.94	0.97	0.992
Basic	1.40	31.5	2.07	134	135.3	5921	153.89	0.87	0.90	0.94	0.97	0.993
Ours	1.25	24.5	1.80	130	131.8	5939	152.33	0.89	0.91	0.94	0.97	0.993

6 Conclusion

We have presented a decentralized and highly scalable approach to online job scheduling of malleable NP-hard jobs with unknown processing times. We split our problem into two subproblems, namely the computation of fair job volumes and the assignment of jobs to PEs, and proposed scalable distributed algorithms with $\mathcal{O}(\log m)$ span for both of them. We presented a practical implementation and experimentally showed that it schedules incoming jobs within tens of milliseconds, distributes resources proportional to each job's priority, and leads to near-optimal utilization of resources.

For future work, we intend to add engines for applications beyond SAT into our system. Furthermore, we want to generalize our approach to heterogeneous computing environments and add fault tolerance to our distributed algorithms.

Acknowledgments and Data Availability. The datasets and code generated and/or analyzed during this study are available in the Figshare repository: https://doi.org/10.6084/m9.figshare.20000642 [23]. This project has received funding from the European Research Council (ERC) under the European Union's Horizon 2020 research and innovation programme (grant agreement No. 882500). The authors gratefully acknowledge the Gauss Centre for Supercomputing e.V. (www.gauss-centre.eu) for funding this project by providing computing time on the GCS Supercomputer SuperMUC-NG at Leibniz Supercomputing Centre (www.lrz.de). The authors wish to thank Tim Niklas Uhl as well as the anonymous reviewers for their helpful feedback.

References

1. Ajtai, M., Komlós, J., Szemerédi, E.: Sorting in $\log n$ parallel steps. Combinatorica **3**(1), 1–19 (1983). https://doi.org/10.1109/tc.1985.5009385
2. Alquraan, A., Takruri, H., Alfatafta, M., Al-Kiswany, S.: An analysis of network-partitioning failures in cloud systems. In: Symposium on Operating Systems Design and Implementation, pp. 51–68 (2018)
3. Audemard, G., Simon, L.: Predicting learnt clauses quality in modern SAT solvers. In: International Joint Conference on Artificial Intelligence, pp. 399–404 (2009)
4. Axtmann, M., Sanders, P.: Robust massively parallel sorting. In: Meeting on Algorithm Engineering and Experiments (ALENEX), pp. 83–97 (2017). https://doi.org/10.1137/1.9781611974768.7
5. Blazewicz, J., Kovalyov, M.Y., Machowiak, M., Trystram, D., Weglarz, J.: Preemptable malleable task scheduling problem. IEEE Trans. Comput. **55**(4), 486–490 (2006). https://doi.org/10.1109/tc.2006.58
6. Buisson, J., Sonmez, O., Mohamed, H., Lammers, W., Epema, D.: Scheduling malleable applications in multicluster systems. In: International Conference on Cluster Computing, pp. 372–381. IEEE (2007). https://doi.org/10.1109/clustr.2007.4629252
7. Castro, M., Liskov, B.: Practical byzantine fault tolerance. In: Symposium on Operating Systems Design and Implementation. pp. 173–186 (1999)
8. Cook, S.A.: The complexity of theorem-proving procedures. In: ACM symposium on Theory of Computing, pp. 151–158 (1971). https://doi.org/10.7551/mitpress/12274.003.0036
9. Desell, T., El Maghraoui, K., Varela, C.A.: Malleable applications for scalable high performance computing. Clust. Comput. **10**(3), 323–337 (2007). https://doi.org/10.1007/s10586-007-0032-9

10. Feitelson, D.G.: Job scheduling in multiprogrammed parallel systems (1997)
11. Froleyks, N., Heule, M., Iser, M., Järvisalo, M., Suda, M.: SAT competition 2020. Artif. Intell. **301**, 103572 (2021). https://doi.org/10.1016/j.artint.2021.103572
12. Gropp, W., Lusk, E., Skjellum, A.: Using MPI: Portable Parallel Programming with the Message-Passing Interface, vol. 1. MIT Press, London (1999). https://doi.org/10.7551/mitpress/7056.001.0001
13. Gupta, A., Acun, B., Sarood, O., Kalé, L.V.: Towards realizing the potential of malleable jobs. In: International Conference on High Performance Computing (HiPC), pp. 1–10. IEEE (2014). https://doi.org/10.1109/hipc.2014.7116905
14. Hamadi, Y., Jabbour, S., Sais, L.: ManySAT: a parallel SAT solver. J. Satisf. Boolean Model. Comput. **6**(4), 245–262 (2010). https://doi.org/10.3233/sat190070
15. Heisinger, M., Fleury, M., Biere, A.: Distributed cube and conquer with Paracooba. In: Pulina, L., Seidl, M. (eds.) SAT 2020. LNCS, vol. 12178, pp. 114–122. Springer, Cham (2020). https://doi.org/10.1007/978-3-030-51825-7_9
16. Huang, C., Lawlor, O., Kalé, L.V.: Adaptive MPI. In: Rauchwerger, L. (ed.) LCPC 2003. LNCS, vol. 2958, pp. 306–322. Springer, Heidelberg (2004). https://doi.org/10.1007/978-3-540-24644-2_20
17. Hungershofer, J.: On the combined scheduling of malleable and rigid jobs. In: Symposium on Computer Architecture and HPC, pp. 206–213. IEEE (2004). https://doi.org/10.1109/sbac-pad.2004.27
18. Kleine Büning, M., Balyo, T., Sinz, C.: Using DimSpec for bounded and unbounded software model checking. In: Ait-Ameur, Y., Qin, S. (eds.) ICFEM 2019. LNCS, vol. 11852, pp. 19–35. Springer, Cham (2019). https://doi.org/10.1007/978-3-030-32409-4_2
19. Marques-Silva, J., Lynce, I., Malik, S.: Conflict-driven clause learning SAT solvers. In: Handbook of Satisfiability, pp. 131–153. IOS Press (2009). https://doi.org/10.3233/faia200987
20. Massacci, F., Marraro, L.: Logical cryptanalysis as a SAT problem. J. Autom. Reason. **24**(1), 165–203 (2000). https://doi.org/10.1023/A:1006326723002
21. Ozdemir, A., Wu, H., Barrett, C.: SAT solving in the serverless cloud. In: Formal Methods in Computer Aided Design (FMCAD), pp. 241–245. IEEE (2021). https://doi.org/10.34727/2021/isbn.978-3-85448-046-4_33
22. Sanders, P., Mehlhorn, K., Dietzfelbinger, M., Dementiev, R.: Sequential and Parallel Algorithms and Data Structures: The Basic Toolbox. Springer, Cham (2019). https://doi.org/10.1007/978-3-030-25209-0
23. Sanders, P., Schreiber, D.: Artifact and instructions to generate experimental results for the Euro-Par 2022 paper: "Decentralized Online Scheduling of Malleable NP-hard Jobs". https://doi.org/10.6084/m9.figshare.20000642
24. Sanders, P., Speck, J.: Efficient parallel scheduling of malleable tasks. In: International Parallel and Distributed Processing Symposium, pp. 1156–1166. IEEE (2011). https://doi.org/10.1109/ipdps.2011.110
25. Sanders, P., Speck, J.: Energy efficient frequency scaling and scheduling for malleable tasks. In: Kaklamanis, C., Papatheodorou, T., Spirakis, P.G. (eds.) Euro-Par 2012. LNCS, vol. 7484, pp. 167–178. Springer, Heidelberg (2012). https://doi.org/10.1007/978-3-642-32820-6_18
26. Schreiber, D.: Lilotane: a lifted SAT-based approach to hierarchical planning. J. Artif. Intell. Res. **70**, 1117–1181 (2021). https://doi.org/10.1613/jair.1.12520
27. Schreiber, D., Sanders, P.: Scalable SAT solving in the cloud. In: Li, C.-M., Manyà, F. (eds.) SAT 2021. LNCS, vol. 12831, pp. 518–534. Springer, Cham (2021). https://doi.org/10.1007/978-3-030-80223-3_35

A Bi-Criteria FPTAS for Scheduling with Memory Constraints on Graphs with Bounded Tree-Width

Eric Angel[1], Sébastien Morais[2,3](✉), and Damien Regnault[1]

[1] IBISC, Univ. Evry, Universite Paris-Saclay, 91025 Evry, France
{Eric.Angel,Damien.Regnault}@univ-evry.fr
[2] CEA, DAM, DIF, 91297 Arpajon, France
Sebastien.Morais@cea.fr
[3] LIHPC - Laboratoire en Informatique Haute Performance pour le Calcul et la simulation - DAM Île-de-France, University of Paris-Saclay, Bruyères-le-Châtel, France

Abstract. In this paper we study a scheduling problem arising from executing numerical simulations on HPC architectures. With a constant number of parallel machines, the objective is to minimize the makespan under memory constraints for the machines. Those constraints come from a neighborhood graph G for the jobs. Motivated by a previous result on graphs G with bounded path-width, our focus is on the case when the neighborhood graph G has bounded tree-width. Our result is a bi-criteria fully polynomial time approximation algorithm based on a dynamic programming algorithm. It allows to find a solution within a factor of $1 + \epsilon$ of the optimal makespan, where the memory capacity of the machines may be exceeded by a factor at most $1 + \epsilon$. This result relies on the use of a nice tree decomposition of G and its traversal in a specific way which may be useful on its own. The case of unrelated machines is also tractable with minor modifications.

1 Introduction

In this paper, we study the scheduling problem $Pk|G, mem|C_{max}$ previously introduced in [12] where the number of machines is a fixed constant. This problem is motivated by running distributed numerical simulations based on high-ordered finite elements or volume methods . Such approaches require the geometric domain of study to be discretized into basic elements, called cells, which form a mesh. Each cell has a computational cost, and a memory weight depending on the amount of data (i.e. density, pressure, ...) stored on that cell. Moreover, performing the computation of a cell requires, in addition to its data, data located in its neighborhood[1]. For a distributed simulation, the problem is to assign all the computations to processing units with bounded memory capacities, while

[1] The neighborhood is most of the time topologically defined (cells sharing an edge or a face).

J. Cano and P. W. Trinder (Eds.): Euro-Par 2022, LNCS 13440, pp. 136–151, 2022.
https://doi.org/10.1007/978-3-031-12597-3_9

minimizing the makespan. As an illustration of the previous notions, let us consider Fig. 1(a) where a mesh and its associated computations are assigned onto 3 processing units. Each color corresponds to a processing unit and the total amount of memory needed by each processing unit is not limited to the colored cells but extends to some adjacent cells. An exploded view of the mesh is pictured in Fig. 1(b), where we consider an edge-based adjacency relationship and where the memory needed by each processing unit is equal to both colored and white cells. In practice, efficient partitioning tools are used but the solutions returned by these tools may not respect the memory capacities of the processing units [14].

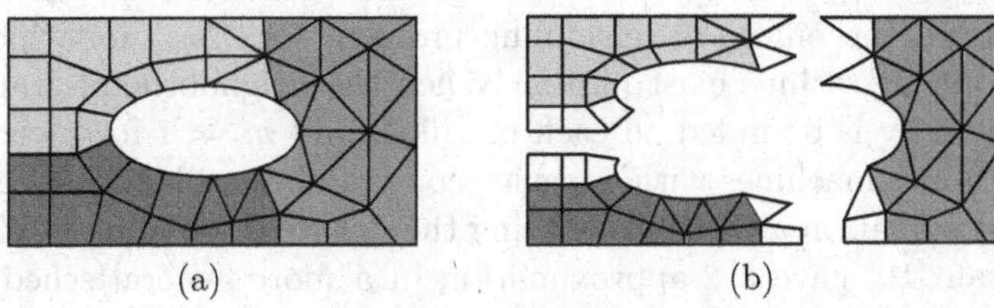

Fig. 1. In *(a)*, a 2D mesh and its computations are assigned onto 3 processing units. In *(b)*, an exploded view of the assignment with an edge-based adjacency relationship.

Formally, the scheduling problem under memory constraints is defined as follows. We have a set of n jobs J, and each job $j \in J$ requires $p_j \in \mathbb{N}$ *units of time* to be executed (computation time) and is associated an amount $m_j \in \mathbb{N}$ of memory. Jobs have to be assigned among a fixed number k of *identical* machines, each machine l having a memory capacity $M_l \in \mathbb{N}$, for $l = 1, \ldots, k$. Additionally we have an undirected graph $G(J, E)$, which we refer to as the *neighborhood graph*. Two jobs $j \in J$ and $j' \in J$ are said to be adjacent if there is an edge $(j, j') \in E$ in G. Moreover, to be processed each job j requires data from its set of *adjacent jobs*, denoted by $\mathcal{N}(j) := \{j' \in J \,|\, (j, j') \in E\}$. For a subset of jobs $J' \subseteq J$, we note $\mathcal{N}(J') := \cup_{j \in J'} \mathcal{N}(j) \setminus J'$ and denote $\mathcal{N}[J'] := \mathcal{N}(J') \cup J'$. When a subset of jobs $J' \subseteq J$ is scheduled on a machine, this machine needs to allocate an amount of memory equal to $\sum_{j \in \mathcal{N}[J']} m_j$, while its processing time is $\sum_{j \in J'} p_j$. The objective is to assign each job of J onto exactly a machine, such that the makespan (the maximum processing time over all machines) is minimized and ensuring that the amount of memory allocated by each machine is smaller than or equal to its memory capacity.

The scheduling problem under memory constraints embraces other well-known **NP**-hard scheduling problems and cannot be solved in polynomial time unless **P** = **NP**. Thus, one could be interested in developing approximation algorithms. An *α-approximation algorithm* (for some $\alpha \geq 1$) for a minimization problem is a polynomial-time algorithm that produces, for any given problem instance I, a solution whose value is at most α times the optimum value. In particular, a *fully polynomial-time approximation scheme* (FPTAS) is a family of $(1+\varepsilon)$-approximation algorithms for all $\varepsilon > 0$ whose time complexity is polynomial in both the input size and $1/\varepsilon$. Considering the scheduling problem under memory constraints, one could wonder if approximation algorithms can be obtained when the memory constraints are relaxed. For $\alpha \geq 1$ and $\beta \geq 1$, an (α, β) *(bi-criteria) approximation algorithm* returns a schedule with objective value at most αC and with memory load at most βM, where C and M, respectively, are the maximum computation time and the memory load of an optimal schedule with respect to the makespan. Following the terminology of [15], a bi-FPTAS for the scheduling problem under memory constraints is a FPTAS which is a bicriteria $(1+\varepsilon, 1+\varepsilon)$ *approximation algorithm*.

Related Problems. When $m_j = 0$ for each job j, the problem $Rk|G, mem|C_{max}$ becomes the scheduling problem $Rk||C_{max}$ for which several approximations algorithms exist [3,6,8]. When the neighborhood graph has no edges, the memory is bounded on each machine, and $m_j = 1$ for each job j, we get the scheduling machines with capacity constraints problem. Zhang et al. [9] gave a 3-approximation algorithm by using the iterative rounding method. Saha and Srinivasan [10] gave a 2-approximation in a more general scheduling setting, i.e. scheduling unrelated machines with capacity constraints. Lately, Keller and Kotov [11] gave a 1.5-approximation algorithm. Chen et al. established an efficient polynomial-time approximation scheme (EPTAS) [13] for this problem and, for the special case of two machines, Woeginger designed a FPTAS [7].

Main Contribution. As the scheduling problem under memory constraints is a generalization of those well-known scheduling problems, a reasonable question is to know whether we can get approximation algorithms, which could depend on some parameters of the neighborhood graph, when the number of machines is a fixed constant. We answered this question in a previous paper [12] by providing a *fixed-parameter tractable* (FPT) algorithm with respect to the path-width of the neighborhood graph, which returns a solution within a ratio of $(1+\varepsilon)$ for both the optimum makespan and the memory capacity constraints (assuming that there exists at least one feasible solution). In this paper we extend this result by providing a bi-FPTAS for graphs with tree-width bounded by a constant[2]. Unlike the FPT algorithm which relies on the numbering of the vertices of the neighborhood graph, the bi-FPTAS takes advantage of a nice tree decomposition of the neighborhood graph and of its traversal in a particular way to bound the algorithm complexity.

Outline of the Paper. We start by briefly recalling in Sect. 2 the definitions of different notions useful in the sequel. We then provide in Sect. 3 an algorithm that computes all the solutions to this problem. This algorithm consists of three steps: build a nice tree decomposition of $G(J, E)$; compute a layout L defining

[2] For sake of readability, the result is presented for two machines but it can be extended to any number of machines, as discussed in the conclusion.

a bottom-up traversal of the nice tree decomposition; and use a dynamic programming algorithm traversing the nice tree decomposition following L. Since the time complexity of this algorithm is not polynomial in the input size, we apply the Trimming-of-the-State-Space technique [1] in Sect. 4 obtaining a bi-FPTAS for graphs with tree-width bounded by a constant. Finally, we give some concluding remarks in Sect. 5.

2 Definitions

Throughout this paper we consider simple, finite undirected graphs. Let us start by defining the notions of tree decomposition, tree-width and nice tree decomposition. The notions of tree decomposition and tree-width were initially introduced in the framework of graph minor theory [2]. For a graph $G(J, E)$, let $J(G) := J$ be its vertices and $E(G) := E$ be its edges. A *tree decomposition* for G is a pair (T, X), where $T := (J(T), E(T))$ is a tree, and $X := (X_u)_{u \in J(T)}$ is a family of subsets of J satisfying the following conditions:

1. For each $j \in J(G)$ there is at least one $u \in J(T)$ such that $j \in X_u$.
2. For each $\{j, j'\} \in E(G)$ there is at least one $u \in J(T)$ such that j and j' are in X_u.
3. For each $j \in J(G)$, the set of vertices $u \in J(T)$ such that $j \in X_u$ induces a subtree of T.

To distinguish between vertices of G and T, the latter are called *nodes*. The *width* of a tree decomposition is $\max(|X_u| - 1 : u \in J(T))$ and the *tree-width* of G, noted $tw(G)$, is the minimum width over all tree decompositions of G. Choosing an arbitrary node $r \in J(T)$ as root, we can make a *rooted tree decomposition* out of (T, X) with natural parent-child and ancestor-descendant relations. A node without children is called a *leaf*. A rooted tree decomposition (T, X) with root r is called *nice* if every node $u \in J(T)$ is of one of the following types:

- **Leaf:** node u is a leaf of T and $|X_u| = 1$.
- **Introduce:** node u has only one child c and there is a vertex $j \in J(G)$ such that $X_u = X_c \cup \{j\}$.
- **Forget:** node u has only one child c and there is a vertex $j \in J(G)$ such that $X_c = X_u \cup \{j\}$.
- **Join:** node u has only two children l and r such that $X_u = X_l = X_r$.

Note that a vertex of $J(G)$ can be forgotten at most once in a node of $J(T)$. Otherwise, it would conflict with the third condition listed in the definition of a tree decomposition. We leverage this property later in the article. There is an alternative definition to the nice tree decomposition where the root r and all leaves u of T are such that $X_r = X_u = \emptyset$. But one can switch from one of these decompositions to the other in a trivial way. A graph $G(J, E)$ is illustrated on Fig. 2(a) and a nice tree decomposition of this graph is presented on Fig. 2(b).

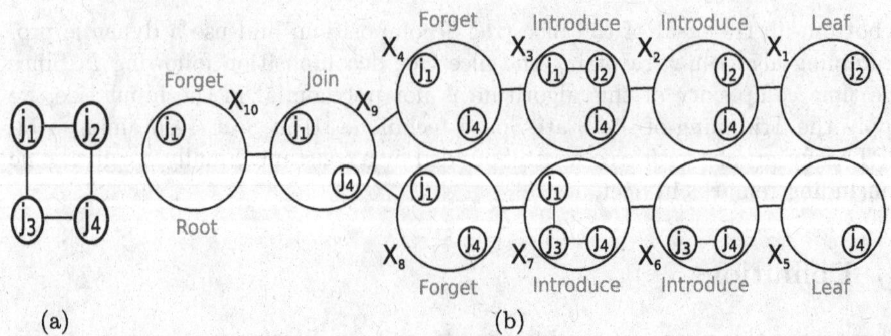

Fig. 2. Example of a graph $G(J, E)$ in (a) and a nice tree decomposition (T, X) of this graph where X is composed of the sets $X_1, \ldots, X_{10}$.

When G is a graph with $tw(G) = h$, where h is any fixed constant, we can compute a tree decomposition of G in linear time with tree-width at most h [5]. Given a tree decomposition (T, X) of $G(J, E)$ of constant width $h \geq 1$, there is an algorithm that converts it into a nice tree decomposition (T', X') with the same width h and with at most $4n$ nodes, where $n = |J(G)|$, in $O(n)$ times (Lemma 13.1.3 in [4]). In the rest of the article, we will consider a nice tree decomposition obtained in this way.

Now, let us introduce the notion of *layout* of a nice tree decomposition (T, X), which is simply a one-to-one mapping $L : J(T) \to \{1, \ldots, |J(T)|\}$. We say that a layout L defines a *bottom-up traversal* of a nice tree decomposition (T, X) if for any edge $\{u, v\} \in E(T)$ such that v is a child of u one has $L(v) < L(u)$. In that case, we say that L is a bottom-up layout.

3 An Exact Algorithm Using Dynamic Programming

Briefly, our algorithm consists of three steps. First, we build a nice tree decomposition (T, X) of the graph $G(J, E)$ with bounded tree-width. Such a tree decomposition can be obtained in polynomial time for graph G with tree-width bounded by a constant (see Sect. 2). Then, we compute a specific layout L defining a bottom-up traversal of the nice tree decomposition. Finally, a dynamic programming algorithm passes through the nodes following the previously defined order L and computes a set $\mathcal{S}_{L(u)}$ of states, which encodes partial solutions for $G_i = (J_i, E_i)$ a subgraph of $G = (J, E)$, for each node $u \in J(T)$. In Sect. 3.1, we start by presenting the dynamic programming algorithm where we detail how the set of states $\mathcal{S}_{L(u)}$ is computed depending on the type of node u. Then, in Sect. 3.2, we give a proof of correctness of our dynamic programming algorithm when the nodes of the nice tree decomposition are traversed in a bottom-up way. Eventually, we compute the complexity of our dynamic programming algorithm when the decomposition is traversed following the layout L. This layout is used to bound the complexity of our algorithm and, being bottom-up, it is compliant with the pre-requisite on proof of completeness.

3.1 The Dynamic Programming Algorithm

The presentation of the dynamic algorithm is done for two machines, but it can be generalized to a constant number k of machines, with $k > 2$. The dynamic algorithm goes through $|J(T)|$ phases. Each phase i, with $i = 1, \ldots, |J(T)|$, processes the node $L^{-1}(i) \in J(T)$ and produces a set $\mathcal{S}_i$ of states. In the sequel, for sake of readability, we use the notation $Z_i := X_{L^{-1}(i)}$. Each state in the state space $\mathcal{S}_i$ encodes a solution for the graph $G_i = (J_i, E_i)$, where $J_i := \cup_{o=1}^{i} Z_o$ with $J_0 = \emptyset$, and $E_i := E_{i-1} \cup E_{Z_i}$ with $E_0 = \emptyset$ and E_{Z_i} the set of all edges in E which have both endpoints in Z_i. For each phase i, we denote by $J_L(i)$ the set of vertices of $J(G)$ which have not been forgotten when going through nodes $L^{-1}(1)$ to $L^{-1}(i)$. For convenience, we note $J_L(0) := \emptyset$. Formally, $J_L(i) := J_i \setminus V_R(i)$, where $V_R(i)$ is the set of vertices that where removed in a Forget node o such that $L(o) \leq i$.

A state $s \in \mathcal{S}_i$ is a vector $[c_1, c_2, c_3, c_4, \mathcal{C}_i]$ where:

- c_1 (resp. c_2) is the total processing time on the first (resp. second) machine in the constructed schedule,
- c_3 (resp. c_4) is the total amount of memory required by the first (resp. second) machine in the constructed schedule,
- $\mathcal{C}_i$ is an additional structure, called *combinatorial frontier*. For a given solution of $G_i(J_i, E_i)$, it is defined as $\mathcal{C}_i := (J_L(i), \sigma_i, \sigma_i')$ where $\sigma_i : J_L(i) \to \{1, 2\}$ and $\sigma_i' : J_L(i) \to \{0, 1\}$ such that $\sigma_i(j)$ is the machine on which $j \in J_L(i)$ has been assigned, and $\sigma_i'(j) := 1$ if the machine on which j is not assigned, i.e. machine $3 - \sigma_i(j)$, has already memorised the data of j. Notice that $J_L(i) \subseteq J_i$ and keeping into memory the combinatorial frontier with respect to $J_L(i)$ rather than J_i is a key point in our algorithm in order to bound its complexity.

In the following, we present how to compute $\mathcal{S}_i$ from $\mathcal{S}_{i-1}$ depending on the type of node $L^{-1}(i)$. For that, we present how states of $\mathcal{S}_i$ are obtained from an arbitrary state $s = [c_1, c_2, c_3, c_4, \mathcal{C}_{i-1}] \in \mathcal{S}_{i-1}$. When $L^{-1}(i)$ is a Leaf node with $Z_i = \{j\}$ or an Introduce node with j the vertex introduced, we note s_a ($a = 1, 2$) the state of $\mathcal{S}_i$ obtained from s and resulting from the assignment of j to machine a, and $\mathcal{C}_i^a$ the combinatorial frontier obtained from $\mathcal{C}_{i-1}$ when j is assigned to machine a.

Leaf. Let $L^{-1}(i) \in J(T)$ be a Leaf of T with $Z_i = \{j\}$. For each state of $\mathcal{S}_{i-1}$ we add at most two states in $\mathcal{S}_i$. If $j \in J_L(i-1)$, it means that j has already been assigned to a machine. Therefore, there is nothing to do and $\mathcal{S}_i = \mathcal{S}_{i-1}$. Now, let us assume that $j \notin J_L(i-1)$. In this case, we must compute two new states taking into account the assignment of j to machine one or two. We have

$$s_a = [c_1 + \delta_{a,1} c_j,\ c_2 + \delta_{a,2} c_j,\ c_3 + \delta_{a,1}\, m_j,\ c_4 + \delta_{a,2}\, m_j,\ \mathcal{C}_i^a]$$

where δ is the Kronecker function ($\delta_{i,j} = 1$ if $i = j$, and $\delta_{i,j} = 0$ otherwise). Since $j \notin J_L(i-1)$, the new combinatorial frontier is obtained by extending $\mathcal{C}_{i-1}$

in adding new information related to j, i.e. $\sigma_i(j) = a$ and $\sigma'_i(j) = 0$. Note that we have $\sigma'_i(j) = 0$ because j was not assigned before phase i and $E_{Z_i} = \emptyset$.

Introduce. Let $L^{-1}(i) \in J(T)$ be an Introduce node of T and $j \in J(G)$ being the vertex introduced. Again, for each state s of $\mathcal{S}_{i-1}$ we are going to add at most two states to $\mathcal{S}_i$ depending on j assignment. However, processing an Introduce node differs from a Leaf because we may have to consider new edges. This happens when $E_i \backslash E_{i-1} \neq \emptyset$. There are two cases to consider. The first one is when $j \in J_L(i-1)$. In that case, job j has already been assigned on machine $a = \sigma_{i-1}(j)$. We add a state in $\mathcal{S}_i$ for every state s in $\mathcal{S}_{i-1}$. Let F_a and F'_a be the set of edges such that

$$F_a = \{\{j, j'\} \in E_{Z_i} : a \neq \sigma_{i-1}(j') \text{ and } \sigma'_{i-1}(j') = 0\}, \quad (1)$$

$$F'_a = \{\{j, j'\} \in E_{Z_i} : a \neq \sigma_{i-1}(j') \text{ and } \sigma'_{i-1}(j) = 0\}. \quad (2)$$

The set F_a represents the new edges in E_{Z_i} inducing additional amount of data on machine a. The set F'_a represents the new edges in E_{Z_i} inducing that m_j must be added on the machine not processing j. Note that some edges in E_{Z_i} may have already been considered in a previous node and that they can't be a part of F_a or F'_a. Thus, we have

$$s_a = [c_1,\ c_2,\ c_3 + \delta_{a,1}\alpha_i^1 + \delta_{a,2}\beta_i^1,\ c_4 + \delta_{a,2}\alpha_i^2 + \delta_{a,1}\beta_i^2,\ C_i^a]$$

where $\alpha_i^a = \sum_{\{j,j'\} \in F_a} m_{j'}$ and $\beta_i^a = m_j\, I[\![F'_a \neq \emptyset]\!]$ where $I[\![A]\!]$ is the indicator function which returns one if condition A is satisfied and zero otherwise. Finally, the combinatorial frontier of the new state s_a is obtained from that of s by updating, if necessary, the information of j and vertices j' such that $\{j, j'\} \in F_a$. If we have $F'_a \neq \emptyset$, it means that j was not memorised by machine $3-a$ in state s. However, this is no longer the case for s_a as new edges have been taken into account leading us to $\sigma'_i(j) = 1 \neq \sigma'_{i-1}(j)$. If we have $F_a \neq \emptyset$, then some vertices processed by machine $3-a$ were not memorised by machine a in state s. Again, this is no longer the case in s_a following the inclusion of new edges leading us to $\sigma'_i(j') = 1 \neq \sigma'_{i-1}(j')$ for every vertex j' such that $\{j, j'\} \in F_a$.

Now, if $j \notin J_L(i-1)$ then we add two states in $\mathcal{S}_i$ for every state $s \in \mathcal{S}_{i-1}$. For $a = 1, 2$, we have

$$\begin{aligned} s_a = [&c_1 + \delta_{a,1}\, p_j,\ c_2 + \delta_{a,2}\, p_j, \\ &c_3 + \delta_{a,1}(m_j + \alpha_i^1) + \delta_{a,2}\beta_i^1,\ c_4 + \delta_{a,2}(m_j + \alpha_i^2) + \delta_{a,1}\beta_i^2,\ C_i^a]. \end{aligned}$$

The way to obtain the first four coordinates of each new state in $\mathcal{S}_i$ is similar to the case where $j \in J_L(i-1)$ except that we have to add p_j and m_j on the machine processing j. In the case of the combinatorial frontier, updates defined for $j \in J_L(i-1)$ also apply and we have to add information related to j since it was unknown so far. The added data is $\sigma_i(j) = a$ and $\sigma'_i(j) = I[\![\exists j' \in Z_i : \{j, j'\} \in E_{Z_i} \text{ and } \sigma_{i-1}(j') \neq a]\!]$.

Forget. Let $L^{-1}(i) \in J(T)$ be a Forget node of T and $j \in J(G)$ being the vertex forgotten. This type of node is easier to handle than previous ones since we do not have to deal with new vertex or edges. The only thing to do is to withdraw j from the combination frontier. Thus, for each state $s \in \mathcal{S}_{i-1}$ we add a state $s' \in \mathcal{S}_i$ where the combinatorial frontier of s' is equal to that of s from which information on j was removed.

Join. Let $L^{-1}(i) \in J(T)$ be a Join node of T. This type of node is even simpler to deal with than the previous one. Once again, there are no new vertex or edges to handle. Moreover, we do not forget any vertex. For each state $s \in \mathcal{S}_{i-1}$ we add s to $\mathcal{S}_i$. Thus, we have $\mathcal{S}_i = \mathcal{S}_{i-1}$.

Our algorithm ends up by returning the state $s = [c_1, c_2, c_3, c_4, \mathcal{C}_{|J(T)|}] \in \mathcal{S}_{|J(T)|}$ with $c_3 \leq M_1$, $c_4 \leq M_2$ and such that $\max\{c_1, c_2\}$ is minimum.

3.2 Algorithm Correctness

Now, let us present the proof of correctness of our dynamic programming algorithm when the nodes of the nice tree decomposition are traversed in bottom-up. We will prove our algorithm correctness by maintaining the following invariant: the states in $\mathcal{S}_i$ encode all the solutions for the graph $G_i = (J_i, E_i)$, defined at Sect. 3.1.

Initialization. Let us start with the first node encountered. Let $G_0 = (J_0, E_0)$ be an empty graph and $\mathcal{S}_0$ be the set composed of the single state $[0, 0, 0, 0, \mathcal{C}_0]$ where $\mathcal{C}_0$ does not store information. The nodes being traversed in bottom-up, the first node encountered is a Leaf. Let $j \in J(G)$ be the vertex such that $Z_1 = \{j\}$. Since $j \notin J_L(0)$ we have $\mathcal{S}_1 = [(p_j, 0, m_j, 0, \mathcal{C}_1^1), (0, p_j, 0, m_j, \mathcal{C}_1^2)]$ where, for $a = 1, 2$, $\mathcal{C}_1^a$ is such that $\sigma_1(j) = a$ and $\sigma_1'(j) = 0$. These two states encode the assignment of j on machines one and two when considering the graph $G_1 = (J_1, E_1)$. Moreover, the combinatorial frontier obtained allows us to keep in memory potentially necessary knowledge for graphs of which $G_1 = (J_1, E_1)$ is a sub-graph. Thus the invariant is correct for the first node.

Maintenance. Now let us assume that the invariant holds for $L^{-1}(i-1) \in J(T)$ and let us prove that it is still correct for $L^{-1}(i) \in J(T)$.

Leaf. Let $L^{-1}(i) \in J(T)$ being a Leaf with $Z_i = \{j\}$. If $j \in J_L(i-1)$ then our algorithm states that $\mathcal{S}_i = \mathcal{S}_{i-1}$. In that case, the invariant holds because $G_i = (J_i, E_i)$ is equal to $G_{i-1} = (J_{i-1}, E_{i-1})$. Now, if $j \notin J_L(i)$ then our algorithm adds two new states in $\mathcal{S}_i$ for every state in $s \in \mathcal{S}_{i-1}$ to take into account the assignment of j to machine one and two. Each new state is obtained by adding p_j and m_j according to the assignment of j and the associated combinatorial frontier is obtained by extending the combinatorial frontier of s with information on j assignment, i.e. $\sigma_i(j) = a$ and $\sigma_i'(j) = 0$. Since we are dealing with a Leaf and $j \notin J_L(i)$ we have $G_i = (V_{i-1} \cup \{j\}, E_{i-1})$. Therefore, the invariant holds.

Introduce. Let $L^{-1}(i) \in J(T)$ being an Introduce node with $j \in J(G)$ being the vertex introduced. If $j \in J_L(i-1)$ then our algorithm adds one new state in

$\mathcal{S}_i$ for every state in $\mathcal{S}_{i-1}$. A new state in $\mathcal{S}_i$ is obtained from a state in $\mathcal{S}_{i-1}$ by adding, if needed, some amount of data on machine one and two. Let $a = \sigma_{i-1}(j)$ and F_a and F'_a be the sets defined in (1) and (2). We note F''_a the set such that $F''_a = E_{Z_i} \backslash (F_a \cup F'_a)$.

Lemma 1. *Let s be a state encoding a solution of a graph $G' = (J', E')$. Then, if we add an edge $e = \{j, j'\}$ such that $j \in J'$, $j' \in J'$ and $e \in F''_a$ then s also encodes a solution of the graph $G' = (J', E' \cup e)$.*

Proof. The proof of this lemma is based on the fact that introducing such edge does not make s inconsistent with graph $G' = (J', E' \cup e)$. Let us begin by noting that adding an edge $e = \{j, j'\} \in F''_a$ does not require to modify the processing times in s to make it a state encoding a solution of $G' = (J', E' \cup e)$. Indeed, since s encodes a solution for $G' = (J', E')$, the processing time induced by the assignment of j and j' has already been encoded. Now, suppose that $e \in F''_a$. Then, we have either j and j' that are assigned to the same machine, or j and j' that are memorised by both machines. In either case, adding such an edge does not require to modify the amount of memory or combinatorial frontier in s to make it a state encoding a solution of $G' = (J', E' \cup e)$. □

On the machine processing j, our algorithm adds $m_{j'}$ for every vertex $j' \in J_i$ such that $\{j, j'\} \in F_a$. Indeed, since j' is on a different machine than j and that this machine does not memorise j', it is necessary to add $m_{j'}$ on machine $\sigma_{i-1}(j)$ to take into account the edge $\{j, j'\}$. On the machine not processing j, our algorithm adds m_j if there is an edge $\{j, j'\} \in F'_a$. Indeed, as j' is on a different machine than j' and j is not memorised by this machine, it is necessary to add m_j on machine $\sigma_{i-1}(j')$ to take into account the existence of such an edge. Finally, we update the combinatorial frontier information on vertex j if $F'_a \neq \emptyset$ and on vertices j' such that $\{j, j'\} \in F_a$. Therefore, the states returned by our algorithm encode solutions for the graph $G' = (J_i, E_{i-1} \cup F_a \cup F'_a \cup F''_a)$ and the combinatorial frontier is consistent with the addition of new vertices or edges. According to Lemma 1, our algorithm encodes solutions for the graph $G_i = (J_i, E_i)$ since $E_i = E_{i-1} \cup E_{Z_i}$ and $E_{Z_i} = F_a \cup F'_a \cup F''_a$. Thus, the invariant holds.

Now, if $j \notin J_L(i-1)$ the proof of the invariant enforcement is similar to the case where $j \in J_L(i-1)$. The difference lies in the fact that j is not yet assigned. Thus, one must generate two new states in $\mathcal{S}_i$ for each state in $\mathcal{S}_{i-1}$ and the processing time, and amount of memory, of j must be added on the machine processing j.

Forget. Let $L^{-1}(i) \in J(T)$ be a Forget node of T and $j \in J(G)$ being the vertex forgotten. Here, our algorithm generates the states of $\mathcal{S}_i$ by taking those of $\mathcal{S}_{i-1}$ from which it removes information on vertex j from the combinatorial frontier. First, let us note that $G_i = (J_i, E_i)$ is equal to $G_{i-1} = (J_{i-1}, E_{i-1})$ and the invariant holds. Notice that since we traverse T in bottom-up, we know that removing a vertex j implies that all edges linked to it have been explored. Otherwise, it would lead to the violation of a property of the tree decomposition (the third listed in Sect. 2). Therefore, we can stop memorising the information related to vertex j.

Join. Let $L^{-1}(i) \in J(T)$ be a Join node of T. In that case, our algorithm computes $\mathcal{S}_i$ by retrieving the states of $\mathcal{S}_{i-1}$ without modifying them. Since we have $G_i = (J_i, E_i)$ equal to $G_{i-1} = (J_{i-1}, E_{i-1})$ and no modification on the combinatorial frontier is performed, the invariant holds.

Termination. Finally, from the first and second conditions listed in the definition of the tree decomposition, we know that the graph $G_{|J(T)|} = (J_{|J(T)|}, E_{|J(T)|})$ is equal to $G = (J, E)$. Since our invariant is valid for the first node and during the transition from nodes $L^{-1}(i-1)$ to $L^{-1}(i)$, our algorithm returns an optimal solution for the scheduling problem under memory constraints.

3.3 Algorithm Complexity

Let us now evaluate the time complexity of our dynamic programming algorithm. Let $J_L^{max} := \max_{1 \le i \le |J(T)|} |J_L(i)|$. Let $p_{sum} := \sum_{j \in J(G)} p_j$ and $m_{sum} := \sum_{j \in J(G)} m_j$, then for each state $s = [c_1, c_2, c_3, c_4, \mathcal{C}_i] \in \mathcal{S}_i$, c_1 and c_2 are integers between 0 and p_{sum}, c_3 and c_4 are integers between 0 and m_{sum}. The number of distinct combinatorial frontiers is $4^{J_L^{max}}$. Therefore, the number of states is $|\mathcal{S}_i| = O(p_{sum}^2 \times m_{sum}^2 \times 4^{J_L^{max}})$. The dynamic programming algorithm processes all $|J(T)| = O(n)$ nodes of the nice tree decomposition. Each state in a phase can give at most two states in the next phase with a processing time of $O(J_L^{max})$ to compute these states. Recall also that in the algorithm, if two states s and s' have the same components, including the same combinatorial frontier, then only one of them is kept in the state space. The time complexity to test whether two states s and s' are the same is thus proportional to the length of the combinatorial frontier, and is therefore $O(J_L^{max})$. We obtain that the overall complexity of the dynamic programming algorithm is $O(n \times |\mathcal{S}_i| \times (J_L^{max} + |\mathcal{S}_i| J_L^{max})) = O(n \times J_L^{max} \times (p_{sum}^2 \times m_{sum}^2 \times 4^{J_L^{max}})^2)$. Notice that J_L^{max} depends on the chosen layout L, and to minimize this complexity it is therefore important to find a layout L with a small J_L^{max}.

Lemma 2. *There exists a bottum-up layout L of the nice tree decomposition such that $J_L^{max} \le tw(G) \lceil \log 4n \rceil$.*

Proof. To prove that such a layout exists we present an algorithm which, when applied to the root of the nice tree decomposition, computes a bottom-up layout L such that $J_L^{max} \le tw(G) \lceil \log 4n \rceil$. To ease the understanding of certain parts of the proof, these parts will be illustrated on Fig. 3 where a tree with 174 nodes is depicted.

The algorithm works as follows. We perform a depth-first search starting from the root node, and when we have a Join node we first go to the subtree having the greatest number of nodes. With this depth-first search we get a discovery

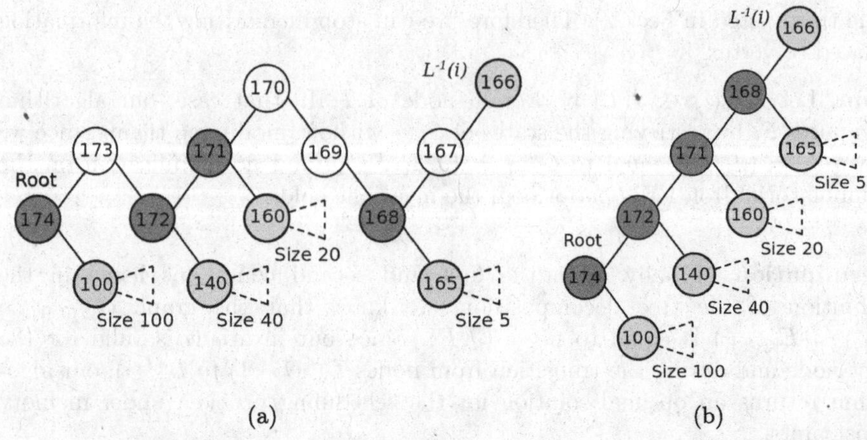

Fig. 3. Illustration of the proof of Lemma 2 on a possible tree with 174 nodes. The tree is labelled with a bottum-up layout L, and for notational convenience we consider that $L^{-1}(i) = i$ for $1 \leq i \leq 174$. Some subtrees are represented by dashed triangles. On Figure (a) is depicted the tree. When considering node 166, the set of critical nodes $A = \{166, 165, 160, 140, 100\}$. All nodes in A, excepting the node 166, are left children of Join nodes, and these Join nodes are on the path $P = \{174, 173, 172, 171, 170, 169, 168, 167, 166\}$ between the root node 174 and the node 166. On Figure (b) is depicted the reduced tree obtained by removing all nodes in P which are not Join nodes, namely R. In each figure, the set of critical nodes A associated to node 166 is green colored and the Join nodes in P are purple colored. (Color figure online)

and finishing times for each node. The labeling is obtained by sorting the nodes in increasing order of their finishing time.

Now, let us analyze J_L^{max} on the layout returned by our algorithm. Recall that we use the notation $Z_i := X_{L^{-1}(i)}$ and let us define the operator $\sqcup$ such that $Z_i \sqcup Z_{i+1} := Z_i \setminus \{j\}$ if $L^{-1}(i+1)$ is a Forget node, with j the vertex forgotten, and $Z_i \sqcup Z_{i+1} := Z_i \cup Z_{i+1}$ otherwise. Notice that $J_L(i) = \sqcup_{o \leq i} Z_o$ and that if we have a set of consecutive nodes $L^{-1}(l)$, $L^{-1}(l+1)$, ..., $L^{-1}(u)$ such that $L^{-1}(i+1)$ is a parent node for $L^{-1}(i)$ ($l \leq i \leq u-1$), then $\sqcup_{i=l}^{u} Z_i = Z_u$. Moreover if this chain is maximal, i.e. $L^{-1}(u+1)$ is not a parent node of $L^{-1}(u)$, then it means that the parent of $L^{-1}(u)$ is a Join node. For any node $L^{-1}(i)$, we have $J_L(i) = \sqcup_{o \leq i} Z_o = \cup_{l \in A} X_l$, with A a set of nodes, of minimum size, that we call *critical*. This set of critical nodes A can be obtained by taking the last node in each maximal chain over nodes $L^{-1}(1)$ to $L^{-1}(o)$. Thus, A is composed of the current node $L^{-1}(i)$ along with other nodes whose parents are Join nodes. Such set A is illustrated in Fig. 3(a) where we consider $i = 166$ and where the nodes composing A are green colored.

For a Join node $L^{-1}(i)$ having two childrens $L^{-1}(l)$ and $L^{-1}(r)$, let denote by $T_l(i)$ and $T_r(i)$ the corresponding subtrees. We will assume that $|T_l(i)| \geq |T_r(i)|$ and therefore during the depth-first search we use, node $L^{-1}(l)$ will be examined before node $L^{-1}(r)$. We say that $L^{-1}(l)$ (resp. $L^{-1}(r)$) is the left (resp. right) children of $L^{-1}(i)$. By the way the depth-first search is performed, all nodes in A, excepting the current node $L^{-1}(i)$, are left children of Join nodes, and these Join nodes are on the path P between the root node and the current node $L^{-1}(i)$. In Fig. 3(a), such path P contains the Join nodes purple colored.

Now, let us bound the number of Join nodes on the path P. First, we construct a reduced graph by removing the nodes of R where R is the set of nodes of P that are not Join nodes. Such a reduced graph is illustrated in Fig. 3(b). By doing this set of deletions, we get a tree with fewer than $4n$ nodes (recall that the nice tree decomposition we started from has at most $4n$ nodes). The number of Join nodes is equal to the length of the reduced path $P \setminus R$ which is $\lceil \log 4n \rceil$. Indeed, starting from the root, each time we go on a node along this path the number of remaining nodes is divided by at least 2.

Thus, we have proved that $|A| \leq \lceil \log 4n \rceil$ for any node $L^{-1}(i)$ labelled with our algorithm. Recall that $J_L(i) = \cup_{l \in A} X_l$, and moreover from the definition of tree-width, we have $|X_l| \leq tw(G)$. Thus, we have $|J_L(i)| \leq tw(G) \lceil \log 4n \rceil$ and the proof is complete. □

Using the previous defined layout, we obtain an overall complexity of our dynamic programming algorithm of $O(p_{sum}^4 \times m_{sum}^4 \times tw(G) \times \log(n) \times n^{2tw(G)+1} \times 16^{tw(G)})$. The time complexity of this dynamic programming algorithm being pseudo-polynomial (because of p_{sum} and m_{sum}), we are going to transform it into a bi-FPTAS.

4 Application of a Trimming Technique

In this Section, we propose a bi-FPTAS derived from the algorithm presented in Sect. 3. To transform the dynamic programming algorithm, we apply an approach for transforming a dynamic programming formulation into a FPTAS. This approach, called the *trimming-the-state-space* technique is due to Ibarra and Kim [1] and consists in iteratively thin out the state space of the dynamic program by collapsing states that are close to each other.

In the approximation algorithm, we are going to trim the state space by discarding states that are close to each other. While carrying these states deletions, we must ensure that the resulting errors cannot propagate in an uncontrolled way. To this end, we characterize a notion of proximity between states. We define $\Delta := 1 + \varepsilon/8n$, with $\varepsilon > 0$ a fixed constant. Let us first consider the first two coordinates of a state $s = [c_1, c_2, c_3, c_4, \mathcal{C}_i]$. We have $0 \leq c_1 \leq p_{sum}$ and $0 \leq c_2 \leq p_{sum}$. We divide each of those intervals into intervals of the form $[0]$ and $[\Delta^l, \Delta^{l+1}]$, with l an integer value getting from 0 to $L_1 := \lceil \log_\Delta(p_{sum}) \rceil = \lceil ln(p_{sum})/ln(\Delta) \rceil \leq \lceil (1 + \frac{8n}{\varepsilon}) ln(p_{sum}) \rceil$. In the same way, we divide the next two coordinates into intervals of the form $[0]$ and $[\Delta^l, \Delta^{l+1}]$, with l an integer value getting from 0 to $L_2 := \lceil \log_\Delta(m_{sum}) \rceil$. The union of those intervals defines a set of non-overlapping boxes. If two states have the same combinatorial frontier and have their first four coordinates falling into the same box, then they encode similar solutions and we consider them to be close to each other.

The approximation algorithm proceeds in the same way as the exact algorithm, except that we add a trimming step to thin out each state space $\mathcal{S}_i$. The trimming step consists in keeping only one solution per box and per combinatorial frontier. Thus, the worst time complexity of this approximation algorithm is $O(L_1^4 \times L_2^4 \times tw(G) \times \log(n) \times n^{2tw(G)+1} \times 16^{tw(G)})$. We therefore get a bi-FPTAS when the tree-width $tw(G)$ is bounded by a constant.

Theorem 1. *There exists a bi-FPTAS for the problem $Pk|G, mem|C_{max}$ when the tree-width of G is bounded by a constant, which returns a solution within a ratio of $(1+\varepsilon)$ for the optimum makespan, where the memory capacity M_i, $1 \le i \le k$, of each machine may be exceeded by at most a factor $(1+\varepsilon)$.*

For sake of readability, the proof is presented when $k = 2$. In the conclusion, we mention the general case when k is any fixed constant. We denote by $\mathcal{U}_i$ (resp. $\mathcal{T}_i$) the state space obtained before (resp. after) performing the trimming step at the i-th phase of the algorithm. The proof of this theorem relies on the following lemma.

Lemma 3. *For each state $s = [c_1, c_2, c_3, c_4, \mathcal{C}_i] \in \mathcal{S}_i$, there exists a state $[c_1^\#, c_2^\#, c_3^\#, c_4^\#, \mathcal{C}_i] \in \mathcal{T}_i$ such that*

$$c_1^\# \le \Delta^i c_1 \text{ and } c_2^\# \le \Delta^i c_2 \text{ and } c_3^\# \le \Delta^i c_3 \text{ and } c_4^\# \le \Delta^i c_4. \tag{3}$$

Proof. The proof of this lemma is by induction on i. The first node we consider is a Leaf of the nice tree decomposition and we have $\mathcal{T}_1 = \mathcal{S}_1$. Therefore, the statement is correct for $i = 1$. Now, let us suppose that inequality (3) is correct for any index $i-1$ and consider an arbitrary state $s = [c_1, c_2, c_3, c_4, \mathcal{C}_i] \in \mathcal{S}_i$. Due to a lack of space, proof of the validity of the Lemma when passing from phase $i-1$ to i is only presented for a node of type Introduce. Note that the proof for other types of nodes can be derived from that of an Introduce node. Let $L^{-1}(i)$ be an Introduce node with $j \in J(G)$ being the vertex introduced. We must distinguish between cases where j belongs to $J_L(i-1)$ and where he does not.

First, let us assume that $j \in J_L(i-1)$. Then s was obtained from a state $[w, x, y, z, \mathcal{C}_{i-1}] \in \mathcal{S}_{i-1}$ and $s = [w, x, y + \delta_{a,1}\alpha_i^1 + \delta_{a,2}\beta_i^1, z + \delta_{a,2}\alpha_i^2 + \delta_{a,1}\beta_i^2, \mathcal{C}_i^a]$ with $a = \sigma_i(j)$. According to the induction hypothesis, there is a state $[w^\#, x^\#, y^\#, z^\#, \mathcal{C}_{i-1}] \in \mathcal{T}_{i-1}$ such that

$$w^\# \le \Delta^{i-1} w\,,\ x^\# \le \Delta^{i-1} x\,,\ y^\# \le \Delta^{i-1} y\,,\ z^\# \le \Delta^{i-1} z. \tag{4}$$

The trimmed algorithm generates the state $[w^\#, x^\#, y^\# + \delta_{a,1}\alpha_i^1 + \delta_{a,2}\beta_i^1, z^\# + \delta_{a,2}\alpha_i^2 + \delta_{a,1}\beta_i^2, \mathcal{C}_i^a] \in \mathcal{U}_i$ and may remove it during the trimming phase, but it must leave some state $t = [c_1^\#, c_2^\#, c_3^\#, c_4^\#, \mathcal{C}_i^a] \in \mathcal{T}_i$ that is in the same box as

$[w^{\#}, x^{\#}, y^{\#} + \delta_{a,1}\alpha_i^1 + \delta_{a,2}\beta_i^1, z^{\#} + \delta_{a,2}\alpha_i^2 + \delta_{a,1}\beta_i^2, \mathcal{C}_i^a] \in \mathcal{U}_i$. This state t is an approximation of s in the sense of (4).

Indeed, its first coordinate $c_1^{\#}$ satisfies

$$c_1^{\#} \leq \Delta(w^{\#}) \leq \Delta(\Delta^{i-1}w) \leq \Delta^i w = \Delta^i c_1, \tag{5}$$

its third coordinate $c_3^{\#}$ satisfies

$$\begin{aligned} c_3^{\#} &\leq \Delta(y^{\#} + \delta_{a,1}\alpha_i^1 + \delta_{a,2}\beta_i^1) \leq \Delta(\Delta^{i-1}y + \delta_{a,1}\alpha_i^1 + \delta_{a,2}\beta_i^1) \\ &\leq \Delta^i y + \Delta(\delta_{a,1}\alpha_i^1 + \delta_{a,2}\beta_i^1) \leq \Delta^i c_3 \end{aligned} \tag{6}$$

and its last coordinate is the same as s. By similar arguments, we can show that $c_2^{\#} \leq \Delta^i c_2$ and $c_4^{\#} \leq \Delta^i c_4$.

Now, let us assume that $j \notin J_L(i-1)$. In that case, the state s was obtained from a state $[w, x, y, z, \mathcal{C}_{i-1}] \in \mathcal{S}_{i-1}$ and either $s = [w + p_j, x, y + m_j + \alpha_i^1, z + \beta_i^2, \mathcal{C}_i^1]$ or $s = [w, x + p_j, y + \beta_i^1, z + m_j + \alpha_i^2, \mathcal{C}_i^2]$. We assume that $s = [w + p_j, x, y + m_j + \alpha_i^1, z + \beta_i^2, \mathcal{C}_i^1]$ as, with similar arguments, the rest of the proof is also valid for the other case. By the inductive assumption, there exists a state $[w^{\#}, x^{\#}, y^{\#}, z^{\#}, \mathcal{C}_{i-1}] \in \mathcal{T}_{i-1}$ that respects (4). The trimmed algorithm generates the state $[w^{\#} + p_j, x^{\#}, y^{\#} + m_j + \alpha_i^1, z + \beta_i^2, \mathcal{C}_i^1] \in \mathcal{U}_i$ and may remove it during the trimming phase. However, it must leave some state $t = [c_1^{\#}, c_2^{\#}, c_3^{\#}, c_4^{\#}, \mathcal{C}_i^1] \in \mathcal{T}_i$ that is in the same box as$[w^{\#} + p_j, x^{\#}, y^{\#} + m_j + \alpha_i^1, z + \beta_i^2, \mathcal{C}_i^1] \in \mathcal{U}_i$. This state t is an approximation of s in the sense of (4). Indeed, its last coordinate $\mathcal{C}_i^1$ is equal to $\mathcal{C}_i$ and, by arguments similar to those presented for $j \in J_L(i-1)$, we can show that $c_o^{\#} \leq \Delta^i c_o$, for $o \in [\![1, 4]\!]$. Thus, our assumption is valid during the transition from phase $i-1$ to i when i is an Introduce node.

Since the proof for the other type of nodes can be derived from the proof of an Introduce node, the inductive proof is completed. □

Now, let us go back to the proof of Theorem 1. After at most $4n$ phases, the untrimmed algorithm outputs the state $s = [c_1, c_2, c_3, c_4, \mathcal{C}]$ that minimizes the value $\max\{c_1, c_2\}$ such that $c_3 \leq M_1$ and $c_4 \leq M_2$. By Lemma 3, there exists a state $[c_1^{\#}, c_2^{\#}, c_3^{\#}, c_4^{\#}, \mathcal{C}] \in \mathcal{T}_n$ whose coordinates are at most a factor of Δ^{4n} above the corresponding coordinates of s. Thus, we conclude that our trimmed algorithm returns a solution where the makespan is at most Δ^{4n} times the optimal solution and the amount of memory for each machine is at most Δ^{4n} its capacity. Moreover, since $\Delta := 1 + \varepsilon/8n$, we have $\Delta^{4n} \leq 1 + \varepsilon$ for $\varepsilon \leq 2$.

So we have presented an algorithm that returns a solution such that the makespan is at most $(1 + \varepsilon)$ times the optimal solution and the amount of memory for each machine is at most $(1 + \varepsilon)$ its capacity. It ends the proof of Theorem 1.

5 Conclusion

Given 2 machines and a neighborhood graph of jobs with bounded tree-width, we have presented an algorithm that returns a solution, where the capacity of the machines may be exceeded by a factor at most $1+\varepsilon$, if at least one solution exists for the scheduling problem under memory constraints. This algorithm consists of three steps: construct a nice tree decomposition of the neighborhood graph; compute a specific bottom-up layout L of the nice tree decomposition; and use a transformed dynamic programming algorithm traversing the nice tree decomposition following L. Using layout L, the output of our algorithm is generated in polynomial time and is such that the makespan is at most $(1+\varepsilon)$ times the optimal solution and the amount of memory for each machine is at most $(1+\varepsilon)$ its capacity.

Although the algorithm is presented for 2 machines, it can be extended to any number of machines as adding machines means increasing the number of dimensions of a state. It would require to modify the combinatorial frontier such that $\sigma_i'(j)$ would be the machines on which j has not been assigned and which have memorized the data of j. This would change the time complexity to $O(n \times L_1^{2k} \times L_2^{2k} \times k \times tw(G) \times log(n) \times n^{2(ktw(G)+1)} \times 16^{ktw(G)} \times k^{4tw(G)})$ where n is the number of phases; $L_1^k \times L_2^k$ is the number of boxes, $L_1^k \times L_2^k \times k \times tw(G) \times log(n)$ is the processing time to compute if the states are the same; and $n^{2(ktw(G)+1)} \times 16^{ktw(G)} \times k^{4tw(G)}$ is the number of distincts combinatorial frontiers.

Now that we have provided a bi-FPTAS for graphs of bounded tree-width, it would be interesting to look at graphs bounded by more generic graph parameters like the clique-width and local tree-width. The latter is all the more interesting as we know that planar graphs have locally bounded tree-width and can be used to model numerical simulations on HPC architectures.

References

1. Ibarra, O.H., Kim, C.E.: Fast approximation algorithms for the knapsack and sum of subset problems. J. ACM **22**(4), 463–468 (1975)
2. Robertson, N., Seymour, P.: Graph minors. I. excluding a forest. J. Comb. Theory Ser. B **35**(1), 39–61 (1983)
3. Lenstra, J.K., Shmoys, D.B., Tardos, E.: Approximation algorithms for scheduling unrelated parallel machines. Math. Program. **46**(3), 259–271 (1990)
4. Kloks, T. (ed.): Treewidth: Computations and Approximations. LNCS, vol. 842. Springer, Heidelberg (1994). https://doi.org/10.1007/BFb0045375
5. Bodlaender, H.L.: A linear time algorithm for finding tree-decompositions of small treewidth. SIAM J. Comput. **25**(6), 1305–1317 (1996)
6. Woeginger, G.J.: When does a dynamic programming formulation guarantee the existence of a fully polynomial time approximation scheme (FPTAS)? INFORMS J. Comput. **12**(1), 57–74 (2000)
7. Woeginger, G.J.: A comment on scheduling two parallel machines with capacity constraints. Discret. Optim. **2**(3), 269–272 (2005)

8. Gairing, M., Monien, B., Woclaw, A.: A faster combinatorial approximation algorithm for scheduling unrelated parallel machines. Theor. Comput. Sci. **380**(1–2), 87–99 (2007)
9. Zhang, C., Wang, G., Liu, X., Liu, J.: Approximating scheduling machines with capacity constraints. In: Deng, X., Hopcroft, J.E., Xue, J. (eds.) FAW 2009. LNCS, vol. 5598, pp. 283–292. Springer, Heidelberg (2009). https://doi.org/10.1007/978-3-642-02270-8_29
10. Saha, B., Srinivasan, A.: A new approximation technique for resource-allocation problems. In: Proceedings of the Innovations in Computer Science (ICS), pp. 342–357 (2010)
11. Kellerer, H., Kotov, V.: A 3/2-approximation algorithm for 3/2-partitioning. Oper. Res. Lett. **39**(5), 359–362 (2011)
12. Angel, E., Chevalier, C., Ledoux, F., Morais, S., Regnault, D.: FPT approximation algorithm for scheduling with memory constraints. In: Dutot, P.-F., Trystram, D. (eds.) Euro-Par 2016. LNCS, vol. 9833, pp. 196–208. Springer, Cham (2016). https://doi.org/10.1007/978-3-319-43659-3_15
13. Chen, L., Jansen, K., Luo, W., Zhang, G.: An efficient PTAS for parallel machine scheduling with capacity constraints. In: Chan, T.-H.H., Li, M., Wang, L. (eds.) COCOA 2016. LNCS, vol. 10043, pp. 608–623. Springer, Cham (2016). https://doi.org/10.1007/978-3-319-48749-6_44
14. Chevalier, C., Ledoux, F., Morais, S.: A multilevel mesh partitioning algorithm driven by memory constraints. In: Proceedings of the SIAM Workshop on Combinatorial Scientific Computing, pp. 85–95 (2020)
15. Nguyen, T.T., Rothe, J.: Bi-criteria approximation algorithms for load balancing on unrelated machines with costs. In: 31st International Symposium on Algorithms and Computation (ISAAC 2020), pp. 1–14 (2020)

Data Management, Analytics and Machine Learning

mCAP: Memory-Centric Partitioning for Large-Scale Pipeline-Parallel DNN Training

Henk Dreuning[1,2](✉), Henri E. Bal[2], and Rob V. van Nieuwpoort[1,3]

[1] University of Amsterdam, Amsterdam, The Netherlands
{h.h.h.dreuning,R.V.vanNieuwpoort}@uva.nl
[2] Vrije Universiteit Amsterdam, Amsterdam, The Netherlands
bal@cs.vu.nl
[3] Netherlands eScience Center, Amsterdam, The Netherlands

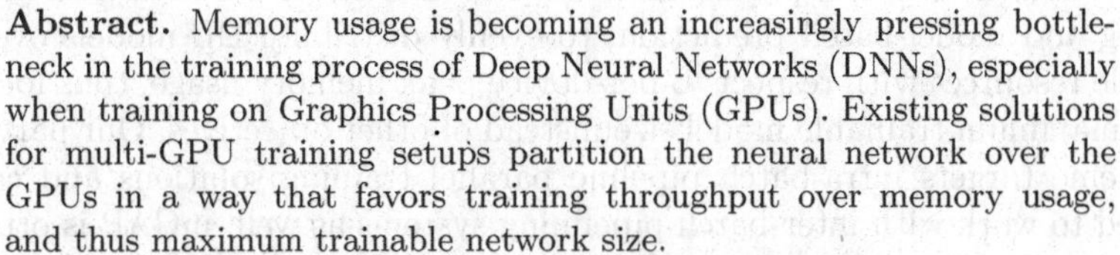

Abstract. Memory usage is becoming an increasingly pressing bottleneck in the training process of Deep Neural Networks (DNNs), especially when training on Graphics Processing Units (GPUs). Existing solutions for multi-GPU training setups partition the neural network over the GPUs in a way that favors training throughput over memory usage, and thus maximum trainable network size.

We propose mCAP, a partitioning solution for pipeline-parallel DNN training that focuses specifically on memory usage. It evenly distributes Deep Learning models over the available resources with respect to per-device peak memory usage. Our partitioning approach uses a novel *incremental profiling* strategy to extract per-layer memory usage statistics. A *model-based predictor* uses the profiling data to recommend a partitioning that balances peak memory usage. Our approach is DL-framework agnostic and orthogonal to existing memory optimizations found in large-scale DNN training systems. Our results show that our approach enables training of neural networks that are 1.55 times larger than existing partitioning solutions in terms of the number of parameters.

Keywords: Deep Learning · Pipeline Parallelism · HPC

1 Introduction

Deep Learning (DL) has facilitated breakthroughs in many application domains, including video analysis, natural language processing and speech recognition. The popularity of neural networks in these domains can be attributed partly to the development of new methods and algorithms, and partly to an increase in available compute power. Increasing the "depth" of neural networks, i.e. the number of hidden layers, often improves the performance of the models, as a deeper network can learn more complex input-output relations. Increased compute power has enabled training of deeper networks and has shortened the development times of neural network architectures.

J. Cano and P. W. Trinder (Eds.): Euro-Par 2022, LNCS 13440, pp. 155–170, 2022.
https://doi.org/10.1007/978-3-031-12597-3_10

However, as DL models, training datasets and individual training samples continue to grow in size, memory usage becomes an increasingly pressing bottleneck in Deep Neural Network (DNN) training. This bottleneck is especially apparent when training on Graphics Processing Units (GPUs), due to their limited memory capacity. To limit memory usage, developers are forced to resort to measures that severely reduce the effectiveness of their solutions, such as downsampling input data, reducing training batch sizes or shrinking DL model sizes. In some cases models cannot even be trained with such measures in place. Examples can be found in research areas such as high resolution image- and video-processing [5,6,15] and natural-language processing [13,16].

In this work, we present mCAP (memory-Centric Approach for Partitioning), a partitioning approach for multi-GPU pipeline-parallel DNN training. Existing pipelined training solutions, such as GPipe [7,9], PipeDream [11,13] and DAPPLE [5] prioritize training throughput when partitioning the model. This creates an imbalance in peak memory usage between devices, leading to a smaller trainable model size. Our partitioning solution uses novel methods, incremental profiling and model-based prediction, to evenly distribute DL models over the available resources with respect to per-device peak memory usage, thus focusing on the maximum trainable model size instead of other objectives. Our partitioning scheme targets intra-batch pipeline parallel training solutions and can be adjusted to work with inter-batch pipelining systems as well. mCAP is orthogonal to memory optimizations found in pipeline-parallel systems, such as efficient scheduling of forward and backward passes [5,13] and more generic optimizations, such as compression, recomputation and swapping of intermediate data to host memory [2,10,19].

Most existing partitioning and placement approaches aim to optimize achieved throughput and do not consider per-GPU memory usage. PipeDream and DAPPLE's planners only focus on equal per-GPU processing time and high throughput. GPipe leaves the task of partitioning the model to the programmer. However, TorchGPipe [9] (an implementation of GPipe in PyTorch) contains an automatic partitioner that optimizes throughput based on measurements of the execution time of the forward pass for each layer of the DL model.

Accurate predictions of per-GPU peak memory consumption are needed for automatic, memory-balanced partitioning. Predicting peak memory consumption is complex, because it is influenced by memory optimizations implemented at different levels of the DNN training software stack. Analytical modeling based on static analysis of the DL model does not capture the effects of these optimizations, making it infeasible to reach accurate predictions of peak memory usage using static techniques. mCAP uses novel profiling and prediction methods to recommend a partitioning with a balanced per-GPU peak memory usage, while automatically capturing the effects of a wide range of memory optimizations at the levels of the DL framework and pipeline-parallel training system.

mCAP **does not affect the convergence speed and accuracy** achieved by the DL model compared to other partitioning approaches, because the weight updates computed during training are not affected by the choice of partitioning.

Concretely, the contributions of this paper are as follows:

- We introduce a novel approach to DNN partitioning for multi-GPU training, focusing purely on reducing peak memory usage to enable the training of larger DL models. By focusing on maximum model size instead of training throughput, we make a different trade-off than existing approaches. We study the effects of this trade-off on training throughput.
- We provide an overview of memory-optimization techniques present in modern DL frameworks and explain the shortcomings of existing attempts to reach balanced peak memory usage across GPUs during DNN training.
- We use a novel profiling method, incremental profiling, for our partitioning.
- We present a prediction based partitioning algorithm that uses the profiling data to obtain balanced peak memory usage between GPUs.
- We demonstrate that our approach enables the training of DL networks that are up to 1.55 times larger than existing partitioning approaches.

2 Background and Related Work

Neural Network Training: the DNN training process consists of iterations in which a forward pass and backward pass are performed for a single batch of input data (a minibatch). When the forward and backward passes have been performed, the weights of the model are updated, which concludes the iteration.

As DNNs continue to grow in size and computational demand, DNN training is now moving towards high-performance computing infrastructures where multiple GPUs can be used simultaneously to train a DNN. State-of-the-art software solutions for multi-GPU training perform pipeline-parallel training.

Figure 1 shows the three layers of the software stack: the DL framework that implements the training operations, the pipelining system that implements pipeline parallelism, and the application layer.

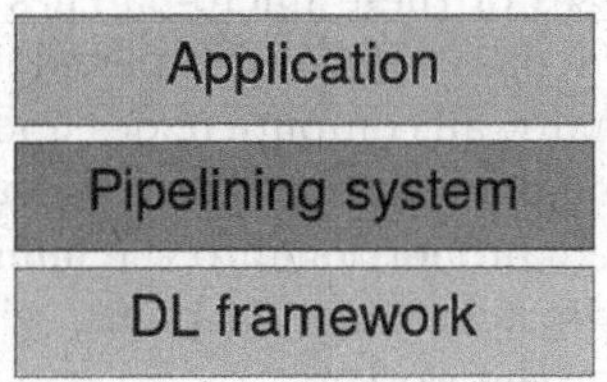

Fig. 1. Pipeline-parallel DNN training software stack

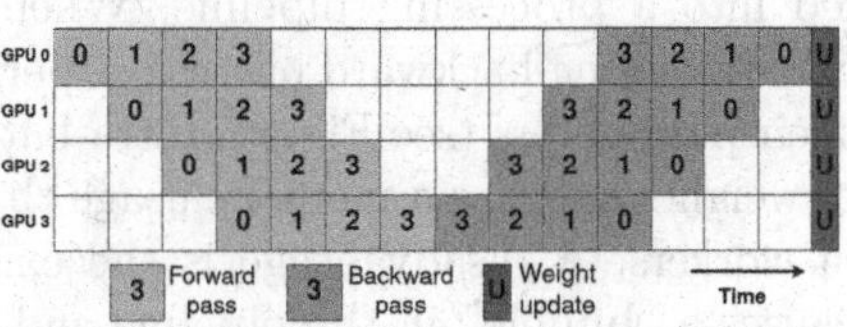

Fig. 2. Pipelined DNN training as performed by GPipe. Numbers indicate microbatch ids.

Existing Memory Optimizations: modern DL frameworks like PyTorch [14] and TensorFlow [1] include optimizations that reduce the memory usage on GPUs. With *early deallocation* of memory, the memory used for forward activations and gradients is released immediately after the backward pass and weight update have been performed for a given layer, instead of for the complete neural network. Another optimization at the level of the DL framework is *activation memory reuse*, in which the memory where activations are stored during the forward pass is re-used to store gradients in the backward pass.

An optimization that is not implemented at the level of the DL framework, but at the level of the pipelining system, is *activation recomputation.* Here forward activations are not kept in memory in between the forward and backward pass of a given layer, but discarded and recomputed again when they are needed during the backward pass.

Several other works have proposed methods to reduce GPU memory usage during training. In [19,22,26], the authors propose methods for memory pooling and swapping (temporarily) unused data (like activations) in GPU memory to main memory. In [2], the authors use Unified Memory capabilities to leverage host memory for out-of-core DNN training. Our approach is orthogonal to such approaches and can be used on top of training systems that implement these optimizations at the level of the DL-framework or the pipelining system.

Pipeline Parallelism: in pipeline-parallel training, the neural network is partitioned over the workers. For each minibatch, each worker performs the forward and backward pass for their part of the network, and activations and gradients are communicated between workers. As a result, the model size is no longer limited by the memory size of a single worker. To increase throughput minibatches are processed in a pipelined fashion. Multiple minibatches (or slices thereof) are consecutively fed into a pipeline, and workers perform forward- and backward-passes on these minibatches.

There are two types of pipeline parallelism. In intra-batch pipelining (such as implemented by GPipe [7,9] and DAPPLE [5]) a single minibatch is split into multiple micro-batches, and the forward passes of these micro-batches are fed into a processing pipeline. When all forward passes have completed, the corresponding backward passes are performed. Finally, all compute nodes update their parameters (see Fig. 2). Intra-batch pipelining does not introduce staleness of weights and has a memory usage that is inversely proportional to the number of workers. A disadvantage is the existence of a synchronization point, which causes a "bubble" in the pipeline and idle time for the workers.

In inter-batch pipelining (such as implemented by PipeDream [11,13]) complete minibatches are fed into the pipeline without splitting them into smaller entities (see Fig. 4). Multiple copies of the model's parameters are kept in memory to make sure forward and backward passes on a particular minibatch are performed with the same parameters. Inter-batch pipelining does not suffer from idle time because there is no system-wide synchronization point. Despite several improvements [13,25], staleness and increased memory usage caused by the need for multiple parameter versions remain disadvantages.

Partitioning Algorithms for Pipeline Parallelism: PipeDream [11] proposes a *planner* specific to inter-batch pipelining that outputs a balanced pipeline in terms of per-stage (GPU) computation time. This is achieved by profiling computation time per layer and estimating communication times with an analytical model. GPipe [7] leaves the task of partitioning the DL model to the programmer. TorchGPipe [9], an implementation of GPipe in PyTorch, provides automatic partitioning based on profiling the computation time needed for the forward pass of each layer. DAPPLE's [5] partitioner tries to achieve high throughput by minimizing the pipeline latency, which is determined by the latency of processing a single minibatch. RaNNC [24] is an intra-batch pipelining framework that performs automatic partitioning using atomic-level, block-level and stage-level partitioning.

All of these partitioning approaches focus on finding the partitioning that achieves the highest throughput. Contrary to existing work, our work proposes a partitioning approach that aims for a balanced pipeline in terms of memory usage, enabling training of larger models. To that end, it models the effects of memory optimizations implemented in the pipelining system, such as activation recomputation. Our approach currently targets intra-batch pipeline parallelism.

Other Large-scale DNN Training Paradigms: MeshTensorflow [20] and Megatron-LM [21] are systems that partition individual tensor operations over multiple accelerators as opposed to layers. Megatron-LM does not provide automatic partitioning and only supports transformer models. In [12], the authors combine tensor partitioning with pipeline parallelism, but do not improve the memory footprint over existing approaches. ZeRO [17] partitions model states over workers to save memory, but focuses on data and model parallelism.

3 Method

We propose mCAP, a partitioning approach for pipeline-parallel DNN training that determines how the DL model is partitioned over the workers (GPUs). Our partitioning approach focuses on achieving balanced peak memory usage across all GPUs during DNN training, to enable the training of larger DL models. By using a novel profiling strategy called *incremental profiling* mCAP automatically captures and models the effects of a wide range of memory optimizations that are present in DL frameworks, such as the ones described in Sect. 2 (early deallocation and activation memory reuse). This makes our approach agnostic to which framework is used at the DL framework layer. Moreover, by combining the incremental profiling strategy with our *model-based prediction algorithm*, mCAP models the memory usage of intra-batch pipelining systems and the optimizations they implement (like activation recomputation).

This section discusses mCAP's design and shows how the combination of *incremental profiling* and our *model-based prediction algorithm* is capable of capturing the memory behavior of intra-batch pipeline-parallel training systems.

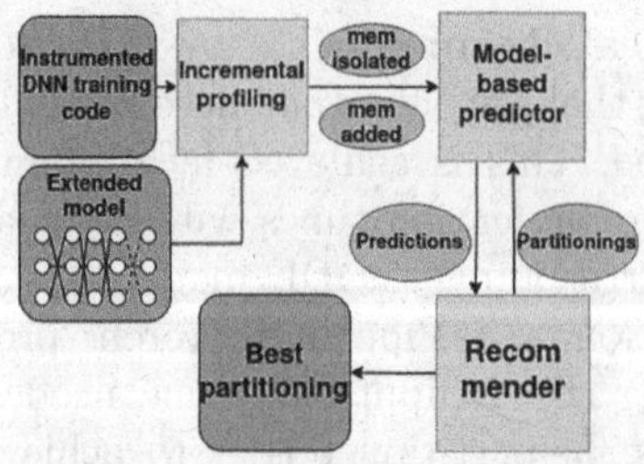

Fig. 3. Overview of mCAP.

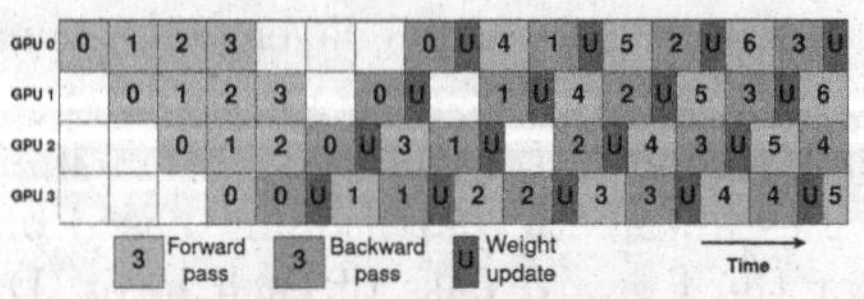

Fig. 4. Pipelined DNN training as performed by PipeDream. Numbers indicate minibatch ids.

Figure 3 shows an overview of our partitioning approach. The approach consists of three parts: incremental profiling, prediction, and recommendation. In the profiling phase, we collect data about the peak memory usage of each GPU during training for several, specifically selected partitionings. From this profiling data, we extract two statistics for each layer in the neural network. In the recommendation phase, these statistics form the input to the predictor, which accurately predicts the memory usage for a set of partitionings generated by the recommender. The recommender applies a search strategy to find the partitioning(s) with the lowest peak memory usage across the GPUs based on the predictions. We explain the workflow step-by-step.

3.1 Profiling

The profiling stage collects per-layer statistics that can be used in the prediction stage. We instrumented pipeline parallel DNN training code to monitor the peak memory usage for each GPU during the training process. Short profiling runs are then performed in the same setup (DL framework, pipelining system, hyper-parameters and hardware) as in the final training run for which we are finding a memory-balanced partitioning. In these profiling runs all training stages are executed: forward passes, backward passes and update steps. Therefore, they automatically capture the effects of memory optimizations at the DL framework level for *all training stages*.

The profiling runs are performed with a specifically selected set of partitionings. The selected set of partitionings is such that for each layer l, we run (with $l > n >= 0$):

(a) a partitioning where layer l is the only one on a GPU, and;
(b) a partitioning where layers n to $l-1$ are placed on a GPU, and;
(c) a partitioning where layers n to l are placed on a GPU.

Figure 5 shows examples of partitionings described by requirements (a), (b) and (c). During selection of these partitionings, we keep n as small as possible.

The above selection requirements ensure that we can extract two metrics for each layer l in the DL model from the profiled data: (1) the peak memory usage when layer l is the only one on a GPU and (2) the effect on peak memory of adding layer l to an existing set of layers on a GPU. We extract the former directly from the partitionings described by requirement (a) and call this metric *mem_isolated*(l), while we extract the latter from the difference in peak memory usage between the partitionings described by requirements (b) and (c), and call it *mem_added*(l). These two per-layer metrics capture the data needed to accurately predict the memory usage for all possible partitionings.

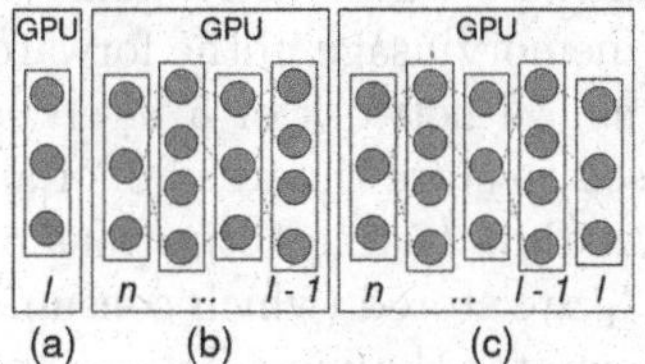

Fig. 5. Examples of partitionings described by requirements (a), (b) and (c).

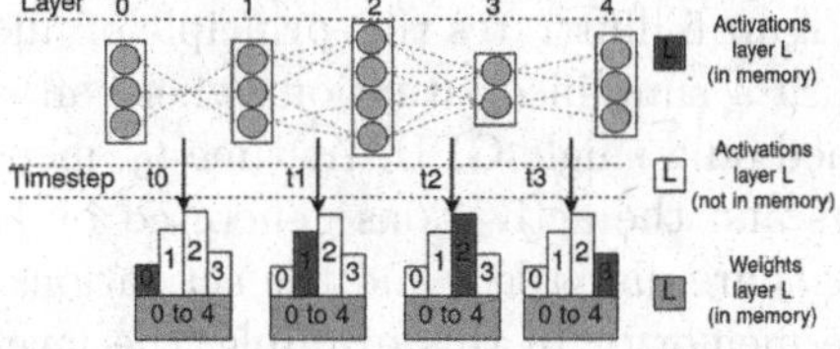

Fig. 6. GPU memory usage for weights and activations during the forward pass.

It is important to make the distinction between *mem_isolated*(l) and *mem_added*(l) because a layer's contribution to peak memory usage depends on its position on the GPU it is assigned to. Inspection of these metrics for AmoebaNet-D(36, 544) showed that the difference between the two metrics is significant, ranging to hundreds of Megabytes per layer. The difference is caused by optimizations such as activation recomputation and the presence of communication buffers to send the activations of the last layer on a GPU to the next GPU in the pipeline. The next subsections show how our predictor models the effects of such optimizations on memory usage, using both metrics as input.

3.2 Peak Memory Usage for Intra-batch Pipelining with Activation Recomputation

This subsection describes how the recomputation optimization implemented in most intra-batch pipelining systems (including TorchGPipe) affects the peak memory consumption. Optimizations such as recomputation do not simply lower the peak memory consumption for each layer individually, but influence peak memory in a more complex manner. We created our prediction algorithm to model such influences of recomputation and other (potentially future) optimizations in intra-batch pipelining systems on peak memory usage.

The peak memory consumption on a GPU in a pipelined system is constituted by two main factors: the memory needed for the weights of the layers hosted by the GPU, and the memory needed for the activations generated by those layers. In intra-batch pipelining, the memory needed for a layer's weights is constant. Recall from Sect. 2 that with activation recomputation, a layer's activations are discarded as soon as the activations for the next layer have been computed. The activations for the former layer are then recomputed when they are needed again in the backward pass. As a result, the amount of memory required to store activations fluctuates during the forward and backward passes of a single microbatch. Hence, the *peak* memory consumption of the GPU is determined by the one layer on the GPU that requires the most memory for its activations.

Figure 6 illustrates this principle of fluctuating memory usage in the forward pass in a simplified situation, where an example neural network of 5 layers is trained on a single GPU. At time t_0, memory is used to store the weights of all layers and the activations generated by layer l_0. At time t_1, the activations of layer l_0 are discarded, and the activations of layer l_1 are stored (which consume more memory). In this example, the layer that generates the most activations is layer l_2, which means the peak memory consumption for this neural network during the forward pass is dictated by that layer. This principle extends to the backward pass in similar fashion.

3.3 Prediction

To find the partitioning with the lowest peak memory usage across all GPUs, we predict the peak memory usage for a set of partitionings. This set is determined by the recommender (see Sect. 3.4) and forms the input to the predictor, together with the per-layer data described in Sect. 3.1. The predictor estimates the peak memory usage for each partitioning in the set as shown in listing 1.1.

Our partitioning algorithm automatically models the effects that different layers have on the peak memory consumption on a GPU, as described in Sect. 3.2, by means of its design. When predicting the memory usage for a given partitioning, it first considers the peak memory usage that is obtained when only the first layer that is assigned to the GPU, is placed (which corresponds to the *mem_isolated* statistic). Figure 7.a illustrates this situation. It then models the changes in peak memory consumption that are caused by adding the remaining layers to the GPU, by adding the *mem_added* statistic layer-by-layer. Two scenarios exist for each added layer: it generates less activations than the preceding one (Fig. 7.b) and the peak memory of the GPU is only affected by the added layer's weights, or it outputs more activations than the preceding layer (Fig. 7.c), and the peak memory usage increases due to the added layer's weights *and* activations.

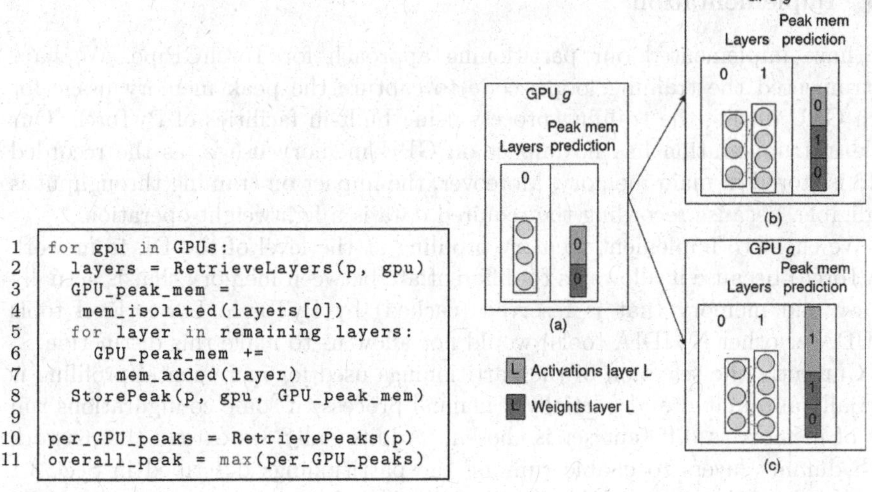

```
for gpu in GPUs:
  layers = RetrieveLayers(p, gpu)
  GPU_peak_mem =
    mem_isolated(layers[0])
  for layer in remaining layers:
    GPU_peak_mem +=
      mem_added(layer)
  StorePeak(p, gpu, GPU_peak_mem)

per_GPU_peaks = RetrievePeaks(p)
overall_peak = max(per_GPU_peaks)
```


Listing 1.1. Peak memory prediction for a given partitioning.

Fig. 7. *Model-based prediction* scenarios.

3.4 Recommendation

mCAP supports two mechanisms to search for the partitioning with the lowest peak memory usage across all GPUs: *Brute-Force (mCAP-BF)* and *Bayesian Optimization (mCAP-BO)*.

mCAP-BF predicts the peak memory usage for all possible $P_{all} = \binom{L-1}{G-1}$ partitionings (where L is the number of layers to partition over G GPUs), and selects the partitioning with the lowest peak memory usage from the prediction outcomes. We apply a tie-breaking rule if there are multiple partitionings with the same lowest predicted peak memory usage. For each remaining candidate, we exclude the GPU with the highest peak memory usage GPU_{peak} in that partitioning and select the candidate that has the best balanced (lowest) peak memory usage across the remaining GPUs. This is a realistic alternative selection criterion if the prediction for GPU_{peak} was inaccurate.

mCAP-BO applies Bayesian Optimization to search for the partitioning with the lowest predicted peak memory usage. Each GPU forms a dimension of the search space and the parameter range is determined by the number of layers that can be placed on the GPU.

The choice between *mCAP-BF* and *mCAP-BO* can be made based on the value of P_{all}. *mCAP-BF* is guaranteed to find the partitioning with the lowest predicted peak memory usage in the search space and is cost efficient enough for limited values of P_{all}. When P_{all} is large (because the DL model has many layers and/or many GPUs are used), it pays off to use *mCAP-BO*. While *mCAP-BO* is not guaranteed to find the partitioning with the lowest peak memory usage from the full search space, it is less expensive in terms of execution time for larger values of P_{all} (see Sect. 4.3).

3.5 Implementation

We have implemented our partitioning approach for TorchGPipe. We have instrumented the training loop's code to capture the peak memory usage for each GPU during the training process using built-in facilities of PyTorch. Our code instrumentation has no impact on GPU memory usage, as the recorded data is stored in main memory. Moreover, the impact on training throughput is negligible, because recording the required data is a lightweight operation.

We chose to implement memory profiling at the level of the DL framework (PyTorch) because it allows us to differentiate between memory that is actually in use and memory that is reserved (cached) by PyTorch. Lower level tools (CUDA or other NVIDIA tools) would not allow us to make this distinction.

Currently the selection of the partitionings used for incremental profiling is partially automated and partially a manual process (if some configurations run out of memory, a different set is chosen). Additionally, we extend the network with dummy layers to enable running the partitionings described in Sect. 3.1 for each layer in the neural network. We plan the implementation of a fully automated version of this process for future work.

We use the DDLBench benchmarking framework [8] to run our experiments. We extended the code of the benchmarking suite and TorchGPipe to parameterize some variables of the training process, such as the partitioning to use. We use *scikit-optimize* to implement the Bayesian Optimization process for the *mCAP-BO* recommendation mode.

Applying mCAP to a different pipelining system or DL framework requires the re-implementation of the instrumentation of the training loop and the parameterization of variables, such as the partitioning to use. These changes can be implemented in approximately 100 lines of code.

4 Experiments

4.1 Experimental Setup

We apply our partitioning approach to two DL models. First, we do experiments with a relatively small neural network, VGG11 [23], to evaluate to what extent mCAP is able to find an optimally memory-balanced partitioning. We then do experiments with a larger, scalable DL model, AmoebaNet-D [18], to see how far we can increase the size of the neural network without running out of memory. We perform this experiment for the partitioning recommended by mCAP and compare the results to the partitioning chosen by TorchGPipe's throughput-oriented partitioner.

We perform multiple experiments using a single DL model with an adjustable size, rather than with multiple different fixed-sized models, because we want to obtain a precise comparison between the maximum trainable model size with mCAP and TorchGPipe's partitioner. We compare to a throughput-oriented partitioner because, to the best of our knowledge, no other memory-oriented partitioners exist for pipeline-parallel training. We do not compare to solutions that are orthogonal to pipeline-parallel training with our partitioning approach. Examples of orthogonal solutions are leveraging host memory to virtually increase the GPU memory size, through activation and weight swapping or Unified Memory techniques [2,19,22,26].

We note that the statistical performance (how fast the neural network learns and achieved accuracy) is not affected by the choice of partitioning. The learning operations performed by the pipelining system are mathematically identical, regardless of the partitioning. We do therefore not explicitly evaluate the statistical performance of the partitioning selected by mCAP. We use randomly generated images of 224×224 pixels as training data in our experiments, consistent with images from the ImageNet dataset [3].

The training runs performed in the profiling stage only have to last a very limited number of epochs and can be performed with a small dataset size. This is because the peak memory usage is steady after the first epoch and the peak memory usage is not dependent on the size of the dataset. In our experiments, the time required for profiling is in the order of minutes per profiling run. The number of required profiling runs is $L - G + 1$. The set of profiling partitionings used in our experiments is: {1-1-1-R, 2-1-1-R, ..., R-1-1-2, R-1-1-1}, where R denotes the remaining layers of the DL model. The time needed by the prediction algorithm ranges from seconds to minutes, depending on the number of possible partitionings and the recommendation mode. We consider this overhead negligible, given that the final run for which we are searching a balanced partitioning typically lasts several days to weeks. Moreover, the aim of our approach is to enable training of larger models, not to increase throughput.

The Bayesian Optimization process of *mCAP-BO* performs 75 iterations, uses *scikit-optimize*'s *gp_hedge* acquisition function with the *sampling* acquisition optimizer, *xi* and *kappa* set to 1000 to favor exploration over exploitation and the default Matérn kernel.

Our experiments are performed on nodes containing 4 NVIDIA Titan RTX GPUs with 24 GB GDDR6 memory. The GPUs are connected to the host through PCIe 3.0 x16. We use PyTorch version 1.5.0 and TorchGPipe as the pipelining system.

4.2 VGG11

We perform experiments with VGG11 to evaluate how accurate our prediction algorithm is. We first use VGG11 because it is a relatively small network (132.9 million parameters) with a limited number of layers (30), so the amount of possible partitionings of the model over 4 GPUs is also limited (3654). It is therefore feasible to perform training runs for all possible partitionings, to get an overview of the memory usage and computational performance for *all datapoints in the partitioning space.* This experiment is only focused on validating that our approach selects a partitioning with a low peak memory usage from the full partitioning space.

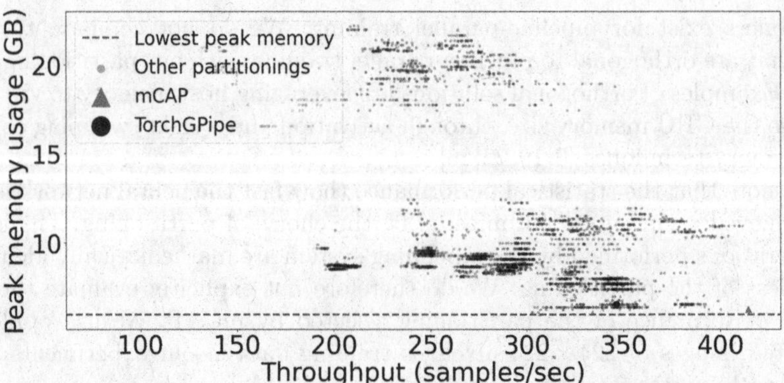

Fig. 8. Memory usage and throughput of all possible partitionings. The partitionings selected by mCAP (yellow) and TorchGPipe (red) are highlighted. (Color figure online)

Figure 8 shows the achieved peak memory usage and throughput of training VGG11 for all possible partitionings on a 4-GPU node, with TorchGPipe. Each run performs 2 training epochs with a training dataset size of 5000 samples, an overall batch size of 1104, consisting of 12 microbatches of 92 samples each, the Stochastic Gradient Descent optimizer with a momentum of 0.9, a weight decay of 1×10^{-4} and a learning rate of 0.1. The partitionings selected by mCAP and TorchGPipe's automatic partitioner are highlighted. Given the limited number of possible partitionings, we use the *mCAP-BF* recommendation mode.

Our approach selects the partitioning (3-3-5-19) with the 3rd-lowest peak memory usage of all partitionings. Our predictor slightly underestimates the peak memory usage of the selected partitioning and deems it equivalent to the partitionings with the lowest peak (the horizontal green line). The tie-breaking rule then works in favor of the selected partitioning. Its peak memory usage is 1.05x higher than the lowest peak, while that is 1.10x for the partitioning selected by TorchGPipe's partitioner. That partitioning (6-2-5-17) achieves 0.84x the throughput of the best performing partitioning, which is the one selected by our approach. These observations confirm that mCAP selects a partitioning from the full partitioning space that has relatively low peak memory usage.

Figure 9.a shows the per-GPU peak memory usage of mCAP's and TorchGPipe's partitioning (predicted and measured). The partitioning selected by mCAP, while being the one with the 3rd-lowest memory usage, is still relatively unbalanced (the standard deviation is 0.95). We attribute this to the small partitioning space of VGG11. Because the network is split at the level of layers and the number of layers in VGG11 is limited, a partitioning with an (almost) perfectly balanced memory usage simply does not exist (the standard deviation of the best performing partitioning amongst the ones with the absolute lowest peak memory usage is still 0.73). We study the memory gain in a more realistic scenario, with a larger network, in Sect. 4.3.

Figure 10 shows a histogram of the error between peak memory usage as predicted by our prediction algorithm and the actual peak memory consumption, for all 3654 possible partitionings. Our predictor is able to predict the peak with an error margin smaller than 14% error in 90% of the cases.

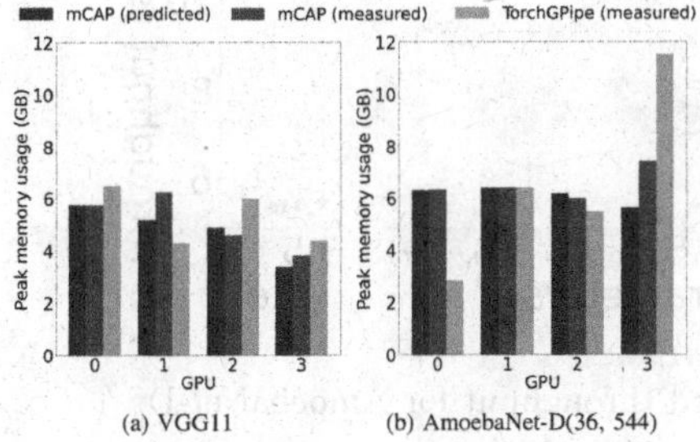

Fig. 9. Per-GPU peak memory usage.

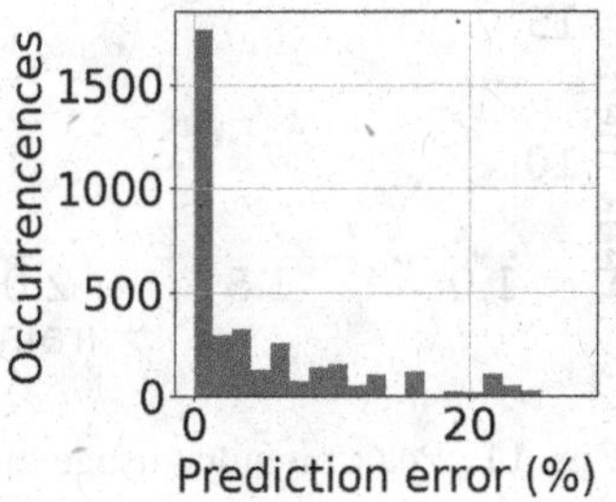

Fig. 10. Prediction error histogram.

4.3 AmoebaNet-D

We now experiment with a larger network (AmoebaNet-D) to see how much reduction in peak memory usage and potential network growth our partitioner realistically achieves.

AmoebaNet-D(L, F) has 2 parameters that determine the size of the neural network: L and F for layers and filters respectively. We first apply our partitioning approach to AmoebaNet-D(36, 544). With these parameters, the neural network has 1.06 billion trainable parameters.

We perform the training runs in this experiment with an overall batch size of 32, consisting of 4 microbatches of 8 samples each. The input data and remaining training- and hyperparameters are identical to the ones used before. We use the *mCAP-BO* recommendation mode (and *mCAP-BF* for reference).

Figure 9.b shows the per-GPU peak memory usage of AmoebaNet-D(36, 544) for mCAP's partitioning (predicted and measured) and TorchGPipe's partitioning. mCAP's partitioning is considerably more balanced in peak memory usage. The measured peak has a standard deviation of 0.53 across all GPUs, while that is 3.15 for TorchGPipe's partitioning. mCAP's partitioning reaches a 35% reduction in peak memory usage compared to TorchGPipe's partitioning.

Our experiments showed that *mCAP-BO* recommends the same partitioning for AmoebaNet-D(36, 544) as *mCAP-BF*, validating the effectiveness of *mCAP-BO* in navigating the search space. It also reduces the prediction time by 2.6x compared to *mCAP-BF* (from 99.5 to 38.8 s). We expect this gain to increase when more GPUs or DNNs with even more layers are used.

Next, we determine how far we can scale the network up with mCAP's partitioning. We use the F (filters) parameter to increase the number of trainable parameters in AmoebaNet-D. To find the maximum value for F that we can train with mCAP's partitioning, we perform a binary search.

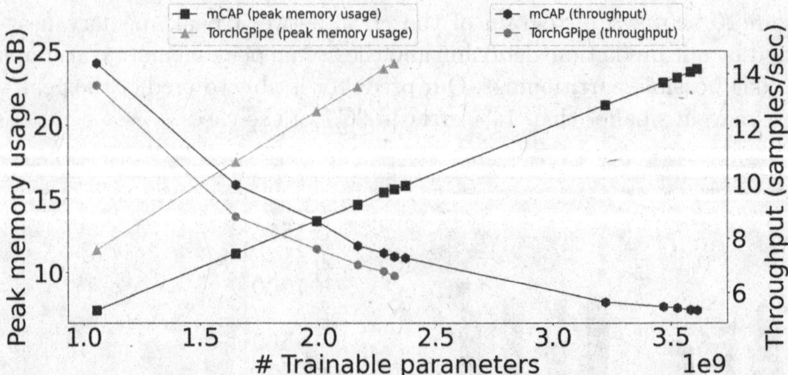

Fig. 11. Peak memory usage and achieved throughput for AmoebaNet-D.

Figure 11 shows the peak memory usage (and throughput) for each successful training run of the binary search, plotted against the network size of AmoebaNet-D. The size of the DL model is expressed in the number of trainable parameters, which is determined by L and F. The peak memory usage is consistently higher for TorchGPipe's partitioning, and grows faster with network size than for mCAP's partitioning. The maximum trainable network size for mCAP's partitioning is 1.55 times larger than for TorchGPipe's partitioning (3.61B vs 2.32B trainable parameters).

Figure 11 also shows the achieved throughput for each value of F used in the scaling experiment. Although it is not our focus, mCAP's partitioning achieves 10.5% higher throughput on average than TorchGPipe's partitioning.

5 Conclusion and Future Work

We proposed mCAP, a partitioning approach for multi-GPU pipeline-parallel DNN training that focuses purely on achieving balanced peak memory usage across GPUs. mCAP uses a combination of incremental profiling and model-based prediction. Through profiling our approach automatically captures the effects of memory optimizations implemented at the DL framework level and can thus (after re-implementation of the memory profiling) be applied in combination with any modern DL framework. mCAP's model-based predictor targets intra-batch pipelining systems and can be easily adjusted to support inter-batch pipelining systems as well. Applying mCAP does not affect the statistical performance compared to other partitioning approaches, because the performed learning operations are mathematically identical.

We demonstrated that mCAP recommends a partitioning with a low peak memory usage from the full partitioning space. mCAP provides the *brute-force* recommendation mode for limited search spaces and the *Bayesian Optimiztion* mode to efficiently find a memory-balanced partitioning in a large search space.

mCAP can train neural networks that are 1.55 times larger than existing partitioning solutions. We plan to automate partitioning selection and network manipulation for the incremental profiling phase for future work. We also plan to port Bayesian Optimization to the GPU to further reduce *mCAP-BO*'s runtime.

Acknowledgements and Data Availability Statement. We would like to thank the anonymous reviewers for their valuable feedback. This work is part of the Efficient Deep Learning (EDL) programme (grant number P16-25), financed by the Dutch Research Council (NWO). This work was carried out on the Dutch national e-infrastructure with the support of SURF Cooperative. The datasets generated during and/or analysed during the current study are available in the Figshare repository: https://doi.org/10.6084/m9.figshare.20000960 [4].

References

1. Abadi, M., et al.: TensorFlow: a system for large-scale machine learning. In: OSDI, pp. 265–283 (2016)
2. Awan, A.A., et al.: OC-DNN: exploiting advanced unified memory capabilities in CUDA 9 and Volta GPUs for out-of-core DNN training. In: HiPC, pp. 143–152. IEEE (2018)
3. Deng, J., et al.: ImageNet: a large-scale hierarchical image database. In: CVPR, pp. 248–255. IEEE (2009)
4. Dreuning, H., et al.: Artifact and instructions to generate experimental results for Euro-Par 2022 paper: mCAP: Memory-Centric Partitioning for Large-Scale Pipeline-Parallel DNN Training (2022). https://doi.org/10.6084/m9.figshare.20000960
5. Fan, S., et al.: DAPPLE: a pipelined data parallel approach for training large models. In: PPoPP, pp. 431–445 (2021)
6. Hara, K., et al.: Learning spatio-temporal features with 3D residual networks for action recognition. In: ICCV Workshops, pp. 3154–3160 (2017)
7. Huang, Y., et al.: GPipe: efficient training of giant neural networks using pipeline parallelism. In: NeurIPS, pp. 103–112 (2019)
8. Jansen, M., et al.: DDLBench: towards a scalable benchmarking infrastructure for distributed deep learning. In: 2020 IEEE/ACM Fourth Workshop on Deep Learning on Supercomputers (DLS), pp. 31–39. IEEE (2020)
9. Kim, C., et al.: Torchgpipe: on-the-fly pipeline parallelism for training giant models. arXiv preprint arXiv:2004.09910 (2020)
10. Mittal, S., Vaishay, S.: A survey of techniques for optimizing deep learning on GPUs. J. Syst. Archit. **99**, 101635 (2019)
11. Narayanan, D., et al.: PipeDream: generalized pipeline parallelism for DNN training. In: SOSP, pp. 1–15 (2019)
12. Narayanan, D., et al.: Efficient large-scale language model training on GPU clusters using Megatron-LM. In: SC21, pp. 1–15 (2021)
13. Narayanan, D., et al.: Memory-efficient pipeline-parallel DNN training. In: ICML, pp. 7937–7947. PMLR (2021)
14. Paszke, A., et al.: PyTorch: an imperative style, high-performance deep learning library. In: NeurIPS, pp. 8026–8037 (2019)
15. Pinckaers, H., Litjens, G.: Training convolutional neural networks with megapixel images. arXiv preprint arXiv:1804.05712 (2018)

16. Raffel, C., et al.: Exploring the limits of transfer learning with a unified text-to-text transformer. arXiv preprint arXiv:1910.10683 (2019)
17. Rajbhandari, S., et al.: ZeRO: memory optimizations toward training trillion parameter models. In: SC20, pp. 1–16. IEEE (2020)
18. Real, E., et al.: Regularized evolution for image classifier architecture search. In: Proceedings of the AAAI Conference on Artificial Intelligence, vol. 33, pp. 4780–4789 (2019)
19. Rhu, M., et al.: vDNN: virtualized deep neural networks for scalable, memory-efficient neural network design. In: MICRO, pp. 1–13. IEEE (2016)
20. Shazeer, N., et al.: Mesh-Tensorflow: deep learning for supercomputers. In: NeurIPS, pp. 10414–10423 (2018)
21. Shoeybi, M., et al.: Megatron-LM: training multi-billion parameter language models using GPU model parallelism. arXiv preprint arXiv:1909.08053 (2019)
22. Shriram, S., et al.: Dynamic memory management for GPU-based training of deep neural networks. In: IPDPS, pp. 200–209. IEEE (2019)
23. Simonyan, K., Zisserman, A.: Very deep convolutional networks for large-scale image recognition. arXiv preprint arXiv:1409.1556 (2014)
24. Tanaka, M., et al.: Automatic graph partitioning for very large-scale deep learning. In: IPDPS, pp. 1004–1013. IEEE (2021)
25. Yang, B., et al.: PipeMare: asynchronous pipeline parallel DNN training. MLSys **3**, 269–296 (2021)
26. Zhang, J., et al.: Efficient memory management for GPU-based deep learning systems. arXiv preprint arXiv:1903.06631 (2019)

Analysing Supercomputer Nodes Behaviour with the Latent Representation of Deep Learning Models

Martin Molan[1(✉)], Andrea Borghesi[1], Luca Benini[1,2], and Andrea Bartolini[1]

[1] DISI and DEI Department, University of Bologna, Bologna, Italy
{martin.molan2,andrea.borghesi3,luca.benini,a.bartolini}@unibo.it
[2] Institut für Integrierte Systeme, ETH, Zürich, Switzerland

Abstract. Anomaly detection systems are vital in ensuring the availability of modern High-Performance Computing (HPC) systems, where many components can fail or behave wrongly. Building a data-driven representation of the computing nodes can help with predictive maintenance and facility management. Luckily, most of the current supercomputers are endowed with monitoring frameworks that can build such representations in conjunction with Deep Learning (DL) models. In this work, we propose a novel semi-supervised DL approach based on autoencoder networks and clustering algorithms (applied to the latent representation) to build a digital twin of the computing nodes of the system. The DL model projects the node features into a lower-dimensional space. Then, clustering is applied to capture and reveal underlying, non-trivial correlations between the features.

The extracted information provides valuable insights for system administrators and managers, such as anomaly detection and node classification based on their behaviour and operative conditions. We validated the approach on 240 nodes from the Marconi 100 system, a Tier-0 supercomputer located in CINECA (Italy), considering a 10-month period.

Keywords: supercomputer monitoring · deep Learning · unsupervised learning · autoencoders · predictive maintenance

1 Introduction

High Performance Computing systems have been steadily rising in size and complexity in the last years, as revealed by the exponential increase of the worldwide supercomputer installation[1]. HPC systems are typically composed by replicating a large number of components, usually, in the order of thousands of computing nodes, each of them constituted of a collection of smaller functional parts, such as CPUs, RAM, interconnections, storage, etc. Even if similar by design, each

[1] https://www.top500.org/.

J. Cano and P. W. Trinder (Eds.): Euro-Par 2022, LNCS 13440, pp. 171–185, 2022.
https://doi.org/10.1007/978-3-031-12597-3_11

computing node is affected by manufacturing variability and variations in the operating conditions. The sheer size and complexity of supercomputers create huge challenges in terms of optimal management of the IT components and their significant energy footprint [1]. The race towards Exascale[2] continues to make these challenges ever more pressing [3–5].

Overall, it is a daunting task for system administrators and facility managers to optimize supercomputer performance and power consumption, identify anomalous behaviors faulty situations, and guarantee systems operate in optimal conditions. The scale of the problem motivates the development of automated procedures for anomaly detection and faulty node identification in current supercomputers and this need will become even more pressing for future Exascale systems [6]. The fact that most of today's HPC computing systems are endowed with monitoring infrastructures [7] that gather data from software (SW) and hardware (HW) components can be of great help toward the development of data-driven automated approaches. Historically, system management was performed through hand-crafted scripts and direct intervention of system administrators; most of the data is stored in log files, and anomalies are investigated a posteriori to find the source of reported problems (e.g., when many users recognize the failure and report it to administrators). At the finer granularity, each core of the processing element is equipped with performance counters which can monitor several micro-architectural events (i.e., cache misses, stalls, throughput) and physical means (i.e., temperature, power consumption, and clock frequency). Processing units as well as the motherboard, the power distribution units, the onboard voltage regulators, the PCIe devices, and the fans are equipped with hardware (HW) sensors and counters. Similarly, software components can provide useful information as well, ranging from the details about jobs submitted by users (e.g., information gathered by job dispatchers such as SLURM [8] or PBS [9]) to software tools performing health-check of various subsystems [10] and I/O monitoring [11].

As the amount of data is overwhelming for human operators, automated processes could be highly beneficial in improving the data center usage to ease the burden of human operators and lower the response time to failures. In this context, Artificial Intelligence (AI) can provide significant benefits, as it allows to exploit the available big data effectively and to create decision support tools for HPC system administrators and facility managers [12,13]. In the past, many works from the literature and the practice demonstrated the possibility to extract useful information using data collected from HPC computing nodes and employing supervised Deep Learning (DL) models [14–16] and semi-supervised ones [17–19]. These methods have been applied to detect nodes' availability, defined as operation without anomalies. Availability and the corresponding error rate (1 minus availability rate) is a key metric of the node's performance, and a target for optimization of the HPC system operation [20]. Due to its importance, we focus on the availability rate in the experimental part of this paper.

---

[2] The supercomputer peak performance is expected to reach the ExaFlops ($10^1 8$) scale in 2023 [2].

Borghesi et al. in [18] show that semi-supervised anomaly detection models trained on individual nodes data outperform a single model trained on multinode data. This suggests that the semi-supervised model can learn differences between nodes even if the nodes share the same design and composition. Theoretically, the learned model encapsulates the node's characteristics, however to the best of our knowledge, no one has ever evaluated the feasibility of using the disparities between trained DL models to evaluate the differences between the behavior of the corresponding nodes. In this work, we answer this question by introducing a novel approach that focuses on the latent representation of the trained DL models (in particular on the coefficients, the weights of the latent layer); the approach can identify clusters that deviate from the overall (node) population's average availability, relying on the DL model parameters.

We focused on a Tier0 supercomputer composed of 985 nodes for which we trained a series of per-node semi-supervised DL models based on autoencoders (AE), as proposed by authors in [19], the state-of-the-art for semi-supervised anomaly and fault detection in HPC systems. We focus on semi-supervised methods as the availability of labels cannot be taken for granted in a supercomputer due to the non-negligible cost of annotating the vast wealth of monitored data. We explored different approaches to extract features from the weights and biases of the latent layer of the AE model. The key idea is to apply a geometric transformation to the weight matrix underlying the latent layer of the trained AEs; we opted to explore a variety of transformations; namely, we compute: (1) the vector of singular values, (2) the singular vector corresponding to the largest singular value, (3) the map of the representative vector (with and without bias), (4) the weights matrix similarity in L1, L2, and absolute L2 norm, (5) the affine (augmented matrix) similarity in L1, L2, and absolute L2 norm. The empirical evaluation demonstrates that the vector of singular values identifies interesting clusters among the different methods to extract salient features from the latent representation.

We propose to use the deviation from population average availability to evaluate the goodness of the clustering results. The vector of singular values, extracted from the weights matrix of the latent layer of the trained autoencoder, identifies two clusters with average overall availability lower than 89% (compared to 96% population average). The proposed method's ability to identify these clusters is significant as the autoencoders have no access to the availability label during training.

2 Related Work

Since anomalies in HPC systems are rare events, the problem of anomaly detection cannot be treated as a classical supervised learning problem [17,21]; the majority of works that treat it in a fully supervised fashion have been tested using synthetic [14,22] or injected anomalies [15]. Instead of learning the properties of both relevant classes, the standard approach is to learn just the properties of the system's normal operation - anything deviating from this normal operation is then recognized as an anomaly. Machine learning models are trained only on normal data to learn the characteristics of the normal operation. This training of ML models on normal data is called *semi-supervised* training [18].

The state-of-the-art for anomaly detection on the HPC system is to train a particular class of neural networks – called autoencoders – in a semi-supervised way [19]. Autoencoders are a specific type of neural networks that are trained to reproduce an input signal while simultaneously learning the most efficient latent representation of the data [23]. The latent representation of the data has a lower dimension than the original data; this lower dimension of the latent layer naturally leads to the idea of using autoencoders as pre-processing step before applying clustering techniques [24–26], as most of the clustering algorithms have worse performance in high-dimensional spaces [27]. The autoencoders are first trained on the whole dataset when using autoencoders as a dimension-reduction step before clustering. Then the dataset is projected (by the encoder part of the network) into a lower-dimensional latent layer [24].

Current approaches that combine clustering and autoencoder neural networks use a single trained autoencoder to encode each instance into a latent space. The state-of-the-art for HPC anomaly detection, however, is to train multiple models (a different model for each node in the system) [19]. The fact that the models trained on individual nodes outperform the model trained on combined data of all nodes [17–19] suggests that there are significant differences between the behavior of the compute nodes and, consequently, the corresponding trained models. Thus, this paper's contribution is to explore the possibility of leveraging the fact that we are training multiple AE models to explore the relationship between the nodes themselves. Specifically, we explore the possibility to extract features from the trained neural networks to perform the clustering of the *whole operation history* of the compute nodes.

3 Methodology

In this section we present the architecture of the proposed approach. We start by providing the probabilistic perspective underlying the foundations of our approach in Sect. 3.1. We then describe in more detail the general architecture (Sect. 3.2) and the proved the more detailed description of the method in Sect. 3.3 and Sect. 3.4.

3.1 Probabilistic Background

The idea of extracting information and comparing trained neural networks extends the standard methodology of statistical modeling where two (or more) populations (or generally a collection of instances) are compared by contrasting parameters of fitted distributions. Comparing the parameters of fitted functions is the key idea underlying the proposed approach. Let us consider as an example the common statistical problem of comparing two populations of individuals - specifically, we want to compare a specific random variable X in two distinct populations (e.g., height in two different countries). The first point of comparison in such cases is to calculate *empirical mean* $\overline{x} = \frac{1}{N}\sum_{i=1}^{N} x_i$ and *empirical variance* $\frac{1}{n-1}\sum_{i=1}^{N}(x_i - \overline{x})^2$. Two populations can be compared by looking at the empirical mean and variance of the random variables of interest (observed variables present inside each population).

The mathematical foundation of comparing mean and variance between two populations is directly in line with the idea of this paper. If we are observing two large populations, we know (from the central limit theorem [28]) that the sum of the variables will tend towards a Gaussian distribution. Two parameters determine Gaussian distribution: expected value μ and variance σ^2 [28]; to fit the Gaussian distribution to the data (population), we thus have to estimate these two parameters. If we fit the distribution via the Maximum Likelihood Estimation (MLE) method, [29], we see that the best estimator for the expected value is *empirical mean* and for variance, the best estimator is *empirical variance.* From the probability theory, we know that the difference of two random Gaussian variables is Gaussian variable with mean that is the difference of means and variance that is the sum of variances [28]. Comparing population mean and population variance is thus actually equivalent to comparing the *Gaussian distributions* fitted to the data.

Another perspective from which to examine the problem of comparing populations is that we fit a *function* to the data (this function being the Gaussian distribution). For some problems - like High Performance Computer (HPC) system monitoring - autoencoders (type of neural networks) achieve state-of-the-art results [18,19]. As autoencoders are the class of functions that best describe this specific class of problems (behavior of compute node in an HPC system), we examine if we can compare the *compute nodes* by comparing the parameters of the fitted autoencoders.

3.2 General Overview of the Approach

Figure 1 reports the block diagram of the proposed methodology. We can identify the following steps:

1. On each node, a separate autoencoder model is trained. Semi-supervised training of per-node autoencoder models is adopted from the state-of-the-art paper [19].
2. After models are trained on each node, features are extracted (as described in Sect. 3.4) from the deep learning models.
3. Based on these extracted features, the similarity between nodes is calculated. Calculation of similarity can be done as the autoencoder projects the input features into a *latent* representation where only the most salient correlations between the input variables are preserved. The similarity measure is calculated by comparing the representation maps - specifically, the parameters of the latent layer.
4. This similarity measure is then used in hierarchical clustering.

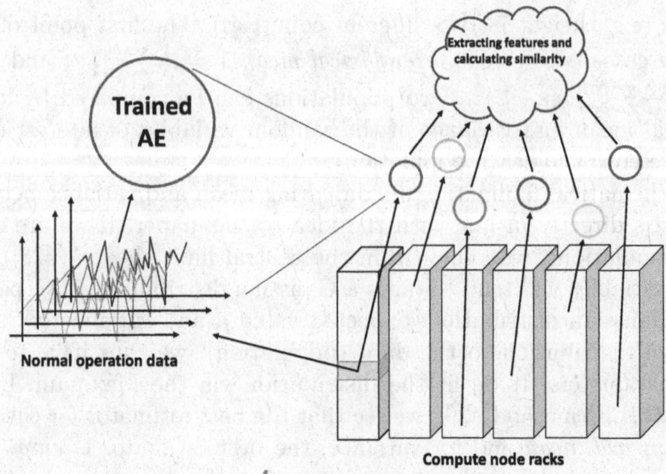

Fig. 1. Data flow schema. On each of the nodes (red in the picture), organized into racks, we train a separate autoencoder model (circles). From these trained models we extract features that are then used in the clustering of nodes. (Color figure online)

3.3 Autoencoder Models

Dense autoencoders are a type of deep neural network, which can be characterized by different topology; those used in this work have a distinct hourglass shape, a choice motivated by the results obtained by previous works in the state-of-the-art[3]. The most relevant information of the network is encoded in the latent layer. In this particular type of autoencoder, the latent layer is the layer in the middle of the network and contains the fewest neurons. It is preceded by the encoder and succeeded by the decoder, each composed of one or multiple layers. The encoder and decoder layers used in this work have a symmetrical architecture, which, generally speaking, is not strictly required. The fundamental role of the network is to efficiently encode the information from the input in a compressed representation in the latent layer. Training of the autoencoder is driven by the reproduction error produced by the decoder; reproduction error, which is the difference between the real input and the reconstructed signal, is minimized during training. The architecture of the network used in this work is presented in Fig. 2. It is adapted from the work by Borghesi et al. [19] where it has been shown to produce state-of-the-art results in detecting anomalies on an HPC system.

The set of autoencoders - as in original work [19] - are individually trained on each node in a semi-supervised setting. Semi-supervised training means that the data for training is filtered of all anomalies and that only the normal instances are used in training the model.

[3] They are also referred to as *contractive autoencoders*.

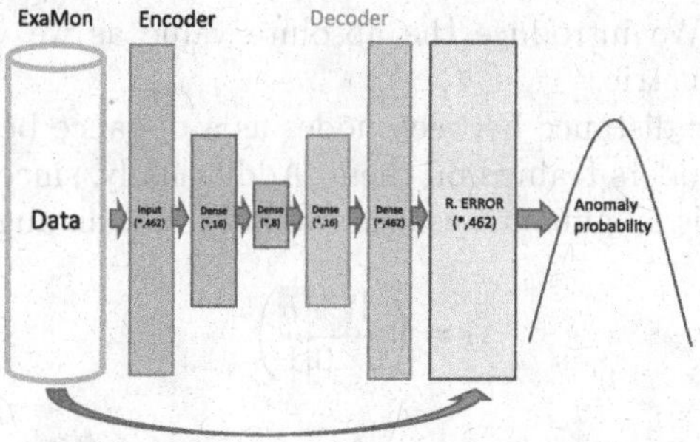

Fig. 2. Architecture of the state-of-the-art model, proposed by [19]. In this paper, relevant information is extracted from the latent layer Dense (*,8). Data is collected for the ExaMon monitoring system [12].

3.4 Feature Extraction

Due to the architecture of the neural network used in this work - as discussed in Sect. 3.3 - we extract the relevant features from each node (each one with its data set); these features are embedded in the weights of the latent layer. The latent layer is described by the weights matrix W and the bias vector $\vec{b}$. The activation of the latent layer is given by $\vec{a}' = f(W\vec{a} + \vec{b})$ where f if a nonlinear activation function. In the next subsections, we will describe different encoding approaches of the latent layer information, which will then be used to extract features.

Singular Value Decomposition. Singular value decomposition represents matrix M as $M = USV^*$ where S is a diagonal matrix containing singular values [30]. In this work, we used singular value decomposition on W, and we extracted the *vector* of singular values (abbreviated to singular values in the future) and a singular *vector* corresponding to the largest singular value (abbreviated singular vector).

Representative Vector. A vector of ones $\vec{1}$ is used as a representative vector as it corresponds to the activation of all neurons in a latent layer. It can serve as a proxy for the transformation of the (linear part) of the latent layer. For each node, we have thus calculated the product of $W\vec{1}$ (abbreviated vector of ones) and $W\vec{1} + \vec{b}$ (abbreviated vector of ones plus bias).

Matrix Measures. In this work, we leveraged the L1 and L2 norms induced in the matrix space (induced by p norms for vectors) [31]. Based on these norms we propose two ways to calculate distance between two matrices: $distance = ||A - B||_p$ and absolute distance $abs\_distance = |||A - B||_p|$ where p is 1 or 2. Since the $L1$ measure is already symmetric, we do not separate a case with absolute distance. We introduce the absolute value as we want our distance measure to be symmetric.

We calculate the distance between nodes as a distance between the weights matrices of autoencoders trained on them. Additionally, since the linear part of the neural network is an affine transform, we introduce an augmented matrix A:

$$A = \left(\begin{array}{c|c} W & \vec{b} \\ \hline 0...0 & 1 \end{array}\right).$$

This matrix A captures the affine transform since $\vec{a}' = W\vec{a} + \vec{b}$ is equivalent to

$$\begin{pmatrix} \vec{a}' \\ 1 \end{pmatrix} = A \begin{pmatrix} \vec{a} \\ 1 \end{pmatrix}.$$

Another way to calculate the distance between nodes is to calculate the distance between an affine transform that is determined by the (affine $W\vec{a} + \vec{b}$) part of the latent layer of the corresponding autoencoder.

3.5 Clustering

The calculated distance between clusters is an input for clustering. In this work, we use agglomerative hierarchical clustering: each instance (in our case node) starts as its cluster. At every step of the iteration, the two closest clusters are connected. The connection between clusters is the closest distance between two instances in corresponding clusters. The combining of clusters is repeated until we reach the predetermined number of clusters.

3.6 Evaluating Clustering

There are several possible measures to evaluate the goodness of the clustering (e.g., Silhouette score) [32]. These scores, however, are not applicable in the scenario explored by this work. We evaluate different possible feature extraction methods from the trained autoencoders; these different feature extraction approaches produce different feature spaces. Thus we cannot compare the clustering score (like Silhouette score) *between different spaces*. For this reason, we evaluate the relevance of our clustering approaches by evaluating how "interesting" the created clusters are.

The interest of clusters is reflected by how well they separate a specific variable. Since clustering is an unsupervised method, it is reasonable to assume that not all clusters will separate the same variable (such clustering would produce distinctly *uninteresting* clusters). However, we expect that there would be at least one cluster where the distribution of the target variable would be significantly different than it is in the whole dataset. In this work, the target variable is system availability. In other words, clusters will separate computing nodes based on the autoencoder model's latent layer encoding in groups having similar availability, thus similar failure rate. We stress that from a practical point of view, this means that an autoencoder model for each node is trained only on "normal" operation samples and contains the information on the likelihood of the node to be available (or not to fail). Clusters of nodes sharing the same failure's likelihood can be used to rationalize the maintenance procedure.

In the whole dataset, the system is available 0.96179% of the time. The most interesting cluster is thus the one where the average availability of a cluster will be as far away from this population average. The best clustering method is the one producing the most interesting cluster.

3.7 Random Sampling Baseline

The relevance of the produced clusters determines the relevance of feature extraction and, consequently, of clustering approaches. Specifically, we observe how well the clusters separate a target variable (in the case of this work, the node's availability). To claim the relevance of the clustering approaches, we compare them to random sampling. We compare how well the target variable is separated by random sampling to how well clustering methods separate it. We are particularly interested in clustering methods that produce clusters and separations that do not (are very unlikely to occur) in random separation.

This paper implemented random clustering by producing a random matrix (of the same size and range as extracted features) that is then passed to clustering algorithms. The produced clusters are thus equivalent to random sampling without replacement. The generation of random clusters is repeated several (in this work 10) times. For each cluster, the distribution of the target variable is calculated; this distribution is then compared to distributions given by clustering methods. In the results (Sect. 4), the range of randomly generated distributions is presented as a box with whiskers plot. Distributions outside the range of random distributions represent interesting patterns uncovered by the clustering method.

4 Results

This section presents the results of the experimental analysis conducted on a tier-0 supercomputer, Marconi100, hosted at CINECA, the largest Italian computing center. The results were conducted on a statistically significant fraction of the supercomputing nodes (more than two hundred) and cover a 10-months time span of production activity of the system.

4.1 Experimental Setting

As explained in the methodology Sect. 3, an individual model was trained on each of the 241 randomly selected nodes of Marconi100. Models were trained semi-supervised, meaning that only normal operation data was used for training. The whole dataset consists of 10 months of operational data collected on Marconi100. The first eight months of the data were used as a training set and the *last two* as a test set. Autoencoder models were trained on the train set. The cluster analysis was performed only on the test set.

The dataset used in this work consists of a combination of information recorded by Nagios (the system administrators tool used to visually check the health status of the computing nodes) and the Examon monitoring systems; the data encompasses the first ten months of operation of the M100 system. The features collected in the dataset are listed in Table 1. In order to align different sampling rates of different reporting services, 15 min aggregates of data points were created. 15 min interval was chosen as it is the native sampling frequency of the Nagios monitoring service (where our labels come from). Four values were calculated for each 15 min period and each feature: minimum, maximum, average, and variance.

Table 1. An anomaly detection model is created only on hardware and application monitoring features. More granular information regarding individual jobs is not collected to ensure the privacy of the HPC system users.

Source	Features
Hardware monitoring	ambient temp., dimm[0-15] temp., fan[0-7] speed, fan disk power, GPU[0-3] core temp., GPU[0-3] mem temp., gv100card[0-3], core[0-3] temp., p[0-1] io power, p[0-1] mem power, p[0-1] power, p[0-1] vdd temp., part max used, ps[0-1] input power, ps[0-1] input voltage, ps[0-1] output current, ps[0-1] output voltage, total power
System monitoring	CPU system, bytes out, CPU idle, proc. run, mem. total, pkts. out, bytes in, boot time, CPU steal, mem. cached, stamp, CPU speed, mem. free, CPU num., swap total, CPU user, proc. total, pkts. in, mem. buffers, CPU idle, CPU nice, mem. shared, PCIe, CPU wio, swap free

Features extracted from trained autoencoders are passed to hierarchical clustering. Hierarchical clustering has been chosen as it only requires the pairwise distance between the instances without making any assumptions about the space induced by the distance measure. The number of clusters is set to 20 for all experiments. A number of clusters is not a tuned parameter; 20 clusters represents roughly 10% of all nodes and is a randomly chosen number.

4.2 Trained Autoencoder

The trained autoencoder is adopted from the current state-of-the-art semi-supervised approach for anomaly detection [19]. The structure of the autoencoder is presented in Fig. 3. The autoencoder used as a binary classifier (form the normalized reconstruction error) on the test set achieves the AUC (area under the receiver-operator characteristic curve) of 0.7602.

Normal operation (the data where the autoencoder is trained) is determined by the label (system availability) provided by the monitoring systems.

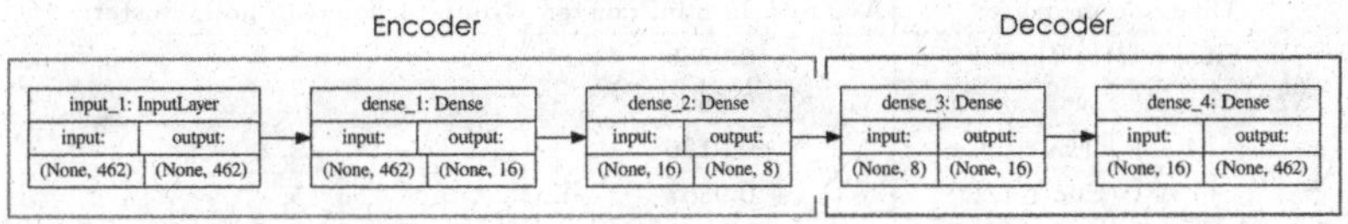

Fig. 3. Architecture of the autoencoder network, adopted from Borghesi et al. [19]

4.3 Cluster Analysis: Normal Operation Percentage

The proposed approach aims to identify interesting clusters of nodes that behave similarly. The similarity in behavior is also reflected in the fact that a cluster will have similar values for at least one relevant feature. In this section, we evaluate the similarity in average availability rate - in other words, we are interested in seeing if the clustering methods can identify clusters with particularly low availability (high failure rate). The average failure rate amongst 241 identified nodes (in the test set) is 0.96179. We wish to identify clusters with significantly lower availability rate.

In Table 2, the minimum average availability rates in a cluster, unidentified by a specific feature extraction approach, are reported. The table shows that the vector of singular values combined by the euclidean distance metric identifies a cluster with the minimum average availability. This availability is also lower than the random method's minimum availability (ever achieved).

In Fig. 4 and Fig. 5 average availability per node is plotted (red dots). Results of random sampling without replacement are presented as a box plot. The average error rate across all nodes (0.96179) is marked with a violet dotted line. Area of values, observed in a random process, are marked with gray. Values *never* observed by the random process are left white.

Analyzing Figs. 4 and 5 we observe that only the vector of singular values produced cluster with averages never observed in random samples.

The clustering method based on a vector of singular values combined with euclidean distance identifies two clusters with particularly low average availability. Such low average availability has also never occurred in a random selection of clusters. Low average availability means that hierarchical clustering based on singular value decomposition of weights matrix produces non-trivial clusters that are extremely unlikely to be matched by a random selection of clusters.

Identifying interesting clusters regarding availability is a non-trivial result as a neural network has no access to that label during training.

This promising result suggests that the created clusters share similar availability, and thus clusters can be created based on autoencoder semi-supervised

Table 2. Minimum average availability within clusters identified by different feature extraction methods. Vector of singular values identifies a cluster with the lowest average availability (highest anomaly rate). This is the most interesting method as it separates the target variable (node availability) the best. None of the proposed methods identify a cluster with a single node.

Distance measure:	Avg ava. in min. cluster:	Num. of nodes in min. cluster:
Sing. vector (Euc.)	0.9286	6
Vector of sing. values (Euc.)	0.8809	7
$W\vec{1} + \vec{b}$ (Euc.)	0.9126	8
$W\vec{1}$ (Euc.)	0.9367	5
W (absolute L2)	0.9191	7
A (absolute L2)	0.9276	5
W (L2)	0.9239	7
A (L2)	0.9124	10
W (L1)	0.9303	8
A (L1)	0.9303	8
Random sampling	0.9021	Not applicable

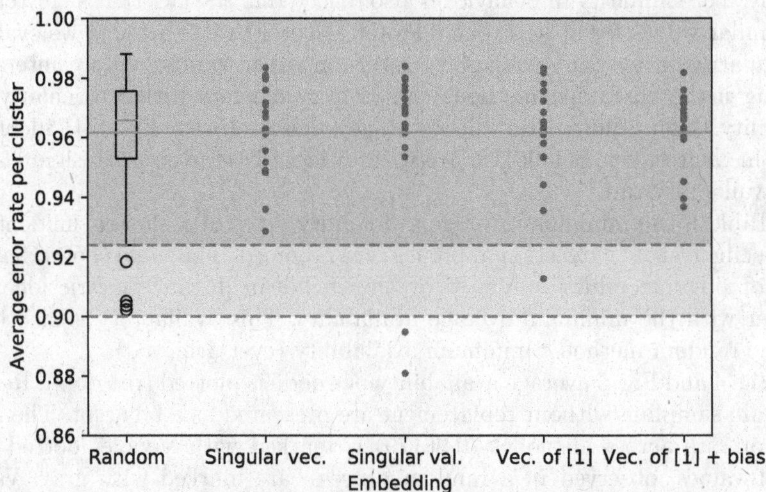

Fig. 4. Average error rate per cluster. Representation of nodes with a vector of singular values identifies two clusters with significantly higher anomaly rate than the whole population. (Color figure online)

models latent layer information. This cluster can then be used during the system's lifetime to create canaries to focus the maintenance over nodes belonging to the same cluster of the canary node.

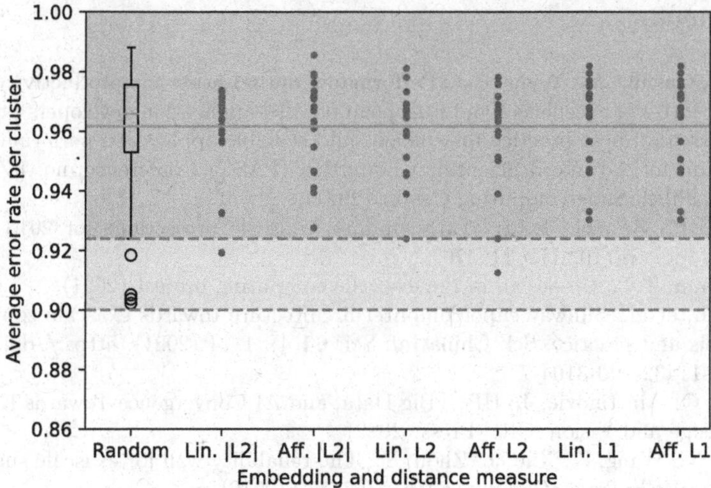

Fig. 5. Average error rate per cluster. Matrix-based feature extraction performs worse than the vector methods. (Color figure online)

5 Conclusions

This work opens the possibility of extracting additional information from the state-of-the-art approach towards anomaly detection in the HPC setting. Besides using per-node autoencoder models for anomaly detection [17–19], it is also possible to construct informative clusters from the parameters of the trained neural networks themselves.

We demonstrate the usefulness of the identified clusters on a concrete example: identifying clusters with the abnormal failure rate. This result is significant as the neural networks, from where the features are extracted, have no *access to that label during training.* Still, our approach can identify two clusters of nodes with lower availability (higher failure rate) than the population average.

We stress the fact that with this approach, clusters can be created based on a model trained on the first month of operations and then applied for the remaining lifetime of the system to focus maintenance to the nodes belonging to the same cluster containing the node which has experienced failures. System administrators focus their regular inspections only on canary nodes, each representative of one cluster.

Acknowledgments. This research was partly supported by the EuroHPC EU PILOT project (g.a. 101034126), the EuroHPC EU Regale project (g.a. 956560), EU H2020-ICT-11-2018-2019 IoTwins project (g.a. 857191), and EU Pilot for exascale EuroHPC EUPEX (g. a. 101033975). We also thank CINECA for the collaboration and access to their machines and Francesco Beneventi for maintaining Examon.

References

1. Garcia-Gasulla, M., Wylie, B.J.: Performance optimisation and productivity for EU HPC centres of excellence (and European parallel application developers preparing for exascale): best practice for efficient and scalable application performance. In: Platform for Advanced Scientific Computing (PASC) Conference, no. FZJ-2022-00887, Jülich Supercomputing Center (2021)
2. Kogge, P., Resnick, D.R.: Yearly update: exascale projections for 2013 (2013). https://doi.org/10.2172/1104707
3. Germann, T.C.: Co-design in the exascale computing project (2021)
4. Gao, J., et al.: Sunway supercomputer architecture towards exascale computing: analysis and practice. Sci. China Inf. Sci. **64**(4), 1–21 (2021). https://doi.org/10.1007/s11432-020-3104-7
5. Terzo, O., Martinovič, J.: HPC, Big Data, and AI Convergence Towards Exascale: Challenge and Vision. CRC Press (2022)
6. Yang, X., Wang, Z., Xue, J., Zhou, Y.: The reliability wall for exascale supercomputing. IEEE Trans. Comput. **61**(6), 767–779 (2012)
7. Stefanov, K.S., Pawar, S., Ranjan, A., Wandhekar, S., Voevodin, V.V.: A review of supercomputer performance monitoring systems. Supercomput. Front. Innov. **8**(3), 62–81 (2021)
8. Yoo, A.B., Jette, M.A., Grondona, M.: SLURM: simple Linux utility for resource management. In: Feitelson, D., Rudolph, L., Schwiegelshohn, U. (eds.) JSSPP 2003. LNCS, vol. 2862, pp. 44–60. Springer, Heidelberg (2003). https://doi.org/10.1007/10968987_3
9. A. P. Works, PBS professional®14.2 plugins (hooks) guide (2017). https://pbsworks.com/pdfs/PBSHooks14.2.pdf
10. Dang, T., Nguyen, N., Chen, Y.: HiperView: real-time monitoring of dynamic behaviors of high-performance computing centers. J. Supercomput. **77**(10), 11807–11826 (2021)
11. Yang, B., et al.: End-to-end {I/O} monitoring on a leading supercomputer. In: 16th USENIX Symposium on Networked Systems Design and Implementation (NSDI 2019), pp. 379–394 (2019)
12. Bartolini, A., et al.: Paving the way toward energy-aware and automated datacentre. In: Proceedings of the 48th International Conference on Parallel Processing: Workshops, ICPP 2019. Association for Computing Machinery, New York (2019). https://doi.org/10.1145/3339186.3339215
13. Wu, N., Xie, Y.: A survey of machine learning for computer architecture and systems. ACM Comput. Surv. (CSUR) **55**(3), 1–39 (2022)
14. Tuncer, O., Ates, E., Zhang, Y., et al.: Online diagnosis of performance variation in HPC systems using machine learning. IEEE Trans. Parallel Distrib. Syst. **30**, 883–896 (2018)
15. Netti, A., Kiziltan, Z., Babaoglu, O., Sîrbu, A., Bartolini, A., Borghesi, A.: A machine learning approach to online fault classification in HPC systems. Future Gener. Comput. Syst. **110**, 1009–1022 (2019)
16. Bose, A., Yang, H., Hsu, W.H., Andresen, D.: HPCGCN: a predictive framework on high performance computing cluster log data using graph convolutional networks. In: 2021 IEEE International Conference on Big Data (Big Data), pp. 4113–4118. IEEE (2021)
17. Borghesi, A., Bartolini, A., et al.: Anomaly detection using autoencoders in HPC systems. In: Proceedings of the AAAI Conference on Artificial Intelligence (2019)

18. Borghesi, A., Bartolini, A., Lombardi, M., Milano, M., Benini, L.: A semisupervised autoencoder-based approach for anomaly detection in high performance computing systems. Eng. Appl. Artif. Intell. **85**, 634–644 (2019). https://doi.org/doi.org/10.1016/j.engappai.2019.07.008. https://www.sciencedirect.com/science/article/pii/S0952197619301721
19. Borghesi, A., Molan, M., Milano, M., Bartolini, A.: Anomaly detection and anticipation in high performance computing systems. IEEE Trans. Parallel Distrib. Syst. **33**(4), 739–750 (2022). https://doi.org/10.1109/TPDS.2021.3082802
20. Netti, A., Shin, W., Ott, M., Wilde, T., Bates, N.: A conceptual framework for HPC operational data analytics. In: 2021 IEEE International Conference on Cluster Computing (CLUSTER), pp. 596–603 (2021). https://doi.org/10.1109/Cluster48925.2021.00086
21. Aksar, B., et al.: Proctor: a semi-supervised performance anomaly diagnosis framework for production HPC systems. In: Chamberlain, B.L., Varbanescu, A.-L., Ltaief, H., Luszczek, P. (eds.) ISC High Performance 2021. LNCS, vol. 12728, pp. 195–214. Springer, Cham (2021). https://doi.org/10.1007/978-3-030-78713-4_11
22. Aksar, B., et al.: E2EWatch: an end-to-end anomaly diagnosis framework for production HPC systems. In: Sousa, L., Roma, N., Tomás, P. (eds.) Euro-Par 2021. LNCS, vol. 12820, pp. 70–85. Springer, Cham (2021). https://doi.org/10.1007/978-3-030-85665-6_5
23. Bank, D., Koenigstein, N., Giryes, R.: Autoencoders, CoRR abs/2003.05991 (2020). arxiv:2003.05991
24. Song, C., Liu, F., Huang, Y., Wang, L., Tan, T.: Auto-encoder based data clustering. In: Ruiz-Shulcloper, J., Sanniti di Baja, G. (eds.) CIARP 2013. LNCS, vol. 8258, pp. 117–124. Springer, Heidelberg (2013). https://doi.org/10.1007/978-3-642-41822-8_15
25. Li, X., Chen, Z., Poon, L.K., Zhang, N.L.: Learning latent superstructures in variational autoencoders for deep multidimensional clustering. arXiv preprint arXiv:1803.05206 (2018)
26. Wang, W., Yang, D., Chen, F., Pang, Y., Huang, S., Ge, Y.: Clustering with orthogonal autoencoder. IEEE Access **7**, 62421–62432 (2019)
27. Alam, A., Muqeem, M., Ahmad, S.: Comprehensive review on clustering techniques and its application on high dimensional data. Int. J. Comput. Sci. Netw. Secur. **21**(6), 237–244 (2021)
28. Davis, B., McDonald, D.: An elementary proof of the local central limit theorem. J. Theor. Probab. **8**(3), 693–702 (1995)
29. Cam, L.L.: Maximum likelihood: an introduction. Int. Stat. Rev./Revue Internationale de Statistique **58**(2), 153–171 (1990). http://www.jstor.org/stable/1403464
30. Fronckova, K., Prazak, P., Slaby, A.: Singular value decomposition and principal component analysis in face images recognition and FSVDR of faces. In: Światek, J., Borzemski, L., Wilimowska, Z. (eds.) ISAT 2018. AISC, vol. 853, pp. 105–114. Springer, Cham (2019). https://doi.org/10.1007/978-3-319-99996-8_10
31. Belitskii, G., et al.: Matrix Norms and Their Applications, vol. 36. Birkhäuser (2013)
32. Murtagh, F., Contreras, P.: Algorithms for hierarchical clustering: an overview. Wiley Interdiscip. Rev. Data Min. Knowl. Disc. **2**(1), 86–97 (2012)

Accelerating Parallel Operation for Compacting Selected Elements on GPUs

Johannes Fett, Urs Kober, Christian Schwarz, Dirk Habich(✉), and Wolfgang Lehner

Database Research Group, Technische Universität Dresden, Dresden, Germany
{johannes.fett,urs.kober,christian.schwarz,dirk.habich, wolfgang.lehner}@tu-dresden.de

Abstract. Compacting is a common and heavily used operation in different application areas like statistics, database systems, simulations and artificial intelligence. The task of this operation is to produce a smaller output array by writing selected elements of an input array contiguously back to a new output array. The selected elements are usually defined by means of a bit mask. With the always increasing amount of data elements to be processed in the different application areas, better performance becomes a key factor for this operation. Thus, exploiting the parallel capabilities of GPUs to speed up the compacting operation is of great interest. In this paper, we present different optimization approaches for GPUs and evaluate our optimizations (i) on a variety of GPU platforms, (ii) for different sizes of the input array, (iii) for bit distributions of the corresponding bit mask, and (iv) for data types. As we are going to show, we achieve significant speedups compared to the state-of-the-art implementation.

Keywords: Compacting · GPU · Optimization · Parallel

1 Introduction

A common observation in different application domains like statistics, database systems, simulations and artificial intelligence is that highly parallel algorithms in these domains usually produce sparse data or data containing unwanted elements [11,16,17]. To achieve a high performance for the following algorithm steps, it is often necessary to compact the data prior to these steps. The parallel breadth first tree traversal is one representative example [17]. Here, the list of open nodes must be pruned of invalid nodes after each traversal step. Otherwise, an exponential explosion of nodes takes place. A second example is the filter operation in database systems to reduce data based on predicates. These filters are usually executed as close to the base data as possible to reduce the effort of subsequent joins or groupings [9]. In all cases, the reduction of the data

J. Cano and P. W. Trinder (Eds.): Euro-Par 2022, LNCS 13440, pp. 186–200, 2022.
https://doi.org/10.1007/978-3-031-12597-3_12

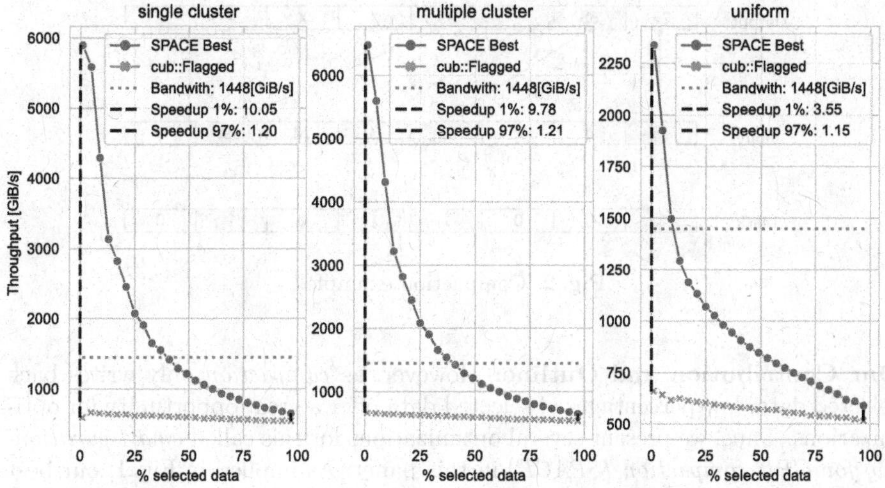

Fig. 1. *SPACE* compared to CUB on A100 Ampere GPU. Uniform, 1 cluster and 32 cluster data distributions for the bit mask. Datatype is unsigned integer 32-bit.

to the selected elements is performed with the *compaction* operation or primitive. This primitive is also denoted as stream compaction, stream reduction, or selection and the task of this primitive is to produce a smaller output array by writing selected elements of an input array contiguously back to a new output array. The selected elements are usually defined by means of a bit mask. With the still increasing amount of data to be processed in the different application domains, high performance for this key primitive is a decisive factor.

In the last decade, GPUs have been increasingly used for highly parallel computations or accelerating specific algorithms and algorithm parts [3,8,10,13]. Thus, exploiting the parallel capabilities of GPUs to speed up the compacting operation is of great interest. For NVIDIA GPUs, the CUB library provides state-of-the-art, reusable software components for every layer of the CUDA programming model [5]. In particular, CUB also provides an efficient implementation for the *compaction primitive* – called `cub::DeviceSelect:Flagged` – as highlighted in Fig. 1. For the illustrated results, we generated a data array and three different bit mask configurations, we varied the percentage of selected elements and we executed the compaction primitive on these settings using a recent NVIDIA GPU A100. One bit mask configuration is called *single cluster* where the selected elements are contiguous in a single cluster. A second bit mask configuration is called *multiple cluster* where the selected elements are contiguous in several clusters and the clusters are uniformly distributed within the bit mask. And the third configuration is denoted as *uniform* because the selected elements are uniform distributed over the bit mask. As shown in Fig. 1, the CUB primitive provides a stably high throughput for all settings, but is not optimized in terms of the percentage of the selected items. That means, the state-of-the-art CUB implementation does not have any specialization for *compaction* with a very low percentage of selected data.

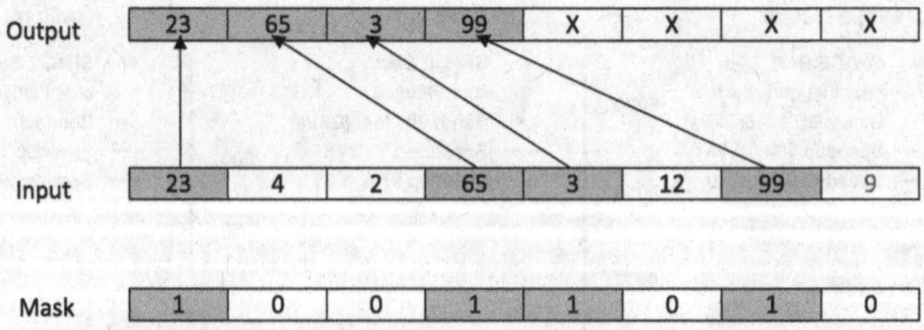

Fig. 2. Compaction example.

Our Contribution and Outline: However, as *compaction* only writes back selected data, low percentages of selected data offer a great opportunity for optimizations. Thus, we present several optimizations for this called *smart partitioning for GPU compaction (SPACE)* in this paper. As implied in Fig. 1, our best performing implementation – denoted as *SPACE Best* in Fig. 1 – clearly outperforms the state-of-the-art CUB implementation. The worst performing bit mask distribution uniform offers a throughput improvement of 3.55x for *SPACE Best* with 1% of data selected. For 97% selected data the improvement remains 1.15x. The best bit mask distribution is single cluster. In this case, *SPACE Best* achieves an improvement of 10.05x and a worst case improvement of 1.2x..

The remainder of this paper is structured as follow: In Sect. 2, we briefly introduce the necessary background. Then, we present our *smart partitioning for GPU compaction (SPACE)* approach in Sect. 3. Afterwards, we present selective results of our exhaustive evaluation. Finally, we conclude the paper with related work in Sect. 5 and a short summary in Sect. 6.

2 Preliminaries

In this section, we introduce all essential preliminary requirements for our work. We start with a clear description of the *compaction* primitive, followed by a classification of possible bit mask configurations and finally, we shortly recap the architecture of NVIDIA GPUs.

2.1 Compaction Primitive

Compaction is a common programming primitive that has a wide range of applications. As illustrated in Fig. 2, the input of the primitive is an input array and a bit mask. The bit mask is used to indicate which elements should be selected. Thus, the number of bits in the bit mask is equal to the number of elements in the input array. Then, the primitive produces a new output array, containing only selected elements from the input data array, which are indicated by bit set to 1 in the bit mask. The most important challenge is that the selected elements have to be written contiguously into the output array as shown in Fig. 2. In case of the NVIDIA GPUs, NVIDIA already ships a library called CUB that offers a performant implementation of the compaction based on a bit mask. The function is called `cub::DeviceSelect::Flagged`.

2.2 Bit Mask Characteristics

The bit mask as input essentially determines how many elements must be written to the output. If the percentage of set ones is small, then only a small amount of values needs to be written out. However, the percentage says nothing about where the set ones are in the bit mask. To be able to specify this more precisely, we examined various algorithms from different application domains and determined the following: On the one hand, there are applications where the set ones are uniformly distributed in the bit masks. On the other hand, there are also applications where the set ones occur contiguously – clustered – in the bit mask. Especially in the case of clustered ones, large parts of the input array can actually be skipped, which can be used for optimizing the *compaction* primitive. However, our experiments from the introduction clearly show that the state-of-the-art CUB implementation does not have such an optimization.

2.3 NVIDIA GPU Architecture and Execution Model

The NVIDIA GPU architecture – considered only in this paper – consists of a set of streaming multiprocessors. Each streaming multiprocessor consists of CUDA cores that are arithmetical logical units and exclusive local memory, which is called shared memory. A larger global memory can be accessed by all streaming multiprocessors. In order to perform calculations on a GPU, a set of threads is spawned and partitioned into work units called blocks. One block can have a maximum of 1024 threads and is assigned to one streaming multiprocessor. Multiple blocks can be assigned to a streaming multiprocessor. Instructions are executed for 32 threads at the same time, which is called a warp. Each streaming multiprocessor has a set of warp schedulers that schedule execution of different warp wide instructions. For example, Turing based GPUs have 4 warp schedulers per block and up to 4 warps can be scheduled at each unit to hide memory access latency. This leads to 16 warps or 512 threads as recommended threads per block [15]. While the basic architecture remains the same across newer GPU generations, there are differences in terms of memory speed, CUDA cores per streaming multiprocessor, shared memory per streaming multiprocessor and total streaming multiprocessors per GPU. As instructions are executed per warp ideally, multiple executions per warp are needed if branching or non-aligned memory access patterns occur.

The execution model is *Single Instruction Multiple Threads (SIMT)*. Unlike *Single Instruction Multiple Data (SIMD)* architectures like AVX512, where one instruction is executed on a vector of elements, GPU threads are able to behave independently from each other. Programs that use CUDA always consist of two parts of code. Host code runs on the CPU and is tasked with managing data transfers and execution of kernels. Device code runs on the GPU and consists of kernel functions. Kernels are C-style functions that execute instructions on data, based on a `ThreadID`. Each kernel is called with a blocksize (number of threads within a block) and a gridsize (total number of blocks). Both parameters together are called a CUDA configuration. Setting the right CUDA configuration is crucial to achieve good performance and varies between different kernels.

3 SPACE - Accelerating Compaction on GPUs

The sequential implementation of the *compaction* operation is straightforward and many programming languages and/or libraries provide such an implementation. However, to implement a parallel version, the most challenging issue is to determine the index positions of the selected elements in the output array. According to [2], a prefix-sum approach works very well for a parallel implementation. This prefix-sum approach works as follows: The input data is partitioned into fixed-sized chunks. As the number of bits in the bit mask is unknown at compile-time, a `popcount` operation is executed on each chunked bit mask to determine the number of set bits. To calculate the offset positions where each chunk starts to write back into the output array, a prefix-sum over the popcounts has to be computed next. The prefix-sum is defined as a sequence of numbers, where each element is generated by adding a number to the last element. Using these offset positions, a parallel write-out to the output array can be performed. Thus, a parallel implementation of the *compaction* primitive consists of the following three phases: **popcount**, **prefix-sum**, and **write-out**.

Since *compaction* only writes back selected data, low percentages of selected data offer a great opportunity for optimizations. Thus, we present an enhanced optimization for this called *smart partitioning for GPU compaction (SPACE)*. *SPACE* is based on the general *prefix-sum* approach with selective optimizations to skip the write-out part of chunks where no elements are selected. These optimizations are beneficial, because *popcount* and *prefix-sum* only perform operations on the bit mask and generate intermediate data, while the *write-out* needs to read the data from the large input array and writes back the final results. In the following, we describe the different variants for each phase.

3.1 Phase Variants for Parallel Implementation

As already introduced, a parallel implementation of the *compaction* primitive consists of three phases: *popcount*, *prefix-sum*, and *write-out*.

Popcount. To calculate a final memory offset on a chunk, it is required to know how many data elements occur before a chunk. This is achieved by performing a *popcount* on the bit mask. A GPU intrinsic function *int__popc(unsigned int x)* [6] counts the bits set to one in a 32 bit wide element. A *popcount* kernel across all chunks is the first operation in *SPACE*.

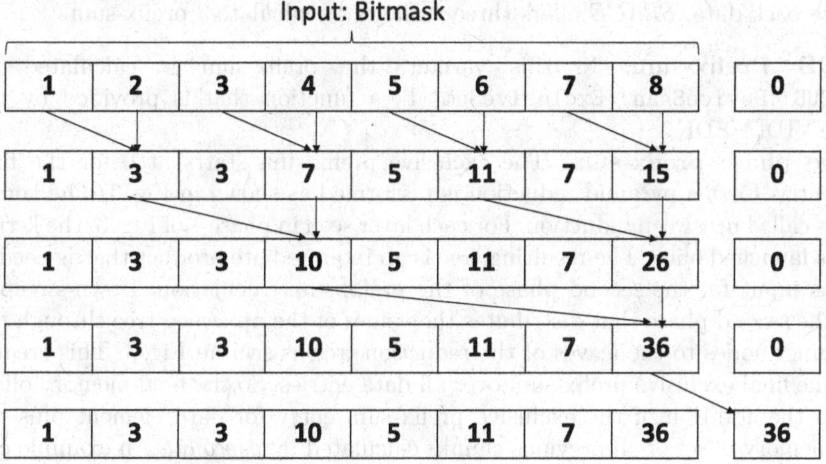

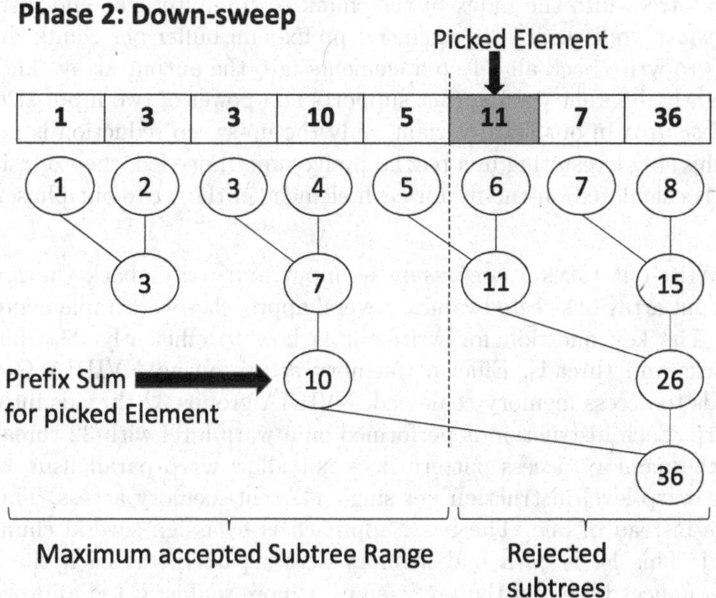

Fig. 3. Two phase prefix-sum is performed. First, up-sweep reduction calculates a partial prefix-sum. A single chunk down-sweep calculation is performed for the highlighted element (black arrow, 11). Below the partial prefix-sum buffer is the intermediate tree from the up-sweep phase. Sub-trees are either rejected or accepted if they fit. The dotted line indicates the maximum range of fitting sub-trees. Thus, the red sub-tree with value 11 is rejected. (Color figure online)

Prefix-sum. Calculating the *prefix-sum* requires the *popcount* intermediate data. The *prefix-sum* consists of all bits that occurred before the specific data element. t is the offset in the output array, where each element needs to start to write back data. *SPACE* offers three variants to calculate a prefix-sum.

CUB Prefix-sum: In this variant, the prefix-sum is calculated by `CUB::DeviceScan::ExclusiveSum` [4], a function that is provided by the NVIDIA SDK.

Two phase prefix-sum: The exclusive prefix-sum starts at 0 for the first entry. First a pyramid reduction is performed as shown in Fig. 3. The kernel is called up-sweep reduction. For each layer seen in phase 1 of Fig. 3, the kernel is launched once. The resulting tree is an intermediate product that is needed as input for the second phase of the prefix-sum calculation. Down-sweep is the second phase that distributes the values of the up-sweep tree through the inner nodes to the leaves of the reduction tree as seen in Fig. 3. This creates the final exclusive prefix-sum over all data entries. So the final memory offset is the addition of the exclusive prefix-sum entry for data element plus the memory offset of all previous chunks calculated by *popcount*. An example can be seen in Fig. 3. The algorithm attempts to fit the highest amount of largest left sided sub-trees into the index of the chunk to compute. The end result of the *two phase prefix-sum* is an exclusive prefix-sum buffer per chunk that can be used to write back all selected elements into the output array. There is also a slightly different version that supports non power of two input sizes.

Partial prefix-sum: In our third variant, only the up-sweep reduction is performed at this stage, resulting in a partial prefix-sum. If needed, the exclusive prefix-sum is calculated on-the-fly for each element in the write-out phase.

Write-out. Write-out takes a *prefix-sum* as input and writes back the final contiguous output array of selected values. Several approaches were implemented for write-out. The key question for write-out is how to efficiently distribute chunks to blocks and threads. Efficient memory access on an NVIDIA GPU requires threads to access memory coalesced. NVIDIA groups 32 threads into a unit called warp. Each instruction is performed on a warp level with 32 threads at a time. If the memory access pattern does not allow warp parallelism, the worst case is a warp level instruction per single element memory access. Thus, 32 instructions instead of one. The basic approach is to assign several chunks to each thread. This leads to a bad memory access pattern, as each thread jumps between indices based on the prefix-sum. A more sophisticated approach assigns chunks to warps instead of threads. While thread level synchronization is expensive, warp level synchronization is not. As a chunk can consist of only not selected elements, the write-out can be skipped for that chunk. This can be checked by performing a *popcount*. As skipping a chunk only needs to read the bit mask and skips reading the larger data array, the amount of memory access can be immensely reduced.

3.2 Overview of SPACE Variants

Based on the above description of the different variants for the three phases, we propose 8 different variants of the SPACE compaction algorithm for GPUs. Each variant shares the basic structure of *popcount*, *prefix-sum*, and *write-out*. Moreover, each implementation variant takes a bit mask and a data array as input as illustrated in Fig. 2. The data can be any datatype between 1 und 8 Byte size which is supported on GPUs. Each bit in the bit mask relates to one data element. Thus, a single bit controls the write out of up to 8 Bytes for double and uint64 data types. Data types smaller than 8 byte lead to a different ratio of bit mask size to data array size. The SPACE variants are:

Variant 1 (base variant approach): A two phase prefix-sum and naive write-out kernel are used. Threads are assigned to one chunk. Each thread calculates one element. No chunk is skipped.

Variant 2 (base variant with skipping): Variant 1 is modified by adding skipping of chunks of not selected elements. A *popcount* kernel that returns 0 bits on a bitmask of an empty chunk indicates which chunks can be skipped.

Variant 3 (asynchronous streamin g): The kernel executions are changed to enable the usage of the CUDA asynchronous streaming API. Distributing kernels across different CUDA streams allow for kernel-level parallelism. However there can be no data dependencies between kernels. Multiple asynchronous CUDA streams are deployed for each kernel that allows concurrent computation.

Variant 4 (optimized read without skipping): Memory access pattern is optimized by using grid striding. Instead of having a thread read additional elements adjacent to each other in memory, the memory access offset per thread is the total number of threads. Adjacent threads attempt to access adjacent data in memory. No calculations are skipped. CUB is used to calculate the exclusive prefix-sum.

Variant 5 (optimized read with skipping and partial prefix-sum): Based on Variant 4, skipping is added and CUB prefix-sum is replaced by the partial prefix-sum algorithm. Only the up-sweep reduction is performed before the write-out kernel and the exclusive prefix-sum is calculated on-the-fly in the write out phase.

Variant 6 (optimized read with skipping and two phase prefix-sum): Like Variant 5, but the prefix-sum is calculated by the two phase prefix-sum algorithm. This leads to a fully calculated exclusive prefix-sum across all elements before the write-out phase.

Variant 7 (optimized read with skipping and CUB based prefix-sum): Like Variant 6, but the prefix-sum is calculated by CUB. CUB is also used to calculate the complete exclusive prefix-sum across all elements.

Variant 8 (optimized read with skipping, optimized write-out and CUB prefix-sum): Like Variant 7 with the addition of an alternative version of the write-out kernel. Write-out kernel aims to write-out at least a warp at once.

Table 1. An overview of evaluated hardware platforms. Version of used build and compilation tools are listed as used in the evaluation.

GPU	GPU Generation	CMake	CUDA	NVCC	G++
A100	Ampere	3.23.0-rc1	11.2	11.2.67	9.3.0-17
RTX 8000 Quadro	Turing	3.22.2	11.5	11.5.119	9.3.0-17
1070 TI	Pascal	3.22.2	11.5	11.5.50	9.3.0-17
3080	Ampere	3.22.2	11.6	11.6.55	9.3.0-17

4 Evaluation

We evaluate our approach on three different data distributions for the bit mask as discussed in Sect. 2. Moreover, the selected bits of a bit mask determine how many percent of the total bits are set to one. All approaches allow adjustable percentages of selected data and are benchmarked across a larger number of different percentages of selected data.

4.1 Implementation

All *SPACE* variants as introduced in the previous sections are implemented in C++ 17 with CUDA 11 and the code is publicly available [14]. CMake is used to build *SPACE* and NVIDIA nvcc is used as compiler. nvcc calls g++ to compile host code. See Table 1 for detailed information about the used compilers and tools across all platforms. CUDA version 10.x and lower are not able to compile *SPACE*, due to the lack of C++17 support.

4.2 Experimental Setup

Data Distributions. Three different bit mask distributions are investigated (i) 1 Cluster, (ii) multiple Cluster, and (ii) uniform. 1 Cluster consists of a single cluster of bits set to 1, while the rest of the bit mask remains zero, thus not selected for output. Multiple cluster distributes several clusters equidistant across the bit mask. The number of clusters varies between 2 and 32 clusters. Uniform is based on a uniform distribution that distributes bits across the whole bit mask. All distributions support any data type that is CUDA compatible and between 1 Byte and 8 Byte large. See Table 2 for an overview of which data types we tested. While the size of the input data array is always set to 1 GiB, this results in different sizes for the bit mask. The size of the bit mask is calculated by dividing 1 GiB by the size of one data element. For example a 1 GiB Array of uint64_t results in 16 MiB bit mask. Elements from the data input array are randomly generated.

Hardware Platforms. We used four different hardware platforms with CUDA 11 as shown in Table 1.

Table 2. Size of evaluated data types and corresponding bit masks.

Data type	Size of Element [Byte]	Total bit mask size [MiB]
u8	1	128
u16	2	64
u32	4	32
u64	8	16
Integer	4	32
Float	4	32
Double	8	16

4.3 Experimental Methodology

As one *SPACE* algorithm consists of several kernel calls, we measure the total runtime of all kernel calls with CUDAevents. The throughput is calculated as

$$throughput = \frac{datasize(bit\_mask[GiB] + input\_data[GiB])}{total\_runtime\_of\_one\_algorithm[s]}$$

This calculation does not account for skipping chunks. As a result, the calculated throughput can exceed the maximum memory bandwidth. The goal of this throughput calculation is to achieve a good comparability of all measured SPACE algorithms and CUB. All data is present on GPU. Data generation is not part of the measurement. Additionally, the input data is partitioned into chunks varying between 512 and 4096 elements.

4.4 Results

In Fig. 4, an overview of the evaluation of all *SPACE* variants is shown. A grid of graphs is shown with different GPUs and data distributions. In each graph, the x-axis show the percentage of selected data and the y-axis depicts the achieved throughput. Percentages of selected data are within 1% and 97% with increments of 4. Variants 1 and 2 overall perform very poorly across all devices. Variant 3 with async CUDA streams outperforms Variants 1 and 2 but is often slower than CUB for higher percentages of selected data. Variants 4,5,6,7 mostly outperform CUB even for very high percentages of selected data, variant 8 is the best performing *SPACE* variant and outperforms all other SPACE variants. Even for higher percentages of selected data Variant 8 outperforms CUB in all cases on the A100 GPU. In case of the Quadro RTX 8000 GPU, CUB is ahead if the percentage of selected data exceeds 71% in a clustering approach, or 21% for uniform distributions. For the 1070 ti, CUB is ahead if the percentage of selected data exceeds 53% in uniform and never for clustering distributions. In case of the 3080 GPU, CUB is slower if percentage of selected data is 81% and smaller for a single cluster. The break even point for uniform is at 33% for a 3080 GPU. The ideal improvement for 1% selected data and single cluster distribution is 12.01x in favor of SPACE variant 8. In case of uniform distribution the improvement for 1% is 3,19x in favor of SPACE variant 8.

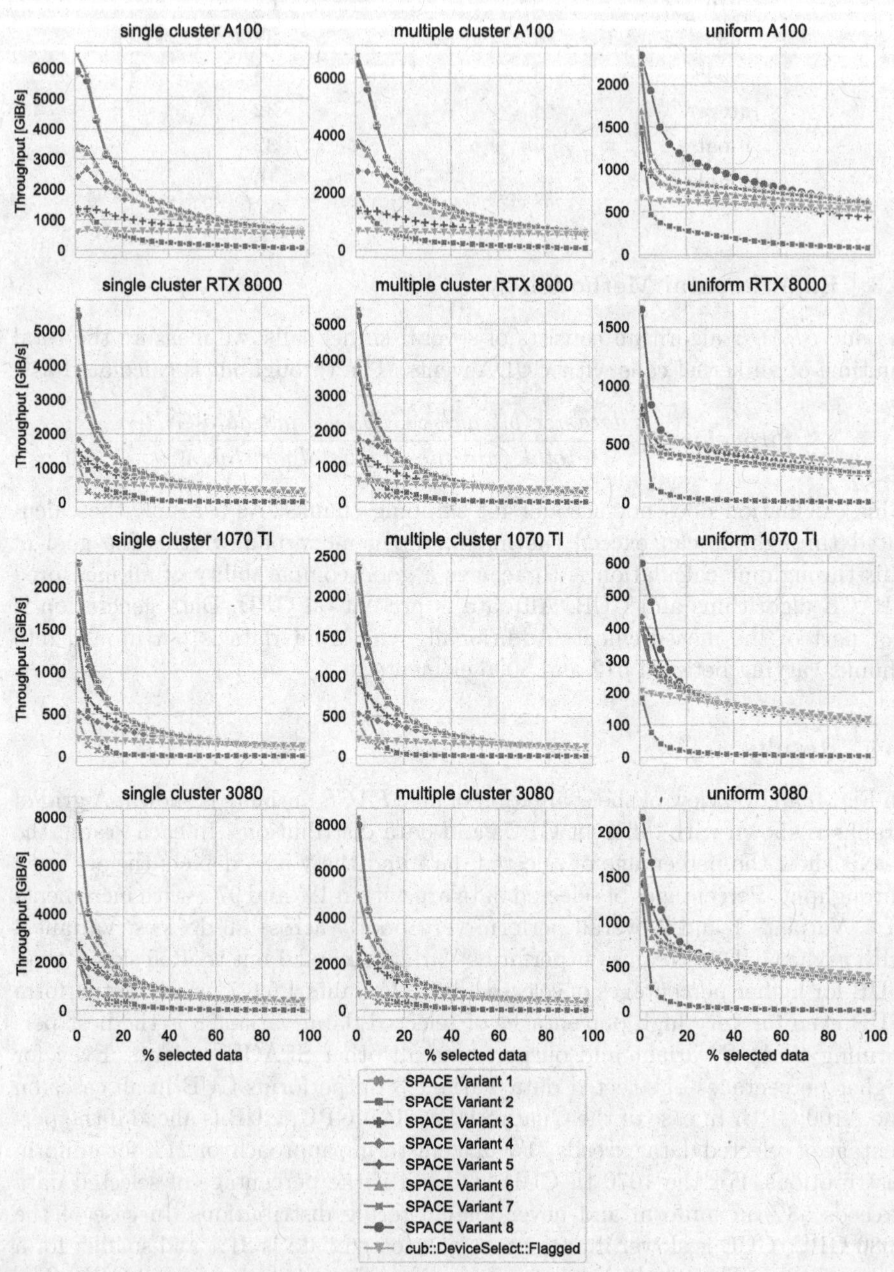

Fig. 4. Overview of all SPACE algorithms for all hardware platforms and data distributions. Datatype is unsigned integer 32 bit.

Very Low Percentages of Selected Data. Figure 5 shows an additional experiment with very low percentages of selected data. All experiments were conducted on a RTX 8000 GPU with 32 bit unsigned integers. Reducing the percentage of selected data further from 1% to 0.1% more than doubles the throughput for both clustering approaches. Uniform reaches above 5000 [GiB/s] only at 10^{-3}%, while both clustering approaches reach it at 0.1%. The highest improvement is achieved for the second lowest percentage of selected data with 10.40x improvement for uniform. CUB achieves 603 [GiB/s] at 10^{-5}% while SPACE 8 reaches 6272 [GiB/s] throughput. In case of single cluster distribution CUB achieves 553 [GiB/s] at 10^{-5}% while SPACE 7 reaches 6647 [GiB/s]. This leads to an improvement of 12.02x in this extremely favorable case. We conclude that decreasing selected data yields diminishing returns. For 10^{-4}% and lower percentages of selected data there is not much improvement to gain. For uniform and single cluster, 10^{-6}% was slightly slower than 10^{-5}%. CUB performs with similar performance across different distributions and percentage of selected data.

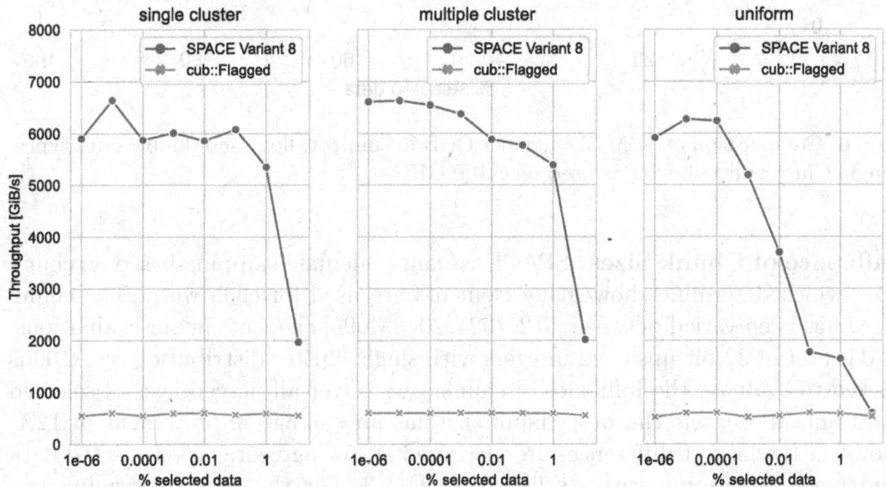

Fig. 5. Very low percentages of selected data in logarithmic scale on x-axis. Measured on RTX 8000. Datatype is unsigned integer 32 bit.

Influence of Data Types. As shown in Table 2, we evaluated our algorithm across 7 different data types. Figure 6 shows the performance of SPACE 8 against CUB for different data types. Skipping is beneficial across all data types. Peak performance for 1% selected items greatly varies between data types. Double achieves 8860 [GiB/s] at 1%, float achieves 5897 [GiB/s] and uint8_t reaches 3313 [GiB/s]. The data type has massive influence on the overall performance. Skipping is beneficial and results in significant improvement compared to CUB across all data types.

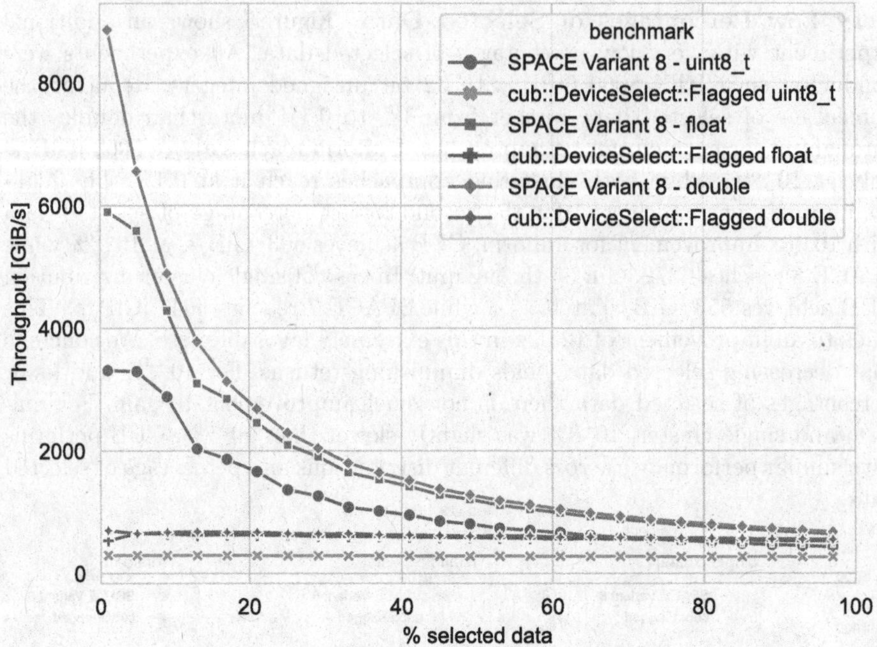

Fig. 6. Comparision of SPACE 8 against CUB for uint8_t, float and double data types. Single Cluster distribution is used on A100 GPU.

Influence of Chunk Sizes. SPACE variants calculate skipping based on chunk size, which determines how many elements are used for each warp. The chunk sized has been varied between [512, 1024, 2048, 4096] elements in our evaluations. A data set of 32 bit unsigned integers with single cluster distribution on A100 is picked to evaluate the influence of chunk sizes. Over all percentages of selected data and all kernels the best chunk size has an average improvement of 12%. However the largest differences are measured at low percentages of selected data and poor performing variants like SPACE 1-3. For the best performing two variants SPACE 7 and SPACE 8 the average improvement from worst to best chunk size is 4.5%. If percentages of selected data below 25% are excluded the average worst to best improvement is reduced to 1.4%. For the best performing variants SPACE 7 and SPACE 8 a chunk size of 512 elements is the fastest choice. SPACE 1 und SPACE 2 achieve the best performance with a chunk size of 4096 elements.

Influence of CUDA Configurations. CUDA Configurations play a significant role for the overall runtime. Each variant consists of a number of different kernel calls. All kernel calls were measured for a large variety of different configurations. The best configurations per kernel were used for our evaluations.

Selection of Datasets. Real world data sets are not included in our experiments. We have shown that the following input characteristics determine the performance of SPACE: data types, bitmask data distribution and percentage of selected data. As our experiments range from worst-case to best-case for all three bit mask characteristics, a real world data set would fit within the current spectrum of parameters. As a consequence, we did not include results on real world data.

5 Related Work

Bakunas et al. classify compaction on GPU into two categories. [1,2]. Atomic based approaches that have a global memory offset index, which all writings threads increment in parallel using atomics, and prefix sum based approaches. On the evaluated NVIDIA Kepler platform, atomics with a single global counter create a major bottleneck. By leveraging warp level parallelism and changing to a prefix-sum based approach, improved performance was achieved compared to global counter atomics. THRUST, an open source compute library is used as part of the algorithm. Merril et al. introduce CUB select if, which computes a compaction based on a selection with a functor to a compare predicate, instead of a bit mask [12]. Their approach outperforms THRUST significantly. The common denominator for all these approaches is, that they do not optimize for low amounts of selected data unlike SPACE.

6 Conclusion and Summary

The goal of SPACE is to offer a specialization that accelerates compaction on GPUs for low percentages of selected data. Skipping memory access to the input data array by analyzing the bit mask is the key idea to gain performance. Great improvements for low amounts of selected data are achieved. In case of 1% the improvement is up to 10.05x. For very low % of selected data the improvement is 12.02x on a NVIDIA Quadro RTX 8000. Depending on the GPU device, our approach is slightly faster than CUB even for data sets that do not benefit from skipping. Source code for all kernels, scripts for experiments, scripts for visualizations and all raw data is provided on our github [14].

Acknowledgements and Data Availability Statement. The datasets and code generated during and/or analyzed during the current study are available in the Figshare repository: https://doi.org/10.6084/m9.figshare.19945469 [7].

This work is funded by the German Research Foundation within the RTG 1907 (RoSI) as well as by the European Union's Horizon 2020 research and innovative program under grant agreement number 957407 (DAPHNE project).

References

1. Bakunas-Milanowski, D., Rego, V., Sang, J., Chansu, Y.: Efficient algorithms for stream compaction on GPUs. Int. J. Netw. Comput. **7**(2), 208–226 (2017)

2. Bakunas-Milanowski, D., Rego, V., Sang, J., Yu, C.: A fast parallel selection algorithm on GPUs. In: 2015 International Conference on Computational Science and Computational Intelligence (CSCI), pp. 609–614. IEEE (2015)
3. Choi, K., Yang, H.: A GPU architecture aware fine-grain pruning technique for deep neural networks. In: Sousa, L., Roma, N., Tomás, P. (eds.) Euro-Par 2021. LNCS, vol. 12820, pp. 217–231. Springer, Cham (2021). https://doi.org/10.1007/978-3-030-85665-6_14
4. CUB: cub::DeviceScan::ExclusiveSum documentation. https://nvlabs.github.io/cub/structcub_1_1_device_scan.html#a02b2d2e98f89f80813460f6a6ea1692b
5. CUB: Main Page. https://nvlabs.github.io/cub/index.html
6. CUB: Main Page. https://docs.nvidia.com/cuda/cuda-math-api/group__CUDA__MATH__INTRINSIC__INT.html
7. Fett, J., Kober, U., Schwarz, C., Habich, D., Lehner, W.: Artifact and instructions to generate experimental results for the euro-par 2022 paper: accelerating parallel operation for compacting selected elements on GPUs. In: European Conference on Parallel Processing. Springer, Heidelberg (2022). http://doi.org/10.6084/m9.figshare.19945469
8. Guo, W., Li, Y., Sha, M., He, B., Xiao, X., Tan, K.: GPU-accelerated subgraph enumeration on partitioned graphs. In: SIGMOD Conference, pp. 1067–1082 (2020)
9. Hertzschuch, A., Hartmann, C., Habich, D., Lehner, W.: Simplicity done right for join ordering. In: 11th Conference on Innovative Data Systems Research, CIDR 2021, Virtual Event, 11–15 January 2021, Online Proceedings (2021)
10. Hu, L., Zou, L., Liu, Y.: Accelerating triangle counting on GPU. In: SIGMOD Conference, pp. 736–748 (2021)
11. Lo, S., Lee, C., Chung, I., Chung, Y.: Optimizing pairwise box intersection checking on GPUs for large-scale simulations. ACM Trans. Model. Comput. Simul. **23**(3), 19:1–19:22 (2013)
12. Merrill, D., Garland, M.: Single-pass parallel prefix scan with decoupled look-back. NVIDIA, Technical report, NVR-2016-002 (2016)
13. Sistla, M.A., Nandivada, V.K.: Graph coloring using GPUs. In: Yahyapour, R. (ed.) Euro-Par 2019. LNCS, vol. 11725, pp. 377–390. Springer, Cham (2019). https://doi.org/10.1007/978-3-030-29400-7_27
14. SPACE Github. https://github.com/yogi-tud/SPACE/
15. Turing Tuning Guide: CUDA Toolkit documentation. https://docs.nvidia.com/cuda/turing-tuning-guide/index.html
16. Ungethüm, A., et al.: Hardware-oblivious SIMD parallelism for in-memory column-stores. In: 10th Conference on Innovative Data Systems Research, CIDR 2020, Amsterdam, The Netherlands, 12–15 January 2020, Online Proceedings (2020). www.cidrdb.org
17. Zhou, K., Hou, Q., Wang, R., Guo, B.: Real-time kd-tree construction on graphics hardware. ACM Trans. Graph. **27**(5), 126 (2008)

Cluster and Cloud Computing

A Methodology to Scale Containerized HPC Infrastructures in the Cloud

Nicolas Greneche[1(✉)], Tarek Menouer[2], Christophe Cérin[1,3], and Olivier Richard[3]

[1] University of Paris 13, LIPN - UMR CNRS 7030, 93430 Villetaneuse, France
{nicolas.greneche,christophe.cerin}@univ-paris13.fr
[2] Umanis Research and Innovation, 92300 Levallois-Perret, France
tmenouer@umanis.com
[3] University of Grenoble Alpes, 38400 Saint-Martin-d'Hères, France
olivier.richard@imag.fr

Abstract. This paper introduces a generic method to scale HPC clusters on top of the Kubernetes cloud orchestrator. Users define their targeted infrastructure with the usual Kubernetes syntax for recipes, and our approach automatically translates the description to a full-fledged containerized HPC cluster. Moreover, resource extensions or shrinks are handled, allowing a dynamic resize of the containerized HPC cluster without disturbing its running. The Kubernetes orchestrator acts as a provisioner. We applied the generic method to three orthogonal architectural designs Open Source HPC schedulers: SLURM, OAR, and OpenPBS. Through a series of experiments, the paper demonstrates the potential of our approach regarding the scalability issues of HPC clusters and the simultaneous deployment of several job schedulers in the same physical infrastructure. It should be noticed that our plan does not require any modification either in the containers orchestrator or in the HPC schedulers. Our proposal is a step forward to reconciling the two ecosystems of HPC and cloud. It also calls for new research directions and concrete implementations for the dynamic consolidation of servers or sober placement policies at the orchestrator level. The works contribute a new approach to running HPC clusters in a cloud environment and test the technique on robustness by adding and removing nodes on the fly.

Keywords: Resource management in HPC Clusters and Clouds · Containers · Scalability · Orchestration · Aggregation and federation of HPC Clusters in the Cloud

1 Introduction

Traditionally, HPC clusters have been all about numerical simulation. Scientists and engineers would model complex systems in software on large-scale parallel clusters to predict real-world outcomes. Financial risk management, computational chemistry, omics (genomics, proteomics, metabolomics, metagenomics,

J. Cano and P. W. Trinder (Eds.): Euro-Par 2022, LNCS 13440, pp. 203–217, 2022.
https://doi.org/10.1007/978-3-031-12597-3_13

and transcriptomics), seismic modeling, and simulating car crashes in software are good examples of numerical simulations. An HPC cluster gathers hardware nodes managed by a single software called the batch scheduler. This scheduler runs scientific workloads on the hardware according to scientists' resource definition constraints. This point results in a very specialized infrastructure designed for massively parallelized applications.

Over the past decade, however, what we consider to be an HPC cluster has broadened considerably. Today, clusters are supposed to involve collecting or filtering streaming data, using distributed analytics to discover patterns in data, or training machine learning models. Usages include, nowadays, interactive workloads and even, for the data science community, "long-running" distributed services such as TensorFlow, Spark, or Jupyter notebooks. As HPC applications have become more diverse, scheduling and managing workloads have evolved. The diversity in applications pushed people to wonder if Cloud systems would be a better computer systems and even if the Cloud would encompass all the categories of scientific issues in a unified way. Our paper is a step in this last direction. It addresses the following challenge: is it possible to execute various HPC job schedulers on the same infrastructure, controlled by a Cloud orchestrator?

The Cloud orchestrator may play a similar role to the HPC batch scheduler. However, the aim is slightly different. They both place active processes on hardware resources, but these processes have a different natures. An HPC cluster is designed to run non-interactive scientific workloads with a beginning and an end. A Cloud orchestrator lets users define a targeted containerized infrastructure and endeavors to satisfy their needs, including restarting failed components. In fact, in system administration, orchestration is the management of computer systems and software, as with the batch scheduler, and the automated configuration and coordination of the computer system.

In a nutshell, we containerized several batch schedulers (OAR [4], SLURM, and OpenPBS in our experiments). These schedulers are hosted on Cloud infrastructure (Kubernetes in our experiments). We attempt to solve the problem of scaling, i.e., dynamically add or remove containerized HPC nodes (we will reference them as workers), without altering neither the Cloud orchestrator nor the HPC scheduler. This work results in a generic method to coordinate Cloud orchestrator and HPC scheduler.

We face many scientific challenges in integrating the new features described above, making the task challenging. First, the targeted Cloud orchestrator for our experiments, Kubernetes, has limited support for the HPC types of workloads[1]. Second, we must check that HPC workloads can run in containers and become Kubernetes friendly. Third, end-users (i.e., people that submit a job to the HPC scheduler) must not be aware that their computations run on a cloudified HPC cluster.

[1] https://kubernetes.io/docs/concepts/workloads/controllers/jobs-run-to-completion/.

The organization of the paper is as follows. Section 2 introduces some related works on HPC cloudification. Section 3 introduce mainlines of our methodology to position our contribution among these works. Section 4 introduces exhaustive experiences that allow the validation of our proposed approach. At last, we introduce future works in Sect. 5.

2 Related Works

In this paper, we propose advanced integration into the Cloud of popular batch schedulers and discuss the suitability of the methodology for the resonance between HPC and Cloud systems. First, we added a degree of difficulty with the ability, for our proposal, to deploy and remove on the fly multiple batch schedulers. More importantly, we developed a layer between the batch scheduler and the Cloud orchestrator that dynamically adds or removes computational nodes, thanks to dedicated mechanisms at the Cloud orchestrator level. Second, we also imposed another constraint for the integration: to modify the orchestrator and batch scheduler sides as little as possible. We mean to count first on the existing mechanisms and not be intrusive in the current architectures. Notice that our work is not related to scheduling jobs or pods but to a generic interposition mechanism to glue HPC and Cloud middlewares.

The IBM Spectrum LSF Suites portfolio [6] redefines cluster virtualization and workload management by integrating mission-critical HPC environments. IBM Spectrum LSF Suites supports organizations using container technologies, including Docker, Shifter, and Singularity. This feature streamlines an application's building, testing, and shipping, enabling an application stack to be deployed on-premises consistently and in the Cloud. IBM Spectrum LSF is not devoted to the containerization of HPC job schedulers.

Kubernetes, commonly stylized as K8s [7] is an open-source container orchestration system for automating software deployment, scaling, and management. Kubernetes aimed to solve an entirely different problem than the traditional problems solved by HPC clusters - delivering scalable, always-on, reliable web services in Google's Cloud. Kubernetes applications are assumed to be containerized and adhere to a cloud-native design approach. Pods which are groups of one or more CRI-O[2] or OCI[3] compliant containers, are the primary constituents of applications that are deployed on a cluster to provide specific functionality for an application. Kubernetes provides features supporting continuous integration/delivery (CI/CD) pipelines and modern DevOps techniques. Health checks give mechanisms to send readiness and liveness probes to ensure continued service availability. Another differentiating feature is that Kubernetes is more than just a resource manager; it is a complete management and runtime environment. Kubernetes includes services that applications rely on, including DNS management, virtual networking, persistent volumes, secret keys management, etc.

---

2 https://cri-o.io/.

3 https://opencontainers.org/.

In [9], the authors address the problem of running HPC workloads efficiently on Kubernetes clusters. They compare the Kubernetes' default scheduler with KubeFlux, a Kubernetes plugin scheduler built on the Flux graph-based scheduler, on a 34- node Red Hat OpenShift cluster on IBM Cloud. They also detail how scheduling can affect the performance of GROMACS, a well-known HPC application, and they demonstrate that KubeFlux can improve its performance through better pod scheduling. In contrast with our work, authors work at the level of one application (GROMACS), whereas we are working on containerizing job-schedulers.

In [2], authors studied the potential use of Kubernetes on HPC infrastructure for use by the scientific community. They directly compared both its features and performance against Docker Swarm and bare-metal execution of HPC applications. They detailed some configurations required for Kubernetes to operate with containerized MPI applications, explicitly accounting for operations such as (1) underlying device access, (2) inter-container communication across different hosts, and (3) configuration limitations. They discovered some rules that showed that Kubernetes presents overheads for several HPC applications over TCP/IP protocol.

In [12] authors argued that HPC container runtimes (Charliecloud, Shifter, Singularity) have minimal or no performance impact. To prove this claim, they ran industry-standard benchmarks (SysBench, STREAM, HPCG). They found no meaningful performance differences between the used environments, except modest variation in memory usage. They invite the HPC community to containerize their applications without concern about performance degradation.

In [16], authors describe a plugin named Torque-Operator. The proposed plugin serves as a bridge between the HPC workload manager Torque and the container orchestrator Kubernetes. The authors also propose a testbed architecture composed of an HPC cluster and a big data cluster. The Torque-Operator enables the scheduling of containerized jobs from the big data cluster to the HPC cluster.

In [13], the authors show the usefulness of containers in the context of HPC applications. They introduce the experience of PRACE (Partnership for Advanced Computer in Europe) in supporting Singularity containers on HPC clusters and provide notes about possible approaches for deploying MPI applications in using different use cases. Performance comparisons between bare metal and container executions are also provided, showing a negligible overhead in the container execution in an HPC context.

In [15] authors' main concern is to define a model for parallel MPI application DevOps and deployment using containers to enhance development effort and provide container portability from laptop to clouds or supercomputers. First, they extended the use of Singularity containers to a Cray XC-series supercomputer and, second, they conducted experiments with Docker on Amazon's Elastic Compute Cloud (EC2). Finally, they showed that Singularity containers operated at native performance when dynamically linking Cray's MPI libraries on a Cray supercomputer testbed. They also concluded that Amazon EC2 environment may be helpful for initial DevOps and testing while scaling HPC applications better suited for supercomputing resources like a Cray.

In [3] authors discuss several challenges in utilizing containers for HPC applications and the current approaches used in many HPC container runtimes. These approaches have been proven to enable the high-performance execution of containers at scale with the appropriate runtimes.

In [14], authors introduce a technique called personal cluster, which reserves a partition of batch resources on the user's demand in a best-effort manner. One individual cluster provides a private cluster dedicated to the user during a user-specified period by installing a user-level resource manager on the resource partition. According to the results obtained in this study, the proposed technique enables cost-effective resource utilization and efficient task management. It provides the user a uniform interface to heterogeneous resources regardless of local resource management software.

In [1], the authors highlight issues that arise when deploying network address translation through containers. In this paper, the authors concentrate on Docker as the container technology of choice and present a thorough analysis of their networking model, focusing on the default bridge network driver used to implement network address translation functionality.

In [10], the authors propose to test container portability on three different state-of-the-art HPC architectures (Intel Skylake, IBM Power9, and Arm-v8) and compare three critical container implementations. From the outcomes of all this, the authors hope to provide system administrators, facility managers, HPC experts, and field scientists with valuable research for guidelines and use-case examples.

3 Methodology

This section describes our methodology from a macro point of view. In the next section, we will go further in implementation details that refer to the micro point of view. The current branch outlines the method not specifically related to the three evaluated HPC schedulers. Our explanation is divided into two parts. First, we enumerate all information users must feed to categorize their Pods. Then, we describe all underlying services that we must develop to configure or reconfigure the containerized HPC infrastructure to match the resources requested by users from Kubernetes. The term "user" relates to the person who defines and instantiates the containerized HPC cluster. The term "developer" is used to determine the person who develops services used for coupling the Cloud orchestrator and the job scheduler.

3.1 Required Information at a User Level

This section is all about users. They describe the Pods composing the targeted containerized HPC clusters, and these Pods can have two roles depending on the hosted service. There are two primary services: schedulers and workers. Schedulers decide where to place the jobs on the infrastructure regarding their resource constraints. The worker is a service on HPC nodes that executes the job. In our method, users must supply essential information in the Pod definition. The listing 1.1 is a shortened example of a set of definitions for Workers. Users write these listings. Let's go on with the comment on this listing to understand the main requirements.

On line 2, we can see that Workers Pods are defined as a `StatefulSet`. A `StatefulSet` is a set of identical Pods that manages stateful applications and guarantees the ordering and uniqueness of these Pods. A `StatefulSet` contains Pods based on identical container specifications. `Statefulset` also maintains a sticky identity for each Pod. The keyword `replicas` (line 9) gives the number of instanced Pods. On line 7, the label `role` informs on the type of Pod (Scheduler or Worker). Here, we have a `worker` Pod. In HPC clusters, homogeneous nodes are frequently gathered in partitions or queues (the denomination may differ from one HPC scheduler to another one). In line 13, we label this set of Pods with `partition` set to `COMPUTE` (a partition is a set of nodes). Line 17 to 21 gives the resource constraint required by the Worker Pod to the Kubernetes orchestrator. Here, we request 2 CPUs. In a nutshell, this example instantiates two Pods with two CPUs each in the COMPUTE partition.

```
1 apiVersion: apps/v1
2 kind: StatefulSet
3 metadata:
4   name: hpc-node
5   namespace: hpc-nico
6   labels:
7      role: worker
8 spec:
9   replicas: 2
10  template:
11    metadata:
12      labels:
13        partition: COMPUTE
14      containers:
15      - name: <my_worker_name>
16        image: <my_hpc_sceduler_image>
17        resources:
18          limits:
19            cpu: "2"
20          requests:
21            cpu: "2"
```

Listing 1.1. Example of a user-defined Worker

3.2 Configuration Services

This section explains services supplied by developers. At a glance, there are two sets of services: initialization and resource polling. These two sets run sequentially, one after the other. When the initialization phase is over, the resource polling starts and lasts until the whole containerized HPC cluster revocation.

The initialization service is an `initContainer` that runs before any Worker or Scheduler Pod. An `initContainer` is a container that runs before any regular container of the Pod. Standard containers start when the `initContainer` ends successfully, i.e., the containerized process exits with return code zero. In our method, the `initContainer` aims at bootstrapping configuration for both Worker and Scheduler Pods. From the scheduler's point of view, this bootstrapping can be mapped to a configuration of a scheduling algorithm, various spool directories, PID file location, etc. From the worker's point of view, the `initContainer` locates the Pod hosting the scheduler.

The resource polling aims to watch the `StatefulSets` set by users and translate them to the containerized HPC cluster, specifically the Scheduler Pod. The resources polling service is a program that connects to the Kubernetes API to get worker Pods' properties. In our previous example described in listing 1.1, the resource polling service will add two nodes with two CPUs each in the `COMPUTE` partition of the scheduler. This program may also restart the Scheduler Pod if it is needed. The resources polling program is embedded in a sidecar container of the Scheduler Pod. A sidecar container is a regular container that interacts with the Pod's main container(s). Most of the time, the interaction is a configuration update, which is the case here. The sidecar container updates the scheduler configuration. For instance, if the user patches his containerized HPC cluster `StatefulSets` to add a worker, the sidecar container automatically updates the scheduler configuration with this newcomer. This hint enables dynamic scaling of the containerized HPC cluster.

These two services, namely initialization and resource polling, are located in containers and deployed aside from the containerized HPC cluster. Consequently, neither HPC schedulers nor Kubernetes the orchestrator need to be modified. The only requirement for our method is adding RBAC policies to enable read access to the Pods' attributes from the Kubernetes API. The containerized HPC cluster can be instanced in a dedicated namespace to mitigate information leaks that may result from such a security policy. Figure 1 sums up all these interactions.

4 Experimentations

4.1 Outline

This section applies our methodology to the three major open-source HPC job schedulers: SLURM, OAR, and OpenPBS. We experience several scenarios to check the consequences of scaling (up or down) workers' containers. We use Kubernetes/CRIO v1.22, SLURM v21.08.5, OAR v2.9, OpenPBS v20.0.1 and OpenMPI v4.1.2. The section aims at highlighting the most relevant points of the approach, making the three implementations similar.

4.2 Micro Description of the Methodology

In this section, we go further in detail on our method implementation. We first discuss the specificities of each HPC job scheduler that impact our methodology. Then, we supply the scaling results of the three containerized HPC clusters.

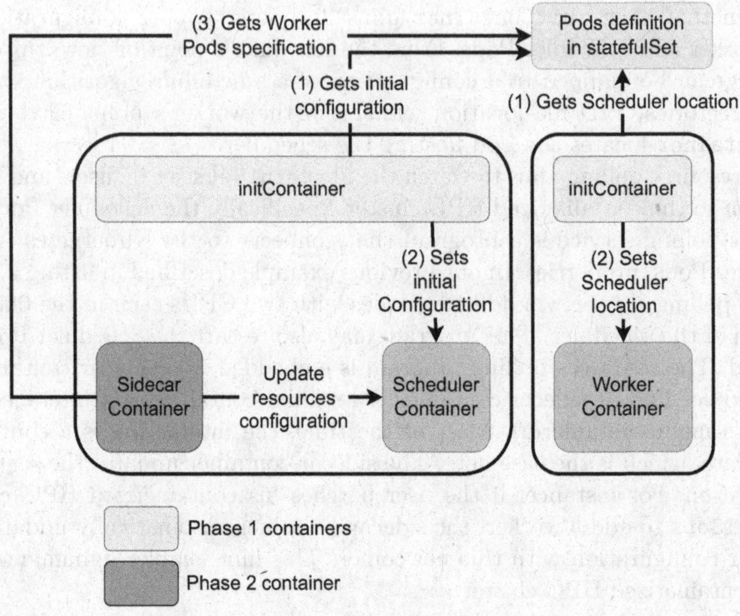

Fig. 1. Methodology: the macro level

SLURM job scheduler is built upon two services: Slurmctld and Slurmd. Slurmctld is the scheduler, and Slurmd is the worker. All HPC nodes are described in a plain text file owned by the scheduler. We configure SLURM in the configless mode: the workers connect to the scheduler to retrieve the configuration. This configuration requires the Munge service to authenticate communications between workers and the scheduler. As a result, scheduler Pod has four containers: an `initContainer`, Slurmctld, Munge, and a sidecar container that generates or updates the configuration file. The worker Pod has three Pods: an `initContainer`, Slurmd, and Munge.

Our contributions are based on introducing `initContainer` for Slurmd and Slurmctld and the Slurmctld's sidecar container. Slurmctld's `initContainer` generates a minimal configuration that enables Slurmctld to start. Slurmd's `initContainer` locates the Slurmctld service to retrieve configuration.

We have an `initContainer` for both Slurmctld and Slurmd Pods. Slurmctld's sidecar container is responsible for configuration updates when nodes are added or suppressed from containerized HPC cluster. SLURM does not support a comprehensive dynamic creation/suppression of his nodes in his current state. However, a relatively safe method is to restart Slurmctld. Then, in configless mode, all attached Slurmd daemons will reread their configuration. This method has limitations, and we will discuss them below.

Consequently, when a modification is detected in the containerized HPC cluster's topology, the sidecar container modifies the configuration file and sends a SIGTERM signal to the Slurmctld process. We use[4] to supervise the Slurmctld process. Thus, when Slurmctld exits due to the SIGTERM reception, Daemontools' manage process restarts it gracefully without crashing the container.

OpenPBS job scheduler hosts several services. The process `pbs_sched` is the scheduler itself, `pbs_comm` handles the High Availability, and `pbs_server.bin` communicates with worker nodes to execute users' jobs. This process also interacts with a Postgres database to store resource descriptions (such as workers' specifications) and job information. We have `pbs_mom` on the worker node, which receives jobs from the PBS server to execute them on the node. The scheduler Pod has three containers: an `initContainer` that creates the configuration file for the PBS server, a container that hosts all the processes composing the PBS server, and the sidecar container that registers or unregister worker from the PBS server's database.

The containerization of OpenPBS follows the same scheme as SLURM. The `initContainer` is likely to be the SLURM's. It creates the configuration file for PBS server Pod and worker Pod. The sidecar container triggers the commands to add or delete resources in the PBS server database at each containerized HPC cluster's topology modification. OpenPBS and SLURM are very close regarding our methodology because they work on the same pattern of server/agent, and these two components are more or less coupled. We now consider a third HPC scheduler called OAR that relies on SSH for interactions between schedulers and workers.

OAR job scheduler is composed of several processes. A central one executes an automaton that reacts to all events from jobs' and nodes' states and initiates appropriate action by launching corresponding processes like scheduling round, job launching, and nodes' checking. All states related to jobs, nodes, and scheduling decisions are stored in a Postgres database. OAR is well suited for containerization because workers and schedulers are loosely coupled, making it easier to deal with synchronization. An `initContainer` in the scheduler

[4] https://cr.yp.to/daemontools.html.

Pod initiates a configuration for the Almighty service that drives OAR cluster resources. An `initContainer` is deployed aside from worker Pods to get the scheduler Pod location. Then, a sidecar container is executed aside from the scheduler server container inside the scheduler Pod to add or remove workers according to resources defined on the `StatefulSets`.

4.3 Experimental Results

We investigate in this section some challenges of doing HPC in the Cloud. The main criterion for addressing them is the robustness of the approach because the behavior of the Cloud system and the applications running under the supervision of the HPC job schedulers is correct when dynamically adding or removing nodes attached to the HPC schedulers. We do not provide a performance metric such as the overhead of the containerization but a measurable quality metric. The proposed approach can scale the containerized clusters dynamically without interfering with already running or scheduled user jobs.

Thus, we explored several scenarios to evaluate how each HPC scheduler behaves when resources (nodes) are added or removed. We qualify the impact on pending and running jobs. For each scenario, we submitted MPI and non-MPI jobs. The MPI job is a Pi computation with a Monte Carlo method. The non-MPI job is a multi-threaded infinite computation. The nature of jobs does not matter, meaning that jobs with MPI communication and without communication are both running correctly. We want to keep nodes busy and generate MPI communications while adding or removing workers' containers on the fly. In Table 1, we have four scenarios that are declined for each of the three evaluated job schedulers. There are two states of jobs regarding the queue of requests in an HPC scheduler: pending (the job is waiting for resources) and running (the job is running somewhere on the HPC cluster nodes). We consider the impact of growth and shrinking workers' containers for each state. In Table 1, a None value means that we do not encounter any problem, also suggesting that the execution was correct.

All the scenarios that we now detail realize a functional validation of our implementation according to our methodology for containerization. This artifact is concerned with Sect. 4 (Experimentations) of our Paper "A methodology to scale containerized HPC infrastructures in the Cloud". The artifact consists of a set of virtual machines from where you can deploy a comprehensive Kubernetes cluster from an Ansible receipt. Then, on this Kubernetes cluster, you can deploy three major HPC schedulers (OpenPBS, OAR, and SLURM) as a set of pods. Sample codes are supplied for each HPC scheduler to check the impact of dynamic growth or shrink of the containerized HPC scheduler on pending and running jobs. This artifact is provided as a single .pdf file containing all URLs required to set up, automatically, the experimental material that runs on the virtual machines. URLs points to an OVA file containing VMs and GitHub repositories that host the Kubernetes Ansible receipt and Dockerfiles, and Kubernetes manifests for each HPC scheduler.

4.4 Impact on Pending Jobs

(1) Workers addition. The first scenario characterizes the state of pending jobs while worker nodes are added. We launch jobs (MPI and non-MPI) on the containerized HPC cluster to consume resources. Then, when it becomes fully occupied, we submit a non-MPI job (i.e., that does not require communications between workers). This job gets the pending state, waiting for resources. We expanded the containerized HPC cluster with additional workers. The pending non-MPI job is scheduled and ends with no errors on each evaluated HPC scheduler. To complete the first scenario, we submit again a bunch of mixed MPI and non-MPI jobs to consume all resources; then, we submit an MPI job. This job is pending.

Furthermore, we expanded the containerized HPC cluster with additional workers. The MPI job is scheduled and fails with SLURM. The reason is that the MPI job is run with srun. The srun command instantiates the MPI communication infrastructure. The first MPI job scheduled on newcomer workers fails. Then, the second will work. When new nodes are added on a SLURM cluster, a reboot of slurmctld and each slurmd service is required. Dynamic nodes addition will be fully supported in the 23.02 version of SLURM[5].

(2) Workers removal. The second scenario characterizes the state of pending jobs while worker nodes are removed. We target free workers (i.e., that does not run any job). We run several jobs to keep the containerized HPC cluster busy. The idea is to have some free workers but not enough to satisfy the requirements of pending jobs. We remove these free workers from the containerized HPC cluster, and the pending jobs are not impacted.

4.5 Impact on Running Jobs

(3) Workers addition. We launch both MPI and non-MPI jobs. While they are running, we add workers. Jobs keep running and end without any errors for each containerized job scheduler. Workers' addition has no impact on running jobs.

[5] https://slurm.schedmd.com/SLUG21/Roadmap.pdf.

(4) Workers removal. We launch both MPI and non-MPI jobs, but we keep some workers free. While jobs are running, we remove free workers. Jobs run and end without any error for each containerized job scheduler, and workers' removal has no impact on running jobs.

Table 1. Results of experimentation

Scenarios	SLURM	OpenPBS	OAR
(1) Impact on pending jobs when resources are added	Fail	None	None
(2) Impact on pending jobs when resources are removed	None	None	None
(3) Impact on running jobs when resources are added	None	None	None
(4) Impact on running jobs when resources are removed	None	None	None

4.6 Short-term Upcoming Perspectives

In our experimentation, we containerized three major HPC schedulers. We evaluated the impact of containerized workers' growth or shrink for each of them. As all scenarios went well (except for the lack of an upcoming feature in SLURM), we demonstrated the potential of building a scalable, fully containerized HPC cluster in Cloud infrastructure. Consequently, a middle-term perspective for our work is to add a controller in Kubernetes that gets the state of containerized HPC cluster's queue. The sidecar containers will act as proxies between this Controller and the HPC scheduler. In our current implementation, the sidecar container adds or manually removes resources without considering the queue's state. In [11], authors introduce fine-grain applicative metrics to autoscale pods in a Kubernetes cluster.

Similarly, a possible enhancement is making our Controller use the queue state as an applicative metric to extend or shrink the containerized HPC cluster automatically. In Fig. 2 we exhibit our targeted architecture at mid-term and according to the previous discussion. The primary enhancement regarding Fig. 1 is the third and fourth steps: *Gets queue state* and *Informs Controller*. These steps will supply metrics to the Controller, allowing him to decide if he must add or remove worker pods.

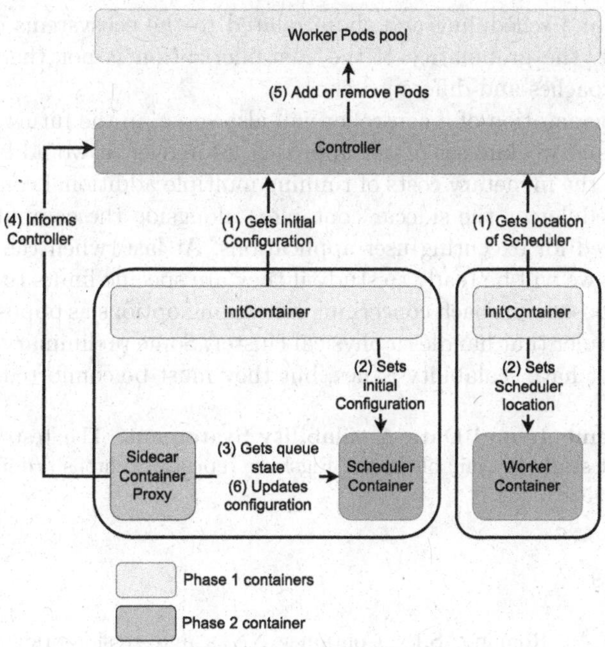

Fig. 2. Evolution of the architecture

5 Conclusion and Long-Term Perspectives

This paper experimented with a method to build scalable containerized HPC clusters in the Cloud. We containerized three central HPC schedulers: SLURM, OpenPBS, and OAR. They all can be jailed in containers, and our experimentation demonstrates that scaling jobs do not impact running or pending jobs (except for SLURM, but this point will be handled in the upcoming release). The next step is to develop a Kubernetes controller to handle the dynamic scaling of the containerized HPC cluster. This specific contribution is part of broader work on mixing HPC and Cloud computing, and studying converged infrastructure. As an example, in [8], we developed a scheduling strategy that gathers containers belonging to the same namespace on the same node. In doing this, we concentrate our effort on scheduling issues for the server consolidation problem. Consolidation is also a tremendous problem in HPC.

Converged computing is a paradigm that aims to offer HPC performance, efficiency, and sophisticated scheduling, with cloud benefits. While orchestration frameworks like Kubernetes offer several advantages such as resiliency, elasticity, portability, and manageability, they are not performance-oriented to the same degree as HPC. Our vision of converged computing is first to put into the Cloud the HPC ecosystems and not the applications supervised by the cloud orchestrator. As pointed out above, through the example of scheduling containers in the same namespace, we separate the concerns related to containers management and scheduling and those related to the ecosystems containerization. In short, the granularity of the containerization is not the same; hence different approaches and different issues.

The implementation of a controller will also serve, in the future, to reinforce the strength and weaknesses of our approach. Moreover, it would be interesting to investigate the monetary costs of running multiple additional containers (e.g., the HPC scheduler or the sidecar container) alongside the compute node containers required for executing user applications. At last, when the controller is implemented, we will be ready to study if they are specific limits to the scalability of the proposed approach concerning scheduling options as opposed to having an HPC scheduler that handles a physical cluster. Some preliminary results show that we do not have scalability issues, but they must be comforted.

Acknowledgements and Data Availability Statement. The testbed used during the current study is available in the Figshare repository: https://doi.org/10.6084/m9.figshare.19952813 [5].

References

1. Amirante, A., Romano, S.P.: Container NATs and session-oriented standards: friends or foe? IEEE Internet Comput. **23**(6), 28–37 (2019)
2. Beltre, A.M., et al.: Enabling HPC workloads on cloud infrastructure using kubernetes container orchestration mechanisms. In: 2019 IEEE/ACM International Workshop on Containers and New Orchestration Paradigms for Isolated Environments in HPC (CANOPIE-HPC), pp. 11–20 (2019)
3. Canon, R.S., Younge, A.: A case for portability and reproducibility of HPC containers. In: 2019 IEEE/ACM International Workshop on Containers and New Orchestration Paradigms for Isolated Environments in HPC (CANOPIE-HPC), Los Alamitos, CA, USA, pp. 49–54. IEEE Computer Society, November 2019. https://doi.org/10.1109/CANOPIE-HPC49598.2019.00012. https://doi.ieeecomputersociety.org/10.1109/CANOPIE-HPC49598.2019.00012
4. Capit, N., et al.: A batch scheduler with high level components. In: Cluster Computing and Grid 2005 (CCGrid05), Cardiff, United Kingdom. IEEE (2005). https://hal.archives-ouvertes.fr/hal-00005106
5. Greneche, N., et al.: Artifact and instructions to generate experimental results for Euro-Par 2022 Conference Proceedings: A Methodology to Scale Containerized HPC Infrastructures in the Cloud, June 2022. https://doi.org/10.6084/m9.figshare.19952813
6. IBM Spectrum LSF - see https://www.ibm.com/downloads/cas/VEO91OVO. Spectrum LSF
7. Kubernetes - see https://kubernetes.io/. k8s
8. Menouer, T., Greneche, N., Cérin, C., Darmon, P.: Towards an optimized containerization of HPC job schedulers based on namespaces. In: Cérin, C., Qian, D., Gaudiot, J.-L., Tan, G., Zuckerman, S. (eds.) NPC 2021. LNCS, vol. 13152, pp. 144–156. Springer, Cham (2022). https://doi.org/10.1007/978-3-030-93571-9_12

9. Misale, C., et al.: It's a scheduling affair: GROMACS in the cloud with the KubeFlux scheduler. In: 2021 3rd International Workshop on Containers and New Orchestration Paradigms for Isolated Environments in HPC (CANOPIE-HPC), Los Alamitos, CA, USA, pp. 10–16. IEEE Computer Society, November 2021. https://doi.org/10.1109/CANOPIEHPC54579.2021.00006. https://doi.ieeecomputersociety.org/10.1109/CANOPIEHPC54579.2021.00006
10. Rudyy, O., et al.: Containers in HPC: a scalability and portability study in production biological simulations. In: 2019 IEEE International Parallel and Distributed Processing Symposium (IPDPS), Los Alamitos, CA, USA, pp. 567–577. IEEE Computer Society, May 2019. https://doi.org/10.1109/IPDPS.2019.00066. https://doi.ieeecomputersociety.org/10.1109/IPDPS.2019.00066
11. Taherizadeh, S., Stankovski, V.: Dynamic multi-level autoscaling rules for containerized applications. Comput. J. **62**(2), 174–197. (2018) ISSN: 0010-4620. https://doi.org/10.1093/comjnl/bxy043. eprint: https://academic.oup.com/comjnl/article-pdf/62/2/174/27736749/bxy043.pdf
12. Torrez, A., Randles, T., Priedhorsky, R.: HPC container runtimes have minimal or no performance impact. In: 2019 IEEE/ACM International Workshop on Containers and New Orchestration Paradigms for Isolated Environments in HPC (CANOPIE-HPC). Los Alamitos, CA, USA, pp. 37-42. IEEE Computer Society, November 2019. https://doi.org/10.1109/CANOPIEHPC49598.2019.00010. https://doi.ieeecomputersociety.org/10.1109/CANOPIE-HPC49598.2019.00010
13. Sande Veiga, V., et al.: Evaluation and benchmarking of singularity MPI containers on EU research e-infrastructure. In: 2019 IEEE/ACM International Workshop on Containers and New Orchestration Paradigms for Isolated Environments in HPC (CANOPIE-HPC). Los Alamitos, CA, USA: IEEE Computer Society, Nov. 2019, pp. 1–10. https://doi.org/10.1109/CANOPIEHPC49598.2019.00006. https://doi.ieeecomputersociety.org/10.1109/CANOPIE-HPC49598.2019.00006
14. Kee, Y.-S., et al.: Enabling personal clusters on demand for batch resources using commodity software. In: 2008 IEEE International Symposium on Parallel and Distributed Processing, pp. 1–7 (2008)
15. Younge, A.J., et al.: A tale of two systems: using containers to deploy HPC applications on supercomputers and clouds'. In: 2017 IEEE International Conference on Cloud Computing Technology and Science (CloudCom). Los Alamitos, CA, USA, pp. 74–81. IEEE Computer Society, December 2017. https://doi.org/10.1109/CloudCom.2017.40. https://doi.ieeecomputersociety.org/10.1109/CloudCom.2017.40
16. Zhou, N., et al.: Container orchestration on HPC systems. In: 2020 IEEE 13th International Conference on Cloud Computing (CLOUD), pp. 34–36. IEEE (2020)

Cucumber: Renewable-Aware Admission Control for Delay-Tolerant Cloud and Edge Workloads

Philipp Wiesner[1](✉), Dominik Scheinert[1], Thorsten Wittkopp[1], Lauritz Thamsen[2], and Odej Kao[1]

[1] Technische Universität Berlin, Berlin, Germany
{wiesner,dominik.scheinert,t.wittkopp,odej.kao}@tu-berlin.de
[2] University of Glasgow, Glasgow, UK
lauritz.thamsen@glasgow.ac.uk

Abstract. The growing electricity demand of cloud and edge computing increases operational costs and will soon have a considerable impact on the environment. A possible countermeasure is equipping IT infrastructure directly with on-site renewable energy sources. Yet, particularly smaller data centers may not be able to use all generated power directly at all times, while feeding it into the public grid or energy storage is often not an option. To maximize the usage of renewable excess energy, we propose Cucumber, an admission control policy that accepts delay-tolerant workloads only if they can be computed within their deadlines without the use of grid energy. Using probabilistic forecasting of computational load, energy consumption, and energy production, Cucumber can be configured towards more optimistic or conservative admission. We evaluate our approach on two scenarios using real solar production forecasts for Berlin, Mexico City, and Cape Town in a simulation environment. For scenarios where excess energy was actually available, our results show that Cucumber's default configuration achieves acceptance rates close to the optimal case and causes 97.0% of accepted workloads to be powered using excess energy, while more conservative admission results in 18.5% reduced acceptance at almost zero grid power usage.

Keywords: admission control · on-site renewable energy · load prediction · resource management · green computing · sustainability

1 Introduction

As the demand for computing continues to grow year by year, so are operating expenses and the associated carbon emissions caused by consuming energy from the public power grid [9]. So far, negative effects could partially be mitigated through advances in hardware efficiency, cooling, and the continuous shift of cloud computing towards highly energy-optimized hyperscale data centers, which already host about 50% of all compute instances [23]. Still, data centers already

J. Cano and P. W. Trinder (Eds.): Euro-Par 2022, LNCS 13440, pp. 218–232, 2022.
https://doi.org/10.1007/978-3-031-12597-3_14

account for more than 1% of global energy consumption and this number is expected to rise further [23] – especially when considering the additional demand of novel domains like the internet of things (IoT), edge and fog computing [32].

To reduce its carbon footprint, the IT industry is pushing to integrate more and more low-carbon energy sources into data centers [1], not least because carbon pricing mechanisms, such as emission trading systems or carbon taxes, are starting to be implemented around the globe [4]. For example, Google plans to operate their data centers solely on carbon-free energy by 2030 [12]. One approach towards more sustainable and cost-effective computing systems in cloud as well as edge environments is directly equipping IT infrastructure with on-site renewable energy sources like solar or wind [18,20]. However, especially smaller compute nodes, such as on-premise installations or edge data centers, are not always able to consume all generated power directly, as depicted in Fig. 1.

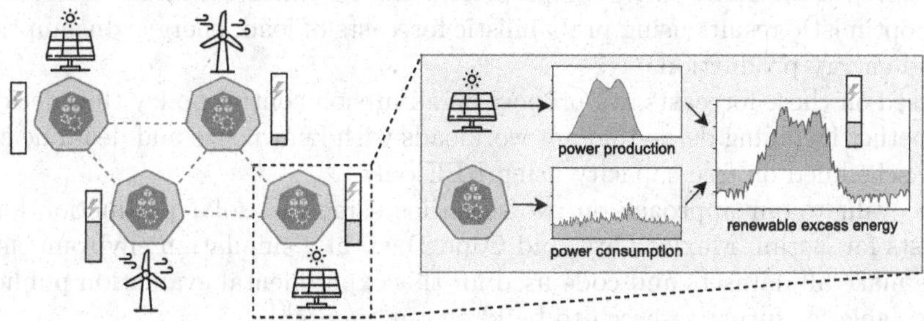

Fig. 1. Problem setting: Renewable excess energy can occur at compute nodes when local demand does temporarily not cover all produced energy.

Energy storage can mitigate this problem to some extent, but is expensive, therefore often not available in sufficient capacity, and may be reserved to ensure operation during power outages. Moreover, storing energy involves power conversion loss, and frequent charging cycles accelerate battery aging [21]. On the other hand, feeding excess energy back to the power grid is often unattractive in practice due to statutory regulations and low compensation. Microgrids address this by directly integrating renewables and energy storage to locally balance excess energy [14]. Such systems can greatly benefit from participants who are flexible and able to adapt their energy consumption to the expected supply.

To make better use of renewable excess energy (REE) occurring close to compute nodes, delay-tolerant workloads originating locally or within the surrounding distributed system should be computed on free computational capacity. Delay-tolerant workloads are common in cloud environments, ranging from machine learning jobs, certain Function-as-a-Service (FaaS) executions, nightly backups and CI/CD runs, and other periodic jobs like generating daily reports [31]. However, they may also occur in otherwise time-critical edge computing environments, such as cache and index updates as well as federated and/or iterative machine learning trainings on locally available data at edge nodes.

We propose Cucumber, an admission control policy for delay-tolerant workloads in resource-constrained compute nodes that have access to renewable energy sources but no access to energy storage. We assume that this infrastructure usually runs high-priority, time-critical workloads with quality of service (QoS) constraints, like user-facing services, but is not always fully utilized. Cucumber admits delay-tolerant workloads to the local system only if they can be computed within their deadlines on free capacity and without the use of grid energy. This leads to increased use of renewable energy sources, hence reducing associated carbon emissions and electricity costs, and contributes to stabilizing the power grid. We furthermore expect Cucumber to be an integral building block of decentralized systems that exploit the varying spatio-temporal availability of renewable energy. Towards this, we make the following contributions:

- we define a method for forecasting free computational capacity that can be powered using REE only. The prediction can be tuned towards conservative or optimistic results using probabilistic forecasts of load, energy consumption and energy production
- based on these forecasts, we propose an admission control policy that decides whether incoming delay-tolerant workloads with known size and deadline can be scheduled on free capacity using REE only
- we evaluate our approach on two scenarios using real solar production forecasts for Berlin, Mexico City, and Cape Town in a simulation environment
- we make all datasets and code used for this experimental evaluation publicly available for future research to build on our results[1]

The remainder of this paper is structured as follows: Sect. 2 reviews related work. Section 3 proposes the admission control policy and explains how we generate forecasts on free computational capacity that can be powered by REE. Section 4 evaluates our approach. Section 5 concludes the paper.

2 Related Work

Carbon-Aware and Renewable-Aware Computing. Incorporating the availability of renewable or low-carbon power into scheduling decisions has been increasingly researched over the last decade. However, many works in this context focus on load migration in geo-distributed settings or optimize for low carbon signals in the public power grid. For example, Google employs a suite of analytics pipelines to defer delay-tolerant workloads if power from the public grid is associated with high carbon intensity [25]. While their work is targeted at large-scale data centers, Cucumber is meant to be deployed in resource-constrained environments with direct access to renewable energy sources. Toosi et al. [27] proposed a load balancer for web applications that increases on-site renewable energy usage at data centers. However, other than Cucumber, their approach is reactive and does not make use of forecasting for better decisions. GreenSlot [10] is a batch job

[1] Github: https://github.com/dos-group/cucumber.

scheduler for data centers with on-site renewable energy sources using hourly predictions of solar energy and optimizes for a low price if grid power usage is unavoidable. Cucumber, on the other hand, aims at using REE only and tries to avoid using any grid power. Aksanli et al. [2] proposed a scheduler using short-term predictions of wind and solar power to reduce grid power usage and the number of canceled jobs. In contrast, Cucumber rejects workloads in danger of violating their deadlines upfront so they can be scheduled elsewhere. The Zero-Carbon Cloud [8] is the only project of which we are aware that aims at exploiting REE by placing data centers close to renewable energy sources. Our approach complements these efforts and opens up a way to distribute workloads in a decentralized manner across their proposed infrastructure by making local decisions about whether or not to accept a job.

Admission Control is a validation process in communication systems to check if sufficient resources are available to, for example, establish a network connection or process a request. Other than most publications on admission control that operates on a network packet level, we consider workloads that can be several minutes or even hours long. Because of this, most related work is in the context of web-based applications or cloud computing where certain requests are prioritized to improve quality of service (QoS) or maximize revenue [7,33]. An admission control policy in green computing was proposed by [13], where a PID controller used in industrial control applications is extended by a hybrid green policy, to reduce grid power usage. Eco-IDC [22] targets energy-aware admission control on a data center level by exploiting electricity price changes while dropping excessive workload if required. Other than these approaches, Cucumber optimizes for utilizing locally available REE while prioritizing time-critical workloads. Furthermore, our approach utilizes probabilistic forecasting methods to be configurable towards more optimistic or conservative admission.

3 Admission Control

Cucumber accepts delay-tolerant workloads based on forecasts of load, power consumption, and power production. A high-level overview and outline of the approach are presented in Fig. 2. This section describes all steps in detail.

3.1 Forecasting Load, Power Consumption, and Power Production

Cucumber uses probabilistic multistep-ahead forecasts to predict time series of probability distributions, which inherent the uncertainty for each observation, to later infer the available REE at different confidence intervals. If no probabilistic forecasts are available, Cucumber can still be operated in its default configuration based on the expected/median forecast.

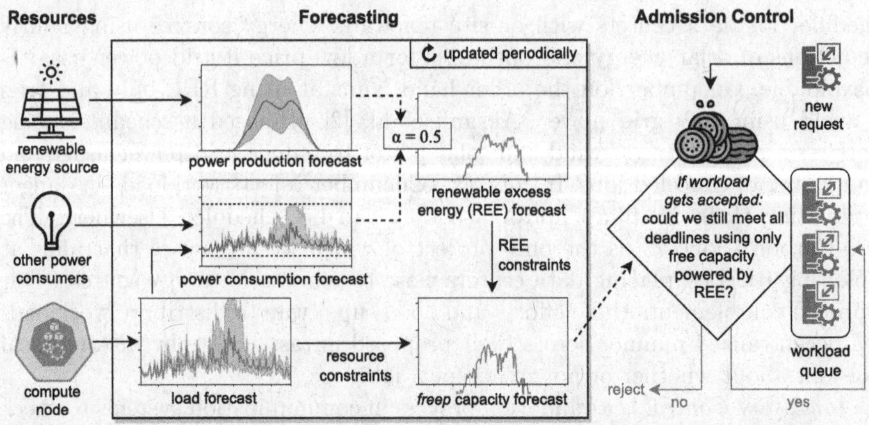

Fig. 2. Cucumber periodically forecasts computational load, power consumption, and power production to compute the *freep* capacity forecast. It determines how much computational capacity will be available in the future, that can be powered using REE only. Based on this forecast and the amount, size, and deadlines of already queued workloads, Cucumber accepts or rejects new workload requests.

Forecasting Computational Load. Load prediction is a widely researched field covering forecasts related to application metrics, such as the number of messages in a stream processing system [11], as well as the utilization of (virtualized) hardware resources like CPU, GPU or RAM. Although load prediction systems are usually formulated as time series forecasting problems based on historical data, they can also take information from other contexts into account. For example, in edge computing use cases like traffic monitoring, additional information on weather, holidays, events, etc. can improve the forecast quality. Whatever type of forecast is most suitable in a concrete use case, Cucumber uses it to identify future time windows with free capacity. Furthermore, these load predictions are used as a factor in the power consumption forecast. In the following, we denote the load of a node as U and any load forecasts as U_{pred}.

Forecasting Power Consumption. The power demand of IT infrastructures can be influenced by many factors like CPU or GPU usage, memory, I/O, and storage access, temperature, etc. While perfect modeling without precise knowledge of workload and infrastructure characteristics is not possible [17], it has been shown that power usage can often be modeled with sufficient accuracy based only on the node's utilization [5] – which usually refers to its CPU usage. In fact, power modeling based on CPU usage only is being used in production at modern hyperscale data centers [24]. For simplicity, here we assume a simple linear power model to convert from a certain load U to the nodes power usage P:

$$P = P_{\text{static}} + U \cdot (P_{\text{max}} - P_{\text{static}}) \tag{1}$$

where P_{static} is the amount of power a node consumes in idle state and P_{max} is the amount of power the node consumes under full load. Besides energy used for computing, the power forecast should also take the expected demand from other co-located consumers into account that are powered by the renewable energy source, like cooling or lighting, to correctly derive the actually available REE.

Forecasting Power Production. Since information on future power production is useful in many domains ranging from high-level application design to low-level grid control, the prediction of variable renewable energy sources like solar panels [6,16] and wind turbines [3,19] is an active field of research. Such models are usually based on weather models for mid- and long-term forecasts as well as, in case of solar, satellite data for short-term forecasts, that enable the observation and movement of clouds [15]. Very short-term models with one-minute resolution can even be based on live video data using sky cameras[2]. As wind and solar power production are known for their high variability, probabilistic prediction methods are especially common in this domain [28,34].

3.2 Deriving the *freep* Capacity Forecast

Based on the previously generated forecasts, we now determine the main input to Cucumber's admission control: the *freep* (free REE-powered) capacity forecast.

For this, we first calculate the REE forecast P_{ree}. If no probabilistic forecasting was used to generate the power production P_{prod} and consumption P_{cons} forecasts, we can directly define $P_{\text{ree}} = \max(0,\ P_{\text{prod}} - P_{\text{cons}})$. If probabilistic forecasting was applied, we now have the possibility to decide that P_{ree} should describe a more optimistic or more conservative view of the future and hence manipulate the behavior of the admission control policy.

However, we need to differentiate between two kinds of probabilistic forecasts. The first contains actual probability distributions for each forecasted observation, which, in practice, is mostly implemented as ensembles of non-deterministic single-value predictions. In this case, the simplest way to build a joint distribution P_{ree} is by randomly sampling from both distributions and subtracting the returned values for power production and consumption. We can then use the quantile function Q to determine a concrete single-valued time series.

$$P_{\text{ree}}^{\alpha} = \max(0,\ Q(\alpha,\ P_{\text{ree}})) \tag{2}$$

where $\alpha \in [0, 1]$ determines how *optimistic* (big α) or *conservative* (small α) our forecasts are. For example, $P_{\text{ree}}^{0.95}$ returns the 95th percentile of P_{ree}.

In the second case, one or both forecasts do not contain the actual distributions but only values for a number of pre-initialized quantiles, usually the median and an upper and lower bound like the 10th and 90th percentile. In this case, we propose a fall-back method as we cannot simply join the distributions:

$$P_{\text{ree}}^{\alpha'} = \max(0,\ Q(\alpha,\ P_{\text{prod}}) - Q(1-\alpha,\ P_{\text{cons}})) \tag{3}$$

[2] https://solcast.com/utility-scale/solar-data-api/super-rapid-solar-farm-forecasts.

where α' can only take certain values determined by the pre-initialized quantiles. Note that using this equation α' holds the same semantic value as α (e.g. big α' represents optimistic forecasts) but no guarantees of actual probability. In the following, we use α and α' interchangeably.

Using the forecasts for computational load U_{pred} and available REE P^{α}_{ree} we can now compute the *freep* capacity forecast U_{freep}, which determines how much of the free capacity in the future can be powered using only REE:

$$U_{freep} = \min(\overbrace{1 - U_{\text{pred}}}^{U_{\text{free}}}, \overbrace{\frac{P^{\alpha}_{\text{max}} - P_{\text{static}}}{P_{\text{max}} - P_{\text{static}}}}^{U_{\text{reep}}}) \tag{4}$$

The *freep* capacity forecast is defined as the minimum of U_{free}, the expected free capacity of the node, and U_{reep}, the expected fraction of capacity that could be REE-powered. If U_{pred} is a probabilistic forecast, it first has to be converted to a single-valued time series, for example using $Q(0.5, U_{\text{pred}})$. The equation for U_{reep} depends on the used power model and it was derived by rearranging the linear power model from Eq. 1.

3.3 Admission Control Policy

Cucumber admits workload requests based on the above derived *freep* capacity forecast and the amount, size, and deadlines of already queued workloads (Fig. 3). For this, all workload requests are expected to provide a job size estimate and a deadline. In practice, deadlines are often provided directly by users or services or can be derived from, for example, application graphs. Estimating the size of jobs is a common problem in scheduling and is usually performed based on previous executions of the same or similar workloads. In the current approach, we do not consider uncertainty in job size estimates, parallelism, or additional resource constraints besides computational load, like memory. However, Cucumber can be extended to consider such factors.

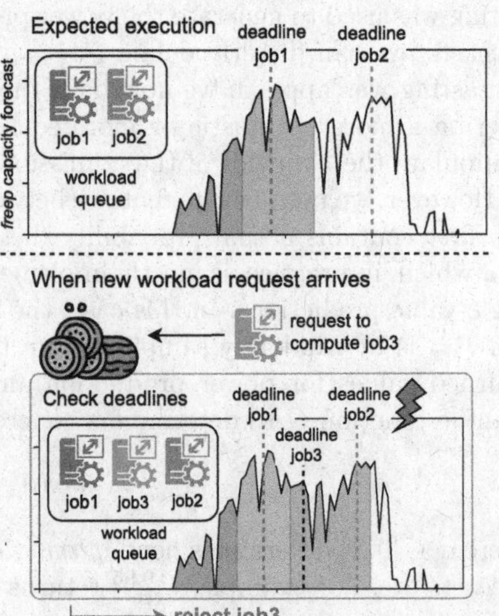

Fig. 3. Cucumber rejects workloads if it expects any future deadline violations using the *freep* capacity forecast.

The approach is agnostic to the applied scheduling mechanism, including multiple levels of priority or preemptive workloads, as long as it can be reliably modeled with the available information. For every incoming request, Cucumber models the expected processing of the queue if the workload was accepted and evaluates if any deadlines are being violated. That is, for each queued workload it progresses in time on the *freep* capacity forecast until the expected (remaining) workload size is covered and then checks if the workload's deadline was violated. If any violation occurs, the request gets rejected, otherwise accepted.

Depending on the number of workload requests and the average queue length, this basic algorithm can become computationally inefficient, since a re-evaluation has to take place for each request. However, performance issues can be mitigated in many ways, for example by grouping jobs with the same or similar deadlines and only evaluation violations per group. Moreover, different heuristics can be applied to decrease the number of re-evaluations, like caching the remaining time and capacity of each group until their deadline, and only performing a full re-evaluation once violations become likely. Concrete performance adjustments depend on the nature of the underlying system, such as the level of parallelization as well as frequency, distribution, and kind of incoming workloads.

3.4 Limiting Power Consumption at Runtime

To ensure that accepted workloads run on REE only, their resource usage needs to be limited at runtime. In practice, there are several ways to approach this, including adjustments of hardware power and speed settings like dynamic voltage and frequency scaling (DVFS). Nevertheless, to propose a simple approach, modern high-level tools or resource orchestration solutions allow for conveniently controlling the usage of resources such as CPU or GPU. For instance, the CPU usage of a process can be limited using tools like *cpulimit*. Likewise, frameworks like Docker and Kubernetes have built-in flags for limiting CPU usage by adapting the settings of a container's *cgroup*. As load U and available REE P_{ree} can be measured periodically at runtime to derive the current U_{gec}, such tools can be used to adjust the node's power consumption to the correct level without inferring with the time-critical baseload. However, the suitability of this simple approach depends highly on the concrete environment and more sophisticated measures might be needed in certain scenarios.

Even when performing admission control at a low α (meaning in conservative mode), conditions at runtime might still be worse than expected. If less REE is available than forecasted, the previously described power limiting could lead to deadline violations of accepted jobs, although there is free computational capacity available. While this behavior might be acceptable in some environments, usually it is more important to meet promised deadlines than ensuring that no grid energy is used at all. To mitigate violations, Cucumber uses the *freep* capacity forecasts at runtime to periodically evaluate whether the currently active jobs can still meet their deadlines. If a running job is expected to violate its deadline, we temporarily stop power limiting and finish it using all free capacity U_{free}. Since also load forecasts are uncertain, deadline violations still cannot be completely ruled out, but will be mitigated as effectively as possible based on the current state of knowledge.

4 Evaluation

We evaluate Cucumber on real datasets over the course of two weeks (January 18–31) using the discrete-event simulation framework SimPy. In total, 36 experiments were conducted: Six admission control policies (three baselines and Cucumber at $\alpha \in \{0.1, 0.5, 0.9\}$) in two scenarios at three solar sites each. All data and simulation code are publicly available as mentioned in Sect. 1.

4.1 Experimental Setup

We want to upfront explain some simplifications we made in our simulation-based evaluation. First, we assume that the reported size of workload requests is always correct, while in practice runtime estimates are often noisy. Yet, we consider this a problem not addressed by Cucumber. Second, we do not explicitly model parallelism but process the workload queue next to the time-critical baseload in sequential order using non-preemptive earliest deadline first (EDF) scheduling. Third, we do not model the energy demand of Cucumber itself. However, we expect its overhead to be very small as forecasts are only updated every 10 min and the admission control itself can be implemented efficiently.

Admission Control Policies. We evaluate six admission control policies for each of the below-described scenarios and solar sites. If deadlines are violated, jobs are not canceled but continue to run until they are completed.

- *Optimal w/o REE* accepts workloads using perfect forecasts for U_{pred} but without considering the availability of REE. It declares the upper bound for accepted jobs without deadline misses but accepts high grid power usage.
- *Optimal REE-Aware* accepts workloads using perfect load and renewable energy production forecasts. It declares the upper bound for accepted jobs without deadline misses and without any grid power usage.
- *Naive* accepts workloads only if there is currently REE available and there is no other workload in process. This approach does not rely on forecasts.
- *Conservative*, *Expected*, and *Optimistic* describe Cucumber admission control using realistic forecasts at $\alpha \in \{0.1, 0.5, 0.9\}$, respectively.

Scenarios. We define two scenarios where each consists of a high-priority baseload and a number of workload requests. Exemplary baseload patterns are depicted in Fig. 4. Since, to the best of our knowledge, trace datasets with information on the delay-tolerance of workloads do not exist yet, we modeled both scenarios based on related real-world datasets:

1. *ML Training* is based on the *cluster-trace-gpu-v2020* dataset from the Alibaba Cluster Trace Program[3], which contains two months of traces from a GPU production cluster [29]. Baseload is modeled using tasks labeled as *worker*,

[3] https://github.com/alibaba/clusterdata.

which are highly variable and hard to predict. Each of the 5477 delay-tolerant workload requests corresponds to an *xComputeWorker* task in the dataset. The size of workloads is determined by the *plan_gpu* property and each workload has to be finished by midnight the day it was issued, meaning deadlines can be anywhere from 0 to 24 h.

2. *Edge Computing*: is based on the NYC Taxi Trip dataset[4] from Dec 2020 and Jan 2021. Baseload is modeled on the number of yellow taxi rides, which is highly seasonal. The 2967 workload requests correspond to long-distance green taxi rides: Every green taxi ride over 10 km length emits a job at *lpep_pickup_datetime* which has to be computed until *lpep_dropoff_datetime*. The median deadline is 41 min. All jobs have the same size.

We generated baseload forecasts by training a DeepAR [26] probabilistic forecasting model[5] on the first 1.5 months of data to then generate 24-h forecasts with a 10-min resolution for every 10-min step in the last two weeks of the datasets. Note, that the arrival rate of workload requests is not forecasted by Cucumber. Power consumption forecasts are derived using Eq. 1 with $P_{\max} = 180\,W$ and $P_{\text{static}} = 30\,W$.

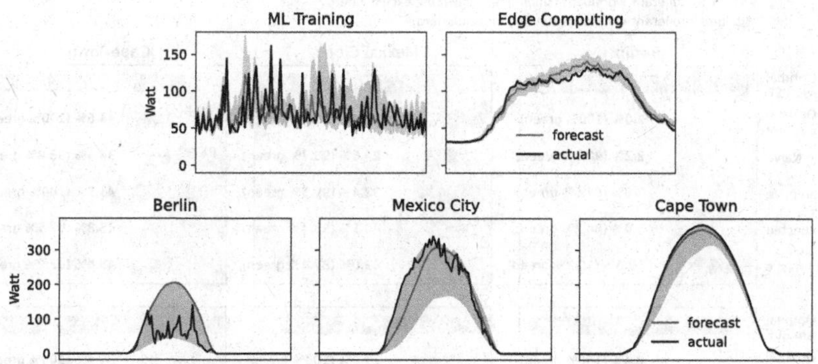

Fig. 4. In red: actual and forecasted baseload power consumption in both scenarios at an exemplary day. In green: exemplary power production at the three solar sites. (Color figure online)

Solar Sites. We assume every compute node has access to a solar panel with 400 W peak production. We collected real solar power production forecasts using the Solcast[6] utility-scale API during the second half of January 2022. Like load forecasts, the solar forecasts cover 24 h in 10-min resolution each and were generated in 10-min intervals. Each forecast contains the median as well as the 10th

[4] https://www1.nyc.gov/site/tlc/about/tlc-trip-record-data.page.

[5] DeepAR parameters: GRU, 3 Layers, 64 nodes, 0.1 Dropout; 20–30 min training time on commodity hardware.

[6] https://solcast.com.

and 90th percentile of expected energy production for each time step. To evaluate the effectiveness of our approach at different geographical locations and during different seasons, we gathered forecasts at three different sites located at different continents and latitudes:

1. *Berlin* during winter (8 h of daylight; 2 h of sunshine)
2. *Mexico City* during the dry season (11 h of daylight; 7 h of sunshine)
3. *Cape Town* during summer (14 h of daylight; 11 h of sunshine)

For orientation, the roughly expected hours of daylight and sunshine in January at each site are listed in parentheses. Exemplary values for each site are displayed in Fig. 4.

4.2 Results

For each experiment, we report the admission control acceptance rate and the fraction of REE that was used to actually power the workloads. Figure 5 illustrates the results.

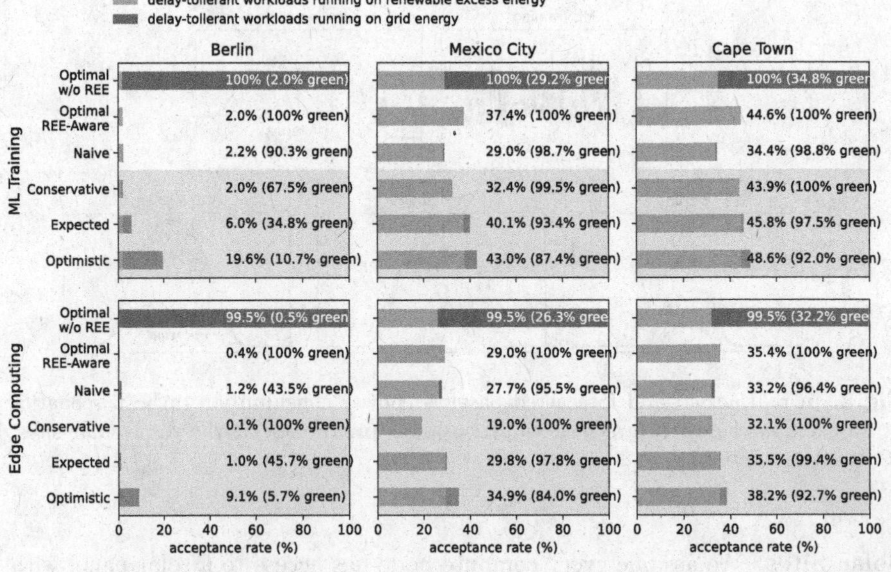

Fig. 5. Acceptance rate of workload requests and the fraction of these workloads that was actually powered via REE during execution (green). (Color figure online)

As expected, *Optimal w/o REE* accepts almost all workload requests at the cost of requiring a substantial amount of grid energy. Worth mentioning is the constant acceptance rate of 100% across all experiments of the ML Training scenario, which is a result of the rather relaxed deadlines. The stricter deadlines in the Edge Computing scenario lead to a slight decrease in acceptance rates. Both baselines utilize perfect forecasts but only *Optimal REE-Aware* considers available REE, which is why is does not use any grid energy across all experiments.

We observe that there was barely any REE available at the Berlin solar site during the observed period. Even *Optimal REE-Aware* accepts only a maximum of 2% of all workloads. Since the uncertainty and error rate of solar forecasts is extremely high at the Berlin site, only *Conservative* forecasts achieved comparably low grid power usage. Admission control based on *Optimistic* and *Expected* forecasts resulted in very low REE usage of 5.7–10.7% and 34.8–45.7%, respectively. Under such conditions, the usage of a forecast-based admission control policy such as Cucumber can hardly be justified, as it does not show improved performance compared to a *Naive* approach.

However, in Mexico City and Cape Town, which had a lot longer days and better weather during January than Berlin, Cucumber clearly outperforms the *Naive* admission control, which achieves 31.1% acceptance rate at 97.3% REE usage in average. Cucumber's *Expected* case configuration maintains almost the same REE usage (97.0%) but increases the acceptance rate to 37.8%, while the *Conservative* configuration manages 99.9% REE usage at an acceptance rate of 31.9%. The trade-off when tuning the forecasts is clearly visible: While *Conservative* admission control results in almost perfect REE coverage, the acceptance rate was on average 18.5% lower.

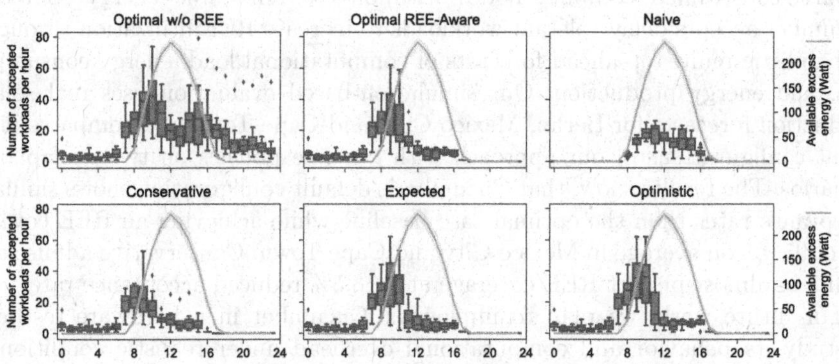

Fig. 6. Aggregated number of accepted workloads per hour for all admission control policies during the ML Training scenario in Mexico City. The orange line indicates the average solar production during a day. (Color figure online)

Figure 6 depicts the aggregated number of jobs per hour for an exemplary solar site on the ML Training scenario (all deadlines are midnight). We observe that the acceptance rate over time differs strongly between the different approaches: Considering that *Optimal w/o REE* describes all workloads that can be accepted without deadline violations, *Optimal REE-Aware* describes the optimal subset that can be computed using only REE. The *Naive* approach cannot exploit this potential, as it only accepts workloads once there is REE available.

The Cucumber admission control, on the other hand, is based on forecasts of REE and hence already accepts workloads before the sun is rising. It can be observed, that in the *Expected* case's behaviour is close to the optimal case and almost all jobs before 11 am get accepted. After that, the number of accepted jobs per hour falls drastically since the forecasted solar energy until midnight is already reserved by queued workloads and forecasts in Mexico City are comparably precise. In *Conservative* mode, Cucumber is more cautious and accepts fewer jobs during early morning hours. However, it accepts additional jobs throughout the day as uncertainty decreases when progressing in time.

We note that *Optimistic* forecasts barely increase REE usage compared to Expected forecasts in most experiments. For example, the acceptance rate for the Edge Computing scenario in Mexico City went up by 16.3%, but the REE usage by only 0.5%, meaning that almost all additionally accepted jobs were powered by grid energy. Furthermore, we note that the *Optimistic* experiments resulted in 1, 5, and 7 deadline misses in the Edge Computing scenario (which has tight deadlines), while none of the other configurations caused any deadline misses. We conclude that users should pick $\alpha > 0.5$ with caution.

5 Conclusion

This paper presents Cucumber, a configurable admission control policy for resource-constrained compute nodes with on-site renewable energy sources. Cucumber accepts delay-tolerant workloads to increase REE utilization through probabilistic multistep-ahead forecasts of computational load, energy consumption, and energy production. Our simulation-based evaluation uses real solar production forecasts for Berlin, Mexico City, and Cape Town and compares different configurations of our approach with baseline policies on two exemplary scenarios. The results show, that Cucumber's default configuration shows similar acceptance rates than the optimal case baseline while achieving an REE coverage of 97.0% on average in Mexico City and Cape Town. Conservative admission results in almost perfect REE coverage at a 18.5% reduced acceptance rate.

For future work, we plan to implement Cucumber in a hardware testbed to study its behavior and computational overhead under realistic conditions. Furthermore, we want to extend the approach to also consider available energy story and make Cucumber part of a decentralized architecture that exploits the spatio-temporal availability of REE in a distributed system via local decisions.

Acknowledgments and Data Availability Statement. The datasets and code generated and analyzed in this paper are available in the Figshare repository: https://doi.org/10.6084/m9.figshare.19984556 [30].

We sincerely thank Solcast for the uncomplicated and free access to their solar forecast APIs. This research was supported by the German Academic Exchange Service (DAAD) as ide3a and the German Ministry for Education and Research (BMBF) as BIFOLD (grant 01IS18025A) and Software Campus (01IS17050).

References

1. Acun, B., et al.: A holistic approach for designing carbon aware datacenters. arXiv:2201.10036 [cs.DC] (2022)
2. Aksanli, B., Venkatesh, J., Zhang, L., Rosing, T.: Utilizing green energy prediction to schedule mixed batch and service jobs in data centers. In: HotPower 2011 (2011). https://doi.org/10.1145/2039252.2039257
3. Alencar, D.B., de Mattos Affonso, C., Oliveira, R.C.L., Rodríguez, J.L.M., Leite, J.C., Filho, J.C.R.: Different models for forecasting wind power generation: case study. Energies **10** (2017). https://doi.org/10.3390/en10121976
4. Bank, W.: State and trends of carbon pricing 2020. Technical report. World Bank, Washington, DC (2020)
5. Barroso, L.A., Hölzle, U.: The case for energy-proportional computing. Computer **40**(12) (2007). https://doi.org/10.1109/MC.2007.443
6. Bright, J.M., Killinger, S., Lingfors, D., Engerer, N.A.: Improved satellite-derived PV power nowcasting using real-time power data from reference PV systems. Solar Energy **168** (2018). https://doi.org/10.1016/j.solener.2017.10.091
7. Chen, X., Mohapatra, P., Chen, H.: An admission control scheme for predictable server response time for web accesses. In: WWW. ACM (2001). https://doi.org/10.1145/371920.372156
8. Chien, A.A., Zhang, C., Nguyen, H.D.: Zero-carbon cloud: research challenges for datacenters as supply-following loads. Technical report CS-TR-2019-08. University of Chicago (2019)
9. Freitag, C., Berners-Lee, M., Widdicks, K., Knowles, B., Blair, G., Friday, A.: The climate impact of ICT: a review of estimates, trends and regulations. arXiv:2102.02622 [physics.soc-ph] (2021)
10. Goiri, I., et al.: Matching renewable energy supply and demand in green datacenters. Ad Hoc Netw. **25** (2015). https://doi.org/10.1016/j.adhoc.2014.11.012
11. Gontarska, K., Geldenhuys, M., Scheinert, D., Wiesner, P., Polze, A., Thamsen, L.: Evaluation of load prediction techniques for distributed stream processing. In: International Conference on Cloud Engineering (IC2E). IEEE (2021). https://doi.org/10.1109/IC2E52221.2021.00023
12. Google: 24/7 by 2030: Realizing a carbon-free future. Technical report, Google (2020)
13. Hazemi, F.A.: A hybrid green policy for admission control in web-based applications. In: SoftCOM. IEEE (2013). https://doi.org/10.1109/SoftCOM.2013.6671846
14. Hirsch, A., Parag, Y., Guerrero, J.: Microgrids: a review of technologies, key drivers, and outstanding issues. Renew. Sustain. Energy Rev. **90** (2018). https://doi.org/10.1016/j.rser.2018.03.040
15. Kallio-Myers, V., Riihelä, A., Lahtinen, P., Lindfors, A.: Global horizontal irradiance forecast for Finland based on geostationary weather satellite data. Solar Energy **198** (2020). https://doi.org/10.1016/j.solener.2020.01.008
16. Khalyasmaa, A.I., et al.: Prediction of solar power generation based on random forest regressor model. In: SIBIRCON (2019). https://doi.org/10.1109/SIBIRCON48586.2019.8958063
17. Koller, R., Verma, A., Neogi, A.: Wattapp: an application aware power meter for shared data centers (2010). https://doi.org/10.1145/1809049.1809055
18. Kordkheili, R.A., Hinkle, T., Gandhi, M., der Pas, N.V., Davari, P.: On-site power generation for data centers. Technical report, Sust. Digital Infrastructure Alliance (2021)

19. Li, Q., et al.: Prediction of power generation of two 30 kw horizontal axis wind turbines with gaussian model. Energy **231** (2021). https://doi.org/10.1016/j.energy.2021.121075
20. Li, W., et al.: On enabling sustainable edge computing with renewable energy resources. IEEE Commun. Mag. **56**(5) (2018). https://doi.org/10.1109/MCOM.2018.1700888
21. Liu, L., Sun, H., Li, C., Li, T., Xin, J., Zheng, N.: Managing battery aging for high energy availability in green datacenters. IEEE Trans. Parallel Distrib. Syst. **28**(12) (2017). https://doi.org/10.1109/TPDS.2017.2712778
22. Luo, J., Rao, L., Liu, X.: Temporal load balancing with service delay guarantees for data center energy cost optimization. IEEE Trans. Parallel Distrib. Syst. **25**(3) (2014). https://doi.org/10.1109/TPDS.2013.69
23. Masanet, E., Shehabi, A., Lei, N., Smith, S., Koomey, J.: Recalibrating global data center energy-use estimates. Science **367** (2020). https://doi.org/10.1126/science.aba3758
24. Radovanovic, A., Chen, B., Talukdar, S., Roy, B., Duarte, A., Shahbazi, M.: Power modeling for effective datacenter planning and compute management. IEEE Trans. Smart Grid (2021). https://doi.org/10.1109/TSG.2021.3125275
25. Radovanovic, A., et al.: Carbon-aware computing for datacenters. IEEE Trans. Power Syst. (2022). https://doi.org/10.1109/TPWRS.2022.3173250
26. Salinas, D., Flunkert, V., Gasthaus, J., Januschowski, T.: Deepar: probabilistic forecasting with autoregressive recurrent networks. Int. J. Forecast. **36**(3) (2020). https://doi.org/10.1016/j.ijforecast.2019.07.001
27. Toosi, A.N., Qu, C., de Assunção, M.D., Buyya, R.: Renewable-aware geographical load balancing of web applications for sustainable data centers. J. Netw. Comput. Appl. **83** (2017). https://doi.org/10.1016/j.jnca.2017.01.036
28. Verbois, H., Rusydi, A., Thiery, A.: Probabilistic forecasting of day-ahead solar irradiance using quantile gradient boosting. Solar Energy **173** (2018). https://doi.org/10.1016/j.solener.2018.07.071
29. Weng, Q., et al.: MLaaS in the wild: workload analysis and scheduling in large-scale heterogeneous GPU clusters. In: NSDI, vol. 22 (2022)
30. Wiesner, P.: Artifact and instructions to generate experimental results for the Euro-Par 2022 paper: "cucumber: renewable-aware admission control for delay-tolerant cloud and edge workloads". Figshare: https://doi.org/10.6084/m9.figshare.19984556
31. Wiesner, P., Behnke, I., Scheinert, D., Gontarska, K., Thamsen, L.: Let's wait awhile: how temporal workload shifting can reduce carbon emissions in the cloud. In: Middleware2021. ACM (2021). https://doi.org/10.1145/3464298.3493399
32. Wiesner, P., Thamsen, L.: LEAF: simulating large energy-aware fog computing environments. In: 5th International Conference on Fog and Edge Computing (ICFEC). IEEE (2021). https://doi.org/10.1109/ICFEC51620.2021.00012
33. Yuan, H., Bi, J., Tan, W., Li, B.H.: CAWSAC: cost-aware workload scheduling and admission control for distributed cloud data centers. IEEE Trans. Autom. Sci. Eng. **13**(2) (2016). https://doi.org/10.1109/TASE.2015.2427234
34. Zhang, H., Liu, Y., Yan, J., Han, S., Li, L., Long, Q.: Improved deep mixture density network for regional wind power probabilistic forecasting. IEEE Trans. Power Syst. **35**(4) (2020). https://doi.org/10.1109/TPWRS.2020.2971607

Multi-objective Hybrid Autoscaling of Microservices in Kubernetes Clusters

Angelina Horn[1(✉)], Hamid Mohammadi Fard[2], and Felix Wolf[2]

[1] Cronn GmbH, Bonn, Germany
angelina.horn@cronn.de

[2] Technical University of Darmstadt, Darmstadt, Germany
{hamid.fard,felix.wolf}@tu-darmstadt.de

Abstract. The cloud community has accepted microservices as the dominant architecture for implementing cloud native applications. To efficiently execute microservice-based applications, application owners need to carefully scale the required resources, considering the dynamic workload of individual microservices. The complexity of resource provisioning for such applications highlights the crucial role of autoscaling mechanisms. Kubernetes, the common orchestration framework for microservice-based applications, mainly proposes a horizontal pod autoscaling (HPA) mechanism, which, however, lacks efficiency. To hinder resource wastage and still achieve the requested average response time of microservices, we propose a multi-objective autoscaling mechanism. Based on machine learning techniques, we introduce a toolchain for hybrid autoscaling of microservices in Kubernetes. Comparing several machine learning techniques and also our in-house performance modeling tool, called Extra-P, we propose the most adequate model for solving the problem. Our extensive evaluation on a real-world benchmark application shows a significant reduction of resource consumption while still meeting the average response time specified by the user, which outperforms the results of common HPA in Kubernetes.

1 Introduction

The microservices architecture provides a highly flexible approach for design and deployment of cloud native applications. In this architecture, the application is decomposed into a collection of loosely coupled services, which interact over light remote interfaces, such as REST APIs.

Containerization is the major technology to deploy the microservices. In both industry and academia, we could observe a change of focus from virtual machine centric to container centric approaches, in the cloud environments [5]. To manage the life cycle of containers in scale, container orchestration frameworks allow the cloud and application providers to define how to select, deploy, monitor, and dynamically control the configuration of containers inside the cluster.

Usually the load of an application is not distributed equally among all microservices. Thus, we need to scale the microservices individually to meet

J. Cano and P. W. Trinder (Eds.): Euro-Par 2022, LNCS 13440, pp. 233–250, 2022.
https://doi.org/10.1007/978-3-031-12597-3_15

the service level agreement (SLA) and quality of service (QoS). Autoscaling is the solution for efficiently managing microservices, which is very complex for the application developers/owners.

The major autoscaling trend in Kubernetes, the de facto standard for orchestration frameworks, is threshold-based autoscaling such that the users specify a set of fixed conditions for scaling actions. Currently, horizontal pod autoscaling (HPA) is the main scaling approach admitted in the Kubernetes community. Vertical pod autoscaling (VPA) is not widely accepted yet but is becoming more popular. It has been proven that the HPA approach is usually not efficient [1]. Consequently, we need to focus on more fine grained autoscaling approaches.

In this paper, based on machine learning modeling, we propose a hybrid autoscaler such that the resources could be scaled horizontally, vertically or by combination of both approaches. The goal of our autoscaling mechanism is simultaneous optimization of response time and resource usage cost. Based on our scaling mechanism, we proposed, implemented and verified a toolchain for the whole autoscaling MAPE (monitor, analysis, planning and execution) loop [12] in Kubernetes. We compared several performance models in our approach and empirically proposed the most adequate model for this problem. In addition, we compared our approach with the built-in HPA in Kubernetes and observed its competence in real-world problems.

The rest of the paper is organized as follows. In Sect. 2, we review the related work and mention the difference of our approach with the state-of-the-art. We present our proposed autoscaling mechanism and toolchain in Sect. 3. We discuss evaluation of the autoscaling approach in Sect. 4 and finally conclude the paper in Sect. 5.

2 Related Work

Resource provisioning for cloud native applications could be managed at different levels. Resource providers focus on efficient assignment of resources to microservices [6], while application developers guide the orchestrator to manage resources more efficiently. Our focus in this paper is resource provisioning at the developer level.

To better understand the related work compared to our approach, we use the taxonomy presented in [12]. This taxonomy has been proposed for autoscaling of virtual machines (VMs) in the cloud but it would be mainly applicable for autoscaling of microservices at the application level. In this section, we first briefly explain the necessary concepts, from the taxonomy, and then we deeply review some of the remarkable autoscaling approaches proposed for microservices.

Autoscaling is the process of scaling resources for a service in an automated manner. Autoscaling of microservices allows us to allocate more resources for microservices when they are under a hefty load and retake extra resources when the load decreases. In general, resource scaling can be done horizontally, vertically or in a hybrid approach. In horizontal scaling, we add or remove the number

Table 1. Comparing our approach (MOHA) to the related work (*NC* stands for *not clear from the publication*)

Autoscaler	Scaling Methods	Application Architecture	Session Stickness	Scaling Indicators	Resource Estimation	Scaling Timing
[13]	Hybrid	Single tier	Non-sticky	Hybrid	Machine learning	Proactive
[14]	Hybrid	NC	NC	Low-level	Hybrid	Proactive
[7]	Horizontal	NC	NC	High-level	Hybrid	Proactive
[16]	Horizontal	Single tier	Non-sticky	Low-level	Machine learning	Proactive
[1]	Hybrid	Single tier	Non-sticky	Hybrid	Application profiling	Reactive
[4]	Horizontal	Single tier	Non-sticky	High-level	Machine learning	Proactive
[15]	Horizontal	Single tier	Non-sticky	High-level	Machine learning	Proactive
MOHA	Hybrid (plus selective scaling)	SOA	Sticky	Hybrid	Machine learning	Proactive

of resource instances assigned to a service (scaling out/in). In vertical scaling, we increase or decrease the capacity of already assigned resource instance to a service (scaling up/down).

We could categorize autoscaling approaches based on the three web *application architecture* as: single tier, multi tier and service-oriented architecture (SOA). Single tier or single service application is the minimum deployable and scalable component size. Microservices are often referred to as single service applications. Applications that consist of more than one service are respectively called multi tier applications. A commonly used architecture of this type is a three-tier application comprising three services: a frontend, a backend, and a database layer (although databases are usually considered not dynamically scalable and therefore ignored in autoscaling). Finally, SOA describes applications consisting of several independent services that interact through lightweight APIs and are not necessarily connected sequentially with each other.

Session stickiness is another aspect of autoscaling mechanisms. If the intermediate status of interaction between a client and an application is saved, the session is considered stateful or sticky. Most autoscalers limit the scaling cluster to be stateless and to support stateful sessions usually they transform stateful servers into stateless servers before autoscaling, for instance, by moving the session data out of the web servers and store them either at user side or in a shared Memcached cluster [12].

Scaling indicators are the metrics observed in the monitoring phase and are the basis for the actions of autoscalers. They can be divided into low-level and high-level metrics. Low-level metrics are observed in physical or virtual machine layers, such as CPU and memory utilization and cache miss rate. Metrics collected in the application layer are referred to as high-level metrics, such as request rate and response time.

Different approaches are used for *resource estimation* in autoscaling. The most basic and widely adopted approach is rule-based resource estimation. It is described by using a set of predefined rules, made up of conditions and actions. These rules are established mainly by empirical estimations and are hard-coded. Application profiling is another approach that describes the process of testing the saturation of resources, by applying synthetic or recorded workloads on application. Other methods to estimate resources are analytical modeling, in which a mathematical model is composed based on theory and analysis, and machine learning which dynamically models the resource usage.

The *scaling timing* can be either reactive or proactive. With reactive scaling, the autoscaler will only react to a given situation and try to counteract it. In contrast to this, with proactive approaches, an autoscaler tries to avoid certain situations, such as exhaustion of resources, by executing scaling actions in advance. Predictions can be based on given data trends and patterns or external data.

In [13], the authors developed a hybrid autoscaler using model-based reinforcement learning, to guarantee the continuity of the performance of the application while simultaneously minimizing resource wastage. The researchers identified the possible long learning phase as a general problem of existing reinforcement learning approaches.

Autopilot [14] is a hybrid autoscaler developed by Google, designed for their internal cloud. They use an orchestration tool called *Borg*, which manages instances of a job consisting of several tasks. The objective of Autopilot is to reduce the slack (difference between the requested and used resources) of jobs while maintaining stability.

A predictive autoscaling approach based on a long short-term memory (LSTM) neural network was proposed in [7] that provides horizontal scaling, using historical time-series data. LSTM neural networks represent a particular type of recurrent neural networks and are very suitable to predict the next sequence in a time-series data.

A horizontal scaling approach was proposed in [16], which is an ARIMA based autoscaling approach using historical time-series data. It estimates the number of pods based on the predicted load represented by CPU usage. The calculation of the estimated resources is based on the Kubernetes HPA approach. Furthermore, the approach combines the ARIMA method with a signal analysis method.

The autoscaler approach in [1] provides hybrid autoscaling possibilities based on automatic application profiling. The authors evaluated the work based on a set of random workloads which cannot be compared to the behavior of real-world applications.

The horizontal autoscaler proposed in [4] uses RNN (Bi-LSTM) model and only predicts the number of requests. This work is evaluated using a dummy web server and has no resource wastage analysis. Another horizontal autoscaling in [15] similarly uses the number of requests for modeling but ignores the importance of CPU and memory usage. This work also uses a dummy web server that mimics a dataset, for evaluation.

Respecting the taxonomy proposed in [12], we categorized the aforementioned related works and positioned our proposed approach in this taxonomy. As shown in Table 1, these autoscaling approaches present a variety in almost each autoscaling category. They provide a mixture of purely horizontal or hybrid (combination of both horizontal and vertical) scaling capabilities and no

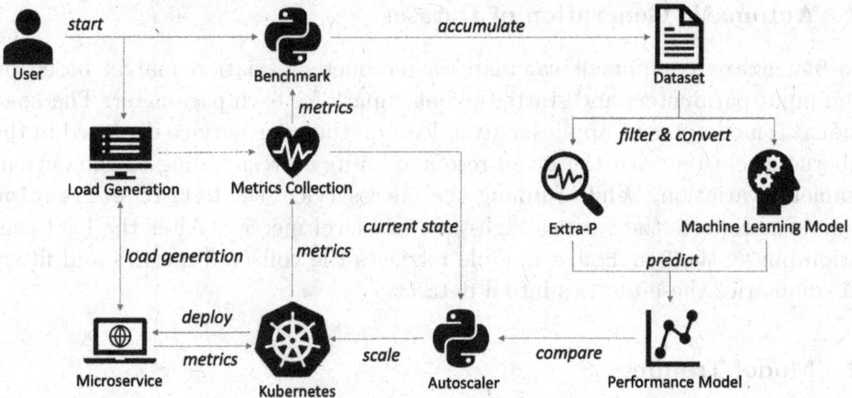

Fig. 1. Architecture of Multi-Objective Hybrid Autoscaling (MOHA)

approach representing a purely vertical autoscaler. The reviewed mechanisms are mostly stateless and need some workaround to cover stateful sessions. Finally, we noticed that none of these works use reference applications in detail. In the cases where an application was described, the application did not represent any real-world reference application but rather a simulated or prototype simple web service. Hence the autoscaling approaches lack real-world comparison, such as connected microservice ensembling.

Compared to the explained autoscaling mechanisms, our proposed approach will be evaluated as service-oriented architecture (SOA) that uses sticky sessions. It uses both high-level and low-level metrics as scaling indicators. The resource needs will be estimated via a machine learning based performance model (see the Sect. 3). Since the performance model is based on historical data, the scaling timing is classified as proactive. We benefit from multiple criteria decision making theory with the flexibility of tuning weights for particular purposes (e.g. scaling data- or compute-intensive services). Finally, our approach provides a flexible hybrid autoscaling such that we could also request for only horizontal or vertical scaling. As analyzed in the Sect. 4, it will achieve the average response time of services, as the QoS defined by the user.

3 Multi-Objective Hybrid Autoscaling

In this section, we explain our proposed toolchain called Multi-Objective Hybrid Autoscaling (MOHA)[1] and the relation between the components. Figure 1 depicts using MOHA in Kubernetes. We explain the components of MOHA by placing those to three main phases: dataset generation, model training and autoscaling approach. In particular, we discuss the machine learning (ML) models and our proposed autoscaling approach.

[1] https://github.com/Angi2412/PodAutoscalingKubernetes.

3.1 Automatic Generation of Dataset

The `Benchmark` component calculates a parameter variation matrix based on given input parameters and starts the benchmark for each parameter. The `Load Generation` component applies a given load on the microservice deployed in the Kubernetes cluster with the given resource limits corresponding to the current parameter variation. While running the microservice, the `Metric collection` component collects the various high- and low-level metrics. After the load generation phase, the `Benchmark` module retrieves the collected metrics and filters and summaries these metrics into a dataset.

3.2 Model Training

The accumulated dataset of performance data, consisting of the gathered metrics must be preprocessed (by scaling samples, as described in the rest of this section) before the `Machine Learning Model` component can use it. After preprocessing, the resulting data can be converted to be used as a training set for `Machine Learning Model` or any other performance modeling tools.

We model the performance of each microservice based on the current load of the service and the resource limits of pods deploying the microservice. The resource limits include CPU and memory limits, and the number of pod replicas, which are the typical input parameters while defining the pods in Kubernetes. Load of the microservice is dynamically represented by requests per second. The outputs (target metrics) of the model are the average response time, CPU usage and memory usage. The average response time models the performance, while CPU and memory usage model resource utilization. Therefore, we could assume that the utilization also reflects the resource wastage, such that if a given resource is not efficiently utilized, then the resource is wasted.

We chose three different ML models and compared them to explore which one is more suitable for the performance model prediction as part of our autoscaling toolchain. The selected ML models are linear regression (LR), support vector regression (SVR) and multi-layer perceptron regressor neural network (MLPRegressor NN). Since regression models can have multiple inputs but only one output, we trained each model for each of the three target variables. Each of the selected ML approaches represents a different complexity level of machine learning and provides advantages and disadvantages for specific use cases, which inspired us to choose them.

The LR model generally provides fast learning and prediction time while also being suited for large datasets. A disadvantage of the LR model is that it performs well only for linear samples. For this approach, we implemented a least-squares and a Bayesian variant, an extended variant of the maximum likelihood estimator, of linear regression.

The SVR model is more stable against outliers than the other models because of its margin approach. Additionally, it provides a wide range of use cases because of the possibility of using several kernel functions based on the dataset behavior. The advantage over the LR model is handling nonlinear coherence but with much higher training time compared to linear regression (more than quadratic to the number of samples).

The MLPRegressor NN model is a neural network that uses backpropagation for training and the square error as the loss function. MLPRegressor NN can also handle non-linear samples while being especially suited for large datasets with several thousands of samples. Furthermore, it provides extensive customizability by offering several activation functions and solvers. Nevertheless, backpropagation has high time complexity and the training time grows with the number of hidden neurons and layers.

Each ML model owns several hyper parameters, including estimation functions, that need to be tweaked for providing the best possible outcome. Thus, we conducted an extensive grid search for each of the models and hyper parameters. The grid search consists of an estimator, a parameter space, a validation scheme, and a score function. The estimator is the ML model, the parameter space specifies a search space for a hyper parameter, and the validation scheme is used to split a given dataset into several smaller datasets. The number of smaller datasets is dependent on the parameter variation resulting from the number of parameters and size of their parameter space. Finally, the score function is used to compare the accuracy of the estimator given a specific parameter variation. In the grid search, each parameter variation is executed on a smaller dataset and then compared to the performance of the others. The output of the grid search is a ranked table of all parameter variations. The described grid search was executed with all three ML models to configure their hyper parameters.

Since we use ML to represent regression then we need to normalize datasets for using distances in the loss functions. We applied the *MinMaxScaler*[2], which scales each sample to a value $1 \leq \alpha \leq 0$. The scaler is fitted onto the training dataset. The inputs and each target use a different scaler instance. These scalers are saved from being usable with new samples. Each time new samples are predicted, the input has to be transformed with the fitted scaler. Furthermore, the predicted values are inversely scaled with the saved target scalers to bring the normalized predicted values into the original ranges.

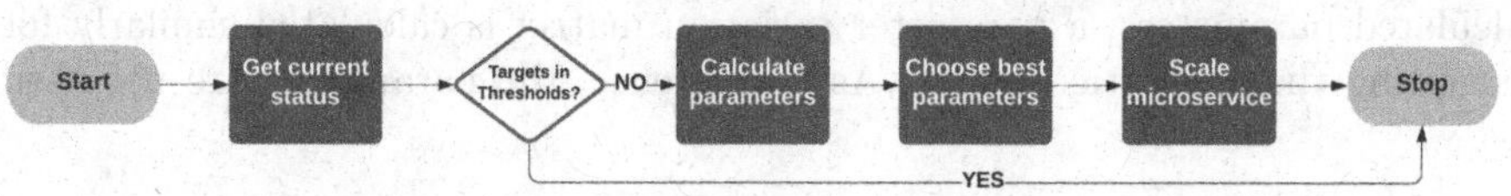

Fig. 2. The autoscaling loop

[2] From the Scikit-learn package (https://scikit-learn.org/).

3.3 Autoscaling Loop

The `Autoscaler` component in Fig. 1 uses the predicted performance model from the previous phase, to choose the proper parameters for improving its target metrics. It gathers the current status of the microservice, checks if resource scaling is necessary and uses the Kubernetes APIs to scale the microservice accordingly.

Every autoscaler follows the *MAPE* (monitoring, analysis, planning and execution) loop [12]. Monitoring is the first step that fetches all the available metrics for a given application. The second step is to analyze the fetched data regarding specific metrics exceeding a given threshold. Considering the metrics measured in the previous step, we need to plan how to proceed for resource provisioning. In the last step of the MAPE loop, the plan must be executed. The MAPE loop is running in a specified time period, which could be, for instance, the application life cycle. The MAPE loop of our autoscaling mechanism is shown by Fig. 2, which is triggered in specific intervals.

First, the Autoscaler gathers the current status of the microservice. It calls the `Prometheus`[3] instances which gathers high-level metrics from the service mesh `Linkerd`[4] and low-level metrics from Kubernetes itself. Then it checks the target metrics. If all targets are in their thresholds, this means that the targets are satisfactory then the loop is exited, and the microservice is not scaled. However, if the threshold is exceeded by any of the three target metrics, the autoscaling loop would proceed. We discussed our precise setting in Sect. 4.

The optimal resource limits for each target are calculated based on the current target values, parameter status and the aimed values. To calculate the number of pods, we rely on the same calculation used in the Kubernetes HPA[5].

Each optimal resource limit ($p_i^{optimal}$) for parameter p_i of the web service, is calculated based on the desired target value ($t_i^{desired}$) and the current status ($p_i^{current}$ and $t_i^{current}$), as follows:

$$p_i^{optimal} = \lceil p_i^{current} \cdot \frac{t_i^{current}}{t_i^{desired}} \rceil \tag{1}$$

The number of optimal parameters is calculated by *number of parameters* to the power *number of targets*, which in our autoscaler is 27 ($= 3^3$). Based on these calculated parameters, a parameter variation matrix is calculated similarly for generating the synthetic dataset. As a difference, the parameters are not used

3 https://prometheus.io.
4 https://linkerd.io.
5 https://kubernetes.io/docs/tasks/run-application/horizontal-pod-autoscale/.

as ranges but used as discrete values. For calculating the parameter variation, the optimal CPU limit that is calculated based on the memory usage as well as the optimal memory limit that is calculated based on the CPU usage are neglected because of their missing correlation. Considering this removal, our parameter variation matrix includes 12 ($= 3 \times 2 \times 2$) parameter variations. This approach limits the possible decision space of parameter variation, ensuring that only sufficient parameter variations are considered.

Then the parameter matrix is scaled by the same *MinMaxScaler* used to train the machine learning models. Furthermore, for each parameter variation, all three target metrics are predicted by the trained models. The resulting predictions are then scaled inversely to represent their original units.

The array with the predicted targets is then handed over to TOPSIS [9], which is a multiple criteria decision making (MCDM) method. The TOPSIS selects the most suitable target set, considering the weights and criteria. Therefore, the criteria for the TOPSIS are always as minimizing the average response time, maximizing the CPU and memory usage, minimizing the CPU and memory limit, and minimizing the number of pods. Based on what result is desired, the weights of each criterion can be adjusted. Moreover, the output of the MCDM is a ranked list of the targets, with the rank specifying how well a target set fulfils the weighted criteria. Since the ranked list of targets is stated in their original order, it is possible to get the best-ranked target set index and its corresponding parameter variation.

Consequently, the best chosen resource limits are used to scale the microservice with the Kubernetes API. In contrast to the pod update method used in the synthetic dataset generation, the updated pod is not recreated but patched. This approach ensures that the rolling update function of Kubernetes is used. The rolling update functionality ensures no downtime and, therefore, no loss of requests while a pod is scaled [10]. Additionally, a readiness probe is implemented in the deployment YAML file of the scaled microservice. If a pod is added to the deployment in horizontal scaling, the traffic is only redirected to the new pod once it is ready. The readiness is checked by making an HTTP request to a specific rest endpoint of the microservice that responds with the status 200 when it is reachable. In vertical scaling, a new pod with the updated resources is created and checked if it is ready before the previous pod is deleted.

Finally, the autoscaling loop is finished and adds a new run of itself to the Python scheduler with the set scaling time.

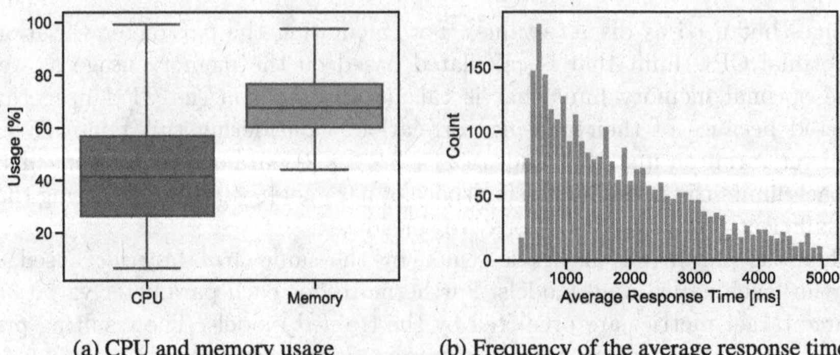

(a) CPU and memory usage (b) Frequency of the average response time

Fig. 3. Target metrics

4 Evaluation

We extensively evaluated our proposed approach including the autoscaling loop and the MOHA toolchain. We used the Scikit-learn[6] and Scikit-Criteria[7] packages to implement the machine learning models and the TOPSIS functionalities, respectively. In continue, we first present the experimental setup and then we analyze the achieved results.

4.1 Experimental Setup

We generated a dataset consisting of 3,125 samples with five variations for each parameter in the ranges of [300 m, 500 m][8] for CPU limit, *[400Mi, 600Mi]*[9] for memory limit and *[1–5]* for replicas. The dataset was split (by randomly shuffling) into the training dataset consists of 75% and the test dataset consists of 25% of the entire dataset.

To be more clear, we depicted a summary of the target metrics of the generated dataset in Fig. 3. The boxplots in Fig. 3a show that we have the possibility of both upscaling and downscaling, as needed. The frequency histogram in Fig. 3b illustrates that the dataset includes various response times, concluding different (light to heavy) loads, were generated.

Each machine learning approach was trained and tested on the same datasets. To ensure comparability between the machine learning algorithms, the used training and test datasets were scaled with the MinMaxScaler. Moreover, for each algorithm, a grid search was performed to tune its hyperparameters.

The threshold for the average response time describes the maximum value that the average response time should not exceed. Respecting the suggestion from [11], this threshold was considered as 1 s. To avoid CPU throttling and

[6] https://scikit-learn.org/.

[7] https://scikit-criteria.readthedocs.io/.

[8] m stands for millicore.

[9] Mi stands for mebibyte.

out of memory errors, we should notice that the resources must not be fully utilized. Therefore, the thresholds for CPU and memory usage were set to a minimum of 70% and a maximum of 90%. In contrast to the average response time, the desired CPU and memory usage is the mean value of the minimum and maximum threshold, being 80% in this case.

4.2 The Benchmark Setup

There are several microservices-based benchmark applications, such as robot-shop[10] and the SockShop[11]. But considering the limitation of the applications, e.g. lack of heavy resource usage, we chose the TeaStore[12] to evaluate our approach. The TeaStore is a microservice-based application representing an e-commerce platform, which was intentionally developed for studying microservice behavior [8].

The TeaStore already provides a profile set for real-world user behavior, but this does not include buyer behavior and is implemented as a closed workload model, with no control on arrival rate of service requests. Thus, we reimplemenetd the given user behavior with minor differences to the original profile, which includes randomized buyer behavior. Furthermore, the provided user behavior for the load testing tool JMeter[13] was changed into an open workload behavior that generates a given number of requests per second.

A user after visiting the landing page of the store, performs a login action with a random username. Afterwards, the user visits a random category and product, which the user puts in its cart. This sub loop is repeated randomly up to five times. When all products are in the cart, it is randomly decided if the user buys them or not. Furthermore, the user visits its profile page and finally logs out.

The synthetic dataset was created with a constant number of requests per second, modeling a constant load on the system. The maximum number of requests per second is varied during the dataset generation to generate more diversity in the dataset. Therefore, this load pattern represents only a scenario for upscaling the resource limits. The constant load pattern is suited for the synthetic dataset generation because it provides performance insight from the load on the microservice with a specific resource specification.

We created a custom load pattern based on an adjustable number of requests per second. This dynamic load starts with a constantly increasing load from 1 request per second until reaching a maximum of 1000 requests per second. This increase phase has a duration of three and half minutes. The load of the maximum number of requests per second stays constant for three more minutes. After that, the load is decreased until reaching 1 request per second. Similarly, this decrease happens in a duration of three and half minutes. The profile represents

[10] https://github.com/instana/robot-shop.

[11] https://github.com/helidon-sockshop/sockshop.

[12] https://github.com/DescartesResearch/TeaStore.

[13] https://jmeter.apache.org/.

a more realistic load pattern than the constant load pattern used for the dataset generation. It provides periods of increase in requests per second and includes periods of load decrease. Therefore, it is suited for the evaluation runs of the autoscaler by providing up-, down-, in- and out-scaling scenarios and a scenario in which no scaling is necessary.

Table 2. Phase one - Accuracy comparison

Model	**LR**			**SVR**			**MLPRegressor NN**		
Target	Response time	CPU usage	Memory usage	Response time	CPU usage	Memory usage	Response time	CPU usage	Memory usage
MSE	0.01	0.01	0.00	0.01	0.01	0.00	0.01	0.01	0.00
R^2	0.55	0.78	0.90	**0.72**	**0.87**	**0.94**	0.56	0.78	0.90

Table 3. Phase two - Qualitative comparison

Model	**CPU limit [m]**	**Memory limit [Mi]**	**Pods (average)**	**Response time [ms]**	**CPU usage [%]**	**Memory usage [%]**
LR	537.78	**439.85**	2.10	**796.96**	69.32	**78.81**
SVR	**437.47**	460.11	**1.60**	1,344.74	**70.46**	77.41
MLPRegressor NN	583.72	501.44	3.47	1,704.66	66.29	56.65
Extra-P	643.68	578.4	5.25	1,466.55	49.12	52.63

4.3 Experimental Results

In this section, we analyze the results achieved by our autoscaling toolchain, using the three machine learning models (LR, SVR and MLPRegressor NN) and the Extra-P model [3]. The results are then compared with the Kubernetes HPA's results.

We divided our analysis into three phases, each of them having a different focus. In the first phase, each machine learning approach is trained on the synthetically generated dataset and then their speed of training, speed of prediction and prediction accuracy are compared. In the second phase, we evaluate the results of using ML and Extra-P models in the MOHA toolchain, considering simultaneously minimizing average response time and resource consumption. In the third phase, the horizontal pod autoscaling of SVR is compared to the standard Kubernetes HPA to observe how the performance of our proposed approach outperforms an already established autoscaling approach.

Phase One. Since the least squares and the Bayesian variant of the LR delivered precisely the same values, the Bayesian variant is further referred to as LR. To measure the speed of the ML algorithms, we considered an accuracy of 17 decimal digits that were shown by rounding to 4 digits. In our experiments, we observed that the LR algorithm has by far the lowest training time of only 0.7 ms, while the MLPRegressor NN has a much higher training time of 0.2 s. Furthermore, the SVR presents the highest training time of all algorithms with around 0.39 s. The LR model's prediction time is very short such that after our rounding it could be assumed to be nearly zero. Similar to the training time, the MLPRegressor is the second fastest algorithm with a prediction time of 1.4 ms, while the SVR model has the highest prediction time of 25 ms.

The prediction accuracy was measured with the Mean Squared Error (MSE) and the coefficient of determination (R^2) metrics [2]. The MSE measures the average squared error between the predicted and the actual value. It is always a positive value. The closer the value is to zero, the better the estimator. The coefficient of determination provides a measure of the probability that the model predicts an unknown sample. The R^2 score can be between infinite negative and one. Here the best value is one, while zero would indicate an estimator that always predicts the expected value regardless of the input. The results of the comparison are shown in Table 2. The best metric value of a target is highlighted.

In summary, it can be concluded that the LR algorithm is the fastest algorithm of all, regarding the training and prediction time but it is the least accurate one. Moreover, the MLPRegressor NN is slower than the LR but slightly more accurate. Furthermore, it scores the same MSE values as the LR and SVR. Finally, the SVR is much slower than the other two methods but results in a much better R^2 score throughout every target. It is, therefore, the most accurate machine learning method of the methods compared. However, considering the importance of prediction accuracy and the fact that the scaling decision is not made every second, the higher prediction time of the SVR could be practically neglected.

Phase Two. We compare the ML and Extra-P models, embedded into the MOHA toolchain. The comparison is divided into qualitative and quantitative comparisons.

Qualitative Comparison. We calculated the average of parameters and targets. The Extra-P resource estimation equations were created using its multi-parameter model that uses the median and the refined approach of the current version of the application.

The results of the comparison are summarized in Table 3. Here, all parameters and target values represent the average except for the response time represented by its median. The median response time is chosen to get a more outlier free impression of the behavior. Moreover, the TOPSIS decision maker's weights are chosen to be balanced: the average response time is weighted with 0.5 while all resources related weights sum up to 0.5. The scaling time for each approach is set to 1 min, allowing up to ten scales per evaluation run.

We observed that the LR model achieves the lowest median response time despite scoring the least accuracy in the prediction of the average response time. Additionally, it scores the highest average memory usage. Furthermore, the prediction with the MLPRegressor NN scores the highest and, therefore, worst response time. The SVR-based autoscaler does use the lowest average CPU limit and number of pods while also showing the highest average CPU usage. It is especially noticeable that Extra-P is scoring the worst values in each metric except for the median response time. This result can be caused by the fact that Extra-P was not initially designed to make precise predictions but rather to find scaling bugs in the performance behavior of a system. Finally, the MLPRegressor NN shows in no metric, except for the median response time, the best or worst value. It can therefore be considered average.

The scaling behavior of all models are shown in the Fig. 4. For each approach, a visualization of each parameter was conducted over the time of the evaluation run (in minutes). As shown, SVR uses considerably less resources, considering the number and the resource capacity of pods, while meeting the specified average response time.

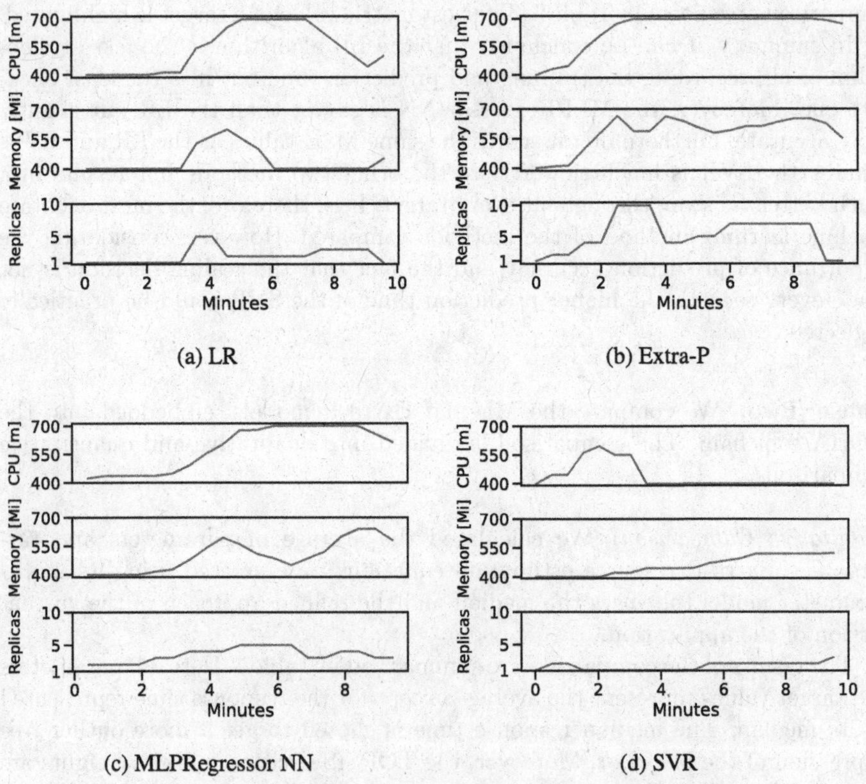

Fig. 4. Scaling behavior

Quantitative Comparison. Since the microservice-based applications usually run on public cloud environments, analyzing the monetary cost of running applications on commercial public clouds makes perfect sense. In continue, based on the published resource prices from the Google Cloud[14], we estimated and compared the cost of running the benchmark application using different autoscaling approaches. To estimate the cost of resources, we assume that the Google Kubernetes server is located in Frankfurt, Germany (Europe-west3). Moreover, the resource prices per hour and a total utilization of 24 h per day are assumed. Consequently, one vCPU (1000 m) costs 0.0573$ per hour, while one gigabyte of memory (≈953Mi) costs 0.0063421$ per hour. To calculate each of the resource costs per hour, the average resource limits of the evaluation run are converted to the corresponding units, multiplied by the corresponding prices, and extrapolated to one hour. Finally, the resource costs are summarized and extrapolated to 24 h to result in the total resource costs per day in the US dollar.

The results of the cost estimation are shown in Table 4. The SVR-based approach shows the lowest costs of CPU and memory resources and therefore, it is the approach with the lowest total resource costs of 6.48$ per day. The Extra-P approach results in a high total resource cost of 30.72$, as the most expensive approach among all.

Table 4. Phase two - Quantitative comparison (cost per day)

Model	**CPU [$]**	**PMemory [$]**	**Total [$]**
LR	9.36	0.96	10.32
SVR	**5.76**	**0.72**	**6.48**
MLPRegressor NN	16.8	1.68	18.48
Extra-P	27.84	2.88	30.72

Table 5. TOPSIS weight variations

Model	$\mathbf{W}_{response\ time}$	$\mathbf{W}_{resources}$
SVR-HPA$_t$	0.9	0.1
SVR-HPA$_r$	0.1	0.9
SVR-HPA$_b$	0.5	0.5

In summary, we could conclude that the SVR-based approach provides the fewest number of pods, highest resource usage and therefore, lowest resource cost. Moreover, although it scores a higher median response time than the LR, its response time still meets the requested QoS. The Extra-P based model scored worst in the described approach because of its very high resource costs and insufficient median response time.

Phase Three. We compared the horizontal scaling ability of the SVR-based approach with the Kubernetes HPA. For the sake of compatibility, we implemented the Kubernetes HPA approach in Python. The HPA follows the same

[14] https://cloud.google.com/kubernetes-engine/pricing.

process similar to the other approaches for gathering the current status and uses the resource estimation of the Kubernetes HPA. The HPA estimates the required number of pods based on the current number of pods and the used target metric. It then decides to take the maximum number of pods calculated from all target metrics. In the case of the novel implemented autoscaler approach, the calculated CPU and memory limits are neglected in the resource estimation process to only use the horizontal scaling capabilities of the approach.

Table 6 presents the results of the comparison. We set the CPU limit to 300 m and memory limit to 400 Mi. The maximum number of requests per second was set to 1000, in 1 min as scaling time, with the maximum number of pods limited to 10.

To study the impact of criteria's weights on the results, several weight distributions of the TOPSIS, following different goals, are compared (see Table 5). SVR-HPA$_t$ favors minimizing the response time, while SVR-HPA$_r$ tends to minimize resource wastage instead. For comparison reasons, SVR-HPA$_b$ representing the balanced weight distribution from phase one is also considered.

It can be observed that the SVR-HPA$_r$ and the Kubernetes HPA use the lowest number of pods. The response time optimized approach uses the most pods, while the balanced approach uses only slightly more pods than the resource optimized and the Kubernetes HPA approach. Furthermore, the resource optimized approach has the lowest median response time.

Overall, the balanced SVR-based approach scores the lowest cost total value and is, therefore, the most beneficial approach of the compared approaches considering the balance of minimizing the response time violations and the total resource wastage.

Table 6. Phase three - SVR-based HPA vs. the Kubernetes HPA

Model	Pods	Response time [ms]	CPU usage [%]	Memory usage [%]	Total cost [$]
SVR-HPA$_t$	5.55	1141.75	41.36	66.03	8.75
SVR-HPA$_r$	**1.95**	**170**	29.42	**70.09**	3.63
SVR-HPA$_b$	2.15	455.2	**47.35**	62.01	**3.11**
Kubernetes HPA	**1.95**	214.93	34.49	68.56	3.40

We could especially distinguish that SVR-HPA$_r$ shows the best median response time even though the intentional weight distribution was not optimized. Furthermore, it shows less CPU usage but more memory usage than the other approaches. In contrast to the resource optimized approach, the response time optimized approach results in the highest median response time of all approaches. This behaviour could be explained by the high number of pods used. It could be possible that the registry web service, responsible for distribution of requests, creates extra overhead for distributing workload to more pods and causes increase of median response time.

All in all, it can be concluded that the SVR-based autoscaling approach shows better results in horizontal pod autoscaling than the Kubernetes HPA when the weight distribution is chosen correctly. Furthermore, the developed approach allows the possibility to tweak its behavior by adjusting its weight distribution to its requirements.

5 Conclusion

Uncontrolled deployment of microservices can cause resource wastage or degrade the performance of applications. In this paper, we propose an autoscaling approach and a toolchain, called MOHA, designed for hybrid autoscaling of microservices in Kubernetes that scale pods horizontally, vertically or in a hybrid way aiming simultaneously decreasing the response time and the resource consumption. We evaluated our approach for three machine learning approaches, namely linear regression (LR), support vector regression (SVR) and the multi-layer perceptron regressor neural network (MLPRegressor NN), and also a performance modeling tool, called Extra-P. We observed that SVR operates better for our problem. Conducting the variant workloads for our experiments on a benchmark application, called TeaStore, confirms the scalability of our proposed toolchain. Moreover, we observed that the horizontal scaling capabilities of the SVR-based approach competes very well with the default Kubernetes HPA for the cost of resource usage while our approach provides much better response time for microservices. We believe that our open source toolchain can be practically used for real-word microservice-based applications and by far decreases the resource usage costs while meeting the QoS for average response time.

Acknowledgements. We acknowledge the support of the European Commission and the German Federal Ministry of Education and Research (BMBF) under the EuroHPC Programme ADMIRE (GA No. 956748, BMBF funding No. 16HPC006K). The EuroHPC Joint Undertaking (JU) receives support from the European Union's Horizon 2020 research and innovation programme and GER, FRA, ESP, ITA, POL and SWE. This research was also supported by the EBRAINS research infrastructure, funded by the European Union's Horizon 2020 Framework Programme for Research and Innovation under the Specific GA No. 945539 (Human Brain Project SGA3), and is partly funded by the Federal Ministry of Education and Research (BMBF) and the state of Hesse as part of the NHR Program.

References

1. Balla, D., Simon, C., Maliosz, M.: Adaptive scaling of Kubernetes pods. In: NOMS 2020–2020 IEEE/IFIP Network Operations and Management Symposium, pp. 1–5 (2020)
2. Botchkarev, A.: A new typology design of performance metrics to measure errors in machine learning regression algorithms. Interdiscip. J. Inf. Knowl. Manag. **14**, 45–76 (2019)
3. Calotoiu, A.: Automatic empirical performance modeling of parallel programs. Ph.D. thesis, Technische Universität Darmstadt (2018)
4. Dang-Quang, N.M., Yoo, M.: Deep learning-based autoscaling using bidirectional long short-term memory for Kubernetes. Appl. Sci. **11**(9) (2021)

5. Fard, H.M., Prodan, R., Wolf, F.: A container-driven approach for resource provisioning in edge-fog cloud. In: Brandic, I., Genez, T.A.L., Pietri, I., Sakellariou, R. (eds.) ALGOCLOUD 2019. LNCS, vol. 12041, pp. 59–76. Springer, Cham (2020). https://doi.org/10.1007/978-3-030-58628-7_5
6. Fard, H.M., Prodan, R., Wolf, F.: Dynamic multi-objective scheduling of microservices in the cloud. In: IEEE/ACM 13th International Conference on Utility and Cloud Computing (UCC), pp. 386–393 (2020)
7. Imdoukh, M., Ahmad, I., Alfailakawi, M.G.: Machine learning-based auto-scaling for containerized applications. Neural Comput. Appl. **32**(13), 9745–9760 (2019). https://doi.org/10.1007/s00521-019-04507-z
8. Von Kistowski, J., Eismann, S., Schmitt, N., Bauer, A., Grohmann, J., Kounev, S.: Teastore: a micro-service reference application for benchmarking, modeling and resource management research. In: 2018 IEEE 26th International Symposium on Modeling, Analysis, and Simulation of Computer and Telecommunication Systems (MASCOTS), pp. 223–236 (2018)
9. Kolios, A., Mytilinou, V., Lozano-Minguez, E., Salonitis, K.: A comparative study of multiple-criteria decision-making methods under stochastic inputs. Energies **9**(7) (2016)
10. Midigudla, D.: Performance analysis of the impact of vertical scaling on application containerized with Docker, Kubernetes on Amazon web services EC2 (2019)
11. Nielsen, J.: Usability Engineering. Morgan Kaufmann, Burlington (1994)
12. Qu, C., Calheiros, R.N., Buyya, R.: Auto-scaling web applications in clouds: a taxonomy and survey. ACM Comput. Surv. **51**(4), 1–33 (2018)
13. Rossi, F., Nardelli, M., Cardellini, V.: Horizontal and vertical scaling of container-based applications using reinforcement learning. In: 2019 IEEE 12th International Conference on Cloud Computing (CLOUD), pp. 329–338 (2019)
14. Rzadca, K., et al.: Autopilot: workload autoscaling at google, pp. 1–16. EuroSys 2020, Association for Computing Machinery, New York, NY, USA (2020)
15. Toka, L., Dobreff, G., Fodor, B., Sonkoly, B.: Machine learning-based scaling management for Kubernetes edge clusters. IEEE Trans. Netw. Serv. Manag. **18**(1), 958–972 (2021)
16. Zhao, A., Huang, Q., Huang, Y., Zou, L., Chen, Z., Song, J.: Research on resource prediction model based on Kubernetes container auto-scaling technology. In: IOP Conference Series: Materials Science and Engineering, vol. 569, pp. 1–8. IOP Publishing (2019)

Theory and Algorithms for Parallel and Distributed Processing

Two-Agent Scheduling with Resource Augmentation on Multiple Machines

Vincent Fagnon[1], Giorgio Lucarelli[2], Clément Mommessin[3(✉)], and Denis Trystram[1]

[1] Univ. Grenoble Alpes, CNRS, INRIA, Grenoble INP, LIG, Grenoble, France
{vincent.fagnon,denis.trystram}@inria.fr
[2] LCOMS, University of Lorraine, Metz, France
giorgio.lucarelli@univ-lorraine.fr
[3] University of Leeds, Leeds, UK
c.mommessin@leeds.ac.uk

Abstract. We are interested in this paper in studying how to schedule tasks in an extreme edge setting, where some sensors produce data and subsequent tasks are executed locally. They are interacting with some external tasks submitted by a superior authority in the cloud. We first model such a system as a problem of scheduling two sets of tasks, each associated with its own objective. The tasks of the first set are released on-line, they can be preempted and the target objective is the minimization of the mean flow-time. The tasks of the second set are known beforehand and cannot be preempted. The objective is to execute them before a common deadline.

Due to strong lower bounds on the competitive ratio of this problem, we use the technique of resource augmentation to cope with these limitations. Specifically, our analysis is based on both speed augmentation and rejection. First, we give a general lower bound for the problem, even in the case of speed augmentation and rejection. Then, we propose a competitive algorithm and analyze its performance using dual fitting.

Keywords: Online Algorithm · Competitive Analysis · Edge Computing · Preemptive Scheduling · Resource Augmentation · Dual Fitting

1 Introduction

Today, the computing systems are evolving in a continuum of cloud/fog/edge. These systems are always more complex, since they are composed of various types of computing devices. The diversity of the digital components that compose such systems creates new problems in the perspective of managing efficiently the execution of tasks. Most data produced by sensors at the extreme edge should be processed immediately and the analysis of data should be done locally, close to the sensors [21]. Most of these data only have an interest in the local

J. Cano and P. W. Trinder (Eds.): Euro-Par 2022, LNCS 13440, pp. 253–267, 2022.
https://doi.org/10.1007/978-3-031-12597-3_16

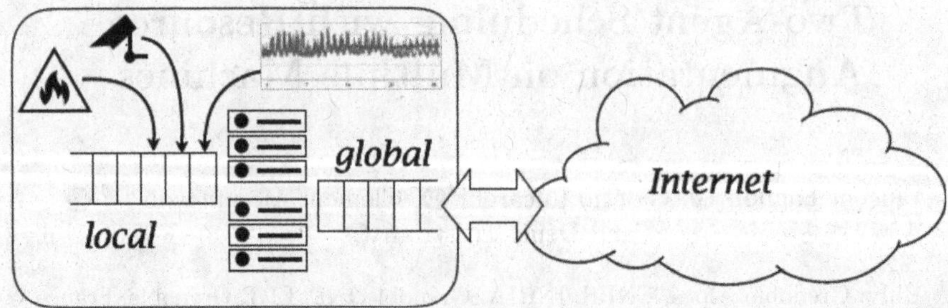

Fig. 1. Schematic view of a smart building with multiple sensors (fire detector, motion sensor, video surveillance, sound analysis, etc.) and a link to the Internet (Cloud services, weather forecast data, information collected around in the smart city, etc.). The tasks associated to the sensors are collected in a local queue and the external tasks are put in a global queue. Both are managed by the computing units of the smart building.

environment where they are produced, and their lifespan is short. Thus, they should be analyzed immediately. When no analysis is performed, the available computing units can be utilized for external or off-loaded computing, such as volunteer computing [5].

In this work, we target a computing system composed of multiple computing units connected to some sensors. For instance, think of a smart building with a centralized control and processing units like the one described in Fig. 1. A classical edge infrastructure is composed of several of such computing systems, but we will restrict our focus on a single one. Informally, there are two types of tasks to execute in this example, and each type is associated to a distinct objective as it will be described in more details in the next section.

1.1 Problem Description

The characteristics of the two types of tasks, each type associated with an agent, are the following:

- The first agent manages the tasks that are generated locally by the sensors. We call these tasks *local* or *dynamic* as they arrive on-line, and we should process them as soon as possible. The release time of a local task is not known in advance, but its processing time is known at the time it is released. The target objective of the first agent is to minimize the total flow-time of these tasks. Due to locality and their usually small processing time and memory consumption, the preemption (without migration) of these tasks is allowed.
- The second type of tasks corresponds to the external tasks submitted per batch. We call them *global* or *static* as they are submitted off-line. The processing of such tasks is known, and the objective is to complete this set of tasks in a reasonable amount of time, typically before a common deadline that is fixed, regarding the total computational load during the batch. From their

nature and possibly large memory consumption compared to local tasks, a global task cannot be preempted. However, we allow the rejection of a global task during its execution, if this is needed to keep a good overall performance of the system. Intuitively, a rejected global task will be re-submitted in a subsequent batch in the same or in another targeted computing system.

The tasks of both agents are sequential. The overall problem is thus to interleave both sets of tasks on the set of computing machines in the *best* possible way with respect to the target objectives. To summarize, the inputs of the corresponding scheduling problem are as follows:

- m identical machines,
- $n^{\mathcal{L}}$ local tasks and $n^{\mathcal{G}}$ global tasks,
- p_j the processing time of task j.

The objective is to minimize the sum flow-time of the local tasks, i.e., the total time that a local task remains in the system, such that a global deadline is respected for the global tasks.

1.2 Contributions and Organization

In the single agent case, the on-line flow-time minimization problem can be solved to optimality on a single machine if preemptions are allowed, but it is hard to approximate with $m \geq 2$ machines [14], or in the off-line setting if preemptions are not allowed [7,13]. These inapproximability results led to analyze the problem in the context of *resource augmentation*, where more power is given to the algorithm, as for instance allowing the algorithm to use more processors or higher speed than the optimal. In the case of speed augmentation, we assume the algorithm is using machines with a speed of $1+\epsilon$, while the optimal solution is based on a machine speed of 1, where $\epsilon \geq 0$ is a constant. Using these resource augmentation models, we can achieve performance guarantees that depend on the value of ϵ [9,12,22].

With the introduction of tasks from the global agent, we show in this paper that it is hard to approximate the flow-time objective for the local tasks, even though their preemption is allowed and resource augmentation is used. Specifically, any on-line algorithm which uses $(1+\epsilon_s)$-speed machines should reject at most k global tasks to achieve a competitive ratio in $O\left((1-\frac{2k}{n^{\mathcal{G}}})\mathcal{W}\right)$, where $\mathcal{W}$ is the ratio between the total work load of the global tasks and the total work load of the local tasks.

On the positive side, we propose an algorithm to solve the addressed two-agent scheduling problem under the resource augmentation model, with both rejection and speed augmentation. Then, we analyze the competitive ratio of the algorithm using the dual fitting approach [4]. In particular we prove that our algorithm is $(1+\epsilon_s)$-speed and $\max\left\{\frac{\mathcal{W}}{\epsilon_s\epsilon_r}+\frac{1+\epsilon_s}{2\epsilon_s}, \frac{1+\epsilon_s}{\epsilon_s}\right\}$-competitive by rejecting a fraction of global tasks depending on a parameter ϵ_r, where $\epsilon_s > 0$ and $0 < \epsilon_r < 1$.

The organization of the paper is as follows: We start by presenting a brief state of the art about the two-agent scheduling problem, the flow-time minimization problem and resource augmentation models in Sect. 2. Section 3 gives a formal definition of the problem and the notations used throughout the paper, and Sect. 4 presents our lower bound. In Sect. 5, we introduce the competitive algorithm for solving the two-agent scheduling problem and analyze its competitive ratio with the dual fitting approach in Sect. 6. Section 7 ends the paper, with concluding remarks and discussions.

2 Related Work

The work presented in this paper can be seen as an extension of the two-agent scheduling problem by considering that the tasks of one agent arrive on-line.

The problem of two-agent scheduling has been introduced by Agnetis et al. [2]. Their seminal paper was dedicated to scheduling two sets of non-preemptive tasks competing to execute on a single machine, where each agent aims at minimizing its own objective function based on the completion time of its tasks (maximum, sum, due dates, etc.). The authors considered two ways for solving the problem: First, by minimizing an objective function while keeping the second objective under a threshold and, second, by finding the set of non-dominated pairs of objective values on the Pareto front. Later, Agnetis et al. [1] extended this work to other multi-agent scheduling problems including the execution on parallel machines.

One can find in the literature many variants of the two-agent scheduling problem, for example considering a chain of tasks for each agent [3], tasks with due dates [8,24], or with an additional setup time when a task of one agent is processed directly after a task of the second agent [15].

In a similar setting, Baker and Smith [6] studied the problem of two or three agents on a single machine, where each agent has its own objective function to minimize. However, they considered the single objective approach by minimizing a linear combination of the objective of each agent. Liu et al. [16] also considered the problem with tasks arriving off-line with release times, with the objective of minimizing a linear combination of the maximum completion times (makespan) of both agents. Saule and Trystram [23] focused on the problem of an arbitrary number of agents scheduling jobs on parallel machines, where the objective of an agent is either the minimization of the makespan or the sum of completion time of its tasks. They proposed inapproximability bounds and approximation algorithms with performance ratios depending on the number of agents.

Our problem may also be considered as an extension of the problem of total flow-time minimization of on-line tasks on parallel machines, under the additional constraint of the off-line scheduling of tasks from a second agent.

For the flow-time minimization problem, it is well known that the *Shortest Remaining Processing Time* (SRPT) policy gives an optimal schedule for on-line tasks on a single machine. Unfortunately, the optimality of SRPT does not hold in our context with a second agent, as will be shown in Sect. 4. When $m \geq 2$

machines are considered, the problem becomes NP-hard [10], and Leonardi and Raz [14] showed that SRPT is $O(\min\{\log(P), \log \frac{n}{m}\})$-competitive, where P is the ratio between the maximum and minimum processing time of the tasks, and n the number of tasks. They also showed that no on-line algorithm could achieve a better competitive ratio.

Such strong results on the inapproximability of scheduling problems motivated the introduction of the *resource augmentation* model, where an on-line algorithm is given more power when comparing to the optimal. Such models can be considered with *speed augmentation* [12], *machine augmentation* [22] or *rejection* [9].

In the context of scheduling on a single machine, Feng et al. [11] studied the common two-agent problem of Agnetis et al. with the additional feature that jobs can be rejected with a given penalty to the objective value of the corresponding agent. In the on-line setting, Lucarelli et al. also introduced the speed augmentation and rejection models to the total (weighted) flow-time minimization problem on unrelated [17,18,20] and related machines [19]. The authors proposed several algorithms whose competitiveness was proved using the dual fitting technique. We will use the same approach in the analysis of our algorithm in Sect. 5.

3 Problem Formulation and Notations

We consider a set $\mathcal{M}$ of m identical machines on which to execute two sets of sequential tasks having different settings. The first set $\mathcal{L}$ is composed of $n^{\mathcal{L}}$ *local tasks* that are submitted on-line, while the second set is composed of $n^{\mathcal{G}}$ *global tasks* that are submitted off-line. Only local tasks can be preempted, but migration between machines is not allowed. For a given task j, we denote by r_j its release time and by p_j its processing time on a machine, only known at the time the task is being released. Note that the release time is 0 for all global tasks, since they are off-line.

Given a schedule, we denote by F_j the flow-time of a local task j, defined as the difference between its completion time and its release time. The objective is to minimize the sum flow-time of all local tasks, under the constraint that all global tasks have completed before a common deadline $d^{\mathcal{G}}$. We also consider that the release time of any local task is bounded above by $d^{\mathcal{G}}$. This deadline, defined as

$$d^{\mathcal{G}} = \frac{1}{m} \cdot \left(\sum_{j \in \mathcal{G}} p_j - \max_{j \in \mathcal{G}}\{p_j\} \right) + \max_{j \in \mathcal{G}}\{p_j\} + \sum_{j \in \mathcal{L}} p_j,$$

guarantees that a schedule interleaving local and global tasks is always feasible. Notice however that, since local tasks are released over time, the value of $d^{\mathcal{G}}$ is not known beforehand by the algorithm.

Under the resource augmentation model, we introduce the coefficients of speed augmentation $\epsilon_s > 0$ and rejection $0 < \epsilon_r < 1$. An algorithm to solve the addressed problem can use machines with speed $1+\epsilon_s$ times faster than that of an optimal adversary, and can reject a number of global tasks bounded by an ϵ_r-fraction of the number of local tasks.

We define below some additional notations used in the next sections. In a partial schedule, $\mathcal{Q}_i^{\mathcal{L}}(t)$ denotes the set of local tasks assigned to machine i, but not completed at time t. This set includes all the local tasks waiting to be executed on machine i, as well as the task currently being executed at time t, if it is local. Note that, upon arrival of task j at time r_j and assigned to machine i, we assume that it is immediately added to $\mathcal{Q}_i^{\mathcal{L}}(r_j)$. Since preemption of local tasks is allowed, $p_j^{rem}(t)$ denotes the remaining processing time of task j at time t. Finally, for a given instance of the problem, we denote by $\mathcal{W} = \sum_{j\in\mathcal{G}} p_j / \sum_{j\in\mathcal{L}} p_j$ the ratio between the total workload of the global tasks and the total workload of the local tasks.

4 A Lower Bound

Theorem 1. *Let $\epsilon_s \leq \frac{1}{3}\cdot\frac{\mathcal{W}-3}{3\mathcal{W}+3}$ and $k \in \{1,2,\ldots,\frac{n^{\mathcal{G}}}{2}\}$, where $n^{\mathcal{G}}$ is the number of global tasks. Any online algorithm which uses $(1+\epsilon_s)$-speed machines should reject at least k global tasks to have a competitive ratio in $O\left((1-\frac{2k}{n^{\mathcal{G}}})\mathcal{W}\right)$.*

Proof. We consider an instance with a single machine, consisting of $2Z$ global tasks that are split evenly into two sets of tasks of respective processing times $X/3$ and $2X/3$. We partition the time into Z phases, each one of length $X+1$: the phase ℓ corresponds to the time interval $[(\ell-1)(X+1), \ell(X+1))$, for each $\ell = 1,2,\ldots,Z$. Let $b_\ell = (\ell-1)(X+1)$, $1 \leq \ell \leq Z$, denote the beginning of phase ℓ. In order to well distinguish the phases, a burst of Y local tasks of processing time 0 is released online at every time $\ell(X+1)$, $1 \leq \ell \leq Z$. Moreover, in each phase there is an arrival of a single local task of processing time 1, whose release time will be defined later. We have two cases to consider:

Case 1: If the online algorithm decides to execute one global task of processing time $X/3$ (say G_1) and one global task of processing time $2X/3$ (say G_2) in each phase ℓ, $1 \leq \ell \leq Z$.

If the algorithm decides to execute G_1 before G_2, then the earliest time at which the execution of G_1 can finish in the algorithm's schedule is $b_\ell + \frac{X}{3(1+\epsilon_s)}$, since the algorithm has access to a machine which executes the tasks at speed $1+\epsilon_s$. After the completion of G_1, the algorithm will start G_2 at some time $t \geq b_\ell + \frac{X}{3(1+\epsilon_s)}$. Then, the adversary decides to release the local task L at time $b_\ell + \frac{2X}{3}$ and the flow time of L will be at least $\frac{X-2X\epsilon_s+3}{3(1+\epsilon_s)}$, if G_2 is not rejected; otherwise the flow time of L will be $\frac{1}{1+\epsilon_s}$. The optimal solution executes the tasks in the order G_2, L and G_1, resulting in a flow-time of 1.

If the algorithm decides to execute G_2 before G_1, then let $t \geq b_\ell$ be the starting time of G_2. Then, the adversary decides to release the local task L at time $\frac{X}{3}$ and the flow time of L will be at least $\frac{X-X\epsilon_s+3}{3(1+\epsilon_s)}$, if G_2 is not rejected; otherwise the flow time of L will be $\frac{1}{1+\epsilon_s}$. The optimal solution executes the tasks in the order G_1, L and G_2, resulting in a flow-time of 1.

Assuming that the algorithm decides to reject the corresponding task G_2 in exactly k phases, then its total flow time is at least $\frac{k}{1+\epsilon_s} + (Z-k)\frac{X-2X\epsilon_s+3}{3(1+\epsilon_s)} = (Z-k)\frac{\mathcal{W}(1-2\epsilon_s)}{3(1+\epsilon_s)} + \frac{Z}{1+\epsilon_s}$, since $\mathcal{W} = X$. On the other hand, the total flow time of the optimal schedule is Z. Then, by rejecting k global tasks, the competitive ratio will be at least $\frac{Z-k}{Z}\frac{\mathcal{W}(1-2\epsilon_s)}{3(1+\epsilon_s)} + \frac{1}{1+\epsilon_s} = \Omega\left(\frac{Z-k}{Z}\mathcal{W}\right)$.

Case 2: Otherwise, there is a phase during which two global tasks of processing time $2X/3$ are partially executed. Hence, there exists a phase ℓ, at the beginning of which a global task started in the previous phase $\ell-1$ will be executed for at least $q = \frac{1}{1+\epsilon_s}\frac{4X}{3} - (X+1)$ time. Then, the burst of local tasks arrived at time $(\ell-1)(X+1)$ will have a total flow-time at least qY. Note that in this case the arrival of local tasks of processing time 1 is not important and we can assume w.l.o.g. that the algorithm will execute all of them just upon their arrival, getting a total flow-time for them equal to Z. On the other hand, the optimal solution will be as in the previous case having a total flow time equal to Z. Therefore, the competitive ratio in this case will be $\Omega(Y)$, which can be chosen large enough such that the first case dominates.

5 An Algorithm for the Two-Agent Problem

The algorithm is denoted by $\mathcal{A}$ and described as follows.

Initialization: At start, we consider a queue of global tasks $\mathcal{Q}^{\mathcal{G}}$ initialized with all the global tasks sorted in an arbitrary order. For each machine $i \in \mathcal{M}$, we initialize an empty queue of local tasks $\mathcal{Q}_i^{\mathcal{L}}$.

Local Task Allocation: Upon submission of a local task j, we allocate it to the machine i that minimizes

$$\lambda_{ij} = \sum_{\substack{l \in \mathcal{Q}_i^{\mathcal{L}}(r_j): \\ p_l^{rem}(r_j) \le p_j}} p_l^{rem}(r_j) + \sum_{\substack{l \in \mathcal{Q}_i^{\mathcal{L}}(r_j): \\ p_l^{rem}(r_j) > p_j}} p_j \tag{1}$$

and denote by λ_j this quantity. Intuitively, we put the task j on the machine minimizing the increase in the total flow-time induced only by the tasks in $\mathcal{Q}_i^{\mathcal{L}}$.

Task Execution: For each machine i, the tasks in $\mathcal{Q}_i^{\mathcal{L}}$ are executed in the *Shortest Remaining Processing Time* order. Note that if a newly arrived task is shorter than the local task currently being executed, then preemption occurs and the remaining part of the current task is put back in $\mathcal{Q}_i^{\mathcal{L}}$.

If $\mathcal{Q}_i^{\mathcal{L}}$ becomes empty, then we remove a task from $\mathcal{Q}^{\mathcal{G}}$ and execute it on i, until no more global tasks are left. By not introducing idle times in the schedule before all global tasks are processed, we ensure that the last global task will complete before the common deadline $d^{\mathcal{G}}$. Note that global tasks are removed from the queue in an arbitrary order.

Rejection Policy for Global Tasks: If at any time there are more than $\frac{1}{\epsilon_r}$ local tasks in the local queue of a machine currently executing a global task, we decide to reject that task. Note that such a rejection can only happen when a local task is released. This way, we ensure that no more than $\epsilon_r \cdot n^{\mathcal{L}}$ global tasks are rejected in total.

6 Analysis by Dual Fitting

We analyze our algorithm by dual fitting [4]. We first provide an expression of the total flow-time achieved by the algorithm in Sect. 6.1 and give a linear programming formulation of our problem in Sect. 6.2, as well as the corresponding relaxed dual program. Then, in Sect. 6.3 we propose an assignment of the dual variables based on the choices made by our algorithm. In Sect. 6.4, we prove that this assignment satisfies the dual constraints and we give the competitive ratio of our algorithm.

6.1 Algorithm's Flow-Time

First, let Δ_j be the increase in the total flow-time of the current solution of our algorithm incurred by the dispatch of a local task j on machine i. This value corresponds to the flow-time of the task j, plus the increase in flow-time of all tasks being delayed by the arrival of j. Following our scheduling and rejection policies, and assuming the task k was being executed at time r_j, the detailed definition of Δ_j is expressed as follows:

$$\Delta_j = \begin{cases} \text{If k}(\in \mathcal{G}) \text{ is rejected:} \\ \quad -\dfrac{p_k^{rem}(r_j)}{1+\epsilon_s} \cdot |\mathcal{Q}_i^{\mathcal{L}}(r_j) - 1| + \displaystyle\sum_{\substack{l \in \mathcal{Q}_i^{\mathcal{L}}(r_j): \\ p_l^{rem}(r_j) \le p_j}} \dfrac{p_l^{rem}(r_j)}{1+\epsilon_s} + \sum_{\substack{l \in \mathcal{Q}_i^{\mathcal{L}}(r_j): \\ p_l^{rem}(r_j) > p_j}} \dfrac{p_j}{1+\epsilon_s} \\ \text{If k}(\in \mathcal{G}) \text{ is not rejected:} \\ \quad \dfrac{p_k^{rem}(r_j)}{1+\epsilon_s} + \displaystyle\sum_{\substack{l \in \mathcal{Q}_i^{\mathcal{L}}(r_j): \\ p_l^{rem}(r_j) \le p_j}} \dfrac{p_l^{rem}(r_j)}{1+\epsilon_s} + \sum_{\substack{l \in \mathcal{Q}_i^{\mathcal{L}}(r_j): \\ p_l^{rem}(r_j) > p_j}} \dfrac{p_j}{1+\epsilon_s} \\ \text{If k}(\in \mathcal{L}) \text{ is preempted:} \\ \quad \dfrac{p_j}{1+\epsilon_s} + \displaystyle\sum_{\substack{l \in \mathcal{Q}^{\mathcal{L}}(r_j): \\ p_l^{rem}(r_j) > p_j}} \dfrac{p_j}{1+\epsilon_s} \\ \text{If k}(\in \mathcal{L}) \text{ is not preempted:} \\ \quad \displaystyle\sum_{\substack{l \in \mathcal{Q}_i^{\mathcal{L}}(r_j): \\ p_l^{rem}(r_j) \le p_j}} \dfrac{p_l^{rem}(r_j)}{1+\epsilon_s} + \sum_{\substack{l \in \mathcal{Q}^{\mathcal{L}}(r_j): \\ p_l^{rem}(r_j) > p_j}} \dfrac{p_j}{1+\epsilon_s} \end{cases}$$

Note that, due to speed augmentation, any value of processing time for our algorithm is divided by $(1+\epsilon_s)$.

By definition, the total flow-time of local tasks achieved by the algorithm is equal to the sum of Δ_j for all local tasks. Due to the rejection policy, the impact of global tasks on the total flow-time of local tasks is limited. There cannot be more than $\frac{1}{\epsilon_r}$ local tasks in the queue during the execution of a global task, so a global task j will contribute at maximum to $\frac{p_j}{\epsilon_r(1+\epsilon_s)}$ on the total flow-time of the algorithm. Therefore, we have the following:

$$\sum_{j\in\mathcal{L}} F_j = \sum_{j\in\mathcal{L}} \Delta_j \leq \sum_{j\in\mathcal{L}} \left(\sum_{\substack{l\in\mathcal{Q}_i^{\mathcal{L}}(r_j):\\ p_l^{rem}(r_j)\leq p_j}} \frac{p_l^{rem}(r_j)}{1+\epsilon_s} + \sum_{\substack{l\in\mathcal{Q}_i^{\mathcal{L}}(r_j):\\ p_l^{rem}(r_j)>p_j}} \frac{p_j}{1+\epsilon_s} \right) + \sum_{j\in\mathcal{G}} \frac{p_j}{\epsilon_r(1+\epsilon_s)} \tag{2}$$

6.2 Linear Programming Formulation

We define a decision variable $x_{ij}(t)$ which is equal to 1 if the task $j \in \mathcal{L}\cup\mathcal{G}$ is running on machine $i \in \mathcal{M}$ at time $t \geq 0$, and 0 otherwise. By convention, we assume that $x_{ij}(t) = 0$ for local tasks when $t < r_j$.

Consider this linear programming formulation, with the constant $\Gamma \geq \frac{1}{2}$:

$$\text{min.} \quad \sum_{i\in\mathcal{M}}\sum_{j\in\mathcal{L}} \int_{r_j}^{\infty} \left(\frac{(t-r_j)}{p_j} + \Gamma\right) x_{ij}(t)dt$$

$$\text{s.t.} \quad \sum_{i\in\mathcal{M}} \int_{r_j}^{\infty} x_{ij}(t)dt \geq p_j \qquad \forall j \in (\mathcal{L}\cup\mathcal{G}) \tag{3a}$$

$$\sum_{j\in(\mathcal{L}\cup\mathcal{G})} x_{ij}(t) \leq 1 \qquad \forall i \in \mathcal{M},\ \forall t \geq 0 \tag{3b}$$

$$\sum_{i\in\mathcal{M}} \int_0^{\infty} \left(\frac{t}{p_j} + \frac{1}{2}\right) x_{ij}(t)dt \leq d^{\mathcal{G}} \qquad \forall j \in \mathcal{G} \tag{3c}$$

$$x_{ij}(t) \in \{0;1\} \qquad \forall i \in \mathcal{M},\ \forall j \in (\mathcal{L}\cup\mathcal{G}),\ \forall t \geq 0$$

Constraint (3a) verifies that each task $j \in \mathcal{L}\cup\mathcal{G}$ is executed for at least p_j units of time, Constraint (3b) indicates that a machine can execute at most one task at any moment $t \geq 0$, and the left-hand side of Constraint (3c) computes the completion time of a global task j.

Note that the quantity $\int_{r_j}^{\infty} \frac{(t-r_j)}{p_j} x_{ij}(t)dt$ in the objective function corresponds to the well-known fractional flow-time of the job j [4]. This is a lower bound to the flow-time of j. Moreover, with $\Gamma = \frac{1}{2}$, the objective value of an optimal solution for the linear program is at most the flow-time of an optimal schedule for our problem [4]. During our analysis, we will use a larger value of Γ and the objective value of the program will be at most $(\Gamma + \frac{1}{2})$ that of the optimal value of the problem.

Note also that the above formulation does not exactly model the addressed problem, as it does not forbid preemption of global task or their migration between machines. Instead, the formulation is a relaxation, but it is sufficient to analyse our algorithm and prove its approximation ratio via dual fitting and resource augmentation.

After relaxing the integrality constraint on the variables $x_{ij}(t)$ in the primal program, its dual program can be expressed as follows.

$$\max. \sum_{j\in\mathcal{L}\cup\mathcal{G}} \alpha_j p_j - \sum_{i\in\mathcal{M}} \int_0^\infty \beta_i(t)dt - \sum_{j\in\mathcal{G}} d^{\mathcal{G}} \gamma_j$$

$$\text{s.t. } \alpha_j - \beta_i(t) - \left(\frac{t-r_j}{p_j} + \Gamma\right) \leq 0 \quad \forall i\in\mathcal{M},\ \forall j\in\mathcal{L},\ \forall t\geq r_j \tag{4a}$$

$$\alpha_j - \beta_i(t) - \left(\frac{t}{p_j} + \frac{1}{2}\right)\gamma_j \leq 0 \quad \forall i\in\mathcal{M},\ \forall j\in\mathcal{G},\ \forall t\geq 0 \tag{4b}$$

$$\alpha_j \geq 0 \quad \forall j\in(\mathcal{L}\cup\mathcal{G})$$

$$\beta_i(t) \geq 0 \quad \forall t\geq 0,\ \forall i\in\mathcal{M}$$

$$\gamma_j \geq 0 \quad \forall j\in\mathcal{G}$$

6.3 Dual Variables

For the purpose of the analysis via dual fitting, we define the variables of the dual program according to the decisions taken by the algorithm.

We define the first dual variable for local tasks as $\alpha_j = \frac{\lambda_j}{(1+\epsilon_s)p_j} + \Gamma$. Note that the value of α_j is only set at the arrival of j, and it does not change afterward. For the other variables, we define $\alpha_j = 0$ and $\gamma_j = 0$ for any global task j; and $\beta_i(t) = \frac{|\mathcal{Q}_i^{\mathcal{L}}(t)|}{1+\epsilon_s}$, $\forall t\geq 0$.

6.4 Competitive Analysis

With the two following lemmas, we show that our definition of the dual variables leads to a feasible solution of the dual program.

Lemma 1. *For every every machine $i\in\mathcal{M}$, every local task $j\in\mathcal{L}$ and every time $t\geq r_j$, the dual constraint (4a) is satisfied, that is:*

$$\alpha_j - \beta_i(t) - \left(\frac{t-r_j}{p_j} + \Gamma\right) \leq 0$$

Proof. First of all, the constant term Γ in the α_j is compensated with the Γ of the constraint. By multiplying all remaining terms by $(1+\epsilon_s)p_j$, we have to prove:

$$\lambda_j - |\mathcal{Q}_i^{\mathcal{L}}(t)|\cdot p_j - (1+\epsilon_s)(t-r_j) \leq 0$$

If more local tasks arrive after j, the quantity $|\mathcal{Q}_i^{\mathcal{L}}(t)|$ will increase and the constraint will be easier to satisfy. For this reason, we assume that there is no other task arrival after j. Thus $|\mathcal{Q}_i^{\mathcal{L}}(t)|$ can only decrease over time, when a task finishes its execution. Moreover, due to the dispatching policy of local tasks we have $\lambda_j \leq \lambda_{ij}$.

Assume that a task k is currently being executed at time r_j and finishes at time $t' = r_j + \frac{p_k^{rem}(r_j)}{1+\epsilon_s}$. For any time $t \in [r_j, t')$, $|\mathcal{Q}_i^{\mathcal{L}}(t)|$ will remain constant and it is sufficient to prove the constraint at the beginning of the interval, when $t = r_j$. We have

$$\lambda_{ij} \leq \sum_{\substack{l \in \mathcal{Q}_i^{\mathcal{L}}(r_j): \\ p_l^{rem}(r_j) \leq p_j}} p_j + \sum_{\substack{l \in \mathcal{Q}_i^{\mathcal{L}}(r_j): \\ p_l^{rem}(r_j) > p_j}} p_j = |\mathcal{Q}_i^{\mathcal{L}}(r_j)| \cdot p_j$$

and thus the constraint is satisfied for any time t in this interval.

Let now k' be the first task in $\mathcal{Q}_i^{\mathcal{L}}(r_j)$ after k, such that when k finishes its execution at time t' then k' starts executing during the interval $\left[t', t' + \frac{p_{k'}^{rem}(r_j)}{1+\epsilon_s}\right)$. Again, it is sufficient to verify the constraint at the beginning of the interval, at time $t' = r_j + \frac{p_k^{rem}(r_j)}{1+\epsilon_s}$. We have

$$\begin{aligned} \lambda_{ij} &\leq p_k^{rem}(r_j) + \sum_{\substack{l \in \mathcal{Q}_i^{\mathcal{L}}(r_j) \setminus \{k\}: \\ p_l^{rem}(r_j) \leq p_j}} p_j + \sum_{\substack{l \in \mathcal{Q}_i^{\mathcal{L}}(r_j): \\ p_l^{rem}(r_j) > p_j}} p_j \\ &= p_k^{rem}(r_j) + |\mathcal{Q}_i^{\mathcal{L}}(t')| \cdot p_j \end{aligned}$$

and

$$p_k^{rem}(r_j) - (1+\epsilon_s)(r_j + \frac{p_k^{rem}(r_j)}{1+\epsilon_s} - r_j) \leq 0.$$

Thus, the constraint is satisfied for any t in the interval.

A similar reasoning for every time interval during the execution of any local task in $\mathcal{Q}_i^{\mathcal{L}}(r_j)$ can be made. Note that, if a global task was rejected on the arrival of the local task j, it would not change the above reasoning. Hence, the dual constraint (4a) is satisfied for any time $t \geq 0$.

Lemma 2. *For every machine $i \in \mathcal{M}$, every global task j and every time $t \geq 0$, the dual constraint (4b) is satisfied, that is:*

$$\alpha_j - \beta_i(t) - (\frac{t}{p_j} + \frac{1}{2})\gamma_j \leq 0$$

Proof. The smallest possible value of $\beta_i(t)$ is when the queue of local tasks is empty. Thus, for any t we have $\beta_i(t) \geq 0$. Provided that $\alpha_j = 0$ and $\gamma_j = 0$ the dual constraint (4b) is satisfied.

Recall that F_j denotes the flow-time of task j in the schedule produced by algorithm. Then, the following lemma shows the relation between the total flow-time of local tasks achieved by the algorithm and the objective value of the dual program.

Lemma 3. *Given our definitions of α_j, $\beta_i(t)$ and γ_j, the dual objective value verifies:*

$$\sum_{j\in\mathcal{L}\cup\mathcal{G}} \alpha_j p_j - \sum_{i\in\mathcal{M}} \int_0^\infty \beta_i(t)dt - \sum_{j\in\mathcal{G}} d^{\mathcal{G}}\gamma_j \geq \frac{\epsilon_s}{1+\epsilon_s}\sum_{j\in\mathcal{L}} F_j$$

Proof. With our definition of α_j (recall $\alpha_j = 0,\ \forall j \in \mathcal{G}$) we have

$$\begin{aligned}
\sum_{j\in\mathcal{L}\cup\mathcal{G}} \alpha_j p_j &= \sum_{j\in\mathcal{L}} \left(\sum_{\substack{l\in\mathcal{Q}^{\mathcal{L}}_{i*}(r_j):\\ p_l^{rem}(r_j)\leq p_j}} \frac{p_l^{rem}(r_j)}{1+\epsilon_s} + \sum_{\substack{l\in\mathcal{Q}^{\mathcal{L}}_{i*}(r_j):\\ p_l^{rem}(r_j)>p_j}} \frac{p_j}{1+\epsilon_s} + \Gamma\cdot p_j \right) \\
&\quad + \frac{1}{1+\epsilon_s}\left(\sum_{j\in\mathcal{G}} \frac{p_j}{\epsilon_r} - \sum_{j\in\mathcal{G}} \frac{p_j}{\epsilon_r} \right) \\
&\geq \sum_{j\in\mathcal{L}} F_j + \Gamma\cdot\sum_{j\in\mathcal{L}} p_j - \sum_{j\in\mathcal{G}} \frac{p_j}{\epsilon_r(1+\epsilon_s)},
\end{aligned}$$

where the inequality holds due to Eq. (2).

With the definition of $\beta_i(t)$, we have:

$$\sum_{i\in\mathcal{M}} \int_0^\infty \beta_i(t)dt = \sum_{i\in\mathcal{M}} \int_0^\infty \frac{|\mathcal{Q}_i^{\mathcal{L}}(t)|}{1+\epsilon_s}dt = \frac{1}{1+\epsilon_s}\sum_{j\in\mathcal{L}} F_j$$

Recall the notation $\mathcal{W} = \frac{\sum_{j\in\mathcal{G}} p_j}{\sum_{j\in\mathcal{L}} p_j}$, which is the ratio between the total work load of the global tasks and the total work load of the local tasks. By choosing

$$\Gamma = \max\left\{\frac{\mathcal{W}}{\epsilon_r(1+\epsilon_s)}, \frac{1}{2}\right\},$$

and knowing that $\gamma_j = 0,\ \forall j \in \mathcal{G}$, the objective value of the dual program can be expressed as follows:

$$\begin{aligned}
&\sum_{j\in\mathcal{L}\cup\mathcal{G}} \alpha_j p_j - \sum_{i\in\mathcal{M}} \int_0^\infty \beta_i(t)dt - \sum_{j\in\mathcal{G}} d^{\mathcal{G}}\gamma_j \\
&\geq \sum_{j\in\mathcal{L}} F_j + \Gamma\cdot\sum_{j\in\mathcal{L}} p_j - \sum_{j\in\mathcal{G}} \frac{p_j}{\epsilon_r(1+\epsilon_s)} - \frac{1}{1+\epsilon_s}\sum_{j\in\mathcal{L}} F_j \\
&= \frac{\epsilon_s}{1+\epsilon_s}\sum_{j\in\mathcal{L}} F_j + \Gamma\cdot\sum_{j\in\mathcal{L}} p_j - \sum_{j\in\mathcal{G}} \frac{p_j}{\epsilon_r(1+\epsilon_s)} \\
&\geq \frac{\epsilon_s}{1+\epsilon_s}\sum_{j\in\mathcal{L}} F_j
\end{aligned}$$

We now have enough to conclude on the competitive ratio of our algorithm.

Theorem 2. *For any $0 < \epsilon_r < 1$ and $\epsilon_s > 0$, the algorithm $\mathcal{A}$ is $(1 + \epsilon_s)$-speed, $\max\left\{\frac{\mathcal{W}}{\epsilon_s \epsilon_r} + \frac{1+\epsilon_s}{2\epsilon_s}, \frac{1+\epsilon_s}{\epsilon_s}\right\}$-competitive and rejects at most $(\epsilon_r \cdot n^{\mathcal{L}})$ global tasks.*

Proof. From the three previous lemmas we know that the dual variables as we defined them form a feasible solution of the dual program, and that the objective value of the dual program is an upper bound of the total flow-time achieved by the algorithm multiplied by a constant factor. From the rejection policy, a global task is rejected the first time when there are more than $\frac{1}{\epsilon_r}$ local tasks waiting in the queue. Thus, no more than $\epsilon_r \cdot n^{\mathcal{L}}$ global tasks are rejected. By definition, the algorithm uses a machine with speed $(1 + \epsilon_s)$ times the machine speed of an optimal solution.

It remains to express the relation between the total flow-time of our algorithm with that of an optimal solution. As $\Gamma \geq \frac{1}{2}$, the objective value of the primal program is at most $\Gamma + \frac{1}{2}$ times the flow-time of an optimal solution, denoted by OPT. Finally, using the duality theorem, we can write the relation:

$$\frac{\epsilon_s}{1+\epsilon_s} \cdot \sum_{j \in \mathcal{L}} F_j \leq (\Gamma + \frac{1}{2}) \cdot OPT$$

$$\frac{\sum_{j \in \mathcal{L}} F_j}{OPT} \leq \max\left\{\frac{\mathcal{W}}{\epsilon_s \epsilon_r} + \frac{1+\epsilon_s}{2\epsilon_s}, \frac{1+\epsilon_s}{\epsilon_s}\right\}$$

and the theorem follows.

7 Concluding Remarks

We introduced in this paper a new scheduling problem with two agents targeting each a different objective. As far as we know, it is the first time a mixed off-line/on-line setting was studied for this problem. We provided a lower bound on the competitive ratio of any algorithm for solving the problem, and proposed an algorithm with a proof of its competitive ratio via dual fitting under a resource augmentation framework (speed and rejection).

The objective of the global tasks is taken as a constraint, while its value is specified by the scheduling policy of global tasks. Using List Scheduling in our case, the common deadline was taken as the classical Graham's bound plus the total work load of the local tasks. It is possible to refine the value of the deadline in accordance with a change in the scheduling policy of global tasks in the algorithm $\mathcal{A}$: Using any algorithm $\mathcal{X}$ for $P||C_{max}$ with known approximation ratio ρ to construct a fixed allocation of global tasks to the machines prior to the submission of any local task, it is guaranteed that a value of the deadline $d^{\mathcal{G}} = C^{\mathcal{X}}_{max} + \sum_{j \in \mathcal{L}} p_j$ will be respected. Doing so, the dynamic allocation of global tasks is lost, but it gives a "bi-objective" vision to the problem: the minimization of both the total flow-time of local tasks and the global deadline.

Going further with the model, we believe it is possible to remove the speed augmentation, which is only used in the algorithm's analysis, as it was successfully done in another work on a single agent problem with on-line tasks [17].

Another interesting perspective is to extend the model to the weighted case, or with related/unrelated machines.

Acknowledgment. This work was partly supported by the french ANR Energumen project 18-CE25-0008, by the research program on Edge Intelligence of the MIAI@Grenoble Alpes (ANR-19-P3IA-0003), and by the EPSRC funded project EP/T01461X/1 "Algorithmic Support for Massive Scale Distributed Systems".

References

1. Agnetis, A., Billaut, J.-C., Gawiejnowicz, S., Pacciarelli, D., Soukhal, A.: Multiagent Scheduling. Springer, Heidelberg (2014). https://doi.org/10.1007/978-3-642-41880-8
2. Agnetis, A., Mirchandani, P.B., Pacciarelli, D., Pacifici, A.: Scheduling problems with two competing agents. Oper. Res. **52**(2), 229–242 (2004)
3. Agnetis, A., Nicosia, G., Pacifici, A., Pferschy, U.: Scheduling two agent task chains with a central selection mechanism. J. Sched. **18**(3), 243–261 (2015). https://doi.org/10.1007/s10951-014-0414-9
4. Anand, S., Garg, N., Kumar, A.: Resource augmentation for weighted flow-time explained by dual fitting. In: Proceedings of the 23rd ACM-SIAM Symposium on Discrete Algorithms, pp. 1228–1241. SIAM (2012)
5. Anderson, D.P.: BOINC: a system for public-resource computing and storage. In: Proceedings of the 5th IEEE/ACM International Workshop on Grid Computing, pp. 4–10. IEEE Computer Society (2004)
6. Baker, K.R., Smith, J.C.: A multiple-criterion model for machine scheduling. J. Sched. **6**(1), 7–16 (2003)
7. Chekuri, C., Khanna, S., Zhu, A.: Algorithms for minimizing weighted flow time. In: Proceedings of the 33rd ACM Symposium on Theory of Computing, pp. 84–93 (2001)
8. Cheng, C., Li, S., Ying, K., Liu, Y.: Scheduling jobs of two competing agents on a single machine. IEEE Access **7**, 98702–98714 (2019)
9. Choudhury, A.R., Das, S., Garg, N., Kumar, A.: Rejecting jobs to minimize load and maximum flow-time. J. Comput. Syst. Sci. **91**, 42–68 (2018)
10. Du, J., Leung, J.Y.T., Young, G.H.: Minimizing mean flow time with release time constraint. Theoret. Comput. Sci. **75**(3), 347–355 (1990)
11. Feng, Q., Fan, B., Li, S., Shang, W.: Two-agent scheduling with rejection on a single machine. Appl. Math. Model. **39**(3), 1183–1193 (2015)
12. Kalyanasundaram, B., Pruhs, K.: Speed is as powerful as clairvoyance. J. ACM **47**(4), 617–643 (2000)
13. Kellerer, H., Tautenhahn, T., Woeginger, G.: Approximability and nonapproximability results for minimizing total flow time on a single machine. SIAM J. Comput. **28**(4), 1155–1166 (1999)
14. Leonardi, S., Raz, D.: Approximating total flow time on parallel machines. J. Comput. Syst. Sci. **73**(6), 875–891 (2007)
15. Li, S.-S., Chen, R.-X., Feng, Q.: Scheduling two job families on a single machine with two competitive agents. J. Comb. Optim. **32**(3), 784–799 (2015). https://doi.org/10.1007/s10878-015-9902-x
16. Liu, P., Gu, M., Li, G.: Two-agent scheduling on a single machine with release dates. Comput. Oper. Res. **111**, 35–42 (2019)

17. Lucarelli, G., Moseley, B., Thang, N.K., Srivastav, A., Trystram, D.: Online non-preemptive scheduling on unrelated machines with rejections. In: Proceedings of the 30th Symposium on Parallelism in Algorithms and Architectures, SPAA, pp. 291–300. ACM (2018)
18. Lucarelli, G., Moseley, B., Thang, N.K., Srivastav, A., Trystram, D.: Online non-preemptive scheduling to minimize weighted flow-time on unrelated machines. In: 26th Annual European Symposium on Algorithms, ESA. LIPIcs, vol. 112, pp. 59:1–59:12 (2018)
19. Lucarelli, G., Moseley, B., Thang, N.K., Srivastav, A., Trystram, D.: Online non-preemptive scheduling to minimize maximum weighted flow-time on related machines. In: 39th IARCS Annual Conference on FSTTCS. LIPIcs, vol. 150, pp. 24:1–24:12 (2019)
20. Lucarelli, G., Thang, N.K., Srivastav, A., Trystram, D.: Online non-preemptive scheduling in a resource augmentation model based on duality. In: 24th Annual European Symposium on Algorithms, ESA. LIPIcs, vol. 57, pp. 63:1–63:17 (2016)
21. Nguyen, D.C., Ding, M., Pathirana, P.N., Seneviratne, A., Li, J., Poor, H.V.: Federated learning for internet of things: a comprehensive survey. IEEE Commun. Surv. Tutor. **23**, 1622–1658 (2021)
22. Phillips, C.A., Stein, C., Torng, E., Wein, J.: Optimal time-critical scheduling via resource augmentation. In: Proceedings of the 29th ACM symposium on Theory of Computing, pp. 140–149 (1997)
23. Saule, E., Trystram, D.: Multi-users scheduling in parallel systems. In: 23rd IEEE International Symposium on Parallel and Distributed Processing, (IPDPS), pp. 1–9 (2009)
24. Yin, Y., Wang, D., Cheng, T.C.E.: Due Date-Related Scheduling with Two Agents. UOR, Springer, Singapore (2020). https://doi.org/10.1007/978-981-15-2105-8

IP.LSH.DBSCAN: Integrated Parallel Density-Based Clustering Through Locality-Sensitive Hashing

Amir Keramatian(✉), Vincenzo Gulisano, Marina Papatriantafilou, and Philippas Tsigas

Chalmers University of Technology, Gothenburg, Sweden
{amirke,vincenzo.gulisano,ptrianta,tsigas}@chalmers.se

Abstract. Locality-sensitive hashing (LSH) is an established method for fast data indexing and approximate similarity search, with useful parallelism properties. Although indexes and similarity measures are key for data clustering, little has been investigated on the benefits of LSH in the problem. Our proposition is that LSH can be extremely beneficial for parallelizing high-dimensional density-based clustering e.g., DBSCAN, a versatile method able to detect clusters of different shapes and sizes.

We contribute to fill the gap between the advancements in LSH and density-based clustering. We show how approximate DBSCAN clustering can be *fused* into the process of creating an LSH index, and, through parallelization and fine-grained synchronization, also utilize efficiently available computing capacity. The resulting method, IP.LSH.DBSCAN, can support a wide range of applications with diverse distance functions, as well as data distributions and dimensionality. We analyse its properties and evaluate our prototype implementation on a 36-core machine with 2-way hyper threading on massive data-sets with various numbers of dimensions. Our results show that IP.LSH.DBSCAN effectively complements established state-of-the-art methods by up to several orders of magnitude of speed-up on higher dimensional datasets, with tunable high clustering accuracy through LSH parameters.

1 Introduction

Digitalized applications' datasets are getting larger in size and number of features (i.e., dimensions), posing challenges to established data mining methods such as clustering, an unsupervised data mining tool based on similarity measures. Density-based spatial clustering of applications with noise (DBSCAN) [11] is a prominent method to cluster (possibly) noisy data into arbitrary shapes and sizes, without prior knowledge on the number of clusters, using user-defined similarity metrics (i.e., not limited to the Euclidean one). DBSCAN is used in many applications, including LiDAR [25], object detection [20], and GPS route analysis [33]. DBSCAN and some of its variants have been also used to cluster high dimensional data, e.g., medical images [4], text [32], and audio [10].

J. Cano and P. W. Trinder (Eds.): Euro-Par 2022, LNCS 13440, pp. 268–284, 2022.
https://doi.org/10.1007/978-3-031-12597-3_17

The computational complexity of traditional DBSCAN is in the worst-case quadratic in the input size [26], expensive considering attributes of today's datasets. Nonetheless, indexing and spatial data structures facilitating proximity searches can ease DBSCAN's computational complexity, as shown with KD-trees [5], R-trees [15], M-trees [8], and cover trees [6]. Using such structures is sub-optimal in at least three cases, though: (i) skewed data distributions negatively affect their performance [20], (ii) the *dimensionality curse* results in exact spatial data structures based on deterministic space partitioning being slower than linear scan [34], and (iii) such structures only work for a particular metric (e.g., Euclidean distance). In the literature, the major means for enhancing time-efficiency are those of parallelization [2,3,13,24,33] and approximation [12], studied alone or jointly [20,21,33]. However, state-of-the-art methods target Euclidean distance only and suffer from skewed data distributions and the dimensionality curse.

Locality-sensitive hashing (LSH) is an established approach for approximate similarity search. Based on the idea that if two data points are close using a custom similarity measure, then an appropriate hash function can map them to equal values with high probability [1,9,17], LSH can support applications that tolerate *approximate* answers, close to the accurate ones *with high probability*. LSH-based indexing has been successful (and shown to be the best known method [17]) for finding similar items in large high-dimensional data-sets. With our contribution, the `IP.LSH.DBSCAN` algorithm, we show how the processes of approximate density-based clustering and that of creating an LSH indexing structure can be *fused* to boost parallel data analysis. Our novel fused approach can efficiently cope with high dimensional data, skewed distributions, large number of points, and a wide range of distance functions. We evaluate the algorithms analytically and empirically, showing they complement the landscape of established state-of-the-art methods, by offering up to several orders of magnitude speed-up on higher dimensional datasets, with tunable high clustering accuracy.

Organization: Section 2 reviews the preliminaries. Section 3 and Sect. 4 describe and analyse the proposed `IP.LSH.DBSCAN`. Section 5 covers the empirical evaluation. Related work and conclusions are presented in Sect. 6 and Sect. 7, respectively.

2 Preliminaries

System Model and Problem Description. Let `D` denote an *input* set of `N` points, each a multi-dimensional vector from a domain $\mathcal{D}$, with a unique identifier `ID`. `Dist` is a distance function applicable on $\mathcal{D}$'s elements. The *goal* is to partition `D` into an a priori unknown number of disjoint clusters, based on `Dist` and parameters `minPts` and ϵ: `minPts` specifies a lower threshold for the number of neighbors, within radius ϵ, for points to be clustered together.

We aim for an efficient, scalable parallel solution, trading approximations in the clustering with reduced calculations regarding the density criteria, while targeting high accuracy. Our evaluation metric for efficiency is *completion time*. Accuracy is measured with respect to an exact baseline using *rand index* [31]: given two clusterings of the same dataset, the *rand index* is the ratio of the number of pairs of elements that are either clustered together or separately in both clusterings, to the total number of pairs of elements. Regarding concurrency guarantees, a common consistency goal is that for every parallel execution, there exists a sequential one producing an equivalent result.

We consider multi-core shared-memory systems executing K threads, supporting `read`, `write` and `read-modify-write` atomic operations, e.g., `CAS` (Compare-And-Swap), available in all contemporary general purpose processors.

Locality Sensitive Hashing (LSH)
The following defines the *sensitivity* of a family of LSH functions [17,23], i.e., the property that, with high probability, nearby points hash to the same value, and faraway ones hash to different values.

Definition 1. *A family of functions* $\mathcal{H} = \{\mathtt{h} : \mathcal{D} \to \mathtt{U}\}$ *is* $(\mathtt{d_1}, \mathtt{d_2}, \mathtt{p_1}, \mathtt{p_2})$*-sensitive for distance function* Dist *if for any* p *and* q *in* $\mathcal{D}$ *the following conditions hold: (i) if* $\mathtt{Dist}(\mathtt{p},\mathtt{q}) \le \mathtt{d_1}$*, then* $\Pr_{\mathcal{H}}[\mathtt{h}(\mathtt{p}) = \mathtt{h}(\mathtt{q})] \ge \mathtt{p_1}$ *(ii) if* $\mathtt{Dist}(\mathtt{p},\mathtt{q}) \ge \mathtt{d_2}$*, then* $\Pr_{\mathcal{H}}[\mathtt{h}(\mathtt{p}) = \mathtt{h}(\mathtt{q})] \le \mathtt{p_2}$*. The probabilities are over the random choices in* $\mathcal{H}$*.*

A family $\mathcal{H}$ is useful when $\mathtt{p_1} > \mathtt{p_2}$ and $\mathtt{d_1} < \mathtt{d_2}$. LSH functions can be *combined*, into more effective (in terms of sensitivity) ones, as follows [23]:

Definition 2. *(i) AND-construction: Given a* $(\mathtt{d_1}, \mathtt{d_2}, \mathtt{p_1}, \mathtt{p_2})$*-sensitive family* $\mathcal{H}$ *and an integer* M*, we can create a new LSH family* $\mathcal{G} = \{\mathtt{g} : \mathcal{D} \to \mathtt{U}^{\mathtt{M}}\}$ *by aggregating/concatenating* M *LSH functions from* $\mathcal{H}$*, where* g(p) *and* g(q) *are equal iff* $\mathtt{h_j}(\mathtt{p})$ *and* $\mathtt{h_j}(\mathtt{q})$ *are equal for all* $\mathtt{j} \in \{1, \cdots, \mathtt{M}\}$*, implying* $\mathcal{G}$ *is* $(\mathtt{d_1}, \mathtt{d_2}, \mathtt{p_1}^{\mathtt{M}}, \mathtt{p_2}^{\mathtt{M}})$*-sensitive; (ii) OR-construction: Given an LSH family* $\mathcal{G}$ *and an integer* L*, we can create a new LSH family* $\mathcal{F}$ *where each* $\mathtt{f} \in \mathcal{F}$ *consists of* L $\mathtt{g_i}$*s chosen independently and uniformly at random from* $\mathcal{G}$*, where* f(p) *and* f(q) *are equal iff* $\mathtt{g_j}(\mathtt{p})$ *and* $\mathtt{g_j}(\mathtt{q})$ *are equal for at least one* $\mathtt{j} \in \{1, \cdots, \mathtt{L}\}$*.* $\mathcal{F}$ *is* $(\mathtt{d_1}, \mathtt{d_2}, 1-(1-\mathtt{p_1}^{\mathtt{M}})^{\mathtt{L}}, 1-(1-\mathtt{p_2}^{\mathtt{M}})^{\mathtt{L}})$*-sensitive assuming* $\mathcal{G}$ *is* $(\mathtt{d_1}, \mathtt{d_2}, \mathtt{p_1}^{\mathtt{M}}, \mathtt{p_2}^{\mathtt{M}})$*-sensitive.*

LSH structure: An instance of family $\mathcal{F}$ is implemented as L hash tables; the i-th table is constructed by hashing each point in D using $\mathtt{g_i}$ [9,17]. The resulting data structure associates each *bucket* with the values for the keys mapping to its index. LSH families can associate with various distance functions [23].

LSH for Euclidean distance: Let u be a randomly chosen unit vector in $\mathcal{D}$. A hash function $\mathtt{h_u}(\mathtt{x})$ in such a family is defined as $\lfloor \frac{\mathtt{x}\cdot\mathtt{u}}{\epsilon} \rfloor$, where $\cdot$ is the inner product operation and ϵ is a constant. The family is applicable for any number of dimensions. In a 2-dimensional domain, it is $(\epsilon/2, 2\epsilon, 1/2, 1/3)$-sensitive.

LSH for angular distance: Let u be a randomly chosen vector in $\mathcal{D}$. A hash function $\mathtt{h_u}(\mathtt{x})$ in such a family is defined as $\mathtt{sgn}(\mathtt{x}\cdot\mathtt{u})$. The family is $(\theta_1, \theta_2, 1-\frac{\theta_1}{\pi}, 1-\frac{\theta_2}{\pi})$-sensitive, where θ_1 and θ_2 are any two angles (in radians) such that $\theta_1 < \theta_2$.

Related Terms and Algorithms DBSCAN: partitions D into an a priori unknown number of clusters, each consisting of at least one *core-point* (i.e., one with at least `minPts` points in its ϵ-radius neighbourhood) and the points that are *density-reachable* from it. Point q is density-reachable from p, if q is *directly reachable* from p (i.e., in its ϵ-radius neighbourhood) or from another core-point that is density-reachable from p. Non-core-points that are density-reachable from some core-point are called *border points*, while others are noise [26]. DBSCAN can utilize any distance function e.g., Euclidean, Jaccard, Hamming, angular [23]. Its worst-case time complexity is $\mathcal{O}(\texttt{N}^2)$, but in certain cases (e.g., Euclidean distance and low-dimensional datasets) its expected complexity lowers to $\mathcal{O}(\texttt{N} \log \texttt{N})$, through indexing structures facilitating range queries to find ϵ neighbours [26].

HP-DBSCAN [13]: Highly Parallel DBSCAN is an OpenMP/MPI algorithm, super-imposing a hyper-grid over the input set. It distributes the points to computing units that do local clusterings. Then, the local clusters that need merging are identified and cluster relabeling rules get broadcasted and applied locally.

PDS-DBSCAN [24]: An exact parallel version of Euclidean DBSCAN that uses a spatial indexing structure for efficient query ranges. It parallelizes the work by partitioning the points and merging partial clusters, maintained via a *disjoint-set* data structure, also known as *union-find* (a collection of disjoint sets, with the elements in each set connected as a directed tree). Such a data structure facilitates *in-place* `find` and `merge` operations [18] avoiding data copying. Given an element p, `find` retrieves the root (i.e., the *representative*) of the tree in which p resides, while `merge` merges the sets containing two given elements.

Theoretically-Efficient and Practical Parallel DBSCAN [33]: Via a grid-based approach, this algorithm identifies core-cells and utilizes a union-find data structure to merge the neighbouring cells having points within ϵ-radius. It uses spatial indexes to facilitate finding neighbourhood cells and answering range queries.

LSH as index for DBSCAN: LSH's potential led other works ([27,35]) to consider it as a plain means for neighbourhood queries. We refer to them as VLSHDBSCAN.

3 The Proposed IP.LSH.DBSCAN Method

IP.LSH.DBSCAN utilizes the LSH properties, for parallel density-clustering, through efficient fusion of the indexing and clustering formation. On the high level, IP.LSH.DBSCAN hashes each point in D, into multiple hash-tables, in such a way that with a high probability, points within ϵ-distance get hashed to the same bucket at least once across all the tables. E.g., Fig. 1a shows how most nearby points in a subset of D get hashed to the same buckets, in two hash tables. Subsequently, the buckets containing at least `mintPts` elements are examined, to find a set of *candidate core-points* which later will be filtered to identify the real *core-points*, in terms of DBSCAN's definition. In Fig. 1a, the core-points are shown as bold points with a dot inside. The buckets containing core-points are characterized as *core buckets*. Afterwards, with the help of the hash tables, ϵ-neighbour core-points get merged. E.g., the core-bucket in the rightmost hash table in Fig. 1a contains two core-points, indicating the possibility that they

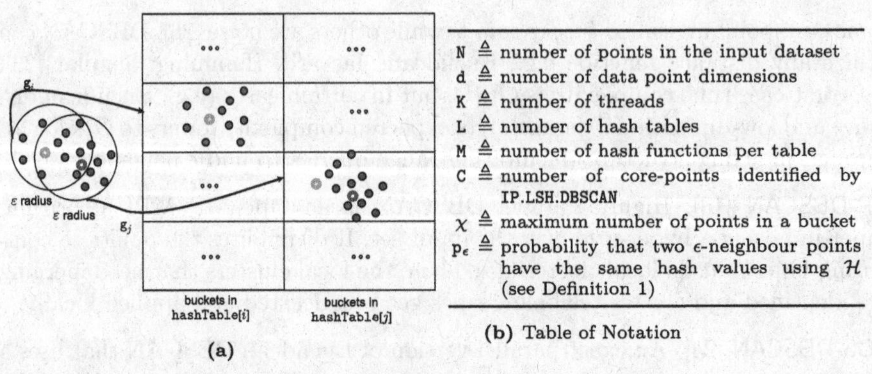

N	≜	number of points in the input dataset
d	≜	number of data point dimensions
K	≜	number of threads
L	≜	number of hash tables
M	≜	number of hash functions per table
C	≜	number of core-points identified by IP.LSH.DBSCAN
χ	≜	maximum number of points in a bucket
p_ϵ	≜	probability that two ϵ-neighbour points have the same hash values using $\mathcal{H}$ (see Definition 1)

(b) Table of Notation

Fig. 1. 1a shows nearby points get hashed to the same bucket at least once across hash tables, whp. Core-points are the bold ones with a dot inside.

are within each other's ϵ-neighbourhood, in which case they get merged. The merging is done using a forest of union-find data structures, consisting of such core-points, that essentially represent core buckets. As we see later, multiple threads can work in parallel in these steps.

Key Elements and Phases. Similar to an LSH structure (cf. Sect. 2), we utilize `L` hash tables (`hashTable`[1], $\cdots$, `hashTable`[`L`]), each constructed using `M` hash functions, chosen according to distance metric `Dist` and threshold ϵ (see Sect. 2, Sect. 4).

Definition 3. *A bucket in any of the hash tables is called a* candidate core-bucket *if it contains at least* `minPts` *elements. A* candidate core-point `c` *in a candidate core-bucket* `ccb` *is defined to be the closest (using function* `Dist`*) point in* `ccb` *to the centroid of all the points in* `ccb`*; we also say that* `c` represents `ccb`*. A candidate core bucket* `ccb`*, whose candidate core-point* `c` *has at least* `minPts` *neighbours within its* ϵ*-radius in* `ccb`*, is called a* core-bucket*. A* Core-forest *is a concurrent union-find structure containing core-points representing core buckets.*

Lemma 1. *Given a core bucket, its corresponding core-point* `c` *is a* true core-point *according to DBSCAN.*

The above follows from the definition of core-point in Definition 3. Next, we present an outline of IP.LSH.DBSCAN's phases, followed by a detailed description of its parallelization and pseudo-code.

In phase I (*hashing and bucketing*), for each i, each point p in D is hashed using the LSH function g_i and inserted into hashTable[i]. Furthermore, the algorithm keeps track of the buckets containing at least minPts, as candidate core buckets. In phase II (*core-point identification*), for each candidate core-bucket, the algorithm identifies a candidate core-point. If at least minPts points in a candidate core-bucket fall within the ϵ-neighbourhood of the identified candidate core-point, the latter is identified as a true core-point (see Lemma 1) and inserted into the core-forest as a singleton. In phase III (*merge-task identification and processing*), the algorithm inspects each core-bucket and creates and performs a *merge task* for each pair of core-points that are within each others' ϵ-neighbourhood. Hence, the elements in the core-forest start forming sets according to the merge tasks. In phase IV (*data labeling*), the algorithm labels the points: a core-point gets assigned the same clustering label as all the other core-points with which it forms a set in the core-forest. A border point (i.e., a non-core-point located in the ϵ-radius of a core-point) is labeled the same as a corresponding core-point, and all the other points are considered noise.

Parallelism and Algorithmic Implementation. We here present the parallelization in IP.LSH.DBSCAN (Algorithm 1), targeting speed-up by distributing

Algorithm 1. Outline of IP.LSH.DBSCAN

```
Input: dataset D, threshold minPts, radius ε, nr. of hash tables L, nr. of hash functions per table
  M, metric Dist, nr of threads K; Output: a clustering label for each point in D
let D be logically partitioned into S mutually disjoint batches
hashTable[1],···,hashTable[L] are hash tables supporting concurrent insertions and traversals
candidateCoreBuckets and coreBuckets are empty sets supporting concurrent operations
let hashTasks be a S × L boolean array initialized to false, indicating the status of hash tasks
  corresponding to the Cartesian product of S batches and L hash tables
let G = {g : S → U^M} be an LSH family suitable for metric Dist, and let g_1, ···, g_L be hash
  functions chosen independently and uniformly at random from G (Definition 2)
for all threads in parallel do
  phase I: hashing and bucketing
    while the running thread can book a task from hashTasks do
      for each point p in task.batch do
        let i be index of the hashTable associated with task
        hashTable[i].insert(key = g_i(p), value = ptr(p))
        bucket=hashTable[i].getBucket(key = g_i(p))
        if bucket.size() ≥ minPts then candidateCoreBuckets.insert(ptr(bucket))
  phase II: core-point identification (starts when all threads reach here)
    for each ccb in candidateCoreBuckets do
      let c be the closest point in ccb to ccb points' centroid
      if |{q ∈ ccb such that Dist(c, q)}| ≥ minPts then
        c→ corePoint := TRUE and insert c into the core-forest
        coreBuckets.insert(ccb)
  phase III: merge-task identification and processing (starts when all threads reach here)
    while cb := coreBuckets.pop() do
      let core be the core-point associated with cb
      for core-point c ∈ cb such that Dist(core, c) ≤ ε do merge(core, c)
  phase IV: data labeling (starts when a thread reaches here)
    for each core bucket cb do
      let core be the core-point associated with cb
      for each non-labeled point p in cb do
        if p→ corePoint then p.idx = findRoot(p).ID
        else p.idx = findRoot(core).ID
```

the work among K threads. We also aim at in-place operations on data points and buckets (i.e., without creating additional copies), hence work with pointers to the relevant data points and buckets in the data structures.

Phase I (*hashing and bucketing*): To parallelize the hashing of the input dataset D into L hash tables, we (logically) partition D into S mutually disjoint batches. Consecutively, we have S × L *hash tasks*, corresponding to the Cartesian product of the hash tables and the data batches. Threads can *book* a hash task and thus share the workload through `hashTasks`, which is a boolean S × L array containing a *status* for each task, initially `false`. A thread in this phase scans the elements of `hashTasks`, and if it finds a non-booked task, it tries to *atomically book* the task (e.g., via a CAS to change the status from `false` to `true`). The thread that books a hash task $\mathtt{ht}_{\mathtt{b,t}}$ hashes each data point p in batch b into `hashTable[t]` using hash function $\mathtt{g}_{\mathtt{t}}$. Particularly, for each point p, a key-value pair consisting of the hashed value of p and a pointer to p is inserted in `hashTable[t]`. As entries get inserted into the hash tables, pointers to buckets with at least `minPts` points are added to `candidateCoreBuckets`. Since the threads operate concurrently, we use hash tables supporting concurrent insertions and traversals. Algorithm 1 l.8–l.14 summarizes Phase I.

Phase II (*core-point identification*): Here the threads identify core-buckets and core-points. Each thread atomically pops a candidate core bucket `ccb` from `candidateCoreBuckets` and identifies the closest point to the centroid of the points in `ccb`, considering it as a candidate core-point, `ccp`. If there are at least `minPts` points in `ccb` within ϵ-radius of `ccp`, then `ccp` and `ccb` become core-point and core-bucket, respectively, and `ccp` is inserted in the core-forest and the `ccb` in the `coreBucekts` set. This phase, shown in Algorithm 1 l.15–l.20, is finished when `candidateCoreBuckets` becomes empty.

Phase III (*merge-task identification and processing*): The threads here identify and perform merge tasks. For each core-bucket `cb` that a thread successfully books from the set `coreBuckets`, the thread `merges` the sets corresponding to the associated core-point with `cb` and any other core-point in `cb` within ϵ distance. For merging, the algorithm uses an established concurrent implementation for disjoint-sets, with *linearizable* and *wait-free* (i.e., the effects of concurrent operations are consistent with the sequential specification, while the threads can make progress independently of each other) `find` and `merge`, proposed in [18]. This phase, shown in Algorithm 1 l.21–l.24, completes when `coreBucekts` is empty.

Phase IV (*data labeling*): Each non-labeled core-point in a core-bucket gets its clustering label after its root ID in the core-forest. All other non-labeled points in a core-bucket are labeled with the root ID of the associated core-point. The process, shown in Algorithm 1 l.25–l.30, is performed concurrently for all core-buckets.

4 Analysis

This section analytically studies IP.LSH.DBSCAN's accuracy, safety and completeness properties, and completion time. We provide sketch proofs to save space, but formal proofs can be found in [19]. Figure 1b summarizes the notations.

Accuracy Analysis

Let p_ϵ be the probability that two given points with maximum distance ϵ have the same hash value using $\mathcal{H}$ (see Definition 1). Lemma 1 shows that any point identified as a core-point by IP.LSH.DBSCAN is a true core-point in terms of DBSCAN. The following Lemma provides a lower bound on the probability that IP.LSH.DBSCAN identifies any DBSCAN core-point.

Lemma 2. *Let* c *be a DBSCAN's core-point. The probability that* IP.LSH.DBSCAN *also identifies* c *as a core-points is at least* $1-\left(1-\frac{1}{\chi}p_\epsilon^{M(minPts-1)}\right)^L$, *where* χ *denotes the maximum number of points in any bucket.*

Proof. (sketch) First note that with M hash functions per table (i.e., the AND construction in Definition 2), the probability that two given points with maximum distance ϵ *collide* into the same hash bucket in a fixed hash table is p_ϵ^M. The probability that c gets identified as a core-point in a fixed hash table is at leaset $\frac{1}{\chi}p_\epsilon^{M(minPts-1)}$ because at least minPts-1 ϵ-neighbours of c must get hashed to b, and c should be the closest point to the centroid of the points in b. Finally, the probability that c gets identified as a core-point in at least one hash table is computed as the complement of the probability that c does not get identified as a core-point in any hash table.

Lemma 2 shows that the probability of identifying any DBSCAN core-point can be made arbitrarily close to 1 by choosing sufficiently large L.

Lemma 3. *Let* c_1 *and* c_2 *be two core-points identified by* IP.LSH.DBSCAN.

1. *If* $\mathtt{Dist}(c_1, c_2) > \epsilon$, *then* IP.LSH.DBSCAN *does not merge* c_1 *and* c_2.
2. *If* $\mathtt{Dist}(c_1, c_2) \leq \epsilon$, *then the probability that* IP.LSH.DBSCAN *merges* c_1 *and* c_2 *is at least* $2p_\epsilon^M - p_\epsilon^{2M}$.

Proof. (sketch) 1. follows directly from IP.LSH.DBSCAN's algorithmic description (see Algorithm 1 l.24). 2. follows from calculating the probability that c_2 hashes into the same bucket in which c_1 is the representative, and vice-versa.

Safety and Completeness Properties

At the end of phase IV, each set in the core-forest maintained by IP.LSH.DBSCAN contains a subset of density-reachable core-points (as defined in Sect. 2). Two disjoint-set structures ds_1, ds_2 are *equivalent* if there is a one-to-one correspondence between ds_1's and ds_2's sets. The following lemma implies that the outcomes of single-threaded and concurrent executions of IP.LSH.DBSCAN are equivalent.

Lemma 4. *Any pair of concurrent executions of* IP.LSH.DBSCAN *that use the same hash functions, produce equivalent core-forests at the end of phase IV.*

Proof. (sketch) Considering a fixed instance of the problem, any concurrent execution of IP.LSH.DBSCAN identifies the same set of core-points and core-buckets with the same hash functions, hence performing the same set of merge operations. As the concurrent executions of merge operations are linearizable (see Sect. 3) and merge operation satisfies the associative and commutative properties, the resulting sets in the core-forest are identical for any concurrent execution.

It is worth noting that *border points* (i.e., non-core-points within the vicinity of multiple core-points) can be assigned to any of the neighbouring clusters. The original DBSCAN [11] exhibits the same behaviour as well.

Completion Time Analysis

Lemma 5. *[adapted from Theorem 2 in [18]] The probability that each* findRoot *and each* merge *perform* $\mathcal{O}(\log \mathtt{C})$ *steps is at least* $1 - \frac{1}{\mathtt{C}}$*, where* C *is the number of identified core-points by* IP.LSH.DBSCAN.

Corollary 1. *The expected asymptotic time complexity of each* findRoot *and each* merge *is* $\mathcal{O}(\log \mathtt{C})$.

Lemma 6. *The expected completion time of phase I is* $\mathcal{O}(\frac{\mathtt{LMNd}}{\mathtt{K}})$*; phase II and phase III is bounded by* $\mathcal{O}(\frac{\mathtt{LN}\log \mathtt{C}}{\mathtt{K}})$*; phase IV is* $\mathcal{O}(\frac{\mathtt{N}\log \mathtt{C}}{\mathtt{K}})$.

Theorem 1. *The expected completion time of* IP.LSH.DBSCAN *is* $\mathcal{O}(\frac{\mathtt{LMNd}+\mathtt{LN}\log \mathtt{C}}{\mathtt{K}})$.

Theorem 1 is derived by taking the asymptotically dominant terms in Lemma 6. It shows IP.LSH.DBSCAN's expected completion time is inversely proportional to K and grows linearly in N, d, L, and M. In common cases where C is much smaller than N, the expected completion time is $\mathcal{O}(\frac{\mathtt{LMNd}}{\mathtt{K}})$; In the worst-case, where C is $\mathcal{O}(\mathtt{N})$, the expected completion time is $\mathcal{O}(\frac{\mathtt{LMNd}+\mathtt{LN}\log \mathtt{N}}{\mathtt{K}})$. For this to happen, for instance, ϵ and minPts need to be extremely small and L be extremely large. As the density parameters of DBSCAN are chosen to detect meaningful clusters, such choices for ϵ and minPts are in practice avoided.

On the memory use of IP.LSH.DBSCAN: The memory footprint of IP.LSH.DBSCAN is proportional to $(\mathtt{LN} + \mathtt{Nd})$, as it simply needs only one copy of each data point and pointers in the hash tables and this dominates the overhead of all other utilized data structures. Further, in-place operations ensure that data is not copied and transferred unnecessarily, which is a significant factor regarding efficiency. In Sect. 5, the effect of these properties is discussed.

Choice of L and M: For an LSH structure, a plot representing the probability of points hashing into the same bucket as a function of their distance resembles an inverse s-curve (x- and y-axis being the distance, and the probability of hashing to the same bucket, resp.), starting at 1 for the points with distance 0, declining with a significant slope around some threshold, and approaching 0 for far apart points. Choices of L and M directly influence the shape of the associated curve, particularly the location of the threshold and the sharpness of the decline [23]. It is worth noting that steeper declines generally result in more accurate LSH structures at the expense of larger L and M values. Consequently, in IP.LSH.DBSCAN, L and M must be determined to (i) set the location of the threshold at ϵ, and (ii) balance the trade-off between the steepness of the decline and the completion time. In Sect. 5, we study a range of L and M values and their implications on the trade-off between IP.LSH.DBSCAN's accuracy and completion time.

5 Evaluation

We conduct an extensive evaluation of IP.LSH.DBSCAN, comparing with the established state-of-the-art algorithms. Our implementation is publicly available [19]. Complementing Theorem 1, we measure the execution latency with varying number of threads (K), data points (N), dimensions (d), hash tables (L), and hash functions per table (M). We use varying ϵ values, as well as Euclidean and angular distances. We measure IP.LSH.DBSCAN's accuracy against the exact DBSCAN (hence also the baseline state-of-the-art algorithms) using rand index.

Setup: We implemented IP.LSH.DBSCAN in C++, using POSIX threads and the concurrent hash table of Intel's threading building blocks library (TBB). We used a c5.18xlarg AWS machine, with 144 GB of memory and two Intel Xeon Platinum 8124M CPUs, with 36 two-way hyper-threaded cores [33] in total.

Tested Methods: In addition to IP.LSH.DBSCAN, we benchmark PDSDBSCAN [24], HPDBSCAN [13], and the exact algorithm in [33], for which we use the label TEDBSCAN (Theoretically-Efficient and Practical Parallel DBSCAN). As the approximate algorithms in [33] are generally not faster than their exact counterpart (see Fig. 9 and discussion on p. 13 in [33]), we consider their efficiency represented by the exact TEDBSCAN. We also benchmark VLSHDBSCAN, our version of a single-thread DBSCAN that uses LSH indexing, as we did not find open implementations for [27,35]. Benchmarking VLSHDBSCAN allows a comparison regarding the approximation degree, as well as the efficiency induced by IP.LSH.DBSCAN's "fused" approach. Section 2 covers the aforementioned algorithms.

Evaluation Data and Parameters
Following common practices [13,28,33], we use datasets with different characteristics. We use varying ϵ but fixed minPts, as the sensitivity on the latter is significantly smaller [28]. We also follow earlier works' common practice to abort any execution that exceeds a certain bound, here 9×10^5 sec (more than 24 h). We introduce the datasets and the chosen values for ϵ and minPts as well as the choices for L and M, based on the corresponding discussion in Sect. 4 and also the literature guidelines (e.g., [23] and the reference therein). The *default* ϵ values are shown in *italics*.

TeraClickLog [33]: Each point in this dataset corresponds to a display ad by Criteo with 13 integer and 26 categorical features. We use a subset with over 67 million points, free from missing features. Like [33], we only consider the integer features, and we choose ϵ from $\{\mathit{1500}, 3000, 6000, 12000\}$ and minPts 100.

Household [12]: This is an electricity consumption dataset with over two million points, each being seven-dimensional after removing the date and time features (as suggested in [12]). Following the practice in [12,33], we scale each feature to [0,10000] interval and choose ϵ from $\{1500, \mathit{2000}, 2500, 3000\}$ and minPts 100.

GeoLife [36]: From this GPS trajectory dataset, we choose ca 1.5 million points as selected in [20], containing latitude and longitude with a *highly skewed* distribution. We choose ϵ from $\{\mathit{0.001}, 0.002, 0.004, 0.008\}$ and minPts 500, like [20].

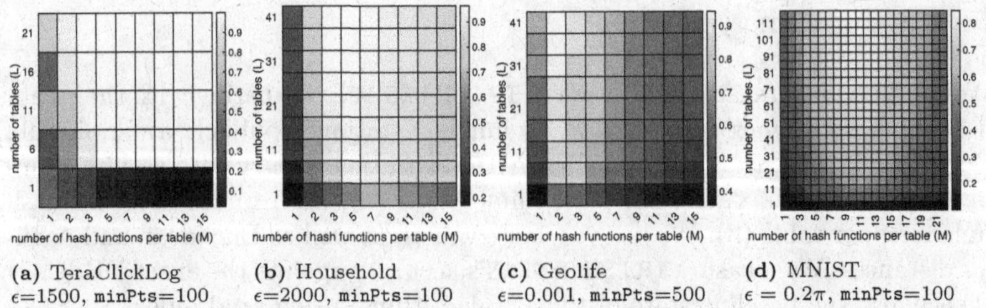

(a) TeraClickLog ϵ=1500, minPts=100 (b) Household ϵ=2000, minPts=100 (c) Geolife ϵ=0.001, minPts=500 (d) MNIST $\epsilon = 0.2\pi$, minPts=100

Fig. 2. Visualizing the rand index accuracy of IP.LSH.DBSCAN as a function of L and M

MNIST: This dataset contains 70000 28×28-pixel hand-written and labelled 0–9 digits [22]. We treat each record as a 784-dimensional data point, normalizing each point to have a unit length (similar to [30]). We utilize the angular distance. Following [29], we choose ϵ from $\{0.18\pi, 0.19\pi, \mathit{0.20\pi}, 0.21\pi\}$ and minPts 100.

The heat-maps in Fig. 2a–Fig. 2d visualize IP.LSH.DBSCAN's rand index accuracy as a function of L and M. For TeraClickLog (Fig. 2a), {L = 5, M = 5}, {L = 10, M = 5}, and {L = 20, M = 5} give 0.98, 0.99, and 1 accuracies, respectively. For Household (Fig. 2b), {L = 5, M = 5}, {L = 10, M = 5}, and {L = 20, M = 5} give 0.92, 0.94, and 0.95 accuracies, respectively. For GeoLife (Fig. 2c), {L = 5, M = 2}, {L = 10, M = 2}, and {L = 20, M = 2} give 0.8, 0.85, and 0.89 accuracies, respectively. For (Fig. 2d) dataset, {L = 58, M = 9}, {L = 116, M = 9}, and {L = 230, M = 9} give 0.77, 0.85, and 0.89 accuracy, respectively, computed with respect to the actual labels.

Experiments for the Euclidean Distance

Completion Time with Varying K: Figure 3a, Fig. 3b, and Fig. 3c show the completion time of IP.LSH.DBSCAN and other methods with varying K on TeraClickLog, Household, and Geolife datasets, respectively. PDSDBSCAN runs out of memory on TeraClickLog for all K and on GeoLife for $K \geq 4$, and none of HPDBSCAN's executions terminate within the 9×10^5 sec threshold. For the reference, in Fig. 3, the completion time of single-thread VLSHDBSCAN is provided as a caption for each dataset, except for TeraClickLog as its completion time exceeds 9×10^5 sec. The results indicate the benefits of parallelization for work-load distribution in IP.LSH.DBSCAN, also validating that IP.LSH.DBSCAN's completion time behavior is linear with respect to L, as shown in Theorem 1. For higher dimensionality, challenging the state-of-the-art algorithms, IP.LSH.DBSCAN's completion time is several orders of magnitude shorter.

Completion Time with Varying ϵ: The left Y-axes in Fig. 4a, Fig. 4b, and Fig. 4c show the completion time of IP.LSH.DBSCAN and other tested methods using 36 cores with varying ϵ values on TeraClickLog, Household, and Geolife datasets, respectively. PDSDBSCAN crashes by running out of memory on TeraClickLog and GeoLife for all ϵ, and none of HPDBSCAN's executions terminate within the 9×10^5 sec threshold. The right Y-axes in Fig. 4a, Fig. 4b, and Fig. 4c show

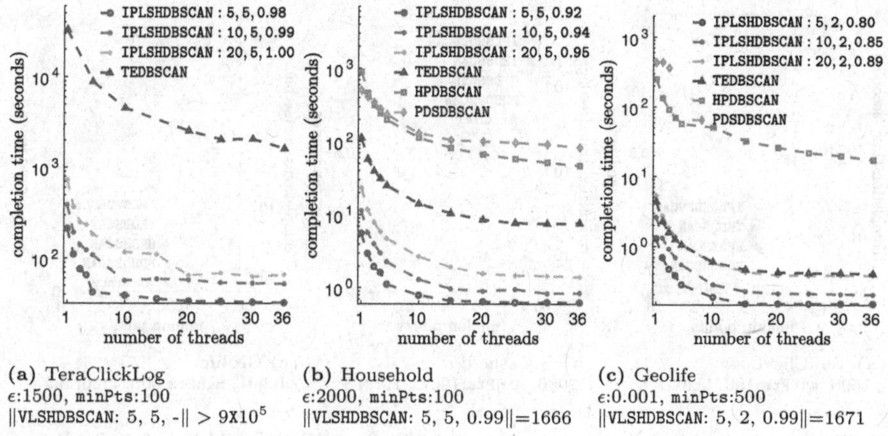

(a) TeraClickLog
ϵ:1500, minPts:100
||VLSHDBSCAN: 5, 5, -|| > 9X10[5]

(b) Household
ϵ:2000, minPts:100
||VLSHDBSCAN: 5, 5, 0.99||=1666

(c) Geolife
ϵ:0.001, minPts:500
||VLSHDBSCAN: 5, 2, 0.99||=1671

Fig. 3. *Completion time with varying* K. *The comma-separated values corresponding to* IP.LSH.DBSCAN *and* VLSHDBSCAN *show* L, M, *and the rand index accuracy, respectively. PDSDBSCAN crashes by running out of memory in 3a for all* K *and for* $K \geq 4$ *in 3c. In 3a no HPDBSCAN executions terminate within the* 9×10^5*-sec threshold.*

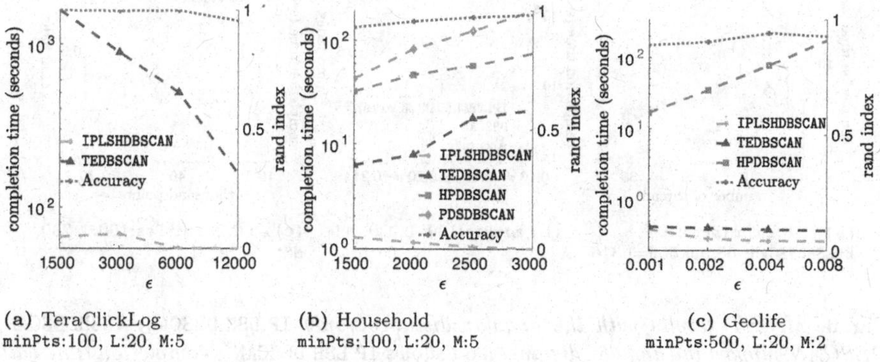

(a) TeraClickLog
minPts:100, L:20, M:5

(b) Household
minPts:100, L:20, M:5

(c) Geolife
minPts:500, L:20, M:2

Fig. 4. *Completion time using varying* ϵ *with 36 cores. PDSDBSCAN crashes by running out of memory in 4a and 4c for all* ϵ. *None of HPDBSCAN's executions terminate within the* 9×10^5 *sec threshold in 4a. Right Y-axes show* IP.LSH.DBSCAN*'s rand index.*

the corresponding rand index accuracy of IP.LSH.DBSCAN. The results show that in general the completion time of IP.LSH.DBSCAN decreases by increasing ϵ. Intuitively, hashing points into larger buckets results in lower merge workload. Similar benefits, although with higher completion times, are seen for TEDBSCAN. On the other hand, as the results show, completion time of many classical methods (such as HPDBSCAN and PDSDBSCAN) increases with increasing ϵ.

Completion Time with Varying N: The left Y-axes in Fig. 5a, Fig. 5b, and Fig. 5c show the completion time of the bench-marked methods using 36 cores on varying size subsets of TeraClickLog, Household, and Geolife datasets, respectively.

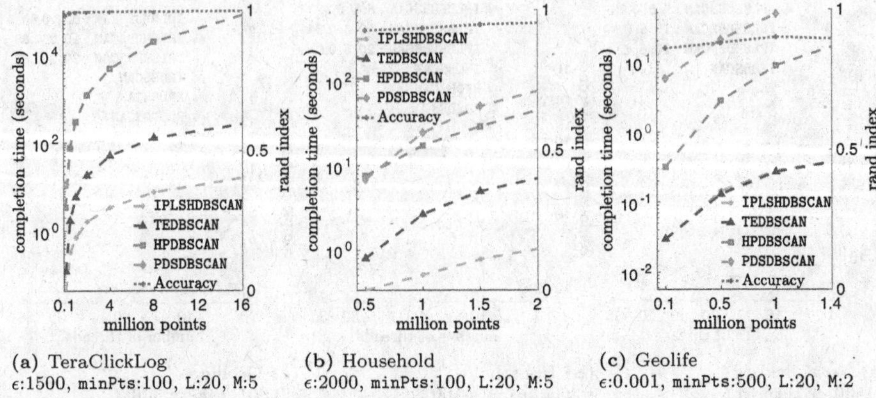

(a) TeraClickLog
ϵ:1500, minPts:100, L:20, M:5

(b) Household
ϵ:2000, minPts:100, L:20, M:5

(c) Geolife
ϵ:0.001, minPts:500, L:20, M:2

Fig. 5. *Completion time with varying* N *using 36 cores. PDSDBSCAN runs out of memory in* 5a *with* N > *0.1 million points and with* N > *1 million points in* 5c. IP.LSH.DBSCAN *and* TEDBSCAN *coincide in* 5c. *Right Y-axes show* IP.LSH.DBSCAN*'s rand index.*

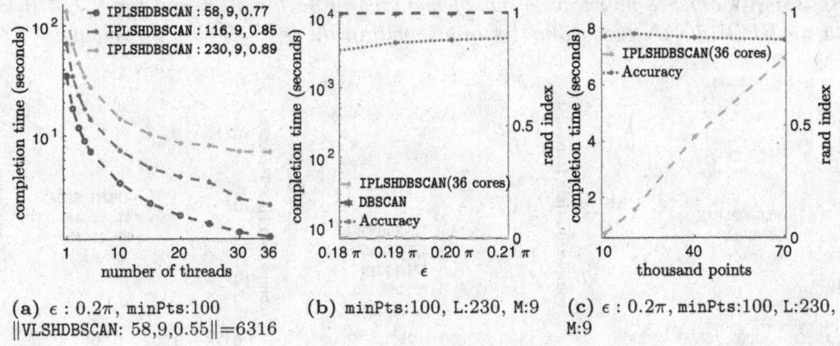

(a) ϵ : 0.2π, minPts:100
||VLSHDBSCAN: 58,9,0.55||=6316

(b) minPts:100, L:230, M:9

(c) ϵ : 0.2π, minPts:100, L:230, M:9

Fig. 6. *MNIST results with the angular distance (only* IP.LSH.DBSCAN, VLSHDBSCAN, *DBSCAN support the angular distance).* 6a *shows* IP.LSH.DBSCAN*'s completion time with varying* K. *The left Y-axes in* 6b *and* 6c *respectively show* IP.LSH.DBSCAN*'s completion time with varying* ϵ *and* N, *using 36 cores. The right Y-axes in* 6b *and* 6c *show the associated accuracy, computed with respect to the actual labels.*

PDSDBSCAN runs out of memory on TeraClickLog subsets with N > 0.1 million points and GeoLife subsets with N > 1 million points. The results empirically validate that completion time of IP.LSH.DBSCAN exhibits a linear growth in the number of data points, complementing Theorem 1. The right Y-axes in Fig. 5a, Fig. 5b, and Fig. 5c show the corresponding rand index accuracy of IP.LSH.DBSCAN.

Experiments for the Angular Distance. For significantly high number of dimensions, as a side-effect of dimensionality curse, the Euclidean distance among all pairs of points is almost equal [23]. To overcome this, we use angular distance. We only study methods that support such a distance: IP.LSH.DBSCAN,

VLSHDBSCAN, and DBSCAN. Here accuracy is calculated against the actual labels. Figure 6a shows completion time with varying K. The left Y-axes in Fig. 6b and Fig. 6c respectively show completion time with varying ϵ and N, using 36 cores. The right Y-axes in Fig. 6b and Fig. 6c show the associated accuracies. Note IP.LSH.DBSCAN's completion time is more than 4 orders of magnitude faster than a sequential DBSCAN and more than 3 orders of magnitude faster than VLSHDBSCAN. Here, too the results align and complement Theorem 1's analysis.

Discussion of Results. IP.LSH.DBSCAN targets high dimensional, memory-efficient clustering for various distance measures. IP.LSH.DBSCAN's completion time is several orders of magnitude shorter than state-of-the-art counterparts, while ensuring approximation with tunable accuracy and showing efficiency for lower dimensional data too. In practice, IP.LSH.DBSCAN's completion time exhibits a linear behaviour with respect to the number of points, even for skewed data distributions and varying density parameters. The benefits of IP.LSH.DBSCAN with respect to other algorithms increase with increasing data dimensionality. IP.LSH.DBSCAN scales both with the size of the input and its dimensionality.

6 Other Related Work

Having compared IP.LSH.DBSCAN with representative state-of-the-art related algorithms in Sect. 5, we focus on related work considering approximation. Gan et al. and Wang et al. in [12,33] proposed approximate DBSCAN clustering for low-dimensional Euclidean distance, with $\mathcal{O}(\mathtt{N}^2)$ complexity if $2^{\mathtt{d}} > \mathtt{N}$ [7]. The PARMA-CC [20] approach is also suitable only for low-dimensional data. VLSHDBSCAN [27,35] uses LSH for neighbourhood queries. However, the LSH index creation in IP.LSH.DBSCAN is embedded into the dynamics of the clusters formation. IP.LSH.DBSCAN iterates over buckets and it applies merges on core-points that represent bigger entities, drastically reducing the search complexity. Also, IP.LSH.DBSCAN is a concurrent rather than a single-thread algorithm. Esfandiari et al. [10] propose an almost linear approximate DBSCAN that identifies core-points by mapping points into hyper-cubes and counting the points in them. It uses LSH to find and merge nearby core-points. IP.LSH.DBSCAN integrates core-point identification and merging in one structure altogether, leading to better efficiency and flexibility in leveraging the desired distance function.

7 Conclusions

IP.LSH.DBSCAN proposes a simple and efficient method combining insights on DBSCAN with features of LSH. It offers approximation with tunable accuracy and high parallelism, avoiding the exponential growth of the search effort with the number of data dimensions, thus scaling both with the size of the input and its dimensionality, and dealing with high skewness in a memory-efficient way. We expect IP.LSH.DBSCAN will support applications in the evolving landscape of cyberphysical system data pipelines to aggregate information from large, high-dimensional, highly-skewed data sets [14,16]. We also expect that this methodology can be used for partitioning data for other types of graph processing and as such this direction is worth investigating as extension of `IP.LSH.DBSCAN`.

Acknowledgements and Data Availability Statement. Work supported by SSF grant "FiC" (GMT14-0032); VR grants "HARE" (2016-03800), "Relaxed Concurrent Data Structure Semantics for Scalable Data Processing" (2021-05443), "EPITOME" (2021-05424); Chalmers AoA frameworks Energy and Production, proj. INDEED, and WP "Scalability, Big Data and AI". The source code generated for the current study is available in the Figshare repository https://doi.org/10.6084/m9.figshare.19991786 [19].

References

1. Andoni, A., Indyk, P.: Near-optimal hashing algorithms for approximate nearest neighbor in high dimensions. Commun. ACM **51**(1), 117–122 (2008). https://doi.org/10.1145/1327452.1327494
2. Andrade, G., Ramos, G.S., Madeira, D., Oliveira, R.S., Ferreira, R., Rocha, L.: G-DBSCAN: a GPU accelerated algorithm for density-based clustering. In: International Conference on Computational Science. ICCS 2013. Procedia Computer Science, vol. 18, pp. 369–378. Elsevier (2013). https://doi.org/10.1016/j.procs.2013.05.200
3. Arlia, D., Coppola, M.: Experiments in parallel clustering with DBSCAN. In: Sakellariou, R., Gurd, J., Freeman, L., Keane, J. (eds.) Euro-Par 2001. LNCS, vol. 2150, pp. 326–331. Springer, Heidelberg (2001). https://doi.org/10.1007/3-540-44681-8_46
4. Baselice, F., Coppolino, L., D'Antonio, S., Ferraioli, G., Sgaglione, L.: A DBSCAN based approach for jointly segment and classify brain MR images. In: 37th International Conference of the IEEE Engineering in Medicine and Biology Society, EMBC 2015, pp. 2993–2996. IEEE (2015). https://doi.org/10.1109/EMBC.2015.7319021
5. Bentley, J.L.: K-d trees for semidynamic point sets. In: 6th Symposium on Computational Geometry, pp. 187–197. ACM (1990). https://doi.org/10.1145/98524.98564
6. Beygelzimer, A., Kakade, S., Langford, J.: Cover trees for nearest neighbor. In: 23rd Conference on Machine Learning. ICML 2006, pp. 97–104. ACM (2006). https://doi.org/10.1145/1143844.1143857
7. Chen, Y., Tang, S., Bouguila, N., Wang, C., Du, J., Li, H.: A fast clustering algorithm based on pruning unnecessary distance computations in DBSCAN for high-dimensional data. Pattern Recogn. **83**, 375–387 (2018). https://doi.org/10.1016/j.patcog.2018.05.030
8. Ciaccia, P., Patella, M., Zezula, P.: M-tree: an efficient access method for similarity search in metric spaces. In: VLDB 1997, 23rd International Conference on Very Large Data Bases, pp. 426–435. M. Kaufmann (1997). http://www.vldb.org/conf/1997/P426.PDF
9. Datar, M., Immorlica, N., Indyk, P., Mirrokni, V.S.: Locality-sensitive hashing scheme based on p-stable distributions. In: 20th Symposium on Computational Geometry. SCG 2004, pp. 253–262. ACM (2004). http://doi.acm.org/10.1145/997817.997857

10. Esfandiari, H., Mirrokni, V.S., Zhong, P.: Almost linear time density level set estimation via DBSCAN. In: 35th AAAI Conference on Artificial Intelligence AAAI 2021, pp. 7349–7357. AAAI Press (2021). https://ojs.aaai.org/index.php/AAAI/article/view/16902
11. Ester, M., Kriegel, H., Sander, J., Xu, X.: A density-based algorithm for discovering clusters in large spatial databases with noise. In: 2nd Conference on Knowledge Discovery and Data Mining (KDD-96), pp. 226–231. AAAI Press (1996). http://www.aaai.org/Library/KDD/1996/kdd96-037.php
12. Gan, J., Tao, Y.: On the hardness and approximation of Euclidean DBSCAN. ACM Trans. Database Syst. **42**(3), 14:1–14:45 (2017). https://doi.org/10.1145/3083897
13. Götz, M., Bodenstein, C., Riedel, M.: HPDBSCAN: highly parallel DBSCAN. In: Workshop on Machine Learning in High-Performance Computing Environments, MLHPC 2015, pp. 2:1–2:10. ACM (2015). https://doi.org/10.1145/2834892.2834894
14. Gulisano, V., Nikolakopoulos, Y., Cederman, D., Papatriantafilou, M., Tsigas, P.: Efficient data streaming multiway aggregation through concurrent algorithmic designs and new abstract data types. ACM Trans. Parallel Comput. (TOPC) **4**(2), 1–28 (2017)
15. Guttman, A.: R-trees: a dynamic index structure for spatial searching. In: 1984 SIGMOD International Conference on Management of Data, pp. 47–57. ACM Press (1984). https://doi.org/10.1145/602259.602266
16. Havers, B., Duvignau, R., Najdataei, H., Gulisano, V., Koppisetty, A.C., Papatriantafilou, M.: Driven: a framework for efficient data retrieval and clustering in vehicular networks. In: 35th International Conference on Data Engineering (ICDE), pp. 1850–1861. IEEE (2019)
17. Indyk, P., Motwani, R.: Approximate nearest neighbors: towards removing the curse of dimensionality. In: 30th ACM Symposium on the Theory of Computation, pp. 604–613. ACM (1998). https://doi.org/10.1145/276698.276876
18. Jayanti, S.V., Tarjan, R.E.: A randomized concurrent algorithm for disjoint set union. In: 2016 ACM Symposium on Principles of Distributed Computating ACM (2016). https://doi.org/10.1145/2933057.2933108
19. Keramatian, A., Gulisano, V., Papatriantafilou, M., Tsigas, P.: Artifact and instructions to generate experimental results for the Euro-Par 2022 paper: "IP.LSH.DBSCAN: Integrated Parallel Density-Based Clustering Through Locality-Sensitive Hashing" (2022). https://doi.org/10.6084/m9.figshare.19991786
20. Keramatian, A., Gulisano, V., Papatriantafilou, M., Tsigas, P.: PARMA-CC: parallel multiphase approximate cluster combining. In: 21st International Conference on Distributed Computing and Networking, pp. 20:1–20:10. ACM (2020). https://doi.org/10.1145/3369740.3369785
21. Keramatian, A., Gulisano, V., Papatriantafilou, M., Tsigas, P.: MAD-C: multi-stage approximate distributed cluster-combining for obstacle detection and localization. J. Parallel Distrib. Comput. **147**, 248–267 (2021)
22. Lecun, Y., Bottou, L., Bengio, Y., Haffner, P.: Gradient-based learning applied to document recognition. Proc. IEEE **86**(11), 2278–2324 (1998). https://doi.org/10.1109/5.726791
23. Leskovec, J., Rajaraman, A., Ullman, J.D.: Mining of Massive Datasets, 2nd edn. Cambridge University Press (2014). http://www.mmds.org/
24. Patwary, M.M.A., Palsetia, D., Agrawal, A., Liao, W., Manne, F., Choudhary, A.N.: A new scalable parallel DBSCAN algorithm using the disjoint-set data structure. In: SC Conference on High Performance Computing Networking, Storage and Analysis, SC 2012, p. 62. IEEE/ACM (2012). https://doi.org/10.1109/SC.2012.9

25. Rusu, R.B., Cousins, S.: 3D is here: point cloud library (PCL). In: IEEE International Conference on Robotics and Automation, ICRA. IEEE (2011). https://doi.org/10.1109/ICRA.2011.5980567
26. Schubert, E., Sander, J., Ester, M., Kriegel, H.P., Xu, X.: DBSCAN revisited, revisited: why and how you should (still) use DBSCAN. ACM Trans. Database Syst. **42**(3), 19:1–19:21 (2017). http://doi.acm.org/10.1145/3068335
27. Shiqiu, Y., Qingsheng, Z.: DBSCAN clustering algorithm based on locality sensitive hashing. J. Phys. Conf. Series **1314**, 012177 (2019). https://doi.org/10.1088/1742-6596/1314/1/012177
28. Song, H., Lee, J.: RP-DBSCAN: a superfast parallel DBSCAN algorithm based on random partitioning. In: 2018 SIGMOD International Conference on Management of Data, pp. 1173–1187. ACM (2018). https://doi.org/10.1145/3183713.3196887
29. Starczewski, A., Goetzen, P., Er, M.J.: A new method for automatic determining DBSCAN parameters. J. Artif. Intell. Soft Comput. Res. **10**(3), 209–221 (2020). https://doi.org/10.2478/jaiscr-2020-0014
30. Sundaram, N., et al.: Streaming similarity search over one billion tweets using parallel locality-sensitive hashing. VLDB Endow. **6**(14), 1930–1941 (2013). http://www.vldb.org/pvldb/vol6/p1930-sundaram.pdf
31. Wagner, S., Wagner, D.: Comparing clusterings- an overview (2007)
32. Wang, X., Zhang, L., Zhang, X., Xie, K.: Application of improved DBSCAN clustering algorithm on industrial fault text data. In: 18th IEEE International Conference on Industrial Information, INDIN, pp. 461–468. IEEE (2020). https://doi.org/10.1109/INDIN45582.2020.9442093
33. Wang, Y., Gu, Y., Shun, J.: Theoretically-efficient and practical parallel DBSCAN. In: 2020 SIGMOD International Conference on Management of Data, pp. 2555–2571. ACM (2020). https://doi.org/10.1145/3318464.3380582
34. Weber, R., Schek, H., Blott, S.: A quantitative analysis and performance study for similarity-search methods in high-dimensional spaces. In: VLDB 1998, 24rd International Conference on Very Large Data Bases, pp. 194–205. M. Kaufmann (1998). http://www.vldb.org/conf/1998/p194.pdf
35. Wu, Y.P., Guo, J.J., Zhang, X.J.: A linear DBSCAN algorithm based on LSH. In: International Conference on ML and Cybernetics, vol. 5, pp. 2608–2614 (2007). https://doi.org/10.1109/ICMLC.2007.4370588
36. Zheng, Y., Xie, X., Ma, W.: GeoLife: a collaborative social networking service among user, location and trajectory. IEEE Data Eng. Bull. **33**(2), 32–39 (2010). http://sites.computer.org/debull/A10june/geolife.pdf

GraphGuess: Approximate Graph Processing System with Adaptive Correction

Morteza Ramezani(✉), Mahmut T. Kandemir, and Anand Sivasubramaniam

Pennsylvania State University, State College, USA
{morteza,kandemir,anand}@cse.psu.edu

Abstract. Graph-based data structures have drawn great attention in recent years. The large and rapidly growing trend on developing graph processing systems focuses mostly on improving the performance by preprocessing the input graph and modifying its layout. These systems usually take several hours to days to complete processing a single graph on high-end machines, let alone the overhead of pre-processing which most of the time can be dominant. Yet for most graph applications the exact answer is not always crucial, and providing a rough estimate of the final result is adequate. Approximate computing is introduced to trade off accuracy of results for computation or energy savings that could not be achieved by conventional techniques alone. In this work, we design, implement and evaluate GraphGuess, inspired from the domain of approximate graph theory and extend it to a general, practical graph processing system. GraphGuess is essentially an approximate graph processing technique with adaptive correction, which can be implemented on top of any graph processing system. We build a vertex-centric processing system based on GraphGuess, where it allows the user to trade off accuracy for better performance. Our experimental studies show that using GraphGuess can significantly reduce the processing time for large scale graphs while maintaining high accuracy.

Keywords: Graph Processing · Approximate Computing

1 Introduction

Nowadays graph-based data are pervasive, with applications including search engines, social and biological networks and financial systems. Studies [29] have pointed out that graph-based data structures constitute more than 25% of all enterprise data. Graph sizes are increasing rapidly and they consist of billions of nodes and edges with relatively random patterns, posing significant challenges to computer systems and architecture. Hence, efficient batch processing or serving instantaneous interactive queries on these graphs becomes a challenge in the big data era. Observing this need, several graph processing frameworks [13,14,19] have been introduced to reduce the programming burden and avoid the need for extensive optimizations for each and every application.

Most prior graph processing systems try to find the "exact answer" in a resource-efficient and timely manner. However, in many real world applications

J. Cano and P. W. Trinder (Eds.): Euro-Par 2022, LNCS 13440, pp. 285–300, 2022.
https://doi.org/10.1007/978-3-031-12597-3_18

(especially in the large-scale data analytics domain), the exact answer may not be necessary all the time, and one can usually tolerate some amount of error. For example, web search engines are most often interested only in the first few tens or hundreds of pages of what users are looking for, disregarding the rest [16,17]. Also, in a financial security application where the goal is to find fraudulent activity patterns, it is good enough to just capture a rough estimate of the number of times the pattern occurs [9]. Such characteristics of many modern graph applications can allow the system to trade off accuracy for execution efficiency. Motivated by this, in this paper, we pursue approximate computing techniques for a spectrum of graph applications where we strive to provide faster and more efficient output with high quality results.

The fundamental question in approximation is the relationship between the amount of data processed and the associated accuracy of the final results. Based on this relationship, typically, the solutions either run the algorithm on a portion of data (sampling) or run a part of the algorithm (task skipping, interpolation) on the entire data, to achieve a reasonable approximation of what actual results would be. Unlike the other types of data structures, the randomness of graphs makes it difficult to exploit specific properties in the data that may help isolate them for conventional sampling and/or subsetting of the processing.

While the system side of graph processing community has been focusing on running the exact algorithms [6,13–15], the theoretical side has come up with a large body of graph approximation techniques, which try to provide a mathematical bound for the solution. Yet such approaches can impose a huge burden on the programmer to design and implement new and complex graph algorithms. There exist few prior works aiming at practical aspects when approximating graph application executions [4,8–10,24]. However, such existing approaches not only rely on offline preprocessing, which imposes a huge overhead and is unfeasible in many cases where the graph structure changes rapidly, but also are not general and mainly target a limited type of applications.

Motivated by these limitations of prior approaches and ever-growing importance of graph applications, in this work, we propose GraphGuess, a run-time adaptive approximation model for graph processing systems which: (i) requires minimal preprocessing and change to the original graph and applications to figure out what data to include in the computation; (ii) adapts dynamically to the graph structure and application at hand; (iii) preserves characteristics of the original graph and increases the output accuracy; and (iv) significantly reduces the volume of computation performed compared to the exact graph computation. Although our evaluations are confined to static graphs in this paper, GraphGuess is certainly applicable to dynamic graphs as well.

2 Graph Processing Systems

2.1 Think Like a Vertex

Traditionally, processing a large graph required significant developer efforts to design and implement an optimized version of the algorithm. Upon increasing interest in the applications with underlying graph-based data structures, this task has become increasingly more challenging and inefficient. Several general-purpose graph processing frameworks have been introduced and evaluated in recent years to improve the programmability of graph applications, focuses mainly on performance and/or scalability. These frameworks include, but not limited to, vertex-centric [6,14,15], edge-centric [22], data-centric [20], matrix operation based [28] and task based [12]. Among all these models, the idea of "*think like a vertex*" or *vertex-centric* programming model has seen significant interest and widespread deployment in recent works [7,13,14], and is our model of choice.

Vertex-centric model is an iterative approach that executes a so-called *vertex program* that includes one or more user-defined functions (*udf*) for each vertex in every iteration. To eliminate the overhead of unnecessary computations in vertices that have not seen any updates, the concept of *active vertices* is employed, where a list of vertices is maintained to keep the vertices that have received an update in the previous iteration for sub-setting the processing (i.e., reducing its scope in the next iteration). *Gather-Apply-Scatter* (GAS) [14] is one of the widely used vertex-centric models, which consists of three main phases that are executed in each iteration. First, in the *Gather* phase, a vertex reads from all incoming edges and reduces them to a single value. Next, in the *Apply* phase, a vertex uses the reduced value to compute its own property. Lastly, in the *Scatter* phase, each vertex propagates its new value over all out-going edges. A sample program in a vertex-centric model is shown in Algorithm 1.

Algorithm 1. An example of vertex-centric algorithm with Gather-Apply-Scatter (GAS) model

```
for each Vertex v do
    for each incoming Edge e do
        new_property ← GATHER(e)
    property ← APPLY(new_property)
    for each outgoing Edge e do
        SCATTER(e)
```

2.2 Preprocessing the Graph

While vertex-centric models provide ease of programming, their performance can still throttle as the graph size increases. However, due to the random nature of the graph, as the number of edges increases, the system suffers from poor spatial locality when accessing the vertex properties. Also, a processed (destination) vertex is unlikely to be processed again before most of the other vertices (low temporal locality). Hence, the system performance still suffers from an under-performing cache, and cannot benefit from any known prefetching techniques [2]. Finally, real world graphs are known to follow the power-law distribution and have skewed degree nodes, which makes synchronization in shared-memory systems problematic [5]. As a result, many existing frameworks focus on optimizing the data layout, by preprocessing the graph and reordering the vertices and/or edges. Preprocessing the graph can improve the locality of the input and increase the performance at run time. However, altering and rewriting the original graph requires several iterations over the entire graph, which may exceed the actual running time of the application itself, making these methods impractical [18].

2.3 Approximate Analysis

Approximate computing has gained much popularity in big data processing systems in recent years. Several techniques are used to run the application approximately including, running the application on a smaller portion of the dataset ("sampling") or running the program partially on the entire data ("task skipping"). Note that, in either case, there is an underlying assumption that data are independent and the accuracy will improve (linearly) with more data or more tasks processed. The same holds true for the area of hardware-based approximation [11] as well, where data representation is approximated (e.g., via quantization) in favor of performance, bandwidth, storage, or power gains.

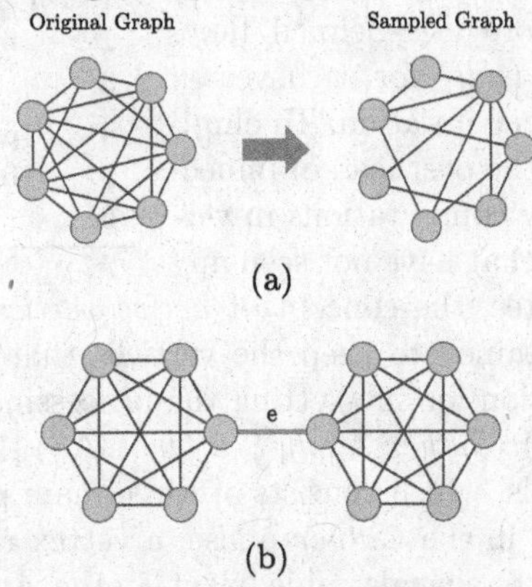

Fig. 1. (a) *Sparsifying* with uniform sampling with $\sigma = 0.5$. (b) Example of Dumbbell, where random uniform sampling may end up not choosing e.

Reducing the size of the input graph or skipping part of the process are promising solutions for certain problems in graph processing. However, unlike other types of data structures, there is a dependency between data elements (vertices) in the graph, where an error in a single vertex (as a result of approximation, for example) can propagate to the entire application. There have been several works in the theory community on graph approximation algorithms [1, 3,17,21,27]. In most cases, the proposed approximation algorithms are variants of the corresponding original algorithms, with proper changes to reduce their running times, while bounding the error through randomization. However, since such approaches are very "algorithm-specific", they are not readily applicable in existing general graph processing systems that are used today to run a wide variety of applications.

Generating a smaller graph or *graph summarization* techniques are introduced to speed up graph processing. Among these methods, sampling, similar to approximate analysis, is one key idea in theoretical graph approximation, commonly referred to as *graph sparsification*. In this approach, a set of edges (or vertices) are selected randomly from the original graph, to reduce the amount required processing. A parameter determines the degree of sparsification, and the accuracy of the result depends on this parameter. An example of random uniform sampling is illustrated in Fig. 1(a). Apart from sparsification, other graph summarization techniques such as graph sketching [23] and graph compression [4,25] have been proposed in recent years. In addition, a few graph approximation frameworks have been developed to alleviate the performance bottleneck of large graph processing [9,10,24]. Shang et al. [24] propose an automatic approximation for graph computing, which targets compiler-level optimization rather than runtime system optimization. ASAP [9] targets approximate graph pattern mining (finding pattern in graphs). More recently, V-Combiner [8] is proposed with a similar goal as graph sketching techniques. V-Combiner consists of an initial step to create an approximate graph with fewer vertices (and edges) and a delta graph to use during the recovery phase in order to compute the output for missing vertices. Similar to the previous methods, this technique depends on building a couple of new graphs, which means a large memory burden in addition to the preprocessing overhead.

2.4 When Graph Approximation Fails

While sparsification reduces the graph size, the reduced graph may *not* necessarily preserve all essential properties of the original graph which are critical for the target application. One such problem can be seen in Fig. 1(b), which is referred to as the "dumbbell graph". In this case, uniform sampling can omit edge e which attaches the two parts of the graph, leading to serious errors in the algorithms that rely on this edge (e.g., graph connectivity). To make sure that edge e is chosen, one may need to sample several times, which is usually quite inefficient and makes random uniform sampling error prone. Spielman et al. [27] proposed a sparsification technique based on the degree of the nodes. However, this method may also fail in some scenarios [26].

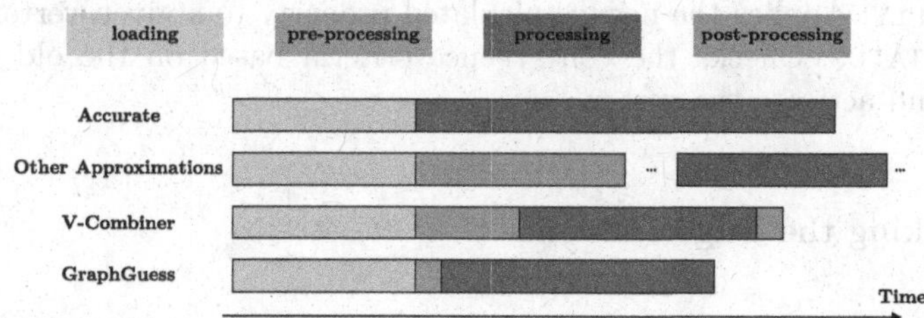

Fig. 2. General timeline of executing a program on graph processing systems.

To solve the problem of leaving out very important edges when sampling, Spielman et al. [26] use importance for edges or "effective resistance" that is taken into account when sparsifying the graph. In a graph, the effective resistance of an edge e is equal to the probability that the edge e appears in a random spanning tree. Although a quite powerful metric, computing effective resistance for *all* edges in a given large graph can introduce excessive overheads at preprocessing time [8,27].

In Fig. 2, we show the timeline of running several graph approximation techniques for an algorithm on a relatively large graph (we scale the figure for better presentation). Clearly, graph summarization and V-Combiner are still suffering from the same type of problem, where the additional overhead is justifiable if the algorithm runs for a large number of iterations. In this paper, inspired by the existing works in graph theory, we introduce GraphGuess, which requires minimal preprocessing, with no need for a new graph. The performance benefits of GraphGuess come mainly from reduced number of edges, which has been shown as a main factor in slowing down the graph processing systems [8–10,24], while its higher accuracy is due to adaptive correction. Furthermore, GraphGuess provides flexibility that allows integration with all types of graph algorithms and requires minimal changes to the front-end applications.

3 GraphGuess

3.1 Programming Model

The programming model used in GraphGuess is closely similar to that in the vertex-centric model discussed earlier in Sect. 2. Such a design makes our framework significantly easier to adapt to the existing applications. Here, for the sake of simplicity, we use *pull-based* vertex-centric model. Note however that GraphGuess is not limited to any specific underlying model and can be easily adapted to the others. The functions defined in the GraphGuess programming interface and their descriptions are provided below, alongside an example of PageRank implementation using this interface shown in Algorithm 2.

- GG-Gather: Gathers property from incoming edges in each iteration and computes a local function. The red line here is the minimal change required in user-program introduced by GraphGuess.
- GG-Apply: Applies the newly calculated property to a given vertex.
- GG-VStatus: Checks the convergence criteria based on the old and new values and activate the vertex.

3.2 Tracking the Edge Influence

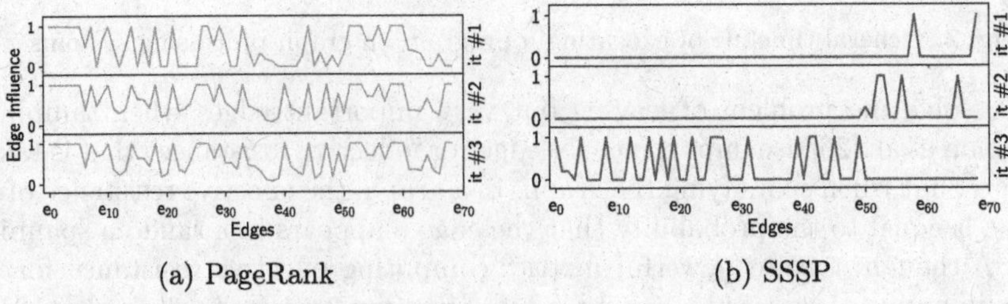

Fig. 3. The edge influence for 3 iterations on (a) PageRank and (b) SSSP

To avoid the high preprocessing overheads, GraphGuess tries to find the importance of edges dynamically at runtime using the concept of *edge influence*.

Algorithm 2. PageRank using GraphGuess API

```
1: procedure GG-GATHER(vertex u, vertex v)
2:     old_value ← u.property
3:     u.property ← v.property / v.degree + u.property
4:     return (u.property - old_value) / u.property        ▷ Return the Edge Influence

5: procedure GG-APPLY(vertex u, value property)
6:     u.old_property ← u.property
7:     u.property ← (1-d)/N + d × property

8: procedure GG-VSTATUS(vertex u)
9:     if |u.old_property − u.property| > ϵ then u.active ← True
10:    else u.active ← False

11: procedure GG-ESTATUS(edge e, value influence, value threshold)
12:    if influence > threshold then e.active ← True
13:    else e.active ← False
```

In each iteration, the calculations at a given vertex are impacted by the "influence" of the edges, i.e., a function of the property of other end vertices. If one could track this importance (*edge influence*), it would be possible to dynamically figure out whether that edge should continue to be used in subsequent iterations as well. This is also a natural way to exploit user-defined functions that get computed at each vertex, rather than artificially try to identify the importance of the edges offline. In other words, regardless of the type of the algorithm (distance, value propagation, etc.) GraphGuess would be able to automatically extract the *edge influence* information. To achieve this flexibility, one can slightly modify the `GG-Gather()` function in the vertex-centric model from Algorithm 2 to capture the influence of each edge (Line 4). This additional information can be passed through to the main method in the processing system, and be used for the future iterations, details of which will be discussed later in Sect. 3.3.

Figure 3(a) illustrates the *edge influence* for all edges in a small, synthetically-generated graph running PageRank algorithm for 3 iterations (one figure for each iteration), using the modified `GG-Gather()` in Algorithm 2. As shown, those edges which provide higher influence would continue to have higher impact in future iterations as well. Thus, one can eliminate the edges that are not contributing significantly to the final result, to reduce the number of processed edges within each iteration. This technique has been previously proposed in the work by McSherry [16] as an optimization "*solely*" for the PageRank algorithm. While PageRank showed a relatively non-changing edge influences across iterations, that may not necessarily be the case in other applications. For instance, Fig. 3(b) shows the edge influences for the SSSP algorithm in which *not* all vertices are active all the time, as it is a traversal algorithm. Consequently, the *edge influence* values depend not only on their source and destination, but also on the iteration. As mentioned before, the criteria for determining "importance" will itself vary, in general, across applications. As a result, a single criteria may not suffice for tracking edge importance, and it is much more practical to let the user determine the criteria as part of the programming exercise.

3.3 Runtime Modes

While the vertex (user) program for GraphGuess requires minor changes, the underlying processing system in GraphGuess, which is completely oblivious to the developers, still needs a few modifications to accommodate the approximate computing capability. One of our main goals in GraphGuess is to avoid any unnecessary preprocessing and building new graphs. Hence, we include a *flag* for each edge in the graph to determine if the edge is active or not. Next, we define the following two running modes for GraphGuess.

- **Accurate Mode:** This is the default setting, where each vertex reads data from all incoming edges (regardless of their active flag) and executes the corresponding functions.
- **Approximate Mode:** Each vertex only reads and processes data from its "active" incoming edges and disregards the rest.

In the *approximate mode*, each vertex deals with fewer edges, thereby reducing the total number of processed edges and less processing time. However, this also means that vertices do not have access to the *edge influence* values for those inactive edges. To figure out whether those missing edges continue to be immaterial in the computation, we define the concept of a *superstep*, in which the system switches back to the *accurate mode*, enabling each vertex to pull information from *all* its incoming edges.

3.4 Adaptive Correction

In GraphGuess, the system starts in the *approximate mode* where a subset of edges is deactivated, similar to graph sparsification, discussed in Sect. 2.4. A control parameter, $\boldsymbol{\sigma}$ (*sparsification parameter*) controls the number of active edges, with a higher value of $\boldsymbol{\sigma}$ indicating more active edges. We want to emphasize that the overhead of this part is negligible and in fact it can be done while loading the graph into the system. The system continues in the *approximate mode* for $\boldsymbol{\alpha}$ iterations (*approximate window*), and then performs a *superstep*, where it transitions to the *accurate mode* to adaptively correct the initial edges selection. At the end of a *superstep*, GraphGuess can determine and activate new "qualified" edges, based on the computed *edge influence* and a threshold $\boldsymbol{\theta}$ (*influence threshold*). This is done in a user defined function, `GG-EStatus()`, example of which is shown in Algorithm 2. The process continues in the next iteration with all activated edges.

This approach can be seen as a coarse-grain active list technique introduced in the original vertex-centric model. However, here, in addition to activating vertices based on their property change, for each vertex, its edges are activated based on the *edge influence* computed in the superstep. Furthermore, we drop the edges with minimal influence to reduce the number of processed edges in the system. We only pick the edges that meet the influence threshold ($\boldsymbol{\theta}$), and discard the rest. That is, after performing a superstep, GRAPHGUESS only activates the qualified edges and deactivate the rest, regardless of whether they were active before or not. Figure 4 illustrates the Vertex Point of View (*VPV*) evolution time-line of this approach, by showing the number of edges processed across iterations for a single vertex.

In a large graph, performing a single superstep iteration may not suffice to capture the changes that gradually ripple through the graph. Motivated by this observation, we propose to use periodic supersteps in GRAPHGUESS and control the frequency using the same approximate window parameter. More specifically, $\boldsymbol{\alpha}$ controls how long it takes before another superstep should take place, as shown in Fig. 4 ❷. Note that, a smaller value of $\boldsymbol{\alpha}$ means more frequent superstep executions and results in better accuracies; however, it also imposes higher overheads on the system. While one could have different parameters for controlling the first superstep and their recurrence, and vary them through the course of running the algorithm, we find that using the same parameters provides a good enough accuracy-performance trade-off.

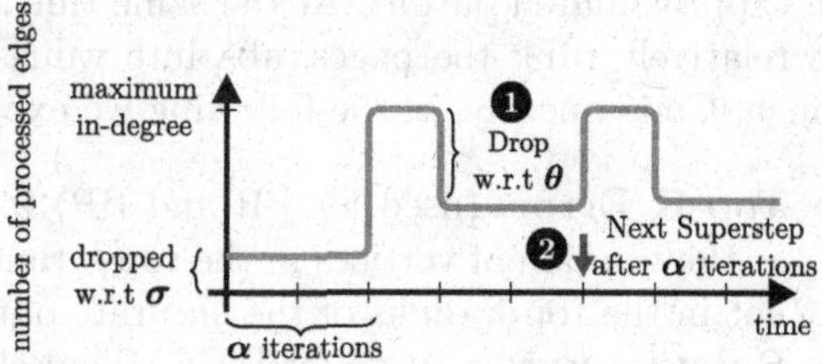

Fig. 4. Time-line of running GRAPHGUESS

4 Applications and Error Criteria

4.1 Applications and Datasets

As discussed before, GRAPHGUESS is application domain agnostic and can work with any target application. Most current graph benchmark suites include popular graph algorithms, including graph traversal, property computing, and pattern mining. Based on that and due to limited space, we selected Single Source Shortest Path (**SSSP**), Weakly Connected Components (**WCC**) Page Rank (**PR**), and Belief Propagation (**BP**). We also chose a wide variety of graph workloads: Wikipedia (**WP**), LiveJournal (**LJ**), Twitter (**TW**) and Friendster (**FS**).

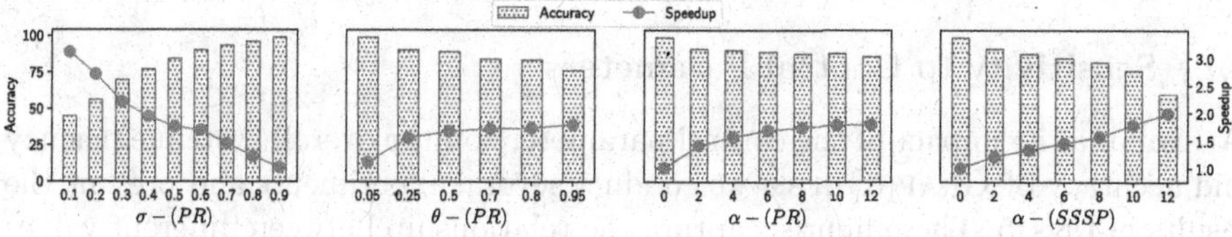

Fig. 5. The impact of GRAPHGUESS parameters on the accuracy and speedup of the system running on Wikipedia. The left y-axis shows the accuracy and the right y-axis shows the speedup and the x-axis represents the value of the parameter. (Color figure online)

4.2 Error Metrics

Unlike non-graph based approximations where determining the error is relatively straightforward, defining error metrics in approximated graph applications is not trivial. Consider PageRank for instance, where the algorithm itself includes a control knob for error (convergence rate), which can also be used for evaluating the approximated output. At the same time, since the intention of PageRank is to relatively rank the pages, absolute values for the rank may not matter too much. Consequently, in the following we explore different evaluation metrics.

- **Top-K Error:** (used for PR and BP) Similar to [17] this metric is defined as the fraction of vertices in the top-k ranks of approximated output that are not in the top-k ranks of the accurate output.
- **Relative Error:** (used for WCC) The relative error is the ratio of the difference between the accurate and the approximate value to the accurate value.
- **Stretch Error:** (used SSSP) Borrowed from graph theory, the stretch factor is applicable in most distance-based graph applications and defined as the ratio of the approximated value to the accurate value for each vertex.

For the sake of better representation, in all of our evaluations we use accuracy, ranging from 0% to 100%, which is defined as $(1 - \text{error}) \times 100$.

5 Experimental Evaluations

Implementation and Setup: We implemented GraphGuess on top of a vertex-centric graph processing platform in C++ and parallelized using the shared memory API OpenMP. Note that, in principle, GraphGuess can be integrated into any other graph processing system (including those with a pre-processing mechanism), with minimal changes in the API. We use the accurate execution as the *baseline*, and measure the speedup and accuracy compared to this baseline. For a fair comparison, we also implemented the user functions for all of our benchmark applications for GraphGuess and all other baselines. In all our experiments, unless otherwise stated, we run the experiment for the same number of iterations five times and report the mean value for the metrics. To determine the effective performance of GraphGuess, we only measure the execution time of processing and pre-processing parts of the application.

5.1 Sensitivity to Control Parameters

To examine the impact of the control parameters on the overall system efficiency and accuracy of GraphGuess, we conduct several experiments and present the results in Figs. 5. These figures capture the relationship between different values of control parameters (x-axis) and speedup on the right y-axis (red line) and accuracy on the left y-axis (blue bars) compared to the accurate baseline. In each setting, we fix all other control parameters and selectively vary the desired parameter (indicated on the bottom of each figure) to observe its effect. We ran the applications on *Wikipedia* dataset for a fixed number iterations to get a fair comparison. Due to space constraints, we show the results only for PageRank and SSSP in one instance.

Figure 5(σ) plots the speedup-accuracy comparison, for different values of the sparsification parameter ($\boldsymbol{\sigma}$). The value of $\boldsymbol{\sigma}$ is varied from 0.1 to 0.9 in 0.1 increments, where 0 represents the case where no edge is active and 1 represents the case where all edges are active. Clearly, one can expect better accuracy from the system when $\boldsymbol{\sigma}$ has a higher value, but at the same time the performance would be degraded. Figure 5(σ) confirms this expectation, and with $\sigma = 0.1$ the accuracy is about 40% with speedup up to 3×, whereas with a higher value $\sigma = 0.9$, the accuracy increases significantly while the performance improvement ending up being as good as the accurate mode.

The influence threshold or $\boldsymbol{\theta}$, can also affect both accuracy and speedup, as demonstrated in Fig. 5(θ). More specifically, a lower value of $\boldsymbol{\theta}$ makes it easier for an edge to get activated – as a result the system processes more edges and achieves higher accuracy. On the other hand, with higher threshold values, the edges are only being activated if they make *significant influence* at the supersteps, thus, the system in this case *trades off* accuracy for performance. Figure 5(θ) also reveals that, when $\boldsymbol{\theta}$ is changed from 0.05 to 0.5 both performance and accuracy change significantly, whereas a change of threshold from 0.5 to 0.8 has a relatively low impact on the performance, while resulting in less accuracy, due to limited number of processed edges.

Figure 5($\alpha - PR$) plots the impact of changing the value of $\boldsymbol{\alpha}$ (superstep frequency) for the PageRank algorithm. Earlier in Fig. 3(a), we saw that for PageRank, the distribution of edge influence is more or less uniform throughout the execution of the algorithm. As a result, the specific starting point (or frequency) for a superstep does not affect the accuracy in any significant way. It can be seen here that changing $\boldsymbol{\alpha}$ does not affect the accuracy considerably, compared to the previous results, while doing so can change the speedup. However, this is not always the case, especially when the algorithm traverses the graph and vertices get activated later.

An example of such behavior is in the SSSP algorithm, the results of which are given in Fig. 5($\alpha - SSSP$). Previously, Fig. 3(b) showed that, in this application, the edge influences do not follow the same pattern throughout the time; hence, the time at which a superstep is performed matters more than the PageRank case. It can be concluded from this figure that the different values of $\boldsymbol{\alpha}$ impact both error and performance considerably. In general, to handle all types of application behaviors in GraphGuess, we use the combination of control parameters $\boldsymbol{\sigma}$, $\boldsymbol{\theta}$, and $\boldsymbol{\alpha}$.

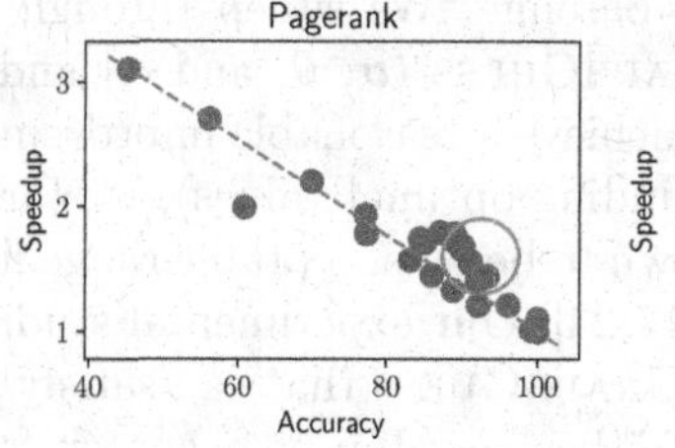

Fig. 6. Accumulated parameter analysis to determine fair value for control parameters.

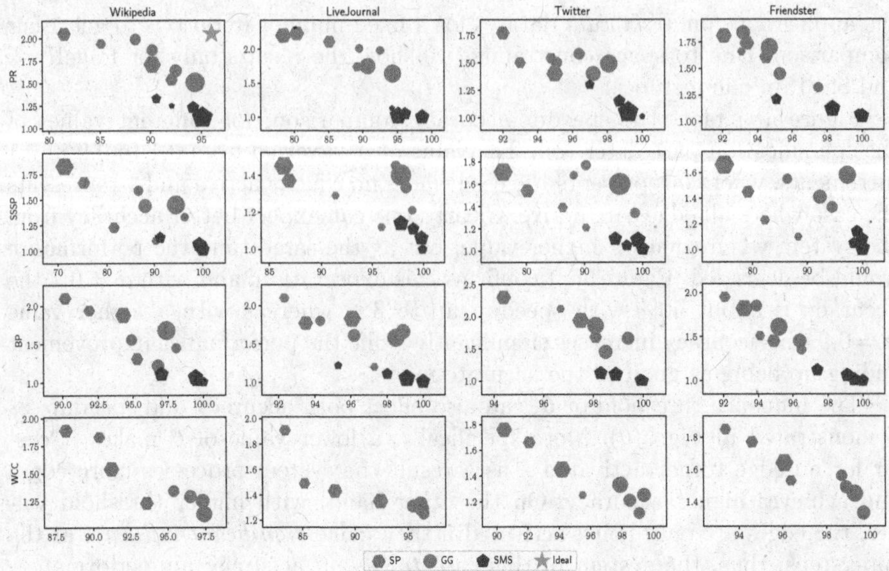

Fig. 7. Speedup (y-axis) vs accuracy (x-axis) for three different running modes with various control parameters. For better visibility, we combined closer points into larger filled area. The ideal spot is only marked in the first figure and same for all applications/dataset.

5.2 Evaluation of Performance and Accuracy

To select the best parameters for our evaluations we refer to our earlier observation in Sect. 5.1. Figure 6 demonstrates the accumulated speedup-vs-accuracy for various configurations for PageRank on Wikipedia dataset. To save space, we only show PageRank in this figure, however we can see a similar pattern. Here, the x-axis represents the accuracy and the y-axis shows the speedup over the baseline. We sweep through various values for each control parameter in GraphGuess ($\boldsymbol{\sigma}$, $\boldsymbol{\theta}$, and α) and report the results as points in these figures. To achieve a reasonable improvement-error ratio (while eliminating the overhead of finding optimal values), we target about 90%–95% accuracy which has been shown to be an acceptable range in several previous graph approximation studies [8,17,24]. Our experimental studies reveal that there exists a set of parameters in GraphGuess that can satisfy this goal (though may not be the ideal setting for either speedup or accuracy for all applications). Therefore, for our experiments discussed below, we selected the parameters within the red circle for all other workloads and applications.

We compare the speedup and accuracy of GraphGuess against a *baseline*, which is the traditional "accurate" vertex-centric system. In addition, to assess the need for mode switching (between approximate vs accurate) in GraphGuess, we introduce two static schemes which are special cases of GraphGuess. The first scheme is a variant of graph sparsification, referred to as *SP* henceforth, where the application starts by deactivating the edges based on the parameter σ, and continues processing in this mode until the end. Note that, unlike previous studies [4,8], there is no need to build a new graph and we use the underlying GRAPHGUESS framework to process the graph. The second scheme, Static Mode Switch(*SMS*), uses a *combination* of the approximate and accurate modes. Similar to *SP*, this scheme starts in *approximate mode*, however after performing a superstep it stays in the *accurate mode* for the remaining iterations.

Figure 7 compares the performance-accuracy trade-off in three aforementioned schemes (*SP*, *SMS*, and *GG*) for all four applications and datasets. We use a similar setting as Fig. 6, where the x-axis shows the accuracy and the y-axis represents the speedup. However, for better visibility here, we apply the kd-tree algorithm on the points for each scheme and cluster closer points into a larger filled areas. Note that a larger area captures the fact that more points ended up in the corresponding region. We also show the ideal spot (our goal), with a gold star in PR (Wiki), where the speedup and accuracy are the highest.

In the case of PR and BP, we see that using *SP* achieves a significantly higher speedup, but the accuracy is lower, due to the missing edges. Using *SMS*, the performance improvement is limited, depending on when we switch back to the accurate mode. Clearly, *SMS* achieves high accuracy, but there is no promising performance improvement over the baseline. For instance, the accuracy of *SP* on *Twitter* dataset is closer to that of *SMS*, due to its higher density. Whereas, on more sparse graphs like *LiveJorunal,* using *SP* ends up in a lower accuracy. On the contrary, when using *GG*, we can see higher speedups with accuracy coming closer to that of *SMS*.

In SSSP, *SP* performs well in terms of speedup, and its resulting accuracy is lower compared to the other two schemes. That is, the missing edges in *SP* can exacerbate the error, since the error from one node can propagate to many other nodes. *SMS* achieves a higher accuracy in SSSP compared to *SP*, as expected; however, the accuracy can vary depending on the start of the accurate mode. This also can hinder the performance of the *SMS* scheme. In comparison, *GG* brings the best of both worlds, and helps us achieve an accuracy which is very similar to that of *SMS*, and a performance which is very close to that of *SP*.

Table 1. Comparison of speedup (Spd) and accuracy (Acc) between GG and others

Alg (Dataset)		PR (LJ)	PR (TW)	PR (FS)	BP (LV)	BP (TW)	BP (FS)	AVG
GG	Spd (×)	1.64	1.49	1.66	1.68	1.85	1.62	1.66
	Acc (%)	94.32	98.12	94.74	96.69	98.08	95.29	96.20
SP	Spd (×)	1.74	1.54	1.81	1.83	1.94	1.81	1.78
	Acc (%)	89.21	94.84	92.19	93.13	97.57	93.64	93.43
VC	Spd (×)	1.45	1.34	1.12	1.20	1.16	1.29	1.26
	Acc (%)	87.15	95.36	91.63	94.41	97.91	93.41	93.31

In WCC, the vertex property is defined as the *Connected Component ID* of the vertex residing in. Consequently, the influence estimate is a binary decision – whether the ID is changed or not. This implementation of WCC application forces the influence values to be either 0 or 1. Hence *GG* and *SMS* end up exhibiting the same behavior; so, we only show *GG* in this figure. As can be observed in Fig. 7, *GG* performs much better (as far as error is concerned) compared to *SP*, with a lower speedup. This also proves that *GG* is more flexible in terms of application, and can be applied in various settings depending on the need.

Overall Performance and Accuracy: We compare the speedup and accuracy values achieved by GraphGuess against a recent approximate graph processing system, V-Combiner [8]. While in this paper we are aiming at minimal pre-processing, we include V-Combiner due to its lower overhead compared to the alternative methods. Note also that V-Combiner only supports specific types of graph applications such as PR and BP, while GraphGuess can support any graph algorithm implemented on current graph processing systems. We also include sparsification (*SP*) as a special case of GraphGuess without adaptive correction, as discussed earlier in Sect. 5.2.

Table 1 shows the speedup and accuracy for GraphGuess, Sparsification, and V-Combiner, on PR and BP, using three different datasets on top 10 best configurations. It is to be noted that V-Combiner does not support SSSP and WCC. From this experiment, we observe that Sparsification has the best speedup, close to 72% on average, at the cost of lower accuracy. However, V-Combiner suffers from lower speedup due to mandatory pre-processing, which involves additional graphs creation and the recovery phase. The performance gain of V-combiner on average is about 26% compared to the baseline, while it maintains an acceptable accuracy. Finally, our proposed approach, GraphGuess, closes the gap between these two with a speedup of up to 85% and 58% on average, while maintaining a higher accuracy compared to the other two methods.

6 Concluding Remarks

This paper presents GraphGuess, a novel attempt at approximating graph processing with a simple extension to current APIs. Inspired by the ideas from graph theory and approximation analysis, GraphGuess implements an adaptive approximate graph processing strategy that requires no time-consuming preprocessing and can be applied to any graph processing system. GraphGuess preserves the main characteristics of the graph using adaptive correction and provides sufficient flexibility in modulating different control parameters. In this work, we vary these control parameters to achieve performance-accuracy tradeoffs, and our experimental studies show that GraphGuess achieves up to 1.85× speedup while maintaining high accuracy compared to an accurate baseline.

Acknowledgements. This work was supported in part by CRISP, one of six centers in JUMP, a Semiconductor Research Corporation (SRC) program sponsored by DARPA and NSF grants 1909004, 1714389, 1912495, 1629915, 1629129, 1763681.

References

1. Abraham, I., Durfee, D., Koutis, I., Krinninger, S., Peng, R.: On fully dynamic graph sparsifiers. In: 2016 IEEE 57th Annual Symposium on Foundations of Computer Science (FOCS), pp. 335–344. IEEE (2016). https://doi.org/10.1109/FOCS.2016.44
2. Ahn, J., Hong, S., Yoo, S., Mutlu, O., Choi, K.: A scalable processing-in-memory accelerator for parallel graph processing. ACM SIGARCH Comput. Archit. News **43**(3), 105–117 (2016). https://doi.org/10.1145/2749469.2750386
3. Bernstein, A., et al.: Fully-dynamic graph sparsifiers against an adaptive adversary. arXiv preprint arXiv:2004.08432 (2020)
4. Besta, M., et al.: Slim graph: practical lossy graph compression for approximate graph processing, storage, and analytics. In: Proceedings of the International Conference for High Performance Computing, Networking, Storage and Analysis, pp. 1–25 (2019). https://doi.org/10.1145/3295500.3356182
5. Capelli, L.A., Hu, Z., Zakian, T.A.: iPregel: a combiner-based in-memory shared memory vertex-centric framework. In: Proceedings of the 47th International Conference on Parallel Processing Companion, pp. 1–10 (2018). https://doi.org/10.1145/3229710.3229719
6. Ching, A.: Giraph: production-grade graph processing infrastructure for trillion edge graphs. ATPESC, ser. ATPESC 14 (2014)
7. Gonzalez, J.E., Low, Y., Gu, H., Bickson, D., Guestrin, C.: Powergraph: distributed graph-parallel computation on natural graphs. In: OSDI, p. 2 (2012)
8. Heidarshenas, A., Yesil, S., Skarlatos, D., Misailovic, S., Morrison, A., Torrellas, J.: V-Combiner: speeding-up iterative graph processing on a shared-memory platform with vertex merging. In: Proceedings of the 34th ACM International Conference on Supercomputing, pp. 1–13 (2020). https://doi.org/10.1145/3392717.3392739
9. Iyer, A.P., Liu, Z., Jin, X., Venkataraman, S., Braverman, V., Stoica, I.: {ASAP}: Fast, approximate graph pattern mining at scale. In: 13th {USENIX} Symposium on Operating Systems Design and Implementation ({OSDI} 18), pp. 745–761 (2018)
10. Iyer, A.P., et al.: Bridging the gap: towards approximate graph analytics. In: Proceedings of the 1st ACM SIGMOD Joint International Workshop on Graph Data Management Experiences & Systems (GRADES) and Network Data Analytics (NDA), p. 10. ACM (2018). https://doi.org/10.1145/3210259.3210269
11. Jevdjic, D., Strauss, K., Ceze, L., Malvar, H.S.: Approximate storage of compressed and encrypted videos. ACM SIGOPS Operat. Syst. Rev. **51**(2), 361–373 (2017). https://doi.org/10.1145/3037697.3037718
12. Kulkarni, M., Pingali, K., Walter, B., Ramanarayanan, G., Bala, K., Chew, L.P.: Optimistic parallelism requires abstractions. ACM SIGPLAN Notices **42**(6), 211–222 (2007). https://doi.org/10.1145/1250734.1250759
13. Kyrola, A., Blelloch, G.E., Guestrin, C.: GraphChi: large-scale graph computation on just a pc. In: 11th {USENIX} Symposium on Operating Systems Design and Implementation ({OSDI} 12). USENIX (2012)

14. Low, Y., Gonzalez, J.E., Kyrola, A., Bickson, D., Guestrin, C.E., Hellerstein, J.: GraphLab: a new framework for parallel machine learning. arXiv preprint arXiv:1408.2041 (2014)
15. Malewicz, G., et al.: Pregel: a system for large-scale graph processing. In: Proceedings of the 2010 ACM SIGMOD International Conference on Management of Data, pp. 135–146. ACM (2010). https://doi.org/10.1145/1807167.1807184
16. McSherry, F., Isard, M., Murray, D.G.: Scalability! but at what cost? In: HotOS, vol. 15, p. 14. Citeseer (2015)
17. Mitliagkas, I., Borokhovich, M., Dimakis, A.G., Caramanis, C.: Frogwild!-fast pagerank approximations on graph engines. arXiv preprint arXiv:1502.04281 (2015)
18. Mukkara, A., Beckmann, N., Abeydeera, M., Ma, X., Sanchez, D.: Exploiting locality in graph analytics through hardware-accelerated traversal scheduling. In: 2018 51st Annual IEEE/ACM International Symposium on Microarchitecture (MICRO), pp. 1–14. IEEE (2018). https://doi.org/10.1109/MICRO.2018.00010
19. Nai, L., Xia, Y., Tanase, I.G., Kim, H., Lin, C.Y.: GraphBIG: understanding graph computing in the context of industrial solutions. In: 2015 SC-International Conference for High Performance Computing, Networking, Storage and Analysis, pp. 1–12. IEEE (2015). https://doi.org/10.1145/2807591.2807626
20. Nguyen, D., Lenharth, A., Pingali, K.: A lightweight infrastructure for graph analytics. In: Proceedings of the Twenty-Fourth ACM Symposium on Operating Systems Principles, pp. 456–471. ACM (2013). https://doi.org/10.1145/2517349.2522739
21. Qiao, M., Cheng, H., Chang, L., Yu, J.X.: Approximate shortest distance computing: a query-dependent local landmark scheme. IEEE Trans. Knowl. Data Eng. **26**(1), 55–68 (2012). https://doi.org/10.1109/ICDE.2012.53
22. Roy, A., Mihailovic, I., Zwaenepoel, W.: X-stream: edge-centric graph processing using streaming partitions. In: Proceedings of the Twenty-Fourth ACM Symposium on Operating Systems Principles, pp. 472–488. ACM (2013). https://doi.org/10.1145/2517349.2522740
23. Sarlós, T., Benczúr, A.A., Csalogány, K., Fogaras, D., Rácz, B.: To randomize or not to randomize: space optimal summaries for hyperlink analysis. In: Proceedings of the 15th International Conference on World Wide Web, pp. 297–306 (2006)
24. Shang, Z., Yu, J.X.: Auto-approximation of graph computing. In: Proceedings of the VLDB Endowment **7**(14), 1833–1844 (2014). https://doi.org/10.14778/2733085.2733090
25. Shin, K., Ghoting, A., Kim, M., Raghavan, H.: SWeG: lossless and lossy summarization of web-scale graphs. In: The World Wide Web Conference, pp. 1679–1690 (2019). https://doi.org/10.1145/3308558.3313402
26. Spielman, D.A., Srivastava, N.: Graph sparsification by effective resistances. SIAM J. Comput. **40**(6), 1913–1926 (2011). https://doi.org/10.1137/080734029
27. Spielman, D.A., Teng, S.H.: Spectral sparsification of graphs. SIAM J. Comput. **40**(4), 981–1025 (2011). https://doi.org/10.1137/08074489X
28. Sundaram, N., et al.: GraphMat: high performance graph analytics made productive. In: Proceedings of the VLDB Endowment, vol. 8(11), 1214–1225 (2015). https://doi.org/10.14778/2809974.2809983
29. Yuhanna, N., Evelson, B., Hopkins, B., Jedinak, E.: Techradar: enterprise dbms, q1 2014 (2013). https://www.forrester.com/report/TechRadar+Enterprise+DBMS+Q1+2014/-/E-RES106801

Deterministic Parallel Hypergraph Partitioning

Lars Gottesbüren(✉) and Michael Hamann

Karlsruhe Institute of Technology, Karlsruhe, Germany
lars.gottesbueren@kit.edu

Abstract. Balanced hypergraph partitioning is a classical NP-hard optimization problem with applications in various domains such as VLSI design, simulating quantum circuits, optimizing data placement in distributed databases or minimizing communication volume in high performance computing. Engineering parallel partitioning heuristics is a topic of recent research, yet most of them are non-deterministic. In this work, we design and implement a highly scalable deterministic algorithm in the parallel partitioning framework Mt-KaHyPar. On our extensive set of benchmark instances, it achieves similar partition quality and performance as a comparable but non-deterministic configuration of Mt-KaHyPar and outperforms the only other parallel deterministic algorithm BiPart regarding partition quality, running time and speedups.

1 Introduction

The goal of hypergraph partitioning is to divide the vertices into k blocks of bounded size while minimizing the sum of the number of blocks connected by each hyperedge. Heuristic algorithms are used in practice since the problem is NP-hard. There has been a huge amount of research on partitioning, but in recent years, the interest in parallel algorithms has surged due to ever growing problem sizes. With the exception of `BiPart` [16], these algorithms are non-deterministic. Researchers have advocated the benefits of deterministic parallel algorithms for several decades [1,21], including ease of debugging, reasoning about performance, and reproducibility. While some strive for deterministic programming models, we want to leverage randomized scheduling for better performance and thus pursue deterministic algorithms. The goal of this work is to design, implement and evaluate a scalable and deterministically parallel hypergraph partitioning algorithm with state-of-the-art solution quality.

Multilevel Partitioning. The most successful approach for partitioning is the multilevel framework. In the *coarsening* phase the hypergraph is repeatedly contracted (based on vertex clusterings) until it is small enough to compute an *initial partition* with slower algorithms. In the *refinement phase*, this partition is projected through the hierarchy and locally improved on each level. `Mt-KaHyPar` [10] adds a preprocessing phase based on community detection to

J. Cano and P. W. Trinder (Eds.): Euro-Par 2022, LNCS 13440, pp. 301–316, 2022.
https://doi.org/10.1007/978-3-031-12597-3_19

the coarsening phase. Contractions are restricted to vertices in the same community to avoid destroying small cuts [14].

Non-determinism in Local Moving. Typical algorithms for community detection, clustering coarsening and refinement are so-called *local moving algorithms*: given an initial assignment of vertices to groups, visit vertices in random order in parallel, and improve the solution by greedily moving vertices when they are visited. Since vertices are moved right away, the local optimization decisions depend on non-deterministic scheduling decisions. Our approach to incorporate determinism is based on the *synchronous local moving* approach of Hamann et al. [13] to parallelize the Louvain community detection algorithm [2] on distributed memory. Instead of performing moves asynchronously, vertices are split into sub-rounds – using deterministically reproducible randomness. The best move for each vertex in the current sub-round is computed with respect to the unmodified groups. In a second step, some of the calculated moves are approved and performed, and some are denied, for example due to the balance constraint.

Contribution. We propose three deterministic parallel local moving algorithms: for the preprocessing, coarsening and refinement phases of `Mt-KaHyPar`. The algorithmic novelty lies in the details of the approval steps. For example, the refinement approval uses a merge-style parallelization to incorporate non-unit weights. Our algorithm achieves good speedups (28.7 geometric mean, 48.9 max on 64 threads) and similar solution quality as its non-deterministic counterpart (as expected slightly worse overall though). We investigate potential causes for this cost of determinism, finding that the coarsening phase is the most affected. Our algorithm outperforms `BiPart` regarding solution quality, running time and parallel speedups on 98% of the instances.

The paper is organized as follows. In Sect. 2, we introduce concepts and notation. Subsequently, we describe our algorithmic components and the implementation in Sect. 3. In Sect. 4, we analyze the algorithm experimentally via a parameter study and comparison with existing algorithms, before concluding the paper in Sect. 5. Related work is referenced throughout the paper, without a dedicated section.

2 Preliminaries

By $[m]$ we denote the set $\{0, 1, \ldots, m-1\}$ for a positive integer m. We use Python-style slicing notation $A[i : j]$ to denote sub-arrays from index i up to (excluding) index j.

Hypergraphs. A *weighted hypergraph* $H = (V, E, c, \omega)$ is a set of vertices V and a set of hyperedges E with vertex weights $c : V \rightarrow \mathbb{N}$ and hyperedge weights $\omega : E \rightarrow \mathbb{N}$, where each hyperedge e is a subset of the vertex set V. The vertices of a hyperedge are called its *pins*. A vertex v is *incident* to a hyperedge e if $v \in e$. $\mathrm{I}(v)$ denotes the set of all incident hyperedges of v. The *degree* of a vertex

v is $d(v) := |\mathrm{I}(v)|$. The *size* $|e|$ of a hyperedge e is the number of its pins. By $N(v) := \{u \in V \mid \mathrm{I}(u) \cap \mathrm{I}(v) \neq \emptyset\}$ we denote the *neighbors* of v. We extend c and ω to sets in the natural way $c(U) := \sum_{v \in U} c(v)$ and $\omega(F) := \sum_{e \in F} \omega(e)$.

A graph is a hypergraph where each edge has size 2. We use the terms nodes and edges when referring to graphs, and vertices, hyperedges and pins when referring to hypergraphs.

Partitions. A *k-way partition* of a hypergraph H is a function $\Pi : V \to [k]$ that assigns each vertex to a *block* (identifier) $i \in [k]$. We call Π *ε-balanced* if each block V_i satisfies the *balance constraint*: $c(V_i) \leq L_{\max} := (1+\varepsilon)\lceil c(V)/k \rceil$ for some parameter $\varepsilon \in (0, 1)$. For each hyperedge e, $\Lambda(e) := \{V_i \mid V_i \cap e \neq \emptyset\}$ denotes the *connectivity set* of e. The *connectivity* $\lambda(e)$ of a hyperedge e is $\lambda(e) := |\Lambda(e)|$. A hyperedge is called a *cut hyperedge* if $\lambda(e) > 1$. Given parameters ε, and k, and a hypergraph H, the *hypergraph partitioning problem* is to find an ε-balanced k-way partition Π that minimizes the *connectivity metric* $(\lambda - 1)(\Pi) := \sum_{e \in E} (\lambda(e) - 1)\, \omega(e)$. We use the term solution quality for connectivity metric in the experiments. In order to avoid confusion later on, note that, while these concepts are defined as functions, the pseudocodes in this paper treat them as data that are modified as the algorithms iteratively change the partition. A *clustering* (or set of *communities*) $\mathcal{C}$ is a partition without a restriction on the number of blocks.

3 Deterministic Parallel Multilevel Partitioning

In this section, we describe our algorithms. The structure follows the order of the multilevel framework. We introduce the community detection preprocessing in Sect. 3.1, the coarsening in Sect. 3.2, and the refinement in Sect. 3.4.

3.1 Preprocessing

The preprocessing phase detects communities in the hypergraph that are used to guide the coarsening process by restricting contractions to vertices in the same community, as proposed in [14]. We perform community detection on the bipartite graph representation with some modified edge weights to handle large hyperedges. The bipartite graph representation $G = (V_G, E_G)$ of a hypergraph $H = (V, E)$ has the vertices and hyperedges as nodes, and an edge for every pin connecting the vertex and hyperedge. Since this also assigns hyperedges to communities, we restrict the communities to the vertices. The edge weights are set to $w'(v, e) := \frac{\omega(e)|\mathrm{I}(v)|}{|e|}$ or $w'(v, e) := \omega(e)$ for pin $v \in e$ and hyperedge $e \in E$, depending on the density of the hypergraph as described in [14].

Modularity Objective. We heuristically maximize the well-known modularity objective using a synchronous parallel version of the popular Louvain algorithm [2]. The modularity of given communities $\mathcal{C}$ is $\mathcal{Q}(\mathcal{C}) := \mathrm{cov}(\mathcal{C}) - \sum_{C \in \mathcal{C}} \mathrm{vol}(C)^2 / \mathrm{vol}(V_G)^2$. Here, the coverage $\mathrm{cov}(\mathcal{C}) := \sum_{C \in \mathcal{C}} \sum_{u \in C}$

$\sum_{v \in C \cap N(u)} w'(u,v)/\operatorname{vol}(V_G)$ is the fraction of edge weights inside communities. The volume $\operatorname{vol}(u) := \sum_{v \in N(u)} w'(u,v)$ is the sum of incident edge weights of a node (counting self-loops twice), which is extended to node-sets $\operatorname{vol}(X) := \sum_{u \in X} \operatorname{vol}(u)$.

Louvain. The Louvain algorithm starts with each node in its own community. In a round, it visits each node in a random order and greedily maximizes modularity by possibly moving the node to the community of a neighbor. After a fixed number of rounds or if no node has been moved in the last round, the communities are contracted and the algorithm is applied recursively to the contracted graph. This continues until no node has been moved on a level, at which point the community assignment is projected to the input graph.

The gain (modularity difference) of moving a node from its current community to a neighboring community can be computed purely from the weight of incident edges to the target or current community, as well as their volumes. Therefore, it suffices to store and update the volume for each community, and compute the weights to the communities by iterating once over the neighbors of the node.

We randomize the visit order by dividing nodes into random sub-rounds. For each sub-round we calculate the best move for each node in parallel, but only apply volume and community assignment updates after synchronizing.

Volume Updates. One intricacy with updating the community volumes is that adding floating point numbers is not associative, and thus the previous approach [10,20] of applying all updates in parallel with compare-and-swap instructions is non-deterministic. Instead, we have to establish an order in which the volume updates of each community are aggregated. For this, we collect all necessary updates in a global vector, which we lexicographically sort by community (primary key) and node ID (secondary key). Applying the updates is done in parallel for different communities. To reduce the sorting overhead we split the updates into two vectors (addition and subtraction) which are sorted independently in parallel, but applied one after another.

To analyze the work and depth, let V'_G denote the nodes in a sub-round. The work is $\sum_{u \in V'_G} \deg(u) + |V'_G| \log(|V'_G|)$. The depth is linear in the maximum number of moves in or out of a community (sequential volume updates) and the maximum degree $\max_{u \in V'_G}(\deg(u))$ for calculating modularity gains, plus the depth of the sorting algorithm. This is usually poly-logarithmic in $|V'_G|$, but `tbb`'s quick-sort implementation uses sequential partitioning, and thus is linear. We tested a supposedly better sorting algorithm but did not achieve an improvement. The number of moves and degree linear terms in the depth may be reduced to poly-logarithmic by parallelizing the per-vertex gain calculation (parallel for loop over neighbors, atomic fetch-add for weight to neighbor clusters) and aggregating updates within a community in parallel with a deterministic reduce. However, in practice the outer level of parallelism is sufficient.

Algorithm 1: Compute Heavy-Edge Rating

```
Input: vertex u ∈ V
candidates ← ∅
for e ∈ I(u) do
    for v ∈ e do
        if community[u] = community[v]
            if rating[C[v]] = 0
                add C[v] to candidates
            rating[C[v]] += ω(e)/|e|
for C ∈ candidates do
    if weight[C] + c(u) ≤ CW_max and rating[C] > best rating
        store C as best candidate
    rating[C] ← 0
return best candidate
```

3.2 Coarsening

After performing community detection on the bipartite graph representation, we proceed to contracting the actual hypergraph. In the coarsening phase we keep performing coarsening passes over the vertices until only a few vertices remain. We choose this contraction limit $CL = 160 \cdot k$ dependent on k, as in [10]. In each coarsening pass, we perform one round of local moving and then contract the resulting clusters. The objective function for the clustering is the commonly used [10,22] heavy-edge rating function $r(u, C) := \sum_{e \in I(u) \cap I(C)} \frac{\omega(e)}{|e|-1}$ which rewards heavy hyperedges between a vertex u and a potential target cluster C, but penalizes large hyperedges.

Initially, the clustering $\mathcal{C}$ is a singleton clustering, i.e., each vertex is in its own cluster. For each vertex u in a sub-round, we store the best target cluster according to the rating function in an array of propositions $\mathcal{P}$. Algorithm 1 shows pseudocode for calculating the ratings and Algorithm 2 shows pseudocode for one coarsening pass over the vertices. First, we aggregate the ratings in a sparse array indexed by cluster ID and store the potential candidates in a dense vector, before we select the highest-rated candidate and reset the ratings. To save running time, and since their contribution to the rating function is small, we skip hyperedges with size > 1000. This ensures that at most $O(|\mathrm{I}(v)|)$ time is spent for vertex v (though the constant is large) instead of $O(\sum_{e \in \mathrm{I}(v)} |e|)$, which leads to work linear in the number of pins per coarsening pass to compute target clusters. If there are multiple candidates with the same rating, we pick one uniformly at random – to achieve deterministic selection we use a hash-and-combine function seeded with u as a random number generator. In Algorithm 1, we could theoretically parallelize the iteration over neighbors by using atomic fetch-and-add instructions for aggregating the ratings. The check $rating[\mathcal{C}[v]] = 0$ can be faithfully implemented because the atomic instruction returns the value immediately prior to its execution. However, in practice the outer level of parallelism over the vertices is again sufficient.

Algorithm 2: Coarsening Pass

```
randomly split vertices into sub-rounds
C[u] ← u, P[u] ← u : ∀u ∈ V
opportunistic-weight[u] ← c(u) : ∀u ∈ V
for r = 0 to number of sub-rounds do
    for u ∈ V in sub-round r do in parallel
        P[u] ← ComputeHeavyEdgeRating(u)
        opportunistic-weight[P[u]] += c(u)                    // atomic
    M ← ∅                                                      // moves
    for u ∈ V in sub-round r do in parallel
        if opportunistic-weight[P[u]] ≤ CW_max
            C[u] ← P[u]
        else
            add u to M
    sort M lexicographically by (P[u], c(u), u)
    for i = 0 to |M| do in parallel
        if i = 0 or P[M[i − 1]] ≠ P[M[i]]
            for j = i until CW_max exceeded do
                C[M[j]] ← P[M[j]]
            set opportunistic-weight of C[M[i − 1]]
contract clustering C
```

Approving Moves. Since the initial partitioning step must be able to compute a feasible partition, we enforce a maximum weight on the clusters $CW_{\max} := \min(L_{\max}, c(V)/CL)$. To respect this constraint, we filter the target cluster candidates further during the selection. Additionally, some of the calculated moves must be rejected. Therefore, we sort the moves lexicographically by cluster, vertex weight, and lastly vertex ID (for determinism). For each target cluster, we then approve the vertices one by one (in order of ascending weight), and reject all of the remaining moves into this cluster once $CW_{\max}$ would be exceeded. Our implementation iterates over the moves in parallel, and the iteration of the first vertex in the sub-range of a cluster is responsible for performing the moves into the cluster. To drastically reduce the number of moves we have to sort, we employ an optimization, where we already sum up the cluster weights during the target-cluster calculation step using atomic fetch-and-add instructions, and simply approve all moves into a target cluster whose weight will not exceed $CW_{\max}$. Due to this optimization, calculating the target clusters is by far the more expensive step in practice, even though approval requires sorting.

Contraction. The hypergraph contraction algorithm consists of several steps: remapping cluster IDs to a consecutive range (as for graph contraction), generating pin lists of the hyperedges of the contracted hypergraph, removing duplicate hyperedges, and finally assembling the data structure.

We generate the coarse pin list of each hyperedge in parallel, by replacing the vertex ID with the remapped cluster ID and removing duplicate entries. Our version uses a bit-set for de-duplication, but sorting is not much slower. At this stage we already discard hyperedges of size one.

To remove duplicate hyperedges, we use a parallel version of the INRSort algorithm [3]. The INRSort algorithm works as follows. Comparing all hyperedge-pairs for equality is too expensive, so a hash function is used to restrict comparisons to hyperedges with equal hash value and size. For parallelism, hyperedges are distributed across threads using the hash value of their pins [10]. Each thread sorts its hyperedges by their hash value, their size, as well as ID for determinism. In each sub-range with equal hash value and size (consecutive in memory due to sorting), pair-wise comparisons of their pins are performed. Again, we use a bit-set to check for equality, as this was slightly faster than sorting the pins. The running time of the de-duplication algorithm is difficult to analyze, since it depends on the collision rate of the hash function, the number of duplicate hyperedges and their sizes. However, in practice, it is faster than constructing the pin lists and the incident hyperedge lists.

At this point, we have obtained the pin lists of the coarse hypergraph, and now need to construct the list of incident hyperedges at each vertex. For this, we first count the number of incident hyperedges at each vertex, and compute a prefix sum over these values. In a second pass, we write the incident hyperedges into the sub-ranges of the corresponding pins, using an atomic fetch-and-add instruction on the starting position of the sub-range. Finally, we sort the incident hyperedges of each vertex for determinism.

3.3 Initial Partitioning

After the coarsening phase, we compute an initial k-way partition on the coarsest hypergraph. We perform recursive bipartitioning with the multilevel algorithm and thus only need to provide *flat* algorithms for computing initial 2-way partitions. Since the coarsest hypergraphs are *small*, a portfolio of 9 different simple, sequential algorithms [18] is used. Combined with 20 repetitions each for diversity, there is ample parallelism. Each run is followed up with 3 rounds of sequential FM local search [6]. These algorithms are inherently deterministic, however care must be taken when selecting which partition to use for refinement. The primary criteria are connectivity followed by imbalance. As a tie-breaker we use generated tags. In combination with deterministic coarsening and refinement, the overall initial partitioning phase is deterministic.

We do not use the adaptive selection technique for flat bipartitioning algorithms from [11] since it is non-deterministic. Furthermore, in the versions from [10,11], each thread runs one FM round [6] on all of the bipartitions it computes and subsequently one on the best it computed. Since this is non-deterministic, we implemented a version, which maintains a global fixed-size population, and applies FM refinement to each of these. However, this lacked diversity in preliminary experiments, so we instead increase the number of FM rounds run on each bipartition from one to three.

Algorithm 3: Compute Max Gain Move

```
Input: vertex v ∈ V
gains[i] ← 0 ∀i ∈ [k]
internal ← 0
for e ∈ I(v) do
  | if Φ(e, Π[v]) > 1
  |   | internal += ω(e)
  | for block i ∈ Λ(e) do
  |   | gains[i] += ω(e)
j ← arg max_{i∈[k]}(gains[i])
return j, gains[j] − internal
```

3.4 Refinement

In the refinement phase, we take an existing k-way partition (from the previous level or initial partitioning) and try to improve it by moving vertices to different parts, depending on their gain values. The gain of moving vertex $u \in V$ from its current block s to block t is $\text{gain}(u, t) := \sum_{e \in \mathrm{I}(u):\Phi(e,s)=1} \omega(e) - \sum_{e \in \mathrm{I}(u):\Phi(e,t)=0} \omega(e)$. The first term accounts for the hyperedges e for which s will be removed from their connectivity set $\Lambda(e)$, the second term accounts for those where t will be newly added.

Finding Moves. Our refinement algorithm is a synchronous version of label propagation refinement [17]. The vertices are randomly split into sub-rounds. For each vertex in the current sub-round, we compute the highest gain move, and store it if the gain is positive. Algorithm 3 shows pseudocode for computing the gains of a vertex v to all k blocks, and selecting the highest gain move. As an optimization it uses the connectivity sets $\Lambda(e)$ instead of checking the pin counts $\Phi(e, i)$ for each block $i \in [k]$ directly. The gain-calculation phase takes $O(k|V| + \sum_{u \in V} \sum_{e \in \mathrm{I}(u)} \lambda(e))$ work (across all sub-rounds) and $O(k + \max_{u \in V}(\sum_{e \in \mathrm{I}(u)} \lambda(e)))$ depth for each sub-round. The $O(k)$ term per vertex for initializing the gains array and selecting the highest gain can be eliminated by tracking occupied slots and resetting only these, though this is not useful in practice if k is small.

In a second step we approve some of the stored moves, and subsequently apply them in parallel, before proceeding to the next sub-round. This is the interesting part, as just applying all moves does not guarantee a balanced partition.

Maintaining Balance By Vertex Swaps. In this step we perform a sequence of balance-preserving vertex swaps on each block-pair, prioritized by gain. This approach was first introduced in SHP [15], though their work only considers unweighted vertices. For each block-pair $(s, t) \in \binom{[k]}{2}$, we collect the vertices M_{st} that want to move from s to t and M_{ts} from t to s, and sort both sequences descendingly by gain (with vertex ID as tie breaker for determinism). SHP moves the first $\min(|M_{st}|, |M_{ts}|)$ vertices from each sequence. With unit weights this does not change the balance of the partition. However, we have to handle non-unit weights, so we are interested in the longest prefixes of M_{st}, M_{ts}, represented by indices i, j, whose cumulative vertex weights $c(M_{st}[0 : i]), c(M_{ts}[0 : j])$ are equal. This is similar to merging two sorted arrays. We do not have to swap exactly equal weight, as long as the resulting partition is still balanced. For each block, we have a certain additional weight B_t it can take before becoming overloaded. If block-pairs are handled sequentially one after another, we can set $B_t = L_{\max} - c(V_t)$. If they are handled in parallel, we divide this budget (equally) among the different block-pairs that have moves into t.

Again, we denote the prefixes as indices i and j into M_{st} and M_{ts}, respectively. The prefixes i, j are called *feasible* if they satisfy the condition $-B_s \leq c(M_{st}[0 : i]) - c(M_{ts}[0 : j]) \leq B_t$, i.e., swapping the first i, j moves yields a balanced partition. To compute the two longest feasible prefixes of M_{st}, M_{ts}, we simultaneously iterate through both sequences and keep track of the so far exchanged weight $c(M_{st}[0 : i]) - c(M_{ts}[0 : j])$. If $c(M_{st}[0 : i]) - c(M_{ts}[0 : j]) < 0$ and M_{st} has moves left, we approve the next move from M_{st} by incrementing i. Otherwise we approve the next move from M_{ts}. In each iteration we check whether the current prefixes are feasible.

We parallelize this similar to a merge. First, we compute cumulative vertex weights via parallel prefix sums. Then the following algorithm is applied recursively. We binary search for the cumulative weight of the middle of the longer sequence in the shorter sequence. The left and right parts of the sequences can be searched independently. If the right parts contain feasible prefixes, we return them, otherwise we return the result from the left parts. The top-level recursive call on the left parts is guaranteed to find at least $i = j = 0$ (no move applied). If n denotes the length of the longer sequence, this algorithm has $O(\log(n)^2)$ depth and $O(n)$ work.

Since we are interested in the longest prefixes, we can omit the recursive call on the left parts if the prefixes at the splitting points are feasible. Depending on the available budgets B_s, B_t this is fairly likely, since the cumulative weights are as close as possible. Further, we can omit the recursive call on the right parts if the cumulative weight at the middle of the longer sequence exceeds the cumulative weight at the end of the shorter sequence plus the appropriate budget. Note that in this case the binary search finds the end and thus the left recursion takes the entirety of the shorter sequence.

We stop the recursion and run the sequential algorithm if both sequences have less than 2000 elements. This value worked well in preliminary experiments. As we already computed cumulative weights, we instead perform the simultaneous traversal from the ends of the sequences. Since we expect to approve the majority of the saved moves, this is likely faster.

3.5 Differences to BiPart

We now discuss differences between `BiPart` and our algorithm. `BiPart` uses recursive bipartitioning, whereas we use direct k-way, which is superior regarding solution quality [19]. The refinement algorithms are similar, inspired by label propagation [17] and SHP [15]. However, their refinement ignores vertex weights (apply all moves of the shorter sequence and the same number from the longer), which leads to imbalanced partitions that must be repaired by explicit rebalancing. This can be slow and offers little control by how much solution quality degrades. Our refinement guarantees balanced partitions at all stages without rebalancing. Additionally, we use sub-rounds for more accurate gains and active vertex sets [8] for better performance. Furthermore, BiPart uses no mechanism to track actual improvements, whereas we use attributed gains [10] to detect and prevent quality-degrading moves. Their coarsening scheme assigns each vertex to its smallest incident hyperedge (ties broken by ID) and merges all vertices assigned to the same hyperedge. This offers no control over vertex weights and does not rank higher hyperedge weights as more important to not cut. Preventing large vertex weights is important so that initial partitioning can find balanced partitions and there is more leeway for optimization. BiPart uses a parallel version of greedy graph growing [22] for initial partitioning, even though the coarsest hypergraphs are small, where it is feasible to afford parallel diversified repetitions of sequential algorithms.

4 Experiments

Our code is integrated in the Mt-KaHyPar hypergraph partitioning framework. It is written in C++17, uses Intel's tbb library for parallelization and is compiled with g++ version 9.2 with optimization level -O3 and native architecture optimizations. The experiments are run on a 128-core (2 sockets, 64 cores each) AMD EPYC Zen 2 7742 CPU clocked at 2.25 GHz (3.4 GHz turbo boost) with 1 TB DDR4 RAM, and 256 MB L3 cache.

Benchmark Set. We use the established benchmark set of 94 large hypergraphs that was assembled to evaluate Mt-KaHyPar, set B in [10]. Since we have 94 instances, we cannot report instance sizes for each of them, however these statistics are available online[1] in the supplementary material of [10]. We use $k \in \{2, 4, 8, 16, 32, 64\}$, $\varepsilon = 0.03$, and five different random seeds.

The largest instances have between 10^7 and 10^8 vertices and hyperedges, as well as 10^8 to $2 \cdot 10^9$ pins. Dual SAT instances are known for large hyperedges (with up to millions of pins), and hence their corresponding primal counterparts are known for large vertex degrees. Some sparse matrices are even more skewed with a maximum degree of 10^7.

Configurations. We perform 5 rounds of local moving on each level during refinement, 5 rounds before contracting during preprocessing, and one round before contracting during coarsening. We call the algorithm and configuration proposed in this work Mt-KaHyPar-SDet, and the equivalent configuration that uses the existing non-deterministic local moving algorithms Mt-KaHyPar-S, where Det stands for determinism, and S for speed. Additionally, we consider Mt-KaHyPar-D

[1] https://algo2.iti.kit.edu/heuer/alenex21/.

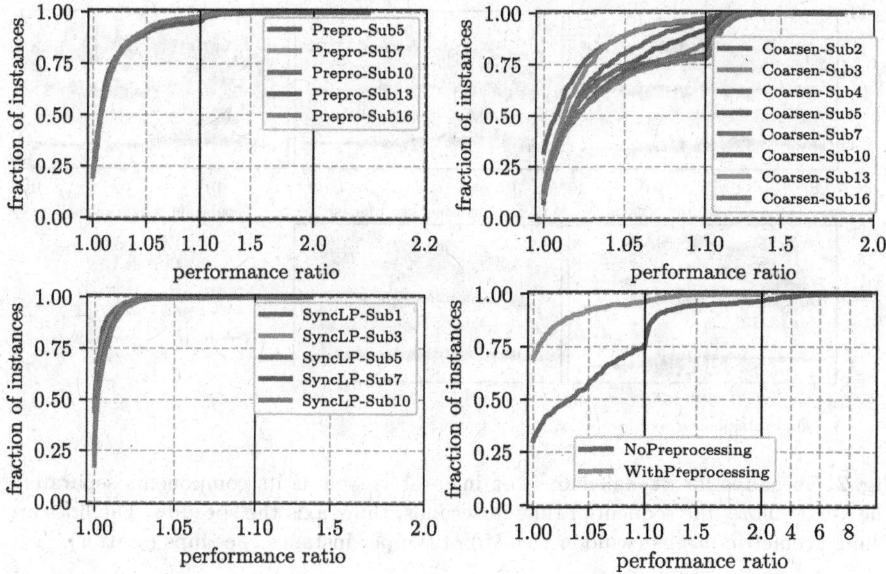

Fig. 1. Impact of the number of sub-rounds and preprocessing.

(default) [10], which has a more advanced refinement algorithm that is difficult to make deterministic.

Performance Profiles. To compare the solution quality of different algorithms, we use *performance profiles* [5]. Let $\mathcal{A}$ be the set of all algorithms we want to compare, $\mathcal{I}$ the set of instances, and $q_A(I)$ the quality of algorithm $A \in \mathcal{A}$ on instance $I \in \mathcal{I}$. For each algorithm A, we plot the fraction of instances (y-axis) for which $q_A(I) \leq \tau \cdot \min_{A' \in \mathcal{A}} q_{A'}(I)$, where τ is on the x-axis. Achieving higher fractions at equal τ-values is considered better. For $\tau = 1$, the y-value indicates the percentage of instances for which an algorithm performs best. To interpret these plots, we either look at how quickly the curve converges towards $y = 1$ (higher is better), or we look at the maximum ratio for certain instance fraction quantiles. To calculate the ratios, we take the average connectivity across different seeds for each instance.

4.1 Parameter Tuning

The supposedly most important parameter is the number of sub-rounds used, as it offers a trade-off between scalability (synchronization after each sub-round) and solution quality (more up-to-date information). In the following, we show that this is actually not a trade-off, as the number of sub-rounds either does not affect solution quality, or using fewer sub-rounds even leads to better quality.

We made an initial guess of 5 sub-rounds for refinement, and 16 sub-rounds for coarsening and preprocessing, which we use as a baseline configuration when

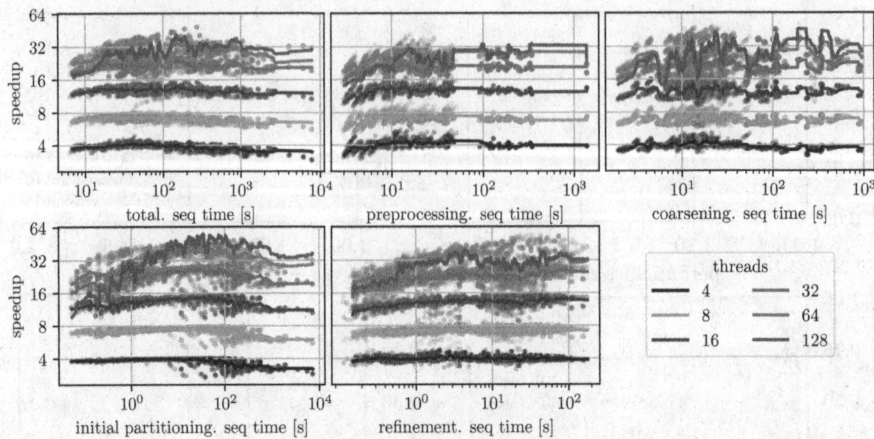

Fig. 2. Speedups for `Mt-KaHyPar-SDet` in total as well as its components separately. The x-axis shows the sequential time in seconds, the y-axis the speedup. The lines are rolling geometric means (window size 50) of the per-instance speedups (scatter).

varying each parameter. Figure 1 shows the performance profiles. The largest impact is on the coarsening phase, where 2 sub-rounds performs the best. Such a small value is surprising, yet one possible explanation is that high-degree vertices attract low-degree vertices too quickly if synchronization happens too frequently. Using only 1 sub-round is excluded here, since the clustering oscillates, which leads to coarsening converging long before the contraction limit is reached and thus initial partitioning takes very long. Furthermore, using 2 sub-rounds is about 12% slower than using 3 sub-rounds in the geometric mean, again due to the same effect. Since it gives only slightly worse solution quality, we choose 3 sub-rounds for coarsening in the main experiments. For preprocessing, there is little impact on solution quality. Here we stick with our original choice of 16 sub-rounds since the floating-point-aggregation handling becomes substantially slower if more vertices are in a sub-round due to the sorting overhead. For refinement, there is again little difference, where 1 sub-round narrowly emerges as the best choice. This is again surprising, as frequently synchronizing should allow for more informed move-decisions. One cause we noticed is that with more sub-rounds the pair-wise swaps did not have sufficiently many moves to balance, as moves from earlier sub-rounds are not considered. Using such moves as back-up could be included in future versions of the algorithm.

In Fig. 1 (bottom right), we show that the preprocessing phase is important for solution quality, which justifies the overhead for the volume updates.

4.2 Speedups

In Fig. 2 we show self-relative speedups of the overall algorithm and the separate components, plotted against the sequential running time on that particular

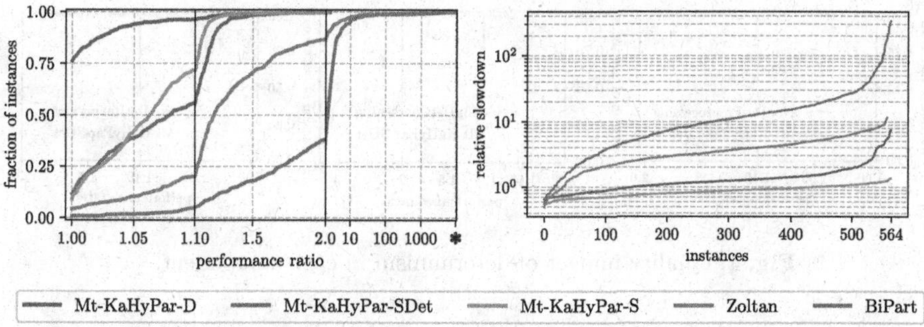

Fig. 3. Left: solution quality of `BiPart`, `Zoltan`, our algorithm `Mt-KaHyPar-SDet` and the existing `Mt-KaHyPar` variants. The ✱ symbol marks segmentation faults (6 instances for `Zoltan`). Right: slowdown relative to our algorithm. The instances on the x-axis are sorted independently.

instance. In addition to the scatter plot, we show rolling geometric means with window size 50. The overall geometric mean speedups of the full partitioning process are 3.91, 7.04, 12.79, 21.32, 28.73, 29.09 for 4, 8, 16, 32, 64, and 128 threads, respectively, and the maximum speedups are 4.9, 8.7, 15.8, 29.1, 48.9, and 72.6. Since our algorithms are memory-bound workload types these are very good results. On about 37% of the runs with 4 threads, and 0.32% of runs with 8 threads, we observe super-linear speedups which occur in all phases except initial partitioning. We identified two reasons for this. First, even sequential runs had running time fluctuations, and as super-linear speedups occur mostly for small sequential times, the speedups are more easily affected. Second, while most of the work performed is deterministic, in all phases except initial partitioning we sort vectors that are filled in non-deterministic order. Sorting algorithms have checks for presorted sub-sequences to speed up execution.

Looking at speedups for the individual phases, we see that most phases exhibit very consistent speedups, even for small sequential running times. Only initial partitioning exhibits sub-par speedups on larger instances, which is due to load imbalance from long running sequential FM refinement.

With 128 threads (only rolling geometric means shown for readability), the running times still improve, though not as drastically. Only small instances show a slight slowdown, predominantly in initial partitioning. Starting at > 64 threads, the second memory socket is used, so some slowdown is expected. We use interleaved memory allocations to cope with NUMA effects as much as possible.

4.3 Comparison with Other Algorithms

Figure 3 (left) shows performance profiles comparing our new algorithm with its non-deterministic variants, the non-deterministic distributed algorithm `Zoltan` [4] as well as the deterministic `BiPart` algorithm [16]. In these experiments, each algorithm is run with 64 threads. As expected, `Mt-KaHyPar-D` performs best, contributing the best solutions on about 75% of the instances,

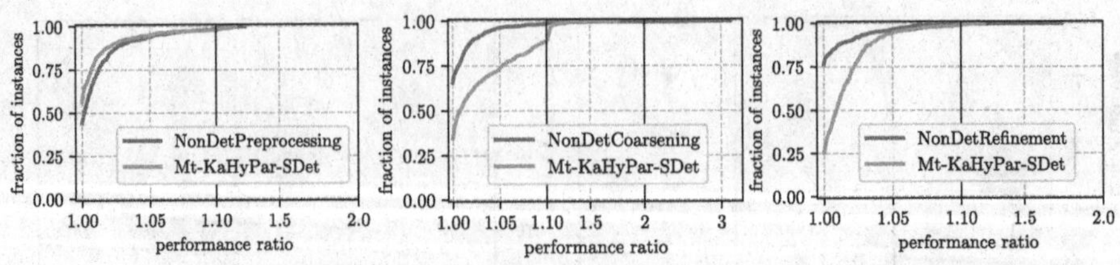

Fig. 4. Quality impact of determinism in each component.

followed by `Mt-KaHyPar-SDet` and `Mt-KaHyPar-S` which are similar, though `Mt-KaHyPar-S` is slightly better as it converges faster towards 1. `BiPart` is far off, contributing only 6 of the best solutions, and its quality is off by more than a factor of 2 on more than 50% of the instances; on some instances even by three orders of magnitude. Zoltan is situated between `BiPart` and `Mt-KaHyPar-S`. In a direct comparison, `Mt-KaHyPar-SDet` computes better partitions than `BiPart` on 551 of the 564 instances with a geometric mean performance ratio of 1.0032 compared to `BiPart`'s 2.3805.

In Fig. 3 (right), we report relative slowdowns, i.e., the running time of the other algorithm divided by running time of the baseline `Mt-KaHyPar-SDet`. `Mt-KaHyPar-S` is faster on all but 158 instances and never by a factor of more than 2. `BiPart` is between *one and two orders of magnitude slower* than the two speed variants of `Mt-KaHyPar`. In the technical report [8], we show instance-wise speedups of `BiPart`, most of which are below 2 and the largest is about 7.

4.4 The Cost of Determinism

In this section, we investigate in which phase the solution quality gets lost, by swapping out one component for its non-deterministic counterpart, in each of the plots in Fig. 4. Interestingly, the biggest quality loss comes from coarsening, whereas deterministic preprocessing even improves quality. The loss in refinement is expected due to the lack of up-to-date gains and the inability to leverage zero gain moves for rebalancing and diversification.

For coarsening, the results are unexpected, particularly because similar local moving algorithms [13] are not as affected by out-of-date gains. One reason for this is that multiple global rounds are performed, where vertices can back out of their first cluster assignment. We only use one round and even prematurely terminate the round to avoid coarsening too aggressively. Performing a second round, where only already clustered vertices may reassess their assignment, may be beneficial and we leave this for future research. Additionally, we unsuccessfully experimented with several features of the non-deterministic coarsening such as adapting hyperedge sizes to the current clustering in the rating function and *stable leader chasing*, where oscillations (vertices joining each other) and cyclic joins are resolved by merging all involved vertices.

5 Conclusion and Future Work

We presented the first scalable, deterministic parallel hypergraph partitioning algorithm. Our experiments show that determinism does incur sacrifices regarding both solution quality and running time compared to the previous non-deterministic version, but these are small enough to justify if determinism is desirable. Future work includes incorporating determinism into additional refinement algorithms, improving performance on multi-socket machines, and implementing these techniques for distributed memory.

For example for flow-based refinement [7,9] this is well within reach, as scheduling on block-pairs can synchronize after each block was involved in a refinement step, and the flow algorithms need not be deterministic since the used cuts are unique. Parallel localized FM seems like a much more difficult target, though a promising approach may be to stick with approving expansion steps at synchronization points. Additionally, handling extremely large k and speeding up initial partitioning is possible by employing the deep multilevel approach [12] instead of recursive bipartitioning during initial partitioning.

References

1. Blelloch, G.E., Fineman, J.T., Gibbons, P.B., Shun, J.: Internally deterministic parallel algorithms can be fast. In: PPoPP 2012. https://doi.org/10.1145/2145816.2145840
2. Blondel, V.D., Guillaume, J., Lambiotte, R., Lefebvre, E.: Fast unfolding of communities in large networks. J. Stat. Mech. Theory Exp. (2008). https://doi.org/10.1088/1742-5468/2008/10/P10008
3. Deveci, M., Kaya, K., Çatalyürek, Ü.V.: Hypergraph sparsification and its application to partitioning. In: ICPP 2013, pp. 200–209 (2013). https://doi.org/10.1109/ICPP.2013.29
4. Devine, K.D., Boman, E.G., Heaphy, R.T., Bisseling, R.H., Catalyürek, Ü.V.: Parallel hypergraph partitioning for scientific computing. In: IPDPS 2006. https://doi.org/10.1109/IPDPS.2006.1639359
5. Dolan, E.D., Moré, J.J.: Benchmarking optimization software with performance profiles. Math. Program. **91**(2), 201–213 (2002). https://doi.org/10.1007/s101070100263
6. Fiduccia, C.M., Mattheyses, R.M.: A Linear-Time Heuristic for Improving Network Partitions. In: DAC 1982. https://doi.org/10.1145/800263.809204
7. Gottesbüren, L., Hamann, M., Wagner, D.: Evaluation of a flow-based hypergraph bipartitioning algorithm. In: 27th European Symposium on Algorithms (ESA), pp. 52:1–52:17 (2019). https://doi.org/10.4230/LIPIcs.ESA.2019.52
8. Gottesbüren, L., Hamann, M.: Deterministic parallel hypergraph partitioning. arxiv preprint (2021). https://arxiv.org/abs/2112.12704
9. Gottesbüren, L., Hamann, M., Schlag, S., Wagner, D.: Advanced flow-based multilevel hypergraph partitioning. In: 18th International Symposium on Experimental Algorithms, SEA 2020, 16–18 June 2020, Catania, Italy, pp. 11:1–11:15 (2020). https://doi.org/10.4230/LIPIcs.SEA.2020.11

10. Gottesbüren, L., Heuer, T., Sanders, P., Schlag, S.: Scalable shared-memory hypergraph partitioning. In: ALENEX 2021, pp. 16–30 (2021). https://doi.org/10.1137/1.9781611976472.2
11. Gottesbüren, L., Heuer, T., Sanders, P., Schlag, S.: Shared-memory n-level hypergraph partitioning. arxiv preprint (2021). https://arxiv.org/abs/2104.08107
12. Gottesbüren, L., Heuer, T., Sanders, P., Schulz, C., Seemaier, D.: Deep multilevel graph partitioning. In: Mutzel, P., Pagh, R., Herman, G. (eds.) 29th Annual European Symposium on Algorithms, ESA 2021, 6–8 September 2021, Lisbon, Portugal (Virtual Conference). LIPIcs, vol. 204, pp. 48:1–48:17. Schloss Dagstuhl - Leibniz-Zentrum für Informatik (2021). https://doi.org/10.4230/LIPIcs.ESA.2021.48
13. Hamann, M., Strasser, B., Wagner, D., Zeitz, T.: Distributed graph clustering using modularity and map equation. In: EuroPar 2018 (2018). https://doi.org/10.1007/978-3-319-96983-1_49
14. Heuer, T., Schlag, S.: Improving coarsening schemes for hypergraph partitioning by exploiting community structure. In: SEA 2017. https://doi.org/10.4230/LIPIcs.SEA.2017.21
15. Kabiljo, I., et al.: Social hash partitioner: a scalable distributed hypergraph partitioner (2017). https://doi.org/10.14778/3137628.3137650
16. Maleki, S., Agarwal, U., Burtscher, M., Pingali, K.: BiPart: a parallel and deterministic multilevel hypergraph partitioner. In: PPoPP 2021. https://doi.org/10.1145/3437801.3441611
17. Raghavan, U.N., Albert, R., Kumara, S.: Near linear time algorithm to detect community structures in large-scale networks. Phys. Rev. E **76**(3), 036106 (2007). https://doi.org/10.1103/PhysRevE.76.036106
18. Schlag, S.: High-quality hypergraph partitioning (2020)
19. Simon, H.D., Teng, S.: How good is recursive bisection? SIAM J. Sci. Comput. **18**(5), 1436–1445 (1997). https://doi.org/10.1137/S1064827593255135
20. Staudt, C.L., Meyerhenke, H.: Engineering parallel algorithms for community detection in massive networks. IEEE Trans. Parallel Distrib. Syst. **27**(1), 171–184 (2016). https://doi.org/10.1109/TPDS.2015.2390633
21. Steele, G.L.: Making asynchronous parallelism safe for the world. In: Allen, F.E. (ed.) POPL 1990, pp. 218–231. ACM Press (1990). https://doi.org/10.1145/96709.96731
22. Catalyürek, Ü.V., Aykanat, C.: Hypergraph-partitioning-based decomposition for parallel sparse-matrix vector multiplication. IEEE Trans. Parallel Distrib. Syst. (1999). https://doi.org/10.1109/71.780863

Parallel and Distributed Programming, Interfaces, and Languages

OmpSs-2@Cluster: Distributed Memory Execution of Nested OpenMP-style Tasks

Jimmy Aguilar Mena(✉), Omar Shaaban, Vicenç Beltran, Paul Carpenter, Eduard Ayguade, and Jesus Labarta Mancho

Barcelona Supercomputing Center, Barcelona, Spain
jimmy.aguilar@bsc.es

Abstract. State-of-the-art programming approaches generally have a strict division between intra-node shared memory parallelism and inter-node MPI communication. Tasking with dependencies offers a clean, dependable abstraction for a wide range of hardware and situations within a node, but research on task offloading between nodes is still relatively immature. This paper presents a flexible task offloading extension of the OmpSs-2 programming model, which inherits task ordering from a sequential version of the code and uses a common address space to avoid address translation and simplify the use of data structures with pointers. It uses weak dependencies to enable work to be created concurrently. The program is executed in distributed dataflow fashion, and the runtime system overlaps the construction of the distributed dependency graph, enforces dependencies, transfers data, and schedules tasks for execution. Asynchronous task parallelism avoids synchronization that is often required in MPI+OpenMP tasks. Task scheduling is flexible, and data location is tracked through the dependencies. We wish to enable future work in resiliency, scalability, load balancing and malleability, and therefore release all source code and examples open source.

1 Introduction

The dominant programming approach for scientific and industrial computing on clusters is MPI+X. While there are a variety of approaches within the node, described by the "X", such as OpenMP, OmpSs, OpenACC and others, the *de facto* standard for programming multiple nodes is MPI. In all cases the program must combine two fundamentally different programming models, which is difficult to get right [29,30]. The tasking approach of OpenMP and OmpSs offers an open, clean and stable way to improve hardware utilization through asynchronous execution while targeting a wide range of hardware, from SMPs, to GPUs, to FPGAs. This paper extends the same approach, of OmpSs-2 tasking, to multiple nodes. We develop OmpSs-2@Cluster, which provides a simple path to move an OmpSs-2 program from single node to small- to medium-scale clusters. We also present the runtime techniques that allow overlapping of the construction of the distributed dependency graph, efficient concurrent enforcing of dependencies, data transfers among nodes, and task execution.

J. Cano and P. W. Trinder (Eds.): Euro-Par 2022, LNCS 13440, pp. 319–334, 2022.
https://doi.org/10.1007/978-3-031-12597-3_20

A number of research groups are looking into tasks as a model for all scales from single threads and accelerators to clusters of nodes, as outlined in Sect. 7. Our approach is unique, in that, in many cases, a functional multi-node version of an existing OmpSs-2 program can be obtained simply by changing the configuration file supplied to the runtime system. The meaning of the program are defined by the sequential semantics of the original program, which simplifies development and maintenance. All processes use the same virtual memory layout, which avoids address translation and allows direct use of existing data structures with pointers. Improvements beyond the first version can be made incrementally, based on observations from performance analysis. Some optimizations that are well-proven within a single node, such as task nesting to overlap task creation and execution, [26] are a particular emphasis of OmpSs-2@Cluster, since they clearly have a greater impact when running across multiple nodes, due to the greater node-to-node latency and larger total number of execution cores.

The program is executed in distribution dataflow fashion, which is naturally asynchronous, with no risk of deadlock due to user error. In contrast, MPI+X programs often use a fork–join model, due to the difficulty in overlapping computation and communication [30]. We show how well-balanced applications have similar performance to MPI+OpenMP on up to 16 nodes. For irregular and unbalanced applications like Cholesky factorization, we get a 2× performance improvement on 16 nodes, compared with a high performance implementation using MPI+OpenMP tasks. All source code and examples are released open source [9].

2 Background

OmpSs-2 [7–9] is the second generation of the OmpSs programming model. It is open source and mainly used as a research platform to explore and demonstrate ideas that may be proposed for standardization in OpenMP. The OpenMP concept of data dependencies among tasks was first proven in OmpSs. Like OpenMP, OmpSs-2 is based on directives that annotate a sequential program, and it enables parallelism in a dataflow way [27]. The model targets multi-cores and GPU/FPGA accelerators. This decomposition into tasks and data accesses is used by the source-to-source Mercurium [5] compiler to generate calls to the Nanos6 [6] runtime API. The runtime computes task dependencies and schedules and executes tasks, respecting the implied task dependency constraints and performing data transfers and synchronizations.

OmpSs-2 differs from OpenMP in the thread-pool execution model, targeting of heterogeneous architectures through native kernels, and asynchronous parallelism as the main mechanism to express concurrency. Task dependencies may be discrete (defined by start address), or regions with fragmentation [26].

OmpSs-2 extends the tasking model of OmpSs and OpenMP to improve task nesting and fine-grained dependences across nesting levels [2,26]. The `depend` clause is extended with `weakin`, `weakout` and `weakinout` dependency types, which serve as a linking point between the dependency domains at different nesting levels, without delaying task execution. They indicate that the task does

Table 1. Key features of OmpSs-2@Cluster

Feature	Description
Sequential semantics	Simplifies development, porting, and maintenance. Tasks can be defined at any nesting level and can be offloaded to any node
Common address space	Simplifies porting of applications with complex data structures by supporting pointers and avoiding address translation
Distributed dataflow execution	Task ordering and overlapping of data transfers with computation are automated, reducing synchronizations and avoiding risk of deadlock
Distributed memory allocation	Informs runtime that memory is only needed by subtasks, reducing synchronization and data transfers. Provides data distribution affinity hint
Minimizing of data transfers	The `taskwait on` and `taskwait noflush` directives help minimize unnecessary data transfers
Early, late or auto release of dependencies	A tradeoff between parallelism and overhead is exposed through control over the release of dependencies
Cluster query API and scheduling hint	Optional ability to instruct the runtime to control detailed behavior and optimize decisions

not itself access the data, but its nested subtasks may do so. Any subtask that directly accesses data needs to include it in a `depend` clause in the non-weak variant. Any task that delegates accesses to a subtask must include the data in its `depend` clause in at least the weak variant. This approach enables effective parallelization of applications using a top-down methodology. The addition of weak dependences exposes more parallelism, allows better scheduling decisions and enables parallel instantation of tasks with dependencies between them.

3 OmpSs-2@Cluster Programming Model

The main features of OmpSs-2@Cluster are summarized in Table 1. Like OmpSs-2 on an SMP, tasks are defined by annotations to a program with *sequential semantics*, and offloadable tasks can be nested and defined at any nesting level. There is a *common address space* across cluster nodes, with data mapped to the same virtual address space on all nodes. As long as the task's accesses are described by dependencies, any data allocated on any node can be accessed at the same location on any other node. There is sufficient virtual address space on all modern 64-bit processors to support up to 65k cores with a typical 2 GB/core footprint. Almost any OmpSs-2 program can therefore be executed using OmpSs-2@Cluster and, conversely, if new features are ignored or implemented with a stub, any OmpSs-2@Cluster program is a valid OmpSs-2 program. This property minimizes porting effort and allows re-use of existing benchmarks.

Figure 1 shows an optimized matrix–matrix multiplication kernel using OmpSs-2@Cluster. Execution starts on node 0, which runs `main` as the first task. The example offloads one task per node then subdivides the work among the cores using a `task for`. The outer task with weak dependencies is an optimization to allow subtask creation to be overlapped with task execution, as shown in Sect. 6 (results). In general, the program as a whole is executed in a *distributed dataflow* fashion, with data transfers and data consistency managed by the runtime system. Data location is passed through the distributed dependency graph.

```
void matmul(double *A, const double *B, const double *C, int dim, int ts)
{
  int rowsPerNode = dim / nanos6_get_num_cluster_nodes();

  for(int i = 0; i < dim; i += rowsPerNode) {
    #pragma oss task label("weakmatvec") \
      weakin(A[i*dim; rowsPerNode*dim]) weakin(B[0; dim*dim]) \
      weakout(C[i*dim; rowsPerNode*dim])
    {
      #pragma oss task for label("taskformatvec") \
        in(A[i*dim; rowsPerNode*dim]) in(B[0; dim*dim]) \
        out(C[i*dim; rowsPerNode*dim])
      for(int j = i; j < i + rowsPerNode; j += ts) {
        cblas_dgemm(CblasRowMajor, CblasNoTrans, CblasNoTrans,
                    ts, dim, dim, 1.0, &A[j * dim], dim,
                    B, dim, 0.0, &C[j * dim], dim);
      }
    }
  }
}
```

Fig. 1. OmpSs-2@Cluster program: optimized dense matrix–matrix multiply, using a weak parent task to overlap task creation and execution.

Compared with OmpSs-2 on SMP, OmpSs-2@Cluster has one new requirement for correctness (full dependency specification) and a few programming model extensions to improve performance. Only a minor revision to the compiler is required to support these new features.

Full Dependency Specification: offloadable tasks (see below) require a full dependency specification, i.e., `in`, `out`, and `inout` dependencies must specify all accesses, rather than just the constraints needed for task ordering. This is the only reason that a valid OmpSs-2 program may not be a valid OmpSs-2@Cluster program, as in SMP systems accesses that are not needed to resolve dependencies may be omitted. This is not a new issue because a similar requirement exists for accelerators with separate memory spaces.

Distributed Memory Allocation: The new distributed malloc, `nanos6_dmalloc`, is an alternative memory allocation primitive for large data structures manipulated on multiple nodes. This call expresses three important distinguishing characteristics. Firstly, since the data is intended to be manipulated by concurrent tasks on several nodes, it can be assumed that the data is not used by the enclosing task, only its subtasks or descendants, similarly to a weak dependency. Secondly, since large allocations are infrequent and use significant virtual memory, it is efficient to centralize the memory allocator, as the overhead is tolerable and it leads to more efficient use of the virtual memory. Thirdly, it is a convenient place to provide a data distribution hint. The data distribution hint is communicated to all nodes, and is intended to help the scheduler improve load balance and data locality, using information from the programmer, if available. The hint does not mandate a particular data distribution, only the data affinity. The scheduler can take account of both the affinity and current location, depending on the chosen scheduling policy.

Minimising of Data Transfers: OmpSs-2@Cluster adds the `noflush` clause for taskwaits, in order to separate synchronization from data dependency.

The contents of the memory allocated by `nanos6_dmalloc` and weak dependencies are by default noflush, so that tasks can wait for their child tasks without copying data that is not needed. The `noflush` variant is also useful for timing parts of the execution. When only a subset of locally-allocated data is needed by the enclosing task, the dependency and data transfer can be expressed using `taskwait on`.

Early, Late or Auto Release of Dependencies: As per the OmpSs-2 specification on SMPs, non-offloaded OmpSs-2@Cluster tasks by default early release all of their dependencies, so that data is passed directly to the successor task without additional synchronization. Late release of dependencies is possible, using the OmpSs-2 `wait` clause, which adds an implicit `taskwait` after the completion of the task body (and release of the stack). On OmpSs-2@Cluster, offloaded tasks by default have auto release of dependencies, which means that early release is supported to successors on the same node, but all other dependencies wait. The alternatives are available through the `wait` and `nowait` clauses.[1]

Cluster Query API: There is also a simple API to read information about the execution environment: `nanos6_get_num_cluster_nodes()` returns the number of processes, and `nanos6_get_cluster_node_id()` returns the current rank.

Scheduling Hint: The runtime schedules tasks, among and within nodes, taking account of current data location and/or affinity from the data distribution hint of `nanos6_dmalloc`. The programmer can override scheduling using the `node` clause on the `task` directive, which can specify the process that will execute the task, mark it as non-offloadable or employ a different scheduling policy.

4 Nanos6 Runtime Implementation

An OmpSs-2@Cluster application is executed in the same way as any MPI program, e.g., using `mpirun` or `mpiexec`. All processes contain a Nanos6 runtime instance, as shown in Fig. 2. The nodes are peers, the only distinction among them being that node 0 executes `main` and it performs runtime operations that require internal collective synchronizations like `nanos6_dmalloc` (which may be called on any node). Each node (including node 0), creates a single "namespace" task, which is the implied common parent of all tasks offloaded to that node. The processes communicate via point-to-point MPI, with a dedicated thread on each node to handle MPI control messages.

During runtime initialization, all processes coordinate to map a common virtual memory region into their virtual address space, organized as in Fig. 3. Each node owns a portion of the local memory region, so that it can allocate stacks and user data without coordinating with other nodes. Similarly, the distributed memory region is available for allocations using `nanos6_dmalloc`. Any data residing in any of these regions can be used by a task on any node. At initialization time only the virtual memory is mapped, physical memory will be allocated on demand, when accessed by a task that executes on the node. Since

[1] Currently `nowait` is available through a Nanos6 API call.

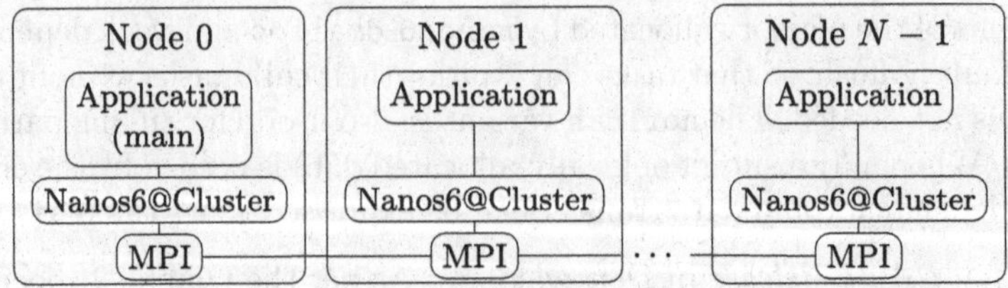

Fig. 2. OmpSs-2@Cluster architecture. Each node is a peer, except that Node 0 runs the `main` task and performs distributed memory allocations.

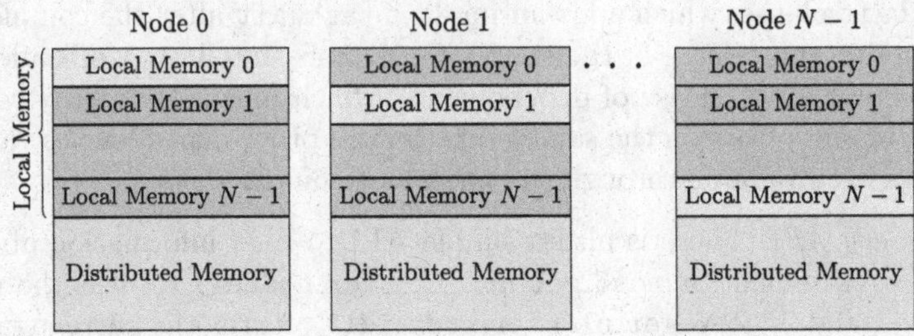

Fig. 3. Runtime memory map, which is common to all processes on all nodes.

all regions are pre-allocated on all nodes, there is no need for temporary memory allocation, address translation or user intervention.

The problem of running the whole program, which is a hierarchy of tasks with dependencies, is conceptually separated into building the distributed dependency graph (Sect. 4.1), tracking dependencies among tasks (Sect. 4.2), scheduling ready tasks for execution (Sect. 4.3), and performing data transfers before executing tasks (Sect. 4.4). All, of course, happen for multiple tasks concurrently.

4.1 Building the Distributed Dependency Graph

Tasks are created by their parent task (which may be `main`). Once tasks become ready, they are allocated to a cluster node. Many offloadable tasks have only weak dependencies, so they are ready immediately and are offloaded in advance (e.g. "weakmatvec" in Fig. 1). This allows concurrent subtask creation on all nodes, overlapped with execution and optimizations to reduce the number of control messages on the critical path. If the task is offloaded, a Task New message is sent from the *creation node*, where the task was first created, to the *execution* node, where it will be executed. This is shown in steps ① and ② in Fig. 4, which illustrates the execution of two offloaded tasks on different nodes sharing an `inout` dependency. The execution node uses the taskInfo information embedded in the message to create and submit the *proxy task* that will execute the task body.

A key design choice of OmpSs-2@Cluster is that no cluster node builds the whole computation graph of the application. Distributing the computation graph across cluster nodes minimizes coordination, thus allowing more potential for scalability. Nodes independently choose whether, and to which node, to offload

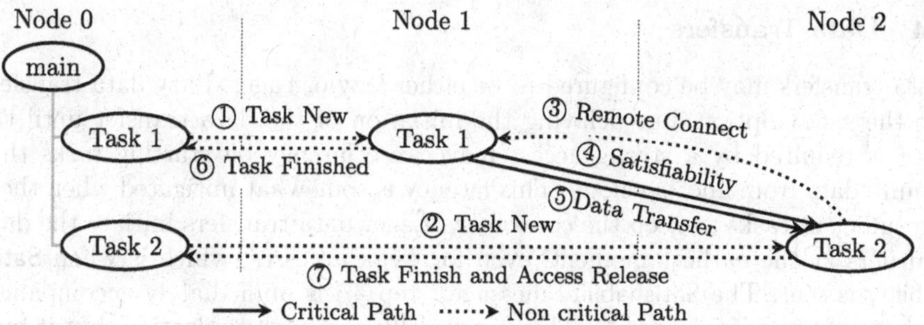

Fig. 4. Direct connection between Task 1 on Node 1 and Task 2 on Node 2. All messages are point to point.

any task created on that node. When a task is offloaded, the predecessor task for each access is known, and in many cases, its execution node is also known.

The identity of the predecessor's execution node is passed through the dependency system as tasks are offloaded. When the task's execution node creates the proxy task, dependencies from a predecessor on the same node are connected inside the namespace task, in the same way as any other sibling tasks. If the predecessor's execution node is different, then a Remote Connect message is sent to the previous node (step ③). Messages to connect the graph are off the critical path and are distributed among the implied nodes with non-blocking point-to-point communications.

4.2 Tracking Dependencies Among Tasks

When tasks complete, dependencies are released by sending point-to-point Satisfiability messages from the predecessor to successor node (step ④). These messages indicate which dependency regions are satisfied and their locations, and the MPI tags for associated eager data sends (see Sect. 4.4). If the access of an offloaded task has no successor on another node, the access is instead released back to the offloader (step ⑦). Write-after-read accesses, i.e. `inout` following multiple `in` accesses, are synchronized at the *creation node*, with satisfiability passed to the `inout` access once all the `in` accesses have released the access back.

4.3 Scheduling Ready Tasks for Execution

When a task becomes ready, the node that created the task decides whether to offload it, and, if so, it decides which node it should be offloaded to. Currently the majority of programs have two levels of nesting: one level across nodes and one level across the cores on the node. These programs have a single level of offloadable tasks, so all offloaded tasks are created on the same node, so no coordination among nodes is required for load balancing. Future work will improve the scheduler to support distributed load balancing among nodes. The scheduling of ready tasks to be executed on a node, whether offloaded or not, is done using the normal Nanos6 scheduler. The scheduler exploits all the cores on the node, and it allows variants of tasks and/or subtasks to execute on accelerators.

4.4 Data Transfers

Data transfers may be configured to be either lazy or eager. Lazy data transfers are the safest option, but delaying the initiation of the data transfer until the data is required by a strong access may cause latency on starting tasks that require data from another node. This latency is somewhat mitigated when there are sufficient tasks to keep the cores busy. Eager data transfers initiate the data transfers at the earliest moment, even for weak accesses, which is when Satisfiability is sent. The Satisfiability message (step ④) is immediately accompanied with a data transfer (step ⑤). This is generally a good optimization, but it may happen that data contained in a weak access is not accessed by any subtask with a strong access, in which case the data transfer would be unnecessary. This situation happens in Cholesky factorization, due to the pattern of the data accesses of the `dgemm` tasks. Since all subtasks are assumed to be created some time in advance, this situation can be detected when a task with weak accesses completes, at which point all subtasks have been created, but no subtask accesses all or part of the weak access. In this case a No Eager Send message is sent to the predecessor. In all cases, when a task completes, the data is not copied back to the parent (write-back) unless needed by a successor task or taskwait. The latest version of the data remains at the execution node until needed.

5 Evaluation Methodology

5.1 Hardware and Software Platform

We evaluate OmpSs-2@Cluster on MareNostrum 4 [4]. Each node has two 24-core Intel Xeon Platinum 8160 CPUs at 2.10 GHz, for a total of 48 cores per node. Each socket has a shared 32 MB L3 cache. The HPL Rmax performance equates to 1.01 TF per socket. Communication uses Intel MPI 2018.4 over 100 Gb/s Intel OmniPath, with an HFI Silicon 100 series PCIe adaptor. The runtime and all the benchmarks were compiled with Intel Compiler 18.0.1, and all the kernels use the same code and same standard BLAS functions from Intel MKL 2018.4.

5.2 Benchmarks

We use simple and optimized variants of four benchmarks all executed in configurations of 2 processes per node (one per NUMA node) from 1 to 16 nodes for a total of 32 MPI processes:

matvec is a sequence of row cyclic matrix–vector multiplications without dependencies between iterations. This benchmark has fine-grained tasks with complexity $O(N^2)$ and no data transfers. It exposes the need to implement and improve the namespace and direct propagation approaches; as well as exhibiting patterns that require reduction and grouping of control messages. The results in Sect. 6 show how this benchmark performs with a simple implementation using a single level of strong tasks vs. an optimized implementation with nested weak and strong tasks.

Table 2. Benchmark characteristics and number of lines of code of kernels.

Benchmark	MPI+ OpenMP		OmpSs-2@Cluster Simple		OmpSs-2@Cluster Optimized	
matvec	MPI point-to-point, OMP parallel for	10	One level strong tasks	11	Nested weak and strong tasks	18
matmul	MPI point-to-point, OMP parallel for	10	Nested only strong tasks	18	Nested weak and strong tasks	18
jacobi	MPI collective gather, OMP parallel for	20	Task for	25	Nested weak and strong tasks with wait clause	30
cholesky	MPI point-to-point OMP Tasks	135	strong tasks	30	Task for, memory reordering and priority	134

matmul is a matrix–matrix multiplication performed to study the behavior with bigger tasks of $O(N^3)$ with a similar access pattern. This benchmark was useful to detect redundant unneeded data transfers negligible with matvec. In this case we compare a simple version with nested strong tasks vs. nested weak and strong tasks to compare the impact of early offloading vs access fragmentation consequence of early release without data transfers or wait clause.

jacobi is an iterative Jacobi solver for strictly diagonally dominant systems. It has the same $O(N^2)$ complexity as matvec, but it has $(N-1)^2$ data transfers between iterations. The objective was to measure the impact of data transfers and control messages to detect optimization opportunities. With this benchmark we detected fragmentation associated with early release and therefore implemented the autowait feature. The simple version uses `task for` (simpler) and the optimized version adds a helper task to reduce control messages and fragmentation.

cholesky is a Cholesky factorization with a complex execution and dependencies pattern. This benchmark performs a higher number of smaller tasks, compared with matmul, and it introduces load imbalance and irregular patterns. The simple version code uses strong tasks and only needs few lines, while the optimized version uses `task for` and memory reordering optimizations to reduce fragmentation and data transfers.

All MPI+OpenMP versions were implemented in two variants, using `parallel for` and OpenMP tasks. The best version was selected and reported in Sect. 6.

Table 2 shows the key benchmark characteristics and the number of lines of code for all implementations. The values consider only the computational parts, ignoring initialization, range specific code and conditions needed in MPI and not required in OmpSs, they also exclude timing, prints and comments. We see that matmul, matvec and jacobi are all small kernels, with no major differences in size. The OmpSs-2@Cluster versions of some of these small benchmarks are larger, due to the enclosing weak task (see Fig. 1), at little increase in complexity.

6 Results

Figure 5 shows the strong scaling results for all the benchmarks. Every experiment was executed 10 times; `jacobi` and `matvec` with 400 iterations each. All points in the graphs include error bars, but in most cases they are hard to see as the standard deviation is usually insignificant.

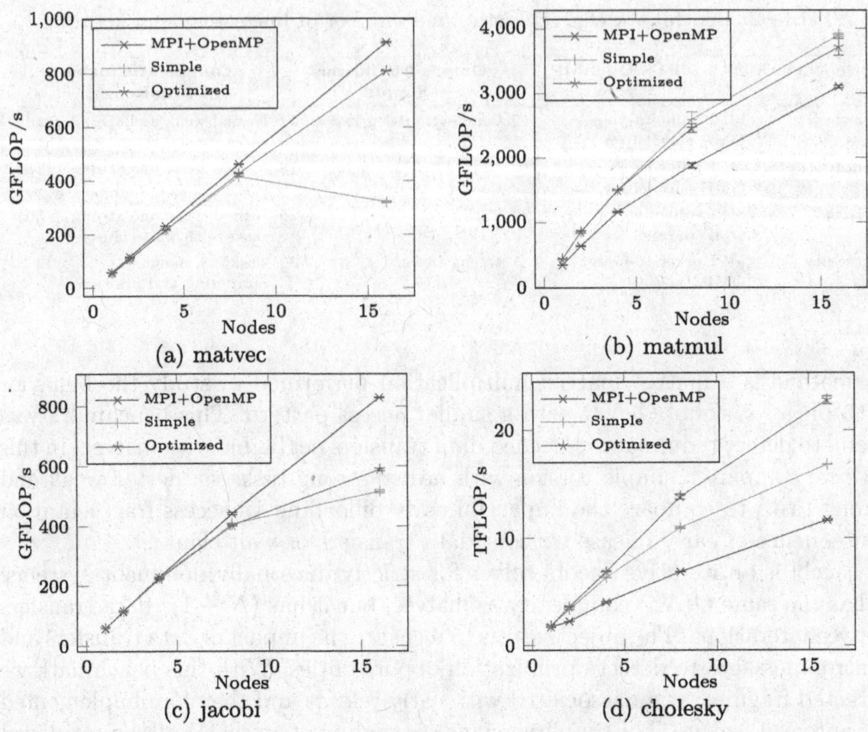

Fig. 5. Strong scaling for OmpSs-2@Cluster and MPI+OpenMP. The x-axis is the number of nodes and the y-axis is the compute throughput in GFLOP/sec.

In all subplots, the x-axis is the number of nodes, from 1 to 16 (see Sect. 5.2), and the y-axis is the performance. We see that the simple (unoptimized) OmpSs-2@Cluster matvec, matmul and jacobi have similar performance to MPI on up to 8 nodes. The optimized code for matvec and matmul has somewhat better performance and is similar to MPI up to 16 nodes. These two benchmarks perform multiple iterations, and do not require data transfers between iterations, so they evaluate the impact of task offload and enforcing of dependencies. On the other hand, jacobi has all-to-all communication, which is optimized using a collective in the MPI implementation but is done with point-to-point transfers by Nanos6. This limits the scalability and is an avenue for future research.

Finally, cholesky has a more complex communication and dependency pattern. Due to asynchronous tasking and early release of dependencies, the OmpSs-2@Cluster implementation achieves better performance than MPI+OpenMP tasks, and it has twice its performance on 16 nodes. The simple OmpSs-2@Cluster implementation of cholesky achieves better performance than MPI + OpenMP with a 4.5× reduction in code size. The optimized OmpSs-2@Cluster code for cholesky has similar length to the MPI+OpenMP version as shown in Table 2.

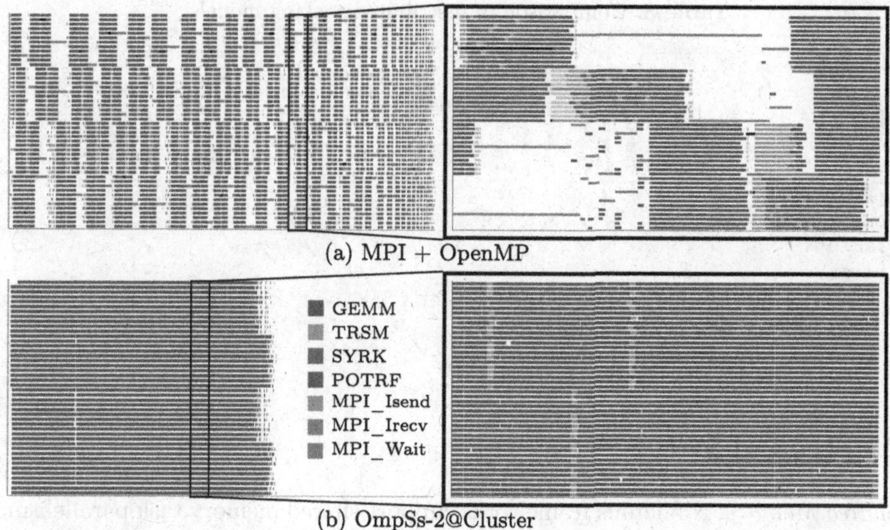

Fig. 6. Paraver/Extrae traces showing synchronization for cholesky: 16384×16384 matrix on four nodes, 12 cores per node

To understand this in more detail, Fig. 6 compares Paraver/Extrae traces for cholesky with MPI + OpenMP vs. optimized OmpSs-2@Cluster. To show an intelligible trace, it is a small example of a 16384×16384 matrix on four nodes, with 12 cores per node. Both traces show a time lapse of 1160 ms since the algorithm start; the zoomed regions are 50 ms. The traces show the BLAS kernels and MPI communications (only non-negligible in the MPI version).

We see that the OmpSs-2@Cluster version has almost 100% utilization, but synchronization among tasks and MPI communication causes the MPI+OpenMP version to have a utilization of only about 50%. As MPI is not task-aware, there are limitations on how MPI calls may be used with OpenMP Tasks to avoid deadlock. Otherwise, tasks in all threads may try to execute blocking MPI calls, occupying all threads even though other tasks may be ready, leading to a deadlock. Resolving this needs synchronization, such as serializing waits or limiting the number of send or receive tasks in every step with artificial dependencies. Figure 6a shows how the waits (gray) stop parallelism between iterations.

On the other hand, Fig. 6b does not show any waits because all communication in OmpSs-2@Cluster is non-blocking. Tasks not satisfied are not ready, so they remain in the dependency system; while ready tasks with pending data transfers, are re-scheduled when they can execute. This approach allows the runtime to concurrently execute tasks from multiple iterations and keep the workers busy while transfers occur. The priority clause is advantageous to prioritize the scheduling of critical-path tasks, in a similar way to OmpSs-2 on SMP, but it is more important for OmpSs-2@Cluster due to the network latency.

Table 3. Comparison of distributed tasking models

Programming model	*Languages*			*Task definition*		*Task discovery*		*Nested tasks*		*Address space*		*Dependencies*		*Depend. graph*			*Location tracking*		
	C	C++	Fortran	From sequential	Explicit	Static	Dynamic	Supported	Offloadable	Common	Different	Flexible	Early release	Distributed	Centralized	Duplicated	Via dependencies	Directory-based	Owner computes
OmpSs-2@Cluster	✓	✓	✓	✓	✓		✓	✓	✓	✓		✓	✓	✓			✓		
OmpSs-1@Cluster	✓	✓	✓	✓	✓		✓	✓	?		✓				✓			✓	
StarPU-MPI	✓	✓			✓		✓	✓			✓	?				✓			✓
DuctTeip		✓			✓		✓	✓			✓					✓		✓	
DASH		✓			✓		✓	✓		✓						✓			✓
PaRSEC	✓	?	✓		✓	✓	✓	?	?		✓					✓			✓
Charm++	✓	✓	✓		✓		✓		✓		✓								

7 Related Work

Shared Memory: Numerous frameworks support shared memory task parallelism with dependencies, with the *de facto* standard being OpenMP version 4.0 or above [23]. **Cilk** [12] is perhaps the first well known task-based programming model, which identifies tasks with the `spawn` keyword and supports synchronization using the `sync` statement. **Cilk++** [21] adds support for parallel loops. **XKappi** [34] also has a directed acyclic graph of tasks like OpenMP. **Wool** [16] is a low overhead library for nested tasks.

Partee [24] is an OmpSs programming model alternative implementation using **BDDT** [33] with strong effort to better handle more fine-grained tasks and irregular dependencies. **Raja** [11] and its associated libraries provide a similar C++11 approach to performance portable programming.

Distributed Memory: Table 3 summarizes the main frameworks for fine-grained distributed memory task parallelism. Most of them wrap or extend existing frameworks for shared memory tasking.

OmpSs-1@Cluster is a variant of OmpSs-1 for clusters of GPUs [13]. It has a similar approach to OmpSs-2@Cluster, but task creation and submission is centralized, dependencies are only among sibling tasks, and address translation is needed for all task accesses. It uses a directory on one node to track all data location, rather than passing the location through the edges of a distributed dependency graph. It has only strong tasks, so it has limited ability to overlap execution with task creation overhead.

StarPU-MPI [3] is the multi-node extension of StarPU. In this model all processes create the same graph of top-level tasks and it uses an owner-computes model as shown in Table 3. Task allocation to nodes and communications for data transfers are at task creation. Posting the receives in advance removes the need of Satisfiability messages, but it implies high memory consumption and some throttling mechanism which limits parallelism discovery [31].

DuctTeip [35] is a distributed task-parallel framework implemented on top of SuperGlue [32]. This approach based on data versioning supports general task graphs to implement common application structures. It divides the computation into levels to build the task graph in parallel. Child tasks are created like the strong tasks of OmpSs-2, so task creation could be on the critical path.

CHAMELEON [20] is a library for fine-grained load-balancing in task-parallel MPI+X applications. The implementation is optimized for responsiveness to changing execution conditions. They do not optimize for strong scaling of task offloading. Data is always copied back to the parent after the task, and it uses a collective distributed taskwait and the OpenMP target construct. **PaRSEC** [18] is a platform for distributed task execution. A front-end compiler generates a parameterized Directed Acyclic Graph (DAG). Tasks can be generated dynamically and could be submitted by other tasks. Dependencies are not just of the DAG type, but they support nesting, concurrent and commutative dependencies, and `weak` and `strong` dependencies. The tasks' data can be described by region dependencies with fragmentation. **DASH** [17] is a C++ template library that extends C++ STL concepts to distributed memory. It is based on a PGAS-based distributed task programming approach. Every process creates a local dependency graph in parallel. The dependencies on non-local memory are automatically resolved by the runtime system. The execution is divided into phases because there is no total ordering on the dependencies among nodes. **Charm++** [25] is a C++-based object oriented programming model for running migratable objects known as "chares". It uses a message-driven runtime model in which methods on chares result in sending a message to the chare, resulting in asynchronous function execution with similarities to task execution.

Legion [10] is a parallel programming system with an OOP syntax similar to C++ based on logical regions to describe the organization of data, with an emphasis on locality and task nesting via an object-oriented syntax. Part of Legion's low-level runtime system uses UPC's GASNet. Other approaches include **COMPSs** [22], which is a Java, C/C++ and Python framework to run parallel applications on clusters, clouds and containerized platforms. The execution granularity is much coarser with data transfer via files. **Pegasus** [15] is another workflow management system that uses a DAG of tasks and dependencies. **GPI-Space** [28] is a fault-tolerant execution platform for data-intensive applications. It supports coarse-grained tasks that helps decouple the domain user from the parallel execution of the problem. **HPX** [19] is an implementation of the ParalleX programming paradigm, with an Active Global Address Space (AGAS) to manage the locality of global objects. **X10** [14] is an object-oriented programming language for high-productivity programming that spawns asynchronous computations, with the programmer responsible for PGAS data distribution.

8 Conclusions

This paper presented OmpSs-2@Cluster, a programming model and runtime system, which provides efficient support for hierarchical tasking from distributed memory to threads. We describe the programming model and runtime optimizations to build the distributed dependency graph, enforce dependencies, perform eager data fetches and execute tasks.

The results show that performance of OmpSs-2@Cluster is competitive with MPI+OpenMP for regular and well-balanced applications. For irregular or unbalanced applications it may be significantly better without increasing the code complexity or sacrificing the programmer productivity. This work opens future work to leverage this model for (a) resiliency, (b) scalability, (c) intelligent multi-node load balancing, and (d) malleability. With this aim, all source code and examples are available open source [9].

Acknowledgements and Data Availability. The datasets and code generated during and/or analyzed during the current study are available in the Figshare repository: [1]. This research has received funding from the European Union's Horizon 2020/EuroHPC research and innovation programme under grant agreement No 955606 (DEEP-SEA) and 754337 (EuroEXA). It is supported by the Spanish State Research Agency - Ministry of Science and Innovation (contract PID2019-107255GB and Ramon y Cajal fellowship RYC2018-025628-I) and by the Generalitat de Catalunya (2017-SGR-1414).

References

1. Aguilar Mena, J., Shaaban, O., Beltran, V., Carpenter, P., Ayguade, E., Labarta Mancho, J.: Artifact and instructions to generate experimental results for the Euro-Par 2022 paper: "OmpSs-2@Cluster: Distributed memory execution of nested OpenMP-style tasks" (2022). https://doi.org/10.6084/m9.figshare.19960721
2. Álvarez, D., Sala, K., Maroñas, M., Roca, A., Beltran, V.: Advanced synchronization techniques for task-based runtime systems, pp. 334–347. Association for Computing Machinery, New York, NY, USA (2021). https://doi.org/10.1145/3437801.3441601
3. Augonnet, C., Aumage, O., Furmento, N., Namyst, R., Thibault, S.: StarPU-MPI: task programming over clusters of machines enhanced with accelerators. In: European MPI Users' Group Meeting, pp. 298–299. Springer, Berlin Heidelberg (2012). https://doi.org/10.1007/978-3-642-33518-1_40
4. Barcelona Supercomputing Center: MareNostrum 4 (2017) System Architecture (2017). https://www.bsc.es/marenostrum/marenostrum/technical-information
5. Barcelona Supercomputing Center: Mercurium (2021). https://pm.bsc.es/mcxx
6. Barcelona Supercomputing Center: Nanos6 (2021). https://github.com/bsc-pm/nanos6
7. Barcelona Supercomputing Center: OmpSs-2 releases (2021). https://github.com/bsc-pm/ompss-releases
8. Barcelona Supercomputing Center: OmpSs-2 specification (2021). https://pm.bsc.es/ftp/ompss-2/doc/spec/
9. Barcelona Supercomputing Center: OmpSs-2@Cluster releases (2022). https://github.com/bsc-pm/ompss-2-cluster-releases
10. Bauer, M., Treichler, S., Slaughter, E., Aiken, A.: Legion: expressing locality and independence with logical regions. In: SC '12: Proceedings of the International Conference on High Performance Computing, Networking, Storage and Analysis, pp. 1–11 (2012). https://doi.org/10.1109/SC.2012.71

11. Beckingsale, D.A., et al.: Raja: portable performance for large-scale scientific applications. In: IEEE/ACM International Workshop on Performance, Portability and Productivity in HPC (P3HPC) (2019). https://doi.org/10.1109/P3HPC49587.2019.00012
12. Blumofe, R., Joerg, C., Kuszmaul, B., Leiserson, C., Randall, K., Zhou, Y.: Cilk: an efficient multithreaded runtime system. J. Parallel Distrib. Comput. **37** (1999). https://doi.org/10.1006/jpdc.1996.0107
13. Bueno, J., et al.: Productive programming of GPU clusters with OmpSs. In: IEEE 26th International Parallel and Distributed Processing Symposium (2012). https://doi.org/10.1109/IPDPS.2012.58
14. Charles, P., et al.: X10: an object-oriented approach to non-uniform cluster computing. In: Proceedings of the 20th Annual ACM SIGPLAN Conference on Object-Oriented Programming, Systems, Languages, and Applications, pp. 519–538. OOPSLA 2005. Association for Computing Machinery, New York, NY, USA (2005). https://doi.org/10.1145/1094811.1094852
15. Deelman, E., et al.: Pegasus: a framework for mapping complex scientific workflows onto distributed systems. Sci. Programm. **13**(3), 219–237 (2005). https://doi.org/10.1155/2005/128026
16. Faxén, K.F.: Wool user's guide. Technical report, Swedish Institute of Computer Science (2009)
17. Fürlinger, K., et al.: DASH: distributed data structures and parallel algorithms in a global address space. In: Software for Exascale Computing-SPPEXA 2016–2019, pp. 103–142. Springer International Publishing (2020). https://doi.org/10.1007/978-3-030-47956-5_6
18. Hoque, R., Herault, T., Bosilca, G., Dongarra, J.: Dynamic task discovery in parsec: a data-flow task-based runtime. In: Proceedings of the 8th Workshop on Latest Advances in Scalable Algorithms for Large-Scale Systems, pp. 1–8 (2017). https://doi.org/10.1145/3148226.3148233
19. Kaiser, H., Heller, T., Adelstein-Lelbach, B., Serio, A., Fey, D.: HPX: a task based programming model in a global address space. In: 8th International Conference on Partitioned Global Address Space Programming Models (2014). https://doi.org/10.13140/2.1.2635.5204
20. Klinkenberg, J., Samfass, P., Bader, M., Terboven, C., Müller, M.: CHAMELEON: reactive load balancing for hybrid MPI+OpenMP task-parallel applications. J. Parallel Distrib. Comput. 138 (2019). https://doi.org/10.1016/j.jpdc.2019.12.005
21. Leiserson, C.E.: The Cilk++ concurrency platform. J. Supercomput. **51**(3), 244–257 (2010). https://doi.org/10.1007/s11227-010-0405-3
22. Lordan, F., et al.: ServiceSs: an interoperable programming framework for the cloud. J. Grid Comput. **12**(1), 67–91 (2013). https://doi.org/10.1007/s10723-013-9272-5
23. OpenMP Architecture Review Board: OpenMP 4.0 complete specifications, July 2013
24. Papakonstantinou, N., Zakkak, F.S., Pratikakis, P.: Hierarchical parallel dynamic dependence analysis for recursively task-parallel programs. In: 2016 IEEE International Parallel and Distributed Processing Symposium (IPDPS), pp. 933–942 (2016). https://doi.org/10.1109/IPDPS.2016.53
25. Parallel Programming Lab, Dept of Computer Science, U.o.I.: Charm++ documentation. https://charm.readthedocs.io/en/latest/index.html

26. Perez, J.M., Beltran, V., Labarta, J., Ayguadé, E.: Improving the integration of task nesting and dependencies in OpenMP. In: 2017 IEEE International Parallel and Distributed Processing Symposium (IPDPS), pp. 809–818 (2017). https://doi.org/10.1109/IPDPS.2017.69
27. Pérez, J., Badia, R.M., Labarta, J.: A dependency-aware task-based programming environment for multi-core architectures. In: Proceedings - IEEE International Conference on Cluster Computing, ICCC, pp. 142–151 (2008). https://doi.org/10.1109/CLUSTR.2008.4663765
28. Rotaru, T., Rahn, M., Pfreundt, F.J.: MapReduce in GPI-Space. In: Euro-Par 2013: Parallel Processing Workshops, pp. 43–52. Springer, Berlin, Heidelberg (2014). https://doi.org/10.1007/978-3-642-54420-0_5
29. Sala, K., Macià, S., Beltran, V.: Combining one-sided communications with task-based programming models. In: 2021 IEEE International Conference on Cluster Computing (CLUSTER), pp. 528–541 (2021). https://doi.org/10.1109/Cluster48925.2021.00024
30. Sala, K., Teruel, X., Perez, J.M., Peña, A.J., Beltran, V., Labarta, J.: Integrating blocking and non-blocking MPI primitives with task-based programming models. Parallel Comput. **85**, 153–166 (2019). https://doi.org/10.1016/j.parco.2018.12.008
31. Sergent, M., Goudin, D., Thibault, S., Aumage, O.: Controlling the memory subscription of distributed applications with a task-based runtime system. In: 2016 IEEE International Parallel and Distributed Processing Symposium Workshops (IPDPSW), pp. 318–327 (2016). https://doi.org/10.1109/IPDPSW.2016.105
32. Tillenius, M.: SuperGlue: a shared memory framework using data versioning for dependency-aware task-based parallelization. SIAM J. Scient. Comput. **37**(6) (2015). https://doi.org/10.1137/140989716
33. Tzenakis, G., Papatriantafyllou, A., Kesapides, J., Pratikakis, P., Vandierendonck, H., Nikolopoulos, D.S.: BDDT: Block-level dynamic dependence analysis for deterministic task-based parallelism. In: Proceedings of the 17th ACM SIGPLAN Symposium on Principles and Practice of Parallel Programming. PPoPP 2012, vol. 47, pp. 301–302. Association for Computing Machinery, New York, NY, USA (2012). https://doi.org/10.1145/2145816.2145864
34. Virouleau, P., Broquedis, F., Gautier, T., Rastello, F.: Using data dependencies to improve task-based scheduling strategies on NUMA architectures. In: European Conference on Parallel Processing, pp. 531–544. Springer (2016). https://doi.org/10.1007/978-3-319-43659-3_39
35. Zafari, A., Larsson, E., Tillenius, M.: DuctTeip: an efficient programming model for distributed task-based parallel computing. Parallel Comput. (2019). https://doi.org/10.1016/j.parco.2019.102582

Generating Work Efficient Scan Implementations for GPUs the Functional Way

Federico Pizzuti[1(✉)], Michel Steuwer[1], and Christophe Dubach[2]

[1] University of Edinburgh, Edinburgh, UK
federico.pizzuti@ed.ac.uk
[2] McGill University, Montreal, Canada

Abstract. Scan is a core parallel primitive. High-performance work-efficient implementations are usually hard-coded, leading to performance portability issues. Performance portability is usually achieved using a generative approach, which decomposes the primitive in simpler, composable parts, expressing the implementation space.

Data parallel functional languages excel at expressing programs as composition of simple patterns. Lift, Furthark, Accelerate have successfully applied this technique to patterns such as parallel reduction and tiling. However, work-efficient parallel scan is *still* provided as a hard-coded builtin.

This paper shows how to decompose a classical GPU work-efficient parallel scan in terms of other data-parallel functional primitives. This enables the automatic exploration of the implementation design space, using a set of simple rewrite rules.

As the evaluation shows, this technique outperforms hand-written baselines and Furthark, a state of the art high performance code generator. In particular, this composable approach achieves a speedup of up to 1.5× over hard-coded implementations on two different Nvidia GPUs.

1 Introduction

Parallel hardware offers great opportunities for performance but is difficult to program. Modern parallel architectures are complex and it is hard for developers to fully exploit their potential. A compiler-oriented approach is highly desirable to exploit these systems automatically.

Data Parallel Functional Code Generators have been shown to be a viable solution in tackling this challenge. Projects such as Lift [20], Futhark [8], and Accelerate [3], are capable of taking a high-level program and automatically generating high-performance implementations, targeting a variety of platforms. Functional representations possess a number of desirable characteristics: the lack of side effects allows one to easily reason about parallelism, the emphasis on function composition maps well to the idea of parallel patterns, and finally the rich type systems allow the expressions of powerful invariants, enabling very sophisticated program optimizations.

J. Cano and P. W. Trinder (Eds.): Euro-Par 2022, LNCS 13440, pp. 335–349, 2022.
https://doi.org/10.1007/978-3-031-12597-3_21

The approach is not without downsides. Many algorithms and applications which are relatively straightforward to implement in a traditional low-level language are not as clearly implemented in a functional style. This includes common application domains and algorithms for which a plethora of well-known implementations are readily available. This gap is due both to the highly constrained nature of functional languages and their relative obscurity in the realm of high-performance code generation for parallel hardware.

The most salient example of such a missing algorithm is *scan*, a core data-parallel control pattern [11]. *Scan* is a crucial component to many application domains, such as linear algebra [14] and computer graphics. There is extensive literature both concerning the algorithmic approaches to the parallelization of scan [4] and the concrete techniques to be used on specific platforms [12,19].

However, in most data-parallel functional code generators, *scan* is either only available as a sequential primitive, such as in the case of Lift compiler, or as a parallel primitive with a black-box implementation, such as in the case of Futhark. While the latter approach offers at least some way to express a program using a *parallel scan*, it requires the compiler authors to provide a handwritten implementation, either precluding the usage of the compiler's own powerful optimization techniques or applying them in an ad-hoc way.

This paper addresses these shortcomings by deriving a functional formulation of *parallel scan*, expressed within a data-parallel functional programming language. As the compiler used has OpenCL as its primary target, the implementation used is optimized for a GPU system. The technique used is based on publicly available code by NVidia [7].

The papers then demonstrates how to decompose a *parallel scan* implementation into a number of *reusable* and *composable* rewrite rules, modeling the algorithm's *optimization space*. These rewrites can be used to optimize arbitrary *scan* calls, rewriting them into a parallel implementation. As the rules model an optimization space, the compiler can automatically explore possible variations, leading to significant performance gains across different GPU architectures. - The automatic derivation of a parallel implementation of scan is a thoroughly studied topic. A generic technique for deriving a scan parallelisation is given in [13]. However, such schemes do not generate *work-efficient* implementations. A parallel algorithm is said to be work efficient if its asymptotic complexity is at most a constant factor away from the best known sequential implementation. To the best of the authors' knowledge, the method presented here is the first to yield a *work-efficient* parallel scan from a high-level specification and suitable for a GPU target.

In summary, this paper makes the following contributions

- presents a functional formulation for a GPU *parallel scan*, based on a number of parallelization strategies.
- decomposes the functional formulation into a number of rewrite rules, modeling a parametric space of parallel scan algorithms that can be mechanically explored to derive efficient GPU scan implementations.
- evaluates the overall effectiveness of the approach, by comparing the generated code it with a handwritten reference implementation and the state-of-the-art parallel code generator Futhark, outperforming both by a factor of 1.5×.

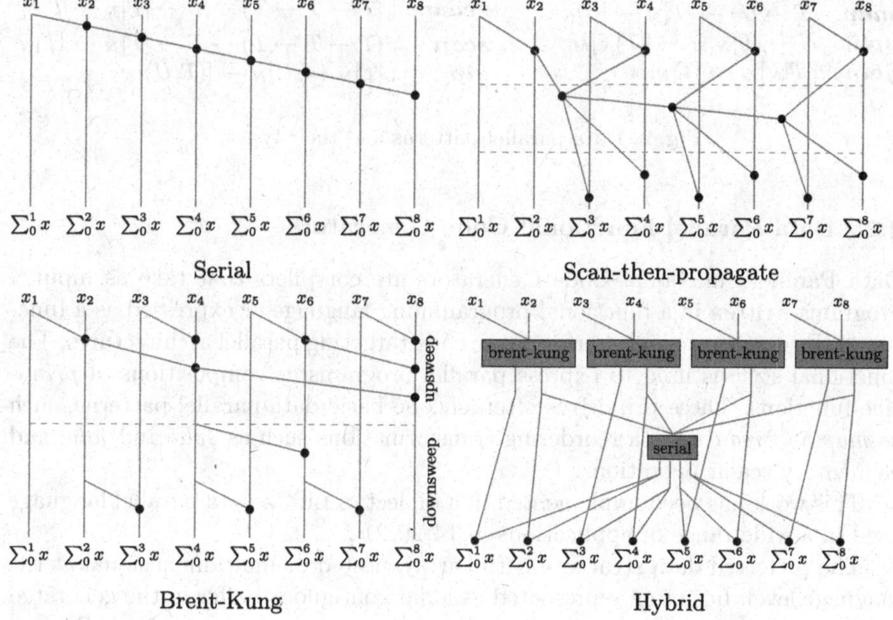

Fig. 1. Scan

2 Background

2.1 Parallel Scan

Scan is one of the fundamental data parallel control patterns [11]. The semantics of scan are illustrated in the following equation:

$$scan(\oplus, x_0, [x_1, \ldots x_n]) = [x_0, x_0 \oplus x_1, \ldots, x_0 \oplus \cdots \oplus x_{n-1}]$$

Given an associative binary operator a starting value and an input sequence, generates a new sequence of n elements in which the i-th item is the result of recursively applying the operator i times.

Being a well-studied operation, there is a wide number of known scan implementations [9], with varying complexity and parallelism. Relevant strategies for this paper include *Serial* scan (Fig. 1a), *Scan-then-propagate* (Fig. 1b) and the *Brent-Kung* scan (Fig. 1c). The latter is both parallel and *work-efficient.*

Additional scan implementations may be derived by combining together different strategies. This is common when implementing parallel scan for devices such as GPUs, and is the approach used by a well-known publicly available NVidia implementation [7]. The algorithm, shown as (Fig. 1d) unfolds on two levels: an outer scan following the scan-then-propagate strategy, and an inner scan implementation parallelized using the *Brent-Kung* approach.

$$\begin{aligned}
&\textit{map} : (T \to U) \to [T]_N \to [U]_N && \textit{reduce} : (T \to T \to T) \to T \to [T]_N \to T \\
&\textit{split} : N \to [T]_{N \cdot M} \to [[T]_N]_M && \textit{scan} : (T \to T \to T) \to T \to [T]_N \to [T]_N \\
&\textit{join} : [[T]_N]_M \to [T]_{N \cdot M} && \textit{zip} : [T]_N \to [U]_N \to [(T, U)]_N
\end{aligned}$$

Fig. 2. Data parallel patterns and their types.

2.2 Data Parallel Functional Code Generators

Data Parallel Functional Code Generators are compilers that take as input a programs written in a functional programming language or expressed as a functional IR to generate high-performance code targeting parallel architectures. The functional style is used to express parallel programs as compositions of *primitive* functions. These primitives often encode basic data-parallel patterns, such as *map* and *reduce*, data reordering transformations such as *split* and *join*, and elementary scalar operations.

This work has been implemented in a dialect of Lift, a data parallel language used in a wide range of applications [6,14,20,21].

The preferred data structure is the array, nested or multidimensional at the language level, but often represented as a flat contiguous buffer in the generated code. As the language is purely functional, arrays are never mutated. Rather, patterns always produce new arrays. It is important to note that most of these transformations are lazy whenever possible, avoiding spurious copies.

Data parallel functional languages tend to have rich type systems. This enables the compiler to statically check invariants that otherwise either go unchecked, or are implemented in terms of dynamic checks at run-time. For example, the length of each arrays is tracked at the type level as a symbolic algebraic expression. In this paper, every array has it's length represented as a symbolic formula. Examples of this can be seen in the patterns described in Fig. 2.

3 Functional Formulation of Work Efficient Parallel Scan

This section presents a work-efficient GPU implementation of parallel scan expressed in the Lift dialect mentioned in the previous section. The code is an adaptation of an handwritten NVidia implementation, whose imperative pseudocode is also shown. Algorithmically, this is a case of hybrid scan, as shown in Fig. 1d, and can be analyzed in terms of the *outer* and *inner* scans.

3.1 Outer Scan

Listing 1 shows the functional formulation of the outer scan side-by-side with the equivalent imperative pseudo-code. The algorithm unfolds in three sections: the block-scan phase, the global scan phase, and then the aggregation phase.

In the block scan phase, the data input is split in blocks of size `BLK`, and each `block_scan` is computed in parallel. `unzip` is then used to separate an

```
parallel for i=0 to BLK do
 block_scan(data[i*N/BLK], &sums[i])
 sequential_scan(sums, global_scan)
 parallel for b=0 to BLK do
 parallel for i=0 to N/BLK do
  data[b*BLK+i] = data[b*BLK+i] + global_scan[b]
```

```
let (data',sums) = data|> split(BLK)|> map(block_scan)|> unzip
let global_scan = sums|> scanSeq(+)
 zip(data', global_scan)|> map(
   (xs, b) => xs|> map(x =>x+b)
 )|> join
```

Listing 1: Imperative pseudo-code and functional expression for the outer scan.

array of `[(partial_scan, sum)]` pairs into a pair of `([partial_scan],[sum])` arrays. This corresponds to the multiple output parameters in the imperative pseudo-code. `global_scan` is implemented sequentially, by calling the `scanSeq` primitive.

Finally, we reach at the aggregation step. The `zip` primitive associates each block's partial scan with the corresponding overall `global_scan`. The outer `map` call operates over these `(block, value)` pairs, adding `value` to every element of `block`. The blocks are concatenated by using `join`, which flattens the array.

It must be remarked that the functional version diverges somewhat from the imperative version, which freely updates arrays in-place, something which is difficult to express in a language that forbids. This has forced the introduction of some intermediate variables, such as `data'` in Listing 1.

3.2 Inner Scan

The inner `block_scan` is more complex to express faithfully in a functional style. Just as in the case of the outer algorithm, we will have to give up on an in-place formulation. However, the inner algorithm performs in-place writes within sequential for loops, which prevents the introduction of intermediate variables.

Listing 2 demonstrates how to remedy the issue in the *upsweep* phase. Notice that the sequential iterations are in fact not dependent on the size of the input but rather the fixed parameter `BLK`: implying the loop can be unrolled. Afterward, we can proceed by introducing the intermediate variables in place of every mutation step. This implies that the *upsweep* phase therefore no longer updates the tree in place. Rather it constructs the tree level by level, storing each successive layer in a different variable.

```
for d=0 to log2(n-1) do
 parallel for k=0 to n-1 by 2^(d+1) do
  x[k+2d] = x[k+2d-1]+x[j+2d]
```

```
// d = 0...
let up_0 = input |> split(2) |> map(+) |> join
// d = 1...
let up_1 = up_0 |> split(2) |> map(+) |> join
//....
let up_n = up_n-1 |> split(2) |> map(+) |> join
```

Listing 2: Imperative pseudo-code and functional expression of *upsweep* phase

With this knowledge, we notice that each iteration produces the next tree layer by summing together adjacent pairs of the previous tree layer, expressed functionally by chaining together the primitives `split(2)|> map(+)|> join`.

Likewise, Listing 3 shows how the *downsweep* phase is unrolled to combine the generated layers in Last-In-First-Out order. We begin the recursion with an array containing a single element, 0. This corresponds to the line `x[n-1]=0` in the imperative code. The layers are then combined, via executing `zip(prev_layer, layer |> split(2))|> map(scan(+, 0))|> join`, which is in fact equivalent to the seemingly-unrelated loop body in the imperative pseudo-code: given two layers, we match together one element of the previous (smaller) layer with two elements of the successive, larger layer, with the pseudo-code lines 10–12 being an in-lined sequential scan. The importance of generalizing this custom-looking code into a *scan* call is shown in Sect. 4.2. Finally, the functional version must return the last tree layer and the block sum value, as the tuple `(down_0, up_n[0])`.

We have now derived a working functional formulation of the GPU work efficient scan, and have encountered some limitations of the functional approach, such as introducing intermediate variables have been introduced for in-place updates – although this limitation can be overcome in certain cases, such as when the intermediate layers are used only once (such as the case for `up_n` and `down_n`. As we will see in the Sect. 6, even when fusion is not possible, these intermediates do not significantly affect the performance of the generated code.

4 Modeling the Optimization Space with Rewrite Rules

The aim of this section is to derive an optimization process capable of mapping uses of the *scan* pattern to work-efficient parallel implementations. We will do so by generalizing the functional formulation presented in Sect. 4.

```
sum = x[n-1]
x[n-1] = 0
for d = log2(n-1) down to 0 do
 parallel for k = 0 to n-1 by 2^(d+1) do
  t = x[k + 2d - 1];
  [k + 2d - 1] = x[k + 2d]
  x[k + 2d] = t + x[k + 2d]
```

```
let down_n = [0]
let down_n-1 =
 zip(down_n, up_n |> split(2)) |>
 map(scanSeq(+)) |> join
....
let down_0 =
  zip(input, up_0 |> split(2)) |>
  map(scanSeq(+)) |> join
(down_0, up_n[0])
```

Listing 3: Imperative pseudo-code and matching functional expression of *down-sweep* phase.

A straightforward way to provide this optimization may be to substitute the handwritten functional implementation for suitable uses of *scan*, or expose it as a standard library function. However, this solutions have several limitations.

Firstly, the handwritten functional implementation makes use of two distinct and orthogonal parallelization strategies: the *scan-then-reduce* and *brent-kung.* It is reasonable to assume that in certain circumstances the compiler should be able to apply the two optimizations independently. For instance, for sufficiently small inputs just parallelizing the outer scan may have acceptable performance.

Moreover, in the course of implementing the functional version, a number of implementation details had to be decided, such as fixing the block size and the depth of the parallel scan tree, which materializes in the source code by influencing the amount of unrolled operations. These choices may not be optimal for many uses of the *scan* primitive. Indeed, in Sect. 6 we will show how significant performance gains can be obtained by supporting a degree of variation in the algorithm used to generate optimized parallel scans.

The goal, therefore, is not just to express an optimization, but rather to *model an optimization space.* We achieve this by using a system of parametric rewrite rules, which the compiler can then use to generate the optimized code, be it on the basis of a set of heuristics, a user-defined specification, or an extensive process of automatic exploration.

scan-then-reduce(BS)

```
match scan(f,zero,input)
if input.size % BS == 0 ↦
 let chunks = split(input, BS) |>
  map(chunk => scan(f,zero,chunk))
 let sums = chunks |> map(reduce(f, zero))
 let scans = scan(f,zero, sums)
 zip(chunks, scans) |> map(
  (chunk, x) => chunk |> map(y => f(x,y)))
```

Listing 4: The *scan-then-reduce* rule parallelizes an abstract scan call.

4.1 Optimization via Rewrite Rules

Functional representations simplify the expression of program transformations using rewrite rules. A rewrite rule is a transformation that matches specified program patterns, rewriting them in accordance with a different pattern. This paper uses Elevate [5], a DSL for expressing rewrite rules in a compositional style. Primitive rules are specified via matching over program fragments, and then larger rules – known as *strategies* – are constructed by composing existing rules using a generic family of *combinator* functions.

In the syntax of the rewrite rules shown here, highlighted code refers to program fragments, while non-highlighted code is the rewrite rule logic – tasked with finding and replacing the such fragments. Rule logic can query type information, such as inspecting the known length of an array, be parameterized by numerical values, and perform simple numerical and logical computation.

Optimizations that are normally implemented ad-hoc within the compiler can therefore be expressed in this generic system. The rest of this section covers in detail the transformations generating *work-efficient parallel scan* implementation from an abstract high-level description.

4.2 Algorithmic Optimization

Scan-then-Reduce. The first rule applied is *scan-then-reduce* (Listing 4). It matches a call to an abstract scan *scan(f,zero,input)*, replacing it with a parallelized version that uses the *scan-then-propagate* algorithm. The parameter BS expresses the block size for the parallel sub-scans. The rule requires the scan's input array to be divisible by BS. This is a necessary correctness check.

Brent-Kung. As seen in Sect. 3.2, the work-efficient block-level scan is an instance of *Brent-Kung* scan, which we also seek to express as a rewrite rule. As we have seen before, a *Brent-Kung* parallel scan recursively computes (*upsweep* phase) or consumes (*downsweep* phase) layers of a tree. In the functional formulation, this iteration is necessarily unrolled, as expressing it as a loop requires mutating the array that stores the tree.

brent-kung-step(BF)

```
match  scan(f,zero,input)
if input.size % BF == 0 ↦
// Upsweep
  let partials = input |> split(BF) |>
   map(chunk => reduce(f, zero, chunk))
// Recursion point
  let rest = scan(f, zero, partials)
// Downsweep
  zip(rest, partials |> split(BF)) |>
   map((r, ps) => scan(f, r ps)) |> join
```

Listing 5: Each application of the rule adds one layer to the parallelization tree.

brent-kung(BF)

```
match  scan(f,zero,input)
if (log(BF, input.size) is whole) ↦
 num_iterations := log(BF, input.size)
 iterate(num_iterations)(
  first(scan)(brent-kung-step(BF))
 ) @  scan(f,zero,input)
```

Listing 6: The rule rewrites an abstract scan into a *brent-kung* parallel scan

This expansion is expressed with recursive rewrite rules. Listing 5 shows the rule for the recursive step. The rule is parameterized by the tree branch factor BF. The rule's body has three parts: first and last are the *upsweep* and *downsweep* phases. In between, the rule inserts an abstract scan call, acting as the recursion point. Based on *brent-kung-step* we can build the full *brent-kung* rule (Listing 6), which expresses the iterative behavior. It inspects the size of the input array in the matched *scan* call to compute the depth of the parallel tree, determining the number of recursive applications of *brent-kung-step*.

The rule uses *combinators*: rules parametrized by other rules. The first combinator is `first(scan)(brent-kung-step(BF))`. It generates a rewrite rule that finds the first instance of `scan`, and rewrites it using `brent-kung-step(BF)`. The `iterate(num_iterations)` combinator then applies this repeatedly. This composition of combinators results in an iterative expansion of the *scan* supplied, each step adding one layer of *upsweep* before the scan and one layer of *downsweep* after the matched *scan* call, while simultaneously shrinking the leftover scan input by a factor of 2.

parallel-scan(BS, BF)

```
match scan(f,zero,input)
 if BS % BF == 0
 if input.size % BS == 0 ↦
    (scan-then-reduce(BS);
    first(scan)(brent-kung(BF))
    ) @  scan(f,zero,input)
```

Listing 7: The *parallel-scan* rule combines parallelization strategies into the complete GPU scan.

Parallel-Scan. We can now express the algorithm for the full GPU parallel scan by combining *scan-then-propagate* and *brent-kung* into a single rule, whose definition is shown in Listing 7. The rule first applies the *scan-then-propagate*, followed by the *brent-kung* rule on the first instance of *scan* encountered.

5 Optimization Space Exploration

5.1 Expressing Scan Variants

As we have seen in the previous section, the *brent-kung* rewrite rule works by recursively expanding a call to scan into a parallel tree computation. Given block size BS and tree branching factor BF, the process is iterated $log_F(BS)$. As a variation, it is possible to terminate this expansion earlier, by parametrizing the *brent-kung* rule by TD, the maximum depth of tree expansion.

The overall optimization from *scan* to *parallel scan* now admits three possible parameters: the tree growth factor BF, the block size BS (obtained from the input parameter type), and the parallelization tree depth TD. These parameters delineate a space of possible optimizations. Given a value for the block size BS, the possible parallel tree depth ranges from $TD = 0$, which generates a fully sequential scan, to $D = log_{BF}(BS)$, yielding the canonical *Brent-Kung scan*. Intermediate values express hybrid versions, such as that shown in Listing 8.

To see why such intermediate optimization points may be of interest, consider that on a GPU target each block maps to an OpenCL work-group. As the value of successive layers depends on that of preceding layers, these must be computed sequentially, introducing a synchronization point. Shrinking the parallel tree depth reduces the amount of synchronization necessary, but also trades away parallel computation for sequential work, growing exponentially as TD decreases by a factor of BF. For small reductions in TD this may be a positive trade-off.

5.2 Exploring Scan Variants

Finding the optimal (BF,BS,TD) triple is not a straightforward task: a sound choice of parameters requires knowledge of the target platform. For example,

```
void block_sum(float output[S], float input[S])
local float up1[8], up2[4], dn2[4], dn1[8];
 parallel for block=0 to S/16
  float* in = &input[16*block];
  float* out = &output[16*block];
  parallel for i=0 to 8
   up1[k] = in[2*i]+in[2*i+1];
  parallel for i=0 to 4
   up2[k] = up1[2*i]+up1[2*i+1];
  dn2[0] = 0;
  for i=1 to 4
   dn2[i] = dn2[i-1]+up2[i];
  parallel for k=0 to 4
   dn1[2*i]=dn2[i]; dn1[2*i+1]=dn2[i]+up1[2*i];
  parallel for k=0 to 8
   out[2*i]=dn1[i]; out[2*i+1]=dn1[i]+in[2*i];
```

Listing 8: Block sum with BF=2, BS=16, TD=2.

when targeting GPUs, the number of local thread used equals BF^{TD}. This value should be larger then the GPU's warp size to avoid needless stalls, but not too large, to minimize synchronization.

The compiler then generates and tests the variations, finding the best triple for the target architecture. In this paper, the search space is sufficiently small that it is practical to exhaustively explore it. Should the search space become large, one can alternatively use a more sophisticated search strategy, such as using an generic autotuner like OpenTuner.

6 Evaluation

This section presents the paper's experimental results. All measurements are performed using the compiler's OpenCL CUDA back-end, targeting version 1.2 of the standard, driver version 10.2.185 and are run on NVidia GeForce GTX 1070 and NVidia A100 GPUs. All times refer to GPU computation time only. The *scans* compute the prefix sum of 32-bit floating-point values.

6.1 Performance of Scan Block Variants

Sect. 5.1 parametrized the *work-efficient parallel scan* generation by the triple of Branching Factor (BF), Block Size (BS) and Tree Depth (TD). This section presents the details of exploring this delimited space of possible variants.

We begin by fixing the value of $BF = 2$, which implies that the parallel iteration tree is a binary tree. For ease of presentation, we introduce the new parameter $SE \in [0, BS]$, indicating the number of Sequentially Scanned Elements.

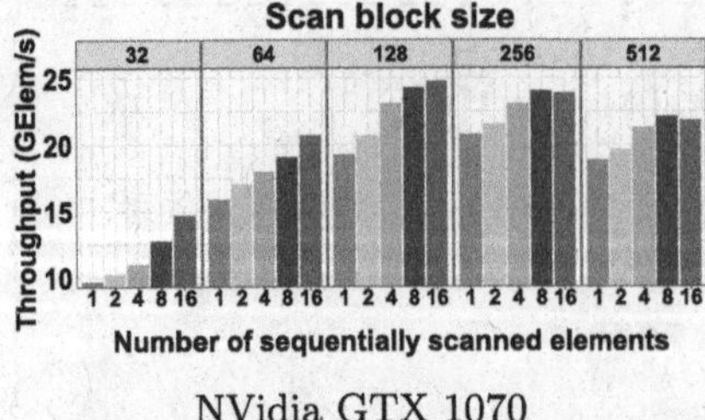

NVidia GTX 1070

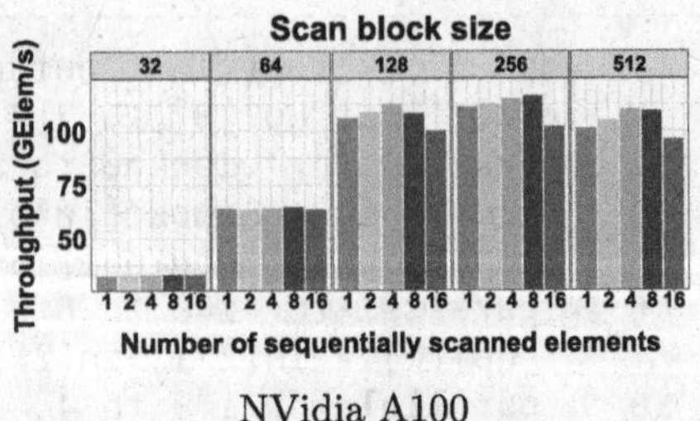

NVidia A100

Fig. 3. Throughput of automatically explored variations of *block_scan*. Each version is parameterized by the scan block size (top) and by the number of elements that are sequentially scanned (bottom).

We wish $SE = 0$ to yield a fully parallel scan, while $SE = BS$ corresponds to an entirely sequential one. This desired behavior corresponds to constraining $TD = log_2(BS - SE)$. The range of sensible values for BS is shaped by the GPU's architecture, as it directly correlates to the amount of local memory required. Here, it ranges from 32 to 512, doubling each step. Fixing BS also allows determining the range of valid SE values: 1 to 16, also doubling each time.

Figure 3 shows the results of exhaustively exploring the space delimited by these constraints. The source program is a prefix sum computation over an array of 25.6 million 32-bit floating-point elements. Executing the whole exploration takes approximately 40 min on the author's commodity hardware platform.

For both GPUs, the best versions have $SE > 4$. This is likely because higher values of SE imply a reduction in synchronization points, as these are required between parallel iterations. The trade-off is only beneficial with larger block sizes, as a small block with positive SE will lead to many of the warp's threads being idle. While the optimal values for SE and BS vary across GPU architectures, our approach can easily adapt to each platform's characteristics.

6.2 End-to-End Comparison

The quality of our approach is evaluated by measuring the end-to-end performance of the generated code. This includes the block-scan as well as the subsequent propagation phases. The comparison covers both the baseline parallel scan shown in Sect. 4 and the result of variant exploration in Sect. 5 with two reference implementation. The first is a handwritten version provided by NVidia [7], and the second is the code produced by the Futhark compiler [8], a state-of-the-art data-parallel functional generator.

The results are shown in Fig. 4. Across both GPUs, the optimized version significantly outperforms both reference implementations. This is in contrast to Futhark, whose performance varies significantly across architectures. By expressing the optimization process via rewrite rules, our compiler can reliably generate high-performance code.

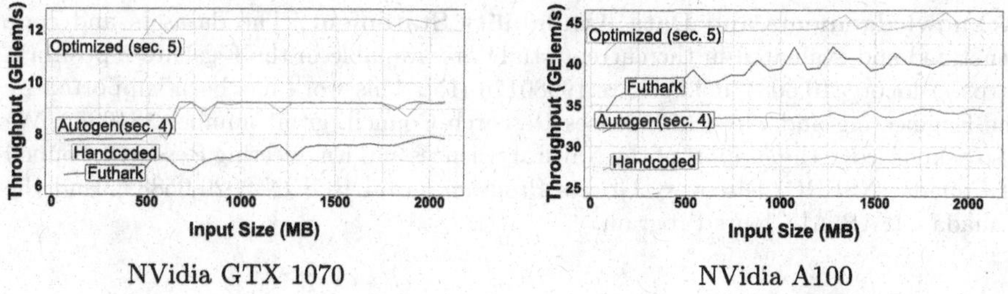

Fig. 4. End-to-end throughput of scan implementations. **Autogen** refers the code generation shown in Sect. 4. **Optimized** refers to the best version obtained in Sect. 5. **Handcoded** is the NVidia optimized version shown in [7], and **Futhark** is the version generated by the Futhark compiler [8].

7 Related Work

Data Parallel Functional Code Generators. A recent trend in the design of high-performance code generators that use functional languages as inputs or internal representations. These include Lift [20,21], Futhark [8], Single-assignment C [18] and Accelerate [3]. These compilers leverage the properties of a functional style to generate high-performance code for GPUs and other accelerators.

Rewrite Rules & Optimization Spaces. The use of rewrite rules to express optimizations is well attested in the literature. We expressed our rewrite rules via the Elevate [5], which has also been similarly used for image processing applications [10]. The Spiral [16] compiler spearheaded using rewrite rules to optimize Digital Signal Processing applications in the SPL [22] language.

Petabricks [1] has been used to explore the design space of optimization for sorting algorithms. The use of an auxiliary language to model optimizations has similarities in Halide [17] schedules.

Parallel Scan. There is a wide literature concerning the use of scan in parallel programs, starting from the seminal work of Blelloch [2]. Much work has gone into producing parallel implementation for the GPUs, from early CUDA implementations [7] to libraries such as CUDPP [19] and CUB [12]. Parallel scan is also a topic of relevance in the functional programming community. In particular [4,13], which show algorithms to derive parallel scan implementations.

8 Conclusion

This paper presented a functional formulation of work-efficient parallel scan. We have decomposed it in a series of rewrite rules, modeling an optimization space. Exploring this space yields efficient implementations across GPUs from the same high-level source, consistently outperforming both an hand-written implementation and state of the art code generator, with up to 1.5x improvement.

Acknowledgements and Data Availability Statement. The datasets and code generated and evaluated in the current study are available in the Figshare repository: https://doi.org/10.6084/m9.figshare.19980176 [15]. This work has been supported by the Engineering and Physical Sciences Research Council, grant number 1819353. We also acknowledge the support of the Natural Sciences and Engineering Research Council of Canada (NSERC) Discovery Grants Program [grant RGPIN-2020-05889], and the Canada CIFAR AI Chairs Program.

References

1. Ansel, J., et al.: Petabricks: a language and compiler for algorithmic choice. ACM SIGPLAN Notices **44**(6), 38–49 (2009). https://doi.org/10.1145/1542476.1542481
2. Blelloch, G.E.: Scans as primitive parallel operations. IEEE Trans. Comput. **38**(11), 1526–1538 (1989). https://doi.org/10.1109/12.42122
3. Chakravarty, M.M.T., Keller, G., Lee, S., McDonell, T.L., Grover, V.: Accelerating Haskell array codes with multicore GPUs. In: POPL-DAMP (2011). https://doi.org/10.1145/1926354.1926358
4. Elliott, C.: Generic functional parallel algorithms: Scan and FFT. In: Proceedings of the ACM on Programming Languages, vol. 1, no. ICFP, pp. 1–25 (2017). https://doi.org/10.1145/3110251
5. Hagedorn, B., Lenfers, J., Koehler, T., Gorlatch, S., Steuwer, M.: A language for describing optimization strategies. arXiv preprint arXiv:2002.02268 (2020). https://doi.org/10.48550/arXiv.2002.02268
6. Hagedorn, B., Stoltzfus, L., Steuwer, M., Gorlatch, S., Dubach, C.: High performance stencil code generation with lift. In: CGO (2018). https://doi.org/10.48550/arXiv.2002.02268
7. Harris, M., Sengupta, S., Owens, J.D.: Parallel prefix sum (SCAN) with CUDA. GPU Gems **3**(39), 851–876 (2007)
8. Henriksen, T., Serup, N.G.W., Elsman, M., Henglein, F., Oancea, C.E.: Futhark: purely functional GPU-programming with nested parallelism and in-place array updates. In: PLDI (2017). https://doi.org/10.1145/3062341.3062354
9. Hinze, R.: An algebra of scans. In: International Conference on Mathematics of Program Construction, pp. 186–210 (2004). https://doi.org/10.1007/978-3-540-27764-4_11
10. Koehler, T., Steuwer, M.: Towards a domain-extensible compiler: optimizing an image processing pipeline on mobile CPUs. In: CGO (2021)
11. McCool, M., Reinders, J., Robison, A.: Structured Parallel Programming: Patterns for Efficient Computation. Elsevier, Amsterdam (2012). https://doi.org/10.1145/2382756.2382773
12. Merrill, D., Garland, M.: Single-pass parallel prefix scan with decoupled look-back. Technical report NVR-2016-002, NVIDIA (2016)
13. Morita, K., Morihata, A., Matsuzaki, K., Hu, Z., Takeichi, M.: Automatic inversion generates divide-and-conquer parallel programs. In: PLDI (2007). https://doi.org/10.1145/1273442.1250752
14. Pizzuti, F., Steuwer, M., Dubach, C.: Generating fast sparse matrix vector multiplication from a high level generic functional IR. In: CC (2020). https://doi.org/10.1145/3377555.3377896

15. Pizzuti, F., Steuwer, M., Dubach, C.: Artifact and instruction for replication of experiments in the Europar '22 paper titled: "generating work efficient scan implementations for GPUs the functional way" (2022). https://doi.org/10.6084/m9.figshare.19980176
16. Puschel, M., et al.: Spiral: code generation for DSP transforms. Proc. IEEE (2005). https://doi.org/10.1109/JPROC.2004.840306
17. Ragan-Kelley, J., Barnes, C., Adams, A., Paris, S., Durand, F., Amarasinghe, S.P.: Halide: a language and compiler for optimizing parallelism, locality, and recomputation in image processing pipelines. In: PLDI (2013). https://doi.org/10.1145/2499370.2462176
18. Scholz, S.: Single assignment C: efficient support for high-level array operations in a functional setting. J. Funct. Program. (2003). https://doi.org/10.1017/S0956796802004458
19. Sengupta, S., Harris, M., Garland, M., et al.: Efficient parallel scan algorithms for gpus. Technical report NVR-2008-003, NVIDIA, Santa Clara, CA, **1**(1), 1–17 (2008)
20. Steuwer, M., Fensch, C., Lindley, S., Dubach, C.: Generating performance portable code using rewrite rules: from high-level functional expressions to high-performance OpenCL code. In: Fisher, K., Reppy, J.H. (eds.) ICFP (2015). https://doi.org/10.1145/2784731.2784754
21. Steuwer, M., Remmelg, T., Dubach, C.: Lift: a functional data-parallel IR for high-performance GPU code generation. In: CGO (2017)
22. Xiong, J., Johnson, J., Johnson, R., Padua, D.: SPL: a language and compiler for DSP algorithms. ACM SIGPLAN Not. **36**(5), 298–308 (2001). https://doi.org/10.1145/378795.378860

Automatic Parallelization of Python Programs for Distributed Heterogeneous Computing

Jun Shirako[1(✉)], Akihiro Hayashi[1], Sri Raj Paul[2], Alexey Tumanov[1], and Vivek Sarkar[1]

[1] Georgia Institute of Technology, Atlanta, GA 30332, USA
{shirako,ahayashi,atumanov3,vsarkar}@gatech.edu
[2] Intel Corporation, Austin, TX 78746, USA
sriraj.paul@intel.com

Abstract. This paper introduces a new approach to automatic ahead-of-time (AOT) parallelization and optimization of sequential Python programs for execution on distributed heterogeneous platforms. Our approach enables AOT source-to-source transformation of Python programs, driven by the inclusion of type hints for function parameters and return values. These hints can be supplied by the programmer or obtained by dynamic profiler tools; multi-version code generation guarantees the correctness of our AOT transformation in all cases.

Our compilation framework performs automatic parallelization and sophisticated high-level code optimizations for the target distributed heterogeneous hardware platform. It introduces novel extensions to the polyhedral compilation framework that unify user-written loops and implicit loops present in matrix/tensor operators, as well as automated selection of CPU vs. GPU code variants. Finally, output parallelized code generated by our approach is deployed using the Ray runtime for scheduling distributed tasks across multiple heterogeneous nodes in a cluster, thereby enabling both intra-node and inter-node parallelism.

Our empirical evaluation shows significant performance improvements relative to sequential Python in both single-node and multi-node experiments, with a performance improvement of over 20,000× when using 24 nodes and 144 GPUs in the OLCF Summit supercomputer for the Space-Time Adaptive Processing (STAP) radar application.

Keywords: Parallelizing compilers · Python language · Parallel computing · Heterogeneous computing · Distributed computing

1 Introduction

Multiple simultaneous disruptions are currently under way in both hardware and software, as we consider the implications for future parallel systems. In hardware, "extreme heterogeneity" has become critical to sustaining cost and performance

J. Cano and P. W. Trinder (Eds.): Euro-Par 2022, LNCS 13440, pp. 350–366, 2022.
https://doi.org/10.1007/978-3-031-12597-3_22

improvements with the end of Moore's Law, but poses significant productivity challenges for developers. In software, the rise of large-scale data science and AI applications is being driven by domain scientists from diverse backgrounds who demand the programmability that they have come to expect from high-level languages like Python. While this paper focuses on Python as an exemplar of modern high-productivity programming, the approach in this paper is equally applicable to other high-productivity languages such as Julia [3].

A key challenge facing domain scientists is determining how to enable their Python-based applications to use the parallelism inherent in both distributed and heterogeneous computing. A typical workflow for domain scientists is to experiment with new algorithms by starting with smaller datasets and then moving on to larger datasets. A tipping point is reached when there is a need to use intra-node parallelism with multiple cores and accelerators such as GPUs, and another tipping point is reached when the dataset size becomes too large to be processed within a single node.

One approach to dealing with these tipping points is to rely on experienced programmers with a deep "ninja level" expertise in computer architecture and code optimization for accelerators and inter-node communication who use low-level programming languages such as C/C++. However, this approach is a non-starter for many domain scientists due to the complexity and skills required. For example, even though Python bindings for MPI [6] have been available for many years, there has been very little adoption of these bindings by domain scientists. An alternate approach is to augment a high-productivity language with native libraries that include high-performance implementations of commonly used functions, e.g., functions in the NumPy [14] and SciPy [20] libraries for Python. However, fixed library interfaces and implementations do not address the needs of new applications and algorithms. Yet another approach is to develop and use Domain Specific Languages (DSLs); this approach has recently begun showing promise for certain target domains, e.g., PyTorch and TensorFlow for machine learning, Halide for image processing computations, and TACO for tensor kernels. However, the deliberate lack of generality in DSLs poses significant challenges in requiring domain scientists to learn multiple DSLs and to integrate DSL kernels into their overall programming workflow, while also addressing corner cases that may not be supported by any DSLs.

In this paper, we make the case for new advances to enable productivity and programmability of future HPC platforms for domain scientists. The goal of our system, named `AutoMPHC`, is Automation of Massively Parallel and Heterogeneous Computing. It aims to deliver the benefits of distributed heterogeneous hardware platforms to domain scientists without requiring them to undergo any new training. As a first step towards this goal, this paper introduces a novel approach to automatic ahead-of-time (AOT) parallelization and optimization of sequential Python programs for execution on distributed heterogeneous platforms, which supports program multi-versioning for specializing code generation to different input data types and different target processors. The optimized code

```
def kernel(self, float_n: float, data: list, corr: list, mean: list, stddev: list):
    ...
    for i in range(0, self.M-1):
        corr[i][i] = 1.0
        for j in range(i+1, self.M):
            corr[i][j] = 0.0
            for k in range(0, self.N):
                corr[i][j] += (data[k][i] * data[k][j])
            corr[j][i] = corr[i][j]
    corr[self.M-1][self.M-1] = 1.0
```

Fig. 1. PolyBench-Python `correlation`: List version (default)

```
1  from numpy.core.multiarray import ndarray
2  ...
3  def kernel(self, float_n: float, data: ndarray, corr: ndarray, mean: ndarray, stddev: ndarray):
4      ...
5      corr[np.diag_indices(corr.shape[0])] = 1.0
6      for i in range(0, self.M - 1):
7          corr[i,i+1:self.M] = (data[0:self.N,i] * data[0:self.N,i+1:self.M].T).sum(axis=1)
8      tril_indices = np.tril_indices( n=self.M, m=self.M, k=-1 )
9      corr[tril_indices] = corr[triu_indices]
10     corr[self.M - 1, self.M - 1] = 1.0
```

Fig. 2. PolyBench-Python `correlation`: NumPy version

Table 1. Execution time of `correlation` benchmark (dataset = large on Titan Xp workstation equipped with Intel i5-7600 4-core CPU and NVIDIA Pascal GPU)

List version	NumPy version	`AutoMPHC` (input: List)	`AutoMPHC` (input: NumPy)
152.5 [sec]	2.212 [sec]	0.1760 [sec]	0.07163 [sec]

is deployed using the Python-based Ray runtime [10] for scheduling distributed tasks across multiple heterogeneous nodes in a cluster.

As a simple illustration of our approach, consider two versions of the Poly-Bench [1] `correlation` benchmark shown in Figs. 1 and 2. The first case represents a list-based pattern implemented using three explicit Python loops that access elements of lists (as surrogates for arrays), which might have been written by a domain scientist familiar with classical books on algorithms such as [16]. The second case represents a NumPy-based pattern with one explicit loop and a two-dimensional array statement in line 7 of Fig. 2, which might have been written by a domain scientist familiar with matrix operations. A unique feature of our approach is the ability to support both explicit Python loops and implicit loops from NumPy operators and library calls in a unified optimization framework. The performance results for this example in Table 1 show that the NumPy-based version of the `correlation` benchmark performs better than the list version, while our approach (which can be applied to either style of input) performs significantly better than both. Additional performance results are discussed in Sect. 5.

In summary, this paper makes the following contributions:

- A novel approach to automatic ahead-of-time (AOT) parallelization and optimization of sequential Python programs for execution on distributed heterogeneous platforms. Our approach is driven by the inclusion of type hints for function parameters and return values, which can be supplied by the programmer or obtained by dynamic profiler tools; multi-version code generation guarantees the correctness of our AOT transformation in all cases.
- Automatic parallelization and high-level code optimizations for the target distributed heterogeneous hardware platform, based on novel extensions to the polyhedral framework that unify user-written loops and implicit loops present in matrix/tensor operators, as well as automated selection of CPU vs. GPU code variants.
- Automatic code generation for targeting the Ray runtime to schedule distributed tasks across multiple heterogeneous nodes in a cluster.
- An empirical evaluation of 15 Python-based benchmarks from the PolyBench suite on a standard GPU-equipped workstation, and multi-node evaluation of the Space-Time Adaptive Processing (STAP) radar application in Python. Both evaluations show significant performance improvements due to the use of `AutoMPHC`. In the case of STAP, the performance improvement relative to the original Python code was over 20,000× when using 24 nodes and 144 GPUs (6 GPUs/node) in the OLCF Summit supercomputer.

2 Background

2.1 Intrepydd Compiler

The Intrepydd programming language [30] introduced a subset of Python that is amenable to ahead-of-time (AOT) compilation into C++. It is intended for writing kernel functions rather than complete or main programs. The C++ code generated from Intrepydd kernels can be imported into a Python application or a C++ application.

A key constraint in the Intrepydd subset of Python is the requirement that Intrepydd function definitions include type annotations for parameters and return values. Given these type annotations, the Intrepydd compiler statically infers the types of local variables and expressions. The Intrepydd tool chain includes a library knowledge base, which specifies type rules for a wide range of standard library functions used by Python programs. As discussed in the following sections, the `AutoMPHC` system extends the Intrepydd tool chain to serve as a Python-to-Python optimization and parallelization system; there is no C++ code generated by the current version of `AutoMPHC`.

It is important to note that Intrepydd also includes extensions to standard Python to enable C++ code generation. These extensions include statements with explicit parallelism (e.g., `pfor` for parallel loops) and special library functions. In contrast, `AutoMPHC` does not rely on any of these extensions. All input code to `AutoMPHC` and all output code generated by `AutoMPHC` can be executed on standard Python implementations.

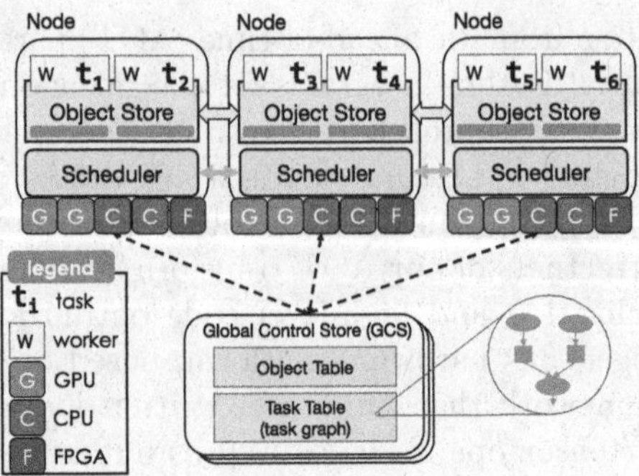

Fig. 3. `AutoMPHC` distributed runtime architecture.

2.2 Ray Runtime

We use Ray [10] as the base distributed runtime framework. Ray features a number of properties beneficial for `AutoMPHC`. First, the ability to simultaneously support both *stateless* and *stateful* computation—one of its key research contributions useful for a heterogeneous mix of CPU and GPU compute. Stateless computation, in the form of side-effect free tasks, is best suited for processing large data objects or partitions on numerous CPU resources. Stateful computation is beneficial for GPU tasks. We create tasks for this distributed runtime by *automatically* compiling selected regions of code into Ray tasks. Each Ray task then can be spawned asynchronously. A full directed acyclic graph (DAG) of such task instantiations is dynamically constructed and submitted for execution without waiting for intermediate computation results. It enables `AutoMPHC` to (a) hide the latency of task instantiation and propagation to workers for execution, (b) extract pipeline parallelism, and, (c) extract parallelism from the partial order of the dynamically constructed directed acyclic task graph. As Ray tasks are instantiated, they return immediately with a future-like construct, called an ObjectID—an object handle that refers to a globally addressable object. The object is eventually fulfilled and can be extracted with a blocking `ray.get(object_id)` API. We note that the distributed object store (Fig. 3) used for the lifecycle of these objects is immutable—a property that elides the need for expensive consistency protocols, state coherence protocols, and other synchronization overheads needed for data correctness. Further, DAG parallelism alleviates the need for expensive MPI-style distributed barriers and, therefore, does not suffer from the otherwise common straggler challenges—an important property for heterogeneous compute at scale. Finally, data store and the deterministic nature of the task graph jointly enable fault tolerance, as any missing object in the graph can be recomputed by simply replaying the sub-graph leading up to and including the object's parent vertex. This mechanism can be triggered automatically and comes with minimal overhead on the critical path of a task [29].

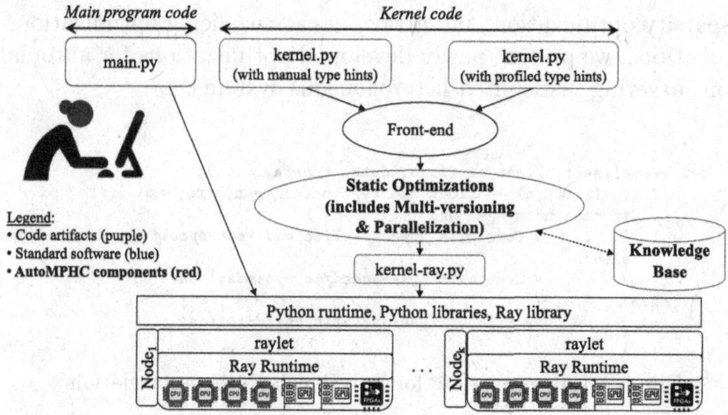

Fig. 4. Overall design of AutoMPHC system

3 Overview of Our Approach

Figure 4 summarizes the overall design of our proposed AutoMPHC system. User-developed code is a combination of *main program code* and *kernel code*, where the former is unchanged while the latter is optimized by AutoMPHC via automatic ahead-of-time (AOT) source-to-source transformations. Both execute on a standard Python runtime along with Ray and other libraries used by the application. There are two forms of kernel code supported by our system—one in which type annotations are manually provided by the user, and another in which type annotations are obtained by a type profiler such as MonkeyType. In both cases, the type annotations serve as *hints* since multi-version code generation guarantees the correctness of our AOT transformations in all cases (whether or not the actual inputs match the type annotations).

The kernel functions with type annotations (hints) are first translated by the Front-end to an Abstract Syntax Tree (AST) representation implemented using the standard Python Typed AST package [19]. The core optimizations in AutoMPHC are then performed on the AST, including multi-version code specialization (Sect. 4.1), polyhedral optimizations (Sect. 4.2), and generation of distributed parallel code using Ray tasking APIs along with generation of heterogeneous code using selective NumPy-to-CuPy conversion (Sect. 4.3). These Static Optimizations benefit from the use of the AutoMPHC Knowledge Base, which includes dataflow and type information for many commonly used library functions. The transformed code is then executed on a distributed heterogeneous platform using standard Python libraries in addition to Ray.

4 Optimizations

The AutoMPHC compiler is an extension of Intrepydd compiler [30], which supports type inference and basic optimizations including loop invariant code motion, sparsity optimization, and array allocation/slicing optimizations. In the following sections, we present newly developed optimizations for automatic parallelization targeting distributed heterogeneous systems.

```
def kernel(self, float_n: float, data: ndarray, ...):
    if type(float_n) == float and type(data) == ndarray and ...:
        if data.ndim == 2 and ... :
            ... # Code with type-specific and rank-specific optimizations
        else:
            ... # Code with type-specific optimizations
    else:
        ... # Code without type-specific optimizations
```

Fig. 5. Multi-versioning for PolyBench-Python correlation

4.1 Program Multi-versioning for Specialized Code Optimizations

Multi-versioning is an approach to data-aware optimizations, which generates multiple code versions specialized under certain conditions at compile-time and selects a proper code version at runtime. In our framework, we consider two classes of conditions, *legality-based* and *profitability-based*. All the conditions are organized as decision trees, where legality conditions are located at higher levels while profitability conditions are at lower levels in general.

The legality conditions are mainly used to verify the data type annotations attached on function parameters and returns. In our approach, the type annotations are used as hints and the compiler speculatively performs optimizations assuming these hints are correct. For example, the accuracy of array rank/dimensionality inference, which is derived from the type hints, is critical to the polyhedral optimizations (Sect. 4.2). In contrast, array element types may be less critical in some cases since AutoMPHC generates untyped Python code as output (unlike Intrepydd, which generated typed C++ code). In general, since these type annotations can be different from the actual types at runtime, the multi-versioning code generation introduces runtime checks of annotated/inferred types and ranks for specialized code version while ensuring correct behavior for others, as shown in Fig. 5.

The profitability conditions can cover a broad range of conditions/scenarios related to runtime performance rather than correctness. As described later, the AutoMPHC compiler can generate two versions of optimized kernels, one for CPUs and the other for GPUs. The runtime condition used to select between these two versions is a typical example of a profitability condition (Sect. 4.3).

4.2 Polyhedral Optimizations

Polyhedral compilation has provided significant advances in the unification of affine loop transformations combined with powerful code generation techniques [4,27,31]. However, despite these strengths in program transformation,

Table 2. NumPy examples in library knowledge base

Library function	Domain	Semantics and dataflow
transpose_{2D}	(i_0, i_1)	$R[i_0, i_1] := A_1[i_1, i_0]$
$\text{mult}_{1D,2D}$	(i_0, i_1)	$R[i_0, i_1] := A_1[i_1] \times A_2[i_0, i_1]$
sum_{1D}	(0)	$R := \Sigma_k A_1[k]$
$\text{sum}_{2D,axis=1}$	(i_0)	$R[i_0] := sum_{1D}(A_1[i_0, :])$
$\text{dot}_{2D,2D}$	(i_0, i_1)	$R[i_0, i_1] := sum_{1D}(mult_{1D,1D}(A_1[i_0, :], A_2[:, i_1]))$
$\text{fft}_{2D,axis=1}$	(i_0)	$R[i_0, :] := fft_{1D}(A_1[i_0, :])$

the polyhedral frameworks lack support for: 1) dynamic control flow and non-affine access patterns; and 2) library function calls in general. To address the first limitation, we have extended the polyhedral representation of Static Control Parts (SCoPs) to represent unanalyzable expressions as a compound "black-box" statement with approximated input/output relations. To address the second limitation, we took advantage of our library knowledge base to obtain element-wise dataflow relations among function arguments and return values (see examples in Table 2). These unique features enable the co-optimization of both explicit loops and implicit loops from operators and library calls in a unified optimization framework, as detailed in the rest of this section.

Given SCoP representation extracted from the Python IR, the `AutoMPHC` polyhedral optimizer, which is built on the PolyAST [22,23] framework, computes dependence constraints and performs program transformations. Finally, the optimized SCoP representation is converted back to Python IR with the help of the library knowledge base for efficient library mapping.

Intra-node Parallelization: The optimization goal for the intra-node level is to generate sufficient parallelism to fully utilize efficient multithreaded libraries such as BLAS-based NumPy and CuPy. Our modified PolyAST [23] algorithm applies loop distribution to split different library calls into different loops while maximizing the iteration domain (i.e., amount of computation) that can be mapped to a single library function call. The SCoP-to-Python-IR generation stage leverages the library knowledge base to select the most efficient combination of available library functions for each statement when available.

Figure 6a shows the computationally dominant code region in the PolyBench-Python `correlation` NumPy benchmark, which has a `for` loop enclosing a sequence of NumPy function calls: 2-D array transpose overlapping `T` operator; 1-D×2-D array multiply overlapping `*` operator, and 2-D array summation `sum` to produce 1-D result. Based on the type inference results, the polyhedral phase first identifies these library functions with specific types and array ranks. As shown in Table 2, the library knowledge base provides the element-wise dataflow information and operation semantics of these functions, which are used to extract the SCoP information and semantics of each statement (Fig. 6b). Note that: both explicit and implicit loops are unified in a triangular iteration domain; and the element-wise dataflow and semantics are summarized as the statement body, `corr[i0, i1] = sum(mult(data[:, i0], data[:, i1]))`.

```
for i in range(0, M-1):
    corr[i, i+1:M] = (data[0:N, i] * data[0:N, i+1:M].T).sum(axis=1)
```

(a) Original code fragment

```
Domain: {S[i0, i1] : 0 <= i0 < M - 1 and i0 + 1 <= i1 < M}
Read:   {S[i0, i1] -> data[any1, i0], data[any2, i1] : 0 <= any1, any2 < N}
Write:  {S[i0, i1] -> corr[i0, i1]}
Body:    S[i0, i1] :: corr[i0, i1] = sum(mult(data[:, i0], data[:, i1]))
```

(b) Extracted polyhedral information (SCoP)

```
tmp1 = np.dot(data[0:N, 0:M].T, data[0:N, 0:M])
corr[0:M-1, 0:M] = np.triu(tmp1[0:M-1, 0:M], k=1)
```

(c) Transformed code fragment by intra-node polyhedral optimization

Fig. 6. Kernel from the PolyBench-Python correlation

Given the statement body, the SCoP-to-Python-IR generation stage selects the combination of matrix-matrix multiplication `numpy.dot` and 2-D transpose `T` as the best mapping, followed by `numpy.triu` to update only the triangular iteration domain (Fig. 6c). As discussed in Sect. 5.2, this transformation sufficiently increases the intra-node parallelism per library call and contributes to significant improvements for several benchmarks.

When the input program is written only with explicit loops, e.g., the List version in Fig. 2, our approach extracts similar SCoP and generates similar code, but with necessary conversions between List and NumPy array data types.

Inter-node Parallelization: The optimization policy for inter-node level is equivalent to the original PolyAST [23] algorithm that maximizes outermost level parallelism, while incorporated with our data layout transformation approach [24,25] to reduce the total allocated array sizes and data movement across Ray tasks. Analogous to two-level parallelization for GPUs [22], our polyhedral optimizer selects different *schedules* – i.e., compositions of loop transformations and parallelization – for inter-node and intra-node levels individually; and integrates them into the final schedule via loop tiling.

Figures 7a and 7b respectively show the computational kernel of the STAP radar application and the extracted SCoP information. The explicit loop with statement S and the `fft` call of statement T are handled as 1-D iteration domains while 2-D×2-D array multiply of statement U is handled as a 2-D iteration domain. The polyhedral optimizer identifies the outermost level parallelism and computes the inter-node schedule that fuses these statements into a single parallel loop. The transformed code after integrating the inter-node and intra-node schedules is shown in Fig. 7c, where `pfor` is an intermediate parallel loop construct that is implemented using Ray tasks.

```
for idx in range(numPulses):
    ...
    beamforming[idx,:] = np.squeeze(np.matmul(steerVector11, dataCube)) # S
d_X = np.fft.fft(beamforming, fftSize, axis=1) # T
d_Y = d_X * d_matchFilterMultiply # U
```

(a) Original code fragment

```
Domain: {S[i0]        : 0 <= i0 < numPulses}
        {T[i0]        : 0 <= i0 < numPulses}
        {U[i0, i1] : 0 <= i0 < numPulses and 0 <= i1 < fftSize}
Body:    S[i0]        :: beamforming[i0, :] = ...
         T[i0]        :: d_X[i0, :] = fft(beamforming[i0, :])
         U[i0, i1] :: d_Y[i0, i1] = d_X[i0, i1] * d_matchFilterMultiply[i0, i1]
```

(b) Extracted polyhedral information (read/write omitted due to space)

```
pfor t1 in range(0, numPulses, __tile_size):  # Parallel loop across nodes
    up1 = min(t1 + __tile_size, numPulses)
    for c1 in range(t1, up1):
        ...
        beamforming[c1,:] = np.squeeze(np.matmul(steerVector11, dataCube)) # S
    d_X = np.fft.fft(beamforming[t1:up1, :], fftSize, axis=1) # T
    d_Y = d_X * d_matchFilterMultiply # U
```

(c) Transformed code fragment by inter-node polyhedral parallelization

Fig. 7. Kernel from the STAP Signal Processing Application

4.3 NumPy-to-CuPy Conversion and Parallelized Code Generation

After the polyhedral phase, the program multi-versioning pass (Sect. 4.1) is applied to the *pfor* parallel loops and generates both sequential and parallel versions. The profitability condition, which makes the decision on whether the loop should be distributed across nodes via the Ray runtime, is generated by a simple cost-based analysis and summarized as a threshold expression using loop counts. This analysis also includes the profitability check of the CuPy conversion for a given sequence of NumPy library calls. The current implementation takes an all-or-nothing approach for NumPy-to-CuPy conversion in a code region, and more fine-grained control, e.g., per-array decisions, is a topic for future work.

To generate Ray-based distributed code from a high-level *pfor* loop, the polyhedral phase provides the following supplemental information related to data access and NumPy-to-CuPy conversion.

`pfor (output =` $\{var_{out_1} : type_{out_1}, var_{out_2} : type_{out_2}, ...\}$,
`input =` $\{var_{in_1} : type_{in_1}, var_{in_2} : type_{in_2}, ...\}$,
`transfer =` $module\_name$)

The `output` and `input` clauses respectively specify the produced and referenced variables by the *pfor* loop and their corresponding types, while the `transfer` clause indicates the possibility of NumPy-to-CuPy conversion based on the polyhedral dataflow analysis and library compatibility.

4.4 Important Packages Used in AutoMPHC Tool Chain

Our AutoMPHC compilation flow is built on top of the Python Typed AST package [19], which serves as the baseline IR to perform fundamental program analyses and transformations such as type inference, loop invariant code motions, and constant propagations. For the polyhedral optimizations presented in Sect. 4.2, we employ the islpy package, the Python interface to the Integer Set Library (ISL) [28] for manipulating sets and relations of integer points bounded by linear constraints. Beside the polyhedral representations using islpy, we employ sympy [26] to analyze symbolic expressions observed in the Typed AST.

Table 3. Hardware Platform Information (per node) and software versions

Per node	Cori-GPU	Summit	Titan Xp (workstation)
CPU	2 × Intel Xeon Gold 6148 @ 2.40 GHz (40 cores/node)	2 × IBM POWER9 @ 3.1 GHz (44 cores/node)	1 × Intel i5-7600 CPU @ 3.50 GHz (4 cores)
GPU	8 × NVIDIA Tesla V100	6 × NVIDIA Tesla V100	1 × NVIDIA Pascal
Memory	384 GB	512 GB	15 GB
Interconnect	InfiniBand + PCIe (CPUs-GPUs) + NVLink (GPUs)	InfiniBand + NVLink (CPUs-GPUs, GPUs)	PCIe (CPU-GPU)
Python/NumPy/CuPy	3.7.3/1.16.4/7.4.0	3.7.3/1.16.0/7.4.0	3.6.9/1.19.5/7.2.0
Ray	0.8.4	0.7.7	0.8.4

Table 4. PolyBench-Python baselines: Execution time in second (dataset = large)

	2 mm	3 mm	atax	bicg	correlation	covariance	doitgen	gemm
List Default [sec]	224.4	356.2	0.6578	0.6730	152.5	305.7	54.46	147.4
List Pluto [sec]	205.2	337.9	0.8381	0.8304	152.1	153.8	54.45	191.5
NumPy [sec]	0.0214	0.03252	0.002516	0.002447	2.212	3.813	0.1250	0.01789
	gemver	gesummv	mvt	symm	syr2k	syrk	trmm	
List Default [sec]	1.510	0.3068	0.8710	140.4	171.4	96.66	91.10	
List Pluto [sec]	1.453	0.3154	0.8714	140.5	137.9	81.73	93.27	
NumPy [sec]	0.04676	0.001074	0.002537	1.656	2.667	0.7839	0.8499	

5 Experimental Results

5.1 Experimental Setup

We use a standard GPU-equipped workstation, Titan Xp, for single-node experiments (Sect. 5.2) and two leading HPC platforms, NERSC Cori [11] and OLCF Summit [8] supercomputers, for multi-node experiments (Sect. 5.3). The single-node specification of these platforms is summarized in Table 3. For Summit, we manually built Ray and its dependencies from scratch because there is currently no out-of-the-box Python Ray package for the POWER processor.

5.2 Single-node Results (PolyBench)

We first evaluate the impact of our polyhedral optimizations using PolyBench-Python [1], which is the Python implementation of PolyBench [15], a widely used benchmark kernels for compiler evaluations. We use a total of 15 benchmarks shown in Table 4, which are well suited to our current library-oriented optimization strategy. The evaluation of other 15 benchmarks is a topic for future work that supports hybrid Python/C++ code generation.

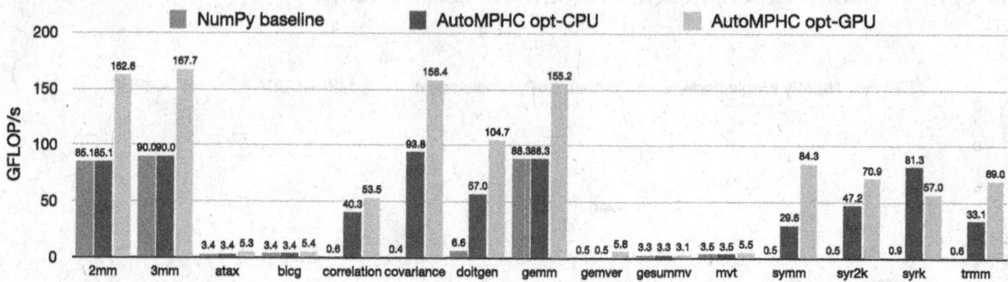

Fig. 8. PolyBench-Python performance on NVIDIA Titan Xp (dataset = extra large)

PolyBench Python provides a variety of benchmark implementations, including the default List version, the optimized List version by the Pluto polyhedral compiler [4], and the NumPy version. Table 4 shows the execution time of these versions using the "large" datasets. While the Pluto optimization improves the performance, NumPy version largely outperforms List versions for all cases.

In the following experiments, we use NumPy version as the baseline of our comparison, and "extra large" dataset to ensure sufficient execution time. Note that "extra large" and "large" respectively refer to the first and second largest datasets. Figure 8 shows the GFLOP/s of three experimental variants:

- NumPy baseline: the original NumPy implementation from PolyBench.
- AutoMPHC opt-CPU: the CPU optimized version by AutoMPHC framework.
- AutoMPHC opt-GPU: the GPU optimized version by AutoMPHC framework enabling NumPy-to-CuPy conversion.

Comparing the NumPy baseline and AutoMPHC opt-CPU versions, our polyhedral optimization gives 8.7× – 212.4× performance improvements for `correlation`, `covariance`, `doitgen`, `symm`, `syr2k`, `syrk`, and `trmm`, while showing comparable performance for other benchmarks. Enabling NumPy-to-CuPy conversion, i.e., AutoMPHC opt-GPU version, further improves the performance for most benchmarks with the exception of `gesummv` and `syrk`. In this evaluation, our profitability conditions always selected GPU variants. The improvement of CPU/GPU selection based on offline profiling is an important topic for future work.

5.3 Multi-node Results (STAP)

We demonstrate the multi-node performance of our AutoMPHC compiler framework using one of our target applications in the signal processing domain, namely the Space-Time Adaptive Processing (STAP) application for radar systems [9]. The problem size used for STAP is to evaluate the analysis of 144 data cubes for the CPU case; and 2304 data cubes for the GPU case, where each data cube has # pulses per cube = 100, # channels = 1000, and # samples per pulse = 30000. The throughput performance required for real-time execution is 33.3 [cubes/sec]. We compare four experimental variants as listed below:

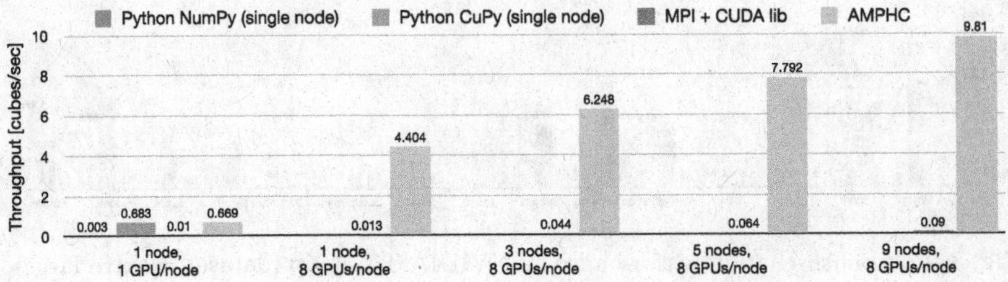

Fig. 9. STAP radar application performance on NERSC Cori supercomputer

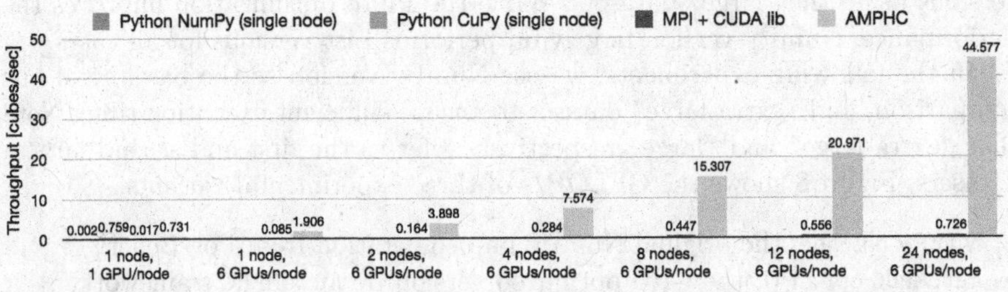

Fig. 10. STAP radar application performance on OLCF Summit supercomputer

- Python NumPy: The original single-node CPU implementation.
- Python CuPy: CuPy-based single-node GPU implementation, manually ported from the original Python NumPy version.
- MPI+CUDA lib: MPI C/C++ and CUDA library-based multi-node GPU implementation, manually ported from the Python CuPy version by a domain expert with past experience in MPI and C/C++ programming.
- AutoMPHC: Automatic parallelization by the AutoMPHC compiler of the original Python NumPy version, running on the Ray distributed runtime.

Figures 9 and 10 show the throughput performance, i.e., number of data cubes processed per second, respectively on Cori and Summit clusters. Given the Python NumPy version as input, the AutoMPHC compiler automatically parallelized the major computation kernel and mapped it to GPUs via NumPy-to-CuPy conversions. This significantly improves the throughput performance, resulting in comparable single-GPU performance with the manually ported CuPy implementation on both clusters. The MPI+CUDA lib version shows significantly worse performance compared to the AutoMPHC version. The major performance bottleneck of this variant lies in the unoptimized data transfers among CPUs and GPUs. Although the majority of computation in the MPI+CUDA lib version is covered by CUDA-based libraries such as `cufft`, the interleaving of C-based CPU code with the CUDA-based GPU library calls resulted in a large amount of CPU/GPU data transfers. Optimizing these data transfers would have required deep (ninja-level) experience with CUDA programming as well as sufficient time for performance tuning. In contrast, the AutoMPHC version shows good multi-node scalability with performance of up to 44.58 [cubes/sec] using 24 nodes on Summit, which exceeds 33.3 [cubes/sec] of the domain-specific throughput requirement for the real-time radar systems. The AutoMPHC version also achieves 4.40 [cubes/sec] of single-node performance on Cori while the multi-node scalability is more limited than that on Summit. This stems from the difference in network, i.e., Summit's NVLink (50 GB/s) vs. Cori's PCIe 3.0 (16 GB/s).

Breakdown on CPU-GPU Interconnect Performance: In the parallelized STAP code by AutoMPHC, each parallel task performs the computation on the GPU-side and returns a few gigabytes of the result via device-to-host (D2H) data transfers. We developed a synthetic benchmark that mimics the behavior of the D2H transfers in our AutoMPHC-parallelized STAP application and evaluated its impact on the overall performance. Because `nvprof` could not profile the GPU part invoked from the Ray distributed runtime, our D2H benchmark is implemented using OpenMP+CUDA and spawns parallel threads to simultaneously perform the D2H transfers. The benchmarking results, i.e., timings to complete D2H data transfer using all GPUs of a single node, are summarized as:

- Cori: 8 GPUs per node, PCIe 3.0 (16 GB/s)
  - 6 cubes (2.4 GB) per GPU – 39.563 s
  - 16 cubes (6.4 GB) per GPU – 150.224 s
- Summit: 6 GPUs per node, NVLink (50 GB/s)
  - 6 cubes (2.4 GB) per GPU – 3.251 s
  - 16 cubes (6.4 GB) per GPU – 8.791 s

The results clearly show that simultaneously transferring back large amounts of data significantly degrades the D2H bandwidth of PCIe 3.0 on Cori. As expected, NVLink on Summit largely outperforms PCIe 3.0 in terms of D2H data transfers, which is why NVLink contributed to the good scalability of the AutoMPHC-generated code on the Summit system.

6 Related Work

There are a number of compilation frameworks for enhancing Python performance, most notably Numba [13], PyPy [17] and Pyston [18] which use just-in-time compilation; and Cython [5], Nuitka [12], and Shed Skin [21] which use source-to-source translation and native compilation. As an example of loop-aware optimizations, PyPy's Tracing JIT [2] enables common subexpression elimination and memory allocation removal within loops, based on the interpreter execution traces. Numba, implemented as a Python library, dynamically translates a subset of Python code into machine code via LLVM-based JIT compilation. Despite the rich set of optimization passes in LLVM framework, the low-level translated code is not amenable to a large segment of the LLVM optimizations including the polyhedral optimizations by Polly [7]. While all these efforts aim to improve performance through generating native code, to the best of our knowledge, none of them has leveraged high-level abstractions of Python source program for AOT compilation as in our approach.

7 Conclusions

This paper describes `AutoMPHC` —a programming system designed to deliver the benefits of distributed heterogeneous hardware platforms to domain scientists who naturally use high-productivity languages like Python. In our approach, the parameters and return values of kernel Python functions are annotated with type hints, manually by users or automatically by profiling tools. Based on these type hints, the `AutoMPHC` compiler performs automatic AOT parallelization, based on advanced polyhedral optimizations, CuPy-driven GPU code generation, and Ray-targeted heterogeneous distributed code generation and execution. The correctness of our AOT parallelization is guaranteed by multi-version code generation, since code versions with type-specific optimizations are executed only when the actual runtime types match the type hints. Our empirical evaluations using PolyBench-Python for workstation performance and the STAP radar application for heterogeneous distributed performance show significant performance improvements, e.g., up to 358× improvement for PolyBench and up to 20,000× improvement for the STAP radar application, relative to baseline NumPy-based implementations. Opportunities for future work include hybrid Python/C++ code generation, fine-grained NumPy-to-CuPy conversion, and profile-based CPU/GPU runtime selection.

Acknowledgments. This material is based upon work supported by the Defense Advanced Research Projects Agency (DARPA) under Agreement No. HR0011-20-9-0020. This research used resources of the Oak Ridge Leadership Computing Facility, which is a DOE Office of Science User Facility supported under Contract DE-AC05-00OR22725. Also, this research used resources of the National Energy Research Scientific Computing Center, which is supported by the Office of Science of the U.S. Department of Energy under Contract No. DE-AC02-05CH11231.

References

1. Abella-González, M.A., Carollo-Fernández, P., Pouchet, L.N., Rastello, F., Rodríguez, G.: Polybench/python: Benchmarking python environments with polyhedral optimizations. In: Proceedings of CC 2021 (2021). https://doi.org/10.1145/3446804.3446842
2. Ardö, H., Bolz, C.F., FijaBkowski, M.: Loop-aware optimizations in pypy's tracing jit. SIGPLAN Not. **48**(2), 63–72 (2012). https://doi.org/10.1145/2480360.2384586
3. Bezanson, J., Karpinski, S., Shah, V.B., Edelman, A.: Julia: a fast dynamic language for technical computing. CoRR abs/1209.5145 (2012)
4. Bondhugula, U., Acharya, A., Cohen, A.: The pluto+ algorithm: a practical approach for parallelization and locality optimization of affine loop nests. ACM Trans. Program. Lang. Syst. 38(3), April 2016. https://doi.org/10.1145/2896389
5. Cython (2007). https://cython.org/
6. Dalcin, L., Fang, Y.L.L.: mpi4py: status update after 12 years of development. Comput. Sci. Eng. (2021). https://doi.org/10.1109/MCSE.2021.3083216
7. Grosser, T., Größlinger, A., Lengauer, C.: Polly - performing polyhedral optimizations on a low-level intermediate representation. Parallel Process. Lett. **22**(4), 1250010 (2012)
8. LCF Summit supercomputer (2019). https://www.olcf.ornl.gov/olcf-resources/compute-systems/summit/
9. Melvin, W.L.: Chapter 12: Space-time adaptive processing for radar. Academic Press Library in Signal Processing: Volume 2 Comm. and Radar Signal Proc. (2014)
10. Moritz, P., et al.: Ray: a distributed framework for emerging ai applications. In: Proceedings of OSDI 2018 (2018)
11. NERSC Cori supercomputer (2016). https://docs.nersc.gov/systems/cori/
12. Nuitka (2012). https://nuitka.net/pages/overview.html
13. Numba (2012). https://numba.pydata.org/
14. NumPy (2006). https://numpy.org/
15. PolyBench: The polyhedral benchmark suite. http://www.cse.ohio-state.edu/~pouchet/software/polybench/
16. Press, W.H., Teukolsky, S.A., Vetterling, W.T., Flannery, B.P.: Numerical Recipes 3rd Edition: The Art of Scientific Computing. 3 edn. (2007)
17. PyPy (2019). https://pypy.org/
18. Pyston (2014). https://blog.pyston.org/
19. Python typed AST package (2019). https://pypi.org/project/typed-ast/
20. SciPy (2001). https://www.scipy.org/
21. Shed Skin (2012). https://shedskin.github.io/
22. Shirako, J., Hayashi, A., Sarkar, V.: Optimized two-level parallelization for gpu accelerators using the polyhedral model. In: Proceedings of CC 2017 (2017). https://doi.org/10.1145/3033019.3033022
23. Shirako, J., Pouchet, L.N., Sarkar, V.: Oil and water can mix: An integration of polyhedral and ast-based transformations. In: Proceedings of SC'14 (2014). https://doi.org/10.1109/SC.2014.29
24. Shirako, J., Sarkar, V.: Integrating data layout transformations with the polyhedral model. In: Proceedings of IMPACT 2019 (2019)
25. Shirako, J., Sarkar, V.: An affine scheduling framework for integrating data layout and loop transformations. In: Proceedings of LCPC 2020 (2020). https://doi.org/10.1007/978-3-030-95953-1_1
26. SymPy (2017). https://www.sympy.org

27. Verdoolaege, et al.: Polyhedral parallel code generation for CUDA. ACM Trans. Archit. Code Optim. **9**(4), 54:1–54:23 (2013). https://doi.org/10.1145/2400682.2400713
28. Verdoolaege, S.: isl: an integer set library for the polyhedral model. In: Mathematical Software - ICMS 2010 (2010). https://doi.org/10.1007/978-3-642-15582-6_49
29. Wang, S., et al.: Lineage stash: Fault tolerance off the critical path. In: Proceedings of the ACM Symposium on Operating System Principles (SOSP'19), SOSP 2019 (2019)
30. Zhou, T., et al.: Intrepydd: Performance, productivity and portability for data science application kernels. In: Proceedings of Onward! '20 (2020). https://doi.org/10.1145/3426428.3426915
31. Zinenko, O., et al.: Modeling the conflicting demands of parallelism and temporal/spatial locality in affine scheduling. In: Proceedings of CC 2018 (2018). https://doi.org/10.1145/3178372.3179507

Multicore and Manycore Parallelism

A Hybrid Piece-Wise Slowdown Model for Concurrent Kernel Execution on GPU

Bernabé López-Albelda, Francisco M. Castro, Jose M. González-Linares, and Nicolás Guil(✉)

Department Computer Architecture, University of Málaga, Málaga, Spain
nguil@uma.es
http://www.ac.uma.es

Abstract. Current execution of kernels on GPUs allows improving the use of hardware resources and reducing the execution time of co-executed kernels. In addition, efficient kernel-oriented scheduling policies pursuing criteria based on fairness or Quality of Service can be implemented. However, achieved co-executing performance strongly depends on how GPU resources are partitioned between kernels. Thus, precise slowdown models that predict accurate co-execution performance must be used to fulfill scheduling policy requirements. Most recent slowdown models work with Spatial Multitask (*SMT*) partitioning, where Stream Multiprocessors (*SMs*) are distributed among tasks. In this work, we show that Simultaneous Multikernel (*SMK*) partitioning, where kernels share the *SMs*, obtains better performance. However, kernel interference in *SMK* occurs not only in global memory, as in the *SMT* case, but also within the *SM*, leading to high prediction errors. Here, we propose a modification of a previous state-of-the-art slowdown model to reduce median prediction error from 27.92% to 9.50%. Moreover, this new slowdown model is used to implement a scheduling policy that improves fairness by 1.41x on average compared to even partitioning, whereas previous models reach only 1.21x on average.

Keywords: Concurrent Kernel Execution · Simultaneous Multikernel · Slowdown model · Fairness Scheduling

1 Introduction

Current Graphic Processing Units (GPUs) provide high computational power and memory bandwidth and are able to execute thousands of threads at a time to exploit the data parallelism that can be found in application kernels. Threads are organized in Cooperative Threads Arrays (*CTAs*), also called thread blocks, that are launched into the available Streaming Multiprocessors (*SM*).

Despite this large amount of computing resources, kernel execution can saturate some of them, harming the execution efficiency. In this situation, resources are also wasted as no further speedup can be achieved. With concurrent execution of kernels, those wasted resources can be assigned to another kernel, which

J. Cano and P. W. Trinder (Eds.): Euro-Par 2022, LNCS 13440, pp. 369–384, 2022.
https://doi.org/10.1007/978-3-031-12597-3_23

allows improving the use of hardware resources and reducing the total execution time of co-executed kernels. In addition, efficient kernel-oriented scheduling policies that pursue criteria based on fairness or Quality of Service can be implemented.

Concurrent kernel execution reveals specially useful in GPU servers, where applications running on CPUs offload specific functions to GPUs in order to take advantage of the device performance. In these environments, it is likely to have several independent kernels ready to run concurrently on the same GPU. In this context, several works have been published that try to improve the way kernels are scheduled on GPUs.

Previous works have proposed two possible ways of allocating resources to kernels. On the one hand, using Spatial Multitask (SMT) a subset of the available SMs is assigned to a kernel so that all the CTAs of that kernel are run in that subset [1]. On the other hand, Simultaneous Multikernel (SMK) assigns CTAs belonging to different kernels to each SM, replicating the same assignation scheme at each SM [2,3]. A recent and exhaustive survey of SMT and SMK approaches can be found in [4].

The co-execution performance achieved is highly dependent on how GPU resources are partitioned between the kernels. Thus, precise slowdown models that accurately predict the co-execution performance relative to running the kernel alone (single-execution) must be used to fulfill scheduling policy requirements. Researchers have employed several approaches to predict the slowdown of co-executing kernels. All of these approaches fall into two main categories [5]. Methods belonging to the first category rely on information obtained from hardware counters to make the prediction [6–8]. However, the impact of interference between co-executing kernels is difficult to model and, consequently, the prediction is not accurate [9]. In the second category, we find methods that build a prediction model applying machine learning techniques using representative kernel datasets [10]. However, the computational complexity of the model inference is high and, furthermore, the accuracy of the prediction is very dependent on the training set employed.

A recent method, called Hybrid Slowdown Model (HSM) [5], which takes characteristics of both categories, is able to predict the performance achieved by compute and memory-bound co-executing kernels following an SMT distribution scheme. However, we have noticed that the above model incurs high prediction errors when the SMK distribution scheme is employed. We also note that the SMK distribution typically achieves better performance for different scheduling policies than SMT. In this paper, we propose a modification of HSM that allows building a more accurate slowdown model for the SMK distribution of concurrent kernel CTAs. Thus, the main contributions of this work are the following:

- We compare the SMK and the SMT distribution schemes in terms of the average normalized turn-around time and the system throughput.
- We add a piece-wise approximation method to the HSM model to improve slowdown prediction. We call this model $HPSM$.

- We use *HPSM* to implement a fairness-based *CTA* allocation policy, and compare it to *HSM*.

The rest of the paper is organized as follows. Section 2 discusses some simple experiments that motivated us to conduct this research. In Sect. 3, we analyze the inaccuracy sources of current slowdown models and propose some modifications to obtain more precise predictions. In the next section, a thorough experimentation is conducted with memory-bound and compute-bound kernels to show the generalization capabilities of our approach. Then, Sect. 5 presents relevant related works and, finally, we present the conclusions of our work in Sect. 6.

2 Motivation

Kernel execution on a GPU may not scale well due to architecture constraints and saturation of computational resources caused by, for example, pipeline stalls on RAW dependencies (in compute-bound kernels) or L1-cache trashing (in L1-cache sensitive kernels) [2]. Another type of saturation can occur with memory-bound kernels since they can saturate the global memory bandwidth before all the possible *CTA*s are allocated to the *SM*s. One way to deal with saturation problems is to reduce the number of *CTA*s of the saturating kernels assigned to the *SM*s and, to maintain high GPU utilization, concurrently schedule *CTA*s from another kernel with different resource needs. Thus, in this section we perform experiments with two kernels: *GCEDD*, a compute-bound kernel, and *RED*, a memory-bound kernel (see Table 2 for more details), to evaluate their performance. Each of these kernels can saturate some computational resources before all the *CTA*s have been assigned, limiting the maximum performance they could achieve.

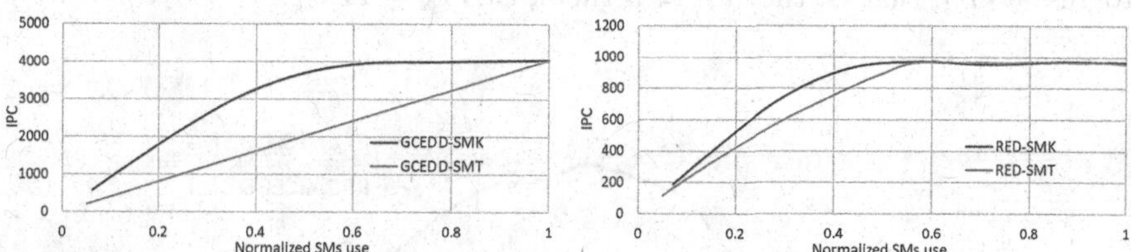

Fig. 1. IPC achieved by a single execution of *RED* and *GCEDD* kernels using a variable number of *CTA*s.

In our first experiment, we compare the behavior of *SMT* and *SMK* distributions when only a single kernel is executed to test the effect of saturation on performance. Thus, we gradually increase the number of used resources by using more *SMs*, in the *SMT* case, or by allocating more *CTA*s to each *SM*, in the case of *SMK*. In the left graph of Fig. 1, we show the instruction per clock (*IPC*) achieved by *GCEDD* (a compute-bound kernel) as more device resources are utilized. It can be observed that the IPC values of SMT execution of $GCEDD$ are linear with the number of SMs [5]. However, when SMK allocation scheme is employed, the IPC values for intermediate resource usage are higher and there is almost no gain after allocating more than 60% of the maximum number of *CTA*s that fit in each SM. Thus, SMT launches all the possible kernel *CTA*s on the assigned SMs and the achieved IPC obtained on each SM is limited by the intensive use of shared resources on the SM. In contrast, since SMK distributes *CTA*s evenly across all SMs, maximum performance can be achieved using a low number of *CTA*s running on each SM, thereby reducing the pressure over other resources such as global memory.

Similarly, the right graph in Fig. 1 shows the IPC obtained by a memory-bound kernel, RED. Using both allocation schemes, the kernel achieves a similar IPC in the saturation zone, indicating that the kernel has reached its maximum memory bandwidth. However, in the non-saturated area, SMK gets higher IPC values since the execution of memory access instructions is distributed among all the available SM instead of being restricted to a subset of these SMs, probably saturating load/store buffers in the SM.

Now, we are going to analyze the behavior of both kernels when they are co-executed. A performance metric of kernel co-execution is the system throughput (STP) [11]. The expression of STP for a set of K co-executing kernels is given by

$$STP = \sum_{k=1}^{K} \frac{IPC_k^{shared}}{IPC_k^{alone}} \tag{1}$$

where IPC_k^{shared} and IPC_k^{alone} indicate the number of instructions per cycle obtained by the kernel when running in co-execution with other kernels and the number of instructions per cycle when executing alone (all the GPU resources assigned to the kernel), respectively. Each summation term is called normalized progress (NP), that is, the NP of kernel k is $NP_k = IPC_k^{shared}/IPC_k^{alone}$.

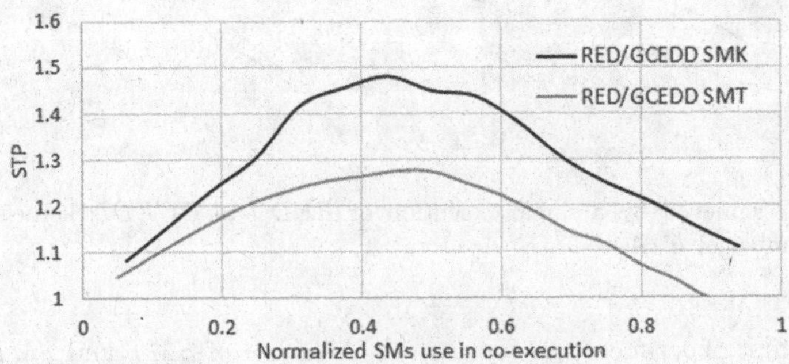

Fig. 2. Normalized progress obtained during the single co-execution of RED and $GCEDD$ kernels for different SM resource partitioning.

Figure 2 illustrates the achieved STP for RED and $GCEDD$ (the higher the better). On the abscissa axis we indicate the normalized value of *CTA*s launched by RED. $GCEDD$ is using the remaining GPUs resources to launch as many *CTA*s as possible. STP depends not only on the assigned SM resources, but also on the interference between co-executing kernels caused by the use of other shared resources (functional units, load/store queues, global memory row buffers, etc.). Thus, for SMT, where all the resources of the SM are assigned to one kernel, the interference appears at the global memory level, since co-executing kernels will compete for global memory resources. With SMK, in addition to the memory conflicts mentioned above, interferences also appear within the SM when *CTA*s from different kernels are allocated in the SM. Comparing the results obtained for the allocation schemes SMT and SMK, we can observe that SMK achieved higher scores than SMT. Following the reasoning that we exposed to explain the results of Fig. 1, we can argue that SMK performs better because *CTA*s of the same kernel located in the same SM do not compete with each other as intensively as in the SMT scheme. We will show in Sect. 4 that this reasoning can be generalized to all pairs of kernels that we have studied.

It can also be observed that STP takes very different values depending on the number of *CTA*s that are executed by each kernel simultaneously. These STP values range from 1.0 to 1.36 for SMT, and from 1.0 to 1.47 for SMK. However, the CTA partition that achieves the highest STP is not known in advance, since it depends on the interference among kernels when using shared resources such as global memory, L1 and L2 caches, load/store queues, functional units, etc.

Therefore, it is possible to improve the use of the computational resources of the GPU by running two or more kernels concurrently. For this, it is necessary to develop a slowdown prediction model for SMK that allows us to establish the best intra-CTA partition to achieve some specific objective in the scheduling policy.

3 Slowdown Model for *SMK*

Looking at Eq. 1, implementing scheduling policies for kernel co-execution based on minimizing turnaround time or co-execution fairness requires knowing both the IPC at execution time, IPC^{shared}, and the IPC achieved by the kernel when executed using all SM resources, that is IPC^{alone}. The value of IPC^{shared} can be obtained by reading some device counters. However, IPC^{alone} must be predicted using a model.

Some slowdown models for kernel co-execution lack the required precision to predict the NP value of a specific co-allocating scheme [2,3,10,12]. In a recent work [5], SMT allocation scheme is used for kernel co-execution and a slowdown model is built using only values extracted from the co-executing kernels. Thus, this model predicts the memory bandwidth of a memory-bound kernel when it is using the GPU alone. The prediction is based on the assumption that the row buffer hit rate of the kernel remains constant for any CTA allocation. In the case of a compute-bound kernel, a simple linear model based on the current allocated *CTA*s is employed. More details of the slowdown model are given below.

3.1 Hybrid Slowdown Model

Zhao et al. [5] proposed a Hybrid Slowdown Model, HSM, that predicts the values of NP for both memory-bound and compute-bound kernels co-executing under a SMT-based allocation scheme. They realized that the effective bandwidth utilization of a memory-bound kernel can be predicted using the Row Buffer Hit rate, RBH, obtained from global memory accesses. Then, the value of NP for memory-bound kernels can be obtained using linear regression and the value of RBH obtained while co-executing with another kernel. They use this model to implement a fairness-aware allocation policy, HSM-Fair.

In order to test the validity of the assumption for the SMK allocation scheme, we have executed alone each kernel in Table 2 and gathered the values of bandwidth utilization and RBH. In Fig. 3 we show the calculated regression line. We have also added the location of pairs (BW utilization, RBH) for several memory-bound kernels to show that the HSM linear regression model fits the data well.

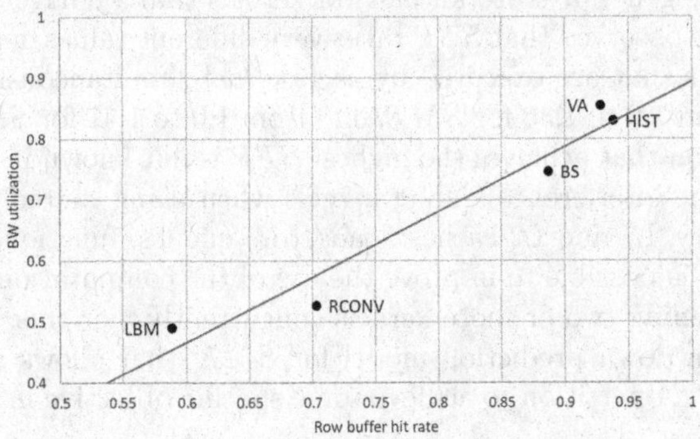

Fig. 3. BW prediction requires to calculate, in advance, a linear model with the linear relation between row buffer hit rate and BW utilization

On the other hand, a compute-bound kernel NP can be predicted using a simple proportional rule given by the following expression:

$$IPC_{cb}^{Alone} = IPC_{cb}^{Shared} \times \frac{R_{cb}^{Alone}}{R_{cb}^{Shared}} \tag{2}$$

where IPC_{cb}^{Shared} is the IPC obtained by the compute-bound kernel while co-executing with another kernel, and R_{cb}^{Alone} and R_{cb}^{Shared} are the computational resources assigned to the kernel during alone and co-execution, respectively. As HSM applies a SMT allocation scheme, R_{cb}^{Alone} is the total number of SMs in the GPU, and R_{cb}^{Shared} is the number of SMs allocated to the compute-bound kernel. Then, NP for compute-bound kernels is given by

$$NP = \frac{R_{cb}^{Shared}}{R_{cb}^{Alone}} \tag{3}$$

The values of the predicted NPs can be used to choose a fair allocation of SMs between the co-running kernels. A fairness metric can be defined as the ratio between the normalized progress of kernels i and j [11]. It can be computed as

$$Fairness = \min_{i,j}(NP_i/NP_j) \tag{4}$$

and the computed value ranges between 0 (no fairness) and 1 (perfect fairness, both kernels progress identically). HSM-Fair starts allocating the same number of SMs to each kernel and predicting NP and $Fairness$. Then, it computes how many SM should be taken from the high-NP kernel and given to the low-NP kernel to result in similar NP for both kernels. This procedure is repeated until the predicted $Fairness$ is higher than a threshold (e.g. 0.9).

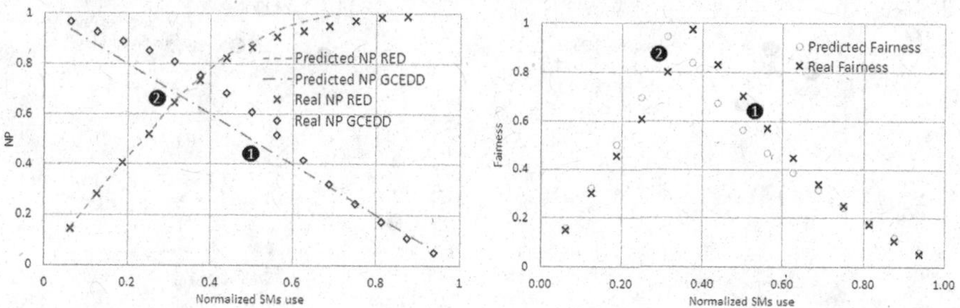

Fig. 4. HSM-fair applied to SMK co-execution of RED and $GCEDD$

Figure 4 shows an example of the application of HSM-Fair to the co-execution of kernels RED and GCEDD using SMK. The left plot shows predicted and actual values of NP for both kernels. The values in the abscissa axis represent the percentage of CTAs allocated to RED, with respect to the maximum number of resident CTAs (16 for RED). Thus, a value at 50% means a configuration with 8 CTAs allocated to RED, and as many CTAs as possible allocated to GCEDD. RED is a memory-bound kernel and there is almost no error in the prediction. GCEDD is a compute-bound kernel and the behaviour of NP is not linear. The right plot shows the predicted and actual fairness for all the configurations. The predicted maximum fairness is to the left of the actual maximum fairness. HSM-Fair starts testing the 50% configuration, annotated with a black circle and the number 1 in the plot. The predicted ($\widehat{NP}$) and actual NP values, alongside the predicted ($\widehat{Fairness}$) and actual $Fairness$ values are shown in Table 1. The prediction error is near 20% but nevertheless, HSM-Fair correctly assumes that more CTAs must be allocated to the compute-bound kernel. Then, the 30% configuration, which allocates 70% of the CTAs to the compute-bound kernel, is tested. HSM-Fair predicts a fairness of 0.949, which is above the threshold of 0.9, therefore it stops searching for a better configuration. Unfortunately, the prediction error is very high and the actual fairness is 0.8. If the threshold were higher and the actual best configuration, at 40%, were tested, HSM-Fair would predict a fairness below the one at 30% and set again this configuration.

3.2 Piece-wise Model for Compute-Bound Kernels

As it has been shown, HSM can predict well memory-bound kernels NP, but fails with compute-bound kernels. Unfortunately, assumptions about linear performance behaviour as resource allocation changes, that work fine for SMT, do not hold for SMK. One of the main reasons is that Eq. 2 fails to predict IPC^{Alone} using IPC^{Shared} at a 50% configuration. In this work we propose a Hybrid Piece-wise Slowdown Model, $HPSM$, that predicts IPC^{Alone} using IPC^{Shared} at the configuration with most CTAs. Then, it predicts how many CTAs should be taken or given to a compute-bound kernel using intervals between already tested configurations.

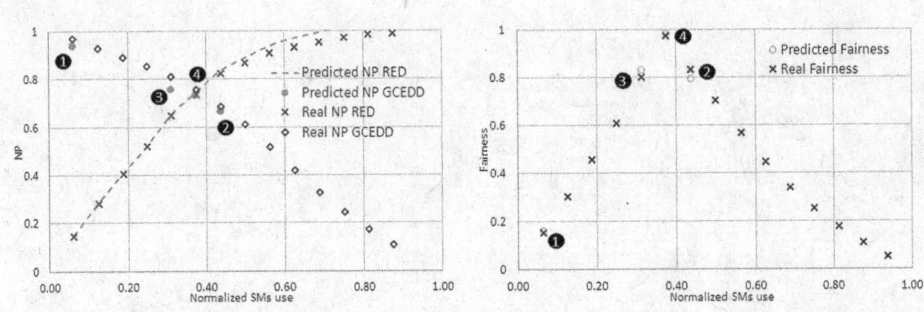

Fig. 5. HPSM-fair applied to SMK co-execution of RED and GCEDD

Figure 5 shows an example of the application of our model to the co-execution of kernels RED and $GCEDD$ using SMK. The left plot shows predicted and actual values of NP for the memory-bound kernel, RED. For $GCEDD$, it only shows the values tested by our method since the prediction of one configuration depends on the configurations already tested. The right plot shows the actual fairness for all the configurations and the predicted values of the configurations tested. Our model starts testing a configuration with just 1 CTA for RED and 15 CTAs for $GCEDD$. IPC_1^{Shared} at that point is used to predict $\widehat{IPC}^{Alone} = \frac{16}{15} \times IPC_1^{Shared}$, thus $\widehat{NP}_1 = \frac{15}{16}$. Table 1 shows the predicted and actual values of both NP and $Fairness$ and, as it can be seen, the prediction errors are very low. Right now, the prediction interval is between IPC_1^{Shared} and 0 (the IPC value with 0 allocated CTAs). HPSM-Fair uses that interval to predict a configuration with 9 CTAs per SM for $GCEDD$. HSM-Fair would predict $\widehat{NP}_2 = 0.562$ but our model corrects the prediction using $\widehat{NP}_2 = IPC_2^{Shared} / \widehat{IPC}^{Alone}$

Table 1. Values for data in Figs. 4 and 5

HSM				
#	$\widehat{NP}$	NP	$\widehat{Fairness}$	$Fairness$
1	0.5	0.611	0.563	0.703
2	0.687	0.810	0.949	0.800

HPSM				
#	$\widehat{NP}$	NP	$\widehat{Fairness}$	$Fairness$
1	0.937	0.967	0.160	0.152
2	0.662	0.683	0.793	0.832
3	0.754	0.810	0.830	0.800
4	0.732	0.755	0.983	0.975

that is closer to the actual value. Now, there are two intervals, one between IPC_1^{Shared} and IPC_2^{Shared}, and another between IPC_2^{Shared} and 0. HPSM-Fair predicts to take more *CTA*s from the compute-bound kernel, thus it uses the first interval to predict a third configuration, at 30%, that coincides with the second configuration tested using HSM-Fair. This time, errors are much lower and HPSM-Fair correctly predicts to try a fourth configuration, at 40%, where the optimal fairness is found.

4 Experimental Results

4.1 Simulated System

We have modified GPGPU-sim v4.0 [13] by adding support for concurrent kernel execution of two kernels using either SMT or SMK based *CTA*s allocation. We have used the Volta Titan V configuration file which models a GPU with 40 clusters with 2 cores each (80 *SM*s), connected to an HBM memory with 3 stacks and 24 channels.

For the SMT implementation we have added a register to the *CTA* scheduler. In this register, the number of *SM*s assigned to the first scheduled kernel is stored, for instance, N. Then, when the *CTA* scheduler checks that a *CTA* belonging to the first kernel needs to be launched, it checks if there are available resources in any *SM* with id going from 0 to N-1. If no room is available, the *CTA* is not scheduled. A similar operation is performed with the second kernel by consulting *SM*s from N to 79. For SMK, two pairs of double counters need to be added per SM. The first pair stores the maximum number of *CTA*s that can be allocated in the *SM* for both kernels. This value can be calculated at compilation time using both kernel requirements (shared memory storage, number of threads and number of registers) and the compute capability of the device. The second pair of counters stores the current count of running *CTA* per kernel. These last counters increase or decrease their values when a new *CTA* of a kernel is scheduled or finishes its computation, respectively. In SMK, a *CTA* of a kernel is scheduled if the current count of *CTA*s running on the *SM* is lower than the maximum number of *CTA*s.

4.2 Workloads

Table 2. Kernels used in the experiments.

Kernel Acronym	Application	CTAs per cluster	Category
HIST	Histogram [14]	16	MB
BS	Black Scholes [14]	32	MB
VA	Vector Addition [14]	16	MB
RED	Reduction [14]	16	MB
RCONV	Rows convolution [14]	64	MB
SRAD	Diffusion algorithm [15]	16	MB
LBM	Lattice-Boltzmann method [16]	20	MB
EULER	Euler3D [15]	10	MB
GCED	Gaussian Canny edge detection [17]	16	CB
PF	Pathfinder [15]	16	CB
MM	Matrix multiplication [14]	16	CB
HS	Hotspot [15]	10	CB
DXTC	DXT Compression [14]	24	CB
BOPTS	Binomial options [14]	32	CB

Experiments have been conducted using different kernels belonging to CUDA SDK [14], Rodinia [15], Parboil [16] and Chai [17] benchmark suites. Table 2 shows the names of the kernels, the maximum number of resident *CTA*s per cluster, and the category they are classified using the procedure explained in [5]. We have taken all the pairs of a memory-bound kernel with a compute-bound kernel to get 48 workloads. We have used them to compare SMK allocation against SMT allocation and the performance achieved by a fair-based allocation policy using our hybrid piece-wise slowdown model. We have simulated each workload by launching both kernels at the same time and stopping when one of them has no new *CTA*s left to allocate.

We have used the metrics defined in [11] to measure performance: Normalized Progress, NP, Average Normalized Turnaround Time, $ANTT$, System Throughput, STP and Fairness. NP_i is defined as the fraction of kernel i alone execution reached during shared execution, $NP_i = IPC_i^{Shared}/IPC_i^{Alone}$. The reciprocal of NP is the normalized turnaround time and it can be used to define $ANTT$, the slowdown due to concurrent execution of kernels i and j,

$$ANTT = \frac{1}{2}\left(\frac{1}{NP_i} + \frac{1}{NP_j}\right) \tag{5}$$

$ANTT$ is a lower-is-better metric. STP quantifies the accumulated progress of kernels i and j under concurrent execution, it is computed using Eq. 1, and is a higher-is-better metric. Finally, we have used the fairness metric defined in Eq. 4.

We have simulated each kernel executing in isolation to obtain reference values for IPC^{Alone}. We have also measured row buffer hits RBH and bandwidth utilization to compute the linear regression model that will be used with HSM and HPSM.

4.3 SMT Vs SMK Comparison

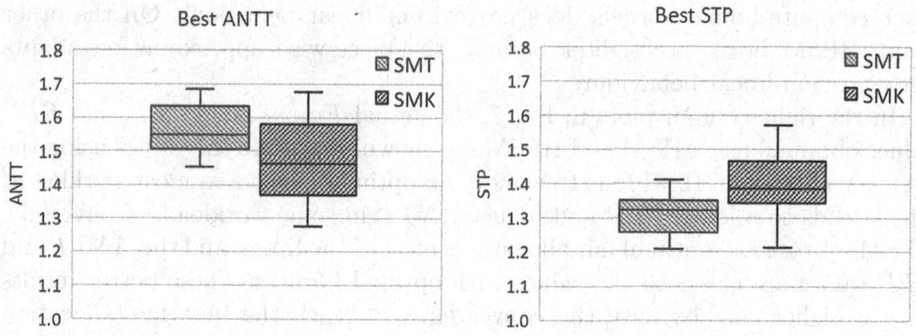

Fig. 6. Boxplots of best $ANTT$ and STP values achieved by SMT and SMK in kernel co-execution.

Each workload has been simulated using every possible SMT and SMK based SM allocation. In SMT, each kernel is allocated with 1 to 39 SM clusters and the other kernel with the remaining ones to complete the 40 clusters. In SMK, each kernel is allocated between 1 and the maximum number of resident CTAs per cluster (see Table 2), and the other kernel with as many CTAs as possible to fill the cluster. Then, we have obtained IPC^{Shared} values for each allocation of each workload and computed $ANTT$ y STP. Finally, we have selected the best values for each workload for both SMT and SMK. Boxplots of these values are shown in Fig. 6 to visualize their statistical properties [18]. On each box, the central mark corresponds to the median, the edges of the box are the 25th and 75th percentiles, and the whiskers extend to the most extreme data points not considered to be outliers (about $\pm 2.7\sigma$ and 99.3% coverage). SMK clearly outperforms SMT in both $ANTT$ and STP. This is mostly due to the fact that, in SMT allocation, CTAs of the same kernel compete for the same resources inside a SM. With SMK allocation there are CTAs from different kernels inside the same SM that may compete for different SM resources, reducing the destructive interference between co-running kernels.

4.4 Fairness Based Policy

In this work, we have proposed HPSM to predict the normalized progress, NP, of kernels executing concurrently. It models memory-bound kernels using the same scheme as HSM and uses a piece-wise approximation to predict NP of compute-bound kernels. These predictions can be used to allocate *CTA*s in a way that meets some criteria such as fairness. Thus, approximation errors can lead to wrong allocations that do not meet the criteria. We measure the approximation error using the percent relative error, $100 \times \frac{|\hat{\alpha}-\alpha|}{\alpha}$, where $\hat{\alpha}$ is the predicted value and α is the actual value.

We have evaluated both HPSM and HSM to obtain prediction errors while computing $Fairness$, $ANTT$, and STP for fairness-based *CTA* allocation. The left column plots in Fig. 7 show boxplots of all these prediction errors. The boxes height for HSM prediction errors is larger because the normalized progress of some compute-bound kernels does not exhibit linear behaviour. On the other hand, HPSM boxes are tighter because the piece-wise approximation adapts better to non-linear behaviour.

In the right column plots in Fig. 7, the actual $Fairness$, $ANTT$, and STP values obtained using HSM and HPSM are shown, alongside the values using the best fair allocation. HSM fails to achieve an optimal fairness in most workloads, which leads to a lower STP and higher $ANTT$ in some workloads. Conversely, HPSM selects near-optimal fair allocations most of the times, and the $ANTT$ and STP values are closer to the values with optimal fairness. These better results have a higher cost because the convergence to reach the best fair allocation is slower. We have measured the number of different allocations tested with each method: HSM tries 2.9 allocations on average, while HPSM goes up to 4.2 because it starts testing allocations in one extreme while HSM starts in the centre.

5 Related Works

Various authors have proposed hardware enhancements to the GPU architecture that improve CKE support using simulation tools such as GPGPUSim [13] or Accel-sim [19]. Adriens *et al.* [1] proposed one of the first hardware modifications to support CKE. They compared spatial multitasking, that is, kernel co-location, with cooperative multitasking, that is, temporal multitasking, and showed the advantages of the former one. Later, an intra-SM *CTA* allocation policy for CKE was proposed in [2], focusing on reducing the resource fragmentation when *CTA*s of different kernels are allocated in a SM. In addition, they also proposed a resource partitioning method that maximizes the throughput. However, it requires an off-line phase, which can take a long number of cycles, to obtain IPC values for each kernel varying the number of *CTA*s per SM. To save time, they proposed to carry out these measurements with several kernels executing concurrently. Wang *et al.* [3] proposed a similar *CTA* allocation strategy but including preemption. This way a new arriving kernel can be allocated by previously evicting *CTA*s belonging to the running kernel. This preemption mechanism allows to implement strategies for improving overall throughput while being fair to co-executing kernels. A productive mechanism to establish the best *CTA* mapping for two concurrent kernels was proposed

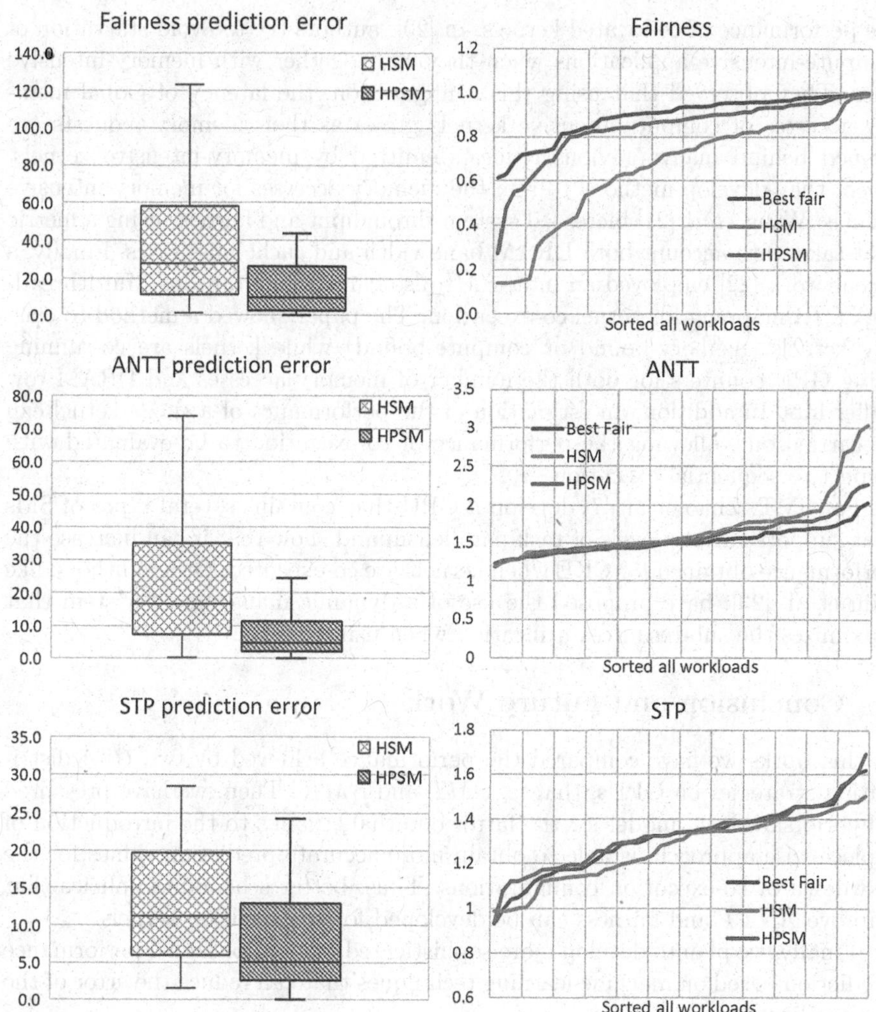

Fig. 7. Left column: boxplots of prediction errors for *Fairness*, *ANTT* and *SMT*. Right column: sorted results obtained with fairness-based *CTA* allocation for all workloads.

in [12]. A heuristic is proposed where different *CTA* mappings are assigned to different groups of *SM*s, thus quickly exploring all possible configurations. This heuristic consists of an iterative process that gradually finds the best co-location configuration by analyzing the IPC values in the *SM*s. In [10], the authors proposed a trained predictor of slowdown for co-located kernels to reduce the overhead produced by the process of finding the best solution. The predictor collects statistics of hardware events of two co-running kernels and estimates their slowdown. Other works have focused on the memory subsystem to increase the performance of co-located kernels. In [20], authors try to avoid starvation of compute-intensive applications when they run together with memory-intensive ones. They observed that using this configuration, the latency of global memory accesses of compute-intensive kernels grows as their memory requests are queued behind many previous requests emitted by memory-intensive kernels. Then, they develop methods to rein the memory accesses for memory-intensive kernels. Wang *et al.* [21] increased system throughput and fairness using a metric that takes into account both DRAM bandwidth and cache miss rates. Finally, a recent work [22] employed an inter-SM (also called Simultaneous Multithreading) CTA mapping for kernel co-execution. The paper showed a method to classify kernels (memory-bound or compute-bound) while kernels are co-running using GPU counters for both the number of memory accesses and DRAM row buffer hits. In addition, an estimation of the performance of a single kernel can be carried out, allowing the performance of co-execution to be evaluated with respect to sequential execution.

For SMT, Zhao et al. [7] develop a GPU that contains several types of SMs that support various levels of task parallelism and show that it can increase the performance obtained for CKE when kernels are co-executed. Other authors, like Kim et al. [23], have proposed the use of a dynamic management system that maximizes the sub-resources utilization when using SMT.

6 Conclusion and Future Work

In this works we have compared the performance achieved by two CTA distribution strategies on GPUs, that is, SMT and SMK. Then, we have presented a hybrid slowdown model for the latter one that, thanks to the introduction of a piece-wise approach, is able to obtain more accurate prediction values for the slowdown of co-execution configurations. Thus, better scheduling policies that improve $ANTT$ and fairness can be developed for co-execution kernels.

Finally, we plan to develop more sophisticated models for kernel performance prediction based on machine learning techniques that can reduce the error of the current linear model.

Acknowledgment. This work has been supported by the Junta de Andalucía of Spain (P18-FR-3130 and UMA20-FEDERJA-059) and the Ministry of Education of Spain (PID2019-105396RB-I00).

References

1. Adriaens, J.T., Compton, K., Kim, N.S., Schulte, M.J.: The case for GPGPU spatial multitasking, In: IEEE International Symposium on High-Performance Comp Architecture, pp. 1–12 (2012). https://doi.org/10.1109/HPCA.2012.6168946
2. Xu, Q., Jeon, H., Kim, K., Ro, W.W., Annavaram, M.: Warped-slicer: efficient intra-sm slicing through dynamic resource partitioning for gpu multiprogramming. In: 2016 ACM/IEEE 43rd Annual International Symposium on Computer Architecture (ISCA), ISCA 2016, pp. 230–242 (2016). https://doi.org/10.1109/ISCA.2016.29

3. Wang, Z., Yang, J., Melhem, R., Childers, B., Zhang, Y., Guo, M.: Simultaneous multikernel gpu: multi-tasking throughput processors via fine-grained sharing. In: IEEE International Symposium on High Performance Computer Architecture (HPCA) 2016, pp. 358–369 (2016). https://doi.org/10.1109/HPCA.2016.7446078
4. Zhao, C., Gao, W., Nie, F., Zhou, H.: A survey of GPU multitasking methods supported by hardware architecture. IEEE Trans. Parallel Distrib. Syst. **33**(6), 1451–1463 (2022). https://doi.org/10.1109/TPDS.2021.3115630
5. Zhao, X., Jahre, M., Eeckhout, L.: HSM: a Hybrid Slowdown Model for Multitasking GPUs, Association for Computing Machinery, pp. 1371–1385 (2020)
6. Zhao, X., Wang, Z., Eeckhout, L.: Classification-driven search for effective SM partitioning in multitasking GPUs. In: Proceedings of the 2018 International Conference on Supercomputing, ICS 2018, pp. 65–75. Association for Computing Machinery, New York 2018. https://doi.org/10.1145/3205289.3205311
7. Zhao, X., Wang, Z., Eeckhout, L.: HeteroCore GPU to exploit TLP-resource diversity. IEEE Trans. Parallel Distrib. Syst. **30**(1), 93–106 (2019). https://doi.org/10.1109/TPDS.2018.2854764
8. Thomas, W., Toraskar, S., Singh, V.: Dynamic optimizations in GPU using roofline model. In: IEEE International Symposium on Circuits and Systems (ISCAS) 2021, pp. 1–5 (2021). https://doi.org/10.1109/ISCAS51556.2021.9401255
9. Hu, Q., Shu, J., Fan, J., Lu, Y.: Run-time performance estimation and fairness-oriented scheduling policy for concurrent GPGPU applications. In: 2016 45th International Conference on Parallel Processing (ICPP), pp. 57–66 (2016). https://doi.org/10.1109/ICPP.2016.14
10. Zhao, W., et al.: Themis: predicting and reining in application-level slowdown on spatial multitasking GPUs. In: IEEE International Parallel and Distributed Processing Symposium (IPDPS) 2019, pp. 653–663 (2019). https://doi.org/10.1109/IPDPS.2019.00074
11. Eyerman, S., Eeckhout, L.: System-level performance metrics for multiprogram workloads. IEEE Micro **28**(3), 42–53 (2008). https://doi.org/10.1109/MM.2008.44
12. Park, J.J.K., Park, Y., Mahlke, S.: Resource management for efficient utilization of multitasking GPUs. In: Proceedings of the Twenty-Second International Conference on Architectural Support for Programming Languages and Operating Systems, ASPLOS 2017, pp. 527-540. ACM, New York (2017). https://doi.org/10.1145/3037697.3037707. http://doi.acm.org/10.1145/3037697.3037707
13. Bakhoda, A., Yuan, G.L., Fung, W.W.L., Wong, H., Aamodt, T.M.: Analyzing CUDA workloads using a detailed GPU simulator. In: IEEE International Symposium on Performance Analysis of Systems and Software 2009, pp. 163–174 (2009). https://doi.org/10.1109/ISPASS.2009.4919648
14. NVIDIA, Cuda sdk code samples, May 2018. https://www.nvidia.com/object/cuda_get_samples_3.html
15. Che, S., et al.: Rodinia: a benchmark suite for heterogeneous computing. In: IEEE International Symposium on Workload Characterization, 2009, IISWC 2009, pp. 44–54 (2009). https://doi.org/10.1109/IISWC.2009.5306797
16. Stratton, J.A., Rodrigues, C., Sung, I.-J., Obeid, N., Chang, L.-W., Anssari, N., Liu, G.D., Hwu, W.-M.W.: Parboil: a revised benchmark suite for scientific and commercial throughput computing. Center for Reliable and High-Performance Computing **127**, 29 (2012)
17. Gómez-Luna, J., et al.: Collaborative heterogeneous applications for integrated-architectures, in: ISPASS, pp. 43–54 (2017). https://doi.org/10.1109/ISPASS.2017.7975269

18. Tukey, J.W.: Exploratory Data Analysis (1977)
19. Khairy, M., Shen, Z., Aamodt, T.M., Rogers, T.G.: Accel-sim: an extensible simulation framework for validated GPU modeling. In: 2020 ACM/IEEE 47th Annual International Symposium on Computer Architecture (ISCA), 2020, pp. 473–486. https://doi.org/10.1109/ISCA45697.2020.00047
20. Dai, H., et al.: Accelerate GPU concurrent kernel execution by mitigating memory pipeline stalls. In: IEEE International Symposium on High Performance Computer Architecture (HPCA) 2018, pp. 208–220 (2018). https://doi.org/10.1109/HPCA.2018.00027
21. Wang, H., Luo, F., Ibrahim, M., Kayiran, O., Jog, A.: Efficient and fair multiprogramming in GPUs via effective bandwidth management. In: IEEE International Symposium on High Performance Computer Architecture (HPCA) 2018, pp. 247–258 (2018). https://doi.org/10.1109/HPCA.2018.00030
22. Zhao, X., Jahre, M., Eeckhout, L.: HSM: a hybrid slowdown model for multitasking GPUs, in: Proceedings of the Twenty-Fifth International Conference on Architectural Support for Programming Languages and Operating Systems, ASPLOS 2020, pp. 1371–1385. Association for Computing Machinery, New York (2020)
23. Kim, J., Cha, J., Park, J.J.K., Jeon, D., Park, Y.: Improving GPU multitasking efficiency using dynamic resource sharing. IEEE Comput. Archit. Lett. **18**(1), 1–5 (2019). https://doi.org/10.1109/LCA.2018.2889042

Parallel Numerical Methods and Applications

Accelerating Brain Simulations with the Fast Multipole Method

Hannah Nöttgen, Fabian Czappa(✉), and Felix Wolf

Laboratory for Parallel Programming, Technical University of Darmstadt, Darmstadt, Germany
hannah.noettgen@stud.tu-darmstadt.de,
{fabian.czappa,felix.wolf}@tu-darmstadt.de

Abstract. The brain is probably the most complex organ in the human body. To understand processes such as learning or healing after brain lesions, we need suitable tools for brain simulations. The Model of Structural Plasticity offers a solution to that problem. It provides a way to model the brain bottom-up by specifying the behavior of the neurons and using structural plasticity to form the synapses. However, its original formulation involves a pairwise evaluation of attraction kernels, which drastically limits scalability. While this complexity has recently been decreased to $O(n \cdot \log^2 n)$ after reformulating the task as a variant of an n-body problem and solving it using an adapted version of the Barnes–Hut approximation, we propose an even faster approximation based on the fast multipole method (FMM). The fast multipole method was initially introduced to solve pairwise interactions in linear time. Our adaptation achieves this time complexity, and it is also faster in practice than the previous approximation.

Keywords: Fast Multipole Method · Brain Simulation · Structural Plasticity · Scalability

1 Introduction

The human brain undergoes constant change not only in children but throughout the whole life [8]. These changes, especially in the form of synapse creation and deletion, are believed to be responsible for a major portion of the brain dynamics. There is overwhelming evidence that structural plasticity, i.e., the change of connectivity of neurons, is responsible for learning, memory creation, and healing after lesions [12,20,23–25]. However, current in vivo imaging techniques cannot create connectivity maps for human brains at a scale comparable to the original [5,12,13]. This leaves a large portion of current research in need of simulations to fill the gap. Many state-of-the-art simulators can mimic very complex behaviors of a single neuron, however, they lack the possibility to let neurons freely connect to others. This task inherently involves solving pairwise interactions. Seeing that the human brain contains 86 billion neurons [6], this

J. Cano and P. W. Trinder (Eds.): Euro-Par 2022, LNCS 13440, pp. 387–402, 2022.
https://doi.org/10.1007/978-3-031-12597-3_24

drastically limits scalability. Many simulators bypass this issue by only allowing already existing connections to be strengthened or weakened (synaptic plasticity), bringing the complexity down to linear in the number of neurons and synapses per neuron.

It is not fully understood how neurons form and delete synapses over time. For a long time, Hebbian Plasticity [19] was the dominant opinion. In recent times, however, homeostatic mechanisms—in which neurons pursue a stable state and thus the whole brain reaches an equilibrium—have been suggested and shown to be accurate [7,10]. One of these mechanisms, the Model of Structural Plasticity [7], predicts the recovery of lesions in mice very well. In a recent publication, Rinke et al. [27] have reduced the quadratic complexity of solving the pairwise interactions to $O(n \cdot \log^2 n)$. They achieved this by utilizing the Barnes–Hut algorithm [3], which has been developed to approximately solve pairwise interactions, which is popular in the context of physics.

We propose another approximation for the pairwise interactions based on the fast multipole method (FMM) [28]. While Barnes–Hut calculates point-area interactions, FMM calculates area-area interactions, reducing the complexity from quadratic to linear. Current in vivo imaging techniques such as [9] cannot precisely locate where synapses begin and end; they can only trace them to a certain area. This, together with the fact that we do not know exactly why a particular neuron formed a (long-reaching) synapse and not its direct neighbor, gives us confidence that this approximation is reasonable.

In this publication, we build on the Barnes–Hut approximation and utilize their distributed algorithm to implement our approximation in terms of the fast multipole method. To summarize, our main contributions are:

- We integrated the fast multipole method into an existing parallel neuron simulation and replaced the Barnes–Hut algorithm, which was responsible for finding synapses.
- We reduced the theoretical complexity from $O(n/p \cdot \log^2 n)$ to $O(n/p + p)$, when n is the number of input neurons and p the number of MPI ranks.
- We measured the influence on performance in practice for different numbers of computing nodes.

The remainder of this paper is structured as follows. We firstly review related work in Sect. 2 before we explain relevant background in Sect. 3. Afterward, we present our algorithm in Sect. 4, and analyze it in terms of theoretical and practical run time with multiple compute nodes in Sect. 5.

2 Related Work

There are many brain simulators freely available, for example, C2 [2], NEST [16], and The Virtual Brain [29]. They allow initial connectivity of neurons to be inserted, and during the simulation, they may strengthen and weaken those. However, they do not create new connections.

This way, their connectivity update step has complexity $O(n \cdot m)$, where n is the number of neurons and m is the number of synapses per neuron. The latter term is most often bounded (e.g., at most 1000 synapses per neuron), and thus, it is linear in the number of neurons.

Structural plasticity—the way in which neurons grow new and delete old synapses—has gained track in recent years; see [31] for an overview of the current state of the art. A simple model for structural plasticity, proposed by van Ooyen et al. [30], achieves this by defining the outreach of a neuron to be a circle around its center. The individual neurons form synapses proportional to the overlapping area whenever two such circles overlap. This model requires linear time for the connectivity update, but it lacks the possibility of connecting neurons while omitting a third neuron between them. The Model of Structural Plasticity (MSP) [7], on which this publication is based, overcomes this limitation by calculating the connection probability dependent on the distance of neurons.

In the MSP, the likelihood of a synapse forming between two neurons with positions p_1, p_2, is proportional to $\texttt{exp}(-||p_1 - p_2||_2^2/\sigma)$, with a scaling constant $\sigma > 0$. This way, the greater the distance between two neurons is, the smaller the likelihood of a connection between them is. Rinke et al. [27] used this insight to approximate the influence of a whole area of neurons far away with the Barnes–Hut algorithm [3]. They achieved this by inserting the neurons into an octree and calculating the attraction to inner nodes whenever possible (thus skipping the need to calculate the attraction to all neurons in the induced subtree). This way, they reduced the complexity of calculating $O(n^2)$ interactions (n again the number of neurons) to $O(n \cdot \log^2 n)$.

The fast multipole method (FMM) [17,28] is another way of approximating pairwise interactions. Instead of only combining the affecting elements (neurons, particles, etc.) at the calculation's source side, they also group the affected elements at the target side. This way, they can approximate the pairwise interactions in linear time using Hermite and Taylor expansions [14,15]. This is used quite successfully in physics, including astrophysics [11] and particle simulation [1]. There exists many accelerated FMM implementations both with GPUs and MPI, for example [18,26,32]. However, they focus on a fixed-level attraction, i.e., in contrast to us, they don't need to resolve the attractions down to a object–object level.

3 Background

In this section, we repeat the arguments and definitions from previous publications to be partially self-contained. This includes the initial publication for the Model of Structural Plasticity [7], the one that introduced the fast multipole method we use [17], and the publication that introduced the Barnes–Hut approximation to the MSP [27].

3.1 The Model of Structural Plasticity

The Model of Structural Plasticity [7] describes how neurons change their plasticity over time, i.e., how they form new and delete old synapses. It consists of three different phases:

The update of electrical activity, the update of synaptic elements, and the update of synapses. An overview of the used model parameters can be seen in Table 1.

Update of Electrical Activity. In the step to update the electrical activity, all neurons calculate their current activity. This can be done by neuron models such as the one proposed by Izhikevich [21], the FitzHugh–Nagumo model [22], or as in our case, a Poisson spiking neuron model (the same as in [27]).

In our model, the activity, on the one hand, strives exponentially to a resting potential (resting potential: 0.05, constant of decay: 5); on the other hand, it is constantly increased by a small background activity (0.003) and the input of all connected neurons (those neurons that form a synapse from their axon to the dendrite of the neuron in question) that spiked in the last update step by a fixed amount (5e−4). Then a uniformly distributed value from $[0, 1]$ is drawn, and if this value is smaller than the current activity, the neuron spikes. If a neuron spikes, it does not spike again for a fixed number of steps (refractory period: 4).

Update of Synaptic Elements. In the update step, each neuron updates its intercellular calcium level. The calcium level decays exponentially (constant of decay: 1e−5), while if a neuron spiked in that simulation step, it is increased by a fixed value (1e−3).

After the neuron has updated its calcium, it uses this to determine the amount of change to its synaptic elements. We use the same Gaussian growth curve as originally proposed in [7], setting the right intersection (the target value) to 0.7, the left intersection (the point at which the elements start to grow) to 0.4 for axons, and 0.1 for dendrites, and the scaling parameter to 1e−4 (maximum attained value). The neuron updates the number of axons and dendrites by the calculated amount.

Update of Synapses. Every time a neuron updates its synapses (once every 100 updates of activity and synaptic elements), it checks its number of synaptic elements. If it now has fewer elements than synapses (the elements are continuous, the synapses discrete), it chooses synapses randomly, notifies the connected neurons, and deletes them. It does so for both the dendrites with the incoming synapses and the axons with the outgoing synapses.

After the deletion phase, if a neuron has at least one vacant axon, it searches for another neuron with one vacant dendrite to connect to. For each vacant axon (i), it calculates the probability of connecting to a vacant dendrite (j) by

$$K(i, j) = \mathbf{exp}\Big(\frac{-||\mathbf{pos}_i - \mathbf{pos}_j||_2^2}{\sigma}\Big) \tag{1}$$

Table 1. Overview of the model parameters used in the executions and tests. A more detailed description of the model and the parameters can be found in [7].

Name	Symbol	Value
Resting potential	x_0	0.05
Membrane potential constant of decay	τ_x	5
Background activity	I	0.003
Increase in calcium per spike	β	5e−4
Calcium constant of decay	τ_{Ca}	1e−5
Gaussian growth curve right intersection	ϵ	0.7
Gaussian growth curve left intersection (axons)	η_A	0.4
Gaussian growth curve left intersection (dendrites)	η_D	0.1
Growth scaling parameter	μ	1e−4
Probability kernel standard deviation	σ	750

and chooses one such vacant dendrite ($\sigma = 750$ as in [7]). These requests are gathered (this takes quadratic time) and sent to the neurons with vacant dendrites. Those resolve potential conflicts, and a new synapse is formed whenever possible.

3.2 A Distributed Octree

In [27], Rinke et al. introduced a distributed octree to overcome the memory limitations inherent to large simulations. The problem is that only a limited number of octree nodes can be held in memory. In order to be able to simulate more neurons and thus achieve the desired order of magnitude, many MPI ranks are required. They recursively divide the simulation domain into eight cells until a cell contains at most one neuron. Inner nodes of the octree store the sum of vacant elements of all their children and the combined position (the centroid), which is just the weighted average position of the children. The octree is updated in a step-wise fashion: All ranks update their subtrees, then exchange the branch nodes, and calculate the shared upper portion afterward. They insert all neurons into a spatial octree, where every MPI rank is responsible for 1, 2, or 4 subtrees. All ranks share the same upper portion of the octree (heights 0 to $\log(8, p)$ where p is the number of ranks), and if a rank i requires information of a neuron on rank j, it downloads them lazily.

3.3 Mathematical Formulation of the Fast Multipole Method

Assuming there is a set of points in space, we consider a split into M sources $s_1, \ldots, s_M$ (in our case the neurons that have a vacant dendrite) and N targets (the neurons that have a vacant axon) $t_1, \ldots, t_N$. If a neuron has vacant axons as well as vacant dendrites, it is included in both sets M and N. The general form of an n-body problem is [4]:

$$u(t) = \sum_{i=1}^{M} \omega_i \cdot K(t, s_i) \tag{2}$$

$\omega_i \in \mathbb{R}$: The weight of the point s_i.

$K : (\mathbb{R}^3 \times \mathbb{R}^3) \to \mathbb{R}$: A kernel that calculates the interaction between t and s_i.

This formula gives the total attraction $u(t)$ for a vacant axon. If a neuron has more than one vacant axon, we multiply $u(t)$ with that number. In order to calculate $u(\cdot)$ for every target t_j, this function must be calculated N times, which results in a total complexity of $O(N \cdot M)$. If every source is also a target, i.e., $N = M$, this scales quadratically.

The general form of Eq. 2 fits the attraction formula of the MSP (cf. Eq. 1), with ω_i being the number of vacant dendrites of a neuron and $u(t)$ being the force of attraction to an axon of a neuron at position t.

Notation. A multi-index $\alpha = (n_1, n_2, n_3)$ is a tuple of three natural numbers (including zero). For any multi-index and any vector $t = (x, y, z) \in \mathbb{R}^3$, we define the following operations:

$$|\alpha| = n_1 + n_2 + n_3 \tag{3}$$

$$\alpha! = n_1! \cdot n_2! \cdot n_3! \tag{4}$$

$$t^\alpha = x^{n_1} \cdot y^{n_2} \cdot z^{n_3} \tag{5}$$

For our adapted fast multipole method we often use multi-indices in combination with sums. For example, $\sum_{\alpha \geq p}$ or $\sum_{0 \leq \alpha \leq p}$ stands for three nested sums with $n_1, n_2, n_3 \geq p$ or $0 \leq n_1, n_2, n_3 \leq p$, respectively.

Approximations of Attraction Kernel. In general the MSP sums over Gaussian functions. We can approximate the attraction of multiple neurons in a box and group the sources and targets together. For each such box (S for a box of sources, T for a box of targets), we need to calculate the centroid with respect to its sources s_C and its targets t_C. Using the function $h(\alpha, x)$ (the same as in [17] Eq. 8) and $\delta = \sigma^2$, Eq. 2 with the Gaussian kernel of Eq. 1 has the following Taylor series (using a multi-index β):

$$\begin{aligned} u(t) &= \sum_{0 \leq \beta} B_\beta \cdot \left(\frac{t - t_C}{\sqrt{\delta}} \right)^\beta \\ B_\beta &= \frac{(-1)^{|\beta|}}{\beta!} \cdot \sum_{j=1}^{M} \omega_j \cdot h\left(\beta, \frac{s_j - t_C}{\sqrt{\delta}} \right) \end{aligned} \tag{6}$$

We can truncate the outer series from Eq. 6, i.e., sum only up to some fixed β. The approximation error depends on the box side length, which is determined by the box's level in the octree. Furthermore, the number of calculated terms and the number of sources that are approximated have an influence on the approximation error. Overall, the calculation of one coefficient B_β from Eq. 6 has complexity $O(M)$, and crucially they are shared for all targets in the box. In addition, Eq. 6 must be calculated for N target points with k coefficients. This results in a complexity of $O(k \cdot M + k \cdot N)$ for a interaction between one target box and one source box.

Alternatively, we can also approximate Eq. 1 with Hermite coefficients A_α, where the same argument as before applies (with multi-index α). The complexity to calculate this expansion is also $O(k \cdot M + k \cdot N)$ for k coefficients:

$$u(t) = \sum_{0 \leq \alpha} A_\alpha \cdot h\left(\alpha, \frac{t - s_C}{\sqrt{\delta}}\right)$$
$$A_\alpha = \frac{1}{\alpha!} \cdot \sum_{j=1}^{M} \omega_j \cdot \left(\frac{s_j - s_C}{\sqrt{\delta}}\right)^\alpha \tag{7}$$

4 Algorithm Description

To determine which neurons form synapses with each other, we must calculate the forces of attraction between the target and source neurons (note here that a "source" and "target" are used differently in the literature: The "source" neuron is the one with the axon, however, it is the "target" of the attraction). Therefore, we create an n-body problem on top of the kernel in Eq. 1 in order to apply the series expansions already presented:

$$u(t) = \sum_{j=1}^{M} \omega_j \cdot \exp\left(\frac{-\|t - s_j\|_2^2}{\sigma^2}\right), \tag{8}$$

where ω_j is the number of vacant dendritic elements of the j-th neuron. Furthermore, we use the same distributed octree as in [27]. In our version—compared to the Barnes–Hut inspired one—we also need to calculate the centroid of the inner nodes with respect to the axons. For this, we increased the size of the octree nodes from 200 Bytes to 264 Bytes (2× 32 Byte for the axon positions, which consist of 24 Bytes vector and a flag).

Algorithm 1 shows the implementation for finding suitable neurons. For the initialization of the stack (Line 2), we first collect all roots of the subtrees and then find another subtree-root as the target for each of them, as described in the paragraph below. We push the source–target pairs onto the stack and then process the elements of the stack until it is empty. Whenever we want to form a synapse, we save the source and target ids and send them to the MPI rank of the target. Each rank collects these requests, chooses locally which to accept (to avoid too many synapses, e.g., five axons want to connect to two dendrites), and sends the answers back.

Initialization of the Stack. Every MPI rank does the following: For each of its subtree-roots, choose a target with `choose_target` (cf. Algorithm 2) with the global root as initial target. Fix the subtree-root and only unpack the targets until the target is at the same level as the subtree-root. Put these pairs on the stack.

```
find_synapses():
    init(stack)
    while (! stack.empty()):
        source_node, target_node = stack.pop()
        if (source_node.is_leaf && target_node.is_leaf):
            form_synapse(source_node, target_node)
        else if (source_node.is_leaf):
            new_target = choose_target(source_node, target_node.children)
            stack.push(source_node, new_target)
        else if (target_node.is_leaf):
            new_source = choose_source(source_node.children, target_node)
            stack.push(new_source, target_node)
        else: foreach (new_source in source_node.children)
                new_target = choose_target
                    (new_source, target_node.children)
                stack.push(new_source, new_target)
```

Algorithm 1: Pseudo code of the method `find_synapses`. `choose_target` and `choose_source` are shown in Algorithm 2.

Choice of Target Node. This method calculates the attractiveness of the target neurons to the source neuron. It does so by first determining if it needs to evaluate the formula directly or if it can use an approximation (Taylor or Hermite). It then calculates the attractiveness of the children of the target and chooses one randomly, proportional to their attractiveness. In addition, the method needs two constants `c1` and `c2`, which determine when a Taylor or a Hermite expansion is used as it is easier to evaluate the attractions directly if the number of dendrites and axons is small.

4.1 Complexity

For the complexity, it is enough to determine how often `choose_target` is called. We assume a balanced octree and start with the serial version. Starting at level 0, the root must determine a target for each of its children, so it calls `choose_target` 8 times and thus spawns 8 new pairs to consider. For each of the newly created pairs, the same applies, they spawn (up to) 8 new tasks, and in general, processing level k of the octree spawns 8^k tasks. As the tree is balanced its height is $\log(8, n)$ for n neurons, so it spawns $8, 64, \ldots, n/8, n$ tasks, i.e., linear in the number of neurons.

choose_target itself either performs a direct pair-wise calculation (with quadratic complexity) or one of the FMM approximations (with linear complexity). In our instance, however, choose_target has a constant complexity because the number of sources and targets is at most 8.

For the parallel version, we have to initialize the stack first. This requires choosing a target node for each subtree-root on the same level, which is $\log(p)$ for p the number of MPI ranks. Once we have found the pairs, we can apply the serial version to n/p neurons, so the overall complexity is $O(n/p + \log p)$. Gathering the branch nodes beforehand has complexity $O(p)$, so the overall complexity of the connectivity update is $O(n/p + p)$.

```
choose_target(source_node, target_node):
    probabilities = [ ]

    for (i = 0; i < target_node.number_children; i++):
        child = target_node.children[ i ]

        if (source.is_leaf || child.is_leaf):
            probabilities[ i ] = direct_calculation()

        else if (child.get_number_dendrites() > c1
           && source_node.get_number_axons() > c2):
            probabilities[ i ] = calculate_hermite_expanison()

        else if (child.get_number_dendrites() > c1):
            probabilities[ i ] = calculate_taylor_expanison()

        else:
            probabilities[ i ] = direct_calculation()

    total_probability = sum(probabilities)
    rand = uniform_random(0, total_probability)
    index = upper_bound(probabilities, rand)

    return target_node.children[index]
```

Algorithm 2: choose_target calculates the probability for source_node to connect to each child of target_node. It chooses the method based on the number of vacant axons and dendrites. It then picks one target neuron randomly with chances proportional to the calculated probabilities. choose_source works analogously with swapped roles of source_node and target_node. In our case, c1 = 70 and c2 = 70.

5 Evaluation

Our proposed algorithm trades time against freedom of choice; the complexity of finding the target neurons is lower than for the adapted Barnes–Hut algorithm, however, we lose some freedom of choice for the synapses. Previously, with the Barnes–Hut algorithm, each axon searched its own dendrite, so if a neuron had two vacant axons, they could connect to dendrites with a large distance between them as they could be in different nodes. In our algorithm, both axons are always in the same box, so their choice will be the same throughout the whole process. This also affects axons on neurons that are close to each other—if they are in the same box on level l, their choice of boxes coincides on every level $i = 0, \dots, l-1$. This, in turn, means that every neural network that was calculated with the fast multipole method can also be calculated with the Barnes–Hut algorithm, but not vice versa.

All calculations for this research were conducted on the Lichtenberg 2 high-performance computer of the TU Darmstadt. One compute node has 2 Intel Xeon Platinum 9242 processors (with disabled hyper-threading), 384 GB main memory, and the interconnection is a 100 GBit/s InfiniBand. We always tested the algorithm with 500 000 simulation steps (5000 connectivity updates) and a network with only excitatory neurons.

From a neuroscientific point of view, we investigated the following observable metrics for both the Barnes–Hut and the fast multipole method inspired algorithms:

1. The average calcium concentration of the neurons (together with the standard deviation) to see how well both algorithms allow the neurons to reach a local equilibrium.
2. The number of formed synapses to see how well the overall simulation reaches a global equilibrium.

Figure 1 shows the average calcium of the neurons (together with its standard deviation), and Fig. 2 shows the total number of created synapses for one run of $p = 64$ MPI ranks and $n = 320\,000$ neurons. With our proposed algorithm, the average calcium is nearly indistinguishable from the Barnes–Hut algorithm, however, its standard deviation is slightly higher. Our algorithm trails the previous version slightly when it comes to the total number of formed synapses. This is due to more collisions, resulting in more rejections, so we need more simulation steps to connect all vacant axons. Furthermore, the total number of synapses is less for our algorithm. The reason is that a neuron generally grows more dendrites than axons. If the synapses now cluster more (due to the restricted freedom of choice), some neurons receive more synapses than they want—so they delete some again.

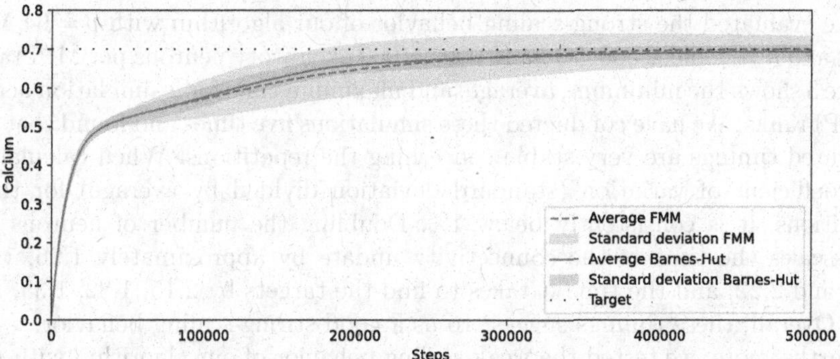

Fig. 1. The average calcium (solid lines) and its standard deviation (light area) for both algorithms (Barnes–Hut in solid purple, fast multipole method in dashed orange). The target calcium is 0.7 (thinly dashed black line). $p = 64$ MPI ranks, $n = 320\,000$ neurons, and 500 000 simulation steps (5000 connectivity updates). (Color figure online)

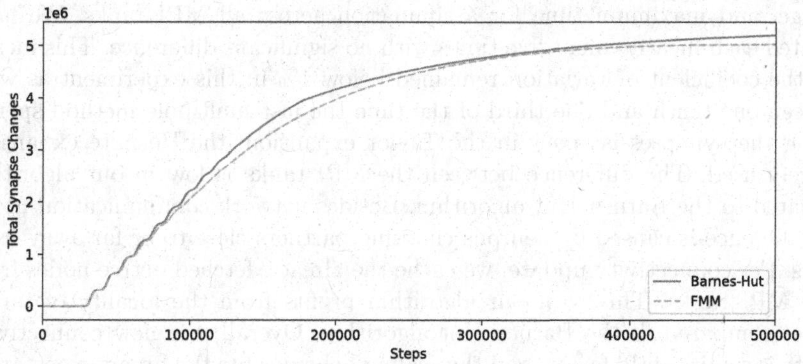

Fig. 2. The total number of synapses for both algorithms. $p = 64$ MPI ranks, $n = 320\,000$ neurons, and 500 000 simulation steps (5000 connectivity updates).

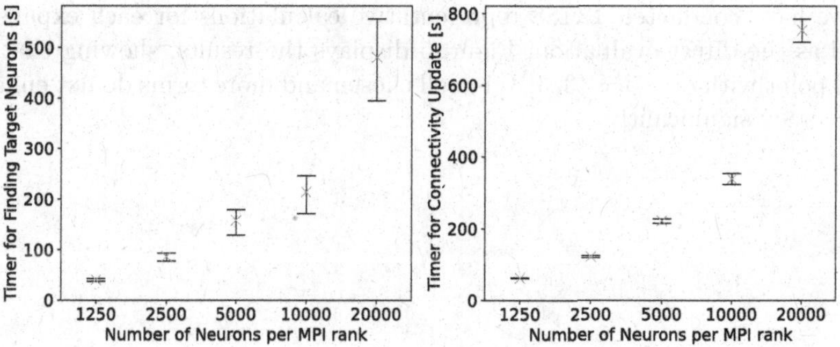

Fig. 3. The timings for the strong scaling experiments with $p = 64$ MPI ranks and 500 000 simulation steps (5000 connectivity updates). We give the minimum, average, and maximum time across the different ranks. All timings are in seconds.

We evaluated the strong-scaling behavior of our algorithm with $p = 64$ MPI ranks and $n = 1\,250, 2\,500, 5\,000, 10\,000, 20\,000$ excitatory neurons per MPI rank. Figure 3 shows the minimum, average, and maximum time for a simulation across all MPI ranks. We have conducted these simulations five times and found that the generated timings are very stable concerning the repetitions. When calculating the coefficient of variation (standard deviation divided by average) for these repetitions, it is consistently below 1%. Doubling the number of neurons per rank scales the time of the connectivity update by approximately 1.96, 1.81, 1.53, and 2.22, and the time it takes to find the targets by 2.15, 1.82, 1.35, and 2.25. Overall, these timings suggest to us a good strong-scaling behavior.

Furthermore, we tested the weak-scaling behavior of our algorithm with $n = 5000$ neurons per MPI rank (as in the previous publication which introduced the Barnes–Hut approximation [27]) and with $p = 1, 2, 4, 8, 16, 32, 64$ MPI ranks. For the timings, we investigated the overall time for the connectivity update, the time it takes to find the target neurons, and for the fast multipole method also the time it takes to compute the expansions. Figure 4 shows the minimum, average, and maximum time for a simulation across all MPI ranks. We have repeated each measurement five times with no significant difference. This means that the coefficient of variation remained below 1% in this experiment as well. Between one tenth and one third of the time the fast multipole method spends finding the synapses is spent in the Taylor expansion; the Hermite expansion is rarely used. The difference between the MPI ranks is low in our algorithm compared to the Barnes–Hut algorithm. Besides network communication noise, this difference is caused by neurons choosing partners close to or far away from others. Per connectivity update, we cache the already fetched octree nodes from other MPI ranks. This way, our algorithm profits from the locality of target choices compared to the Barnes–Hut algorithm. Overall, the new connectivity update is significantly faster, and the scaling behavior fits the broad expectation of $O(n/p + p)$.

Lastly, we evaluated the influence of the parameters β from Eq. 6 and α from Eq. 7, i.e., the points at which we cut of the evaluation of the infinite series. For this, we have conducted 12 188 representative calculations for each expansion, as well as the direct evaluation. Figure 5 displays the results, showing that our cut-off point with $\alpha = \beta = (3, 3, 3)$ is well chosen and more terms do not enhance the accuracy significantly.

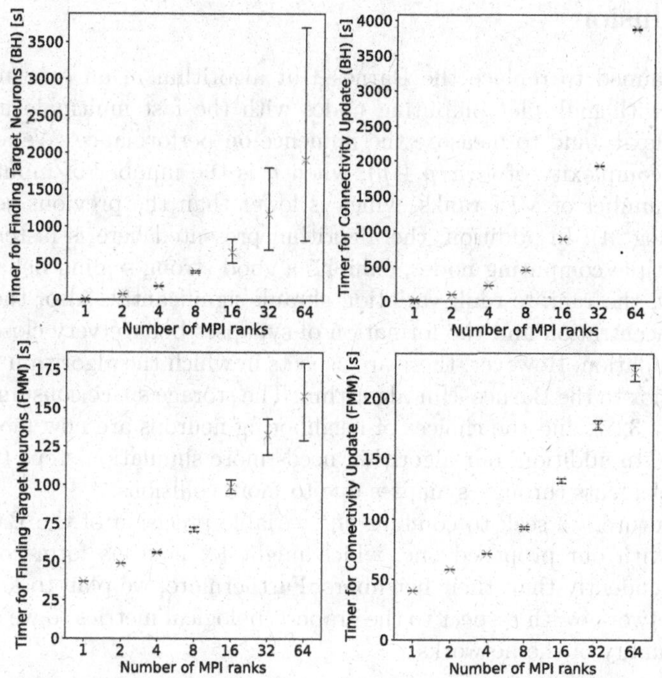

Fig. 4. The timings of different methods of the simulation for $p = 1, 2, 4, 8, 16, 32, 64$ MPI ranks and 500 000 simulation steps (5000 connectivity updates). For each method we give the minimum, average, and maximum time across the different MPI ranks. All timings are in seconds.

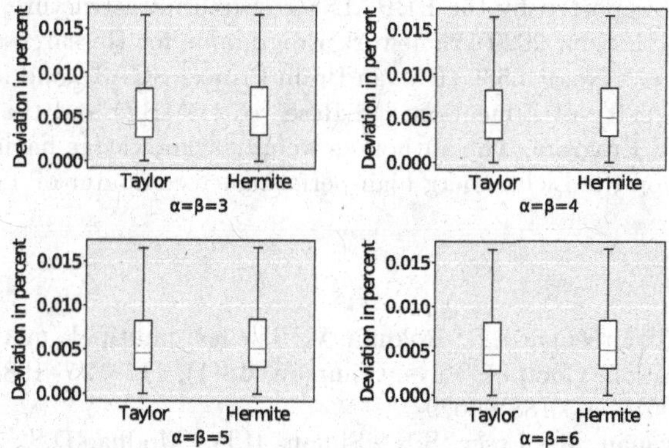

Fig. 5. The deviation in percent between the directly evaluated attraction and the corresponding Hermite and Taylor expansions, gathered from 12 188 representative boxes. The red line is the median, the box indicates the 0.25 and 0.75 quartile, the interval indicates the minimum and maximum after removing all outliers. A value is an outlier if it is larger then the 0.75 quartile + 1.5 times the inter-quartile range. The number of outliers for the Taylor expansions were 1830, 1834, 1833, and 1833, and there were consistently 1753 outliers for the Hermite expansions. The largest outliers were below 0.125%. (Color figure online)

6 Conclusion

This work aimed to replace the Barnes–Hut algorithm in an existing neuron simulation with multiple computing nodes with the fast multipole method of lower complexity and to measure the influence on performance. We achieved a theoretical complexity of $O(n/p + p)$, when n is the number of input neurons and p the number of MPI ranks, which is lower than the previous complexity of $O(n/p \cdot \log^2 n)$. In addition, the algorithm presented here is faster in practice on multiple computing nodes, exhibits a good strong-scaling behavior, and additionally, the rank-to-rank variation shrank significantly. Also, the internal calcium concentration and the formation of synapses behave very closely to the original simulation. However, there are aspects in which the algorithm presented here is inferior to the Barnes–Hut algorithm. The storage space consumption has increased by 32%, and the choices of neighboring neurons are now more similar than before. In addition, our algorithm needs more simulation steps to connect all vacant elements through synapses due to more collisions.

In the future, we seek to combine the variable precision of the Barnes–Hut algorithm with our proposed one, which might let neurons form connections more independently than their neighbors. Furthermore, we plan to analyze the resulting networks with respect to the graph-topological metrics so we can assess the functionality of the networks.

Acknowledgments. We acknowledge the support of the European Commission and the German Federal Ministry of Education and Research (BMBF) under the EuroHPC Programme DEEP-SEA (955606, BMBF Funding No. 16HPC015). The EuroHPC Joint Undertaking (JU) receives support from the European Union's Horizon 2020 research and innovation programme and GER, FRA, ESP, GRC, BEL, SWE, UK, CHE. This research was also supported by the EBRAINS research infrastructure, funded by the European Union's Horizon 2020 Framework Programme for Research and Innovation under the Specific GA No. 945539 (Human Brain Project SGA3), and is partly funded by the Federal Ministry of Education and Research (BMBF) and the state of Hesse as part of the NHR Program. The authors gratefully acknowledge having conducted a part of this study on the Lichtenberg high-performance computer of TU Darmstadt.

References

1. Ambrosiano, J., Greengard, L., Rokhlin, V.: The fast multipole method for gridless particle simulation. Comput. Phys. Commun. **48**(1), 117–125 (1988). https://doi.org/10.1016/0010-4655(88)90029-X
2. Ananthanarayanan, R., Esser, S.K., Simon, H.D., Modha, D.S.: The cat is out of the bag: cortical simulations with 109 neurons, 1013 synapses. In: SC 2009. Association for Computing Machinery, New York (2009). https://doi.org/10.1145/1654059.1654124
3. Barnes, J., Hut, P.: A hierarchical o (n log n) force-calculation algorithm. Nature **324**(6096), 446–449 (1986). https://doi.org/10.1038/324446a0
4. Beatson, R., Greengard, L.: A short course on fast multipole methods. Technical report, Department of Mathematics and Statistics, University of Canterbury and Courant Institute of Mathematical Sciences, New York University (1997)

5. Beaujoin, J., et al.: Post-mortem inference of the human hippocampal connectivity and microstructure using ultra-high field diffusion MRI at 11.7 T. Brain Struct. Funct. **223**(5), 2157–2179 (2018). https://doi.org/10.1007/s00429-018-1617-1
6. Berlin, C.U.: Brain simulation section (2019). https://www.brainpreservation.org/content-2/connectome/. Accessed June 2021
7. Butz, M., van Ooyen, A.: A simple rule for dendritic spine and axonal bouton formation can account for cortical reorganization after focal retinal lesions. PLOS Comput. Biol. **9**(10), 1–21 (2013). https://doi.org/10.1371/journal.pcbi.1003259
8. Butz, M., Wörgötter, F., Ooyen, A.: Activity-dependent structural plasticity. Brain Res. Rev. **60**, 287–305 (2009). https://doi.org/10.1016/j.brainresrev.2008.12.023
9. Chen, X., Wang, Y., Kopetzky, S.J., Butz-Ostendorf, M., Kaiser, M.: Connectivity within regions characterizes epilepsy duration and treatment outcome. Hum. Brain Mapp. **42**(12), 3777–3791 (2021). https://doi.org/10.1002/hbm.25464
10. Dammasch, I.E., Wagner, G.P., Wolff, J.R.: Self-stabilization of neuronal networks. Biol. Cybern. **54**(4), 211–222 (1986). https://doi.org/10.1007/BF00318417
11. Dehnen, W.: A fast multipole method for stellar dynamics. Comput. Astrophys. Cosmol. **1**(1), 1–23 (2014). https://doi.org/10.1186/s40668-014-0001-7
12. Diaz-Pier, S., Naveau, M., Butz-Ostendorf, M., Morrison, A.: Automatic generation of connectivity for large-scale neuronal network models through structural plasticity. Front. Neuroanat. **10**, 57 (2016). https://doi.org/10.3389/fnana.2016.00057
13. Dodt, H.U., et al.: Ultramicroscopy: three-dimensional visualization of neuronal networks in the whole mouse brain. Nat. Methods **4**(4), 331–336 (2007). https://doi.org/10.1038/nmeth1036
14. Eylert, B.: Praktische Mathematik für Informatiker. Telematiker und Ingenieure, Wildau (2014)
15. Friedrich, H., Pietschmann, F.: Numerische Methoden: ein Lehr- und Übungsbuch, 2. auflage edn. De Gruyter Studium, Berlin (2020)
16. Gewaltig, M.O., Diesmann, M.: Nest (neural simulation tool). Scholarpedia **2**(4), 1430 (2007)
17. Greengard, L., Strain, J.: The fast gauss transform. SIAM J. Sci. Stat. Comput. **12**(1), 79–94 (1991). https://doi.org/10.1137/0912004
18. Gumerov, N.A., Duraiswami, R.: Fast multipole methods on graphics processors. J. Comput. Phys. **227**(18), 8290–8313 (2008). https://doi.org/10.1016/j.jcp.2008.05.023
19. Hebb, D.O.: The Organization of Behavior: A Neuropsychological Theory. Psychology Press, London (2005)
20. Holtmaat, A., Svoboda, K.: Experience-dependent structural synaptic plasticity in the mammalian brain. Nat. Rev. Neurosci. **10**(9), 647–658 (2009). https://doi.org/10.1038/nrn2699
21. Izhikevich, E.M.: Simple model of spiking neurons. IEEE Trans. Neural Netw. **14**(6), 1569–1572 (2003). https://doi.org/10.1109/TNN.2003.820440
22. Izhikevich, E.M., FitzHugh, R.: Fitzhugh-Nagumo model. Scholarpedia **1**(9), 1349 (2006)
23. Keck, T., Mrsic-Flogel, T.D., Vaz Afonso, M., Eysel, U.T., Bonhoeffer, T., Hübener, M.: Massive restructuring of neuronal circuits during functional reorganization of adult visual cortex. Nat. Neurosci. **11**(10), 1162–1167 (2008). https://doi.org/10.1038/nn.2181
24. Kleim, J.A., et al.: Synapse formation is associated with memory storage in the cerebellum. Proc. Natl. Acad. Sci. **99**(20), 13228–13231 (2002). https://doi.org/10.1073/pnas.202483399

25. Kleim, J.A., Hogg, T.M., VandenBerg, P.M., Cooper, N.R., Bruneau, R., Remple, M.: Cortical synaptogenesis and motor map reorganization occur during late, but not early, phase of motor skill learning. J. Neurosci. **24**(3), 628–633 (2004). https://doi.org/10.1523/JNEUROSCI.3440-03.2004
26. Lashuk, I., et al.: A massively parallel adaptive fast-multipole method on heterogeneous architectures. In: Proceedings of the Conference on High Performance Computing Networking, Storage and Analysis, pp. 1–12 (2009). https://doi.org/10.1145/1654059.1654118
27. Rinke, S., Butz-Ostendorf, M., Hermanns, M.A., Naveau, M., Wolf, F.: A scalable algorithm for simulating the structural plasticity of the brain. J. Parallel Distrib. Comput. **120**, 251–266 (2018). https://doi.org/10.1016/j.jpdc.2017.11.019
28. Rokhlin, V.: Rapid solution of integral equations of classical potential theory. J. Comput. Phys. **60**(2), 187–207 (1985). https://doi.org/10.1016/0021-9991(85)90002-6
29. Sanz Leon, P., et al.: The virtual brain: a simulator of primate brain network dynamics. Front. Neuroinform. **7** (2013). https://doi.org/10.3389/fninf.2013.00010
30. van Ooyen, A., van Pelt, J.: Activity-dependent neurite outgrowth and neural network development. In: Van Pelt, J., Corner, M., Uylings, H., Lopes Da Silva, F. (eds.) The Self-Organizing Brain: From Growth Cones to Functional Networks, Progress in Brain Research, vol. 102, pp. 245–259. Elsevier (1994). https://doi.org/10.1016/S0079-6123(08)60544-0
31. Van Ooyen, A., Butz-Ostendorf, M.: The Rewiring Brain: A Computational Approach to Structural Plasticity in the Adult Brain. Academic Press, London (2017)
32. Yokota, R., Barba, L., Narumi, T., Yasuoka, K.: Petascale turbulence simulation using a highly parallel fast multipole method on GPUs. Comput. Phys. Commun. **184**(3), 445–455 (2013). https://doi.org/10.1016/j.cpc.2012.09.011

High-Performance Spatial Data Compression for Scientific Applications

Ronald Kriemann[1](✉), Hatem Ltaief[2], Minh Bau Luong[3], Francisco E. Hernández Pérez[3], Hong G. Im[3], and David Keyes[2]

[1] Max Planck Institute for Mathematics in the Sciences, Leipzig, Germany
rok@mis.mpg.de

[2] Extreme Computing Research Center, KAUST, Thuwal, Saudi Arabia
{Hatem.Ltaief,David.Keyes}@kaust.edu.sa

[3] Clean Combustion Research Center, KAUST, Thuwal, Saudi Arabia
{minhbau.luong,francisco.hernandezperez.1,Hong.Im}@kaust.edu.sa

Abstract. We implement an efficient data compression algorithm that reduces the memory footprint of spatial datasets generated during scientific simulations. Storing regularly these datasets is typically needed for checkpoint/restart or for post-processing purposes. Our lossy compression approach, codenamed `HLRcompress` (https://gitlab.mis.mpg.de/rok/HLRcompress), combines a hierarchical low-rank approximation technique with binary compression. This novel hybrid method is agnostic to the particular domain of application. We study the impact of `HLRcompress` on accuracy using synthetic datasets to demonstrate the software capabilities, including robustness and versatility. We assess different algebraic compression methods and report performance results on various parallel architectures. We then integrate it into a workflow of a direct numerical simulation solver for turbulent combustion on distributed-memory systems. We compress the generated snapshots during time integration using accuracy thresholds for each individual chemical species, without degrading the practical accuracy of the overall pressure and temperature. We eventually compare against state-of-the-art compression software. Our implementation achieves on average greater than 100-fold compression of the original size of the datasets.

Keywords: Algebraic/Binary Compression · Scientific Datasets · Hierarchical Matrices

1 Introduction

Over the three last decades, the High-Performance Computing (HPC) community has witnessed a billion-fold improvement in computational power, thanks to hardware technology scaling. This extreme scaling may however translate into architectures over-provisioned in floating-point units. While high computational throughput is often beneficial for scientific applications in sustaining performance, data movement remains the main bottleneck. Indeed, memory bandwidth has not similarly benefited, which creates imbalanced situations where

J. Cano and P. W. Trinder (Eds.): Euro-Par 2022, LNCS 13440, pp. 403–418, 2022.
https://doi.org/10.1007/978-3-031-12597-3_25

the system cannot supply data at the pace required by the computational hardware. This challenge is further exacerbated when the applications need to fetch data from/to remote storage media. The current hardware landscape may transform scientific applications into an I/O-bound regime of execution. Data compression has become a popular solution to address bandwidth starvation and improve the performance of I/O operations. In particular, binary compression approaches [14,28] have been successful in mitigating the overheads of data motion needed for performing checkpoint/restart, post-processing purposes such as visualization, or reducing the storage footprint of archived scientific data.

In this paper, we combine an algebraic spatial data compression method based on Hierarchical Low-Rank (HLR) approximation techniques [15,21,22] using standard linear algebra operations with binary compression. It employs various algebraic compression methods, e.g., Singular Value Decomposition (SVD), Randomization SVD (RSVD), Rank-Revealing QR (RRQR), or Adaptive Cross-Approximation (ACA), and relies on vendor-optimized scientific libraries for performance and portability. With the addition of binary compression, we further adapt the number representation to the accuracy and optimize the compression level. We demonstrate the capabilities of `HLRcompress`, including robustness and versatility, using synthetic datasets. We illustrate the effectiveness of our approach on several shared-memory systems and show the compression rate and performance superiorities relative to state-of-the-art compression methods. Furthermore, we incorporate `HLRcompress` into a turbulent combustion simulation. We compress the generated domain solutions during time integration for each individual chemical species for post-processing purposes, without degrading the practical accuracy of the overall pressure and temperature fields. We achieve more than 100-fold compression rate compared to the full dataset, outperforming SZ [14] by 29%, MGARD [1] by 58% and ZFP [28] by 820% for the total memory savings. Compared to similar algebraic compression methods, the compression ratio is 3X better without sacrificing runtime.

The remainder of the paper is as follows. Section 2 provides the necessary background on low-rank matrix approximations. Section 3 positions our work among existing compression techniques. Section 4 provides the algorithmic formulation, the complexity, the error analysis, and the implementation details of `HLRcompress`. We showcase compression rates and performance results in Sect. 5 on synthetic and real datasets and discuss future work in Sect. 6.

2 Background

Low-rank compression of dense data has long been used for representing dense matrices in the context of integral and partial differential equations in the form of *hierarchical matrices* ($\mathcal{H}$-matrices) [21,22]. The goal is to attain (log-)linear arithmetic and memory storage complexity. Various optimizations of these have been developed, e.g., by using shared and nested bases for the low-rank factors in the $\mathcal{H}^2$-matrix format [7,18] or for highly oscillatory data with Directional-$\mathcal{H}^2$ [8] or Butterfly factorization [27]. Other formats simplify the structure of the hierarchy, e.g., the TLR/BLR format [26,35] with a flat block layout or the Hierarchically Off-Diagonal Low-Rank (HODLR) [2]) and Hierarchically Semi-Separable (HSS) [12,37] formats, with hierarchical blocks only along the diagonal. Common to all low-rank schemes is a reordering of the rows and columns of the matrix such that neighboring rows/columns correspond to spatially neighbored (data) points. Different methods exist to perform this initial step, e.g., via binary space partitioning [23]. For other problems this reordering is based on graph distances [17] or purely algebraic properties of the matrix [38]. After the permutation of the matrix rows and columns, the actual identification of low-rank blocks is normally based on an *admissibility condition*, which is again often based on spatial data, e.g., diameters and distances of subsets of the geometry [19,20]. Once identified, a candidate block for low-rank representation can be approximated using different algorithms, e.g., SVD/RRQR, randomized methods [24], ACA [6], CUR [34] or interpolation decompositions [11].

Unfortunately, for the compression of spatial data the above mentioned admissibility condition is not usable as it requires each row and column to be associated with a spatial position. However, in the case of 2D spatial datasets the matrix entry itself corresponds to a spatial position, with rows and columns just being separate parts, i.e., for the position $(x, y) \in \mathbb{R}^2$ a row corresponds to the x-part and a column to the y-part.

3 Related Work

By using the rank computed by any of the above mentioned low-rank approximation schemes, one can directly determine if a given sub-block has low-rank property. Such a method for multi-dimensional data was introduced in [15], which is a generalization of the coarsening algorithm for $\mathcal{H}$-matrices described in [16]. They employ an *adaptive* procedure by recursively partitioning the block structure of the data and approximating it in a bottom-up way by a (tensor) low-rank representation with respect to a user-defined accuracy $\varepsilon > 0$. For the 2D case, this is structurally identical to `HLRcompress`. A top-down approach (HALR) for an adaptive admissibility of matrices from partial differential equations is described in [36]. There, for a matrix block, a low-rank approximation is computed with a user-defined accuracy *and* a maximal permitted rank. If such an approximation exists, the block is considered as low-rank approximable, if not, its sub-blocks are tested. Using SVD for the low-rank approximation, HALR can guarantee accuracy though with a cubic runtime complexity. To limit the computational cost, ACA [6] is chosen instead as it only requires the matrix coefficients for the chosen rows and columns. However, there are known cases where it overlooks parts of a matrix, which results in bad approximation [9]. In fact, the ACA based version of HALR fails to compute an accurate approximation of the spatial data studied in this work. Furthermore, the goal of HALR of generating low-rank blocks as soon as possible in the hierarchy is not optimal for compression as it may result in blocks with a larger rank. A more fine-grained representation with low-rank blocks of a much smaller rank may be more efficient. Global tensor decomposition and HOSVD is used in TuckerMPI [3] and in TThresh [4] for multi-dimensional data, but with the same high runtime complexity as a global SVD in the 2D case. Furthermore, it may result in non-optimal compression if no global low-rank properties are present in the data. MGARD [1] is another compressor based on techniques from algebraic multigrid methods and as such also employing an hierarchical approach. Unfortunately, it showed compression problems when using high accuracy for the datasets in Sect. 5. Other error-bounded lossy compression methods are ZFP [28] and SZ [14]. ZFP decomposes d-dimensional data into blocks of size 4^d and then represents the floating point data in an optimized way such that either a user-defined (bit-) rate or accuracy is guaranteed. SZ applies a curve-fitting method for the full dataset for compression. The additional lossy compression of low-rank data is also used in TThresh for the tensor data and investigated in [30] for a global SVD based compression. MGARD uses additional lossless compression on the binary multigrid data.

In this work, we introduce `HLRcompress`, a high-performance, parallel implementation of an algebraic data compression using hierarchical low-rank (HLR) approximations with additional binary compression based on ZFP on various hardware platforms. We highlight the versatility, the numerical robustness, and the performance scalability on 2D spatial datasets generated from a synthetic testcase. We then deploy `HLRcompress` into a combustion application and prove its effectiveness in improving the I/O performance of the post-processing phase, without degrading the practical accuracy of the domain solutions.

4 Hierarchical Low-Rank Data Compression

4.1 Problem Definition and Adaptive Procedure

We consider the 2D case, i.e., we have a set of N data points $d_{ij} \in \mathbb{R}$ with $i \in I := \{0, \ldots, m-1\}, j \in J := \{0, \ldots, n-1\}$ and $m \cdot n = N$. For simplicity, we assume that the indices i and j correspond to the spatial position $(i \cdot h_x, j \cdot h_y)$ with step widths $h_x, h_y > 0$. With this definition, the data d_{ij} forms a $m \times n$ matrix D.

As in [15,16], we assume a hierarchical partitioning $\mathcal{T}$ of D. If not given, it can easily be constructed by recursively starting at $(I, J) \in \mathcal{T}$ and splitting each block (τ, σ) of $\mathcal{T}$ with $\tau = [i_\tau^0 : i_\tau^{\ell-1}], \sigma = [j_\sigma^0 : j_\sigma^{k-1}]$, $0 < \ell < m$, $0 < k < n$, into four (almost) equal sized sub-blocks: $\begin{pmatrix} (\tau_0, \sigma_0) & (\tau_0, \sigma_1) \\ (\tau_1, \sigma_0) & (\tau_1, \sigma_1) \end{pmatrix}$, with $\tau_0 = [i_\tau^0 : i_\tau^{\ell/2-1}], \tau_1 = [i_\tau^{\ell/2} : i_\tau^{\ell-1}]$ and $\sigma_0 = [j_\sigma^0 : j_\sigma^{k/2-1}], \sigma_1 = [j_\sigma^{k/2} : j_\sigma^{k-1}]$. The process stops if $\min(\#\tau, \#\sigma) \leq n_{\text{tile}}, n_{\text{tile}} > 0$. The size of n_{tile} is typically chosen to optimize performance but also has an influence on the memory efficiency of the method. The blocks in $\mathcal{T}$ form a tree with (I, J) being the root and with children $(\tau_0, \sigma_0), (\tau_0, \sigma_1), (\tau_1, \sigma_0), (\tau_1, \sigma_1)$ for all inner nodes $(\tau, \sigma) \in \mathcal{T}$. Let $\mathcal{L}$ be the set of leaves of $\mathcal{T}$.

The compression starts by computing a low-rank approximation $U_{\tau,\sigma} V_{\tau,\sigma}^H$ for all blocks $D_{\tau,\sigma} := D|_{\tau,\sigma}$ with $(\tau, \sigma) \in \mathcal{L}$. This approximation is computed with respect to a given precision $\varepsilon > 0$: $\|D_{\tau,\sigma} - U_{\tau,\sigma}V_{\tau,\sigma}^H\| \leq \varepsilon\|D_{\tau,\sigma}\|$. Let $k_{\tau,\sigma}$ be the corresponding rank, i.e., $U_{\tau,\sigma} \in \mathbb{R}^{\#\tau \times k_{\tau,\sigma}}$ and $V_{\tau,\sigma} \in \mathbb{R}^{\#\sigma \times k_{\tau,\sigma}}$. If $k_{\tau,\sigma} < \min(\#\tau, \#\sigma)/2$, the representation of $D_{\tau,\sigma}$ via $U_{\tau,\sigma}V_{\tau,\sigma}^H$ uses less memory compared to the full dense representation. In this case, the low-rank format is kept. Otherwise, the full data is stored. Here, a too small value of n_{tile} may favor full data representation as a very small rank is required to switch to low-rank approximation.

In the next step, neighboring low-rank matrices are merged together. For this, let (τ,σ) be a non-leaf block in $\mathcal{T}$ and with low-rank sub-blocks $D_{\tau_i,\sigma_j} = U_{\tau_i,\sigma_i}V_{\tau_j,\sigma_j}^H, 0 \leq i,j < 2$. This can also be represented as

$$\begin{aligned} D_{\tau,\sigma} &= \begin{pmatrix} U_{\tau_0,\sigma_0} & U_{\tau_0,\sigma_1} & 0 & 0 \\ 0 & 0 & U_{\tau_1,\sigma_0} & U_{\tau_1,\sigma_1} \end{pmatrix} \cdot \begin{pmatrix} V_{\tau_0,\sigma_0} & 0 & V_{\tau_1,\sigma_0} & 0 \\ 0 & V_{\tau_0,\sigma_1} & 0 & V_{\tau_1,\sigma_1} \end{pmatrix}^H \\ &=: \widehat{U}_{\tau,\sigma} \cdot \widehat{V}_{\tau,\sigma}^H. \end{aligned}$$

Using low-rank truncation, $\widehat{U}_{\tau,\sigma}\widehat{V}_{\tau,\sigma}^H$ can be again approximated up to ε by another low-rank matrix, i.e., $[\widetilde{U}_{\tau,\sigma}, \widetilde{V}_{\tau,\sigma}] := \text{truncate}\left(\widehat{U}_{\tau,\sigma}, \widehat{V}_{\tau,\sigma}\right)$, with rank $\widetilde{k}_{\tau,\sigma}$. If the memory requirements for $\widetilde{U}_{\tau,\sigma}\widetilde{V}_{\tau,\sigma}^H$ are less than the combined memory of the smaller low-rank matrices, i.e., if $\widetilde{k}_{\tau,\sigma} < \frac{\sum_{i,j=0}^{1} k_{\tau_i,\sigma_j}}{2}$, then the merged and truncated low-rank matrix is kept. Otherwise, we keep the low-rank blocks of the level below. The same strategy is also applied for dense blocks, e.g., if all sub-blocks are dense, they are merged to form a larger block, thereby preventing a too fine-grained representation. If no merging is performed, the data of the sub-blocks is finalized and will not be changed anymore.

Instead of a 2×2 subdivision per block, more sub-blocks may be used, though this typically increases the joined rank of all sub-blocks in the merging phase and may lead to a higher cost of that stage.

We further apply lossy binary compression to the low-rank factors $U_{\tau_i,\sigma_j}, V_{\tau_i,\sigma_j}$, $0 \leq i,j < 2$, (or the data of dense blocks) while maintaining the approximation error. For this we use ZFP because it proved very robust with respect to the input data due to the small chunks (4^d with d being the problem dimension) to which it applies compression[1]. With this, all computations may be performed in double (or single) precision but the final memory representation is still optimal with respect to the user defined accuracy ε.

This merging process is repeated for all blocks starting from the leaves until either no low-rank approximation with a sufficiently small rank can be found or the root of $\mathcal{T}$ is reached, in which case D is approximated by a global low-rank matrix. The full procedure is shown in Algorithm 1 in the form of a recursion starting at D, with **approxlr** a general low-rank approximation algorithm (e.g. SVD, RRQR, etc.) and **truncate** a low-rank truncation procedure.

[1] Using SZ resulted only in a small compression benefit or even worse compression rates, leading to the assumption that the curve fitting algorithm of SZ seems to work best with the original uncompressed data and not the data already compressed by low-rank approximation.

Algorithm 1: HLRcompress.

```
function HLRcompress(M, ε, n_tile)
  [n, m] := size(M);
  if min(n, m) ≤ n_tile then
    { Compression Phase }
    [U, V] := approxlr(M, ε);
    if mem(Ũ) + mem(Ṽ) < n · m then
      return Ũ, Ṽ;
    else
      return M;
  else
    for 0 ≤ i, j < 2 :
      rs := [i · n/2 + 1 : (i + 1) · n/2];
      cs := [i · m/2 + 1 : (i + 1) · m/2];
      M_ij := HLRcompress(M(rs, cs), ε, n_tile);
    { Merging Phase }
    if M00, M01, M10, M11 all low-rank then
      U := ( U_0,0  U_0,1  0      0     )
           ( 0      0      U_1,0  U_1,1 );
      V := ( V_0,0  0      V_1,0  0     )
           ( 0      V_0,1  0      V_1,1 );
      [Ũ, Ṽ] := truncate(U, V);
      if mem(Ũ, Ṽ) < Σ_{i,j=0}^{1} mem(M_ij) then
        return Ũ, Ṽ;
    elif M00, M01, M10, M11 all dense then
      return M;
    for 0 ≤ i, j < 2 :
      if M_ij is low-rank or dense then
        zfp_compress( M_ij );
    return ( M00  M01 )
           ( M10  M11 );
```

Let $\widetilde{D} = (\widetilde{d}_{ij})_{i=0,j=0}^{m-1,n-1}$ be the result of Algorithm 1. Note that the coefficients $\widetilde{d}_{ij}$ are only implicitly given if the corresponding block is stored as a low-rank matrix. Let also $\widetilde{\mathcal{T}}$ be the resulting partitioning, i.e., with leaves $\widetilde{\mathcal{L}}$ of $\widetilde{\mathcal{T}}$ defined by the merging stage. By construction, $\widetilde{\mathcal{T}}$ is a sub tree of $\mathcal{T}$.

4.2 Error Bounds

In Algorithm 1, a single accuracy parameter ε is used for all blocks. However, this only guarantees a local error bound. To satisfy a global accuracy, the local precision has to be adapted. For this, we want to bound the error in the Frobenius norm $\|D - \widetilde{D}\|_F \le \varepsilon \|D\|_F$ We assume that the error is uniformly distributed throughout the full matrix, i.e., $\forall 0 \le i < m, 0 \le j < n : |d_{ij} - \widetilde{d}_{ij}| \approx \delta$, for some $\delta \ge 0$. This yields $\sum_{i=0}^{m-1} \sum_{j=0}^{n-1} (d_{ij} - \widetilde{d}_{ij})^2 \approx \sum_{i=0}^{m-1} \sum_{j=0}^{n-1} \delta^2 = mn\delta^2$ and hence $\delta \le \frac{\varepsilon \|D\|_F}{\sqrt{mn}}$. Because the aforementioned assumption also implies $\|D_{\tau,\sigma} - \widetilde{D}_{\tau,\sigma}\|_F = \delta\sqrt{\#\tau\#\sigma}$, we can define the local (absolute) error bounds as: $\varepsilon_{\tau,\sigma} := \delta\sqrt{\#\tau\#\sigma}$. These local precisions are used for the initial compression as well as for the low-rank truncation during the merge phase.

4.3 Runtime Complexity

For simplicity, we assume the square case, i.e., $m = n$, where n is a power of 2. Furthermore, we use SVD as the most time consuming low-rank approximation algorithm for the initial compression of the leaves in $\mathcal{T}$ and also for the low-rank truncation while merging sub-blocks. Since there are $n/n_{\text{tile}} \cdot n/n_{\text{tile}}$ leaves and the SVD has runtime complexity of $\mathcal{O}(n_{\text{tile}}^3)$, the leaf compression takes $\mathcal{O}\left(\frac{n}{n_{\text{tile}}} \cdot \frac{n}{n_{\text{tile}}} \cdot n_{\text{tile}}^3\right) = \mathcal{O}(n_{\text{tile}} \cdot n^2)$. For the merging phase, we assume a maximal rank of half the block size up to the root. For a single merge step for a block of size $n' \times n'$ with $n_{\text{tile}} < n' \le n$ and rank $k' = \frac{n'}{2}/2$ for the sub-blocks, this results in truncation cost of $\mathcal{O}(k'^2 n'/2 + k'^3) = \mathcal{O}(n'^3)$. Summing up all merges for all $\log n - \log n_{\text{tile}}$ level, this yields $\sum_{i=0}^{\log n/n_{\text{tile}}} 4^i \left(\frac{n}{2^i}\right)^3 = n^3 \sum_{i=0}^{\log n/n_{\text{tile}}} \frac{1}{2^i} = \mathcal{O}\left(n_{\text{tile}} \cdot n^2\right)$, which is identical to the initial compression. However, as this is the worst case scenario for the merging phase, it is expected that normally the compression of the leaf blocks is the most time-consuming part of the algorithm.

4.4 Implementation Details

Algorithm 1 is a typical reduction algorithm and, as such, is easily parallelizable, i.e., each recursive call of `HLRcompress` is a separate, independent task, spawning further sub-tasks. This is also used in the actual implementation which uses Intel TBB or OpenMP. Furthermore, as most of the computational work is expected to be performed during the initial compression stage of the $m/n_{\text{tile}} \times n/n_{\text{tile}}$ leaves, an almost perfect parallel speedup is expected. In case of load imbalance, OpenMP dynamic scheduling may mitigate the resulting overheads. However, the hierarchical compression method can also be formulated to handle each layer separately, starting at the leaf level. Standard loop parallelization can be used per level to compress or merge blocks. Such a level-by-level algorithm creates opportunities for *batch operations* on GPUs. Indeed, the initial compression is an easy candidate for batching as the block size is (nearly) identical and compression has to be performed for all leaves. The sub-block merging phase on the other hand may witness a wide range of different ranks and a highly irregular structure, which makes efficient use of batch functions difficult. However, we expect the largest gains by accelerating this first stage of the algorithm.

5 Performance Results

Environment Settings. We launch our performance benchmarking campaign on two shared-memory x86 systems. The first system is a two-socket 36-core Intel Ice Lake 8360Y. The second system is a two-socket 64-core AMD Epyc Rome 7702. We rely on GCC 10.2/10.3 compilers, link against sequential Intel MKL v2021.2/v2020.0[2] for high-performance linear algebra operations, and use TBB v2020.1/v2021.2 for thread parallelism, respectively. Both servers have 512 GB of main memory with 54 MB/256 MB L3 cache size per socket for Intel and AMD systems, respectively. The Intel system hosts an NVIDIA A100 40 GB GPU with CUDA 11.2. We refer to each system by their respective vendor name. Unless stated otherwise, all computations are performed on AMD Epyc in double precision arithmetic and we report performance average out of five runs. We use ZFP v0.5.5, SZ v2.1 and MGARD v1.0. For SZ, we set best compression mode with relative error bound. ZFP is configured to use fixed-accuracy mode with the same block-wise accuracy as for low-rank compression or δ from Sect. 4.2 if applied globally as this ZFP compression mode is designed for absolute error. MGARD is configured for relative error with additional lossless compression (`CPU_Lossless`), which yielded best results. We also include results for compression by HLR alone, as used in [15], to demonstrate the improvements by the additional ZFP compression.

[2] AVX2 code path via MKL_DEBUG_CPU_TYPE=5 on AMD Epyc.

5.1 Logarithmic Kernel

This example is a modified version of the classical 1D model problem for $\mathcal{H}$-matrices [10]. The dataset $D^{\log} = (d_{ij}^{\log})_{i,j=0}^{n}$ is defined as $d_{ij}^{\log} = \log |x_i - x_j|_2$, with $x_i, 0 \leq i < n$, uniformly distributed over the 2D unit circle, i.e., $x_i = (\sin ih, \cos ih), h := 2\pi/n$ (Fig. 1). $D^{\log}$ becomes singular along the diagonal and at the lower left and upper right corner. This dataset is smooth away from the diagonal singularity resulting in very good low-rank properties, yielding large low-rank blocks after compression corresponding to a long running merging phase. The resulting partitioning depends on the user-defined accuracy ε, as shown in Fig. 2 (top). The numbers in the various (green) low-rank blocks are the corresponding rank while red blocks signal dense storage. Compression rates for the pure HLR compression, `HLRcompress`, ZFP and SZ are shown in Fig. 2 (middle). For HLR and `HLRcompress`, we use SVD for low-rank approximation/truncation and a tile size of $n_{\text{tile}} = 32$, which yields best results though the compression rates for $16 \leq n_{\text{tile}} \leq 256$ are very similar. For all compression algorithms, we choose the same overall relative accuracy. Because of the smoothness, the compression gets better with a larger problem size. This is also true for the SZ compression algorithm for $\varepsilon = 10^4$. For a higher accuracy, the SZ compression rate seems to stagnate. ZFP also shows a better compression for smoother data though the rate only decreases slowly. Furthermore, the benefit of ZFP in `HLRcompress` is clearly visible compared to HLR compression alone. The runtime shown in Fig. 2 (bottom) is very similar throughout the tested precisions, indicating only a small increase in ranks with an increased accuracy, typically seen for smooth datasets. SZ compression shows a much larger runtime compared to the other algorithms with the main reason being that parallelization is not supported for 2D datasets. Although comparing elapsed time is unfair, our compression rate remains superior to SZ. The fastest compression is achieved with ZFP, which also supports OpenMP, however it also shows the worst compression rates. The theoretical complexity of $\mathcal{O}(n^2)$ for `HLRcompress` (see Sect. 4.3) is also confirmed by these tests; see the black lines in the bottom three panels of Fig. 2.

Fig. 1. Dataset of logarithmic model problem.

Due to the nature of the algorithm, `HLRcompress` shows performance scalability independent on the CPU vendor, as seen in Table 1. On Intel, `HLRcompress` shows a nearly perfect speedup, whereas it is slightly reduced on AMD. However, when using only 36 cores per socket on the AMD system, the parallel speedup is almost linear with 33X/65X, similar to the Intel system. This seems to indicate a bandwidth saturation with the larger number of cores on the AMD system as both systems have an identical memory bandwidth. The AMD system exhibits a better time to solution than Intel thanks to a larger L3-cache per core ratio, which enables `HLRcompress` to better exploit the higher L3 cache bandwidth [29].

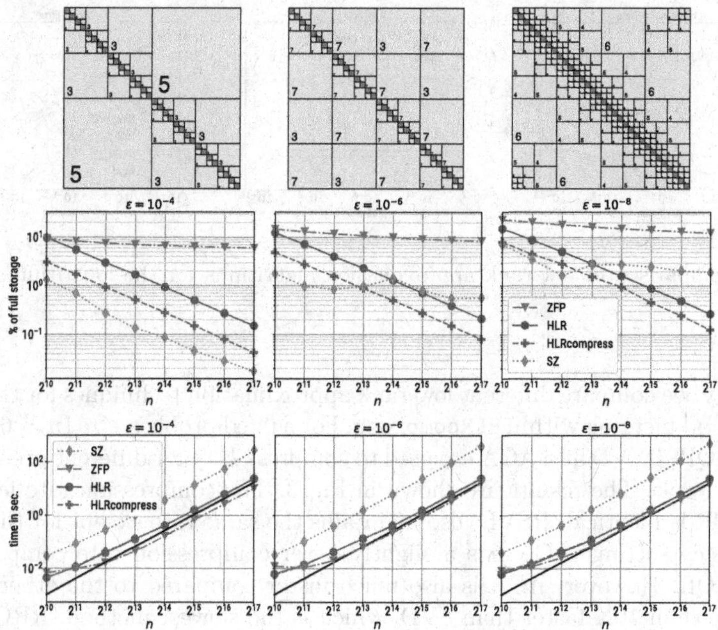

Fig. 2. Hierarchical partitioning (top), compression rates (middle) and runtime (bottom) with precisions $\varepsilon = 10^{-4}$, $\varepsilon = 10^{-6}$ and $\varepsilon = 10^{-8}$ (left to right).

Table 1. Runtime (T)/Speedup (S) for n = 131.072 on different CPUs.

Socket	#cores	T	S
Intel	36	74.43 s	36X
2x Intel	72	37.51 s	71X
AMD	64	43.21 s	49X
2x AMD	128	22.75 s	93X

Table 2. NVIDIA/AMD runtimes for (a) compression/(b) merging stages.

Matrix size n	8.192	16.384	32.768	65.536
(a) NVIDIA	0.04 s	0.16 s	0.65 s	2.70 s
(a) AMD	0.12 s	0.38 s	1.47 s	5.62 s
(b)	0.03 s	0.12 s	0.31 s	0.99 s

Moreover, as discussed in Sect. 4.4 for the initial compression, batching functions should be considered to maintain high occupancy on GPUs. Table 2 reports time breakdown of the compression/merging phases on the AMD and NVIDIA systems. We rely on the SVD implementation of the cuSolver library for the compression of the leaf blocks on the GPU device, while performing the merging phase on the CPU host. For smaller problems, the merging phase still dominates the computation. However, the trend changes for an increasing problem size and is expected to go on. The maximum size of the problem is limited by the GPU main memory. We can see the NVIDIA A100 GPU outperforms the AMD system by a factor of two. The main reason for the rather small speedup is that the batched SVD on the GPU is based on Jacobi SVD (`gesvj`) whereas on the CPU the faster `gesvd` LAPACK function is used. Nevertheless, it shows the potential of GPUs for the compression stage.

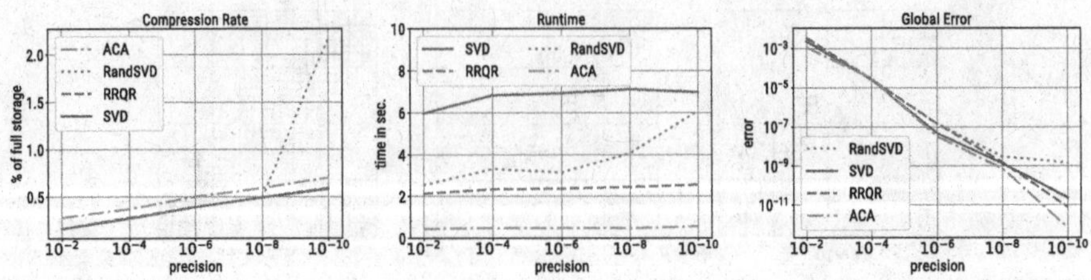

Fig. 3. Comparison of low-rank approximation algorithms for the logarithmic model problem.

Finally, we compare different low-rank approximation techniques for the compression and merging within `HLRcompress`. For a fixed problem size ($n = 65.536$), SVD, RRQR, RSVD and ACA are used to compress $D^{\log}$ for different pre-defined accuracy levels. The results are shown in Fig. 3. The compression rate for SVD and RRQR is identical. RSVD also maintains the same rate except for the highest accuracy setting. ACA has a slightly lower compression rate compared to SVD/RRQR. However, ACA is also much faster compared to the other methods, more than 10X faster than SVD, which is the slowest method. RRQR and RSVD follow in between. The global accuracy is very similar between all low-rank approximation algorithms. However, RSVD fails to achieve the given accuracy for $\varepsilon = 10^{-10}$. In this case, ACA actually surpasses all other methods. Because of the smoothness of the dataset, ACA is expected to converge fast with a small rank.

Thanks to this behaviour, the HALR algorithm from [36] based on ACA is even faster than `HLRcompress`, as it stops recursion earlier in the tree, with only a slightly worse compression rate compared to HLRcompress (for $n = 4096$ 3% for `HLRcompress` vs. 4% for HALR). With SVD instead of ACA, the same compression ratio as with `HLRcompress` is achieved but with a much higher runtime (52s for HALR vs. 0.03s for HLRcompress).

5.2 The Wave Equation

The global low-rank properties of the logarithmic kernel example are normally not present in typical data sets. To look into the compression behavior of HLR-compress for more realistic data we choose the time dependent wave equation defined by $\frac{\partial^2 u}{\partial t^2} - \Delta u = f$ in $\Omega \times [0, T], u(x, t) = g$ on $\partial\Omega \times [0, T]$, and $u(x, 0) = \frac{\partial u(x,0)}{\partial t} = 0$ in Ω, with $\Omega = [-\pi, \pi]^2, T > 0$ and $g = \sin(8\pi t)$ for $x = (x_0, x_1)$ with $x_0 = -\pi$ and $|x_1| < 0.1$, 0 otherwise. The simulation dataset was generated by using deal.II v9.3.2 [5] and we use the same ZFP setting as in the logarithmic model problem.

In the beginning, most data is zero (Fig. 4, top) while at the end, the interfering waves (Fig. 4, bottom) may lead to more localized features of the data set, possible degrading compression rates. Also, the spatial resolution has an important influence on the low-rank compression as a too low resolution leads to data not smooth enough for efficient global low-rank compression.

First, we look how the compression rates vary depending on the timestep as they are shown in Fig. 5 (left). In the beginning, due to most data being zero, the compression is best and declines with increasing timesteps. Here, HLRcompress is about twice as efficient as just HLR compression. The compression rate behaviour of SZ and ZFP is similar to HLR but by a factor of about 9 (SZ) and 15 (ZFP) worse than HLRcompress. For all compression algorithms the same global accuracy of $\varepsilon = 10^{-8}$ was chosen.

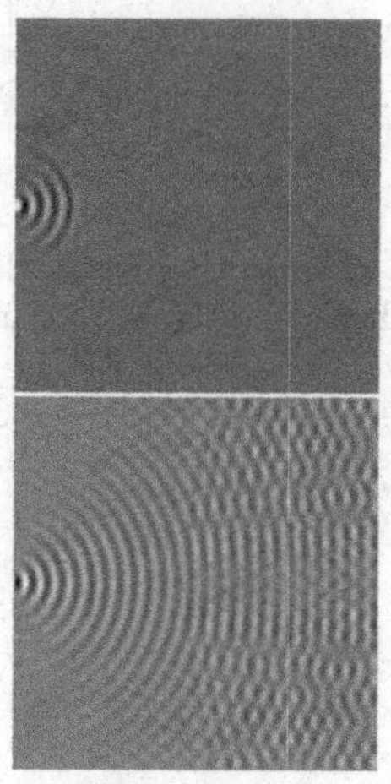

Fig. 4. Simulation dataset for the wave equation at the beginning (top) and end (bottom).

For HLR, HLRcompress and ZFP the runtime changes only little with respect to the timestep. Only in the very beginning of the simulation, the zero data approximation could be computed faster. SZ shows here a stronger dependence on the data with an increasing runtime up to the middle of the simulation. Again, ZFP shows the fastest runtime.

The importance of smooth data for low-rank approximations can best be seen in Fig. 5 (right) as the compression gets better with a higher spatial resolution, especially for the oscillating data at the end of the simulation which can not be compressed with the coarsest stepwidth but almost reaches the same level of compression as for the zero data at the simulation start with the finest stepwidth.

For comparing the different low-rank approximation methods we choose the solution at the end of the simulation as it shows the most chaotic properties, with the results shown in Fig. 6. The most obvious difference to the logarithmic problem is the accuracy of ACA, which completely fails to achieve the user-defined accuracy, which is owed to the unsmooth data. For this example, the top-down approach from [36] also fails when using ACA. All other methods are very similar in terms of compression rate and global error. However, randomized SVD needs a much larger runtime compared to SVD and RRQR to achieve these results.

5.3 Turbulent Combustion

Large-scale turbulence, combustion and detonation simulations pose a significant challenge due to the presence of a wide range of length and time scales, requiring overly fine spatial and temporal resolutions to resolve highly intermittent localized phenomena, which results in intensive checkpoint output data and extensive computational resources. Multidimensional simulations of super-knock phenomena in combustion devices are examples that require such highly

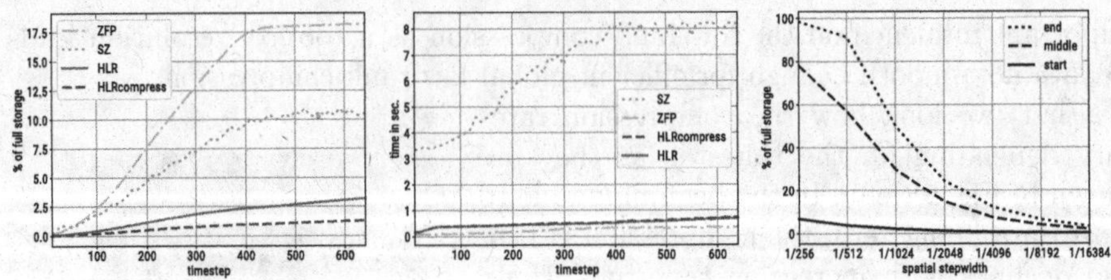

Fig. 5. Compression rates (left) and runtime (center) depending on the timestep and dependence on spatial resolution (right) for the wave equation.

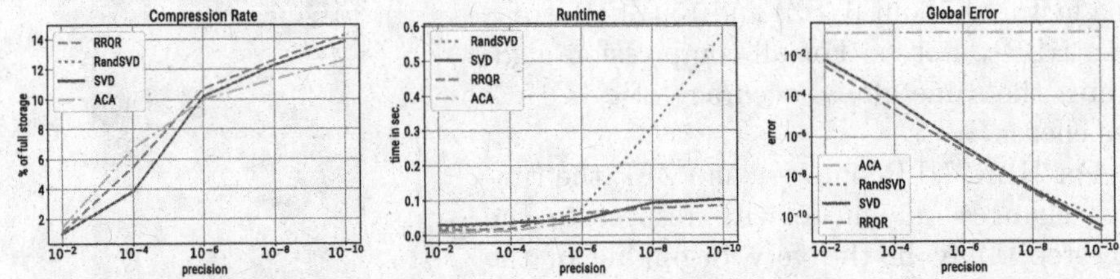

Fig. 6. Comparison of low-rank approximation algorithms for the wave equation.

intensive I/O and computational resource requirements [31–33]. These simulations may unravel the mechanism of abnormal combustion phenomena in devices under extreme high-load operating conditions. We perform experiments using the MPI-only KARFS code [13,25] compiled with Intel on a Cray XC40 distributed-memory system using 512 two-socket Intel Haswell nodes.

Figure 7a shows a detonation front with a peak pressure of $\approx$ 750 bar, while Fig. 7b shows the mass fraction of representative chemical species in the ethanol oxidation mechanism, spanning a wide spectrum of values. To fully resolve the complex structure of a detonation wave under high load, a typical grid cell size $\sim$1 μm is needed. Additionally, an extremely short-time step is also needed to resolve the temporal evolution of the chemical species.

Figure 7c shows the temporal evolution of the maximum pressure in the entire computational domain, monitored with an interval of 0.5 ns, that drastically changes in its amplitude due to shock-shock collisions, as seen in the pressure contour. A necessary high frequency of saving output data is activated prior to the onset of detonation, which permits capturing the subsequent development of the detonation process. The data generated during this stage constitutes $\sim$80% of the entire simulation data. The data size for a single checkpoint of a detonation using 2D direct numerical simulation (DNS) is typically $\sim$100 GB with $\sim$4.2 million grid points. We monitor a total number of 44 primitive variables (temperature, pressure, velocities, and chemical species).

If no compression is performed, a single run may generate $\sim$100 TB. Although these I/O operations account for a negligible portion of the overall KARFS' profile for the 2D testcase, the per-user storage quota may become a bottleneck,

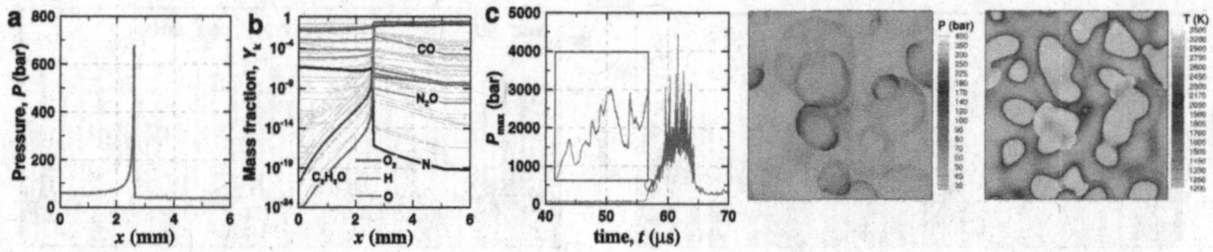

Fig. 7. **a** Pressure, **b** mass fraction of species across of a detonation wave, **c** temporal evolution of the maximum pressure from a 2D simulation. The inset in **c** and pressure and temperature contours indicate the onset of detonation.

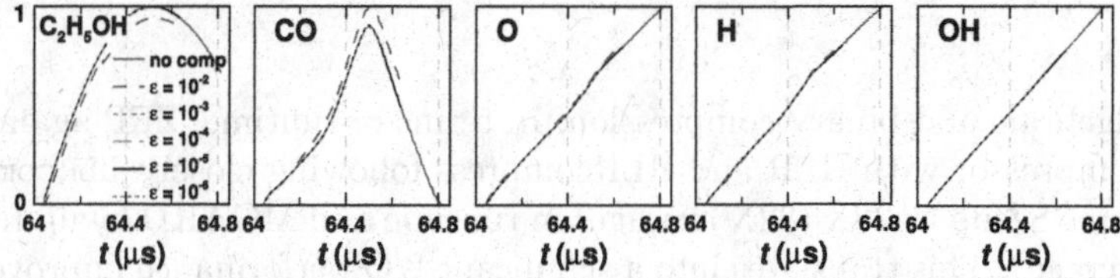

Fig. 8. Temporal evolution of the standard deviation of the normalized mass fraction of key species, i.e., fuel (C_2H_2OH), CO, O, H and OH.

not to mention the I/O-intensive post-processing phase needed to perform the offline analysis and identify abnormal combustion phenomena. This critical context justifies the integration of `HLRcompress` into KARFS. Each MPI process creates an instance of `HLRcompress` on the shared-memory node that generates the compressed datasets at runtime using OpenMP, as explained in Sect. 4.4, with limited impact on KARFS. Subsequently, KARFS stores the snapshots into the filesystem as before but now they are reduced in size, eventually alleviating the I/O performance and storage constraints during post-processing.

Figure 8 shows that the compression with $\varepsilon = 10^{-2}$ has a noticeable effect on the mass fraction of major species, i.e., fuel (C_2H_2OH) and CO, as compared to that of radicals (O, H, and OH) due to their short lifetime and thin reaction layer. All in all, the compression with $\varepsilon \leq 10^{-3}$ can still reproduce the profiles of all the primitive solution variables for the 1500 snapshots, as if no compression is applied. Figure 9 shows relative compression rates and runtime for a single timestep of the combustion simulation captured during the detonation using $\varepsilon = 10^{-4}$ with HLRcompress being the reference. We use RSVD since the numerical error is identical to SVD/RRQR, while achieving best compression rate and performance with $n_{\text{tile}} = 256$. `HLRcompress` achieves more than 100-fold compression rate compared to the full dataset.

The total memory compression for all species with `HLRcompress` is 29% better compared to SZ, with a very high compression for the inert N_2. As before, ZFP exhibits the worst compression with 9X more than HLRcompress. MGARD [1], which is applicable to this dataset due to the relaxed accuracy setting, achieves a compression 58% worse than HLRcompress. The addition of ZFP within HLR-compress yields a 3.5X better compression, clearly indicating the ideal combina-

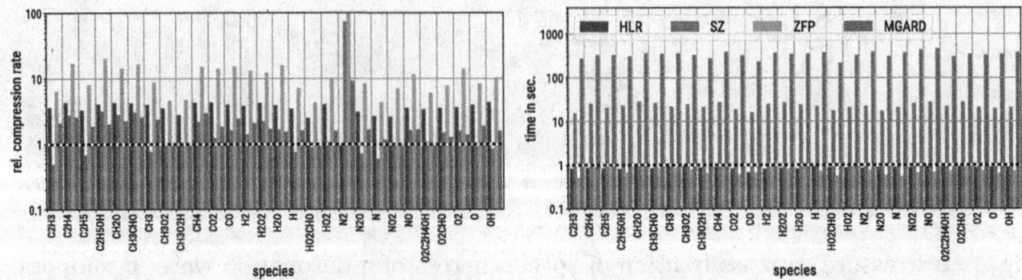

Fig. 9. Relative compression rates/runtimes per species compared to HLRcompress for one timestep of combustion simulation.

tion of algebraic and binary compression. In terms of runtime, ZFP again is the fastest compressor with HLR and HLRcompress following closely. `HLRcompress` outperforms SZ up to 28X (22X average) in runtime and MGARD by up to 465X (360X average). This translates into a significant I/O performance improvement, while analyzing the snapshots during the post-processing phase. When using ACA as the low-rank approximation scheme, `HLRcompress` is only able to compute an accurate result for a single species. For all other species, the accuracy is typically at least one order worse than requested, which also holds for the top-down HALR approach from [36]. This shows the lack of numerical robustness of ACA when dealing with non-smooth datasets.

6 Conclusion and Future Work

We highlight the performance superiority of a novel hybrid data compression algorithm, combining HLR compression schemes with ZFP binary compression, thereby outperforming state-of-the-art binary compression techniques alone on x86 parallel systems. To our knowledge, this is the first time that feasibility of lossy data compression in high-fidelity combustion datasets is demonstrated. We perform the preliminary steps in supporting GPUs into `HLRcompress`, though the current implementation of batched (Jacobi) SVD from cuSolver has limitations. Other compression algorithms need to be used on the GPU, e.g., RRQR, RSVD, and ACA. Besides planning to extend our `HLRcompress` software to high-dimensional spatial datasets within the combustion application and beyond (e.g., climate/weather applications), we would like to study the interplay between spatial and time compression of datasets generated during the detonation and autoignition. Finally, we would like to enhance the arithmetics of the PDE solvers for each chemical species by engaging `HLRcompress` beyond data compression.

Acknowledgments. For computer time, this research used `Shaheen-2` Supercomputer hosted at the Supercomputing Laboratory at KAUST.

References

1. Ainsworth, M., Tugluk, O., Whitney, B., Klasky, S.: Multilevel techniques for compression and reduction of scientific data - the univariate case. Comput. Vis. Sci. **19**, 65–76 (2018)
2. Ambikasaran, S., Foreman-Mackey, D., Greengard, L., Hogg, D.W., O'Neil, M.: Fast direct methods for Gaussian processes. IEEE Trans. Pattern Anal. Mach. Intell. **38**(2), 252–265 (2015)
3. Ballard, G., Klinvex, A., Kolda, T.G.: TuckerMPI: a parallel C++/MPI software package for large-scale data compression via the tucker tensor decomposition. ACM Trans. Math. Softw. **46**(2) (2020)
4. Ballester-Ripoll, R., Lindstrom, P., Pajarola, R.: TTHRESH: tensor compression for multidimensional visual data. IEEE Trans. Vis. Comput. Graph. **26**(9), 2891–2903 (2020). https://doi.org/10.1109/TVCG.2019.2904063
5. Bangerth, W., Hartmann, R., Kanschat, G.: deal.II - A general-purpose object-oriented finite element library. ACM Trans. Math. Softw. **33**, 24 (2007)
6. Bebendorf, M.: Approximation of boundary element matrices. Numer. Math. **86**(4), 565–589 (2000)
7. Börm, S.: Efficient Numerical Methods for Non-local Operators: $\mathcal{H}^2$-Matrix Compression, Algorithms and Analysis, vol. 14. European Mathematical Society (2010)
8. Börm, S.: Directional $\mathcal{H}^2$-matrix compression for high-frequency problems. Numer. Linear Algebra Appl. **24** (2017)
9. Börm, S., Grasedyck, L.: Hybrid cross approximation of integral operators. Numer. Math. **101**, 221–249 (2005)
10. Börm, S., Grasedyck, L., Hackbusch, W.: Hierarchical matrices. Preprint, Max Planck Institute for Mathematics in the Sciences (2003)
11. Börm, S., Hackbusch, W.: $\mathcal{H}^2$-matrix approximation of integral operators by interpolation. Appl. Numer. Math. **43**, 129–143 (2002)
12. Corona, E., Martinsson, P.G., Zorin, D.: An $O(N)$ direct solver for integral equations on the plane. Appl. Comput. Harmon. Anal. **38**(2), 284–317 (2015)
13. Desai, S., Yu, J.K., Song, W., Luong, M.B., et al.: Direct numerical simulations of reacting flows with shock waves and stiff chemistry using many-core/GPU acceleration. Comput. Fluids **215**, 104787 (2021)
14. Di, S., Cappello, F.: Fast Error-bounded lossy HPC data compression with SZ. In: 2016 IEEE International Parallel and Distributed Processing Symposium (IPDPS), pp. 730–739 (2016)
15. Ehrlacher, V., Grigori, G., Lombardi, D., Song, H.: Adaptive hierarchical subtensor partitioning for tensor compression. SIAM J. Sci. Comput. **43**, 139–163 (2021)
16. Grasedyck, L.: Adaptive recompression of $\mathcal{H}$-matrices for BEM. Computing **74**, 205–223 (2004)
17. Grasedyck, L., Kriemann, R., LeBorne, S.: Parallel black box $\mathcal{H}$-LU preconditioning for elliptic boundary value problems. Comput. Vis. Sci. **11**(4–6), 273–291 (2008)
18. Hackbusch, W., Khoromskij, B., Sauter, S.A.: On $\mathcal{H}^2$-Matrices. In: Bungartz, H.J., Hoppe, R.H.W., Zenger, C. (eds.) Lectures on Applied Mathematics, pp. 9–29. Springer, Heidelberg (2000). https://doi.org/10.1007/978-3-642-59709-1_2
19. Hackbusch, W., Khoromskij, B.: A sparse $\mathcal{H}$-matrix arithmetic. Part II: application to multi-dimensional problems. Computing **64**, 21–47 (2000)
20. Hackbusch, W., Khoromskij, B., Kriemann, R.: Hierarchical matrices based on a weak admissibility criterion. Computing **73**, 207–243 (2004)

21. Hackbusch, W.: A sparse matrix arithmetic based on $\mathcal{H}$-matrices. Part I: introduction to $\mathcal{H}$-matrices. Computing **62**, 89–108 (1999)
22. Hackbusch, W.: $\mathcal{H}^2$-Matrices: Algorithms and Analysis, vol. 49. Springer, Heidelberg (2015). https://doi.org/10.1007/978-3-662-47324-5
23. Hackbusch, W., Khoromskij, B.N.: $\mathcal{H}$-matrix approximation on graded meshes. In: Whiteman, J.R. (ed.) Proceedings of the 10th conference on Mathematics of Finite Elements and Applications X, MAFELAP 1999, pp. 307–316 (2000)
24. Halko, N., Martinsson, P.G., Tropp, J.A.: Finding structure with randomness: probabilistic algorithms for constructing approximate matrix decompositions. SIAM Rev. **53**(2), 217–288 (2011)
25. Hernández Pérez, F.E., et al.: Direct numerical simulations of reacting flows with detailed chemistry using many-core/GPU acceleration. Comput. Fluids **173**, 73–79 (2018)
26. Keyes, D.E., Ltaief, H., Turkiyyah, G.: Hierarchical algorithms on hierarchical architectures. In: Proceedings of PASC, pp. 1–11 (2020)
27. Li, Y., Yang, H., Ying, L.: Multidimensional butterfly factorization. Appl. Comput. Harmon. Anal. **44**, 737–758 (2018)
28. Lindstrom, P.: Fixed-rate compressed floating-point arrays. IEEE Trans. Vis. Comput. Graph. **20**(12), 2674–2683 (2014)
29. Ltaief, H., Cranney, J., Gratadour, D., Hong, Y., Gatineau, L., Keyes, D.: Meeting the real-time challenges of ground-based telescopes using low-rank matrix computations. In: Proceedings of the International Conference for High Performance Computing, Networking, Storage and Analysis, SC 2021 (2021)
30. Luo, H., et al.: Identifying latent reduced models to precondition lossy compression. In: 2019 IEEE International Parallel and Distributed Processing Symposium (IPDPS), pp. 293–302 (2019)
31. Luong, M.B., Desai, S., Hernández Pérez, F.E., et al.: Effects of turbulence and temperature fluctuations on knock development in an ethanol/air mixture. Flow Turbul. Combust. **106**, 575–595 (2021)
32. Luong, M.B., Desai, S., Hernández Pérez, F.E., et al.: A statistical analysis of developing knock intensity in a mixture with temperature inhomogeneities. Proc. Combust. Inst. **38**, 5781–5789 (2021)
33. Luong, M.B., Im, H.G.: Direct numerical simulation of preignition and knock in engine conditions. In: Gupta, A.K., De, A., Aggarwal, S.K., Kushari, A., Runchal, A.K. (eds.) Advances in Energy and Combustion. GET, pp. 311–336. Springer, Singapore (2022). https://doi.org/10.1007/978-981-16-2648-7_14
34. Mahoney, M.W., Drineas, P.: CUR matrix decompositions for improved data analysis. Proc. Natl. Acad. Sci. **106**(3), 697–702 (2009)
35. Mary, T.: Block low-rank multifrontal solvers: complexity, performance, and scalability. Ph.D. thesis, Paul Sabatier University, Toulouse, France (2017)
36. Massei, S., Robol, L., Kressner, D.: Hierarchical adaptive low-rank format with applications to discretized PDEs (2021). https://arxiv.org/abs/2104.11456
37. Rouet, F.H., Li, X.S., Ghysels, P., Napov, A.: A distributed-memory package for dense hierarchically semi-separable matrix computations using randomization. ACM Trans. Math. Softw. (TOMS) **42**(4), 27 (2016)
38. Yu, C.D., Levitt, J., Reiz, S., Biros, G.: Geometry-oblivious FMM for compressing dense SPD matrices. In: Proceedings of the International Conference for High Performance Computing, Networking, Storage and Analysis, SC 2017 (2017)

Author Index

Printed in the United States
by Baker & Taylor Publisher Services